# A Learner's Dictionary of English Idioms

Isabel McCaig
Martin H Manser

Oxford University Press

Oxford University Press
Walton Street, Oxford OX2 6DP

Oxford New York Toronto Delhi Bombay
Calcutta Madras Karachi Petaling Jaya
Singapore Hong Kong Tokyo Nairobi
Dar es Salaam Cape Town Melbourne
Auckland

and associated companies in
Berlin Ibadan

OXFORD and OXFORD ENGLISH are trade marks of
Oxford University Press

ISBN 0 19 431254 2



First published 1986
Fifth impression 1991



Typeset in Great Britain by
Promenade Graphics Limited, Cheltenham.

Printed in Hong Kong

# About this dictionary

Idioms are a very important part of the English language: you may be told that if you want to *go far* you should *pull your socks up* and use your *grey matter*. An idiom is a phrase which you cannot understand by putting together the meanings of the words in it. For example, *pull your socks up* has nothing to do with socks or pulling them up, but means 'improve your behaviour'.

This dictionary is for intermediate learners of English who want a clear explanation of the common idioms that are used in contemporary English. You will find over 5500 idioms clearly explained, nearly all with one or more examples of how they are commonly used.

# How to use this dictionary

## Order of entries

Idioms are in alphabetical order according to the first of the most important words in each, and this 'key word' is printed in *italic* type:

**like *anything***
**a *bag* of nerves**
***change* one's tune**

Because it is sometimes difficult to decide which is the key word, there are many cross-references to guide you to the right place in the Dictionary. For example, if you look up *humble pie* at *humble* you will find

***eat* humble pie ⟶ *eat***

which means that the idiom is defined at *eat*. Cross-references will also help you when there are different versions of an idiom: if you look up *climb on the bandwagon* at *climb*, you will find

***climb* on the bandwagon ⟶ *jump*/climb on the bandwagon**

which means that you will find the idiom at *jump*.

Note that *be* is rarely counted as part of an idiom: you should therefore look for ***ill* at ease** rather than ***be* ill at ease**, for example.

Within each group of idioms with the same key word, idioms are listed alphabetically according to the words after the key word, taking one word at a time. **A**, **an**, and **the** are counted for this purpose, but words which are normally replaced by others when an idiom is actually used (**sb**, **sth**, **sb's**, **sth's**, **one**, **one's**, **oneself**, and **etc**) are not. Also, when there are alternatives, only the first is counted. Thus, the order of these entries:

***know*/have all the answers**
**not *know* any better**
***know* sth backwards**
***know* best**

is determined by **all**, **any**, **backwards**, and **best**. **Sb**, **sth**, **one** etc and any words before the key word *are* counted if they are the only difference between two or more idioms:

**at *last***
**at the *last***

***look* up**
***look* sb up**
***look* sth up**

Contractions and hyphenated words are treated as two words:

***how* on earth?**
***how*'s your father**
***how* the hell?**

***knock* off**
***knock*-on effect**
***knock* sb out**

A word in round brackets is counted in the alphabetical ordering only if it is the key word, as in **the *(absolute)* limit**.

## Alternatives

/ and ( ) are used to show that there are different versions of an idiom:

***cut* both/two ways**

means that **cut both ways** and **cut two ways** are both idioms;

***that* (all) depends**

means that **that all depends** and **that depends** are both idioms.

## Stress

The stress in an idiom is normally on the last noun, verb, adjective, or adverb, eg on *bucket* in *kick the bucket*. When this is not so, however, it is shown by ':

**'*small* fry**

Occasionally, , is used to show lighter stress.

## Style labels

These show that some idioms have limited use: amongst others, *(informal)* means that the idiom is used in everyday conversation and would not be used much in writing; *(slang)* indicates a very informal style normally used between people of the same age, especially young people; *(taboo)* describes an idiom that is rude or offensive and is generally best avoided by learners of English.

A label applies also to any alternatives given in the same entry (or in the same numbered section of an entry) unless they are differently labelled.

## Derived words

These are given in some entries: they are mainly nouns and adjectives that take their meaning from the idiom, eg the adjective **back-breaking** from the idiom **break one's back**.

## See also . . .

An idiom given after 'See also' is worth comparing because it either uses some of the same words or has a similar meaning.

## Abbreviations

*adj* adjective
eg for example
etc and so on
*n* noun
*pl* plural
sb somebody
sth something
*US* American
*vb* verb

# A

**from *A* to Z** very thoroughly and in detail: *He's spent four years examining the life cycle of insects, so he knows his subject from A to Z.*

**the *ABC* of sth** the basic facts of a subject: *There are several books available that give you the ABC of home computers.* See also **as easy as ABC.**

***abide* by sth 1** obey or keep a rule or law: *Players must abide by the rules of the game.* **2** accept sth such as a decision or judgment without arguing over it: *The company managers and the unions agreed to abide by the findings of the committee on pay and working conditions.*

**be *above* oneself** ⟶ ***get*/be above oneself**

***above* all (else)** especially; most importantly; in addition to all the other things: *When you choose a new car, see that it's big enough for what you want and that it's economical, but above all else, make sure you can afford it! / Leave everything as you found it, and above all don't forget to lock the door.*

***above* and beyond** more than; in addition to: *Our soldiers did above and beyond what was expected of them, and they will be rewarded accordingly.*

***above*/below par** (of sb's health, performance etc) better/worse than it usually is: *He said he'd been feeling a bit below par for a few weeks but had not realised that there was anything seriously wrong with him until the doctor told him he had cancer.* **not up to par** = below par.

**the *(absolute)* limit** *(informal)* very annoying; intolerable: *You children really are the limit! Why can't you ever arrive on time?*

**on 'no *account*** not for any reason: *On no account must they disturb the hens. / 'You wouldn't like to take my place, would you?' 'On no account* (or *Not on 'any account)!'*

***account* for sb** kill, defeat, or overcome sb: *He hoped to account for two or three of his attackers before he was captured. / 'That's you accounted for, anyway,' I thought, as the heckler sat down without another word to say.*

***account* for sb/sth** keep and give a record of sb/sth: *I have to account for every penny I spend. / With three passengers still not accounted for* (or *still unaccounted for*), *rescue operations continued into the night.*

***account* for sth** be/give a reason or explanation for sth: *If he was in pain that would account for his bad temper. / 'Why did she give up her studies when she was doing so well?' 'I can't account for it either.'*

**on *account* of sb/sth** because of sb/sth: *I can't go, but don't stay in on account of 'me* (or *on 'my account*). */ Flights were delayed on account of the fog.*

**there's no *accounting* for tastes** *(saying)* you cannot guess who or what another person may like.

**by/from 'all *accounts*** ⟶ ***all***

**within an *ace* of (doing) sth** only just fail to do, achieve, or suffer sth: *I was within an ace of punching him, I was so angry. / This sudden change of fortune came when they were within an ace of victory.*

**sb's *Achilles'* heel** a weakness or flaw in an otherwise strong person, organization, defence system etc.

**the '*acid* test (of sth)** a severe test that proves or disproves the worth, ability etc (of sth): *He has done well as a student teacher under supervision. The acid test will come when he has to face a class by himself.*

**catch sb in the *act* (of doing sth)** ⟶ ***catch***

***act*/be one's age** not act in such a foolish, childish way: *Come on, Jenny, stop playing with your food—act your age!*

***act* like a charm** ⟶ ***work*/act like a charm**

**an *act* of God** an event not caused or controlled by man, especially a natural disaster such as a flood or earthquake: *The policy insures your property against acts of God but not against enemy action in war. / He was determined to walk the whole way, and nothing less than an act of God could have stopped him.*

***act*/play the fool** behave in a stupid or playful way intended to amuse: *It was impossible to get a decent game of tennis with Frank acting the fool most of the time.*

***act*/play up** *(informal)* cause trouble in an annoying, tiresome way: *The children are all right with me—they only start acting up when their parents come home.*

**where the '*action* is** ⟶ ***where***

**'*action* stations** (an order to go to) the places in which everybody is ready for action: *Action stations, everyone! The royal party have just arrived outside!*

***actions* speak louder than words** *(saying)* what you do matters more than what you say.

**in *actual* fact** ⟶ **in *fact***

***Adam's* ale** *(old-fashioned or literary)* water.

***Adam's* apple** the part in the front of the neck, especially on a man, which sticks out and moves when a person talks.

***add* fuel to the fire** cause or encourage more activity, a stronger emotion or attitude etc: *In an area where there are already strong feelings about discrimination, the smallest incident seems only to add fuel to the fire and produce even further discontent.* Also **fan the flames (of sth).**

***add* insult to injury** offend sb's feelings as well as cause him (material) loss or damage:

*The tiny sum of money offered in compensation for the damage added insult to injury.*

**(not) *add* up** *(informal)* (not) make sense or seem reasonable: *Why did the gang bother to break in if they could just walk in? It doesn't add up.*

***add* 'up to sth** mean sth: *What all these new restrictions add up to is that I can't invite my friends here any more.*

***admit*/allow of sth** *(formal)* offer scope or opportunity for sth: *The terms of the lease do not admit of sub-letting.*

**to (better etc) *advantage*** in a way that produces a good or profitable result: *You should be spending your time to better advantage (than you do). / It's a lovely picture, but it's not seen to advantage where it is. Why don't you hang it nearer the light?*

**I'm *afraid* ⟶ *I***

***afraid*/frightened of one's own shadow** extremely timid and nervous.

**be *after* sb/sth ⟶ *go*/be after sb/sth**

***after* all 1** finally; in the end; after everything that has gone before: *We looked everywhere for the key and then found it in my coat pocket after all.* **2** contrary to what a person first intends to do or expects to happen: *I think I will have something to eat after all. / We could have left our coats at home—it didn't rain after all.* **3** what is more important in the circumstances (often used with a reason or argument that has been remembered or thought of): *Can't I stay up late tonight? After all, there's no school tomorrow! / You got a fair price for your car. It is six years old, after all.*

**act/be one's *age* ⟶ *act***

**be/come of *age*** be/reach the age when you are legally responsible for your own actions: *When he comes of age, he can do what he wants with the money left to him in his father's will.*

**over/under *age*** too old/young to be employed, join the army, be admitted to a place etc: *At the recruiting office they told him he was over age. / The landlords of pubs have been warned against serving under-age drinkers.*

**pile on the *agony* ⟶ *pile***

***agony* aunt** *(informal)* the woman who answers readers' letters about their personal problems in a newspaper or magazine.

***agree* to differ** allow each other to keep different opinions about sth, especially in order to avoid further argument: *'I don't think you'll ever convince me.' 'OK—let's say we agree to differ, then.'*

**(not) *agree* with sb** (of climates, foods, or activities) (not) suit sb's health or comfort: *Greasy food doesn't agree with me. I always get indigestion afterwards. / A nap after lunch just doesn't agree with me. I always wake up with a headache.*

**(be) *ahead* of one's/its time** (of sb or an idea, invention etc) (be) more advanced than others of his/its period and unlikely to be accepted, except by future generations: *Leonardo da Vinci's notebooks and drawings show him to have had a scientific knowledge that was well ahead of his time.*

**what's sth in *aid* of? ⟶ *what***

**in the *air*** (of a piece of information or idea) going about: *There's a rumour in the air that Siegfried's going to be sacked soon.*

**(up) in the *air*** (of plans or proposals) very uncertain and perhaps never to be carried out: *It could be an interesting trip—but the plan's very much up in the air still, you know; nothing fixed or final.*

**off the *air*** not broadcasting or not being broadcast: *The series you mentioned has been off the air for weeks now. Hadn't you noticed? / 'I can't get Radio Clyde tonight.' 'Oh, it's off the air because of an industrial dispute.'* See also **on the *air*.**

**on the *air*** broadcasting or being broadcast: *He's on the air a lot, that fellow, considering he's a fairly minor politician. / Goodnight from all of us here. BBC-2 will come on the air again at 6.40 for Open University students.* See also **off the *air*.**

**tread/walk on *air* ⟶ *tread***

**put on *airs* ⟶ *put***

***airs* and graces** affected manners to give an impression of great elegance, but in reality often having the opposite effect: *I'm inclined to suspect anybody so full of airs and graces as she is of being insincere.*

**roll in the *aisles* ⟶ *roll***

**an *Aladdin's* cave** a treasure-house; any place where valuable or interesting objects can be found or seen: *He kept for his private pleasure an Aladdin's cave of stolen masterpieces. / London toy shops must seem like Aladdin's caves to children from the country.*

***alive* and kicking** *(informal)* alive and well or active: *'Whatever happened to Fred?' 'He's still alive and kicking: I think he's landed a job somewhere in Africa.'*

**in *all*** as a total quantity or number: *We had only ten litres in all to last us till the end of the week. / 'You must have hundreds of tapes there.' '340 in all.'*

**by/from '*all* accounts** from what people say; from what is in the newspapers etc; as seems generally agreed: *Unemployment is high and from all accounts is going to get worse. / 'I'm sorry you couldn't be there.' 'Me, too. It was a very happy occasion by all accounts.'*

***all* along** from the start until this particular time: *I've said all along that this would happen. / I knew that all along.*

***all* and sundry** everyone; people of any or every kind: *The place would be open to all and sundry if her wishes were fulfilled.*

***all* at once** suddenly: *Everything seemed settled, when all at once he changed his mind.*

**carry *all* before one ⟶ *carry* all/everything before one**

***all* being well** if nothing unforeseen or unfortunate happens: *We'll see you then, all being well, around Christmas.*

**in *all* one's born days** *(informal)* at any time

in your life (usually used when referring to sth unpleasant): *How dare you talk to me like that! I've never been spoken to like that in all my born days!*

**all but** **1** very nearly: *I all but fell into the trap. / He himself was all but bankrupt and so couldn't help us.* **2** all the people or things mentioned except . . . : *All but two of the boys failed the exam.*

**for all sb cares/knows** sb does not care/know: *He can sack me tomorrow for all I care. / That was years ago. He might be dead by now for all anyone knows.*

**in all conscience** truly; without doubt or question: *I can say in all conscience that I've never knowingly harmed anybody.*

**it was all sb could do (not) to do sth** *(informal)* it was very difficult (not) to do sth: *The situation was so desperately sad that the couple found it was all they could do not to cry.*

**(not) be/take all day/morning/afternoon/evening/night** *(informal)* (not) spend too long a time; (not) be too slow (used as a request to hurry up): *Don't be all day choosing your book.* Also **(not) have (got) all day etc.**

**,all day and 'every day** without change or a break over a period of time: *I have to be active—I couldn't sit around all day and every day now I've retired.*

**it/that (all) depends** ⟶ ***depends***

**all dressed up and nowhere to go** *(informal)* wearing your best clothes and ready for an engagement, party etc, but not actually going, for example because of a change of plans; clearly ready for an event which does not take place (usually used humorously).

**be all ears/eyes** *(informal)* pay close attention by listening/looking: *Yes, tell me, I'm all ears!*

**at 'all events** in any case; whatever the circumstances: *We do not have a record of his travels, but he must, at all events, have visited Madagascar during the summer of 1854.*

**(all) for the best** ⟶ ***best***

**on all fours** ⟶ **on one's *hands* and knees**

**be all go** be (a situation where people are) constantly active, energetic, excited etc: *With the election so close, it's all go for the organizers at the moment.*

**all good things (must) come to an end** *(saying)* (said especially in reference to the end of a happy holiday, or meeting with friends etc.)

**be (all) Greek to sb** *(informal)* (of difficult or technical talk or writing) be too hard for sb to understand: *His lecture on the latest developments in electronics was all Greek to me.*

**all hell breaks loose** violent rioting or great, noisy uproar and confusion suddenly start: *When the soldiers fired shots into the crowd, all hell broke loose.*

**(all) hot and bothered** ⟶ ***hot***

**at/till all hours (of the night)** at/till any time between late evening and early morning: *He sat up working till all hours to finish his essay.*

**all 'in** **1** (of a price) with everything included; with no extra to pay: *I'll sell you this car for £10,000 all in. / These are 'all-in prices—room, breakfast, service and tax.* **2** *(informal)* very tired; exhausted: *I'll finish digging that patch tomorrow, Mary. Right now, I'm all in.*

**all in a/the day's work** sth that a person accepts as normal or to be expected in his daily routine or duties: *To a trawlerman, it seems, a soaking is all in a day's work.*

**all in all** **1** taking everything into consideration: *All in all, we've done a good day's work.* **2** the object of (obsessive) devotion and interest: *A man can love his wife without her becoming his all in all.*

**be (all) in the mind** ⟶ ***mind***

**to all intents (and purposes)** in all practical respects; in fact; in every way: *He was treated with kindness but was still to all intents and purposes a slave.*

**when all is said and done** when all the facts are considered: *Half of these costly conferences, when all is said and done, achieve little or nothing.*

**for all one is worth** (do sth) with all your energy and/or concentration: *The thief ran off down the road, so I chased him for all I was worth.*

**all manner of** all kinds of: *The warehouse was stocked with all manner of goods.*

**all my eye and Betty Martin!** ⟶ **my *eye*/foot!**

**all of** *(informal)* (used to emphasize an amount such as an age or distance): *It took us all of four hours to clear out the garage! / It must be all of 1000 kilometres from here to Paris.*

**all of a sudden** *(informal)* suddenly and unexpectedly: *I was sitting reading my book when all of a sudden the lights went out.*

**all one (to sb)** or **all the same (to sb)** make no difference, not matter at all (to sb): *Clearly, it was all one to him whether we approved or not.* Also **one and the same.**

**be ,sb all 'over** be typical of sb; be just the way he is likely to behave: *It was a tactless thing to say, but that's your father all over!*

**be all over sb** welcome, fuss over or flatter sb greatly or too much: *James is the children's favourite uncle. They're all over him as soon as he comes to visit us!*

**be all over bar the shouting** *(informal)* (of sth such as a contest or performance) be (successfully) concluded with only the official announcement, the applause etc to follow: *90% of the votes had been counted, and Macdonald had won—it was all over bar the shouting!*

**all 'over the place/shop** *(informal)* (found, scattered etc) everywhere: *Walk along a main street anywhere and you'll see foreign-built cars all over the shop.*

**of 'all people, places etc** be a particular person, place, thing that is the most/least likely or suitable: *Of all people, you should be the one to sympathize, having just had a similar* *accident yourself. / If it's a rest they need, then why go to London of all places?*

***all* right 1** (a way of agreeing to something, which may be willing or not, as shown by the tone of voice and expression on the face): *'Come for your dinner, Billy.' 'All right, Mum. What are we having today?' / 'May I borrow your camera this afternoon?' asked Bill. 'All right, but don't make a habit of it,' agreed Harry reluctantly.* **2** certainly, without doubt (used at the end of a statement, promise, or threat, to emphasize it): *Jack's an amusing fellow all right. / 'And tell him we're very annoyed.' 'I'll tell him that all right.' / We know their marriage is in a mess all right, but what are we going to do about it?* **3** in good or satisfactory health or condition; uninjured, undamaged, or in working order: *I had a bad cold last week but I feel all right now. / The machine's all right—the trouble is that you don't know how to work it.* This is also a common way of replying to a greeting such as ***How are you?***: *'How are you, June?' 'All right, thanks—and how are you?'* As a question it may itself be a greeting: *'All right?' 'Yes thanks—and you?'* **4** (only just) satisfactory or good enough; well or satisfactorily enough: *'Don't you like the Smiths?' 'Peter's all right, but his wife is a bit of a troublemaker.' / 'Did I do all right?' 'Yes, what you said was splendid!'* **5** (used at the beginning of a sentence to show annoyance and impatience): *All right, there's no need to get so angry with me! / All right, forget I ever came into your life if that's how you feel about me!* **6** Have you understood so far? (used to join parts of an explanation): *So you want to get to the station? OK, you turn left at the end and go straight on at the junction. All right? Go down the hill, and there it is.* Also **right**. See also **it's *all* right; that's/it's *all* right.**

***all* right (with sb)** allowed; convenient (for sb); not an action or arrangement that sb would dislike or object to: *Is it all right to park here? / 'Stay overnight with us.' 'Well, if you're sure that would be all right with your wife, we'd be glad to.'*

**a bit of *all* right** ⟶ ***bit***

**do *all* right for oneself** ⟶ ***do***

**it's *all* right** (used to show discontent, dissatisfaction, or sometimes envy): *'I'm on holiday tomorrow!' 'It's ˌall right for ˈsome, isn't it? I've got to go to work!'* Also **it's all very well:** *It's all very well filing these papers away, but are you ever going to use them again?* See also **that's/it's *all* right.**

**see sb *(all)* right** ⟶ ***see***

**that's/it's *all* right** (used as a response to sb saying thank you or apologizing): *'Thank you for these flowers.' 'Oh, that's all right.' / 'I'm sorry I couldn't come to the party.' 'It's all right—perhaps you'll be able to make it another time.'* See also **it's *all* right.**

***all's* fair in love and war** *(saying)* actions sb would usually be blamed for are excused in love or in war.

***all's* well that ends well** *(saying)* if the final result is good, earlier difficulties or setbacks no longer matter.

**(be) *(all)* square (with sb)** ⟶ ***square***

**(not) as stupid, tired etc as *all* that** (not) as stupid etc as to do sth that has previously been described or suggested: *'You didn't sign the paper, did you?' 'I am not as stupid as all that.' / 'Father can't be nursed at home any longer.' 'Oh, I'm sorry. I didn't realize he was as ill as all that.'*

**(not) *(all)* that good, easy etc** ⟶ ***that***

**and *all* that (jazz)** *(informal)* and more/other things of the same kind, having the same meaning, or of equal (un)importance: *She was very polite and apologetic and all that—said it had all been a misunderstanding. / 'Our grandmother,' said Paul, 'is very keen on good manners, brushing your teeth, keeping your back straight, and all that jazz.' / He knows a lot about politics and all that, but not too much about real life.*

***all* the best!** *(informal)* (a wish that sb will be happy, successful etc, used when saying goodbye, at the end of a letter, or when drinking with sb): *All the best, then, Maria, and we'll see you in a fortnight!*

**be *(all)* the better/worse for sth** ⟶ **be (all, none etc) the *better*/worse for sth**

**of *all* the cheek, nerve etc!** an exclamation of annoyance or disapproval: *Of all the nerve! Some people want everything done for them! / Of all the idiots, leaving his car unlocked in the middle of town!*

**make ˈ*all* the ˈdifference** ⟶ ***make***

***all* the go/rage** very much in fashion: *Electronic games were all the go that year, and every child wanted one for Christmas.*

**for *all* the good sb/sth is/does** sb/sth is so bad or does so little good that . . . : *For all the good the boy's education did him, he might as well have had none.*

***all* the same** nevertheless: *I'm sure your figures will be correct, but I'll check them all the same, if you don't mind.*

**not for *all* the tea in China** ⟶ ***tea***

***all* the world and his wife** large numbers of people, especially assembled as guests, spectators, or holidaymakers: *There was no escape on our little holiday beach! All the world and his wife were there.*

**(not) *all* there** *(informal)* (not) having a right, sane mind or normal intelligence: *One of their boys is not all there, you know. He has to go to a special school. / Anne may be stupid in some respects but she's all there when it comes to money matters.*

***all* things considered** when everything, especially something bad, connected with a situation or event is considered: *The weather was awful for the garden fete, so they did quite well, all things considered, to raise as much as £360.*

**be ˈ*all* things to ˈall men** vary your behaviour or the expression of your opinions, to suit your company or audience.

**be 'all 'thumbs** → **one's *fingers* are all thumbs**

***all* told** with all items counted and included: *'How many?' '60 passengers all told.'*

***all* too common, often etc** much more common etc than a person likes or is right: *The vegetables were overcooked—an all too common fault in British kitchens. / One meets with such courtesy all too seldom.*

**it's *all* 'up with sb/sth** *(informal)* sb is dead or sure to die; sb's career or prosperity is at an end; sth is ended, cannot continue, or must be abandoned: *If he hadn't been wearing a life-jacket it would certainly have been all up with him.*

**it's *all* very well** → **it's *all* right**

***all* very well/fine (but . . . )** good or satisfactory in some respect(s) only: *Camping is all very well if you get good weather.*

**for *all* one's wealth, disadvantages etc** in spite of one's wealth etc: *The Duke, for all his wealth, was a deeply unhappy man. / She's an awful gossip but a good-hearted woman for 'all that.*

***all* work and no play makes Jack a dull boy** *(saying)* it is not healthy to spend all your time working and never relaxing.

**it's *all* yours, theirs etc** *(informal)* I am or would be pleased to have nothing (further) to do with sb/sth: *I'm trying my best to do a difficult job. If anyone wants to take over from me, it's all theirs. / 'There you are, Mr Brown,' she said, taking him into the classroom, 'they're all yours.'*

**(right) up sb's *alley*** → **(right) up sb's *street*/alley**

***allow* of sth** → ***admit*/allow of sth**

**make *allowance*(s) for sb/sth** → ***make***

**in the *altogether*** naked, wearing no clothes: *There they all were, alone on the beach, in the altogether.*

**can/could *always* do sth** be free to do sth; have the option of doing sth: *Make him the offer—he can always say no.*

**any *amount* (of)** → ***any* amount/number (of)**

***amount* to sth** be regarded as sth, especially after all the points have been considered: *The news agency reported that the agreement between the superpowers amounted to an attempt at gaining nuclear superiority. / A promise from her amounts to nothing.*

***ancient*/past history** sth, especially in sb's past, that is no longer relevant or significant: *Tom's first marriage to Stella is ancient history.*

***and* all 1** and other (connected) matters: *What with her job and the 'children and all, Jane's kept pretty busy.* **2** as well; included; too: *They've invited themselves, dog and all, for the weekend. / You can take that smile off your face and all, young Jones.* **3** in spite of; notwithstanding: *Crippled leg and all, he's a lot more active than you are.*

***and* how!** *(informal)* very much so: *'Would you like a place in the team?' 'And how!'*

**an *angel* of mercy** sb who brings help, comfort etc just at the right time: *No sooner had I realized that we didn't have a spare tyre in the car than this man came up, a real angel of mercy, and helped us to mend the puncture.*

***angle*/fish for sth** try to obtain sth such as compliments, an invitation, or information for yourself by hints or other indirect methods: *I could tell from what he was saying that he was fishing for information on what business we were doing with Pane & Co.*

**a horse of *another* colour** → ***horse***

***answer* (sb) back** defend yourself when being accused or criticized; reply rudely to sb, such as a parent, teacher, or boss, who is criticizing you or telling you what to do: *It's easy for the others to blame Jack when he's not here to answer (them) back. / Don't answer back, my lad, and take that grin off your face, too!*

***answer* for sb** say or promise what sb will do: *'Would your husband help?' 'I can't answer for him, but I don't see why not.'*

***answer* for sth** (have to) accept the responsibility or blame for sth: *He has neglected his health and now he has to answer for the consequences. / That poor woman seems more neurotic every time I see her—her husband's got a lot to answer for.*

***answer* to sb (for sth)** try to explain or justify (mis)conduct to sb who may punish you (for sth) (often used as a warning or threat): *If I catch you in here again, it's the police you'll have to answer to.*

**have (got) *ants* in one's pants** → ***have***

***any* amount/number (of)** *(informal)* a large amount/number of: *They were a bit stingy with the sandwiches, but there was any amount of drink. / 'Who wants to watch rubbish like that?' 'Any 'number of people, I assure you.'*

**in '*any* case** anyway; whatever happens or has happened: *I don't yet know who'll bring them or when, but in any case we'll see you get the papers back tomorrow. / The Irish runner got badly bumped in the last lap but wouldn't have won in any case.*

**'*any* day (of the week)** *(informal)* (used to emphasize a strong preference): *I'd rather have him than his brother any day of the week.*

**'*any* day of the week** *(informal)* at any time, as frequently as you want: *You can hear that stuff on the radio any day of the week.*

**,*any* minute, day etc 'now** in the next few minutes, days etc; very soon: *The car will be here any minute now.*

**'*any* old time, place/where, how etc** *(informal)* any time, place, manner etc at all; any time etc that may be convenient for sb, though perhaps not for others: *I told him he could drop in and see us any old time. / I want this job done properly, not any old how.*

**'*anyone's*/'anybody's guess** a matter no one can be sure about: *Who will win is anybody's guess.*

**as easy, clear, quickly etc as *anything*** *(informal)* very easy etc indeed: *'I could climb up there as easy as anything,' boasted Sally. / It* *was only a small gift, but she was as pleased as anything with it.*

**if *anything*** if there is any difference: *I can't really tell who is taller, but Peter is, if anything. / If anything, I think I prefer my old pen as it writes a bit better.*

**like *anything*** *(informal)* very well, much, hard, fast etc: *She ran like anything to catch the bus. / It hurts like anything.*

**more than *anything* (else) (in the world)** → ***more***

***anything* but** certainly not; far from; just the opposite of: *Jack is anything but mean. / I wouldn't say he was generous—anything 'but!*

***anything* doing? 1** *(informal)* is anything happening?: *Anything doing tonight? Do you fancy going to the cinema with me?* **2** *(informal)* can you help?: *I need a lift into town. Anything doing?*

***anything* goes** anything is permitted; there are no rules for work or behaviour: *Don't imagine, because you have more freedom than in most schools, that anything goes. / In our modern society, anything goes.* Note that there is no change of tense: *It will be (*or *It was) a case of anything goes.*

**if *anything* happens to sb** *(euphemistic)* if sb dies, especially in an accident, or is seriously injured.

***anything* 'in it** → **something, anything, nothing etc '*in* it**

***anything* 'in it for sb** → **something, anything, nothing etc '*in* it for sb**

***anything* like** at all near; to any degree (used with a negative, in a question, or in an if-clause): *He isn't anything like as clever as his brother. / If this weekend is anything like the summer camp you've told us about, then it will be fantastic.* Also **anywhere near:** *Your car isn't anywhere near as fast as ours!* Also (with positive forms) **nothing like; nowhere near:** *This exam's nothing like as easy as last year's.*

***anything* out of the ordinary/usual** → ***ordinary***

**come/fall *apart* at the seams** → ***come***

**an *apology* for sth** an example of bad quality of sth: *I'm sorry, but this is rather an apology for lunch—we'll have a good meal this evening.*

**to all *appearances*** apparently; as far as a person can judge from looking at or observing sb/sth: *The house was to all appearances unoccupied. / Although to all appearances a normal healthy child, David suffered from asthma.*

**the *apple* of sb's eye** a person or thing that is dearly loved, especially treasured: *Rosalind is the apple of her father's eye.*

**in *apple*-pie order** neatly and tidily arranged: *I'm sure he'll have left his papers in apple-pie order.*

**tied to his mother's/wife's '*apron* strings** → ***tied***

**(come) out of the *ark*** → ***come***

**cost an *arm* and a leg** → ***cost* (sb) a pretty penny**

**the strong/long *arm* of the law** → ***strong***

**(keep/hold sb/sth) at *arm's* length** → ***keep***

**an *armchair* critic, expert, cricketer etc** a person who offers criticisms about an art, study, or sport, in which he has never actively taken part.

***armed* to the teeth (with sth)** *(informal)* equipped with or carrying many weapons or many articles having a definite purpose: *The tourists stepped out of the coach, armed to the teeth with cameras, binoculars, and guidebooks.*

**up in *arms*** *(informal)* protesting; showing anger, opposition, and disapproval: *Local parents are up in arms about threats to close two of the town's secondary schools.*

***as* and when** whenever; at such times as: *This tap gives you instant hot water as and when required.*

***as* for sb/sth** referring to or turning to the subject of sb/sth: *I like Muriel—but as for George, I wouldn't care if I never saw him again.*

***as* if** (used to show anger at or disapproval of a suggestion, explanation etc): *As if you expect me to believe that! / As if I really cared!*

**it isn't *as* if** or **it's not as if** it is not true that: *It isn't as if he didn't recognize me! I just stood there and he walked straight past!*

***as* if/though I would, anybody could etc** (used to deny a possibility): *'Don't tell the boss I said that, will you?' 'Oh, Alice, as if I would!'*

***as* it is/was** in the state of affairs that exists/existed: *We won't be able to buy a new car this year—we've only got just enough money for a holiday as it is.*

***as* it were** if it may be expressed in this way: *What is shown on television is, as it were, a reflection of what society is like.* Also **so to speak.**

***as* you were** → ***you***

**what more could one *ask?*** → ***what***

***ask* after sb** enquire, through another person, about sb's health and well-being: *Tell Anna I was asking after her.*

***ask* for one's cards** → ***get* one's cards**

***ask* for it** *(informal)* behave in such a way that you deserve to be corrected, scolded, punished: *Been pushed out, has he? Well, he's been asking for it. / 'You're always so sharp with people, aren't you?' 'No, I'm not—only if they ask for it.'*

***ask* for the moon** → ***cry*/ask for the moon**

***ask*/look for trouble** *(informal)* behave in a way that is likely to involve you in trouble, especially an accident, fight, or illness: *They're asking for trouble, leaving young children alone in a house. / You could see right away that they'd come here looking for trouble.* Note that this is usually used in continuous tenses.

***ask* sb in** invite a neighbour, salesman, or casual caller inside your house to discuss sth, have a cup of tea etc: *Don't leave him outside, Peter. Ask him in.*

**if you ˌ*ask* ˈme** in my opinion (usually used when the opinion has not been asked for): *If you ask me, Mark shouldn't have bought that car—it's just not worth it. / 'I don't think you two will ever get on, if you ask me.' 'We weren't asking you, so shut up!'*

***ask* me another** *(informal)* I don't know; I can't answer your question: *'What's the population of Wales?' 'Ask me another.'* Also **don't ask me.**

***ask* sb out** invite sb to a special occasion such as a dinner or party, whether mentioned or not: *We can't come round on Saturday, I'm sorry. We've been asked out to a dance that evening. / Surprise, surprise! So Rob's finally asked you out! I am pleased!*

***ask* sb over/round** invite a friend to come to your house for a meal, drink etc: *Why don't we ask Shirley and Neil round one evening?*

**I ˈ*ask* you** (used to show surprise or other strong feeling): *Well, I ask you! What a nerve that chap has—coming in here and just taking my tape-recorder without my permission! / Not another day when it rains the whole time! I ask you!*

**be sb's for the *asking* ⟶ (can) *have*/get sth for the asking**

**(can) have/get sth for the *asking* ⟶ *have***

**it's *asking* a lot (of/from sb/sth)** you want or expect a lot of, or too much, work, help, or self-sacrifice from sb/sth: *It's asking a lot, I know, but could you go instead of me?* Also **it's a lot to ask (of/from sb/sth):** *A chance to do a day's work for a living wage is not a lot to ask, but it's more than many people get.*

**be *at* sb ⟶ *get*/be at sb**

***at* all 1** to the slightest degree (used with a negative, in a question, or in an if-clause): *I didn't know that at all. / If you're at all unhappy about marrying him, then don't.* **2** anyway; even so: *I'm surprised she came at all.*

**be *at* it** *(informal)* be doing sth such as work: *You've been hard at it for five hours now without a break. Surely you can take half an hour off for a cup of tea and a sandwich?*

**make an *attempt* on sth ⟶ *make***

**make an *attempt* on sb's life ⟶ *make***

**pay *attention* (to sb/sth) ⟶ *pay***

***avoid* sb/sth like the plague** *(informal)* dislike or fear sb/sth intensely and try to avoid him/it: *What's he so frightened of that he avoids women like the plague?*

**have an ˈ*axe* to grind ⟶ *have***

# B

**a *babe* in arms** an infant too young to sit up or crawl about; helpless and/or harmless person: *At the family party there were all ages from babes in arms to great-grandfathers. / When it comes to buying property, he is a babe in arms.*

***babes* in the wood** simple, innocent people who are easily misled or exploited, especially a pair of young lovers or inexperienced partners in a business venture.

**sb's *baby*** *(informal)* (of a task) be sb's responsibility: *That's an invoicing problem—it's Richard's baby.*

**as smooth/soft as a *baby's* bottom ⟶ *smooth***

**behind sb's *back*** when sb is not looking, not present, or not informed, because he would not like or would disapprove of what is said or done: *You shouldn't say nasty things like that about Ruth behind her back. / The boys smoke behind his back.* See also **go behind sb's back.**

**get (sb) off one's/sb's *back* ⟶ *get***

**get on sb's *back* ⟶ *get***

**go behind sb's *back* ⟶ *go***

**on one's *back*** helpless or ill: *That glandular fever really put Sue flat on her back for months.*

**pat sb/oneself on the *back* ⟶ *pat***

**stab sb in the *back* ⟶ *stab***

***back* down** withdraw (the full extent of) a statement, claim, or accusation: *The Prime Minister is not prepared to back down over his threat to withhold the money from the steel industry. / After swearing the process was 100% safe, the manufacturers are now having to back down.*

**be *(back)* in business ⟶ *business***

**sb's *back* is turned** sb is not looking or is not present or informed: *The children laugh at him as soon as his back is turned.*

**one's *back* is up** *(informal)* you feel offended, resentful, or angry: *He started to apologize, but by that time my back was up and I wouldn't listen.* See also ***get*/put sb's back up.**

**see the *back* of sb/sth ⟶ *see***

**at the *back* of sth** the motive or reason for sth: *Fred insists that George can't act, but I think a bit of professional jealousy is at the back of it.*

**like the *back* of a bus** *(informal)* very ugly: *You know Janet Butcher—she looks like the back of a bus!*

**fall off the *back* of a lorry ⟶ *fall***

**the *back* of beyond** an isolated place or one with poor communications and little activity: *After leading a hectic business life in the city, Bob was pleased to be able to retire to the back of beyond.*

**know sth like the *back* of one's hand ⟶ *know***

**have (got) eyes in the *back* of one's head ⟶ *have***

**talk through the *back* of one's head/neck ⟶ *talk***

**at/in the *back* of one's mind** in your

thoughts or memory but not always heeded or not easily recalled: *I think your father knew in the back of his mind that he was being deceived. / There's something else at the back of my mind that I meant to say to you, but it's escaped me for the moment.*

***back* out (of sth)** withdraw from an undertaking, promise, or agreement: *After saying he would serve on the committee, he now wants to back out.*

**take a *back* seat → *take***

**a *back*-seat driver** a passenger who keeps giving the driver advice or instructions about how to control the car; sb who, without authority, interferes with the management of a business, sb's affairs etc.

**fed up (to the *back* teeth) (with sb/sth) → *fed***

**(it's) *back* to the drawing-board** sth must be planned again from the beginning because of failure, revised opinions, or changed circumstances: *The Advertising Standards Authority refused to accept our advertisement, so it's back to the drawing-board to rewrite it.*

**have (got) one's *back* to the wall → *have***

***back* sb up** give sb support; make it known that you agree with sb's argument, claim, or objection: *Can I rely on you to back me up if I propose these changes?*

***back* sth up** supplement sth to make it more effective: *The term's public lectures are backed up by a full programme of small discussion groups.* **back-up** *n, adj*: *We're prepared to give you lots of back-up. / back-up materials.*

**'*backroom* boys** people such as scientists or researchers whose work does not bring them into contact with the public or bring them public acclaim: *It's the backroom boys in the space centre, as well as the astronauts in space, who deserve recognition.*

**a kick up the *backside* → a *kick* in the pants**

***backwards* and forwards** in one direction and then the opposite, repeatedly or often: *He rocked the stone backwards and forwards until it loosened enough to roll out.* Also **back and forth; to and fro:** *His wife had been going back and forth to hospital all week.*

**not (so/too) *bad*** *(informal)* quite good really: *We were surprised that the weather turned out to be not bad after all. / 'How are you feeling today, Rita?' 'Not too bad, thanks!'*

**that can't be *bad*** *(informal)* (an expression of approval): *He's just won second prize in the competition—a weekend abroad!' 'Well, that can't be bad, can it?'*

**(it's) too *bad*** *(informal)* it's unfortunate; it's a pity, but nothing can be done about it: *Too bad that you don't like what I've done—but you'll just have to accept it, that's all. / It really is too bad that the play's been cancelled. / 'It's too bad of you not to have rung me to tell me you were going to be late,' complained Mum indignantly.*

**give a *bad* account of oneself → *give* a good, bad etc account of oneself**

**a *bad*/rotten apple** one of a group of people who is dishonest or disobedient and who has an unfavourable effect on the good ones: *In every police force, there are bound to be a few rotten apples.*

**in sb's *bad*/books → in sb's *good*/bad/black books**

***bad* blood (between sb and sb else)** ill-feeling or enmity between two people: *There's been bad blood between Miss Randall and Mr Smith ever since she was promoted above him.*

**a *bad* egg/lot** *(slang, old-fashioned)* an untrustworthy or dishonest person.

**come to a *bad* end → *come***

**make the best of a *bad* job → *make* the best of sth**

***bad* language** swear words; talk that includes obscene words: *Please don't use bad language in front of the children.* See also **strong language/words.**

***bad*/hard/tough luck!** *(informal)* (an expression of sympathy on sb's misfortune): *So she didn't inherit a penny? That was hard luck, after all the years she'd worked for him!* Also **hard lines!**

***bad* news travels fast** *(saying)* people are quicker to pass on bad news than good news.

**take sth in *bad* part → *take* sth in good/bad part**

**turn up like a *bad* penny → *turn***

**good riddance (to *bad* rubbish) → *good***

**(a) *bad*/poor show!** *(becoming old-fashioned)* (a comment on) sth disappointing, unlucky, to be disapproved of etc: *'I crashed the car yesterday.' 'Oh, bad show!'* See also **(a) *good* show!**

**a *bad* taste in the/one's mouth** a feeling of distaste or disgust about sth you have seen, heard, or taken part in: *The film left a bad taste in his mouth.*

**go from *bad* to worse → *go***

**do sb a *bad* turn → *do* sb a good/bad turn**

***bad* value for money → (good/bad) *value* for money**

**in a *bad* way** in a very poor or dangerous state: *One of the two survivors was in a very bad way when we picked them up.*

**a *bad* workman blames his tools** *(saying)* (said by sb who excuses his own inefficiency by complaining about the quality of his tools or the material he has to work with).

***badly* off → *well*/badly off**

***badly* off (for sth) → *well*/badly off (for sth)**

**in the *bag*** *(informal)* already achieved or certain to be so very soon: *With a three-goal lead and only ten minutes left to play, victory was in the bag.*

**let the cat out of the *bag* → *let***

***bag* and baggage** with all your luggage and/or movable possessions: *His landlady put him out, bag and baggage, the next morning.*

**a *bag* of bones** *(informal)* a very thin or emaciated person.

**a *bag* of nerves** *(informal)* a nervous, easily agitated person.

**a *bag* of tricks** *(informal)* all the equipment that is needed to do sth, especially when this is viewed as having a strangely mysterious effect: *I'll just go and get my bag of tricks from the van and we'll have your television set repaired in no time at all, madam!*

***bags* I (do) sth** *(informal)* I, as first to speak, claim the right to do or have sth in preference to anyone else present: *'The boys can sleep here.' 'Bags I the top bunk,' said Tommy quickly.* Also **I bags . . . :** *I bags the front seat!*

***bags* of** *(slang)* = lots of.

***bail* sb/sth out** → ***bale*/bail sb/sth out**

**a *baker's* dozen** 13.

**in the *balance*** (of events, the future etc) still uncertain and at a critical point where a decision may be taken to follow one of two ways: *The future of the school is still (or still hangs) in the balance.*

**on *balance*** after comparing the value, importance, or merits of two or more things: *Time is money for businessmen, so that on balance the cost of flying is not much greater than that of travelling overland. / 'Isn't he a difficult man to work with?' 'On balance, no. You saw him at his worst that day.'*

**throw sb off his *balance*** → ***throw***

**as *bald* as a coot** completely bald or with no hair on the top of the head.

***bale*/bail sb/sth out** help sb, an organization etc, in need, especially by providing money: *The government decided the only solution was to bale the company out. / In some parts of the country, because of the lack of money, parents want to bail out the schools for their children's sakes, and they have the cash to do this.*

**on the *ball*** *(informal)* shrewd and intelligent either in general or in a particular respect: *He looks rather a simpleton, but he's on the ball when it comes to investing.*

**have (got) the *ball* at one's feet** → ***have***

**the *ball* is in sb's court** sb, having received an offer, challenge etc, must decide what to do or make the next move: *We've shown, by inviting them to Mary's wedding, that we wish to forget our quarrel. The ball is in their court now.*

**a *ball* of fire** a highly competent, lively, and successful person: *Since her appointment, she's reorganized the sales force, halved the company's debts, and worked out a profit-sharing scheme—a real ball of fire, in fact!*

**set/start/keep the '*ball* rolling** → ***set***

**the *balloon* goes up** *(informal)* sth serious, such as a war, begins: *I managed to catch a quick sleep in the afternoon, before the balloon went up, and the battle began in the evening.*

**slip on a *banana* skin** → ***slip***

**jump/climb on the *bandwagon*** → ***jump***

**go with a *bang*** → ***go* with a bang/swing**

***bang* goes sth** *(informal)* that puts an end to a particular plan, hope etc: *The car repairs cost me over a week's pay, so bang goes our evening out at the theatre.*

***bang* one's head against a brick wall** *(informal)* try for a long time to achieve sth, but not be successful; make no progress in an action or enquiry because of an obstruction: *I realized they weren't even listening to my protests. I was just banging my head against a brick wall!*

***bang*/spot on** *(informal)* absolutely accurate in an answer, estimate, or description: *'I suppose you want your money back?' 'You're bang on there, mate.' / What a mimic! His imitations of politicians, in particular, are bang on. / 'Well, I work out the percentage profit on the deal as 31.8%. Does that agree with your figures?' 'Yes, it's spot on; I've checked it on my calculator.'*

***bank* on sb/sth** rely on sb/sth; have confidence that sb will act or sth will happen as expected: *I'm banking on you to support me (or on your support). / 'Is it going to stay dry for our fete this afternoon, Mr Smith?' 'I wouldn't bank on it.'*

**a *baptism* of fire** a difficult or violent introduction to a way of life, profession, or new activity: *His first night on the beat turned out to be a baptism of fire for the young policeman. / The new Defence Secretary faces a baptism of fire over his decision to re-allocate money amongst the different sections of the armed forces.*

**be all over *bar* the shouting** → ***all***

**the *bare* bones of sth** the basic facts of a story, subject etc, without supplementary background, details, or interpretation: *Given only the bare bones of the case, most people would have felt quite sure that Brown had killed his wife.*

**into the *bargain*** as well; in addition: *She gave us a cup of tea and, into the bargain, some useful information. / So I had a nasty fall and broke my watch into the bargain.*

**(not) *bargain* for sth** (not) expect sth; (not) include sth in your plans or arrangements: *We hadn't bargained for such bad weather. / Giving birth to triplets was certainly more than Jill bargained for!*

**wouldn't touch sb/sth with a *barge*-pole** → ***touch***

**sb's *bark* is worse than his bite** *(saying)* sb appears bad-tempered or is apt to scold or threaten but will do no real harm to others.

***bark* up the wrong tree** be mistaken and direct your efforts, enquiries, or accusations towards the wrong person or thing: *Evans may have been the obvious suspect, but I think that the police were barking up the wrong tree that time.*

**have (got) sb over a *barrel*** → ***have***

**behind *bars*** in or into prison: *The thief was caught and spent the next two years behind bars. / He would like to see all such vandals put behind bars.*

**put all one's eggs in/into one *basket*** → ***put***

**off one's own *bat*** *(informal)* independently, without asking for help; voluntarily, without being prompted or forced: *He didn't ask anyone's advice when he wanted to buy a house—he just went ahead and did it off his own bat.*

**not *bat* an eyelid/eye** show no sign of being concerned, disturbed, or dismayed: *He watched the whole grisly proceedings without even batting an eyelid.*

**like a *bat* out of hell** *(informal)* very fast: *If there was a fire, I wouldn't wait to sound the alarm—I'd be off like a bat out of hell!*

**with *bated* breath** scarcely breathing because tense with anxiety, fear, or expectation: *The competitors waited with bated breath for the judges to announce the results.*

**throw the baby out with the *bathwater*** ⟶ ***throw***

**have (got) *bats* in the belfry** ⟶ ***have***

***bawl* sb out** *(slang)* rebuke or scold sb severely, especially in front of others: *He got bawled out by the referee.*

**keep/hold sb/sth at *bay*** ⟶ ***keep***

**the *be*-all and end-all (of)** the whole extent of; the supreme aim or interest of: *He refuses to accept that the be-all and end-all of our existence is a life with God. / Football isn't the be-all and end-all of life, you know.*

***be* that as it may** whether that is true or not (though it probably is): *'It's a film that has been highly praised by the critics.' 'Be that as it may, I didn't enjoy it.'* Also **that's as (it) 'may be.**

**broad in the *beam*** ⟶ ***broad***

**on/off *beam*** having the right or relevant/wrong or irrelevant idea or approach: *You're way off beam with your estimate.*

**on one's/its *beam*-ends** having almost no more money, stocks, or other resources: *Can you lend me some money? I'm on my beam-ends till Friday. / As things are going at present, the whole of British industry will be on its beam-ends in a year or two.*

**not (have) a *bean*** ⟶ ***have***

***bear*/carry one's cross(es)** suffer the trouble(s) that life brings to you: *We all have our crosses to bear. / Blind from birth, he carried his cross bravely.*

***bear* sb down** overcome sb's strength; cause sb hardship (usually used in the passive): *He was borne down by poverty.*

***bear* down on sb/sth** *(formal)* move in a fast, threatening way towards sb/sth: *Enemy ships bore down relentlessly on the small group of boats at the harbour entrance.*

***bear* fruit** produce a good and desired result: *The new teaching methods had borne fruit at last and all the students passed the exam.*

**a '*bear* garden** *(informal)* a place or occasion where there is much noise and rough behaviour: *You can't leave these kids for five minutes without them turning the classroom into a bear garden!*

***bear* heavily on sb** cause hardship or suffering to sb: *The extra responsibilities of his new job bore heavily on his health, and he had several heart attacks.*

**bring sth to *bear* on/upon sb/sth** ⟶ **bring**

***bear* on/upon sth** *(formal)* have relevance to or a significant effect on sth: *How does this bear on what Peter said earlier?*

***bear* sb/sth out** confirm or support sb's statement or a theory, opinion, or suspicion: *I was working late—the office cleaner will bear me out. / The claims made for the fertilizer were not borne out by the results.*

***bear* the brunt (of sth)** bear the heaviest share of an attack, loss, or deprivation: *The private motorist, as usual, has to bear the brunt of the increase in the tax on petrol announced today.*

***bear* up** *(informal)* show courage and ability to cope in hard conditions, grief, or pain: *His widow bore up wonderfully at the funeral. / I try to bear up, but it's awful to have to live in an institution after having had a home of your own.*

***bear* with sb/sth** tolerate sb/sth; excuse or be patient with sb/sth: *I've borne with your drunkenness and bad tempers long enough, and now I'm going to leave you. / If you will bear with me a moment, sir, I should like to explain a little more fully.*

**like a *bear* with a sore head** surly; short-tempered: *Dad's always like a bear with a sore head when he gets up, so nobody asks him a favour till well after breakfast.*

**have a, no, some etc *bearing* on/upon sth** ⟶ ***have***

***beat* a path to sb's door** ⟶ **the *world* beats a path to sb's door**

***beat* a retreat** signal a military retreat; go or run back or away from sb/sth you fear or wish to avoid: *When I saw the bull I beat a hasty retreat!*

***beat* about the bush** talk about a subject indirectly; take too long before saying or asking what is on your mind: *Let's not beat about the bush, Miss Brown. I've sent for you to discuss your work, which has become most unsatisfactory recently.*

***beat* sb at his 'own game** do better than sb in his own special work, skill, or activity; defeat sb by doing as he does, but more successfully: *If you thought someone was cheating you, would you challenge him or try to beat him at his own game?*

***beat* one's brain(s)** ⟶ ***rack*/beat one's brain(s)**

***beat* one's 'brains out** *(informal)* struggle with a long and difficult task: *We've spent months beating our brains out to think of ways of raising more money.* See also ***rack*/beat one's brain(s); *blow*/dash one's/sb's 'brains out.**

***beat* one's breast** display your feelings of guilt, distress, or shame openly (sometimes used to imply that you are too vehement to be sincere): *If anything happens to the children while you're out enjoying yourself, don't come beating your breast to me about it afterwards.*

***beat* sb down** make sb reduce the price he asks for an article: *The car is worth all of what you are asking, so don't let him beat you down for the sake of a quick sale!*

***beat* sb hands down** → ***win* hands down**

***beat* sb/sth hollow** defeat sb completely; be greatly superior to, better than, sb/sth: *The students took on the staff in a game of volleyball and beat them hollow. / I thought I had a nice garden myself but this one beats it hollow.*

***beat* sb/sth into a cocked hat** → ***knock*/beat sb/sth into a cocked hat**

***beat* it** *(slang)* go away: *'Beat it!' the attendant told the boys. 'This is a car park, not a playground.' / The party was getting a bit rowdy for my liking, so I beat it.*

**can you *beat* it/that?** (an exclamation used about sth that is very or unusually annoying, foolish, or stupid): *Can you beat it? They've sent us the wrong size yet again!*

***beat* the drum (for sb/sth)** try to attract public attention to sb/sth: *The Prime Minister has beaten the drum for our exports on a recent trip abroad.*

***beat*/knock the living daylights out of sb** *(slang)* beat sb brutally, showing no mercy: *Jack used to get home drunk from the pub several nights a week and beat the living daylights out of his wife and kids. It's a wonder they're still alive.*

***beat* sb 'to it** *(informal)* get somewhere, invent or discover sth, complete a task, or put a product on the market before sb else does; narrowly defeat a competitor for an award, elected post, or business contract: *I hurried home to tell my wife the good news, but somebody had beaten me to it. / Mr Lowe has scored 25 points but Miss Jones has just beaten him to it with 26.*

***beat* sb up** *(informal)* injure sb with heavy blows from fists, sticks etc: *The store was raided and an elderly night watchman beaten up, shortly after midnight.* **beating-up** *n.*

**a rod/stick to *beat* sb with** → ***rod***

**off the *beaten* track** far away from anywhere that people normally go to: *He lived in a little hut right off the beaten track.*

**it *beats* me (why, how etc)** I cannot understand or explain sth: *It beats me how he can afford it. / What he does with his time beats me.*

**the *beauty* of (doing) sth** the special convenience of or the advantage gained by doing or having sth: *The beauty of (having) a small car is that you can often find a parking space when others can't.*

**'*beauty* sleep** sleep (often used humorously to speak of long sleep that will refresh and restore sb): *Look at the time! You won't get your beauty sleep tonight.* Note that this is usually used with a possessive.

***beaver* away** *(informal)* work very hard, willingly and busily: *He beavers away in his study every evening writing articles for learned journals.* Also **work like a beaver.**

**at sb's *beck* and call** ready or required to obey sb and do just as he wishes: *In return for a home she was expected to be at her aunt's beck and call 16 hours a day.*

***become* of sb/sth** happen to sb/sth (usually preceded by ***what*** or ***whatever***): *Whatever became of old Willy? I've not heard anything about him for years!*

**a *bed* of roses** *(informal)* luxurious, pleasant, or easy conditions of life or work (often used in the negative): *I'm not disappointed because I never expected our marriage to be a bed of roses.* See also **(not) be *roses* all the way.**

**have (got) a *bee* in one's bonnet (about sth)** → ***have***

***beef* about sb/sth** *(slang)* complain about sb/sth: *She's always beefing about her neighbours.*

***beef* sth up** *(informal)* strengthen sth by adding an extra ingredient, further support, or vitality: *The introduction to the book needs beefing up a bit to arouse the reader's interest.*

**make a *bee*-line for sb/sth** go quickly by the most direct way towards sb/sth: *At parties Joe always makes a bee-line for the most attractive girl.*

**have (*been* and) gone and done it (now/again)** → ***gone***

**(not) (all) *beer* and skittles** *(informal)* (not) (all) fun, pleasure, and entertainment: *We call ourselves a Social Club, but it's not all beer and skittles. We do a lot of useful community work. / Once you have a family to support, you'll learn that there's more to life than beer and skittles.*

**the *bees'* knees** *(slang)* sb/sth wonderful, or exactly what you want: *Patricia thinks she is the bees' knees in every way—that's what makes her so insufferable. / A plate of hot soup right now would be the bees' knees, wouldn't it, Sam?* See also **the *cat's* pyjamas/whiskers.**

***beetle* off** *(slang)* go or hurry away: *Why don't you children beetle off and give us some peace?*

**(and) not *before* time** → ***not***

***beg*, borrow, or steal sth** obtain sth by any means you can: *'I haven't got a life-jacket.' 'Then beg, borrow, or steal one—the skipper won't let you on board without one.'*

***beg* the question** *(formal)* assume that the truth of a statement or proposition is also the proof or explanation of it: *Telling a child who asks why his dachshund has short legs that all dachshunds have short legs is begging the question.*

***beg* to differ** *(formal)* claim the right to express an opposite or different opinion (usually used with the first person subject): *'I think we should adopt the manager's proposals.' 'Well, I beg to differ.' / The advertisements stated that the film was suitable for older children; some of us beg to differ.*

**to *begin*/start with 1** for a start; as a first item, statement, reason, when another or others will follow: *The house is not at all suitable. It's too big to begin with and it's too near* *the main road.* **2** originally; at/from the start; before (doing or saying) anything else: *This was marsh land to begin with, but just see what good drainage has done for it. / 'I never really wanted this job.' 'Then why didn't you say so to begin with?'* Also **in the 'first place.**

**fall/be *behind* (with sth)** ⟶ ***fall***

**have (got) bats in the *belfry*** ⟶ ***have***

**(not) *believe* a word of it** or **not believe a word sb says** (not) believe sb/sth at all; (not) trust sb to tell the truth: *Some people say he was a spy during the war, but I don't believe a word of it.*

**(not) *believe* one's ears/eyes** be so surprised at what you hear/see that at first you cannot believe it: *I couldn't believe my ears when the judge announced I'd won! / We could hardly believe our eyes—there he was, our son back home after all those long years!* Note that this is usually used with **can't/couldn't.**

***believe* in sb/sth 1** trust in, have confidence or faith in sb/sth: *You can most certainly believe in Jonathan—he'll never let you down! / When he became unemployed he found he could no longer believe in his own abilities.* **2** be sure that sb/sth that cannot be seen does really exist: *Do you believe in fairies? / He was a deep believer in God.* **3** support the idea of or favour sth: *He believes in giving people a second chance if they fail. / She doesn't believe in sending her children away to boarding-school.*

**would you *believe* it (?/!)** (an exclamation of astonishment, joy, or dismay): *Would you believe it! Somebody has let down all the tyres of my car!*

***believe* it or not** whether you believe it or not (usually used for emphasis without implying real doubt about being believed): *I am still, believe it or not, very nervous about speaking in public. / It's the usual excuse, I know, but—believe it or not—I had to wait 25 minutes for a bus.*

**will *believe* it/that when one sees it** *(informal)* doubt that sth will ever happen or be done: *'John says he'll pay you back the money he owes you on Friday.' 'I'll believe that when I see it!'*

***believe* (you) 'me** you can/should believe me (used to emphasize an assertion, promise, or threat: *He's the worst singer in the world, believe you me. / 'You should write to the firm and complain.' 'Believe you me, I will.'*

**if you, they etc can *believe* ˌthat, you'll, they'll etc believe 'anything** *(informal)* you etc must be very stupid or foolish if you believe that: *My father listened to the party political broadcast with a believe-that-and-you'll-believe-anything look on his face.*

**be saved by the *bell*** ⟶ ***saved***

***bell* the cat** *(old-fashioned)* do sth which is dangerous to yourself in order to help or protect other people: *Somebody must complain to the Manager about the shortage of money in the department, but who's going to bell the cat?*

**have a *bellyful* (of sb/sth)** ⟶ ***have***

***below* par** ⟶ ***above/below par***

**below the *belt*** *(informal)* (of an action, comment, attack etc) unfair; not following the accepted rules: *Giving the workers the sack while they were on strike was very much below the belt. / The boss's rude comments really hit below the belt.*

**under one's *belt*** already achieved in your experience, and so making you feel more confident: *With ten years' experience under his belt, Mark was ready to start his own business. / Once I'd got a couple of good answers under my belt, I didn't feel particularly nervous about the rest of the exam.*

***belt* up** *(slang)* = shut up: *'Belt up!' their father said angrily. 'You do nothing all day but quarrel with each other.'*

**round the *bend*/twist** *(informal)* mad or insane; overwrought with anger, exasperation, worry, or fear: *I always thought he was odd but now I know he's definitely round the bend. / Why can't you do as the doctor tells you? You're driving (or sending) me round the twist the way you're carrying on.*

***bend*/lean/fall over backwards to do sth** try very hard to help, please, or satisfy sb: *Because he was the boy's stepfather he bent over backwards to be good to him.*

**be *bent* on (doing) sth** *(informal)* be determined about (doing/having) sth: *I could tell, the moment they went out, that those two boys were bent on mischief. / If your son is bent on marrying her, then there's not much you can do to stop him.*

**at *best*/worst** taking the most/least favourable or hopeful view: *Smoking is acknowledged to be at best unwholesome and expensive, and at worst lethal. / We'll find somewhere to stay the night. At worst all that can happen is that we'll have to sleep in the car.*

***(all)* for the *best*** a good and beneficial result, though this may not be foreseen: *One never knows what may be for the best in this world. If I'd got the job I wanted I might never have met you.*

**with the *best* (of them)** (can do sth) as well as anyone; as ably as the best in a sport, art, or skill: *He was one of those scholars who can write a learned treatise with the best of them yet can't keep up an ordinary conversation.*

**one's *best* bib and tucker** your best or finest clothes: *Everybody will be wearing their best bib and tucker on Sunday morning.*

**put one's *best* foot forward** ⟶ ***put***

**have (got) the *best* of sth** ⟶ ***have***

**make the *best* of sth** ⟶ ***make***

**the *best* of both worlds** the best or the most attractive or advantageous of two ways of life, policies, or philosophies: *You want the best of both worlds—to live near the town centre for the shops, but far enough away to avoid all the noise and traffic.*

**the *best* of (British) luck (to sb)** *(informal)* (a form of well-wishing; sometimes sarcastic, especially when **British** is included): *'The best of luck to you in your exam,' Peter said as they shook hands on parting. / If your friend thinks he can make a living from writing poetry, the best of British luck to him.* Also **the best of British.**

**the *best*/pick of the bunch** the best of a group of persons or set of things: *Frankly, I don't care for your neighbours. You didn't get the pick of the bunch there, did you?*

**(even) at the *best* of times** (even) when conditions are favourable: *'Perhaps your son feels shy with strangers?' 'Partly that, but he's not very communicative at the best of times.' / 'Even at the best of times I couldn't eat all that!' he protested to the nurse who had brought him the tray.*

**the *best*/better part of sth** the most or the greatest/greater part of sth: *The baby, fortunately, spent the best part of the journey asleep.*

**(not) with the *best* will in the world** (cannot do sth) however much you are willing or eager to try or please: *It's impossible, even with the best will in the world, to satisfy everybody all the time.*

**you *bet!*** → ***you***

***bet* one's bottom dollar on sth** or **bet one's bottom dollar (that) . . .** *(informal)* stake all that you have (left); be or feel certain of/that . . . : *I'd have bet my bottom dollar on his honesty, but I was proved wrong.*

***bet* one's life on sth** or **bet one's life (that) . . .** *(informal)* be or feel certain that sth is a fact or will happen: *I'll bet my life those were imitation pearls. / 'Will you be coming to my party?' 'You (can) bet your life on it* (or *You bet your life I will)!'* Note that it is usually used with ***will, would, can,*** or ***could.***

**change (sb/sth) for the *better*** → ***change* (sb/sth) for the better/worse**

**sb had *better* (do sth)** → ***had***

**take a turn for the *better*** → ***take* a turn for the better/worse**

**to *(better* etc) advantage** → ***advantage***

**have seen/known *better* days** → ***seen***

**be (all, none etc) the *better*/worse for sth** be made better/worse by (doing) sth: *He says they're starving him at that hospital, but at his weight, he'll be all the better for it. / The window frames would be none the worse for a coat of paint.* Note that this idiom is also used with other verbs such as ***look***, ***feel*** and ***seem***. Other adverbs commonly used are ***much***, ***little***, and ***(not) any.***

**sb's *better* half** *(informal)* sb's wife: *We've met Mr Black before but not his better half.*

**against one's *better* judgment** although feeling and thinking that your action, decision, is unwise: *I agreed against my better judgment to let the children go swimming on their own and was very uneasy until they returned.*

***better* late than never** *(saying)* it is better to do sth such as arrive or complete a task late than not do it at all: *Here's a book for your birthday, Jane. I know it was yesterday, but better late than never!*

**see sb/sth in a *better* light** → ***see* sb/sth in a different/better/new light**

***better* luck next time** *(informal)* (a way of comforting sb who has failed in a game, sporting event, examination etc and who may have another chance to succeed).

***better*/worse off** richer/poorer; happier/unhappier; more/less safe, comfortable, or fit: *I've only got a broken leg. There are patients far worse off than me in here. / I'll tell you this: Jack would be better off without a wife than the way he lives now.* **better-off, worse-off** *adj, n*: *houses where the 'better-off (people) live; give it to some 'worse-off fellow.*

**for *better* or (for) worse** whether the result, which may be known or unknown, proves to be good or bad; whatever the possible results are: *I've just left my husband, for better or worse.*

**the *better* part of sth** → **the *best*/better part of sth**

**discretion is the *better* part of valour** → ***discretion***

***better* (to be) safe than sorry** *(saying)* it is better to be over-careful and take precautions that may not be necessary than to risk an accident, illness, or failure that you will regret: *I think I had time to overtake that lorry, but I didn't do so—better safe than sorry.*

***better* the devil you know than the devil/one you don't** *(saying)* it may be better to endure sb or sth bad or unsatisfactory, but which you have learned to cope with, such as a boss, system of government, or personal relationship, than to risk a change for sb/sth entirely unknown.

***between* ourselves, you and me etc** as a secret, as a private matter or confidential information to be shared only by us etc: *I was speaking to him yesterday, and, between ourselves, Mary, I think the man's going off his head. / 'How much money did you lend him anyway?' 'That's between him and me.'* Also *(informal)* **between you, me, and the bedpost/gatepost.**

***betwixt* and between** midway between two kinds, states, or sizes; neither one thing or another but having some qualities of both: *Some of them were clever and some of them very stupid but most were betwixt and between.* Also **in between**: *'Would you call this dress blue or green?' 'It's kind of in between, isn't it?*

**one's best *bib* and tucker** → ***best***

***bide* one's time** wait for a good opportunity or suitable occasion to do sth: *He didn't know whether the police had dismissed him from their enquiries or were biding their time while they collected more evidence.*

***big* brother (is watching you)** the state, through a government department, police force, or surveillance system (knows what you do and will punish, restrict, or reward you accordingly): *We live in a databank society* *where big brother, if not actually watching you, can quickly check on you if he wants to.*

**a/the *big* cheese** *(slang, derogatory)* sb who is, or thinks he is, the most important person in a group: *Stand by, everyone—here comes the big cheese himself!*

**(a) *big* deal** an important transaction or matter; ((*informal)* often used without ***a, the*** etc as an exclamation and often ironically): *He's off to Paris to discuss some big deal with a French manufacturer. / 'I've got a complimentary ticket for the football match on Saturday.' 'Oh, big deal! They've been trying to get rid of them all week.'*

**a *big* fish in a little pond** sb who is important but only in a small community or a minor or limited field of activity. **a little fish in a big pond** sb of no special importance in a large community etc.

**too *big* for one's boots** → ***too***

**a *big* gun/noise/shot** *(slang)* a high-ranking or important person, sometimes implying conceit or self-importance. Also **a bigwig:** *'What does Roger's Dad do?' 'He's a bigwig in one of the nationalized industries. He works somewhere in London.'*

**a *big* hand** *(informal)* enthusiastic applause: *Here he is—James Townley—give him a big hand, ladies and gentlemen.*

**(like) a/one *big* happy family** → ***one***

**what's the *big* idea?** → ***what***

**a '*big* mouth** *(informal)* sb who boasts, promises, or threatens more than he will do, or who claims status or knowledge he does not have: *'Does he really have so much influence in the council?' 'Of course he hasn't—he's just a big mouth.'*

**a *(big)* night out** → **a *night* on the town**

***big* oaks from little acorns grow** → ***tall*/great/big oaks from little acorns grow**

***big* of sb** *(informal)* kind or generous of sb (usually used ironically): *'You can have the window seat if you like.' 'That's big of you—I'd already reserved it!'*

***big* talk/words** *(informal)* boastful talk, promises, or threats: *We've heard all that big talk before from party leaders who promise everything their predecessors have failed to do for the last thirty years. We just don't believe it!*

**the '*big*/'small time** *(informal)* the more/less prestigious and highly-paid levels of the public entertainment business: *Success in a talent-spotting competition brought him a chance to get into the big time.* **big/small-time** *adj*: *a small-time cabaret singer.* **big/small-timer** *n.*

**in a *big*/small way** on a big/small scale; very much or only a little: *Her father was a poultry-farmer in a small way somewhere in Devon.*

**have (got) *bigger* fish to fry** → ***have* (got) other/bigger fish to fry**

**one's eyes are *bigger* than one's belly/stomach/tummy** → ***eyes***

**a clean *bill* of health** → ***clean***

**as smooth as a *billiard* table** → ***smooth***

**like *billy*-(h)o** *(informal)* vigorously, hard, or fast: *He had to work like billy-ho to finish the painting in time. / It was raining like billy-ho.*

***bind*/tie sb hand and foot (to sb/sth)** take away or severely restrict sb's freedom of movement or choice of action: *The daughter can only go out now for an hour or two, and if her aged parents become more senile, then she'll be really bound hand and foot.*

***bind* sb over (to keep the peace)** *(legal)* requires sb to behave as ordered by a judge or magistrate or else appear before the court again: *The younger of the accused was given a suspended sentence, which is the equivalent, in English law, of being bound over to keep the peace.*

**the *bird* has flown** sb has escaped, gone away (before sth planned concerning him can be done): *When the police arrived at his lodgings with a warrant for his arrest the bird had flown.*

**a *bird* of passage** sb who just passes through a place or does not stay there long: *'But you've often been in London!' 'Only as a bird of passage.'*

**a *bird's*-eye view (of)** a view from above, as from the top of a hill, tower or as provided by an aerial photograph or drawing; brief overall survey of: *Bird's-eye views of Welsh castles. / Stuart's course of lectures gives a bird's-eye view of Shakespeare's plays.*

**(strictly) for the *birds*** *(informal)* sth that only stupid, simple, or weak people would believe, like, or want to do or have: *Tommy used to think poetry readings and art exhibitions were strictly for the birds, but he's gradually getting his mind broadened.*

**the *birds* and the bees** *(euphemistic)* matters concerned with sex in human beings, especially as told to children: *Roy is getting a big boy now—isn't it time you had a talk with him about the birds and the bees?* See also **the *facts* of life 1.**

***birds* of a feather (flock together)** *(saying)* people of similar character, habits, or tastes (seek each other's company) (usually said of a person or group of whom you disapprove): *Why blame the boy's friends for the way he behaves? Birds of a feather flock together—he could have other friends if he chose to.*

**in one's '*birthday* suit** *(informal)* wearing no clothes; naked: *Here's a picture of me in my birthday suit, aged three!*

***bit* by bit** slowly, by a gradual process or progression: *Bit by bit the patient's condition improved. / This was money we had saved bit by bit over a period of ten years.*

**not a/one *bit* (of it)** *(informal)* not at all (often used as a reply): *Was she sad when her husband died? Not a bit of it! / 'Do you mind if I borrow your car this afternoon?' 'Not one bit—go right ahead!'*

**take/get the *bit* between one's/the teeth** → ***take***

**a *bit* of a coward, fool etc** *(informal)* rather cowardly, foolish etc: *Joe's a bit of an idiot, don't you think?*

**a *bit* of all right** *(slang)* sb/sth pleasing or that you are glad to have: *'Who is that with George at the bar?' 'I don't know, but she looks a bit of all right to me. / A win on the pools would be a bit of all right for us just at the moment.*

**a *bit* on the side** *(slang)* (an act of) adultery: *Happily married or not, don't tell me you've never wanted a bit on the side!*

***bite*/snap sb's head/nose off** *(informal)* speak to or answer sb in a bad-tempered way: *It was only a suggestion—there's no need to bite my nose off! / If she can't tell people they've filled in the form wrongly without biting their heads off, then she shouldn't be a receptionist.*

***bite* one's lip** (press your lower lip behind your teeth in order to) control the dismay, disappointment, anger, objection you feel you could express: *You could tell she thought the criticism unfair, but she bit her lip and said nothing.*

***bite* one's (finger-)nails** (put or press your fingers to your mouth because you) feel tense with excitement, fear, anticipation, or impatience: *The final sequence with the runaway train had the whole audience in the cinema biting their finger-nails with excitement.* **nail-biting** *adj.* very exciting or tense: *What an exciting film—real nail-biting stuff!*

***bite* off more than one can chew** *(informal)* try or agree to do more than you are able to: *Tom said he could easily build the sun-porch himself, but, as usual, he found he had bitten off more than he could chew.*

***bite* (on) the bullet** realize that you cannot avoid an ordeal or unpleasant truth and accept it with courage or resignation: *He'll have to bite the bullet and pay up.*

***bite* the dust** *(informal)* be killed, defeated, ruined, or finished: *Many more small engineering businesses are likely to bite the dust within the next two years.*

***bite* the hand that feeds one** show ingratitude, harm, or abuse to sb who has helped you.

**the *biter* bit(ten)** sb who means to cheat another person turns out to be cheated himself: *It's much easier for an unscrupulous antique dealer to pass off a fake on you than for you to pass off a fake on him; but sometimes you hear of a case of the biter bit.*

**have/get two *bites* at/of the cherry** ⟶ **have**

***bits* and pieces** various small articles; scraps or fragments: *'Is he going straight to the station from the meeting?' 'No, he'll be back to collect his bits and pieces first.'* Also **bits and bobs; odds and ends.**

**to the *bitter* end** (of a fight or argument) until death or defeat; to the very end, however long it takes: *They won't have an easy victory for we'll fight to the bitter end. / We argued for an hour or more, Bill maintaining to the bitter end that the goal should have been disallowed.*

**a *bitter* pill to swallow** a disappointment, setback, or unpleasant fact that is hard to accept: *His father's refusal to let him study law must have been a bitter pill to swallow.*

**in the *black*** having money in one's account; not in debt: *The state-owned railway company hopes to be back in the black next year.* See also **in the *red*.**

***black* and blue** marked with bruises: *The left side of my face was black and blue for days.*

**in *black* and white 1** (of moral matters) as absolute right or wrong with no grades between them: *My grandmother has very rigid ideas of character and behaviour; she sees everything in black and white.* **2** in print or writing (used especially to state that something is legally binding): *'They're hiring the boat at their own risk, they said.' 'Well, get them to put that down in black and white before they leave.'*

**not as/so *black* as one/it is painted** not as bad as people say or seem to believe: *Most of his employees have been with him five, ten, or even twenty years, so he can't be as black as he's painted* (or *as you paint him).*

**in sb's *black* books** ⟶ **in sb's *good*/bad/black books**

**a *black* day (for sb)** a day or time when sth sad, very unpleasant, or disastrous happens (to sb): *It was a black day for this country when our party lost the election.*

**a *black* eye** an area of severe bruising and swelling around the eye, caused by an accident or deliberate blow: *How did you get that black eye?*

**a *black* look** an angry or disapproving expression on a person's face: *He continued his drunken singing despite black looks from the other passengers.*

**a *black* mark** (against sb) a note in an official record that sb has done sth wrong: *I don't know if the firm will actually sack me for having lost the contract, but it'll certainly be a black mark against me.*

***black* out** lose consciousness for a short time: *Fortunately I managed to get out of the bath before I blacked out.* **blackout** *n*: *The old chap's just had another blackout.*

***black* sth out 1** conceal lights that would make a town, buildings, vehicles etc visible by night from the air or from a distance: *During the war we had to black out our windows and switch off lights before opening an outside door.* **blackout** *n*. **2** halt, stop, or forbid transmission of television or radio programmes or coverage: *Most TV channels have been blacked out for over three weeks owing to an industrial dispute.* **blackout** *n*: *Either the rumoured earthquake never occurred or a strict blackout on information about it has been imposed by the government.*

**(the) *black* sheep (of the family)** a criminal or other person who does wrong; sb who is (considered to be) a disgrace to the family or group to which he belongs: *I'm the black sheep of the family because I didn't want to* *join my brothers and sisters in my father's business.*

**have only (got) oneself to *blame* ⟶ *have***

**a bad workman *blames* his tools ⟶ *bad***

**give sb a *blank* cheque ⟶ *give***

***blaze* a/the trail** mark a route, for example through a forest, for others to follow; be the first to do sth important or interesting that others will learn from and continue with. **trailblazer** *n*.

**(God) *bless* my soul!** *(informal)* (an exclamation of astonishment): *'Look what I've found in the garden, mother.' 'God bless my soul! Who could have dropped a wad of banknotes here?'*

**(God) *bless* your, his etc soul/heart** *(informal)* (an affectionate, or less commonly a religious, comment in connection with sb mentioned): *Your mother, God bless her soul, is the only friend I have. / I see you've done the washing-up for me, bless your heart.* Also *(humorous or ironic)* **(God) bless your, his etc little cotton socks.**

**be *blessed* with sth** *(informal)* have sth good or bad: *I've never been blessed with a good memory, and it's getting worse as I grow older! / Did you say Penelope Pennyfeather? Poor girl, what a name to be blessed with!*

**a *blessing* in disguise** sth that proves to be fortunate and beneficial although not thought to be so at first: *There's no use saying so to Anne just now, but this broken engagement may be a blessing in disguise.*

**there's none so *blind* as those who will not see ⟶ *there's* none so blind/deaf as those who will not see/hear**

**not a *blind* bit of notice, difference etc** no notice etc at all: *'You don't take a blind bit of notice of what I tell you,' the teacher said to the children. / It's not a blind bit of use protesting to your MP.*

**a *blind* date** *(informal)* a social meeting arranged between two people of opposite sexes who have not met before: *'If I bring this girl, do you think John would make up a foursome?' 'He may not be too keen on a blind date but I'll ask him.'*

**turn a *blind* eye (to sth) ⟶ *turn***

**a nod is as good as a wink (to a *blind* horse) ⟶ *nod***

**the *blind* leading the blind** *(saying)* (an example of) sb with as little ability or knowledge as the person he is trying to help or teach: *'George insisted on seeing his pal home safely, but the one's as tipsy as the other.' 'The blind leading the blind, eh?'*

**a/one's '*blind* spot** an area of vision which is blocked from sight; failure in yourself or sb to understand or accept sth.

**on the *blink*** *(slang)* (of an electrical device) not working properly: *I'll have to take the washing to the launderette—our washing machine's on the blink.*

**put/lay one's head on the *block* ⟶ *put***

**be after sb's *blood* ⟶ *want* sb's blood**

**in sb's *blood*** (of an aptitude, inclination, or weakness) part of one's nature, often as an inherited trait: *Born of three generations of sailors, a desire for the sea was in his blood.*

***blood* and thunder** sensational and melodramatic incidents in stories, plays, or films: *blood and thunder novels. / This is a TV series with exotic scenery and plenty of blood and thunder.* Note that this is usually used before a noun, as in the first example.

**one's *blood* boils** *(informal)* you are filled with anger: *My blood boils* (or *it makes my blood boil) when I think of what I have done for them and the way they're treating me now.*

**one's *blood* freezes** or **one's blood runs cold** *(informal)* you are filled with fear or horror: *I saw him start to sway on the edge of the roof and my blood ran cold.* **chill sb's marrow; freeze/chill/curdle sb's blood** fill sb with fear or horror: *She was telling them ghost stories that would freeze anyone's blood, let alone a child's.* **blood-curdling** *adj*. See also ***freeze*/chill sb to the bone/marrow.**

***blood* is thicker than water** *(saying)* family ties are stronger than other relationships: *People may have friends who are very good to them and relatives who are not, but when it comes to making a will you'll find that blood is thicker than water.*

**sb's *blood* is up** *(informal)* sb feels angry and aggressive: *Don't anger him. He's dangerous when his blood is up, and he might break your jaw for you.* **get sb's blood up** make sb angry: *Now don't you get my blood up, I can be much more insulting than you once I start.*

**have (got) sb's *blood* on one's hands ⟶ *have***

**like getting *blood* out of a stone ⟶ *getting***

***blot* one's copybook** spoil your good reputation or record: *He paid back the money he'd stolen and and wasn't sacked. But he'd blotted his copybook and could never hope for promotion. / I blotted my copybook with Mrs Saunders, I'm afraid, when I didn't turn up for her husband's funeral.*

***blow* away the cobwebs** freshen the mind or spirits after a spell of study or confinement: *I often put down my pen and take a 15-minute walk or do a bit of gardening just to blow away the cobwebs.*

***blow* one's/sb's 'brains out** kill oneself/sb by shooting in the head: *He was so depressed he committed suicide—blew his brains out with a shotgun.*

***blow* by blow** with no item omitted when sb is telling what was said or done in the course of a fight, argument, or conversation: *She told me all about her wrangle with her landlord—blow by blow!* **'blow-by-blow** *adj*: *a blow-by-blow account of a football game.*

***blow* sb's/one's cover** *(informal)* discover or reveal the true identity of sb such as a spy: *A secret agent's cover may be blown without his being aware of it and he may be used to pass on false information.*

**strike a *blow* for sth ⟶ *strike***

***blow* hot and cold** *(informal)* alternate between approving of or wanting sth and not doing so; be unable or unwilling to decide for or against sb/sth: *A new opera house was first proposed fifteen years ago, and the city council has been blowing hot and cold about it ever since. / Andrew was the man she really wanted to marry but she grew tired of waiting while he blew hot and cold.*

***blow* it! —› *damn* (it (all))!**

***blow* me (down)!** *(informal)* (an exclamation of astonishment): *'Could you give me a lift home tomorrow night?' 'Blow me down, I was just going to ask* you *for one!'*

***blow* sb's/one's mind** *(informal)* make sb's/one's brain unable to function in a normal and/or rational way: *Young people are blowing their minds on heavy rock music. / These drugs will really blow your mind!* **mind-blowing** *adj.*

***blow* over** pass quickly; (soon) come to an end and be forgotten: *Her fits of temper soon blew over. / I'll stay in baby's room till the thunderstorm blows over.*

***blow* one's own trumpet/horn** praise yourself; boast about your own qualities or abilities: *I don't like blowing my own trumpet,' said Mrs Brown, 'but the office was much better run when I was in charge.'*

***blow* sb/sth sky-high** kill or destroy by means of a large explosion; completely demolish a theory or claim; completely upset plans or hopes: *We'll all be blown sky-high one of these days if you're not more careful about turning the gas off. / It was an ill-considered statement which blew his chances of being re-elected sky-high.* See also ***blow*, send etc sb/sth to kingdom come.**

***blow*, send etc sb/sth to kingdom come** kill by means of a large explosion: *The amount of explosives stored in here is enough to blow them all to kingdom come.* See also ***blow* sb/sth sky-high.**

***blow* one's top** *(informal)* lose your temper and speak or shout angrily: *I expected my father to blow his top when he saw what I'd done to his car.* Also *(slang)* **blow one's cool.** See also ***blow* up 2.**

***blow* up 1** arise; develop: *It sounds as if there's a bit of a breeze blowing up outside. / A major row was about to blow up between the two departments.* Note that this is often used in continuous tenses or the infinitive. **2** *(informal)* lose your temper; become very angry: *I don't know what he said to her, but she blew up and swiped him with her handbag.* See also ***blow* one's top.**

***blow* (sth) up** (cause sth to) explode, fly, or fall to pieces: *This was the last group to cross the bridge before it blew up* (or *it was blown up*).

***blow* sb up** *(slang)* scold or reprimand sb severely: *I suppose you know the boss will blow you up for not reporting this at once?* **ˌblowing-ˈup** *n*: *I got a blowing-up when I came late.*

***blow* sth up 1** enlarge a photograph by a technical process: *I want this photograph blown up on the front of the book, please.* **blow-up** *n.* **2** *(informal)* exaggerate the extent or importance of sth: *How things get blown up! It wasn't a riot—only a few people shouting objections.*

***blow* up in sb's face** *(informal)* (of a plan or expectation) be suddenly completely defeated or changed: *His plans blew up in his face when he heard that Julia had married someone else.*

**(well,) I'll be *blowed*/damned/hanged!** *(slang)* (an exclamation showing amazement or pleasure): *'Well, I'll be damned!' he cried when he'd opened the present, 'I've been trying to get hold of a copy of this book for years!'* Also **(well,) I'll be darned!** *(old-fashioned);* **(well,) I'm blowed/damned/hanged!** See also **I'll be *blowed*/damned/hanged if . . .**

**I'll be *blowed*/damned/hanged if . . .** *(slang)* I'm determined not to do sth; I'm unable to do sth; it certainly isn't true that: *'You must agree that their offer is very reasonable.' 'I'll be damned if I do!'* Also **I'm blowed/damned/hanged if . . .** See also **(well,) I'll be *blowed*/damned/hanged!**

**a bolt from the *blue* or a bolt out of the blue —› a *bolt* from the blue**

**into the *blue*** (depart or disappear) suddenly or unexpectedly; you do not know where to: *And then the white rabbit just vanished into the blue, as quickly as it had appeared.*

**out of the *blue*** (arrive, appear, or act) suddenly or unexpectedly; you do not know where from: *Acquaintances who turn up out of the blue shouldn't expect us to drop everything just to fit in with their plans. / It was then that he asked me, quite out of the blue, to marry him.*

***blue* blood** royal or aristocratic birth or ancestry: *They say she's got blue blood in her veins.* **blue-blooded** *adj*: *He's a genuine blue-blooded aristocrat.*

**a *blue*-collar job, worker etc** manual, skilled, or semi-skilled work etc. See also **a *white*-collar job, worker etc.**

***blue*-eyed boy** a favourite person; sb whom another person thinks cannot do anything wrong (usually used to describe a man or a boy): *The boss gives him all the good jobs and he does them perfectly—he's the real blue-eyed boy at the moment!*

**till one is *blue* in the face** (do sth without result) until you are exhausted or have to stop: *You can argue with John till you're blue in the face about the best way to do something, but he'll never agree with you.*

**once in a *blue moon* —› *once***

**get away with *(blue)* murder —› *get***

**scream, cry etc *blue* murder —› *scream***

**above *board*** open and honest; not secret: *Negotiations for any new contracts must be kept above board.* **above-board** *adj.*

**across the *board*** (of changes in prices, taxes etc) affecting everything or everyone with no exceptions: *The government has decided to* *raise oil prices by 8.2% right across the board.* **across-the-board** *adj*: *an across-the-board increase.*

**take sth on *board* → *take***

**when one's *boat* comes in → when one's *ship*/boat comes in**

**(and) *Bob's* your uncle** *(informal)* (and) everything will be all right or just as desired; the job is done; the problem is solved: *Once you're across the border, Bob's your uncle.*

***body* and soul** in/with all aspects of one's being, both physically and mentally: *She devoted herself body and soul to this mission. / The company don't own me body and soul just because they pay my wages.* See also ***keep* body and soul together.**

**a *body* blow** a disabling blow, shock, injury, or loss to sb/sth: *The decision to build the ship abroad dealt a severe body blow to the home shipbuilding industry. / His self-esteem had suffered a body blow.*

***bog* (sb/sth) down** *(informal)* (cause sb/sth to) become stuck or lodged (in mud etc); (cause sb to) become too heavily involved with work, social obligations etc to do much else: *Some vehicles bogged down and had to be abandoned temporarily. / I must have a part-time secretary if I'm not to get completely bogged down with correspondence.*

**go off the *boil* → *go***

**on the *boil*** *(informal)* in an active or lively condition: *Fresh discoveries kept their enthusiasm on the boil.*

***boil* sth down** reduce the length of a story, report etc by summarizing it: *The article was returned to my desk with a request to boil it down to 1500 words.* **boiled-down** *adj*: *A boiled-down version of the full findings was sent to each shareholder.*

***boil* down to sth** can/may be summarized as sth, often as a conclusion: *I've had your medical report from the hospital; what it boils down to is that they can find nothing much wrong with you.*

***boil* over** become extremely or furiously angry; (of situations) get out of control, explode into war, violence, or open quarrelling: *At this final piece of impudence his resentment boiled over. / They wanted to get out of the country before things boiled over into civil war.*

***boil* up** *(informal)* develop; threaten to occur: *There's trouble boiling up in the factory.*

**be/make so *bold* (as to do sth) → *make***

**as *bold* as brass** impudent(ly), shameless(ly): *As bold as brass, she jumped on the bus ahead of the queue. / He lied to me as bold as brass.*

**put a *bold* face on it → *put* a brave, bold etc face on it**

**make a *bolt*/dash for sth/it → *make***

**a *bolt* from the blue** or **a bolt out of the blue** sth (often unpleasant) that happens very suddenly and unexpectedly: *I had always thought of Sybil as a friend. Her vicious attack on me came as a bolt from the blue.*

***bolt* upright** in a perfectly vertical position; erect; (of a posture) with your back very straight: *The children were told to sit bolt upright in their seats for one minute.*

**near the *bone*/knuckle** (of talk or songs) rather vulgar or indecent in general, or likely to offend or upset a particular listener or audience: *I've heard plenty of jokes nearer the knuckle than that one. / The play, about a man's struggles to avoid bankruptcy, was a bit too near the bone for John's enjoyment.*

**to the *bone*** thoroughly; in every respect: *Prices have been cut to the bone in an effort to attract customers, but it means less profit for the manufacturers.* See also ***freeze*/chill sb to the bone/marrow; *work* one's fingers to the bone.**

**a *bone* of contention** a cause/subject of dispute or quarrelling: *The child, his own interests disregarded, became a bone of contention between his estranged parents. / The interpretation of this passage has always been a bone of contention among academics.*

**have (got) a *bone* to pick with sb → *have***

***bone* up on sth** *(informal)* study or obtain information about a subject, usually quickly for a special purpose: *I shall have to bone up on soil chemistry before the conference.*

**feel sth in one's *bones* → *feel***

**have (got) a bee in one's *bonnet* (about sth) → *have***

**would not say *boo* to a goose → *say***

**bring sb to *book* (for sth) → *bring***

**by the *book*** strictly following, in what you do or say, a set of rules or the usual procedure: *Head office makes decisions and we branch managers have to go by the book.*

**come to *book* (for sth) → *bring* sb to book (for sth)**

**in sb's *book*** according to the experience, information etc of sb: *John was disgusted with them because in 'his book it was more important to play fair than to win.*

**read sb like a *book* → *read***

**take a leaf out of sb's *book* → *take***

**throw the *book* (of rules) at sb → *throw***

**to *boot*** as well; moreover: *He's the ablest guide in the district and an excellent companion to boot.*

**the *boot* is on the other foot/leg** a former or the usual or expected situation or advantage is reversed: *He used to be the one that had to obey orders, but now the boot is on the other foot.*

***boot* sb out (of sth)** *(slang)* dismiss or expel sb from a job, house, club etc: *If there's to be a cutback in staff I'll be one of those to be booted out. / Can you put me up for a few days? My landlady booted me out this morning!*

**pull/lift oneself up by one's own *bootlaces* → *pull*/lift oneself up by one's own bootstraps/bootlaces**

**die in one's *boots* → *die***

**hang up one's *boots* → *hang***

**one's heart is in one's *boots* → *heart***

**too big for one's *boots*** → ***too***
**die with one's *boots* on** → ***die* in one's boots**
**pull/lift oneself up by one's own *bootstraps*** → ***pull*/lift oneself up by one's own bootstraps/bootlaces**
***bore* sb stiff/rigid** *(informal)* bore sb to an extreme or stupefying degree: *That's not my kind of holiday. I'd be bored stiff lying about on a beach all day. / He may be an expert on his subject, but he bored his audience rigid.* Also **bore sb to death/tears;** *(slang)* **bore the pants off sb.**
***bored*, sick etc to death of sb/sth** *(informal)* extremely wearied or annoyed by sb/sth: *I'm getting tired to death of this revising! I do wish the exams were all over!*
***born* and bred** both by birth and upbringing: *Although a Glaswegian born and bred, he was often taken for an Irishman.*
***born* before one's time** likely to have been happier, more successful, better appreciated etc if you had lived in a later age: *He was unfortunate in being born before his time—his contemporaries just couldn't accept his ideas.*
**in all one's *born* days** → ***all***
***born* on the wrong side of the blanket** *(euphemistic, old-fashioned)* born to parents who are not married to each other: *Some of the children of this country's rulers have been born on the wrong side of the blanket.*
***born* with a silver 'spoon in one's mouth** born of rich parents, the heir to a lot of money.
**was/were not *born* yesterday** *(informal)* not be innocent, gullible, and without experience of the world: *Why don't you tell your father? After all, he can probably guess—he wasn't born yesterday, you know.*
**be *borne* in on/upon sb** (of a fact etc) be realized or understood by sb: *Following Jeff and Sybil's retirement, it was borne in on them just how few friends they had outside their jobs.*
**live on *borrowed* time** → ***live***
**burn the candle at *both* ends** → ***burn***
**take one's courage in *both* hands** → ***take***
**(seize/grasp an opportunity) with *both* hands** (take the opportunity of doing or obtaining sth) eagerly and immediately.
**cut *both*/ways** → ***cut* both/two ways**
**have it/things *both* ways** → ***have***
**the best of *both* worlds** → ***best***
**no *bother*** → ***no* trouble, bother, problem etc**
**on the *bottle*** *(informal)* often taking alcoholic drinks: *I see Pat's on the bottle again.*
***bottle* sth up** *(informal)* suppress or hide a strong emotion: *I'd prefer to see her give way to grief than bottle it all up like this. / He managed to keep his anger bottled up until they were alone.*
**at *bottom*** essentially; in reality: *She never seemed to despise her brother's success, but I suspect that at bottom she was a bit jealous.*
**bet one's *bottom* dollar on sth** or **bet one's bottom dollar (that) . . .** → ***bet***
**one's *bottom* drawer** a woman's personal store of clothes, linen etc that are collected towards her marriage: *I've bought some lovely towels at the sale, Mum! I can't make up my mind whether to use them now or put them in my bottom drawer.*
**the *bottom* drops/falls out of the market** trade is at a very low level; a commodity is no longer wanted and has to be sold very cheaply.
**the *bottom* drops/falls out of sb's world** sb loses the basis of his happiness, hopes, or self-confidence: *When his wife left him, the bottom dropped out of his world.*
**the *bottom* line** *(informal)* the important conclusion, judgment or result; crucial fact: *The Prime Minister described the bottom line of the country's negotiating position by declaring that it would contribute no more money to the community.*
**get to the *bottom* of sth** → ***get***
**from the *bottom* of one's heart** sincerely; with genuine affection, gratitude, and sympathy: *I am saying this from the bottom of my heart.*
**scrape (the *bottom* of) the barrel** → ***scrape***
***bottom* out** (of prices etc) reach the lowest point on a scale: *Output is slumping as it did in the 1930s and is not expected to bottom out for two years.*
**knock the *bottom* out of sth** → ***knock***
***bottoms* up!** (an expression used when drinking with sb).
***bounce* back** *(informal)* recover your health, fortune, or success after a great difficulty: *After injuring himself badly in a recent car crash, Jason Janetta has now bounced back into the public eye with this major victory.*
***bounce* sth off sb** *(informal)* talk about an idea etc to sb to get his opinion of it: *Do you mind if I bounce this idea off you?*
**I'll be *bound*** *(becoming old-fashioned)* I am sure (used to emphasize a statement): *Jack won't stay long watching this cricket match; he'll be down at the pub soon, I'll be bound.*
***bound* up in sb/sth** deeply interested in or occupied with sb/sth: *I was so bound up in my book I didn't notice the time. / 'They seem very much bound up in each other.' 'Yes, more like an engaged or newly married couple than the oldsters they are.'*
***bound* up with sth** closely connected with or difficult to separate from sth: *The two countries' political quarrels, bound up as they are with different religious beliefs, will be hard to resolve.*
**a/one's *bounden* duty** a duty or service you feel morally obliged to perform: *She's always helped me in my troubles, so it's my bounden duty to do the same for her now.*
**out of *bounds*** outside the area or areas where soldiers, schoolchildren etc are permitted to go: *After the drowning, the canal was declared out of bounds for Junior School boys.*
***bow* and scrape** behave in an insincere, ser-

vile way that tries to gain favour: *If he had been royalty, the waiters would have been lined up bowing and scraping as he entered. / I'm damned if I'll bow and scrape to him for favours!*

***bow* out (of sth)** resign from a career or important position: *I've busied myself with municipal affairs for forty years, so I think it's time for me to bow out and let younger women take over.*

***bowl* sb over** overwhelm sb with amazement, admiration, dismay, or delight (often used in the passive): *The poor man was quite bowled over by the news of his success. / 'Is it really so beautiful there?' 'It bowled me over, I can tell you.'*

**(fire) a (warning) shot across the/sb's *bows* → *shot***

**oh *boy*!** (an expression of excitement, surprise, or delight): *Oh boy, we've won first prize!* Also **boy, oh boy!**

**the *boys* in blue** *(informal)* policemen.

***boys* will be boys** *(saying)* you must expect boys to be actively adventurous, mischievous, and noisy, and not criticize them too severely for it: *'Why do they have to play such rough games?' 'Oh well, boys will be boys—they've got to get rid of their energy somehow.'*

**have (got) sb/sth on the *brain* → *have***

**sb's '*brain* child** sb's own invention, idea, or scheme which, when adopted or furthered by others, he should be given credit for.

**the '*brain* drain** the considerable loss of a country's qualified scientists, doctors, engineers etc to another country, especially one which pays them better for their work.

***brains* and/or brawn** intelligence and cleverness contrasted with physical strength and athletic ability: *He has brains as well as brawn—off the rugby field he's a doctor in a large hospital.*

***branch* out (into sth)** expand in new directions; start new activities related to your usual business or occupation: *Owing to the reduced demand for sewing-machines, the firm is branching out into other light-engineering products. / The young actor's attempt to branch out as a singer met with little success in this highly competitive field.*

**(not) care/give a *brass* farthing etc (about/for sb/sth) → *care***

**get down to *brass* tacks → *get***

**put a *brave*, face on it → *put* a brave, bold etc face on it**

**step into the *breach* → *step***

**one's *bread* and butter** your means of earning a livelihood: *His novels are far from best-sellers, so he depends on teaching for his bread and butter. / Many solicitors make their bread and butter from doing the legal paperwork for people buying and selling houses—other business they get just comes as a useful addition.*

**know which side one's *bread* is buttered (on) → *know***

***break* and enter** illegally force an entry into a building: *You can have them on a charge of breaking and entering whether they actually stole anything or not.*

***break* away (from sb/sth)** leave or escape from a guard etc suddenly: *When the train stopped in the tunnel, two of the prisoners broke away from their police escort and jumped out.*

***break* away (from sth)** withdraw from membership of a political party, religious denomination, or other established group: *Over 20 MPs have now broken away from their old party to form a new, independent one.* **break-away** *adj, n: a break-away group.*

***break* one's/sb's back** (cause sb to) work extremely or too hard; do a (physically) exhausting task: *I don't see why your mother should break her back dragging refuse-bins around, with you two boys in the house!* **'back-breaking** *adj: a back-breaking job.*

***break* cover → *take/break cover***

***break* down 1** lose self-control and weep from grief, pity, or sentimental emotion: *She didn't want to go to the funeral in case she broke down in front of everybody.* **2** collapse; become so ill that medical advice or treatment is necessary: *If his health is not to break down completely he must get away for a long holiday.* **breakdown** *n: She was off work for three months after a nervous breakdown.* **3** (of cars, machines etc) develop a fault and stop: *Their car broke down on the way here.* **breakdown** *n: Let's hope we don't have a breakdown while we're in this traffic jam.* **4** fail; cease to be effective; be discontinued: *Negotiations between management and trade union officials have broken down, and a strike now seems inevitable.* **breakdown** *n: a complete breakdown of relationships in modern society.*

***break* sth down** overcome opposition, suspicion, fear etc, especially by argument or persuasion: *Local resistance to a nuclear power station on this site will be difficult to break down. / Her sympathetic questioning gradually broke down his reserve.*

***break* (sth) down** analyse sth; present sth in detail or in separate items; (of total figures, results etc) be presented in this way: *The annual insurance premium breaks down into different cover for the building, contents and individually valued items.* **breakdown** *n: The boss wants you to give him a complete breakdown of your expenses claim.*

***break* even** make neither a profit nor a loss as the result of a business deal, a year's trading etc: *I shall have to charge my lodgers more. With present costs, I'm only just breaking even.*

**make a *break* for it → *make***

***break* one's/sb's heart** (cause sb to) feel sorrow or deep distress: *That boy is breaking his mother's heart with his wild ways. / It's a job I would like, but I won't break my heart if I don't get it.* Note that this idiom is often used ironically. **heartbreak** *n: He causes his mother nothing but heartbreak.* **heartbreaking** *adj: a* *heartbreaking story.* **heartbroken** *adj*: *We were heartbroken by the news.*

***break* in 1** interrupt when sb is speaking: *'Not in front of the children,' she broke in hurriedly. / I'm sorry to break in, but you're not telling this the way it really happened.* See also ***break* in on/upon sth.** **2** force an entry into a building, room etc: *These precautions won't keep a determined thief from breaking in but will discourage a casual one.* **break-in** *n*: *That's the third break-in at the warehouse this year.* Also **break into sth:** *Their shop was broken into last night.*

***break* sb/sth in** train and discipline a horse, recruit, or pupil; wear or use sth gradually till it becomes comfortable or adapted to its function: *The chestnut pony isn't thoroughly broken in yet—you'd better ride this one. / I don't want to wear these boots for a long walk till I've broken them in.*

***break* in on/upon sth** interrupt or disturb sth: *The shrill sound of the telephone broke in upon his thoughts.* See also ***break* in 1.**

***break* into sth 1** use part of an amount of money, a high-value note or coin, a supply of food, or a period of time: *Fortunately I haven't yet had to break into the money that Mum lent me. / Could we finish off the old biscuits before we break into a new packet?* **2** change from a slower to a faster pace suddenly: *The horse broke into a gallop, and the young girl fell off.* See also ***break* in 2.**

***break* into laughter, a run, etc** suddenly begin to laugh, run etc: *As soon as she read the letter Marcia just broke into tears.* See also ***break* out in(to) sth; *burst* into tears etc.**

**sticks and stones may *break* my bones but words will never hurt me** ⟶***sticks***

**(not) *break* one's neck (doing sth)** *(informal)* (not) hurry more or try harder than is safe or convenient: *There's no need to break your neck getting here by 5 o'clock. We'll wait for you.*

***break* oneself/sb of (doing) sth** make sb stop doing sth which has become a habit and is harmful or annoying: *Reaching for a cigarette as soon as you wake is a habit you should try to break yourself of.*

***break* off 1** (suddenly) stop talking: *'You see, you could always . . . ,' he broke off as the telephone rang.* **2** stop temporarily; take a short rest from work: *I think we should break off for lunch now.*

***break* sth off** end a relationship or negotiations abruptly: *'I thought they were engaged to be married.' 'So they were, but they've broken it off.' / Peace talks have been broken off, and the delegates are preparing to leave.*

***break* out** (of war, disease etc) start suddenly and/or violently: *Fighting broke out between the clans. / There should be another exit—if fire broke out in the front of the building we'd all be trapped.* **outbreak** *n: Medical experts are still trying to determine the cause of the outbreak.*

***break* out in sth** suddenly show or become covered with sth such as spots on the skin: *His arms have broken out in a rash of red blotches.*

***break* out in(to) sth** suddenly begin to express sth loudly and strongly: *At the appearance of the group, the fans broke out into screams and cries of delight.* See also ***break* into laughter, a run etc; *burst* into tears etc.**

***break* out (of sth)** escape (from a prison etc), especially by using force: *The three prisoners had broken out of gaol and were on the run.* **break-out** *n.*

***break* the back of sth** succeed in completing the largest or hardest part of a task or undertaking: *I won't get this essay finished tonight, but I'd still like to break the back of it before I stop.*

**(not) *break* the bank** *(informal)* (not) leave sb without any money: *'Can you lend me the money for a cup of coffee?' 'Yes—I think I can manage that! It won't break the bank!'*

***break* the ice** ease the formality or tension at a (social) meeting or gathering; take the first steps in informing sb of news, a suggestion etc he may not like: *If you serve drinks as soon as they arrive it will help to break the ice.*

***break* through** make a new discovery or invention in science, art, medicine etc, especially after a lot of research: *It was the Russians who broke through first. / The scientists claim to have broken through in a new field of microbiology.* **break-through** *n: a major break-through.*

***break* up** (of schools, staff, or pupils) disperse for holidays: *When do you break up for Christmas?*

***break* (sth) up 1** (of a meeting, party, or negotiations) (cause to) come to an end with people separating and going away: *As the meeting broke up, there was still no sign of agreement between the oil ministers. / Come on, lads, break it up. Get back on the job. / The police had to be called to break up the demonstration.* **2** (of a relationship or association) (cause to) come to an end: *Because their jobs took them many thousands of miles apart, the couple's marriage began to break up.* **break-up** *n.*

***break* wind** let out air or gas from the stomach or bowels: *Baby often brings up a mouthful of milk when he breaks wind.*

***break* one's word** ⟶***keep*/break one's word**

**all hell *breaks* loose** ⟶***all***

**out of *breath*** not able to breathe easily because of physical effort: *Running for the bus has made me out of breath.*

**under one's *breath*** in a whisper, so that other people cannot hear: *He muttered something under his breath.*

**get one's *breath* back** ⟶***get***

**(not) *breathe* a word (about/of sth)** (not) even mention a secret or private matter: *If either of you breathes a word about our plans outside this room I'll withdraw my support.* Also **not a word (about/of this):** *Not a word to anyone, please.*

***breathe* again/freely** relax because sth which

you were unhappy or anxious about has passed: *Once through the Customs, we could all breathe freely. / On a second reading he found his name on the Pass List and breathed again.*

***breathe* down sb's neck** *(informal)* be (too) close behind sb, as in a race or queue; watch or supervise sb (too) closely: *I can't work with people breathing down my neck the whole time.*

***breathe* one's last** die: *He grew worse, and around 4 a.m. breathed his last.*

**a *breathing* space** time to regain your breath or to pause and rest between one effort, task, or engagement, and the next.

***brew* (sth) (up)** (of a storm, mischief, or trouble) (cause to) start and gather strength: *That sort of talk just brews up trouble. / In the west we could see a storm brewing (up).*

**bang one's head against a *brick* wall** ⟶ ***bang***

**talk to a *brick* wall** ⟶ ***talk***

***bricks* and mortar** buildings; the building trade; house property as an investment: *Those fields are all bricks and mortar now. / Savings depreciate with inflation—put your money into bricks and mortar.*

**make *bricks* without straw** ⟶ ***make***

***bright* and early** early in the morning: *'Yes, it's true. I heard it on the 6.30 news.' 'Goodness! You were up bright and early this morning!'*

**(as) *bright* as a button** intelligent, lively, and alert: *What a pretty child—and bright as a button!*

***bright*-eyed and bushy-tailed** very cheerful, pleased, and proud.

**a *bright* spark** *(informal)* a lively, cheerful, quick-witted person: *I would have thought that some bright spark would have been able to think of a way out of this.*

***bring* sth about** cause sth to happen: *Being over-ambitious brought about his downfall. / 'I would like to meet them.' 'Well, that can easily be brought about.'* See also ***come* about.**

***bring* sb/sth along/on** help a (young) person to improve his abilities; promote the growth of plants etc: *The boy's new teacher has brought him along marvellously. / Too much heat and moisture brings the seedlings on too quickly, and they will not be very hardy.* See also ***come* on 1.**

***bring* sb around (to sth)** ⟶ ***bring* sb (a)round (to sth)**

***bring* sth back 1** remind you of memories of sth: *Do you remember that first night of our holiday in Majorca? That record brings it all back!* See also ***come* back 2. 2** reintroduce or restore a rule, law, or system: *There are still quite a few people who want to bring back the death penalty.* See also ***come* back 3.**

***bring* sb down** cause the defeat or fall of a government, leader etc: *The scandal surrounding the politician's private life was in the end sufficient to bring him down.*

***bring* sb down to earth** or **come down to earth** (make sb) face reality or accept the true facts about himself/oneself or a situation: *'You don't run a hospital on ideals alone,' she said and brought him down to earth with a few practical questions. / He says money isn't important to him but he'd come down to earth with a bump if he couldn't pay his bills.* **down-to-earth** *adj*: sensible, practical, and realistic: *She'll give you some down-to-earth advice, I'm sure.*

***bring* home the bacon** *(informal)* be successful in an undertaking; be the person or means that chiefly earns money for a family, business, or national economy: *The firm wants very much to get this contract, and we're looking to you to bring home the bacon. / I'd like to give all my time to art printing but it's the leaflets, tickets, and so on that bring home the bacon.*

***bring* sb in on sth** let sb have a part in an activity, business venture, or project: *The local people, who are the ones who will be affected by the planned motorway, must be brought in on the proposals from the outset.* See also ***come* in on sth.**

***bring* sth into effect** or **come into effect** (of an arrangement or system) (cause sth to) begin to operate: *The new timetable comes into effect on the first Monday in May.*

***bring*/call sth into play** cause sth to operate, become involved or have an influence: *One touch brings the whole alarm system into play.* See also ***come* into play.**

***bring* sb into the world** give birth to sb: *He says people shouldn't bring children into the world unless they can provide for them. / I didn't ask to be brought into the world.*

***bring* sth off** succeed in a plan or ambition: *It will be a very profitable deal if he can bring it off.* See also ***come* off 2.**

***bring* sb/sth on** ⟶ ***bring* sb/sth along/on**

***bring* sth on** cause sth to begin or happen: *Fears that an oil price war would bring on a worldwide financial collapse shook international markets yesterday.*

***bring* sb out** cause a group of workers to go on strike: *Trade union leaders in the coal mines have decided to bring out their men from Monday.* See also ***come* out 3.**

***bring* sb out (of his shell)** help sb to lose or overcome shyness or reserve: *Sam used to feel awkward with other people, but his wife has brought him out a lot since they married. / 'It's a pity she doesn't drink—a couple of whiskies might bring her out of her shell.'* See also ***come* out of one's shell.**

***bring* sth out 1** reveal or emphasize a colour, shape, or sound: *This old recording doesn't bring out the quality of his voice properly. / You should wear blue more often—it brings out the colour of your eyes.* Note that the object, unless it is a pronoun, usually comes at the end. See also ***come* out 4. 2** make the meaning of sth, or a fact about sth, clear: *An example sentence often helps to bring out the meaning of a phrase. / The advantages and dis-*

*advantages of both methods are clearly brought out in this report.* **3** publish (a book etc); introduce onto the market: *Have you tried the new type of glue that has just been brought out?* See also ***come* out 1.**

***bring* sb out in sth** cause the skin of sb to be covered with spots or marks: *Whenever he eats raspberries, they bring him out in a rash.* See also ***come* out in sth.**

***bring* out sth in sb** cause sb to show a quality of his character: *A crisis of any sort brings out the best in George, who, in general, is a rather quiet person. / Money doesn't usually bring out the generosity in people.*

***bring* sb (a)round (to sth)** convert sb to your own opinion; persuade sb: *You have always said Henry wasn't to be trusted, and I'm gradually being brought round to that belief myself. / Your mother says she won't fly in a small plane, but I dare say we can bring her round.* See also ***come* (a)round (to sth).**

***bring* sb round/to** help sb to regain consciousness after a faint, blow, or anaesthetic: *After his companions brought him to, they walked him up and down for a while.* See also ***come* round/to.**

***bring* the curtain down (on sth)** → ***ring*/bring the curtain down (on sth)**

***bring* the house down** make an audience laugh, applaud or cheer loudly: *A comedy sketch that brings the house down in London might be coolly received elsewhere. / 'Did he sing well?' 'He really brought the house down!'*

***bring* sb to himself** make sb think and behave sensibly after having been foolish or mistaken: *His poverty brought him to himself and he realized he'd been silly to leave home.* Also ***bring* sb to his senses.** See also ***come* to oneself.**

***bring* sth to a head** bring a troubled or dangerous situation to a critical or culminating stage: *The firm was losing business already. Jim's recent alcoholism only brought things to a head.* See also ***come* to a head.**

***bring* sb to account** → ***call*/bring/hold sb to account**

***bring* sth to bear (up)on sb/sth** *(formal)* use sth to control or influence sb/sth: *Trade sanctions can be brought to bear upon those who violate international law. / We must bring all our powers to bear on making a success of this enterprise.*

***bring* sb to book (for sth)** or **come to book (for sth)** *(informal)* (make sb) explain or justify his actions and/or be punished: *This is another of the many acts of vandalism for which nobody was ever brought to book.*

***bring* oneself to do sth** overcome your reluctance to do sth (usually used in the negative): *I dislike him so much I can hardly bring myself to even say, 'Good morning' to him.*

***bring* sb to his feet** or **come to one's feet** (make sb) stand up quickly in order to escape or defend himself/oneself, or to applaud, condemn, or question sth done or said: *They were playing a hand of bridge when cries of 'Fire!' brought them to their feet.* Alternatives to ***come*** include ***get, leap, jump, rise,*** and ***spring***: *As the Managing Director entered the office, all the workers rose to their feet.*

***bring* sth to fruition** (cause sth to) be fulfilled or realized: *I have certain projects in mind but I don't know whether any of them will come to fruition.*

***bring* sb to heel** subdue or control sb so that he obeys your orders or conforms to your wishes: *'My assistant is getting altogether too presumptuous.' 'Then you must bring her to heel or get rid of her.'* **come to heel** be subdued or controlled in this way: *He'll soon come to heel if I get nasty with him.*

***bring* sb to his knees** *(formal)* force sb to submit or to humble himself: *By continuing the strike till their demands are met, the unions hope to bring both employers and government to their knees.*

***bring* sb/sth to life 1** cause sb/sth to become lively, interested, or interesting: *Many of the oldest inmates sat around apathetically all day, and nothing seemed capable of bringing them to life. / The arrival of David and his friends really brought the party to life.* See also ***come* to life 1. 2** describe or portray a character, scene, or period vividly: *The film really brought to life for me what had just been a dry fact in a history book before.* See also ***come* to life 2.**

***bring* sth to light** reveal sth which has been hidden or not known: *Research has brought to light many new facts about the composer's early life.* See also ***come* to light.**

***bring* sb to his senses** → ***bring* sb to himself**

***bring* sth to the boil** or **come to the boil** *(informal)* (cause sth to) reach a climax or a high degree of intensity or excitement: *What really brought matters to the boil was the Secretary's rudeness to the Chairman in public.*

***bring* sb up** provide a home, care, and education for a child; train a child: *She was left a widow with four children to bring up on her own. / I was brought up to be self-reliant.* **brought-up** *adj*: *It's obvious that they're badly brought-up girls.* **upbringing** *n*: *She gave him a good upbringing.*

***bring* sth up 1** mention or call attention to sth: *Can you think of anything else I should bring up at the meeting? / That's not a suitable subject to bring up at the dining-table.* See also ***come* up 2. 2** *(informal)* vomit food etc: *The baby has just brought up his milk again.* See also ***come* up 4.**

***bring* sb up against sb/sth** make sb face or confront sb/sth: *Having to travel to work for four hours each day really brought him up against the problem of time.* See also ***come* up against sb/sth.**

***bring*/draw/pull sb up short/sharply** make sb stop and take notice: *I was dozing off while watching the news on television when news of the bomb attack suddenly pulled me up short.*

***bring* up the rear** come in last; follow at the

end of a procession of people or vehicles: *They marched in a double column with one sergeant leading them and another bringing up the rear.*

***bristle* with sth 1** have or display sth in frightening or impressive numbers: *Only a practised eye could discern that the bushes were bristling with spears. / The Sponsors' List bristled with famous names.* **2** show clearly your aggressive or self-assertive feeling: *The slightest reference to her ex-husband made her bristle with anger.*

**the best of *(British)* luck (to sb)** → ***best***

**it's as *broad* as it's long** the result will be the same, or it makes no difference, whichever of two views or actions you take: *'Will it be cheaper to take the car or go by rail?' 'It's as broad as it's long, I think, for one person travelling alone.'*

**(in) *broad* daylight** (during) the hours of full daylight, considered as conditions more favourable to some activities and less favourable to others: *Though it was now broad daylight no one seemed to be astir in the village as we passed through. / One doesn't expect, after all, to be mugged in broad daylight.*

***broad* in the beam** *(informal)* (of persons) wide in build, especially across the hips.

**a new *broom* (sweeps clean)** → ***new***

**(not) be one's *brother's* keeper** (not) have/feel responsibility for another person's actions or any duty to prevent him either doing or suffering harm: *'Where's the electrician that's working with you? He should be checking this wiring!' 'I'm not my brother's keeper. Look for him yourself!'*

***browned*/cheesed off** *(slang)* bored, jaded, or irritated: *She'd now been describing her trip for a full half-hour and James was looking thoroughly browned off.*

***brush* sb/sth aside 1** push sb/sth aside; thrust sb/sth out of your way: *All obstacles in the army's way were easily brushed aside.* **2** reject or dismiss sb/sth thought to be unimportant: *The cost of the scheme won't matter to him, but there's a stronger objection which he won't be able to brush aside.*

***brush* sb down** *(slang)* scold or reprimand sb. **brushing-'down** *n*: *give sb a good brushing-down.*

***brush* sb off** *(slang)* not allow a relationship or conversation to begin or continue. **'brush-off** *n*: *I was nearly engaged to her once, but I eventually got the brush-off.*

***brush* sth under the carpet** → ***sweep*/brush sth under the carpet**

***brush* up (on) sth** *(informal)* improve your knowledge or skill by revision or practice: *I shall have to brush up my French before our trip to France in the summer.*

***brush* up against sb** *(informal)* meet sb (briefly) by chance: *I must have brushed up against him somewhere before, because I knew his face.*

***prick* the bubble (of sth)** reduce the apparent size, importance etc of sb/sth to its true amount: *Failing his exams badly pricked the bubble of his own self-importance.*

**the *buck* stops here** *(informal)* the responsibility for sth is accepted by this person, group, or office and will not be evaded or shifted on to sb else. See also ***pass* the buck.**

***buck* up** *(informal)* hurry up: *Buck up, David. You're keeping your friends waiting. / If your mother doesn't buck up with that cup of tea she promised us, we'll have to leave without it!*

***buck* (sb) up** *(informal)* (cause sb to) become more cheerful, confident, or vigorous: *The poor lad bucked up a bit when he heard that we too had all failed our driving tests the first time of trying. / People often feel tired and depressed after flu—you need a good holiday to buck you up.*

***buck* up one's ideas** *(informal)* become more alert, diligent, or enterprising: *The girl's nearly 18 now. She'll have to buck up her ideas if she wants to become an engineer—or anything else worthwhile.*

***bucket* down** *(informal)* rain very heavily. Also **come down in buckets.**

***buckle* down to sth** start to work seriously on a task, problem, course of study etc: *After a week spent getting to know each other and allotting duties, the team buckled down to work in earnest. / You could learn your part in one evening if you buckled down to it.* Also **buckle to.**

**nip sth in the *bud*** → ***nip***

**in the *buff*** *(informal)* (of persons) naked: *go swimming in the buff. / I caught a glimpse of her in the buff.*

**as snug as a *bug* in a rug** → ***snug***

***build* bridges with sb** establish a relationship with sb: *The trade union movement wants to build bridges with the government.* **bridge-building** *n.*

***(build)* castles in the air** (think or talk about) plans, hopes, or wishes that you are not likely to carry out or see fulfilled: *They talked of travelling the world together as singer and accompanist. Building castles in the air at least kept their spirits up. / Politicians should stop trying to fool the electorate by promising them castles in the air.*

***build* on sth** use sth as a basis for further progress: *The team hope to build on this year's good performance by being even more successful next year.*

***build* (sth) up** (cause sth to) get bigger, stronger etc: *The traffic begins to build up on the approaches to the city from 8 o'clock onwards.*

***build* sb up 1** develop sb's strength: *You need building up after your stay in hospital—eat good food and get some fresh air. / His trainers started to build him up months before the big fight.* **2** develop the image or reputation of sb, often when the praise is too much or undeserved: *The media have built her up as one of the country's most talented performers, but her friends still know her as 'our Kathy.'*

***build* sth up 1** develop or extend sth gradually from a smaller to a bigger level: *It has taken him many years to build up his business. / I'm gradually building up my stamp collection.* **build-up** *n*: *Most people are concerned about the build-up of nuclear weapons.* **2** develop; cover an area with buildings: *Most of this area was already built up by the time we moved here ten years ago.* **built-up** *adj*: *There is usually a speed limit for traffic in built-up areas.*

**Rome was not *built* in a day** ⟶ ***Rome***

**take the *bull* by the horns** ⟶ ***take***

**a/the *bull's*-eye** the centre ring on a target board; a throw, answer etc that is absolutely accurate: *Whether it was knowledge or guesswork that led to the accusation, it was clear from their reaction that he had hit the bull's-eye* (or *scored a bull's-eye with it*).

***bully* for sb!** *(informal, becoming old fashioned)* well done! (a form of congratulation, often implying either the speaker's jealousy or his doubt about the worth of sb/sth): *'I've passed my exam.' 'Bully for you! Now you can really enjoy your holiday.' / 'John can always trust his wife to agree with him.' 'Bully for him—we're not all so lucky!'*

**things that go *bump* in the night** ⟶ ***things***

***bump*/run into sb** *(informal)* meet sb by chance: *'You'll never guess who I bumped into at the airport.' 'Tell me, then.' / It's strange that though we both live in the same neighbourhood, we hardly ever run into each other.*

***bump* sb off** *(slang)* kill sb: *'What's he in prison for?' 'He bumped off a night-watchman.'*

***bump* sth up** *(informal)* increase a figure or amount: *If he thinks you'll pay more, the salesman will probably bump the price of the car up a bit.*

***bumped*/jumped up** (of persons) having risen or been promoted, suddenly or rather quickly, to a higher social or professional status: *The report refers to our 'Sanitary Engineer'—I must tell Mr Jones the plumber that he's been bumped up! / The secretary resigned when Robert was made Manager, saying she couldn't accept a jumped-up sales clerk as her boss.*

**have (got) a '*bun* in the oven** ⟶ ***have***

**a *bunch* of fives** *(slang)* a blow with your fist: *Mike came nearer and suddenly gave him a bunch of fives in the face.*

***burn* a hole in sb's pocket** ⟶ ***money* burns a hole in sb's pocket**

***burn* one's boats/bridges (behind one)** cut off your means of escape or retreat; commit yourself so firmly to a course of action that you cannot reverse it: *He can't go back to the Corporation for a job. He burned his boats there when he had a big row with his boss just before he left.*

***burn* one's fingers** suffer harm or (financial) loss through being too rash, trusting, or optimistic: *A lot of people have burnt their fingers speculating without the advice of a financial consultant.* Also **get/have one's 'fingers burnt.**

***burn* (oneself) out** *(informal)* ruin your health by overwork, dissipation etc: *A lifestyle that in many cases included the use of drugs resulted in some performers burning (themselves) out* (or *performers being burned out*) *by their early thirties.*

***burn* the candle at both ends** exhaust your energy by too much work and/or social activity, especially when this involves getting up early and going to bed late: *At the end of each term I'd go back home exhausted as someone who'd really burnt the candle at both ends—I'd finished off all my essays and gone to lots of all-night parties, as well.*

***burn* the midnight oil** work or study until very late at night: *I've been burning the midnight oil most nights this week preparing for my exams.*

**a *burning* question** an important question that needs to be answered; subect that is greatly discussed: *Help was on the way, but the burning question was would it be in time?*

***burst* a blood vessel** *(informal)* become very angry or excited: *When I asked Dad for some more money in addition to what he'd already lent me, he really burst a blood vessel.*

***burst* at the seams** *(informal)* be full to the point of breaking open: *Our old offices are bursting at the seams, so we're moving to bigger premises.*

***burst* into tears etc** start to weep suddenly and loudly or violently: *She burst into tears as she read the letter. / At this point in the opera, Sarah, playing Violetta, bursts into song.* See also ***break* into laughter, a run etc; *break* out in(to) sth.**

**(be) *bursting* to do sth** *(informal)* (be) scarcely able to wait to do sth, to restrain oneself from doing sth: *She was just bursting to tell us the news.*

**go for a *Burton*** ⟶ ***go***

***bury*/hide one's head in the sand (like an ostrich)** act as if refusing to see or face a danger or difficulty, hoping it will disappear: *They should have been mobilizing their defences instead of burying their heads in the sand.*

***bury* oneself in sth** become deeply interested and involved in sth: *Sue can really bury herself in a good book.*

***bury* the hatchet** (of two people or groups) agree to become friendly again after a fight or quarrel: *I've shown that I'm willing to bury the hatchet—it's John who won't give in.*

**beat about the *bush*** ⟶ ***beat***

***bush* telegraph** the unofficial spreading of news by one person to another: *You seem to know all the local gossip already. There must be some kind of bush telegraph operating between here and London. / 'The appointment hasn't been announced in the press yet.' 'I know it hasn't—we heard it on the bush telegraph!'*

**hide one's light under a *bushel* → *hide***

**be (back) in *business*** have work, especially after a time when there has been none; have things working to your advantage once more: *I think we'll be back in business soon—that order for tablets for the Third World is going to come in any day now. / We're in business! Now that the switches work OK, let's see if the whole machine works properly.*

**get down to *business* → *get***

**go/be about one's *business* → *go***

**a *busman's* holiday** a holiday spent doing almost the same kind of thing as you do at work: *Taking the family on a weekend at a Scout camp is rather a busman's holiday for a schoolmaster, isn't it?*

**. . . or *bust*** *(informal)* (do or obtain sth or get somewhere) or die, be defeated etc (often used to express determination without serious fear of failure): *I'm going to get that engine working or bust.*

**a *busy* bee** *(informal)* sb who is very busy: *You're a proper busy bee! You're always doing plenty of things, aren't you?*

***butter* sb up** *(informal)* make yourself very pleasant and agreeable to sb; praise or flatter sb in the hope of winning his favour: *Susan's clever, you know. She realizes it pays to butter her father up—he's much softer towards her than he is to the boys.* Also **butter up to sb.**

***butter* wouldn't melt in sb's mouth** *(saying)* sb seems a well-behaved and harmless person (usually implying that his appearance is deceiving): *Fancy her treating a patient like that, and she looks as if butter wouldn't melt in her mouth!*

**know which side one's bread is *buttered* (on) → *know***

**have (got) *butterflies* (in one's stomach/ tummy) → *have***

***button* sth up** *(informal)* conclude or make definite the final details of a plan or arrangement: *Now that we've agreed the terms of the transfer between ourselves, it won't take long for our solicitors to button the whole thing up.*

***(buy)* a pig in a poke** *(informal)* buy sth you have not examined or cannot examine first: *We booked a holiday chalet we saw advertised in a newspaper—buying a pig in a poke, I suppose, but it turned out all right.*

***buy* it** *(slang)* die or be killed: *The doctor shook his head and stood up. 'Bought it, has he?' the ambulance man asked.*

**(not) *buy* it/that** *(informal)* not believe, accept, or tolerate sth: *'Tell her you tried to ring but couldn't get an answer.' 'She won't buy that; my mother may be old but she's not that daft!' / 'The idea seems to be that I do the work and the Director takes the credit. Well, you can tell him I'm not buying it!'*

***buzz* off** *(informal)* go away; leave: *I've enjoyed our chat but now I must buzz off and finish my shopping. / 'We're just watching you, Grandpa.' 'Well, I don't want to be watched when I'm shaving. Buzz off.'*

***by* and by** presently; after a little time: *I keep telling myself that life is bound to get easier by and by, and perhaps it will.*

***by* and large** viewed in a general way; in the main: *There is more mechanization in the fields, but by and large the farmer's life is not much different from what it was 50 years ago.*

**let *bygones* be bygones → *let***

# C

**at sb's *call*** (of people and/or their services) ready to assist or supply sb whenever he orders or asks: *Now understand that we're at your call, day or night, and don't hesitate to ask for help. / With all the experts he has at his call, you would have thought that the Defence Minister would have come better informed.*

**on *call*** (of doctors, rescue teams etc) required to be quickly available for duty if needed: *Do try to come! If you're on call for the hospital that evening you can give them our phone number.*

***call* a spade a spade** name or describe sb/sth plainly and directly: *'The boy has learning difficulties.' 'You mean he's a dunce,' said his father, who liked to call a spade a spade.*

***call* sb's bluff** give sb the chance to do what he says he will or to prove what he claims, and perhaps find that he really won't or can't: *Next time she threatens to resign we'll call her bluff and say, 'Get going, then.' / The owner says he knows where he can get a higher price for his caravan, but I'm tempted to call his bluff and not increase my offer.*

***call* for sth** need or require sth: *The repair work called for greater skill than mine. / 'I told her to mind her own business.' 'That wasn't called for, Sarah* (or *That was quite uncalled for*). *She only wanted to help.'*

**have (got) no, less, more etc *call* for sth → *have***

***call* sth in** request or order the return of sth: *The bank has decided to call in all its loans immediately. / The car company is calling in all Mark II models as it has been discovered that the brakes on that design are defective.*

***call* sth into play → *bring*/call sth into play**

***call* it a day** decide you have done enough (work) for the day and stop: *We can't do any more till the cement hardens. Let's call it a day and go home.*

***call* it quits** agree to end an argument or quarrel at a point where both sides have equal honour, advantage etc.

***call* sb names** or **call names at sb** jeer at or

insult sb with rude or unpleasant names: *In the playground they called him names like 'Fatty' and 'Stinkpot'.*

**(above and) beyond the *call* of duty** *(formal)* used to describe an even greater degree of courage, effort, or self-sacrifice than is usual or expected in a role or profession: *The young policeman later received an award for bravery beyond the call of duty. / It is the little acts of personal kindness that go above and beyond the call of duty that distinguish a dedicated nurse from a merely efficient one.*

**a/the *call* of nature** *(euphemistic)* a need to empty the bladder or bowels: *He had left the meeting to answer a call of nature.*

***call* sb/sth off** order sb to stop doing sth such as attacking or pursuing: *For God's sake, call your dog off before he kills one of those lambs.*

***call* sth off** cancel a plan, arrangement, or business deal before or after it has begun: *Water union leaders last night rejected a request from the government to call off their strike. / The search for the missing climbers was called off last night.*

***call* on sth** (need to) use some supply or resources: *If a problem arises with your car, the engineers can call on a huge, comprehensive back-up service that covers the country.*

***call* sb out** order workers to go on strike: *The miners have stopped work today after being called out by their leaders.*

**(not) have (got) a minute/moment to *call* one's own** ⟶ ***have***

***call* the kettle black** ⟶ **the *pot* calls the kettle black**

***call* the tune/shots** *(informal)* have control of a situation; decide what other people should do: *You'll do it whether you like it or not—I call the tune here.* See also **he who *pays* the piper calls the tune.**

***call*/bring/hold sb to account** *(formal)* require sb to explain his misconduct, error, or failure (and blame or punish him for it): *They terrorize the region, and no one dares call them to account. / Keep the cupboards locked, for it's you that'll be brought to account over anything that goes missing.*

**have (got) no, less, more etc *call* to do sth** ⟶ ***have***

***call* sb up** summon sb to do military or national service: *Jack enlisted soon after war was declared—he didn't wait to be called up.* **call-up** *n, adj*: *Call-up dates for the various age groups were announced in the newspapers.* See also ***join* up.**

***call* sth up** bring back sth such as a memory, scene, or incident to your mind: *The photograph was faded, but what happy memories it called up!*

**don't *call* us, we'll call you** *(informal)* (said by or about sb who is not very interested in meeting or doing business with another person again; the expression refers to telephone calls but implies any means of getting or keeping in touch): *I had hoped we might be friends, but her attitude was clearly one of 'don't call us, we'll call you.'* Also **don't ring us, we'll ring you.**

**the *calm* before the storm** a period of deceptive calm before a violent outburst such as a storm, war, or anger starts: *What the country was experiencing was not peace but just the calm before another storm. / I knew his self-control wouldn't last and hoped to leave in the calm before the storm.*

***camp* sth up** *(informal)* make a play, film, or role exaggeratedly stylized, sentimental, or melodramatic in order to entertain an audience: *The producer wanted to camp the whole thing up and play it for laughs.* **camped-up** *adj*: *a camped-up version of 'Love's Labour's Lost'.*

**in the *can*** *(informal)* already decided, arranged, ready to be used, or put into practice: *I don't need to worry about a grant—my application's been approved so it's in the can.*

***can* it** *(slang)* = shut up: *'Can it, you two!' said their father. 'Any more quarrelling and off you go to bed!'*

**burn the *candle* at both ends** ⟶ ***burn***

**'*cannon* fodder** troops thought of as expendable in the cause of winning a war.

**if the *cap* fits, (wear it)** *(saying)* if you are not named in a criticism or rebuke but feel you deserve to be, then accept it (and try to improve): *'There are too many lazy people in this house.' 'Including me, I suppose?' 'If the cap fits, wear it.'*

**go *cap* in hand** ⟶ ***go***

**to *cap* it all** ⟶ **to *crown*/cap it all**

**. . . with a *capital* A, B, C etc** (used for emphasis to indicate 'very great'): *When I say he's a bore, I mean a bore with a capital B!* See also **. . . with a *small*/little a, b, c, etc.**

**a *carbon* copy of sb/sth** sb/sth that is exactly or extremely like another: *The recent robberies in south London are a carbon copy of those that have occurred in other parts of the capital over the last few months.*

**a *card*-carrying Communist, member etc** a registered member of the Communist party or other (political) group (sometimes said jokingly about sb strongly committed to an opinion or course of action): *He was a card-carrying Communist in the days when there weren't many of them outside the Soviet Union. / A visit to the slaughter-house would turn quite a few of you into card-carrying vegetarians.*

**on the *cards*** *(informal)* likely or possible: *With a railway strike on the cards for next week, flight bookings have been unusually high. / It's quite on the cards that, at his age, your brother will marry again.*

**in *care*** (of children) housed and looked after in a government institution (because their parents are homeless, do not or cannot look after them properly etc): *I was reading an article about children in care. / The social worker recommended that their baby be taken into care.*

**(not) *care*/give a brass farthing etc (about/for sb/sth)** *(old-fashioned)* (not) concern yourself or (not) value, respect or fear sb/sth: *I'm invited, but they won't care a brass farthing whether I come or not.* Alternatives to ***a brass farthing*** are: ***a damn; a fig; a tinker's cuss; two hoots; twopence***: *'Tell her it's inconvenient.' 'Do you really suppose she would care a fig about that?'* / *'Don't you care what you look like?' 'Not two hoots, my dear.'*

***care* for sb/sth** like sb/sth; be pleased to have sth: *Jane seems to like him—I don't care much for him, myself.* / *Would you care for a drink?* Note that this is used with a negative, or as a question with ***would.***

***care* of sb** at the address of a householder, business, firm, or institution (usually written c/o): *I don't know his private address, but a letter sent care of the BBC in London will reach him.*

***care* to do sth** like or be willing to do sth: *John would help, but he's so busy with other things I don't care to bother him.* / *Would you care to take a seat? The manager will be along to see you presently.*

**a *caretaker* government, manager etc** a temporary government etc that acts until a new one is elected or appointed.

**be past/beyond *caring* (about sth)** have reached a stage when you no longer care about or are no longer affected by sth: *She can't hurt him now because he's beyond caring about what she says.* / *'We're coming into port now,' they said—but I felt so ill I was past caring.*

**be on the *carpet*** *(informal)* (be sent for and) receive a scolding or reprimand, especially from an employer or superior: *That's twice Johnson has been on the carpet for exceeding his authority. He won't be excused a third time.* **have sb on the carpet** treat sb in this way.

**sweep/brush sth under the *carpet*** → ***sweep***

**pull the *carpet*/rug (out) from under sb's feet** → ***pull***

***carried* away** so moved, interested, and excited that you cannot keep your thoughts or actions under control: *She let herself be carried away with enthusiasm for the project and promised more than she could do.* / *'We could have a wonderful holiday, redecorate the house, and . . . '. 'Now, now, don't get carried away. We haven't won the money yet!'*

**the *carrot* and/or the stick** reward and/or punishment or persuasion and/or compulsion as methods of getting people to work, behave well, or do as sb wishes: *'I believe in using the carrot instead of the stick in the classroom.' 'I believe in a bit of both.'*

***carry* all/everything before one** be completely successful in a battle, a competition, your career etc: *In three successive tournaments this young player has carried all before him.* / *If their delegates came to the conference expecting to carry everything before them they soon found themselves mistaken.*

***carry*/take coals to Newcastle** bring or provide goods, facilities, or information of a kind in ample supply already: *'I wish I had brought you some of our fresh eggs, but I thought I would be carrying coals to Newcastle.' 'So you might have been. It's only six months since we stopped keeping hens.'* Sometimes shortened to **coals to Newcastle.**

***carry* one's cross(es)** → ***bear*/carry one's cross(es)**

***carry* it/sth off** make a success of sth, especially in a difficult or embarrassing situation: *I suggest we wait to see if we carry off the robbery before we congratulate ourselves.* / *I think he should have apologized for his blunder instead of trying to carry it off with a joke.*

***carry* on** *(informal)* behave in a troublesome, noisy, unsuitable, or suspicious way: *If you children always carry on like this it's no wonder your mother's ill.* **carry-on; ˌcarryings-ˈon** (*pl only*) *n*: *I see some cricketers have started the same carry-on as footballers—hugging each other after a success.* / *Several neighbours have reported strange carryings-on at night.*

***carry* on (with sb)** *(informal)* flirt; have a casual or adulterous love affair (with sb): *'You'll have a grand time in hospital,' she teased, 'living like a lord and carrying on with all the nurses!'* / *How long do you suppose the pair of them had been carrying on before her husband found out?* Note that this is often used in continuous tenses.

***carry* on (with) sth** or **carry on (doing sth)** continue or persevere, in a course of life, work, or action; continue with a task or with what you are doing at a particular time: *Sometimes he got so depressed he felt he couldn't carry on.* / *The rest of the band carried on playing, and few dancers noticed Jim being helped from the stage.* / *I want you to carry on with the antibiotic till the infection is quite cleared up.*

***carry* on sth** conduct or manage a business or trade; conduct or be engaged in a conversation or correspondence: *It was in these premises that my grandfather carried on his ironmonger's business.* / *She is studying both French and German but can't carry on a conversation in either of them.*

***carry* on (about sth)** *(informal)* talk, fuss, complain etc (excessively) about sth: *He carried on about that £5 note he'd lost as if it had been his life's savings.* / *It's little Sarah's pet—she'll carry on something dreadful if her budgie dies.* **carry-on** *n*: *What a carry-on about a few scratches!*

**to *carry* on with** (of material, money, or work) (enough) for present needs or use until more is required or available: *'I'll get more paint sent up from the warehouse for you.' 'No hurry—I've got enough (or plenty) to carry on with.'* Also **to be going on with.**

***carry* out sth 1** conduct or be engaged in sth such as an experiment, an enquiry, or repairs: *Cancer research is being carried out in laboratories all over the world. / There is a shortage of the right personnel to carry out these duties.* **2** fulfil a promise, threat, or purpose; act or perform as planned, ordered, or requested: *The party's promises at election time have not been carried out. / Don't blame us, guv'nor. We're only carrying out orders!*

***carry* the can (for sb/sth)** *(informal)* take the responsibility or blame (instead of sb or for sth that sb has done): *'Will you be my guarantor for a loan?' 'And carry the can if you don't repay it? Not likely!' / The warders who were reprimanded say they have been made to carry the can for faults in the prison system.*

***carry*/win the day** win a battle, contest, or argument; prove to be the strongest influence or consideration: *For once, objectors to a government-backed scheme have carried the day. / I was tempted to lie about my qualifications, but when it came to it, conscience won the day.*

***carry* (the weight of) the world on one's shoulders** (feel that you are) burdened with many heavy responsibilities: *You never see her without that worried look on her face, as if she were carrying the weight of the world on her shoulders.* Also **carry all the troubles of the world on one's shoulders.**

***carry* sb through (sth)** (of sth such as faith in God or family support) help sb to survive a period of illness, danger, or difficulty: *When most people would have given up the struggle, his own will to live carried him through.*

***carry* sth through** complete a process, enterprise, or course of action; act consistently with a belief or policy you have: *She worked hard for these reforms and lived to see them carried through. / Don't set yourself up as a disciplinarian unless you mean to carry it through.*

***carry* sth too, rather etc far** extend a practice beyond right or reasonable limits: *It's rude to refuse a gift. You can carry independence too far. / 'Our dentist's children aren't allowed to eat sweets at all.' 'That's carrying things a bit far, don't you think?'*

**in the *cart*** *(informal)* facing defeat, failure, punishment, or sb's anger: *See you keep quiet about this or you'll land us all in the cart.*

**put the *cart* before the horse** ⟶ ***put***

**give sb *carte* blanche** ⟶ ***give***

***carve* up sth** divide land, an empire etc, especially between the victors in a war: *At the conference the leaders decided how they would carve up the territory of the defeated side.* **carve-up** *n.*

**(just) in *case* (it rains, of trouble etc)** so as to be prepared for sth that may or may not happen: *Somebody should stay here in case John rings. / 'Did John say he would phone?' 'No, but somebody should stay here just in case.'* See also **in *case* of sth.**

**in 'any *case*** ⟶ ***any***

**a *case* in point** sb/sth you mention as a particular example to illustrate a general statement: *Some people only work well under pressure, and our David is a case in point.*

**in *case* of sth** *(formal)* if a difficulty or emergency such as fire occurs: *Instructions for procedure in case of fire are displayed throughout the building. / In case of difficulty, dial 100 for the operator.* See also **(just) in *case* (it rains, of trouble etc).**

***cash* in (on sth)** *(informal)* obtain for yourself (financial) benefit from sth such as a demand for goods, a current fashion, or sb else's misfortune: *During the week of the fair, hotels and boarding-houses cash in on the shortage of accommodation by raising their prices. / 'Your mother got a good price for her house, I hear.' 'Yes, and there'll be at least one member of the family hoping to cash in.'*

***cash* in one's chips** *(slang)* die: *Stop worrying about my health, dear. I don't intend to cash in my chips for a long time yet.*

**the die is *cast*** ⟶ ***die***

***cast* a veil over sth** ⟶ ***draw*/throw/cast a veil over sth**

***cast* about/around for sth** move here and there searching for sth; try to find or think of sth to do or say: *The hounds cast about for a scent, suddenly found it, and were off. / She cast around in her mind for an answer that would satisfy his curiosity.*

***cast*/run an eye (on/over sth, to the left, etc)** glance or look at sb/sth: *'He's so used to staff coming in and out that he never even cast an eye in my direction. I could have walked off with anything.'* Instead of **an eye, one's eye(s)** can be used: *Just run your eye(s) over this list and tell me if anything should be added.*

***cast* in one's lot with sb** ⟶ ***throw*/cast in one's lot with sb**

***cast* light (up)on sth** ⟶ ***throw*/cast/shed light (up)on sth**

***cast* lots (for sth)** ⟶ ***draw*/cast lots (for sth)**

***cast* off** release the ropes and cables that fasten a boat or ship to its docking-place: *We cast off at 0540, just before daybreak.*

***cast* sb off** abandon or reject sb, especially a lover: *Her mother was rather annoyed with her for casting off yet another nice young man.* **cast-off** *n, adj*: *In so small a town he could not always avoid encounters with his cast-offs (or cast-off mistresses).*

***cast* pearls before swine** waste sth valuable or of good quality on sb who cannot appreciate, enjoy, or benefit from it: *'She wants to start an Art Appreciation class here next winter—casting pearls before swine, I'm afraid.' 'Well, you never know till you try.'*

***cast* the first stone (at sb/sth)** *(formal)* be the first person (though others may be ready to join in) to attack openly, criticize or condemn sb/sth.

**(build) *castles* in the air** ⟶ ***build***

**put/set the *cat* among the pigeons** ⟶ ***put***

**fight like *cat* and dog** ⟶ ***fight***

**(play) a *cat*-and-mouse (game) (with sb)** ⟶ ***play***

**a *cat* can/may look at a king** *(saying)* you can't stop anybody looking at or watching another person who is there to be seen, however important that person may be and whether he likes it or not: *'It's rude to stare, you'll embarrass them.' 'I wasn't staring. And even if I was, a cat can look at a king, can't it?'*

**a *cat* has nine lives** *(saying)* cats are very tough and seem able to survive many accidents or hardships (often used in comparisons): *God knows how he's still alive. He's like a cat with nine lives* (or *He must have nine lives like a cat*).

**(not) have (got) a *cat* in 'hell's chance (of doing sth)** ⟶ ***have***

**see which way the *cat* jumps** ⟶ ***see***

**like a *cat* on hot bricks** *(informal)* restless, nervous, or uneasy: *He'll be like a cat on hot bricks till he gets his exam results.*

**let the *cat* out of the bag** ⟶ ***let***

**when the *cat*'s away the mice will play** ⟶ ***when***

**look what the *cat*'s brought/dragged in!** ⟶ ***look***

**the *cat*'s got sb's tongue** sb doesn't speak or answer because he is too shy or timid or doesn't know what to say: *'The cat's got her tongue, I think,' Emma's mother apologized for her, but the little girl hung her head still lower. / Are you deaf or has the cat got your tongue? The Inspector here has asked you a question!*

**the *cat*'s pyjamas/whiskers** *(informal)* sb/sth extremely fine or exactly what you like, need, or want: *'You think it's a good plan, then?' 'It's the cat's whiskers—bound to succeed!'* See also **the *bees'* knees.**

**like the *cat* that ate/stole the cream** *(informal)* well-pleased, smug, or very satisfied: *There he is in the front row, smiling to himself like the cat that stole the cream.*

**(you won't) *catch* sb (doing sth)** *(informal)* sb never does, is not likely ever to do, sth: *He'll want some money for it, of course. You won't catch Henry doing any work without being paid for it!*

**a sprat to *catch* a mackerel/whale** ⟶ ***sprat***

***catch* as catch can** *(informal)* (a situation where) each person advances his own interests, trying to get as much as possible of what he needs or wants himself: *'She's George's girl really, and you're trying to cut him out.' 'So what? It's catch as catch can in this world, you know.'*

***catch* sb's/one's breath** (make sb) gasp, cough, or choke: *Rain soaked him, and the icy wind caught his breath. / The magnificent view made us catch our breath.*

***catch* one's death (of cold)** *(informal)* get such a bad cold you could die (usually said, with no real fear of death, to warn, advise, or complain): *Wrap up well if you must go out. I don't want you catching your death of cold. / It was nearly as wet inside the tents as out. It's a wonder we didn't all catch our deaths.*

***catch* sb's eye** obtain or happen to get sb's notice so that you can communicate in some way: *If you can catch a steward's eye without making too much fuss, beckon him over here.*

***catch*/take sb's fancy** please or attract sb: *Mary seems afraid that if she's not constantly around, some other girl may catch his fancy. / She saw that the picture had taken my fancy and insisted on giving it to me.* Also *(informal)* **tickle sb's fancy.**

***catch* fire 1** start to burn: *She stumbled against the fireguard and her nightdress caught fire.* **2** (of feelings, a plan, a performance etc) become lively or impassioned, show or arouse great interest: *They've launched a national campaign, but if it's ever to catch fire it won't be with speakers like those we've heard today.*

***catch* sb in the act (of doing sth)** discover sb while he is engaged in doing sth criminal or wrong or sth that he doesn't want to be found doing: *The police were tipped off, and they caught him* (or *he was caught*) *in the act of loading the stolen goods into his van. / Aha! Caught in the act! I thought you said you'd given up smoking?* Note that this is often used in the passive.

***catch* it** *(informal)* be punished or scolded: *He'd lost his new school case and torn his trousers, so he didn't half catch it when he got home. / Better get back on the ward. We'll catch it from Sister if she finds us gossiping here.*

***catch* sb napping** surprise, outwit, or gain an advantage over sb because he has not been sufficiently alert, attentive, or well-prepared: *Two publishing firms who had previously turned down this highly successful book admitted they'd been caught napping.*

***catch* on (to sth)** *(informal)* understand what is being said or done; become aware of what a situation or activity really is: *The lawyer explained his position to him, but you could see he still didn't catch on.*

***catch* on (with sb)** *(informal)* become popular or fashionable with the general public or with certain groups: *Nicotine-free cigarettes were put on the market a few years ago but they never really caught on. / Jogging for fitness seems to be catching on with as many middle-aged and elderly people as younger ones.*

***catch* sb on the hop** put or find sb in a situation he is unprepared for; catch or discover sb in error or at fault: *The early start of winter that year caught many cattle-farmers on the hop.*

***catch* sb out** outwit or trick sb in a deal, contest, or argument; show that sb has made a mistake or acted wrongly: *Emily is such a know-all that I was delighted to catch her out on a matter of plain historical fact.*

***catch* sb red-handed** find or capture sb while he is committing a crime or wrongdoing, or with the evidence of it on him: *I've a good* *idea who's stealing from my orchard, but the only way to prove it is to catch them red-handed.*

***catch* the/sb's eye** be easily seen or quickly noticed; have an attractive, interesting, or unusual appearance: *When every kind of packaging competes to catch the eye (of the customer) the total effect is null.* **eye-catching** adj: *an eye-catching design.*

**(not) *catch* the name, what was said etc** (not) hear clearly sth told to you or said within your hearing: *I'm afraid I didn't quite catch your name when we were introduced. / 'Did you catch any of that?' she asked Tom when the voice over the loudspeaker stopped.*

***catch* 22** a difficulty from which a victim cannot escape because the way of escape is blocked by conditions or reasons that were part of the original situation, the result being that there is no real choice in such an absurd predicament: *a catch-22 situation.*

***catch*/take sb unawares** approach or capture sb unexpectedly or when he doesn't know you are there; do or ask sth that finds sb unprepared to deal with it: *He can outrun any of you. Your only chance is to creep up and take him unawares.*

***catch* up (on sth)** bring yourself up to date in information or in your understanding of new ideas and practice: *The conference will be your chance to catch up on the latest developments in the industry.*

***catch* up (on/with sb)** follow sb quickly enough to reach or overtake him; reach the same level in a competition, skill, or course of study as sb who was ahead of you: *The visitors established an early lead in the quiz, and the local team never looked like catching up (on/ with them).* Also **catch sb up:** *You start off with the children and I'll catch you up.*

***catch* up (on/with sth)** do sth you have left undone for lack of opportunity or because you have been neglectful: *It's been a long journey. I'll be better company tomorrow after I've caught up on my sleep. / It seems to me you have a lot of catching up to do before your exam.*

***catch* up on/with sb** (of sth such as age or a secret in the past) have an effect or result that sb can no longer escape: *He's looked much the same for over 30 years, but age has finally caught up with him now.*

***catch* sb with his pants/trousers down** *(informal)* confront, trap, or deceive sb when he is unprepared or not being watchful or attentive: *They maintained full guard in case a second attack should catch them with their trousers down.*

**rain/pour *cats* and dogs** ⟶ ***rain***

**be *caught* short** ⟶ **be *taken*/caught short**

***cause*/create a ripple/stir** cause some talk, interest, surprise etc in an audience, a group or the public: *The possibility of a royal visit caused quite a ripple at the hospital.*

**give *cause* for sth** ⟶ ***give***

***cave* in 1** collapse; fall inwards: *Without these supports the tunnel would cave in.* **cave-in** n: *Subsidence could cause a cave-in.* **2** collapse under difficulties; yield when threatened or opposed: *Those who fight the disease instead of just caving in may prolong their life and can certainly improve the quality of it.*

***cease* fire** stop firing guns, etc in warfare: *The signal was given to cease fire.* **cease-fire** n: *The rebel leader asked for a cease-fire in order to negotiate terms for surrender.*

**know for *certain* that . . .** ⟶ ***know***

**(separate) the *chaff* and/from the wheat/ grain** ⟶ ***separate***

***chalk* sth up** *(informal)* add a success to a record or score: *Our team chalked up yet another fine victory at the weekend.*

***chalk* sth up (to sb** or **on sb's slate)** *(informal)* allow a customer to have credit for sth, especially drinks in a public house: *A whisky and soda—and chalk it up please. / He'll get no more drinks chalked up to him (*or *chalked on his slate) till he pays something on account.*

***champ* at the bit** *(informal)* be impatient and fretful when kept from starting sth you are eager to do: *Hurry up with your goodbyes or Jimmy'll be off without you. He's champing at the bit out there.*

**on the 'off *chance* (that)** ⟶ ***off***

**as *chance* has/had it** *(formal)* as it happens/ happened, fortunately or unfortunately: *'Do you have a room to let?' 'As chance has it, we do. Would you like to see it?' / I was standing by the window, as chance had it, and got cut when it broke.*

**(not) a *chance* in a million** a very unlikely possibility: *If it was on the beach that you lost your ring then there isn't (*or *you haven't) a chance in a million of ever finding it.*

**(not) have (got) a *chance* in hell (of doing sth)** ⟶ **(not) *have* (got) a cat in 'hell's chance (of doing sth)**

***chance* it** *(informal)* take the risk, in deciding to do sth, that you may be unlucky or may not achieve what you want: *I think I'll chance it and park here. It's only for half an hour and the traffic wardens can't be everywhere.* Also **chance one's arm/luck:** *Any marriage is a matter of chancing your luck to some extent.*

**the *chance* of a lifetime** a much greater opportunity for profit or pleasure than you are ever likely to get again: *I've been offered a place in the Baikal ecological survey team—it's the chance of a lifetime!*

***chance* upon sb** meet sb accidentally: *The friends just happened to chance upon each other on holiday in Wales.*

**the *chances* are (that) . . .** it is probable that . . . ; it is more likely than not that . . . : *The chances are the hurricane will blow itself out before it reaches here.*

***change* one's coat** ⟶ ***turn* one's coat**

***change* (sb/sth) for the better/worse** (cause sb/sth to) get better/worse: *This dreadful weather must be spoiling your holiday. Let's hope it will change for the better soon. / If a boy's nature has already been warped by*

*harsh treatment, further punishment may change him for the worse.*
**change hands** (of property or articles) pass from one owner to another: *We still call it 'Joe's Cafe' although it has changed hands twice since Joe had it.*
**change horses in mid-stream** → ***swap* horses in mid-stream**
**a *change* of heart** (an example of) changed opinions and feelings, especially implying that you now behave better or more responsibly or kindly: *'You surprise me—I had the impression your boy was very anti-school.' 'So he was, but he seems to have had a change of heart.'*
**the *change* of life** the menopause in women.
***change* places (with sb)** exchange seats or other actual positions; exchange circumstances or a role in life or work with another person or group: *In the train, a kind person offered to change places so that Emily could sit beside her friend. / The Smiths can afford to go on expensive foreign holidays because they haven't a family to bring up. But I wouldn't change places with them for the world!*
***change* the subject** talk or write about something else for the sake of variety or because to do so would be wise or tactful: *We tried to get him to state his intentions clearly, but he successfully managed to change the subject whenever he felt he was being questioned too closely.*
***change* one's tune** change your opinion about or your attitude towards sb/sth: *'Parents worry too much about their children,' Tom used to say. But he changed his tune when he became a parent himself!*
**(give) *chapter* and verse (for sth)** → ***give***
**a *chapter* of accidents** several minor unfortunate events following one after another in a short period of time: *What a chapter of accidents! It's not been your lucky day, has it?*
**in/out of *character*** (of sb's behaviour or action) characteristic/uncharacteristic of sb; just the sort of thing you would or would not expect him to do: *'I'm sure it was Bill I saw from the bus. He was arguing with a policeman.' 'That's in character, anyway. What a fool he is!' / For Emily to assert herself in that way was completely out of character—she must have been greatly provoked.*
***charge*/pay the earth (for sth)** *(informal)* charge/pay a very high price (for goods or services): *When these vegetables are out of season, you have to pay the earth for them.*
**work/act like a *charm*** → ***work***
***chat* up** *(informal)* talk to sb, especially of the opposite sex, in order to win his or her friendship or have an affair: *Who was that girl I saw you chatting up at the party?*
**on the *cheap*** *(informal)* at a low or reduced price (often implying possible lack of quality): *I didn't mind roughing it a bit when I was younger, but holidays on the cheap are not the kind I want now.*
***cheap*/dear at the price** worth more/less (to sb) than the price paid: *This magnificently illustrated book costs £15 and for the serious student of botany is cheap at the price.*
**keep/hold sb/sth in *check*** → ***keep***
***check* in (at sth)** report and/or register your arrival at an airport or your place of work, or whenever it is authorized or required: *I phoned the hotel and they say our friends haven't checked in yet.* **check-in** *n, adj*: *George knows a way of getting into the hall that avoids the check-in (point).*
***check* out (from sth)** pay your bill and leave a hotel or self-service store; (record when you) finish work: *Remind guests to leave their room keys with the porter when they check out. / Emma checked out from the laboratory as usual, around 4.30.* **check-out** *n*: *Supermarket customers are dissatisfied with having to queue so long at the check-outs.*
***check* up (on sb/sth)** investigate sb's background, behaviour etc in order to learn more about him or to find out what he is doing; test sth, by further examination, in order to see whether facts or figures are correct: *Surely you wouldn't expect to get a post, however humble, in the Foreign Office without them checking up on you. / 'You asked me all these questions before, officer.' 'Yes, madam. I'm just checking up.'* **check-up** *n* a medical examination. Also **check sb/sth out** *(mainly US)*: *Our suspect says the train he was on got into Euston 14 minutes late. Check that out with the station, will you?*
***cheek* by jowl (with)** side by side (with): *If he had known he was to find himself seated cheek by jowl with his old enemy he wouldn't have attended the dinner.*
***cheesed*/browned off** *(slang)* bored, jaded, or irritated: *She'd now been describing her trip for a full half-hour and James was looking throroughly browned off.*
**a *chequered* career/history** a lifetime or long record of ups and downs in fortune, changes of occupation or function, or variety of experiences: *Sailor, waiter, stage-hand, driving instructor—I couldn't list all the jobs old Jack had had, but I rather think a short term or two in prison has formed part of his chequered career.*
**get sth off one's *chest*** → ***get***
**bite off more than one can *chew*** → ***bite***
***chew* sth over** *(informal)* carefully consider a matter or proposed action: *What a difficult question! I'll have to chew it over before I can give you an answer.* Note that this is usually used with ***it***, ***this***, or ***that*** referring to sth already mentioned.
***chew* the cud (of sth)** *(informal)* think about or discuss sth seriously or reflectively: *Well, you've given me a lot to think about. I'll go home now and chew the cud a bit before I make my decision.*
***chew* the fat/rag (about sth)** *(informal)* talk about (recent) events, often in a criticizing or grumbling way: *You know how it is with Bill and Tom. After a rugby match they'll chew the*

*fat for hours.* Note that the subject is usually plural.

**no *chicken* ⟶ *no***

**a *chicken*-and-egg situation** a situation where you do not know which of two connected or interrelated events is the cause of the other. There are variants on this idiom: **which came first, the chicken or the egg?; the chicken and/or the egg:** *If giraffes evolved long necks in order to feed from tree foliage, what did they live on until they did? It's the old problem of the chicken and the egg.*

**'*chicken* feed** sth of little value, especially a small or insufficient amount of money in comparison with a larger sum: *What the government might have to pay out to keep the coal industry going is chicken feed compared with the cost in misery if it collapses.*

***chicken* out (of sth)** *(informal)* take no further part in sth you have planned or started to do when it becomes difficult or dangerous: *Some of those who said they would support strike action chickened out when it came to a vote. / Strong men have been known to chicken out of a visit to the dentist.*

**one's *chickens*, misdeeds etc come home to roost** your misdeeds, especially wrongs done to others, recoil upon yourself: *His neglect of family ties has come home to roost in his old age, for he has nobody to care about what happens to him now.*

**'*child's* play (to sb)** a very easy job or task (for sb): *Filling in my Income Tax forms is child's play compared to what it was when I was self-employed.*

***chill* sb's blood/marrow ⟶ one's *blood* freezes**

***chill* sb to the bone/marrow ⟶ *freeze*/chill sb to the bone/marrow**

**send a *chill* up/down sb's spine ⟶ *send* a chill/shiver up/down sb's spine**

***chime* in (with sth)** *(informal)* add sth to or interrupt a conversation, especially in order to agree: *'A man with your chest shouldn't be smoking at all.' 'That's what I keep telling him, doctor,' his wife chimed in.*

**take sth on the *chin* ⟶ *take***

***chin* up! ⟶ *keep* one's chin/pecker up**

**a *chink* in sb's armour** *(informal)* a weakness or fault that sb has which might allow other people to defeat, criticize, or exploit him: *Nevertheless, she has a chink in her armour. She hasn't got a sense of humour and gets quite rattled when people won't take her seriously.*

***chip* in (with sth) 1** *(informal)* interrupt a conversation etc (with a comment, question, or correction): *Rosemary went on, 'And then the Irishman said to the Englishman . . .'. 'We've heard that one before,' chipped in Ruth.* **2** *(informal)* contribute (a sum of) money or (article of) goods towards a fund, gift, or loan: *The skipper of the 'Sea Star' said his crew would like to chip in if a collection was being made for the pilot's widow.*

**a *chip* off the old block** *(informal)* a person who is very like one of his/her parents in appearance and/or character, especially a son who is like his father.

**have (got) a '*chip* on one's shoulder ⟶ *have***

**the *chips* are down** *(informal)* the situation you are in is serious, urgent, or desperate, and action must be taken that will bring success or failure: *When the BBC started to lose audiences to its rivals, when the chips were down, it used its power and met competition with competition.*

***chips* with everything** *(informal)* conventional, unimaginative food and catering: *Besides providing them with the usual chips with everything, some of the restaurants try to tempt British holidaymakers with local dishes.*

**there's nothing to *choose* between A and B ⟶ *nothing***

***chop* and change** be often changing or changed; (be apt to) alter your plans, methods, or opinions frequently: *I'll never get used to the way the weather chops and changes in Britain. / There's been so much chopping and changing of the timetables since term began, staff are always turning up in the wrong classrooms.* Also **chop about.**

***chuck* sth (in/up)** *(informal)* give up your job or an activity, habit, or task: *She said it was a dead-end job and chucked it in.*

**off one's *chump* ⟶ off one's *head***

***churn* sth out** manufacture goods, provide information, or write, paint, or compose in large, regular quantities (used to imply that the product is of average or poor quality): *In this factory they made nothing but T-shirts, churning them out at the rate of 12,000 a week. / 'Still churning out those serials for women's mags, are you?' 'I make a living. There's no need to sneer.'*

***clam* up** *(informal)* refuse to speak, say any more, or discuss a particular subject: *When Susan realized what their questions were leading to, she simply clammed up.*

***clamp* down on sth** (of governments or people with authority or influence) (try to) prevent, end, or suppress sth: *The government could save more money by clamping down on tax evasion by large and wealthy companies than on false claims for unemployment money.* **clamp-down** *n*: *I can't ring you, you'll have to ring me—there's been a clamp-down on using office telephones for outgoing personal calls.*

***clap*/set/lay eyes on sb/sth** see sb/sth: *I've no idea who she is. I've never clapped eyes on her before. / From the moment he set eyes on the dog, he knew they'd become firm friends.*

**the man on the *Clapham* omnibus ⟶ the *man* in the street**

***clapped* out** *(slang)* (usually of machines or vehicles but occasionally of people or working animals) too worn out for further use or for repair: *She tried to sell me a clapped-out old cooker. 'No thank you,' I said, 'I'd rather pay* *a lot more to get a new one that works properly.'*

**(go) like the *clappers* → *go***

**in a *class* by oneself/itself** without equal among people or things of the same kind; usually much better than others but sometimes *(humorous)* much worse: *The winning competitor was in a class by herself. The difficulty lay in deciding who should be awarded the second and third prizes.* Also **in a class of one's/its own.**

**as *clean* as a new pin** *(informal)* very clean and tidy: *The place is in rather a mess, but don't worry—I'll leave it as clean as a new pin when I go.*

**as *clean* as a whistle** *(informal)* perfectly clean and free from dirt, disease, or rust; (of an action) done very neatly, accurately, or deftly: *Arms inspections were held without warning and if your rifle wasn't as clean as a whistle you'd be punished. / The dog jumped through the hoop as clean as a whistle.*

**a *clean* bill of health** a statement that sb/sth is in a satisfactory, healthy, or fit condition: *The commission's report gave the power station a clean bill of health following the investigation into standards of safety.*

**make a *clean* breast of sth → *make***

***clean* forget** *(informal)* completely forget (to do) sth: *'Get Jenkins to help you.' 'Jenkins is on holiday.' 'So he is—I'd clean forgotten.' / I'm sorry, I was so upset by other things, I clean forgot to give John your message.* Note that this is usually used with a first-person subject and with past tenses.

**have (got) *clean* hands → *have***

***clean* sb out (of sth)** *(informal)* take or use all sb's money; take or buy all sb's stock: *It was found out later that the gang had broken into the home and cleaned the old lady out of her life's savings. / Not all bakers are on strike, but most stores say they were cleaned out of bread within an hour of taking delivery.*

**be *clean* out of sth** *(informal)* have used or exhausted your whole supply of sth: *I could have left my shopping till tomorrow, except I'm clean out of butter—so I'll have to go today.* See also ***run*/be out of sth.**

**show (sb/sth) a *clean* pair of heels → *show***

**a *clean* slate/sheet** a record of work or conduct that contains nothing to discredit you, sometimes with previous faults or offences forgotten: *Investigate as much as you want to! You'll find I have a clean slate as far as my twenty years of administering trust funds is concerned. / When the father comes out of prison the family hope to move to another district where they can start again with a clean slate.* See also ***wipe* the slate clean.**

**(make) a *clean* sweep (of sth)** *(informal)* (organize) a complete change in sth or a removal of unnecessary things; (achieve) a complete victory in sth: *The athletes completed a clean sweep for Britain last night when they became the sixth British club to reach the semi-finals of the three European competitions.*

***clean* up (sth)** *(informal)* make or win money: *The first season's takings meant that he could pay back his bank loan, and by the end of the second he had cleaned up a small fortune.*

***cleanliness* is next to godliness** *(saying)* being clean in your habits is next in importance to having good religious or moral principles (usually said as a joke): *'That girl always seems to be taking a bath!' 'Oh well, cleanliness is next to godliness!'*

**in the *clear*** not or no longer in danger, trouble, or debt, or under suspicion: *Though he's not quite in the clear yet, it's beginning to look as if the patient may pull through.*

**as *clear* as a bell** easily heard; having a pure sound: *This deaf-aid is really wonderful. I can hear you as clear as a bell.*

**as *clear* as crystal** pure and transparent; obvious or very easy to recognize or understand: *Crossword clues that would puzzle me for a whole afternoon are as clear as crystal to him.*

**as *clear* as day(light)/noon(day)** *(informal)* plain to be seen; easy to notice, recognize, or understand: *Although 'No dogs allowed' is printed on the door as clear as day, people frequently come in with one under their arm or on a lead.*

**as *clear* as mud** *(informal)* not clear at all; difficult to understand: *'The instructions are quite clear.' 'They're as clear as mud! Here, let me read them for myself.'*

**have (got) a *clear* head → *have***

***clear* off** *(informal)* go or run away: *Are you kids here to buy something? Because if not, then clear off.*

***clear* out** *(informal)* leave home for another life: *Her husband treats her like dirt. If it wasn't for the children she'd have cleared out long ago.*

***clear* out (of sth)** *(informal)* leave somewhere quickly to avoid danger, difficulty, or inconvenience: *Then the crowd started throwing bottles and cans, so I decided it was time for me to clear out.*

***clear* the air** lessen or get rid of fears, worries, doubts, or suspicions, by talking or arguing about them frankly: *Sulking serves no purpose, but a good row sometimes clears the air. / The work force here is unsettled by rumours. Nobody wants to be made redundant, but some sort of firm statement would at least clear the air.*

***clear* the deck(s) (for action)** (arrange that other people, things, matters etc are out of the way or dealt with and) get ready for a special activity: *'Come when it suits you,' she told the decorators, 'but give me a day or two's warning so that I can clear the decks.'*

***clear* one's throat** cough once or twice, especially to rid your voice of huskiness when speaking: *The lawyer stood up, cleared his throat, and began to address the jury.*

**(be) in a *cleft* stick** (be) in a situation that is difficult or impossible to get out of, to change, or to make progress in: *I was in a cleft stick—the other firm had offered me a better job, but I still felt very loyal to my company.*

**a 'clever Dick ⟶ a 'smart alec(k)**

***climb* down** *(informal)* admit, after having too confidently made a statement, boast, threat, or accusation, that you were mistaken; (be forced to) behave in a less haughty or domineering way: *It took him a while to convince her of his innocence, but eventually she climbed down and apologized for her suspicions.* **climbdown** *n*: *Monday's announcement represented a climbdown from the government's original uncompromising position.*

***climb* on the bandwagon ⟶ *jump*/climb on the bandwagon**

***clip* sb's wings** limit sb's power, influence, or activities: *The bill was seen as an attempt to clip the wings of the trade unions.*

***cloak*-and-dagger** describing (melodramatic or perhaps murderous) espionage or political or international conspiracies: *There's a lot more painstaking fact-gathering work and a lot less cloak-and-dagger stuff in being a foreign agent than the layman imagines.*

**against the *clock*** *(informal)* (work, race, press forward etc) very fast and hard in order to achieve or complete sth by a certain time or before it is too late: *With the other competitors now far behind he was running against the clock to try to break the course record.*

**(a)round the *clock*** for 24 hours; night and day continuously: *Rescue teams have been working around the clock for nearly a week now to try to find any earthquake victims who are still alive.*

**put/turn/set the *clock* back ⟶ *put***

***clock* in/out** record, often by means of an automatic device, the time when you arrive at or leave a place of work. Also **clock on/off.**

**go/run like *clockwork* ⟶ *go***

**keep a *close* eye on sb/sth ⟶ *have* (got) an/one's eye on sb/sth**

***close*/shut one's eyes to sth** pretend that you can't see or don't know sth in order to avoid embarrassment or trouble: *My son has his faults—and I've never closed my eyes to them—but dishonesty isn't one of them. / It seems clear that doctors, perhaps because of difficulty in staffing some wards, had been shutting their eyes to standards of nursing care that would not have been tolerated elsewhere in the hospital.*

**too *close* for comfort ⟶ *too***

***close* in (on/upon sb/sth)** approach or surround sb/sth in a threatening way: *The soldiers advanced slowly, closing in on the remaining enemy fortifications.*

**be *close* on/upon sb's heels ⟶ be *hard*/close on/upon sb's heels**

**at *close* quarters** from/within a very short distance: *'You made a good job of the paintwork.' 'Not so good if you examine it at close quarters, I'm afraid.'*

***close* (the/one's) ranks** (of the members of a community, profession or organization) co-operate closely to protect and defend each other: *Although the family quarrelled a good deal among themselves, they quickly closed ranks against any outsider who criticized or tried to make trouble for one of them.*

**a *close*/open season** a period of the year in which it is illegal/legal to kill or catch certain animals, birds, or fish.

**a *close* shave/thing** an escape from death, injury, capture, failure or loss, by a very narrow margin or at the last possible moment: *He survived the operation, but it was a close thing, as he himself knows.* Also **a close run thing; a narrow shave/squeak.**

***close*/shut/slam the door ((up)on sb/sth)** make it impossible for sb to do sth or for sth to happen or be done; refuse in a hostile or obstinate way to see or talk to sb or to consider his requests or proposals: *When the government applied to become a member of the European Economic Community, de Gaulle firmly slammed the door on us.* Also **close/shut/slam the door in sb's face.**

**hold/keep/play one's *cards* close to one's chest ⟶ *hold***

**sail *close* to the wind ⟶ *sail***

**a *closed*/sealed book (to sb)** sth about which nothing is known either generally or to sb: *I'm afraid geomorphology is a closed book to me.*

**a *closed* book** a subject that need not or should not be enquired into or discussed again (because it relates to an event or situation which has (been) ended): *'Why shouldn't I help? You got me out of a heap of trouble once.' 'Please! That's a closed book—you're not under any present obligation to me for that.'*

**behind *closed* doors** (of a meeting) taking place in private, with the press and public not admitted: *The two men will appear before the disciplinary committee at a hearing to be held behind closed doors.*

**have (got) a *closed* mind (on sth) ⟶ *have***

**a *closed* shop** the practice, ruling, or agreement under which only people who belong to a recognized trade union may be employed in a factory etc or a trade or profession.

**cut one's coat according to one's *cloth* ⟶ *cut***

**under a *cloud*** *(informal)* suspected of a crime or wrongdoing; in disgrace or out of favour (with sb): *His indiscretions became an embarrassment to the department. He was asked for his resignation and left under a cloud.*

**on *cloud* nine** *(informal)* extremely happy: *He's been on cloud nine since he heard he's been offered a job—he starts next week!*

**a (small) *cloud* on the horizon** a sign of trouble to come; sth that may be a threat to your welfare or happiness: *A small cloud on the horizon is giving the booksellers of this* *country some cause for concern—there is a possibility of a tax being imposed on books.*

**have (got) one's head in the *clouds* ⟶ *have***

**be/live in *clover* ⟶ *live***

**be in the *club*** *(informal)* be pregnant: *She'd only had her baby six months when she found she was in the club again.* **get/put sb in the club** make a girl or woman pregnant.

***clutch*/grasp/snatch at straws** seize any chance or cling to any hope, however slight, or rescue from danger or difficulty: *'Perhaps,' said Jack, clutching at straws, 'she wrote a letter I never got. I wonder if I should phone?'* Also **clutch/grasp/snatch at a straw:** *He'd have scorned the idea of faith-healing once. But you know what they say, a drowning man will grasp at a straw.*

**drive/take a *coach* and horses through sth ⟶ *drive***

**haul sb over the *coals* ⟶ *haul***

**heap *coals* of fire on sb's head ⟶ *heap***

**carry/take *coals* to Newcastle ⟶ *carry***

**the *coast* is clear** you can move, do as you plan, safely or freely, for there is nobody or nothing to endanger, hinder, or inconvenience you: *She poked her head out cautiously, looked left and right to make sure the coast was clear, then darted out across the corridor.*

***cock* sth up** *(slang)* do a job badly; spoil sth: *He's such a fool he couldn't even put a shelf up on a wall without cocking it up.* **cock-up** *n.*

**a *cock*-and-bull story** a story, excuse, or explanation that should not be, or is not likely to be, believed: *An old sailor was entertaining tourists with a cock-and-bull story of how he'd saved a whole crew single-handed.*

**knock/beat sb/sth into a *cocked* hat ⟶ *knock***

**warm the *cockles* (of sb's/one's heart) ⟶ *warm***

**a *coffee*-table book** a handsomely produced book, with many illustrations or photographs and only short pieces of text, that may be left lying in a room for casual reading or to interest a guest or visitor.

**a *cog* in the machine/wheel** sb who plays a part that is small or seems insignificant in a large organization or plan: *At the company I feel just a cog in the machine, not really important, if you know what I mean.*

**to *coin* a phrase** (sometimes added jokingly or ironically when you use an established or well-used idiom): *Tell him exactly what you think. Don't, to coin a phrase, mince your words.*

***coin* it in** earn a lot of money for yourself: *They must be really coining it in at that café on the corner. You can hardly get a seat at any time of the day.* Note that this is usually used in continuous tenses.

**pay sb back in his own *coin* ⟶ *pay***

**come in from the *cold* ⟶ *come***

***leave* sb out in the cold** be excluded from or neglected or ignored by a community, group, or activity: *Of the country's three political party leaders, two were invited to take part in the programme but the third was left out in the cold.*

**as *cold* as charity** very cold; (of people or their actions) unfeeling; impersonal: *Her words themselves were not impolite but her manner was as cold as charity.*

**as *cold* as ice** very cold; (of people) unfeeling; callous: *My feet are as cold as ice, nurse. Can I have a hot-water bottle?* **ice-cold** *adj*: *a glass of ice-cold lager.* / *The look she gave him was ice-cold.* Also **as cold as an iceberg; as cold as marble/stone.**

**in *cold* blood** deliberately and calmly; callously: *The innocent victims were shot in cold blood.* **cold-blooded** *adj*: *a cold-blooded murder.*

***cold* comfort** no or very little help, consolation or sympathy: *When you've just had your car stolen it's cold comfort to be told that it happens to somebody every day.*

***cold* feet ⟶ *get* cold feet**

**in the *cold* light of day** in conditions when a situation, or people or things, can be clearly seen or considered: *Never make a decision or a promise under the influence of any kind of strong emotion because, in the cold light of day, you're very likely to regret it.*

**give sb the *cold* shoulder ⟶ *give***

***cold* turkey** *(slang)* the illness/treatment of a narcotics addict when his drug is suddenly withdrawn, not gradually reduced nor replaced by other drugs to relieve distress.

**pour/throw *cold* water on sth ⟶ *pour***

**hot under the *collar* ⟶ *hot***

**a *Colonel* Blimp** a type of politically right-wing or military person with fixed opinions who ignores or opposes political and social change: *You won't meet many Colonel Blimps in today's armed forces.*

**off *colour*** **1** unwell, in less than your usual good health or spirits: *'You're looking a bit off colour yourself, Mrs Young.' 'Oh, I'm all right, doctor—I'll get more rest now that my husband is on his feet again.'* **2** (of a story, remark etc) improper or in bad taste: *They complained about too many off-colour jokes in shows that were advertised as 'suitable for all the family.'*

**see the *colour* of sb's money ⟶ *see***

**nail one's *colours* to the mast ⟶ *nail***

**as brave, mean etc as they *come*** very brave etc: *He'll have everybody thinking he's in the right and you're in the wrong, for Jack's as cunning as they come.*

***come* a cropper** *(informal)* fall (to the ground); meet with failure or a misfortune: *The horse stumbled and its rider came a cropper.*

***come* about** happen: *'Frances broke her arm this morning.' 'Oh, I'm sorry. How did that come about?'* / *I had picked up a hitchhiker a little earlier. Thus it came about that I had a witness to back up my account of the accident.* See also ***bring* sth about.**

***come* across 1** be communicated or understood: *His speech came across very well, I thought. / You've got ideas, but they don't come across clearly enough.* **2** make an impression of a type that is mentioned: *You must make a real effort to come across well in interviews.*

***come*/run across sb/sth** meet or find sb/sth, especially by chance: *It was the most baffling case I'd come across in all my years of medical practice.*

***come* across (with sth)** *(informal)* give or hand over the money, goods, or information that sb wants or thinks he should get: *The kidnappers gave him 24 hours to come across with the ransom money.*

***come* again?** *(informal)* (please) say that again (often implying that you don't understand or can hardly believe what you've been told): *'This is Peter—he's a dermatologist.' 'Come again?' 'A dermatologist—you know, a specialist in diseases of the skin.'*

**not *come* amiss** be welcome, needed, or able to be used: *Some better weather wouldn't come amiss just now.*

***come* and go** exist or be there for a short time and then stop or depart: *Newspapers come and go, and reluctantly, the time has now come for this one to close. / Please feel free to come and go as you please.*

***come*/fall apart at the seams** *(informal)* develop weaknesses or faults; (seem likely to) break up or collapse: *The team evidently need Watson. When he had to go off injured, their performance really started to come apart at the seams.*

***come* around (to sth)** ⟶ ***come* (a)round (to sth)**

***come* as news to sb** ⟶ **be *news* to sb**

***come* back 1** become popular or fashionable again: *I see that long skirts have come back again this year.* **come-back** *n*: *Sassoon is making a come-back next season and hopes to play in the world championships.* **2** return to your memory: *To begin with, I couldn't think where I'd heard the name before—then it all came back; we'd met at college fifteen years ago.* See also ***bring* sth back 1.** **3** (of a rule, law, or system) be reintroduced or restored: *There are some people who would like to see corporal punishment come back in our schools.* See also ***bring* sth back 2.**

***come* back (to sb) (on/with sth)** reply (to sb) (about sth): *Thank you for your enquiry. I'll need to come back to you later on the last two points you raised.*

***come* back at sb** retaliate or respond when sb attacks, criticizes, or tries to outdo you: *Peter had built up a lead of 15 points to 10 but then the Swede came back at him to draw level.* **come-back** *n*: *Be sure to get a written contract. Otherwise you'll have no come-back (or it'll be difficult to come back at them) if the job isn't satisfactory or takes too long.*

***come* before a fall** ⟶ ***pride* goes/comes before a fall**

***come* between sb and sb** interfere with, harm, or destroy the good relationships between two people or groups: *We have been friends for too long to let differences of opinion come between us. / It seemed to George that his wife was trying to come between him and his parents.*

***come* between sb and sth** prevent sb from doing/having sth: *As long as he doesn't let it come between him and his other studies, I see no harm in the boy learning to play the guitar.*

***come* by sth** obtain sth (by effort); (happen to) acquire or receive sth: *Suddenly, he seems to have a lot of money to spend. I hope he came by it honestly. / These days, jobs aren't easy to come by.*

***come* clean** tell the truth about sth, especially after you have been hiding or lying: *It wasn't until after further questioning that she came clean and confessed.*

***come*, come!** (used to urge sb to act or talk in a sensible or reasonable way): *Come, come! We all know that you were in Manchester the day the crime was committed. So you might as well tell the whole story.* Also **come now!**

***come*/fall down about sb's ears** collapse around and/or on top of sb; (of an organisation, plan, or sb's way of life) become totally disrupted or destroyed: *The ceiling, damp and bulging, looked ready to come down about their ears. / At the time his wife left him it felt as if his whole world had fallen down about his ears.*

***come* down in buckets** ⟶ ***bucket* down**

***come* down/out in favour of sb/sth** or **come down/out on the side of sb/sth** choose or decide, especially after consideration, who or what you want, approve of, or support: *After some debate the selection committee came down in favour of the second candidate. / Supplies were running low and that was what finally made us come down in favour of moving on in spite of the weather. / In the argument that followed, my father came down solidly on my side.* **come down/out against sb/sth** decide not to support sb/sth: *The committee's final report has come out against plans for massive investment in the railways.*

***come*/go 'down in the world** become less important in society, your work etc or become poorer: *We may have come down in the world but we're not beggars yet.* **come-down** *n* a loss of importance: *They've found a place for her in another department, but it's a bit of a come-down after being head of her own.* See also ***come*/go 'up in the world.**

***come* down on sb like a ton of bricks** *(informal)* criticize sb very strongly: *If anyone didn't obey orders instantly, the sergeant-major would come down on them like a ton of bricks.*

***come* down to sth** mean sth, when expressed as a fact; be (finally or importantly) a matter of (doing) sth: *People in their situation can't get bank loans. What it comes down to is that you can buy money, like you can anything* *else, if you can afford to. / When it comes down to practising what he preaches, he's not so perfect as many people believe.*

***come* forward** present or announce yourself ready to help, give information etc: *Unless more parents come forward quickly, the youth club will have to close. / The police are appealing to witnesses to the accident to come forward.* **not backward in coming forward** not hesitant or shy in asserting yourself or your opinions or wishes.

***come*/go full circle** come/go and return to the position or situation that you started in: *Years ago, canals were used for transporting heavy goods. Then came the railways and later the motorway system. Now we've (or the situation/wheel has) come full circle in some cases, and it's cheaper to use the canals again.*

***come* hell or high water** whatever the opposition or difficulties may be: *If he says he'll have the third edition out on the streets by 5 o'clock, then, come hell or high water, he will!*

***come* home to roost** →**one's *chickens*, misdeeds etc come home to roost**

***come* in for sth** incur or be the object of praise, blame etc: *The police came in for a lot of criticism over their handling of the situation.*

***come* in from the cold** become involved with, join, or be admitted to a community, group, or activity that you have had no part in before: *In that year too, Spain came in from the cold and became a member of the EEC.* Also **come in out of the cold.**

***come* in handy/useful** be found useful (for a purpose or on some occasion or occasions): *I'll take those sacks if you don't want them. They'll come in handy for putting the garden rubbish in.*

***come* in on sth** have a part in an activity, business venture, or project: *Sounds an interesting scheme—can I come in on it?* See also ***bring* sb in on sth.**

***come*, get etc in on the ground floor** *(informal)* become involved at the beginning of a plan: *Reg's investment paid off: he came in on the ground floor and saw the value of his money double in two years.*

***come* in with sb** have a part in a business venture or in sharing the cost of sth with sb: *'Johnson has the relevant experience and says he'd like to join the team.' 'Well that's OK—we'll ask him to come in with us and invest some capital in the company.'*

***come* into sth** inherit (a sum of) money or property: *His niece, Sheila, is his only living relative. I expect she'll come into his fortune when he dies.*

***come* into one's own** find full use and/or get recognition for your merits, talents, or capabilities: *It wasn't until late in life, when her children had all grown up, that Rachel really came into her own and led a truly fulfilled life.*

***come* into play** (begin to) operate, be active, or have an effect or influence: *Unless pride and obstinacy come into play, common sense tells you when to give up a struggle.* See also ***bring*/call sth into play.**

***come* it (over sb)** *(informal)* try to impress, persuade, or deceive sb in the hope of getting his attention, respect, sympathy etc: *We're as good as she is though she tries to come it over us.* Also **come the old soldier, stern parent etc:** *I suggested to George that coming the heavy father wasn't the best way to handle that boy of his.*

***come* it (rather, a bit etc) strong** *(informal)* exceed what is suitable or necessary in what you say or do about sb/sth: *'According to my mother, they live like pigs.' 'Live like pigs is coming it a bit strong. Their place is extremely untidy but not really dirty.'*

***come* of sb** happen to sb: *Whatever came of your friend at college? You've not said anything about him for some time.*

***come* of sth** result from (doing) sth: *It's only a temporary job they're giving me, but it's a start, and something good may come of it.' / 'They both turned on me.' 'That's what comes of interfering in other people's quarrels!'*

***come* of age** →**be/come of *age***

***come* off 1** (of an event) take place: *My trip to Paris never came off. Business got in the way.* Note that this is usually used in the negative or interrogative. **2** (of a plan, trick, experiment, or effort) be successful: *Fortunately for him, the scheme never came off.* See also ***bring* sth off.**

***come* off best, well, worst etc** emerge or escape from a fight or dispute in a way that is mentioned: *The other wrestler was far more agile so it was clear who was going to come off worse.*

***come* off it!** don't talk nonsense!; don't say what you know is untrue!: *'I can't afford to run a car.' 'Oh, come off it! You could run two cars on what you spend on drink and cigarettes!'*

***come* on 1** improve; make progress: *His French has come on well since he joined the conversation class. / 'Your peas are coming on.' 'Yes, I'm hoping for a good crop this year.'* Also **come along.** See also ***bring* sb/sth on. 2** (especially of a condition that will continue till it runs its natural course) begin: *We must set up camp before night comes on. / I think I have a cold coming on.* **3** (used to encourage or persuade sb to do sth): *Stop larking around and do as you're told. Come on now! / Come on, if you want that lift home, or we'll go without you! / 'What's wrong? Something is troubling you, I can see.' 'Nothing's wrong and nothing is troubling me.' 'Oh, Frank—come on!'* Also **come along.**

***come* on/upon sb/sth** encounter or find sb/sth: *A chap that was out walking his dog came upon him lying drunk at the side of the road, got him on his feet again, and steered him home.*

***come* out 1** be published or produced: *His latest novel came out in September.* See also ***bring* sth out 3. 2** (of a secret, fact, or truth) become known or public: *It soon came out that he'd been telling a pack of lies.* **3** stop work and go on strike: *The miners are coming out again from next Monday.* See also ***bring* sb out.** **4** (of a picture or a detail) be produced, revealed, or emphasized: *Our holiday photos came out very well. / The tiny carvings come out attractively in the moonlight.* See also ***bring* sth out 1.** **5** (of the working of a sum or puzzle) produce the correct answer or solution: *This sum won't come out, though I can't see what I'm doing wrong.*

***come*/work out at sth** be calculated or calculable at a stated cost or amount: *Your share of the expenses comes out at £14.20. Check the figures if you like. / The recipe says five pounds of sugar to six pounds of fruit. What does that work out at in kilos?*

***come* out at sb's ears** ⟶***have* sth coming out at/of one's ears**

***come* out in sth** have spots, marks etc appear on your skin: *She always comes out in a rash after eating eggs.* See also: ***bring* sb out in sth.**

***come* out in the wash** *(informal)* come right or be put right without real harm done: *'Things will be in a proper muddle if both groups arrive together.' 'To begin with, I dare say. But don't worry, it'll all come out in the wash.'*

***come* out of one's shell** lose or overcome your shyness or reserve; speak or behave more freely or boldly than you once did or than you usually do: *Even with kind foster-parents, it took Anna a long time to come out of her shell and become the open friendly little girl you see now.* See also ***bring* sb out (of his shell).**

**(*come*) out of the ark** *(of things, not people or animals)* (be) extremely old: *This wardrobe looks as if it came straight out of the ark.*

***come* out on top** *(informal)* win or be more successful or lucky than another or others; overcome difficulties or disadvantages: *Although I came out on top this time, he's generally a better chess-player than I am.*

***come* out with sth** say sth, especially of an unexpected, unusual, or unsuitable kind: *When told he couldn't be admitted he came out with a string of oaths. / That child has some strange ideas. You never know what he's going to come out with next. / I know something is troubling you. Now (come) out with it!*

***come* over sb** (especially of an unpleasant feeling) take control of sb: *I don't know what came over me just then. I must apologize. I'm not usually so rude! / A wave of dizziness suddenly came over her as she tried to stand up.*

***come* over faint, embarrassed etc** suddenly feel faint etc: *He'd joined in the dancing but came over dizzy and had to sit down. / She would have been offended if she weren't asked to sing for us, so why does she come over all shy when she's invited to?*

***come* rain or (come) shine** whatever the weather is like; whatever happens: *It was my father's custom, come rain or come shine, to take a short walk before breakfast.*

***come* round/to** regain consciousness: *Your husband is just coming round after the anaesthetic, Mrs Brown, and it would be better if he weren't visited till evening. / When she came to she couldn't remember a thing about the accident.* See also ***bring* sb round/to.**

***come* (a)round (to sth)** change your opinion or attitude after consideration or persuasion: *When the planning officers see the conditions for themselves I think they'll come round to our point of view.* See also ***bring* sb (a)round (to sth).**

***come* short (of sth)** ⟶***fall*/come short (of sth)**

***come* to oneself** think or act sensibly after having been foolish or mistaken: *Most of my energy had been spent on the social side of university life. However, after a year and a half of playing around I came to myself and realized that I was wasting my opportunities.* Also **come to one's senses.** See also ***bring* sb to himself.**

***come* to sth 1** result in or reach an indicated amount: *4 times 8 comes to 32. / If the total cost comes to more than that, I'll have to think whether I can afford it.* **2** mean in real content or significance: *All that this long speech came to could have been said in two minutes.* **3** be a case or matter of (doing) sth: *I'm as good a cook as she is except when it comes to (making) pastry.* **come to that** or **if it comes to that** connected with and in addition to sth just mentioned: *You forget I have to live all the year round on what I make in the summer months. You don't do too badly out of the tourist trade yourself, if it comes to that.* **4** (of a situation) reach a point that is mentioned when sb does sth or sth will happen: *He's in hospital for treatment. If it proves necessary, they will operate—but it may not come to that. / Things have come to such a state that if she doesn't leave the firm, I will.*

***come* to a bad end** (live and) die a criminal or in disgrace or misfortune, especially as the result of your own actions: *Neighbours shook their heads over this wild boy and prophesied that he would come to a bad end.*

***come* to a head** (of a course of events, condition of affairs etc) reach a critical or culminating stage: *Matters came to a head at the emergency board meeting yesterday, and all the directors resigned.* See also ***bring* sth to a head.**

**(*come* to) a pretty pass** *(informal)* reach a sad or sorry state: *Things have come to a pretty pass if she says she'll never speak to her brother again.*

***come* to a sticky end** *(informal)* meet an unpleasant fate, especially death: *The chances of coming to a sticky end are perhaps greater in motor-racing than in any other form of sport.*

**all good things (must) *come* to an end** ⟶***all***

***come* to blows** *(informal)* start fighting: *We didn't actually come to blows over who should be the one to meet the royal couple, but it was a near thing.*

***come* to book (for sth)** ⟶ ***bring* sb to book (for sth)**

***come* to fruition** ⟶ ***bring* sth to fruition**

***come* to one's feet** ⟶ ***bring* sb to his feet**

***come* to grief** be destroyed or ruined; meet with failure or a misfortune: *Many ships have come to grief on these rocks.*

***come* to heel** ⟶ ***bring* sb to heel**

***come* to life 1** (of people or (social) occasions) become lively and active instead of dull and passive: *I've seen schoolboys play more interesting soccer. Only for about 15 minutes in the second half did the game really come to life.* See also ***bring* sb/sth to life 1. 2** (of characters or events in history, drama etc) seem as real and vivid as in life or as a present event: *In Sir Walter Scott's novels many of the subsidiary characters come to life in a way that his heroes and heroines rarely do.* See also ***bring* sb/sth to life 2.**

***come* to light** be revealed or discovered: *He planned to be safely out of the country before his misdeeds came to light. / It came to light that Peter had once been a scoutmaster, and he was asked to help in the youth club.* See also ***bring* sth to light.**

***come* to no good** (of people, plans or actions) meet with (deserved) failure or disgrace: *He'll get a five-year sentence at least, this time. I'm sorry, but I'm not surprised. I knew, from when Jim was a boy, that he'd come to no good.*

***come* to nothing** (of plans, promises etc) produce no successful result: *The latest effort to solve the dispute came to nothing. / She's always making threats that don't (*or *that never) come to anything.*

***come* to pass** *(formal)* happen; actually occur as foretold, planned, or hoped for: *They like to think they'll live here permanently when John retires, but I don't think it'll ever come to pass.*

***come* to terms with sb/sth** make or reach an agreement with sb; accept a situation or condition of life and adapt yourself to it as well as you can: *After a period of being rather miserable, Dennis has now come to terms with his disability and has developed other interests.*

***come* to the crunch** ⟶ **if/when it *comes* to the crunch**

***come* to the same thing (as sth)** be the same in meaning and/or result (as sth else): *'But I didn't mean to—it was an accident.' 'It comes to the same thing,' growled my father. 'You broke it and you'll have to pay for a new one.'*

***come* to the worst** ⟶ **if the *worst* comes to the worst**

***come* under sth** become the target of criticism, attack etc: *The new law on citizens' rights has come under a lot of criticism from many different groups in the community.*

***come* under the hammer** ⟶ ***go*/*come* under the hammer**

***come* unstuck** *(informal)* (of plans, arrangements, or relationships) fail; have to be abandoned or changed: *The robbers had a car waiting for their get-away, but that's where their plans came unstuck, as the engine wouldn't start.*

***come* up 1** (of an event etc) happen or arise: *I'll see you at 6 o'clock unless anything urgent comes up in the meantime.* **2** be mentioned or discussed during a conversation or meeting: *I forget now how the subject came up, but we found ourselves talking about childhood holidays. / The raising of the subscription fees is bound to come up at the Annual General Meeting.* See also ***bring* sth up 1. 3** (of a name, number, or coupon) win or have success in a lottery or competition: *They were drawing the raffle tickets, and she hung around to hear if her number came up.* **4** be vomited: *Baby had no sooner finished his feed than it all came up.* See also ***bring* sth up 2.**

***come* up against sb/sth** have to face or contend with sb/sth that is difficult to overcome: *Though we expect to come up against a lot of opposition to these cutbacks, we see no other way of continuing in business.* See also ***bring* sb up against sb/sth.**

***come*/go ˈup in the world** become more important in society, your work etc or become richer: *Don't you want to go up in the world? Are you happy to stay a junior clerk all your life?* See also ***come*/go ˈdown in the world.**

***come* up with sth** have a good idea or plan that will solve a difficulty or problem: *He lands himself in trouble and then expects someone else to come up with a brilliant idea to get him out of it. / I asked for suggestions, but nobody came up with anything useful.*

***come* upon sb/sth** ⟶ ***come* on/upon sb/sth**

***come* sb's way** be offered to sb or be met or acquired by sb, especially by chance or through no special effort of his own: *She's not dissatisfied with her present salary but would welcome any opportunity that came her way to earn more.*

***come* what may** whatever the difficulties and/or results may be: *I can't see them doing themselves any good by it but, come what may, the workers are determined to strike.*

**if/when it *comes* to the crunch** *(informal)* (if/when) trouble or a difficulty can no longer be avoided; if/when the need for or the pressure on sb to make a decision or take action is great enough: *'You talk as if I was helpless,' her father said. 'I don't like looking after myself but, if it comes to the crunch, I can do it.'* Also **(if/when) the crunch comes:** *'I swear that if someone I loved was suffering terribly with a terminal disease I'd find some way of putting them out of their misery.' 'Maybe. But I've heard of people say that, who, when the crunch came, found themselves emotionally incapable of carrying it out.'*

**have (got) sth *coming* (to one)** ⟶ ***have***

**have sth *coming* out at/of one's ears** → ***have***

**have sth in *common* (with sb/sth)** → ***have***

**as *common* as muck** *(informal)* (of people) vulgar or coarse in their speech or manners: *She'll work in the kitchen and not meet the hotel guests. As long as she's honest and a good worker, I don't care if she's as common as muck.*

***common*-or-garden** *(informal)* common, ordinary, and usual: *'I've been hearing about your lovely new home.' 'What lovely new home? It's just a common-or-garden three-bedroomed suburban semi.'*

**in *common* with sb/sth** as is also true of or as is the case with sb/sth: *The hospital buildings, in common with many others in this country, are sadly out of date.*

**the *company* sb keeps** the kind of people you mix with (often used to imply that the company is superior): *The local village lad never quite managed to come to terms with the company he had to keep in his new job in the city.* See also **keep sb company.**

**beyond *compare*** *(formal)* beyond comparison, without equal: *The moonlit scene was beautiful beyond compare.*

**in *concert* (with sb/sth)** in a combination of voices, sounds, or efforts; together with sb: *Murmurs of approval rose in concert from all parts of the hall. / Ideally, the decision should be reached by management working in concert with trade unions' representatives.*

**the *concrete* jungle** a modern city, thought of as an unfriendly, bewildering, or dangerous place.

***conjure* sth up** suggest or evoke a picture in the mind of sb: *The speaker's words conjured up visions of an ideal society in the future. / The music conjures up memories of that holiday we had in Greece.*

**in all *conscience*** → ***all***

**of (great, some, no etc) *consequence*** (very, quite, not etc) important: *They are arguing about trifles when there are matters of greater/more consequence to discuss. / There was nobody there of any consequence.*

**a *conspiracy* of silence** an agreement among people with certain information not to let it be publicly known: *There might have been no epidemic but for the conspiracy of silence, designed to protect the tourist trade, about the first few cases diagnosed.*

**keep/be in *contact* (with sb)** → ***keep*/be in touch/contact (with sb)**

**lose *contact* (with sb)** → ***lose* touch/contact (with sb)**

**(can't) *contain* oneself** (can't) keep your excitement, anger, delight, curiosity etc under control: *I don't lose my temper easily, but at this fresh piece of rudeness I could no longer contain myself. / 'Did he get out of the hole, Mummy?' 'Did the little dog get out?' cried the children. 'Just contain yourselves a minute and I'll come to that.'*

***contemplate* one's navel** think deeply about sth, while doing nothing practical or useful.

**beneath *contempt*** **1** worse than contemptible, because so shameful, dishonourable, or disgusting: *Stealing the money was bad enough. Trying to get someone else accused of it was beneath contempt.* **2** not worth showing or expressing contempt for, because so petty, stupid, or ridiculous: *'He hasn't replied to my criticisms. He probably considers them beneath contempt.'*

**a *contradiction* in terms** a statement or description combining two words or phrases that cancel each other in meaning: *They call their project 'a peace offensive,' which seems to me a contradiction in terms.*

**on the *contrary*** quite the opposite (of sth said or suggested): *'Didn't you find the Smiths rather boring?' 'On the contrary, I enjoyed their company very much.' / I feel I always know what Margaret thinks or is likely to do. My younger daughter, on the contrary, is often a puzzle to me.*

**to the *contrary*** in opposition to, or contradiction of, sth said or proposed: *How is it that when I give an opinion about anything, you always find something to say to the contrary? / Unless you hear from me to the contrary, expect me on Friday about 6 o'clock.*

***cook* sb's goose** *(informal)* ruin sb's plans, prospects, or chances of success: *Thanks for the advice. Now that we know what he wants to do we'll find a way to cook his goose.*

***cook* the books** *(informal)* make false records of the accounts of a business, especially in order to take money illegally: *The two directors of the company had been cooking the books, a local court heard yesterday. They were both given sentences of two years.*

***cook* up sth** *(informal)* invent a story or excuse for a special purpose or occasion: *I'll have to give them a reason for not going, but don't worry—I'll cook something up.*

**that's the way the '*cookie* crumbles** → ***way***

**what's *cooking*?** → ***what***

**too many *cooks* spoil the broth** → ***too***

**as *cool* as a cucumber** (of people) very cool or calm, especially when the opposite might be expected, for example on a hot day or in a difficult situation: *In contrast to the glistening sunbathers around her, she wore a long-sleeved white dress with a shady hat, and looked as cool as a cucumber.*

***cool* it** *(informal)* speak or behave in a less aggressive, excited, or exaggerated way: *His friends were holding him back and telling him to cool it, but he broke free and punched the barman on the nose.*

***cool* off** *(informal)* become less excited or angry or interested in sb: *I'm going out for a walk to cool off. / Her new boyfriend soon cooled off when he found out she had false teeth.* **cooling-off** *adj*: *The report into the dis-*

*pute recommended a cooling-off period of a month before negotiations should resume.*

**not much *cop*** *(informal)* of slight or no value or advantage: *'What do you think of the book?' 'It's not much cop, really.'*

***cop* it 1** *(informal)* be punished or scolded: *You'll cop it from the boss if he finds you in here making tea just now.* **2** *(informal)* die; be killed or injured: *'I hear old Matthew's copped it.' 'I'm sorry about that, but it was coming, wasn't it?' / Her nose is broken, but better than that if she'd copped it in the eye.*

**to the *core*** completely, right through, in every way: *Some people talk as if the whole police force was rotten to the core with bribery and corruption. /He's a Welshman to the core.*

***cork* sth up** *(informal)* suppress a (natural) emotion or reaction: *Why don't you ever lose your temper, or tell people you love them, or have a good cry, instead of keeping everying all corked up?*

**(a)round the *corner*** quite close, soon to happen: *Those engaged in the research believed that success was just around the corner when funds ran out and the laboratory was forced to close.*

**out of the *corner* of one's eye 1** by chance, though you are not looking in that or any particular direction: *'I only saw him out of the corner of my eye as I drove past, you know. It might have been Dick and, then again, it might not.* **2** intentionally, though secretly or so as not to appear to be looking: *Taking a seat where she could watch the group out of the corner of her eye, she opened her newspaper and pretended to read it.*

***corner* the market (in sth)** buy or produce all, or a very great proportion of, a commodity, so that you can control its price and conditions of sale; create a wide demand for a talent, ability, or service you offer: *Johnson could afford to undercut his competitors in painting and decorating till they were forced out of business from lack of orders. Now that he has cornered the market for miles around, he's put his prices up.*

**the *corridors* of power** the places where important decisions in government, big business, or international or public affairs, are made or influenced.

**to one's *cost*** as a result of having suffered loss, harm etc: *Nobody should try to be their own lawyer, as I know to my cost.*

**to sb's *cost*** causing sb loss, harm, or other disadvantage as a result: *The climbers had been advised not to set out until the weather improved—advice which, to their cost, they ignored.*

***cost*/earn/make/pay/spend a bomb** *(informal)* cost, earn, or spend a lot of money: *Our new car certainly cost a bomb!*

***cost* (sb) a pretty penny** cost a lot of money: *'I had to have a whole new roof.' 'That must have cost you a pretty penny, I'm sure.'* Also *(informal)* **cost (sb) an arm and a leg; cost (sb) the earth/moon.**

**at all *costs*** regardless of the price, effort, or penalty involved: *He's determined to have his own way at all costs.*

***cotton* on (to sth)** *(informal)* realize sth; understand or become fully aware of sth: *'The children won't know what to do. They've never played the game before in their lives.' 'Well, they can start now. They'll soon cotton on.' / Jack had been having an affair with this woman for quite a time before his wife cottoned on to what was happening.*

**(God) bless your, his etc (little) *cotton* socks ⟶ (God) *bless* your, his etc soul/heart**

***cough* (sth) up** *(informal)* pay for sth or give money to sb, perhaps unwillingly on request or demand: *I suppose if George can't pay the fine, then his Dad'll cough up.*

**be out for the *count*** be unconscious, either because you are very tired or in boxing: *Joe Pilsy just lay there—he was out for the count.* Also (boxing sense only) **be down for the count.**

**on that etc *count*** with reference to one or a number of accusations or reasons: *Very old people can become extremely disturbed when moved from their homes. On that count alone the government should provide money to get people to come and care for them at home. / Simpson, who had been charged with possession of illegal drugs and obstructing the police in the course of their duty, was found guilty on both counts.*

***count* one's blessings** realize how much you have to be thankful for and so not grumble: *You should count your blessings instead of complaining all the time! You have got a job, a home, a lovely wife, and children, after all!*

**not *count* one's chickens (before they're hatched)** *(informal)* not be confident of getting a result, realizing an ambition etc until it really happens: *'Well, we can forget about buying vegetables or soft fruit this summer,' Tom said, 'There'll be plenty for our friends, too.' 'Now, don't count your chickens* (or *let's not count our chickens) before they're hatched,' his wife told him.*

***count* sb/sth in/out** include/exclude sb/sth in/from a total of people or things: *The host and hostess forgot to count themselves in when they told the caterer to set 40 places. / If Johnson's going on this trip you can count me out. We don't get on.*

***count* on sb/sth** trust sb to give help or support or to do as he promises; rely on sth to be consistent or effective or to maintain a required standard: *As neighbours we don't visit each other much socially but we know we can count on each other for help in an emergency. / I think the weather will hold steady for a day or two but I wouldn't count on it.*

***count* the cost** consider carefully what the risks, penalties, or disadvantages may be before you take action or make a decision: *The offer was attractive financially, but when I sat down and counted the cost in terms of sep-*

*aration from my family and friends, I decided the job was not for me.*

***count* the pennies** be extremely careful about the money you spend and don't spend, because you are either very poor or very mean: *There was no money from the government for bringing up children in those days, and my widowed mother had to count the pennies in her struggle to keep us all fed and clothed.*

**under the *counter*** secretly or illegally: *Jamieson's isn't the first seemingly respectable bookshop to sell banned literature under the counter, you know.*

**a *country* cousin** an unsophisticated person from a country district, especially as a newcomer or visitor to a big city: *No country cousin could get more mixed up about bus routes than our Peter. He's always being taken to places he doesn't want to go.*

**take one's *courage* in both hands** → ***take***

**have (got) the *courage* of one's convictions** → ***have***

**a *course* of action** a planned or considered way of doing, managing, or achieving sth: *Was tear gas really the only course of action open to the police to use in restraining the rioters?*

***cover* a multitude of sins** include, though perhaps hide, a number of faults, (disagreeable) facts, or wrong or undesirable actions; atone for or make you willing to forgive a number of faults etc in sb/sth: *That's how they justify themselves. But 'normal business practice' can cover a multitude of sins.* / *'What he needs is a really capable secretary.' 'Oh, Jenny's not too bad—and anyway, for Jack, a pretty face and a pleasant manner cover a multitude of sins.'*

**under *cover* of (doing) sth** hidden or protected by sth; with a pretence of (doing) sth: *They hoped to penetrate the enemy's defences under cover of darkness.* / *It's a story about an older man who wins the affections of a young girl under cover of visiting her mother.*

**from *cover* to cover** from the beginning to the end of a book, magazine etc: *He gets a motor-racing magazine every month which he devours from cover to cover two or three times before the next issue comes out.*

***cover* up (sth)/(for sb)** hide a true state of affairs from sb entitled to know, sometimes to protect him from punishment: *On the owner's return from abroad, the manager found he could no longer cover up his mismanagement of the estate.* / *The boss will suspect sooner or later. I can't keep covering up for you.* **cover-up** *n*: *The government has changed the method for registering the numbers of unemployed. It's all a big cover-up to hide how much the totals are increasing.*

**till/until the *cows* come home** *(informal)* for an indefinitely long period of time, perhaps for ever: *The old lady hasn't many subjects of conversation but if you let her, she'll talk about her younger days till the cows come home.* See also **till/until *kingdom* come.**

***crack* a joke** make a joke, say sth, or tell a short story that makes people laugh: *His father was a cheery fellow who loved to crack a joke, and John is just like him!*

**have a *crack* at (doing) sth** → ***have***

***crack* down on sb/sth** *(informal)* use your authority to attack, suppress, or prevent sb/sth: *You were too soft with him. In a school like this you have to crack down on troublemakers as soon as they start.* **crack-down** *n*: *A major government crack-down on crime is planned for next month.*

**(at) (the) *crack* of dawn** (at) the first light of day; very early in the morning: *Often she was up before the crack of dawn, seeing to her household chores before setting off to work.* Note that this is almost always used after a preposition.

**a fair *crack* of the whip** → ***fair***

***crack* up** *(informal)* (of people) fail, especially in physical or mental health; (of structures or machines) disintegrate and/or fail in function; (of organizations or business firms) lose power and influence and/or fail financially: *'I was shocked to see the change in your mother.' 'Yes, the old girl's beginning to crack up, I'm afraid.'* / *The British boxer was clearly cracking up by the third round and lasted only two more before the fight was stopped.* **crack-up** *n*: *The crack-up of the political party after such a promising beginning should serve as a warning to any other movement exulting in initial success.*

**be *cracked* up to be good etc** *(informal)* be praised (often used in the negative): *In my opinion, the food in this restaurant is not all it's cracked up to be (or nothing like as good as it's cracked up to be).*

**from the *cradle*** since early childhood: *'Have you known each other long?' 'From the cradle. Our parents shared the same house until it became too small for their growing families.'*

**'*cradle*-snatching** securing the love of or a sexual relationship or encounter with a person very much younger than yourself (sometimes said jokingly about sb seen with a much younger companion): *'That's his daughter he's with at the bar.' 'I thought it would be. Simson's hardly the type to go in for cradle-snatching.'*

**from the *cradle* to the grave** from birth to death; throughout your whole life: *The new government ministry was formed to look after citizens' social welfare from the cradle to the grave.*

***cramp* sb's style** restrict or interfere with the way sb likes to behave or conduct his life or business: *Perhaps she doesn't want children. You know what a sociable girl Lucy is, she may think that having babies would cramp her style.*

***crash* out** *(slang)* spend the night asleep, especially in a makeshift place: *Can I crash out on your floor tonight?*

**be *crawling* with lice etc** *(informal)* be full of or covered with sth such as small insects or animals, especially pests: *The children's heads were crawling with lice.* / *'Do you get many tourists here during the summer months?' 'Many, did you say? In July and August the place is absolutely crawling with them!'*

**be *crazy* about sb/sth** *(informal)* = be mad about sb/sth: *'What a good-looking young man!' 'Yes, half the girls in the village are crazy about him!'* Also used in compound *adj*: *football-crazy*.

***cream* sb/sth off** choose and remove a part, usually the best part: *The television company is worried that firms set up for the new technology will cream off the popular end of the market.*

***create* a ripple/stir** ⟶ ***cause/create* a ripple/stir**

***create*/raise a stink** *(informal)* complain loudly; make a lot of trouble: *'There's a chap on the phone,' she told the manager, 'creating a stink about his car not having been properly serviced.'* Also **kick up a stink.**

**up the *creek*** *(informal)* in trouble; completely wrong: *This data on the computer printout is up the creek—the program can't be right.*

**(on) the *crest* of a/the wave** (at) a favourable stage or high point of sb's personal life or a nation's, industry's etc history: *Pop idols can make a lot of money, but not for ever, and those who invest wisely while they are on the crest of a wave at least make sure of a future for themselves.* / *He was perhaps fortunate to have arrived in Hollywood at a time when the film industry was still riding the crest of the wave.*

**not be *cricket*** *(informal, old-fashioned)* not be a fair or honourable action or way of behaving: *He got £20 from my wife in exchange for a cheque that he knew perfectly well his bank wouldn't honour. That's just not cricket, you know.*

***crime* doesn't pay** *(saying)* crime (as well as being wrong) isn't even profitable, implying that criminals will eventually be caught and punished: *Recent figures show that the police have managed to obtain convictions in only 20% of all reported cases of housebreaking. Who says crime doesn't pay?*

**'*crocodile* tears** feigned tears or weeping; an insincere show of sorrow: *'She cried so bitterly I couldn't go on scolding her.' 'Crocodile tears—that child can turn them on whenever she likes. She'll be just as naughty tomorrow!'* / *'You can't be rude to the relatives.' 'Why not? If they never even visited the old dear while she was alive, what right have they to come and weep crocodile tears at her funeral?'*

***crop* up** *(informal)* happen; occur though not arranged for or expected; happen to be mentioned in the course of a conversation etc: *We'd be happy to have you stay here, but if something more attractive crops up, then don't feel tied to us.*

***cross* a bridge when one comes to it** deal with or be worried about a problem in the future only when it happens and not before: *We'll have to find some more money for Tina's trip abroad next year, but we'll cross that bridge when we come to it.* There are variations on this idiom, such as **not cross one's bridges before one comes to them.**

**as *cross* as two sticks** *(old-fashioned)* very angry or annoyed (about sth): *I wonder what's upsetting Grandma. She's as cross as two sticks this morning.*

**a *cross* between sb/sth and sb/sth** sb/sth doesn't quite fit either of two categories or descriptions but is a mixture of both: *A cross between a sweetheart and a mother—that's what a lot of men would like their wives to be.* / *Like so many young people's first books it's neither an autobiography nor a novel but a sort of cross between the two.*

***cross* my heart (and hope to die)** (a phrase added to emphasize your sincerity in making a promise or in stating what you believe to be true): *'Don't tell anyone else about this, will you?' 'Cross my heart, I won't!'* (Also used in an appeal to sb): *'Of course I love you.' 'Cross your heart; do you really?'*

***cross* sb's path** meet sb (by chance): *I met Mr White at a party once, and a very unpleasant fellow he was. I hope I'll never cross his path again.* **we/our/their paths cross** we etc meet (by chance): *Have a good voyage. It's been a great pleasure to share a holiday with you, and I hope our paths cross again sometime.*

**at *cross*-purposes** having different or opposing aims that lead to misunderstanding: *The doctor I saw was consulting somebody else's medical record. It took us a few minutes to realize we were talking at cross-purposes.*

***cross* swords (with sb)** contend (verbally) or argue with sb: *It's nearly always the same with Meg and me. We start by exchanging opinions and end up crossing swords.*

***cross* the/one's Rubicon** *(formal)* make a decision that cannot be changed; commit yourself to a course of action that you cannot, or do not wish, to change.

**dot the i's and *cross* the t's** ⟶ ***dot***

**at a/the *crossroads*** at a place where a decision has to be made: *The club is at the crossroads—do we try and enlarge our premises or are we going just to accept that numbers will continue to dwindle?*

**as the '*crow* flies** (of a distance) measured in a straight line, not taking road bends, etc into account: *There's a good lake for fishing 5 kilometres from here as the crow flies, though twice as far by road.*

**to *crown*/cap it all** finally, in addition to, and better or worse than what has been already mentioned: *What a day it was! First the news that Peter had found a publisher for his book at last, then I heard I'd won £500, and to crown it all a phone call from Australia announcing the birth of my first grandchild.*

**be *cruel* to be kind** use harsh or painful

methods (because they are the only ones which will be effective) to benefit sb: *I couldn't let the girl marry Jim without telling her he was into drugs in a big way. You have to be cruel to be kind sometimes.*

**have (got) a *crush* on sb** ⟶ ***have***

***cry* blue murder** ⟶ ***scream,* cry etc blue murder**

***cry* buckets** *(informal)* cry very much: *Poor Anne cried buckets when we told her her horse would have to be put down.*

***cry* down sth** belittle sth; make it seem important: *It was typical of Brown that he persisted in crying down his own part in achieving this outstanding success and giving most of the credit to his colleagues.*

***cry*/ask for the moon** want or ask for sth you cannot get or will not be given to you: *Is it really asking for the moon to hope that world peace could eventually be the norm of human existence?* Also **want the moon.**

***cry*/sob one's eyes/heart out** weep bitterly and for a long time: *'Where's Kitty?' 'Upstairs in her room, crying her eyes out no doubt. I've just told her we can't possibly afford to let her go on this riding-school holiday she's been talking about.'*

***cry* off ((doing) sth)** withdraw from an agreement or arrangement you have made to do sth: *'I've decided to invest some capital in this scheme of yours, Harry.' 'You're sure? I don't want you saying yes now and crying off later.' / Our secretary has made the bookings. Anyone who cries off joining the tour now will still have to pay for their tickets.*

***cry* out for sth** obviously need, or be suitable for, sth: *With so many more important matters crying out for his attention, the Chief Constable had no doubt forgotten about my request for an interview. / It was an excellent site that cried out for redevelopment but the owner wouldn't sell.* Also **cry out to be . . . :** *The system under which these appointments were made had long been crying out to be reformed.* Note that this is often used in continuous tenses.

***cry* wolf** alarm people or appeal for help unnecessarily, either deliberately or by mistake: *That boy! If it's not a headache, it's a sore stomach—anything to stay off school. What worries me is that he'll cry wolf once too often and we won't send for a doctor when he really needs one.*

**a *crying* need, shame, scandal etc** an urgent need etc that should be attended to, put right, or stopped very quickly: *They've cut down the number of nursery school places available, when in an underprivileged district like this, there's a crying need for more, not fewer, of them!*

**for *crying* out loud** *(informal)* (used either as an exclamation or to emphasize a statement, usually implying that you feel annoyed, dissatisfied or reproachful): *'For crying out loud!' she said, slamming down the receiver. 'What's the matter?' I asked. 'That's the third time in five minutes somebody has rung me up and asked me if I was the Gas Board.'*

***cry* over spilt milk** ⟶ **it's *no* good/use crying over spilt milk**

**off the *cuff*** without preparation or rehearsal: *I don't know how you can just stand up and give an after-dinner speech off the cuff, like that. I'd have to get it all ready beforehand. / 'Can you tell me the actual number of cases involved?' 'Not off the cuff, but I can find out and let you know.'* **off-the-cuff** *adj: an off-the-cuff remark.*

**a '*culture* vulture** *(informal)* sb who, though not a practising writer, artist, musician etc is always trying to improve his knowledge and appreciation of the arts (said sarcastically about sb with a pretentious interest or as a joke about sb with a genuine one).

**sb's *cup* (of happiness, sorrow etc) is full** *(formal)* sb's happiness, sorrow, emotional feeling etc has reached a peak; sb feels extremely happy, sad etc: *One thing only had been missing from their marriage and now, with the birth of the child, their cup of happiness was full.* Also **sb's cup overflows; sb's cup runs over.**

**(not) be sb's *cup* of tea** (not) be the (kind of) person, thing, or activity that sb likes or is suited to: *Jackson, with his surly manner and scruffy clothes, wasn't everybody's cup of tea, but I liked his wry sense of humour and respected his honesty. / 'My aunt says she'll help with the catering for the fete, but she doesn't want to be in charge.' 'Really? I thought being in charge of anything was just her cup of tea.'*

**the *cupboard* is bare** there is no food, money or resources to supply your needs: *Come along for an hour or two this evening but I can't offer you a meal. We're going on holiday tomorrow and the cupboard is bare.*

**'*cupboard* love** *(informal)* a show of affection for sb from whom you hope to get some material benefit: *'The dog seems specially fond of you, Mary.' 'Cupboard love—I'm the one that feeds him.'*

**(like) the *curate's* egg, (good in parts)** (said of sth that is partly good, partly bad or that is satisfactory in some ways and not in other ways): *'Is it an interesting book?' 'Nothing special but like the curate's egg, good in parts. The dialogue's often quite amusing.'*

***come* to book (for sth)** ⟶ ***bring* sb to book (for sth)**

***curiosity* killed the cat** *(saying)* asking questions about, or interfering in, what doesn't concern you can be dangerous or have unfortunate results (often used as a warning or teasing reply to a question you choose not to answer): *'Peter blistered his fingers lifting a casserole lid to see what was cooking.' 'Serves him right; doesn't he know that curiosity killed the cat?' / 'Are you two thinking of getting married, by any chance?' 'Now, now! Curiosity killed the cat!'*

***curry* favour (with sb)** try to win sb's approval, so that you may gain some advantage for yourself, for example by flattery or giving presents: *In business or in politics you can get so far by currying favour with your bosses but never to the top.*

**be *curtains* for sb/sth** *(informal)* be the death or the end of sb/sth: *'If this damn thing explodes now,' the sergeant said, 'it'll be curtains for all of us.'*

**the *customer* is always right** *(saying)* a sensible trader does not contradict or argue with customers (in case he loses their custom): *Although it's the general principle in this store that the customer is always right, always check with the supervisor before you exchange or replace goods for anyone.*

***cut* a caper** *(informal)* dance or jump about, especially from joy or pleasure; behave in a foolish, excited, or exaggerated way: *Susie ran out to tell us the good news. Your mother was so delighted she clapped her hands and cut a caper in the middle of the road.* Also **cut capers.**

***cut* a dash** present a stylish, bold appearance and so impress others: *Dressed up so smartly in his new naval uniform, he cut quite a dash.*

***cut* a fine, poor etc figure** have a fine etc appearance: *'There's no doubt,' the colonel said, 'that a pretty woman on a nice horse cuts a dashing figure.' / A tall, elegant man, he would cut a distinguished figure in any group of people.*

**to *cut* a long story short** (a phrase introduced by a speaker or writer when he intends to omit details from his account of events or a situation): *I asked him for an explanation. All this I'm telling you had been going on for six months without her husband suspecting. In the end, somebody told him, and to cut a long story short, he kicked his wife out of the house, gave her lover a proper beating-up, and found himself in the police station on a charge of assault.*

**a *cut* above sb/sth** rather better than or in some degree superior to sb/sth: *This is a cut above the usual run of glossy magazines, indeed. I congratulate both editor and contributors.*

***cut* and dried** (of matters, arrangements, or opinions) settled and decided in all details and unlikely to change or be changed: *By the end of the evening they had their plans for carrying out the robbery all cut and dried with nothing, they thought, left to chance.*

**the *cut* and thrust (of sth)** the vigorous exchange of opinions; the use of moves and counter-moves: *He enjoys the cut and thrust of business competition.*

***cut* back (on) sth** reduce an amount of sth consumed, produced, or spent: *'Cut back on fats as much as possible,' the doctor told her, 'but otherwise you can have a normal diet.' / Farmers in the region have been advised to cut back wheat production in favour of other crops.* **cutback** *n: Owing to the government cutbacks, the facilities in some universities have had to be reduced.*

***cut* both/two ways** (of an argument, action, or situation) have an effect that works both for and against a desired result or the interests of two people or parties: *Manufacturers and producers who want to have certain imports banned should remember that restrictions cut both ways, and we cannot afford to lose the foreign markets for many other commodities.*

***cut* one's coat according to one's cloth** spend within the limit of what money you have; do or produce sth within the limits of what material is available: *'The bank is asking us to reduce our overdraft, and I don't know what to do.' 'You could try cutting your coat according to your cloth. Do you really need, for instance, to send your children to an expensive private school?'*

***cut* corners** do sth in the quickest, easiest, or cheapest way, usually with a less satisfactory result than if you had spent more time, trouble, or money: *Don't be tempted to cut corners when doing a home decorating job. Proper preparation of surfaces for repapering and painting is as important as the final stages.*

***cut* sb dead** show your dislike or scorn of sb you know by an action such as pretending not to see him or not returning his greeting: *'Your wife has just cut me dead in the street.' 'Don't you believe it! She must have been in a hurry, or thinking of something else, and just didn't notice you.'*

***cut* down (on) sth** reduce your consumption or expenditure of sth: *Now that we're no longer earning, we'll have to cut down our expenses. / He'd soon lose weight if he cut down on all those snacks before meals. / 'Cigarette, Betty?' 'Not just now, thanks. I'm trying to cut down.'*

***cut* sb/sth down to size** show that sb is less important and powerful than he or others may think; make sth seem less important, serious, or difficult than was previously thought: *I've met him—a self-important young upstart who badly needs to be cut down to size.*

***cut* sb in** *(informal)* include sb in a group engaged in a (profit-sharing) business or activity: *If you're serious, the pair of you, about taking over this pub in the High Street, what about cutting me in too?*

***cut* in (on sb)** (of a driver) overtake a car, lorry etc and then suddenly turn dangerously into its path: *If he hadn't tried to cut in (on us), then the accident would never have happened.*

***cut* it fine/close** allow only the minimum of time, money, space, or material needed for a purpose: *'You mad fool!' Jane screamed at him. 'I admit I cut it close that time,' he said, 'I shouldn't really try to pass buses on the inside.' / You should leave soon. It takes 30 minutes to drive to the airport—and you don't want to cut it too fine.*

***cut* it out** *(informal)* stop doing what you're doing, because it is wrong, foolish, or annoying: *'I've had enough of your snivelling,' her mother told her. 'Cut it out or leave the* *room!' / 'Hey, cut it out!' Jake said. 'That's my girl and you keep your hands off her!'*

***cut* one's losses** give up an unprofitable business or other activity before you incur even greater loss or harm: *We might have struggled on a bit longer in the hope that trade would pick up, but when the council doubled the rates on our premises we decided to cut our losses and get out.*

***cut* no ice (with sb)** not impress or influence people or a particular person or group: *That domineering manner of yours may do very well in the classroom, but it cuts no ice here with me. / Peter would like to see some changes in the curriculum, but as a junior lecturer he doesn't cut much ice.*

***cut* sb/sth off 1** (of sth such as a flood or enemy soldiers) cause sb/sth to become separated: *Many villages in isolated areas have been cut off by the snow for more than a week now.* **2** interrupt a supply of power to sb/sth: *If you don't pay your gas bill within a month, then you may be cut off.*

***cut* off one's nose to spite one's face** do sth out of bad temper or hurt pride that harms yourself and is against your own interests: *Keeping your class in after school is cutting off your nose to spite your face because you have to stay in with them!*

***cut* out** stop working, sometimes as part of an automatic system: *The engine cut out suddenly just as we came to the junction. / The central-heating system cuts out by itself when the temperature reaches a certain level.* **cut-out** *n, adj*: *a cut-out device.*

**(be) *cut* out for sb/sth** (be) well suited in character or ability to sb, a job, profession, or activity: *I'll join you, but only as a spectator. I'm not cut out for athletic pursuits. / Whatever made the lad enlist in the first place? He's just not cut out for a soldier* (or *not cut out to be a soldier*).

***cut* sb/sth short** interrupt or stop sb who is speaking or a talk or remark: *'Did Jenkins say whether he'd marked the history papers yet?' 'No, and I was going to ask him, but our conversation was cut short by the bell.'*

***cut* sth short** shorten sth that is or seems too long; shorten sth that should have been longer: *The script is too long. See if you can cut it short by two minutes. / We'll have to cut our stay short, I'm afraid. That phone call was to say that my wife's mother has been taken seriously ill.'*

***cut* one's teeth on sth** learn or gain experience from sth (perhaps, but not necessarily, when you are young): *Steve is no newcomer to rock-climbing. As a boy he cut his teeth on the cliffs of his island home.*

***cut* one's throat** adopt a course of action, through folly, which can only bring harm to yourself: *We'll take over your business and you can be manager. We can't stop you carrying on going it alone, of course, though you'd be cutting your own throat. / If you stay on in business, we'll be cutting each other's throats.*

**could *cut* the air/atmosphere with a knife** can feel that the emotional tension, embarrassment etc shared by a group of people is very great: *As soon as John came in—with Elaine, uninvited of course, on his arm—the conversation stopped and you could have cut the air with a knife.*

***cut* the cackle** *(informal)* start doing the actual business or work rather than just talk about it; stop talking about unnecessary matters and come to the central point: *Cut the cackle, man! We know what the situation is. You're here to tell us what you mean to do about it.*

***cut* the ground from under sb's feet** leave sb without the means of, or reason or argument for, doing as he intended: *He had gone to the meeting expecting a lot of opposition, so it rather cut the ground from under his feet when his proposals met with no objections at all.* Also **cut the ground from under sb.**

***cut* sb to the quick** hurt sb's feelings; offend sb deeply: *The widow had done her best to give her children a comfortable home, and it cut her to the quick to hear them compare it unfavourably with what they saw in their friends' houses.*

**be *cut* up (about/over sth)** *(informal)* grieve, be distressed: *We used to say that Moira had no heart, but she was very cut up when her mother died* (or *very cut up over the death of her mother*).

***cut* up nasty/rough** *(informal)* behave or react in an angry, bad-tempered, or violent way: *I didn't like asking Jo for another loan, but my landlady had cut up very nasty when I asked her if she could wait a few more days for the rent.*

# D

**be a *dab* hand at (doing) sth** *(informal)* be skilful at or experienced in (doing) sth: *The film is about an old lady who is a dab hand at persuading airlines to let her travel free.*

***dabble* in sth** spend some time on an activity or hobby, but not be seriously involved in it: *'I'm a writer, really—I only dabble in photography.'*

**be at *daggers* drawn (with sb)** be enemies and ready to fight and quarrel: *He was at daggers drawn with his sister.*

**one's *daily* bread** the food you need or receive each day; your means of living generally: *Each one of us has to earn our daily bread somehow.*

**the/one's *daily* dozen** *(old-fashioned)* a few

physical exercises done every day to keep yourself fit.

**the *daily* round** the common tasks or duties of a working day.

***dam* sth up** *(informal)* control your strong feelings, often of anger, so tightly that you do not show them: *It isn't good to keep all your bitterness dammed up—it'll have to come out sooner or later.*

**what's the *damage*? → *what***

**the *damage* is done** *(informal)* it's too late to stop or prevent sth unpleasant happening: *I wish you hadn't said I'd go. Oh well, the damage is done, and I suppose I'll have to now.*

***damn* (it (all))!** *(slang)* (used to express very strong feeling, in an argument, protest etc): *But damn it all, you must see what I'm getting at!* Also **blow it!; darn it!** *(old-fashioned);* **dash it (all)!** *(old-fashioned);* **hang it (all)!** *(old-fashioned): 'Where did you put the keys, dash it?'*

***damn* all** *(slang)* nothing at all; so little as to be nothing: *If that's what they do with the money they collect, they'll get damn all from me next time they come round.*

***damn* me** *(slang)* (used to express surprise, anger etc): *Damn me, if it isn't Sarah Carpenter over there!* Also **stone me!**

**the boss, Harry etc be *damned*** *(slang)* the boss etc is to be defied, rejected, or ignored: *'You know the supervisor says you shouldn't use this room.' 'The supervisor be damned! Why on earth shouldn't I?'*

**I'll be *damned* if . . . → I'll be *blowed*/damned/hanged if . . .**

***damp* sth down 1** cause a fire to burn more slowly, especially by reducing the flow of air to it: *You can damp down the boiler when the water has got hot.* **2** make a strong feeling such as enthusiasm less forceful: *The Prime Minister's intervention in the dispute was seen as an attempt to damp down speculation about any extra money that the management might offer.*

**a *damp* squib** an event, statement etc that is intended to be exciting or interesting but fails in its effect: *The publishers expected the publication of his latest book to make a great impression, but in reality the launch turned out to be something of a damp squib.*

**put a *damper* on sb/sth → *put***

**a *damsel* in distress** *(humorous)* a young woman who needs help in a practical difficulty: *Pete seems to have a knack of rescuing damsels in distress stranded at the roadside.*

**'*danger*/'dirty money** extra payment in addition to usual wages for doing particularly dangerous/dirty work.

***dangle* sth before sb** or **dangle sth in front of sb** offer sth attractive to sb, to try to persuade him to do sth: *The party candidates dangled a new deal on jobs and pay in front of the voters to get their support.*

**a *Darby* and Joan** a faithful, loving, old married couple: *My parents are a real Darby and Joan—there's no company they enjoy better than each other's.* **a Darby and Joan club** a social club for old people.

**(just) sb *dare*!** (a way of discouraging sb from doing sth): *So he'd defy my orders, would he? Let him dare!* Also **don't sb dare!** Note that usually pronouns, not names, are used in this idiom.

**how *dare* sb (do sth)? → *how***

**I *dare* say → *I***

**a leap/shot in the *dark* → *leap***

**be in the *dark* (about sth)** not know anything at all (about sth) because no one has told you: *I'm afraid I'm completely in the dark about what you're discussing. Could you explain it to me?*

**keep/leave sb in the *dark* (about sth) → *keep***

**not/never *darken* sb's door again** *(informal)* not/never enter a building etc, because one is very unwelcome: *Go—now—and never darken my door again, as long as you live!*

**a *dark* horse** sb who is secretive or reserved about his activities, plans, abilities, or feelings: *Of course Susan always was something of a dark horse. But I never dreamt she could play the piano as well as she did tonight!*

**be a *darling* (and do sth)!** *(informal)* (a way of asking sb to do sth you want him to do): *Be a darling, Freddie, and make me a cup of tea.* Alternatives to ***a darling*** are: ***an angel; a dear.*** Note that this idiom and its variants are used mainly by women.

***darn* it! → *damn* (it (all))!**

***dash* one's/sb's brains out** kill oneself/sb by smashing the skull open: *He fell over the cliff and dashed his brains out on the rocks below.*

**make a *dash* for sth/it → *make* a bolt/dash for sth/it**

***dash* sb's hopes** cause sb to abandon his hopes of doing or getting sth: *Any remaining hopes that a start would be made to the new museum this year were dashed yesterday when the council announced its plans to spend less money on the arts.*

***dash* it! → *damn* (it (all))!**

***dash* sth off** write a letter or article very quickly and without thinking about it much: *I'm not one of those people who can dash off a book in just a few days; I have to take it all very slowly.*

**out of *date*** old-fashioned; of or like older times: *I find this dictionary is rather out of date and doesn't have the modern, technical words I want. / It's difficult to tell some people that they have out-of-date methods.*

**to *date*** up to and including the present time: *To date, we've received 40 bookings for the holiday, so we're doing quite well.*

**up to *date*** modern, current, or the most recent; of or like the present time: *I like to keep up to date with the newest developments in medicine. / Is this an up-to-date copy of the Register?*

***Davy* Jones's locker** the bottom of the sea,

thought of as the place where drowned men and ships go to.

**the *dawn* chorus** the burst of bird-song at dawn: *I love to lie awake early on a summer's day and listen to the dawn chorus.*

***dawn* on sb** (of a fact or idea) become clear to sb: *It slowly dawned on her that she really was very seriously ill. / The extent of the damage caused by the fire is just beginning to dawn on them.*

**'any *day* (of the week) ⟶ *any***

**sb is 60, 70 etc if he's a *day* ⟶ *if***

**in sb's *day*/time** at the time when sb was alive, working, or in a position of authority: *In 'my day, you wouldn't have been allowed to speak to your boss like that. / Just think what a penny would have bought in 'Grandpa's time!*

**not be sb's *day*** *(informal)* be a day when many unfortunate things happen to sb: *Poor Harriet! It's just not been her day. She didn't feel well in the morning; when she went shopping she found she'd left her purse at home; and, to cap it all, her car broke down!*

**that'll be the *day* ⟶ *that***

**in this *day* and age ⟶ *this***

**'all *day* and 'every day ⟶ *all***

***day* and night** through all or most of the 24 hours of the day: *She cared for her husband day and night in the closing months of his life.* Also **night and day.**

***day* 'in, day 'out** every day, month etc: *It rained day in, day out on our holiday.* Alternatives to ***day*** are ***month; week; year.***

**any minute, *day* etc now ⟶ *any***

**the *day* of days ⟶ a *red*-'letter day**

**the *day* of reckoning** the day or time when good actions or success and bad actions or failures will be made known (and have to be suffered for): *The day of reckoning for this government will come later at the time of the election.*

**'any *day* of the week ⟶ *any***

**all in a/the *day's* work ⟶ *all***

***daylight* robbery** *(informal)* a price or charge that you think is excessive: *The prices that garage charges for doing car repairs are daylight robbery, you know!*

**sb's/sth's *days* are numbered** *(informal)* the life, use etc of sb/sth is coming to an end soon: *If he goes on behaving like that, then I think his days in this job will be numbered.*

***dead* and buried/gone** dead, especially for a long time, long-forgotten: *Long after I'm dead and gone, you'll still be carrying on the same as you ever were. / Why bring up old quarrels that have lain dead and buried for years?*

**as *dead* as a/the dodo** no longer in existence; very old-fashioned: *The days when the only opportunity for a girl to meet young men was in their parents' front room are as dead as a dodo.*

**as *dead* as a doornail** completely dead with no hope of reviving: *The soldier just lay there. 'He's as dead as a doornail,' muttered the lieutenant.*

***dead* beat** *(informal)* exhausted, especially after working too hard: *Honestly, I'm dead beat! I shouldn't have tried to finish off all the decorating today! It was too much.* **'deadbeat** *n* sb who does not have the will to work and who does not contribute to the community.

**over sb's *dead* body** *(informal)* not if sb can prevent sth happening (used to express opposition): *'They want to use our front garden to widen the road!' 'Over my dead body!' / The trade union leader said that any further closures to coal pits would be over his dead body.*

**a *dead* cert** sth that will certainly happen, win etc: *Go-getter is a dead cert in the 3 o'clock race. I've put all my money on the horse!*

***dead* drunk, easy, good etc** extremely drunk etc: *I bet it's dead easy to break into one of those safes!*

**a *dead* duck** a plan, idea etc that is abandoned or is certain to fail: *In his article he wrote that breakfast television was bound to prove a dead duck because it offered a service for which there was no demand.* See also **a *lame* duck.**

**(at) a *dead* end** (at) a point where no more progress can be made: *Lack of further clues meant that the investigation came to a dead end.* **dead-end** *adj*: *a dead-end job.*

**a *dead* heat** a case of two or more people, horses etc coming to the finish of a race or competition at exactly the same time.

**stop (sb) *(dead)* in his tracks ⟶ *stop***

**a *dead* loss** *(informal)* sb/sth from whom no profit or benefit can be obtained: *It's no use asking Pete to mend the tap. He's an absolute dead loss as far as doing odd jobs round the house is concerned! I've never known anyone so inept!*

**(in) the *dead* of (the) night** or **at (the) dead of night** (in) the quietest, darkest hours of the night: *The creaking timbers of the old house took on an eerie feeling at dead of night.*

**be a *dead*/real ringer for sb/sth** *(slang)* be extremely like sb/sth: *I can't tell the difference! He's a dead ringer for the Prime Minister!*

**wouldn't be seen *dead* with sb/sth, in sth etc ⟶ *seen***

**as *deaf* as a post** completely or extremely deaf: *She's just turned 90 and is as deaf as a post.*

**there's none so *deaf* as those who will not hear ⟶ *there's* none so blind/deaf as those who will not see/hear**

**turn a *deaf* ear to sth ⟶ *turn***

**fall on *deaf* ears ⟶ *fall***

***deal* with sb** treat an offender, especially by punishing him: *Your father will deal with you when he gets home!*

***deal* with sb/sth** have contact, especially in business, with a person or organization: *They're a difficult firm to deal with—always late in sending the money. / For some years I've found Mr Kemp very pleasant to deal with, so I suggest you speak to him.*

***deal* with sth 1** have as its subject; be concerned with; cover; discuss: *In this week's lecture I want to deal with the geography of the country, and then next week we'll move on to the historical aspects. / The financial details are dealt with very clearly in this chapter.* **2** give your attention to a problem, complaint, or enquiry and do what is necessary; take action on: *The problem of unemployment must be dealt with urgently. / Which office deals with complaints about high rents?*

***dear* at the price** → ***cheap*/dear at the price**

**for *dear* life** *(informal)* very strongly, as if trying to preserve or defend your own life: *There was an explosion—I stood still for a moment and then ran for dear life!*

***dear* me!** (a mild expression of anxiety, sympathy, concern etc): *Dear me! It's started to rain and I've just hung out the washing!* Also **dear, dear!; oh dear!**

**be in at the *death*/kill** *(informal)* be present at the time when the climax of sth unpleasant happens: *'Did you see how they settled their differences?' 'Yes, I was in at the kill when Jane really gave Ann a piece of her mind.'*

**catch one's *death* (of cold)** → ***catch***

**on one's *death*-bed** as you are dying: *You can still ask forgiveness for your sins, even on your death-bed.*

**sound the *(death)* knell of sb/sth** → ***sound***

**be the *death* of sb** *(informal)* be the cause of much harm or worry to sb (often used in an annoyed or humorous way): *These fast cars will be the death of me, I'm sure. / You children are such terrors! You'll be the death of me one day!*

**bored, sick etc to *death* of sb/sth** → ***bored***

**at *death's* door** near to dying: *For some days, William lay at death's door.*

**like *death* warmed up** *(informal)* very unwell: *'How are you today?' 'I feel awful—like death warmed up! But I'm still going to work!'*

**between the devil and the *deep* blue sea** → ***devil***

***deep* down** far into your thoughts; in reality as opposed to appearance: *I know what it is, Ann—deep down you feel that the money you've earned is yours and that it doesn't belong to both of us. / She's very generous deep down, but this only comes out when you get to know her.*

**go off the *deep* end** → ***go***

**throw sb in at the *deep* end** → ***throw***

**(in) *deep* water(s)** (in) profound, dangerous, or complicated matters or affairs: *The speaker was getting into deep water trying to justify the council's policy in the face of some very tough opposition from the hecklers.*

**of the *deepest* dye** of the worst kind: *He was a villain of the deepest dye.*

**one *degree* under** → ***one***

**by *degrees*** gradually; little by little: *The country's economy won't get better overnight but will only improve by degrees.*

***delight* in doing sth** enjoy; take (unkind) pleasure in doing sth: *I think that Elizabeth sometimes delights in teasing her little brother.*

***deliver* the goods** *(informal)* do what is expected of you; fulfil your promise: *The art world is full of people who are creative geniuses. But what we need is people who will deliver the goods.*

**in *demand*** popular; wanted by many people: *Mr Nobbs is a good speaker and is often in demand for after-dinner speeches. / The new magazine-style books are in great demand at the moment.*

**(*demand* etc) one's pound of flesh** → ***pound***

**make a *dent* in sb/sth** → ***make***

***depend* on/upon sb/sth 1** believe confidently that sb/sth will be reliable: *You can depend on her to arrive* (or *her arriving) on time. / They knew that Steve could be depended on for his support—he'd always helped them in the past. / If I were you, I wouldn't depend on my co-operation in the future—I'm not sure I'll have enough money to back you.* **2** get money, food, or other support from sb/sth: *The country depends on money earned from its copper exports as its main source of income. / What will happen if I have to leave this job? I've got a wife and three kids depending on me!*

***depend* on/upon sth** follow directly or logically from: *A successful interview depends on a number of things: having confidence, being interested, and giving good answers, for example. / 'But is it right to send people to prison?' 'It all depends (on) what you mean by right!'* See also **it/that (all) *depends*.**

**(you can) *depend* on/upon it** you can be sure of this; without a doubt: *I'll be there be meet you—you can depend on it, Susie! / Depend upon it, my lad, your work had better start improving or there'll be trouble ahead!*

**it/that (all) *depends*** perhaps; possibly: *'Would you marry him if he asked you?' 'I might. It all depends.'*

**in *depth*** thoroughly: *In contrast to other more general examinations of the history of Anglo-French relations, I intend to treat the matter in depth.* **in-depth** *adj*: *His book is the first exhaustive in-depth study in this area.*

**out of one's *depth*** *(informal)* in a situation that is beyond your knowledge, understanding, or ability: *It looks as if the speaker is getting out of his depth trying to answer the questions—I hope the meeting will finish soon to give him a break.*

***descend* on/upon sth** arrive or attack suddenly or in an overwhelming way: *All my relatives from Manchester unexpectedly descended upon us last weekend!*

***descend* to (doing) sth** make yourself so low morally that you do sth; lower yourself: *They say he even descended to lying to his wife and family.*

**have (got) *designs* on/upon sb/sth** → ***have***

**leave sb to his own *devices*** → ***leave***

**be a *devil*!** *(informal)* (an encouragement to

sb to be bold on this one occasion): *Go on Jane—be a devil! Splash out on a new dress for once!*

**between the *devil* and the deep blue sea** *(saying)* having a choice of two alternative situations, both of which are unpleasant: *The enemy was getting closer. The bridge over the ravine was rotten. Caught between the devil and the deep blue sea, he hesitated as to where to turn next.*

**a/the *devil* of a job, nuisance, fellow etc** *(informal, becoming old-fashioned)* an extreme example of sb/sth; often difficult or unpleasant: *We had the devil of a time trying to get the roots of that tree out of the ground.*

**a/the *devil's* advocate** sb who raises objections to sth, although he may agree with it, especially in order to test the arguments for it: *He'd seemed against the idea, but when it was accepted, it was clear he'd been playing the devil's advocate and was as keen as everyone else.*

**have (got) the *devil*'s own luck** → ***have***

**the *devil* take sb/sth** *(old-fashioned)* (an expression of annoyance with sb/sth): *Oh, the devil take it! I've forgotten to phone Aunt Sally!* Also **to the devil with sb/sth.**

**(the) *devil* take the hindmost** *(saying)* let everyone look after his or her own interest, safety etc: *I admire the orderly way the British queue up everywhere. Back home we just push and shove, and the devil take the hindmost.*

**there'll be the '*devil* to pay** → ***there***

**better the *devil* you know than the devil/one you don't** → ***better***

**no *dice*** → ***no***

***dice* with death** take unnecessary risks and come near to killing yourself: *The motorbike riders love to dice with death on this circuit.*

**well, I never *(did)*!** → ***well***

**well, *did* you ever?** → ***well***

***die* away** (of a sound or voice) gradually become weaker or fainter until no longer heard: *The shouts of the crowd died away as they all went home.*

***die* down** (of wind, fire, or strong feelings) become less strong: *The weather men say the gales are now dying down. / The fuss over who really won the competition took days to die down.*

***die* hard** take a long time to die or disappear: *Old traditions die hard, and I for one would hate to see many of our customs fall into disuse.* **die-hard** *adj*: *die-hard attitudes.* **diehard** *n* sb who continues to hold principles which may be out of date.

***die* in one's boots** *(becoming old-fashioned)* die while still going about your daily business or duties: *I don't want to leave my job and retire—I'd prefer to die in my boots.* Also **die with one's boots on.**

**the *die* is cast** *(saying)* a decision, risk etc has been taken and cannot be cancelled or reversed: *It was done. The die had been cast. He had gambled all his money on this business venture. But doubts still lingered in his mind as to whether it was the right thing to do.*

***die* laughing** *(informal)* laugh to the point of exhaustion: *Did I laugh when he told us what happened? It was so funny I nearly died laughing!'*

***die*/fall/drop like flies** die/collapse in very large numbers: *The epidemic was so bad that one week we scarcely had time to bury all the people—they were dying like flies. / It was so hot in the hall that people were dropping like flies.*

***die* out** become extinct, disappear, or no longer be practised: *Many species of wild animals are in danger of dying out. / The weather forecast said that showers would gradually die out later in the afternoon. / The British custom of remembering Guy Fawkes' plot to blow up Parliament every 5 November shows no signs of dying out.*

***die* the death** *(informal)* stop working or having an effect; come to a sudden end: *She gave a poor performance in her latest film and soon found that her theatre career died the death.*

***die* with one's boots on** → ***die* in one's boots**

**a *different* ball-game** *(informal)* be a separate matter, issue etc: *'But if Washington learnt the lessons of Vietnam, why are they involved in Central America?' 'Central America? Don't you see—that's a completely different* (or *a whole new) ball-game!'*

**a horse of a *different* colour** → **a *horse* of another colour**

**see sb/sth in a *different*/better/new light** → ***see***

**a *different* kettle of fish** *(informal)* sb/sth quite different from sb/sth else previously mentioned: *You may be able to read French well but you'll see it's quite a different kettle of fish to speak it fluently.* See also **a fine/nice/pretty kettle of fish.**

**sing a *different* song/tune** → ***sing***

**(be) on a different *wavelength*** → **(be) on the same, a different etc *wavelength***

***dig* one's heels in** *(informal)* stubbornly refuse to give way on a point of principle: *A number of councils have dug their heels in over the question of reducing spending to comply with the government's request.*

**beneath sb's *dignity*** seeming so unimportant or unpleasant that sb thinks he cannot do it: *I'm sure it would be beneath your dignity to play with your younger brother, wouldn't it, Sarah!' Jean called out to her daughter.*

**stand on one's *dignity*** → ***stand***

**take a *dim*/poor view of sb/sth** → ***take***

***din* sth into sb** repeatedly urge sb to remember or be guided by sth; instil: *I've had such ideals dinned into me all my life, so I know what's right, even if I don't always do it!*

***dine* out on sth** *(informal)* have a dinner that is paid for by someone else, because of your achievements, reputation, or conversation: *He's been dining out for years on that story of how he climbed the Eiger.*

**by *dint* of** through; as a result of (doing) sth: *By dint of sheer hard work, she managed to pass all her exams.*

***dip* into sth 1** *(informal)* take money from sth: *Mark had to dip into his savings to pay for the car repairs.* **2** *(informal)* read passages from a book or books, but not in a planned or thorough way: *I've not had time to read your book properly yet, but I've dipped into it and what I've seen looks good!'*

**wash (one's) *dirty* linen in public** ⟶ ***wash***

**'*dirty* money** ⟶ **'*danger*/'dirty money**

**a *dirty* old man** *(informal)* a man who thinks too much about sex in a way that is thought improper for his age.

**do the *dirty* on sb** ⟶ ***do***

**a *dirty*/rotten/mean trick** a mean or dishonest action that causes sb else to suffer: *I don't want any of your dirty tricks when we play the game this time—like moving the pieces when you think I'm not looking!*

***disagree* wth sb** (of food or a climate) have a bad effect on one's health etc: *She used to eat bananas until they started to disagree with her.*

***discretion* is the better part of valour** *(saying)* it is often wiser to be cautious than be courageous or take unnecessary risks.

***dish* sth out 1** *(informal)* distribute; give to different people in turn: *Maria, can you dish the vegetables out, please? / After the question papers had been dished out we had to wait ages for the headmaster to come before we could start the exam.* **2** *(informal)* give sth such as advice, criticism, or punishment to different people, often in a rather careless way: *As a social worker, she only seems to be happy when she's dishing out advice to everyone she meets—whether they need it or not! / He can't take punishment, but he sure knows how to dish it out!*

***dish* sth up** *(informal)* present sth, especially information, to sb in an unattractive and repetitive way: *Why do the television companies dish up the same boring mixture of old films and repeats all the time?*

**it/that will never *do*** or **it/that won't do** ⟶ ***that***

***do* a sb** *(informal)* do or behave as sb did or would do: *Now don't go and do a Mr Carpenter on us. He left at very short notice, and it took me months to find a replacement.*

***do* a bunk** *(informal)* go away without warning from your house etc, especially to avoid trouble: *The police came round to question Joe about the money, but the whole family had already done a bunk.*

***do* sb a favour** do sth to help sb, often when you are not asked to do so: *Steve was broke, and to do his hosts a favour* (or *to do a favour for his hosts*) *he used to help in the garden and take the dog for a walk.* Also used as a rude request: *Do me/us a favour, will you Rod! Go outside to play your trumpet—we're fed up with it in here!*

***do* sb a good/bad turn** perform a kindly action when not asked to, or do sth that displeases sb: *He's always very helpful—ready to do anyone who needs it a good turn.*

***do* a moonlight (flit)** *(informal)* leave a place quickly and in secret to avoid paying debts: *When the rent collector called, she found they had done a moonlight flit.*

***do* sb/sth a power/world of good** *(informal)* be very helpful or beneficial to sb/sth: *A few days by the seaside did us a world of good. It really refreshed us all!*

***do* a 'roaring trade** be very successful in selling particular goods: *That café right outside the exhibition centre is doing a roaring trade in refreshments for the crowds.*

**not *do* a stroke (of work)** not do any work at all: *Every time my wife goes away, I never do a stroke of work in the house. So she comes back to find dust everywhere and lots of dirty washing.*

***do* all right for oneself** *(informal)* make a success of your life generally or in some particular way: *I know you never grudged the money you gave us, Father. But now that we're doing all right for ourselves, you must allow us to start paying you back.* Also **do well for oneself.**

***do* as I say, not as I do** *(saying)* follow my advice, not my example.

***do* as/what one is told** be obedient to what your parents, teachers etc tell you to do: *Come on now, children, do as you're told and get on with your work!*

***do* as you would be done by** *(saying)* you should treat other people in the way that you would like to be treated by them. See also **do by sb; *hard* done by.**

***do* away with sb** *(informal)* kill sb: *They say she did away with herself by taking an overdose of pills.*

***do* away with sth** *(informal)* abolish; put an end to sth such as a law or tradition: *The government wants to do away with the middle level of administration in the civil service, to save money.*

***do* badly for sth** ⟶ ***do* well/badly for sth**

**can't/couldn't *do* better than do sth** be right, wise, or well-advised to do sth: *For looking at houses to buy in this area, you couldn't do better than buy our local weekly property guide.*

**would *do* better to do sth** it would be more advantageous or profitable if you did sth: *So you want to go to Jacks' to buy a new car? You'd do better to try that new garage in Manchester.*

***do* bird/porridge/time** *(slang)* serve a prison sentence: *He's doing time for armed robbery.* Also *(not slang)* **serve time.**

***do* one's bit** take one's share or responsibility in a task: *Simon, you're not doing your bit! Come on, help!*

***do* by sb** treat sb in a way that is mentioned: *I always do quite well by Mr Hart.* See also **do as you would be done by; *hard* done by.**

**not *do* sth by halves** do sth that you are engaged in thoroughly: *George was not a man* *to do things by halves. He would either refuse to support the venture at all or send us a large cheque for it.*

***do*/try one's damnedest (to do sth)** or ***do*/try one's damnedest for sb** *(informal)* do everything in your power (to do sth or to help sb): *Sylvia may have won the cup for the best orchid for the last four years, but I'm certainly going to do my damnedest to see she doesn't this year.*

***do* sb/sth down** *(informal)* try to make sb/sth appear small, mean, unimportant etc; humiliate: *I wouldn't trust Max—he's been known to do his best friend down. / It seems to be fashionable these days to do down your own country.*

**can't *do* enough** be tirelessly willing or eager to be of service to sb, a cause etc: *Of course they'd prefer a home of their own, but I assure you their hosts can't do enough to make them feel wanted there.*

***do* for sb** *(informal)* clean and keep a house tidy for sb: *Mrs Burns from the other side of town does for them, Mondays and Thursdays.*

***do* for sth** *(informal)* manage to use instead of something that is not available: *What would we do for entertainment if there weren't any television?*

***do* good** act with kind helpfulness, sometimes in a showy way: *Religious people are often thought to be the type of folks who go about doing good—helping old ladies across roads, being decent to your neighbours, and so on.* **do-gooder** *n (usually derogatory)*: *do-gooders who poke their noses into other people's business.*

***do* (sb/sth) good** improve the health or happiness of sb or the condition of sth: *A week's convalescence by the sea would do you good, I think. / You could try complaining about the poor postal service, but I don't think it'll do any good.* Also used ironically in the idiom **much good may it do sb:** *Oh damn him! Let him have the lawn mower if he says it's his! And much good may it do him!* See also ***do* sb/sth a power/world of good.**

***do* one's homework** *(informal)* make appropriate preparations or find out the necessary facts or possibilities before answering questions, starting a business etc: *A good politician must always make sure he has done his homework before going to a meeting where the audience will ask questions.*

***do* sb/oneself in** *(slang)* kill sb: *I heard that some thugs came along and did the old lady in. / I feel so desperate I could do myself in.*

***do* it** ⟶ ***do* the trick/job**

***do*/hear/see it all** *(informal)* have a long and varied experience of life or sth specific: *She was 48 and had had a succession of jobs—as careers go, she'd done it all. / After a few years in practice, a doctor has heard it all.* Note that this is usually used in the past tense.

***do* it yourself** do practical jobs in a home such as decorating or carpentry yourself rather than paying a tradesman to do them: *There's no point in getting a builder in to do such a simple thing. Why not do it yourself?* **DIY; do-it-yourself** *adj*: *The new DIY store in town has everything in the way of tools and materials that the home handyman needs.*

***do* sb/sth justice** or **do justice to sb/sth** give sb/sth the treatment, acknowledgment, praise etc that is deserved: *The fact that we had eaten an hour earlier meant that we couldn't do full justice to her excellent cooking.*

***do*/try one's level best** try as hard as you can to do sth: **I'll do my level best to come, but I'm not making any promises.**

***do* one's nut** *(slang)* lose one's temper and self-control: *The boss will do his nut if he finds out that you've wasted so much of the firm's money!*

***do* or die** make a definite or desperate attempt to do sth: *I'm determined to win first prize, do or die!*

***do* sth out 1** *(informal)* make a room clean or tidy: *I spent the morning doing out the bedrooms and going shopping.* **2** *(informal)* decorate or redecorate a room, house etc: *You should have seen how awful the house was when we bought it! We had to do it out from top to bottom.*

***do* sb out of sth** *(informal)* prevent sb from having sth, often by cheating or neglect: *Paying workers to do overtime is doing other people out of a job. / I should have got some money when Dad died, but the taxman did me out of it!*

***do* sb over** *(slang)* attack and beat sb severely: *Poor old Mike had to spend a week in hospital after the gang did him over at the football match.*

***do* sth over** clean or decorate the surface of a cooker, room etc: *The paintwork is beginning to flake. It'll need doing over soon.*

***do* one's own thing** *(informal)* allow your natural abilities, tastes, feelings etc to guide what you do and how you live.

***do* porridge** ⟶ ***do* bird/porridge/time**

***do* sb/sth proud** honour sb/sth in a generous, lavish way that is thought fitting: *Your new book got good write-ups in quite a few magazines. They really did you proud!*

***do*'s and don'ts** *(informal)* detailed instructions: *This book is a useful guide to the do's and don'ts of home freezing.*

***do* something for sb/sth** *(informal)* improve the appearance of sb/sth: *You know that hat really does something for you!*

***do* one's stuff** *(informal)* do what you are expected to do: *I don't mind how little or much you practise, as long as you do your stuff in the actual performance.*

***do* the dirty on sb** *(informal)* be disloyal to sb, especially by betraying him: *Harry felt that his fellow students had done the dirty on him by telling the lecturer he'd cheated in the exam.*

***do* the honours** act as host; perform the main social duties appropriate to the occasion: *'Would you like to do the honours?' Marge* *asked Ralph, passing him the carving knife, 'You always carve our joints of beef so well!'*

***do* the right thing** behave in a way that is proper or wise: *'Should we have waited until morning to phone you, doctor?' 'No, you did the right thing. He needs to go into hospital right away.'*

***do* the spadework** perform the tasks that are necessary before a project can begin properly: *Before the conference, he did a lot of spadework, urging the other delegates to follow his point of view, so that at the conference itself, his suggestion was implemented.*

***do* the trick/job** accomplish what is desired; be sth that finally solves a problem or has the required effect: *'That should do the trick!' Norman said, as he finished putting tar over the cracks in the roof, 'There shouldn't be any more leaks now!'* Also **do it.**

***do* sth to death** *(informal)* weaken or destroy the effect of sth by doing it too often: *All the life and originality has gone out of this play—it's really been done to death.*

**it was all one could *do* (not) to do sth** ⟶ ***all***

***do* time** ⟶ ***do* bird/porridge/time**

***do* sb/sth up** make sb, especially yourself or your face, more beautiful or attractive by putting powder, lipstick etc on: *She spent an hour doing herself up before the party.*

***do* (sth) up** (of sth such as a coat, pair of trousers, button, or zip) (cause to) fasten: *This coat does up at the back. / Not many children of his age can do up the buttons on a coat.*

***do* sth up 1** *(informal)* renovate, modernize, or redecorate sth such as a room or an old building: *You know you'll have to do up that cottage if you decide to buy it—I don't think anyone has looked after it for years. / We had the back bedroom done up very cheaply last year.* **2** pack a collection of things together into a parcel: *Can you pass me the brown paper and string, please, so I can do up these books properly?*

***do* well for oneself** ⟶ ***do* all right for oneself**

***do* well/badly for sth** *(informal)* obtain or have a large/small number of sth: *At Christmas, the staff at the hotel do very well for tips. / We didn't do too badly for replies to our advertisement, when you think how much our books actually cost.*

***do* well to do sth** find it in your own interests to do sth mentioned: *You'd do well to remember what happened last year at the exhibition and prepare more carefully this year. / Those who think they can pass this exam without doing any work will do well to think again!*

***do* what one is told** ⟶ ***do* as/what one is told**

**could/can *do* with sth** *(informal)* need or want sth such as a meal, drink, or holiday: *I could just do with something to eat! Would you like something as well? / You look as if you could do with a good night's sleep.*

**what did you etc *do* with sth?** ⟶ ***what***

***do* without (sth)** live, exist, or manage without sth: *You simply can't do without sleep for a long time. / If we can't afford to buy a car, then we'll just have to go without, that's all.* See also **could/can *do* without sth.**

**could/can *do* without sth** *(informal)* not require and resent having sth such as an unkind comment or interference: *We can do without that kind of advice, thank you very much. / I could have done without her ringing up just as I was going out.*

***do* wonders/miracles** ⟶ ***work*/do wonders/miracles**

**can/could *do* worse than do sth** be sensible or right to do sth: *If you want to save a small amount each month, you could do a lot worse than put it in the latest national savings investment scheme.*

***do* one's worst** be as unpleasant, difficult etc as possible: *Let the weather do its worst! I'm still going out to win this race!*

**in *dock*** *(informal)* in need of and getting a repair; ill, in hospital etc: *'No car today, Max?' 'No, it's in dock.'*

**just what the *doctor* ordered** ⟶ ***just***

**the '*dog* days** the hottest period of summer; a time of boredom, apathy, and inactivity.

**'*dog* ears** the folded down corners on the page of a book, which are the result of handling over a period of time or done deliberately to keep a place in a book: *Don't do that—I don't like books full of dog ears.* **dog-eared** *adj.*

***dog* eat dog** *(informal)* cruel, merciless competition that does not consider loyalty or other people's feelings: *In the cut and thrust of the business world, it's dog eat dog to see who'll survive.*

***dog* sb's footsteps** (of misfortune) seem always to follow sb: *Bad luck seems to have dogged our footsteps from the beginning.*

**in the '*dog* house** *(informal)* out of favour; in disgrace: *I'm in the dog house with the wife at the moment—I forgot it was our wedding anniversary yesterday!*

**a *dog* in the manger** sb who selfishly stops other people from using or enjoying sth which he keeps for himself, although he knows he cannot use or enjoy it. **dog-in-the-manger** *adj*: *a dog-in-the-manger attitude.*

**a *dog's* breakfast/dinner** *(informal)* a mess; piece of work, room, situation etc that has been mismanaged or is very untidy: *This book is awful—poorly written and with many misprints—the problem is what is a publisher doing lending its name to this dog's breakfast? / She came downstairs, looking like a dog's dinner.*

**(not) have (got) a '*dog's* chance (of doing sth)** ⟶ **(not) *have* (got) a cat in 'hell's chance (of doing sth)**

**a '*dog's* life** a lifestyle in which there is not much pleasure or freedom (usually used as an expression of temporary or not serious dissatisfaction): *It's a dog's life working here, having to take orders from Alf all the time.*

'***dog* tired** *(informal)* very tired: *After a hard day's work I usually come home dog tired.*

**what is sb/sth *doing,* (doing sth)?** ⟶ ***what***

***doll* sb up** dress sb, especially yourself, in unusually smart or colourful clothes (usually used of girls and women and sometimes in a derogatory way): *She spent hours dolling herself up for the party.*

**be *done* for** *(informal)* be ruined, be killed or fail: *The supplies are so low that we'll be done for in a few days unless help comes soon. / I think the project is done for—the money's almost gone and we've got no results after three years' hard work.*

***done* in** *(informal)* extremely exhausted: *'What's the matter, Sue? You look pale.' 'I'm absolutely done in, Rose! I just must lie down!'*

**have *done* it 'this time** *(informal)* have done sth very foolish, serious etc that has great effect: *You've really done it this time, haven't you? How are we going to say the window got broken?* Variations on ***this time*** are ***again; now.***

**that's *done* it!** ⟶ ***that's* done/torn it!**

**if one has *done* sth once, one has done it a hundred times** ⟶ ***if***

**(not) the *done* thing** (not) the conventional, approved behaviour, procedure, or etiquette: *'When I was young,' said her grandmother, 'it wasn't the done thing for girls to go to dance halls without a partner.'* Also **(not) done.**

***done* to a turn** (of cooked food) perfectly prepared and neither undercooked nor overcooked: *'How's the Yorkshire pudding, Dad?' 'Delicious, light as a feather, and done to a turn, thanks!'*

**be/have *done* with sb/sth** dissociate yourself from sb/sth; discontinue or no longer permit an activity: *I'm fed up with you lot! I'm done with you for ever! / Why don't we spend another half hour painting and then we'll have done with it.*

***donkey's* years** *(informal)* a very long time: *He's been in that job for donkey's years.*

**the *donkey* work** the hard, boring parts of a task: *Jim looked with pride over the pages of the book. A lot of detailed work had obviously gone into it. He was glad he had only supervised the people who had done all the donkey work. / Why is it always me who has to do the donkey work?*

***don't . . . me*** *(informal)* don't speak to me in the way or call me with the word that is mentioned (used to show annoyance at sth you find offensive): *'Come off it, Jack.' 'Don't "Jack" me—my name's Robinson and that's what you'll call me—Mr Robinson!'*

**(from) *door* to door 1** from the place of departure to your destination: *The journey takes me four and a half hours from door to door.* **2** from one house, flat etc to the next: *The church distributes leaflets from door to door.* **door-to-door** *adj*: *a door-to-door salesman.*

**lay sth at sb's *door*** ⟶ ***lay***

**on one's/sb's *doorstep*** very near to a home, community etc: *It's easy to be concerned with problems across the other side of the world and not see the needs on your (own) doorstep.*

**a *dose*/taste of one's own medicine** treatment of the same kind that you have given sb else: *There is still a large body of opinion that says that the only effective way to deal with violent criminals is to give them a taste of their own medicine.*

**on the *dot*** *(informal)* promptly: *He always finishes work at 4.30 on the dot* (or *on the dot of 4.30*).

***dot* the i's and cross the t's** be meticulously correct in what you do or say; make clear in every detail sth which may be obvious or well enough understood already: *We basically share the same approach to politics, though we differ on a few minor points. So I think we can work together well without first needing to dot all the i's and cross all the t's.*

**sign on the *dotted* line** ⟶ ***sign***

**at the *double*** very quickly; immediately: *The boss wants you to go and see him at the double.*

***double* Dutch** *(informal)* sth that cannot be understood and is meaningless: *This 300-page guide to government services seems to be written in bureaucratic double Dutch to me.*

***double* quick** *(informal)* very quick(ly): *If the machine starts making a hissing noise, then turn it off double quick.* **double-quick** *adj*: *in double-quick time.*

'***double* talk** sth said that is capable of more than one interpretation or that is intended to mean sth opposite to or different from what the words might indicate.

**a *doubting* Thomas** a sceptic; sb who will not believe sth unless he is personally satisfied by its truth or has seen the evidence himself.

***down* and 'out** (of people) having no home or job and living on the streets of a city; very poor. **'down-and-out** *n*: *life among the city's down-and-outs.*

***down* in the dumps** *(informal)* sad, miserable, and discouraged: *Sue lives by herself and tends to feel down in the dumps quite often.*

***down* in the mouth** (looking) unhappy or discouraged: *'Why is she looking so down in the mouth?' 'They say that her pony was ill and had to be put to sleep.'*

**be *down* on sb /sth** disapprove of or be prejudiced against sb/sth: *My father's very down on the present government.* Also *(slang)* **have a down on sb:** *His excuse for poor marks is that his teacher has a down on him.*

***down* on one's luck** having bad luck: *I've been down on my luck for years! When am I going to be rich?'*

***down* to sb/sth** even including the final item of the whole list of people or things: *From the King down to the lowliest servant, it seemed as if all were affected by the plague. / Yes, you've thought of everything down to the tiniest details of what colours the flowers should be!*

**be *down* to sth** have nothing except one or a

few items of a kind mentioned: *I'm down to my last penny*.

***down* tools** stop work, either at the end of the day or as a strike or other protest: *The workers threatened to down tools if the manager didn't take any notice of their demands*.

***down* under** *(informal)* in or to Australia and/or New Zealand.

***down* with sb/sth!** (an exclamation of protest against sb/sth): *Down with exams!* See also: ***up* (with) sb/sth!**

***downhill* all the way** easy and often fast progress, especially after the difficulties are passed: *As I've done three out of the four parts of the course, I hope it'll be downhill all the way from now on.*

***drag* sb/sth down** bring to a low physical or moral level: *The dull routine of life in the office is enough to drag anyone down. / Opening another betting shop would really drag the area down.*

***drag* one's feet/heels** do sth very slowly and with delay, because you are unwilling to be fully committed: *How much longer can the government go on dragging its feet about whether to invest more money in the railways?*

***drag* sb/sth in(to sth)** *(informal)* make sb participate in an activity against his will; make sb/sth the topic of conversation, especially often: *There's no need to drag Julie in. It's just between us. / Why do you always have to drag sex into every conversation?*

***drag* sb's/sth's name etc through the mud/mire** bring dishonour on sb/sth or damage sb/sth's reputation: *The boy was accused of dragging the respected name of the school through the mud.*

***drag* sb up** *(informal)* allow a child to grow up without proper discipline or training (usually used in the passive): *From the way she behaves, you can see how she's been dragged up.*

***drag* sth up** *(informal)* cause sth, especially sth unpleasant, to be remembered: *The newspaper reporter had certainly dragged up some murky details of his past.*

**sow the *dragon's*/dragons' teeth** ⟶ ***sow***

**down the *drain*** *(informal)* wasted or lost: *When John decided not to take up a career as a vet after his parents had spent a lot on a special education, they thought they'd been pouring (or throwing) money down the drain.*

**laugh like a *drain*** ⟶ ***laugh***

***draw* a blank** fail to obtain or discover sth you are searching for or hope to get: *There was no sign of the murder weapon. The police scoured every inch of the wood but drew a blank.*

***draw*/throw/cast a veil over sth** say nothing or no more about sth shameful or unpleasant; (try to) keep sth secret or private: *Death and dying are subjects over which most of us prefer to cast a veil.*

***draw* in/out** (of the hours of daylight) become shorter/longer: *The days are beginning to draw in now that autumn is upon us.*

***draw*/cast lots (for sth)** make chance decide sth, for example by using differently marked papers, or straws or sticks of different lengths: *'Casting lots for promotion would be fairer than the favouritism that goes on in this firm,' she complained bitterly. / If there aren't tickets for all who want to attend then we'll have to draw lots.*

***draw* on/upon sth** use or exploit your knowledge, skill etc: *All those taking part in the seminars will be expected to draw on their own experience in presenting their talks.*

***draw* sb out** help sb to feel less shy or reserved: *Bernie had learnt the gift of drawing people out and making them feel at home from his father.* See also **bring sb out (of his shell).**

***draw* sth out (of sb)** extract a secret, confession, or piece of information from sb: *It took some hours of patient questioning to draw the full story out of him.*

***draw* sth out (of sth)** withdraw money from an account with a bank etc: *I'd like to draw out £100 please.*

***draw* sth up** prepare and write sth such as an agreement or list: *If you give your solicitors precise details of what you want to put in your will, they will then draw up a draft for you to look at.*

***draw* sb up short/sharply** ⟶ ***bring*/draw/pull sb up short/sharply**

***draw* up** (of a vehicle) stop; come to a halt: *A car drew up outside the house and two policemen got out.*

***draw* the line (at sth)** not go beyond a certain limit in your actions or behaviour: *I may tell the occasional small lie at times but I draw the line at downright, blatant dishonesty.*

**work/go like a *dream*** ⟶ ***work***

**not *dream* of doing sth** *(informal)* not consider or even conceive of doing sth (usually used with **would**): *My parents wouldn't dream of having alcohol in the house. / I never dreamed of giving her a kiss.* **undreamed-of** *adj*.

***dream* sth up** *(informal)* devise or create a project, plot etc, especially one that uses a lot of imagination: *What other wild ideas have you dreamed up?*

***dress* sb down** *(informal)* criticize sb strongly for a wrong action. **dressing-down** *n*: *Pete knew that he was in for a good dressing-down from his father for his rudeness.*

***dress* sb up** put on formal clothes for a special occasion; (of children) put on clothes normally worn by other people: *Do we have to dress up for tonight's dinner?* **dressing-up** *adj, n*: *Children love to wear dressing-up clothes.* See also **all dressed up and nowhere to go.**

***dress* sth up** make sth seem more attractive and impressive by adding details etc: *Why did you have to go and dress up the proposal in pompous language? It was all right as it was before you started messing about with it!*

**mutton *dressed* as lamb** ⟶ ***mutton***

***dressed* to kill** *(informal)* wearing your best clothes, especially clothes designed to attract attention: *She went to the party dressed to kill.*

**all *dressed* up and nowhere to go** ⟶ ***all***

***drink* sth in** *(informal)* listen to or look at sth such as a speech or a view very eagerly: *A packed audience just sat there, drinking in every word he spoke, with rapt attention. / Looking out of the hotel window, I paused to drink in the magnificent beauty of the scenery.*

***drink* like a fish** *(informal)* drink too much alcohol as a habit: *He claims that it was the loss of his wife that drove him to drink, but believe you me, he drank like a fish even before that.*

***drink* sb under the table** *(informal)* drink more alcohol than sb else while remaining more sober than him.

***drive*/take a coach and horses through sth** *(informal)* destroy sth in a strong, convincing way: *The wage increase we've been given is three times the government's norm. We've driven a coach and horses right through their pay policy.*

***drive* a hard bargain** effect an exchange of goods and services that is to your own advantage or unfair to the other person: *I wouldn't do business with Jack; he's got the reputation of driving a hard bargain.*

***drive* sb out of his mind/wits** make sb mad or very nervous or worried: *This noise is driving me out of my mind!*

***drive* sb to drink** make sb so desperate that he seeks forgetfulness or relief in drinking: *His neglect of his wife over the years gradually drove her to drink.*

***drive* sb up the wall** *(informal)* make sb mad or very annoyed: *You children are driving me up the wall!*

**as pure as the *driven* snow** ⟶ ***pure***

**what is sb *driving* at?** ⟶ ***what***

**in the *driving* seat** *(informal)* in a position to control or manage a business, administration, or sb's affairs: *With a new man in the driving seat at the top of the company, we can expect some big changes soon.*

***(drop)* a bombshell** *(informal)* (surprise sb with) shocking and unwelcome news: *The chairman really dropped a bomb-shell when he suddenly announced he was to going to resign.*

***drop* a brick/clanger** *(informal)* say or do sth that causes embarrassment: *'I wouldn't know how to behave at a grand occasion like that,' the old man said, 'I'd be dropping bricks the whole time and upsetting people.'*

***drop* a hint** refer indirectly to sth; make a suggestion indirectly and tactfully: *He tried to drop a hint about it being time to leave, but they didn't seem to take any notice.*

***drop* sb a line/note** *(informal)* write a short letter to a friend or casual acquaintance: *We'll drop you a line nearer the time just to confirm the arrangements for the meeting.*

***drop* one's aitches** omit the initial 'h' sound in a word; often used to suggest that sb comes from a low social class: *''e told us to wait be'ind and 'elp clear up.' 'Now, Harry, say that again, without dropping your aitches!'*

***drop* by/in/round** or ***drop* in on sb** *(informal)* pay a casual visit to sb: *Just drop in at any time for a cup of coffee and a chat.*

***drop* dead** *(informal)* **1** die very unexpectedly: *Poor Alf, he went out to post a letter—and dropped dead by the postbox, as suddenly as that.* **2** *(slang)* (an exclamation telling sb to go away and stop bothering you): *Drop dead, will you, Maxine!*

**a *drop* in the ocean/bucket** a tiny amount in comparison to a very much larger amount: *£100 million is a drop in the bucket compared to what is really needed to help these people effectively.*

***drop*/fall into sb's lap** be obtained without any effort by sb: *You won't get a job by just sitting around waiting for one to drop into your lap, you know.*

***drop* like flies** ⟶ ***die/fall/drop like flies***

***drop* names** *(informal)* over-use the names of important people in order to impress other people with your knowledge. **name-dropping** *n*: *First of all I tell new clients a little about our books. Then I do a bit of name-dropping to show them that we do business with influential customers.*

**at the *drop* of a hat** *(informal)* immediately and willingly; with only the slightest encouragement: *He's the sort of person who can sing any song at all at the drop of a hat.*

***drop* off** *(informal)* fall into a light sleep or doze: *I could feel that I was dropping off when suddenly I smelt something burning.*

***drop* sb/sth off** *(informal)* allow sb to get out of a vehicle; set sb/sth down: *Get the taxi to drop you off at the corner of the High Street. / Could you drop the flowers off at Louise's flat when you go to the station, please?*

***drop* out (of sth)** leave or withdraw from a class, activity, or society prematurely: *Sharon dropped out in her second term at college as she got so fed up. / Peter was hoping to join the party going to the ballet, but he's had to drop out at the last minute.* **drop-out** *adj*: *the drop-out rate at college.* **dropout** *n* sb who rejects conventional society.

**the bottom *drops*/falls out of the market** ⟶ ***bottom***

**the bottom *drops*/falls out of sb's world** ⟶ ***bottom***

***drown* one's sorrows** *(informal)* drink alcohol to comfort yourself and forget your troubles: *Wales beat Scotland 3–0, and in the pubs that evening many Scottish fans could be found drowning their sorrows.*

**like a *drowned* rat** extremely wet: *She'd just been out in a storm so came into the house looking like a drowned rat!*

***drum* sth into sb** make sb remember sth by repeating it often; instil: *Respect for their elders was drummed into them from infancy.*

***drum* sb out of sth** expel from a club or association, often in a formal way: *The politi-*

*cians say that their party would never drum anyone out of office for daring to vote against them.*

**drum sb/sth up** summon sth, such as support or enthusiasm; obtain new recruits, business etc: *The purpose of his trip was to try to drum up some support for his ideas.*

**as *drunk* as a lord/newt** *(informal)* very drunk: *He left the pub, singing and swaying as he went, as drunk as a lord.*

**as *dry* as a bone** containing no moisture: *Just feel this wall now I've repaired the damp—it's as dry as a bone!* Also **bone-dry**.

**as *dry* as dust** very boring and tedious: *His lectures are sound all right, but they're as dry as dust.*

**not *dry* behind the ears →*wet* behind the ears**

**a *dry* run →*a dummy/dry run***

***dry* up 1** (of a supply) be completely exhausted: *When our own money dries up we'll just have to borrow.* **2** (of a speaker) become unable to speak, especially because of nervousness: *I'd just got onto the stage . . . and then I dried up . . . I can't explain it.* **3** *(informal)* stop talking (often used in the imperative): *Dry up, will you, you two! I'm fed up with your nattering all the time—I'm trying to do some work here!*

***duck* out (of (doing) sth)** *(informal)* avoid (doing) a duty or obligation: *He always tries to duck out of doing the washing-up.*

**like water off a *duck's* back →*water***

**(take to sth) like a *duck* to water →*take***

**in *due* course** at the proper and right time in the future: *Thank you for your interest. We shall let you know the result of your application in due course.*

**as *dull* as ditchwater** very boring and dreary: *Bestseller or not, the book sounds as dull as ditchwater to me.*

**never a *dull* moment →*never***

**a *dummy*/dry run** an experimental or trial performance of a project or the working of a machine etc: *It was lucky we found the faults on the dummy run; it could have been disastrous if an accident had happened when the machine was operating normally.*

**down in the *dumps* →*down***

**the *Dunkirk* spirit** a refusal to surrender or despair in a time of crisis, maintaining a strong and courageous determination.

***dust* sb down** *(informal)* criticize sb strongly for a wrong action. **dusting-down** *n.*

**shake the *dust* (of sth) off one's feet/shoes →*shake***

**when, till, after etc the *dust* settles** when etc the trouble or confusion aroused by sth has lessened: *As the dust began to settle, some clear facts about the controversial government leak began to emerge.*

***Dutch* courage** *(informal)* courage that is obtained from drinking alcohol: *I'd had four drinks and hoped that my Dutch courage would help me tell my wife what had happened.*

**then/or I'm a *Dutchman*** *(informal)* I shall be very surprised: *If that's not a genuine 16th-century piece, then I'm a Dutchman! / I'm sure that was the King—either that or I'm a Dutchman!*

**(in) *duty* bound (to do sth)** acting in accordance with what you feel to be professional, moral, or social obligations: *I'm duty bound to help her now she's ill—she's been such a good friend to me over the years.*

***duty* calls** one has work to do that cannot be avoided (often used as a reminder to yourself and other people that sth pleasant has to stop): *Ah, duty calls, I'm afraid—I really must go and finish off those letters.*

***dwell* on/upon sth** *(formal)* spend a long time thinking, speaking, or writing about sth: *There's no need to dwell on past glories. What about our future?*

***dyed*-in-the-wool** extreme; totally committed: *He's a dyed-in-the-wool reactionary—there's no changing his opinions!*

**till/until/to one's *dying* day** for as long as one lives: *I swear I won't forgive her till my dying day!*

**be *dying* for sth** or **be dying to do sth** *(informal)* need or want sth very much: *I'm dying for a drink. / She's heard so much about you. She's dying to meet you!*

**be *dying* of sth** *(informal)* be nearly overcome by an extreme feeling of something such as hunger or boredom: *We're all dying of curiosity—come on, tell us what happened!*

# E

**an *eager* beaver** *(informal)* sb who works very hard, willingly, and busily: *Pat comes in here early in the morning and stays on late. He's a real eager beaver!*

**out on one's *ear*** *(informal)* forced to leave a job, room etc suddenly: *You'll be out on your ear unless your work gets a lot better, my lad.*

**play (sth) by *ear* →*play***

**play it by *ear* →*play***

**have (got) an *ear* for sth →*have***

**an '*early* bird** *(informal)* sb who gets out of bed early in the morning or does sth, such as go to work, earlier than most other people.

***early* days yet** rather too soon to come to conclusions or an opinion on sth still developing: *I didn't manage to bring the committee round to my way of thinking, but I knew it was early days yet and I still had some important ideas to put over.*

***earn* a bomb** → ***cost*/earn/make/pay/spend a bomb**

***earn* one's keep** be sufficiently useful, helpful, and profitable to balance any expense incurred: *Though it's expensive to hire and maintain, the new copying machine is earning its keep as we've been able to reduce the number of office staff. / Jill more than earns her keep with the help she gives me around the house.*

**up to one's *ears*/eyeballs/eyes/neck in sth** *(informal)* deeply involved in sth; overwhelmed by sth such as work or problems: *He was up to his eyes in debt.* Also **up to here in sth.** Note that ***here*** is often accompanied by holding a hand at the level of the eyes or neck.

**feel one's *ears* burning** → ***feel***

**keep one's *ear*(s) (close) to the ground** → ***keep***

**prick up one's *ears*** → ***prick***

**not dry behind the *ears*** → ***wet* behind the ears**

**wet behind the *ears*** → ***wet***

**run sb/sth to *earth*/ground** → ***run***

**(not) have (got) an *earthly* (chance) (of doing sth)** → **(not) *have* (got) a cat in 'hell's chance (of doing sth)**

**ill at *ease*** → ***ill***

**(stand) at *ease*** → ***stand***

***easier* said than done** *(saying)* merely suggesting some course of action is very much easier than actually carrying it out.

**as *easy* as ABC** very easy to do: *Surely you can understand how to put the table together—it's as easy as ABC!* Also **as easy as pie; as easy/simple as falling off a log.**

***easy* come, easy go** *(saying)* what has been acquired very easily and quickly may be spent, lost, or wasted.

***easy*/gently/slowly does it** *(informal)* move sth carefully so as not to damage it; deal with sb patiently and sensitively: *Easy does it! Just lift it up a little bit and I think it'll go through the door.*

***easy* money** money earned in return for very little work, trouble, or initial outlay, often implying that some dishonesty is involved: *Taking parties of six to eight people round the bay for an hour at £10 each seems pretty easy money to me.*

***easy* terms** low interest rates on, or a long time in which to repay, a loan to buy goods, services etc, especially in a hire-purchase arrangement: *'Easy terms available' ran the poster across the shop window. 'Why not refurnish your home now?'*

**an *easy* touch** → **a *soft*/easy touch**

***eat*, drink, and be merry** *(saying)* enjoy yourself now, while you can; don't think about the future (usually used to support or disapprove of a selfish, carefree attitude).

***eat* one's head off** *(informal)* eat too much food: *The children came in from their long walk and they're now in the dining-room eating their heads off.*

***eat* one's heart out** grieve bitterly: *She's been eating her heart out ever since her fiancé broke off their engagement last month.*

***eat* humble pie** have to be more respectful or apologetic than you have been before, especially because your opinion or statement has been proved wrong: *I said I would come first in all the races, but not winning any of them really made me eat humble pie.*

***eat* into sth** use part of a supply of money, especially unwillingly: *They found the cost of the holiday was eating into their savings.*

***eat* like a horse** *(informal)* eat well; consume large quantities of food: *My brother Matthew eats like a horse but never puts on weight.*

**I'll *eat* my hat** → ***I***

***eat* out of sb's hand** be completely willing to submit to sb's wishes: *She's really got him eating out of her hand. He'll do absolutely anything she wants!*

***eat* sb out of house and home** eat a lot of food provided by sb at his own home: *These friends of yours are eating us out of house and home! When are they going to leave?*

***eat* the cream** → **like the *cat* that ate the cream**

**won't *eat* you** *(informal)* will not harm you (used as an encouragement to sb who appears frightened): *Come on, Sarah, Father Christmas won't eat you! If you go closer, he'll give you a present!*

***eat* one's words** *(informal)* be forced to withdraw what you have previously said was true, certain etc: *Nick boasted that he'd be picked for the team, but when he wasn't chosen, he had to eat his words.*

**what is *eating* sb?** → ***what***

**on *edge*** nervous, worried, and anxious: *Most people feel on edge before exams.*

**set sb's '*teeth* on *edge*** → ***set***

**on the *edge* of one's chair/seat** absorbed in listening to or watching sth such as a story or play: *The film was so exciting that it had the audience sitting on the edge of their chairs right up to the last moment.*

**have (got) an/the *edge* on/over sb/sth** → ***have***

**to good, little etc *effect*** with a good etc result: *The jewels are displayed in the case to excellent effect, I think. / I try to keep the house tidy, but with the children here, the cleaning I do is all to little effect.*

**to the *effect* that** having a basic meaning or purpose: *A letter was sent to all employees to the effect that the firm would have to close down. / He told me rudely to go immediately, or words to that effect!*

***egg* sb on** *(informal)*encourage sb to do sth, especially sth foolish or risky: *The older children were egging the younger ones on to jump off the tree.*

**have *egg* on one's face** → ***have***

**put all one's *eggs* in/into one basket** → ***put***

**as sure as *eggs* is eggs** → ***sure***

**have one over the *eight*** → ***have***

**at one's *elbow*** very near; within arm's reach: *I've put up shelves before, you know—I don't need anyone at my elbow telling me what to do!*

**'*elbow* grease** *(informal)* effort put into physical work: *Come on, get this floor scrubbed, and put a bit of elbow grease into it!*

**'*elbow* room** sufficient space to move your elbows, sit comfortably etc; freedom to act or function, especially within certain limits: *The narrow seats at the back of the hall were unpopular as they only give a little elbow room. / As an independent school we have enough elbow room to try out new educational methods.*

**an *elder* statesman** sb who has held high office in government, business etc for a long period and who, though he may have retired, is still likely to be asked for opinions and advice.

**in one's *element*** in a situation in which you can be with like-minded people or in surroundings that make you happy: *Sarah's right in her element! Just look at her—laughing and telling jokes with all the men attending to her every whim!*

**at the *eleventh* hour** almost, but not quite, too late to do sth, for sth to be avoided etc: *We were in despair of finding an accompanist to replace Jack Stevens, who had fallen ill; but at the eleventh hour, just as we were thinking of cancelling the performance, we remembered Jill Chapman, so we asked her to take over.* **eleventh-hour** *adj: an eleventh-hour decision.*

***embark* on/upon sth** start a project, campaign etc: *The government has decided it must embark on a new series of cuts in public expenditure.*

***empty* vessels make the most noise** *(saying)* people who lack intelligence or sense are the most talkative and noisy.

**be the *end*** *(informal)* be very annoying; be intolerable: *You children really are the end! / I'd seen a dirty house before, but theirs was the absolute end!*

**in the *end*** finally; after or in spite of everything that has gone before; after other choices etc have been tried (often used of an action that is achieved by perseverance and patience): *I spent hours looking for my keys and found them in the end. / They tried to get him to confess and in the end he gave in.*

**no *end* ⟶ *no***

**on *end*** (of a period of time) in succession: *He just sits there, watching television for hours on end.*

**a(n)/the X to *end* all X's** sth that is of the highest quality: *This is the souvenir to end all souvenirs—you can capture all the excitement of the royal wedding when you buy this record!*

**(not/never) hear/see the *end*/last of sb/sth ⟶ *hear***

**at/to/towards the *end* of one's/its days** during or approaching the last remaining period of one's life or the existence of sth: *He was one of those who shut their eyes to the fact that the colonial system as they had known it was at the end of its days. / She had been a commanding and domineering woman, but her attitude softened towards the end of her days and she became much more agreeable to live with.*

**not know one *end* of sth from the other** or **can't tell one end of sth from the other ⟶ *know***

**cannot see beyond/past the *end* of one's nose ⟶ *see***

**no '*end* of people, a fuss etc ⟶ *no***

**the *end* of one's tether** the position when you have no more patience or strength left: *I've just about reached* (or *come to) the end of my tether. I don't think I can stand any more of your rudeness!*

**at the *end* of the day** when everything has been considered: *At the end of the day we have to work together, so we might as well talk.*

**the *end* of the road/line** the place where an activity has to stop: *The workers see the closure of the pit as the end of the line for mining in this area.*

**light at the *end* of the tunnel ⟶ *light***

**not be the *end* of the world (for sb)** *(informal)* not be completely disastrous for sb: *It wouldn't be the end of the world if you didn't get into college. I'm sure you could find something to do here.*

***end*/wind up (doing sth)** conclude a series of events (by doing sth): *'Did Jane ever get married?' 'Yes, she ended up with that chap she met at university.' / Their marriage finally ended up in the divorce court.*

**(at) the *ends* of the earth** (at) a place or places in the world that is/are, or appear to be, very remote; at a great distance, and almost unknown to the speaker or observer: *I miss my daughter and grandchildren of course, but it's not as if she was at the ends of the earth. I know I can just get on a train and see them all again any time I like.*

***enough* is as good as a feast** *(saying)* what you have got, done etc should be quite sufficient; nothing more is needed (used as a warning).

***enough* is enough** what has been said or done is quite or more than sufficient (usually used as a warning that what is going on must be stopped): *Enough is enough! I don't mind you playing around a bit, but now you've gone too far!*

**(not) *entertain* the idea, suggestion etc** (refuse to) accept or consider an idea etc made by sb else: *I assured you that our firm simply would not entertain the idea of advancing a loan without security.*

**some men etc are more *equal* than others ⟶ *some***

**the *error* of one's ways** the things that you have done wrong because of the way of life you lead: *Visits from a social worker and a vicar while he was in prison helped him see the error of his ways.*

**the *eternal* triangle** the sexual relationship

between one man and two women, or one woman and two men, with the accompanying tensions, jealousy etc.

**on an *even* keel** maintaining steady progress, an undisturbed course of life or action, or a well-balanced emotional state: *After all the recent disturbances in the car industry, the factory managers are now trying to get things back on an even keel as soon as possible.*

**in the *event*** as actually happened; in contrast with what was expected: *Everyone thought that Duckworth wouldn't stand for re-election as chairman but in the event he did.*

**in the *event* of sth** if sth, such as a death or resignation, happens: *In the event of a tie, we'll have to toss a coin to decide who is a winner.*

***ever* so good, well, much etc** *(informal)* very good etc: *Have you tried one of these sweets? They're ever so nice! / As it turned out, the play went off ever so well. / There have been ever so many replies to the advertisement. / I like him ever so.* Note that some speakers consider this usage substandard.

**explore *every* avenue** → ***explore***

***every* bit as good, clever etc** as good etc as; good etc to the same degree as: *Although two years younger, Mark was every bit as intelligent as his older sister.*

***every* cloud has a silver lining** *(saying)* there is some compensation or basis for hope in most troubles or difficulties (often used as an encouragement): *I had to take an easier and less well-paid job, but I was able to spend more time with my family. Every cloud has a silver lining.* This idiom is often adapted or loosely referred to: *At the moment she sees her failure as total disaster and is in no mood to look for silver linings.*

***every* dog has its day** *(saying)* everybody will, at some time in his life or her life, be successful or powerful (often said to encourage yourself or other people at an unsuccessful time).

**on *every* hand** *(formal)* everywhere; on every side: *He had never been in such a predicament. It seemed as though problems lay on every hand.*

***every* last/single woman, piece etc** every woman etc mentioned, not omitting any: *Every single ticket for the concert went within hours of the box office opening.*

***every* man Jack (of sb)** *(informal)* every one of a large number of people, with no exceptions: *I think all the people who run the country are incompetent—every man Jack of them!*

***(every)* now and again/then** → ***now***

***every* other/second man, time etc** excluding the first, third etc, but including the second, fourth etc: *I go there every other day. / Please take out every second sheet of paper and put them in a separate pile.*

***every* so often** → ***(every)* now and again/then**

**at *every* turn** whatever you do, wherever you go: *He's been trying to get his book finished but had encountered all sorts of difficulties at every turn.*

**money, winning etc isn't *everything*** other things matter more than money etc: *Exam results aren't everything, you know, although they're still very important.*

**carry *everything* before one** → ***carry* all/everything before one**

***everything* but the kitchen sink** every possible (movable) object: *She was only coming to stay for a few days, but she brought with her everything but the kitchen sink!*

**have (got) *everything* going for one** → ***have***

***everything* in the garden is lovely** *(saying)* everything is satisfactory, is going well, or could not be better.

**fall on *evil* days** → ***fall* on hard times**

**need, want etc one's head *examined*/examining** → ***need***

**make an *example* of sb** → ***make***

**the *exception* proves the rule** *(saying)* one thing that is different from or against an established belief or theory does in fact emphasize that the belief or theory is true: *Englishmen are supposed to be very reserved, but Pete's the exception that proves the rule—he'll talk to anyone!*

***excuse*/pardon my French** *(humorous)* forgive me for using such offensive language.

***excuse* me 1** (used before you do or say something that might annoy sb or to get sb's attention): *Excuse me, may I come past? / Excuse me, could you tell me the time, please?* **2** (used to apologise for disagreeing with sb or to show annoyance): *Excuse me, but I think you're mistaken. / Excuse me, Sir, but you can't park there!*

**be *expecting*** be pregnant: *I hear Jean's expecting again.*

**at sb's *expense*** or **at one's own expense** with sb/you paying: *The office didn't think I needed a better light by my desk, so I had to buy one at my own expense. / As Joe was travelling at the firm's expense, he got a taxi from the station.*

***expense*/money is no object** *(saying)* there is a lot of money available so it doesn't matter how much sb wants to spend: *Go on—money is no object! Why not buy what you want?*

**at the *expense* of sb/sth** making sb look foolish; making a loss or reduction somewhere else: *Can you remain calm if other people start cracking jokes at your expense? / We could lower the price but only at the expense of quality.*

***explain* sth away** give a reasonable explanation for sth and so remove an objection, sometimes in an embarrassing situation: *I don't think there's any way you can explain away the inconsistencies in your argument. / George was left at the police station trying to explain away how he'd got so many diamonds in his possession.*

***explode* a myth, theory etc** destroy the

basis of what is believed or accepted by many people; show sth to be false: *This new book explodes once and for all the popular myth that a pop star's life is one long series of parties and concerts.*

***explore* every avenue** examine all the means, opportunities, or possibilities that may be available to achieve some aim: *The management have explored every avenue in an effort to find some way to settle the disagreement, but so far their efforts have been in vain.*

**boring, mad etc in the *extreme*** extremely boring etc: *It's puzzling in the extreme just how these books found their way here, I must admit.*

**to *extremes*** to the greatest degree: *You didn't need to go to extremes! We said we'd just drop in for a quick bite to eat and now you've laid on all this magnificent spread for us!*

**my *eye*/foot! ⟶ *my***

**what the *eye* doesn't see (the heart doesn't grieve over) ⟶ *what***

**have (got) an *eye* for sth ⟶ *have***

**an *eye* for an eye (and a tooth for a tooth)** *(saying)* an aggressive act will be met with retaliation of the same kind (used as a warning).

**the *eye* of the storm** the central and strongest point of a storm; main point of a crisis.

**with an *eye* to (doing) sth** with the main or further purpose of doing sth: *They bought up two of the most successful products, clearly with an eye to cornering the market.*

**have (got) an *eye* to/on/for the main chance ⟶ *have***

***eyeball* to eyeball** *(informal)* close together, especially in a fight. **eyeball-to-eyeball** *adj*: *an eyeball-to-eyeball confrontation.*

**up to one's *eyeballs* in sth ⟶ up to one's *ears*/eyeballs/eyes/neck in sth**

**one's *eyes* are bigger than one's belly/stomach/tummy** *(saying)* you are too greedy; you want more food than you can really eat.

**with one's '*eyes* closed/shut** very easily, because of being very familiar with sth: *I could find my way home from here with my eyes shut.*

**up to one's *eyes* in sth ⟶ up to one's *ears*/eyeballs/eyes/neck in sth**

**have (got) *eyes* in the back of one's head ⟶ *have***

**sb's *eyes* nearly pop out of his head** *(informal)* show by signs on your face that you are very surprised: *His eyes nearly popped out of his head when she told him how much it had cost.*

**through the *eyes* of sb** from the viewpoint of sb: *Let us look at the matter through the eyes of a local person, not from the point of view of a bureaucrat from the capital.*

**in the *eyes* of sb/sth** from the opinion, judgment, or authority of sb/sth: *What you're doing may be right in your own eyes, but in the eyes of the law, you're clearly guilty.*

**with one's *eyes* open** fully aware of what you are doing and what the results may be: *If an adoption is to work, then the adoptive parents must go into it with their eyes open.*

# F

**be written all over sb's *face*** or **be written on sb's face ⟶ be *written* all over sb's face**

**close/shut/slam the door in sb's *face* ⟶ *close*/shut/slam the door ((up)on sb/sth)**

**to sb's *face*** directly; in the presence of sb: *Would you really call her a liar to her face?*

**wipe the smile/grin off sb's/one's *face* ⟶ *wipe***

**one's *face* falls** you show by the expression on your face that you are disappointed or dismayed: *When he began to realize how committed he should really be, his face fell, and he knew it was too great a sacrifice for him to make.*

**in the *face* of sth** although confronted by sth: *He was determined to stay calm in the face of all the opposition.*

**on the *face* of it** from the amount of evidence available: *On the face of it, it seems that he's not willing to go because he won't be paid for it, but I think there are probably deeper reasons as well.*

**wipe sb/sth off the *face* of the earth ⟶ *wipe***

***face* the music** *(informal)* accept the unpleasant difficulties, criticism, and consequences that follow your own decision or action: *Paul knew that when his Mum found out he'd been stealing he'd have to face the music and be punished.*

***face* to face (with sb/sth)** in the presence of sb/sth; directly opposite (sb/sth); having to deal with sb/sth: *You'll have to meet this problem face to face. There's no other way. / As he turned the corner, he came face to face with a statue of a woman holding a baby.* **face-to-face** *adj: a face-to-face confrontation.*

***face* up to sth** confront sth such as a responsibility or difficulty, accepting it honestly and courageously: *Finding somewhere to live is just one of the problems they'll have to face up to once they're married.*

**take sb/sth at (his/its) *face* value ⟶ *take***

**and that's a *fact* ⟶ *that***

**in *fact*** really (often used with a statement that strengthens or corrects what has been said): *You say that you're honest but in fact you've* *been known to cheat sometimes.* Also **in actual fact; in point of fact.**

**the *fact* of the matter is (that)** sth is true or most important (used to draw attention to a particular aspect of sth): *He says that a camping holiday wouldn't give his wife a rest, but the fact of the matter is that he doesn't want to go himself.*

**the *facts* of life 1** matters concerned with sex in human beings: *When do you think you should tell your children the facts of life?* See also **the *birds* and the bees. 2** realities of human existence: *Unemployment and inflation seem to be facts of life that we just have to live with these days.*

***fag* sb out** *(informal)* make sb exhausted: *Walking home from town up the hill really fags you out. / I'm fagged out after a day on my feet.*

**without *fail*** with absolute certainty: *You must be here by 10 o'clock without fail, or the coach will leave without you.*

***faint* heart ne'er won fair lady** *(saying)* a timid or easily discouraged person must be bold if he wants to attract the woman he likes.

***fair* and square 1** with no possibility of misjudgment or misunderstanding: *I think we can pin the blame for the defeat fair and square on the chairman—he failed completely to communicate our policies to the voters.* **2** exactly: *The blow hit him fair and square on the chin.*

**a *fair* cop** *(informal)* the act of catching sb committing a crime, error etc, especially when this has been brought about by legitimate means: *If the police trap a professional thief, it's a fair cop, and he may plead guilty, hoping to be smarter the next time.*

**a *fair* crack of the whip** a fair chance to do sth: *The conference speakers thought they'd not really been given a fair crack of the whip—they'd only been allowed five minutes to present a summary of their reports.*

***fair* do's** *(informal)* just treatment or judgment (used as a request that sb be dealt with fairly): *'It's been months since I've heard from John.' 'Come on, Peter, you know he's been ill—fair do's!'*

***fair* enough** *(informal)* that is just or reasonable (used to express agreement): *'I've already gone down £100. I'm afraid I can't drop the price any more than that.' 'Fair enough—I'll write you out a cheque now.' / OK, fair enough! If he wants a fight, then I'll give him one.*

***fair* game** a suitable or proper object that you can exploit, abuse, ridicule, or tease: *It was not done for male lecturers to consider their female students to be fair game.*

**all's *fair* in love and war** ⟶ ***all***

***fair* play** behaviour in a game or competition that conforms to the rules; personal behaviour or business or government procedures that conform to generally accepted principles of justice. **see fair play** ensure that rules are carried out.

**the *fair*/weaker sex** *(humorous)* women.

***fair's* fair** *(informal)* what is being suggested really is just (used as an appeal or a reminder): *You may not like old Jones, but fair's fair, he's still a good worker.*

**a/one's *fair* share of sth** a usual or expected amount, only rarely of anything that is actually shared: *We've all paid our fair share except Delia, who's never got any money.*

**have (got) more than one's *fair* share of sth** ⟶ ***have***

***fair* to middling** *(informal)* less than satisfactory but not very bad: *'How's your day gone?' 'Fair to middling.'*

**a *fairy* godmother** sb who protects, helps etc, especially sb unknown.

**pride goes/comes before a *fall*** ⟶ ***pride***

**ride for a *fall*** ⟶ ***ride***

***fall* about (laughing)** *(informal)* laugh in an uncontrollable way: *The audience were falling about laughing as they watched the clowns performing.*

***fall* apart at the seams** ⟶ ***come*/fall apart at the seams**

***fall* back on sb/sth** go to sb or use sth, especially when other people or things have been tried unsuccessfully: *It's wise always to have some money in the bank to fall back on if times get hard. / I'm pleased I've got my family to fall back on at such a sad time as this.*

***fall* behind (sb)** fail to keep up with other people or competitors: *I don't like to admit it, but it is clear that our company has fallen behind our rivals in the production of quality boxes.*

***fall*/be behind (with sth)** have work still waiting to be done or money still needing to be paid: *He was already behind with his reports before he was ill. / They stopped delivering the equipment as I'd fallen behind with the payments.*

***fall* between two stools** fail to be either of two satisfactory alternatives: *The show fell between two stools—it was neither a complete historical exhibition nor a proper dramatic production.*

***fall* by the wayside** fail to make progress in life; slip into dishonest, less moral ways: *After the series of special meetings, the church had a congregation of 150, but numbers gradually declined to about 100 as some fell by the wayside.*

***fall* down** (of an idea etc) be unsatisfactory because it is wrong or inadequate; (of a person) fail: *The government wants to raise money by offering some shares to the public, but that's where the plan falls down—the public hasn't got enough money to buy them! / When the careers officer talked about interviews, he told us where most people fall down—they don't present themselves properly, they don't ask any questions, and so on.*

***fall* down about sb's ears** ⟶ ***come*/fall down about one's ears**

***fall* flat** fail in its intended or expected effect: *I didn't think the comedian was funny at all—most of his jokes fell completely flat.*

***fall* flat on one's face 1** *(informal)* fall to the ground suddenly and in a clumsy way: *He managed to pull himself up from the wheelchair but promptly fell flat on his face.* **2** *(informal)* (of an attempt) fail, especially ending in a clumsy or undignified way: *It was the first time he'd ever tried to negotiate such a deal, and he really fell flat on his face.*

***fall* for sb/sth** *(informal)* like sb/sth strongly immediately: *As soon as he met Ingrid, he fell for her in a big way.*

***fall* for sth** *(informal)* be easily persuaded into accepting sth such as a story or argument as true: *You didn't fall for his story about him living with beggars in the city, did you? / The old lady fell for the gang's tricks and they stole all her money.*

***fall* foul of sb/sth** have a confrontation or disagreement with sb/sth such as the government or authorities: *Smith had done a lot of shady dealings over the years and had never been discovered, but eventually he went too far and fell foul of the law.*

**the scales *fall* from one's eyes** ⟶ ***scales***

***fall* from grace** lose your position as sb trusted by people in power; become less moral: *He fell from grace after the affair with his secretary became public.*

***fall* in/out** *(military)* form into or leave ranks, as when on parade: *The soldiers fell in on the barrack square.*

***fall* in with sb** happen to meet sb; become acquainted with sb: *On holiday she often falls in with someone staying at the same hotel.*

***fall* in with sth** agree to or comply with sth such as a suggestion or plan: *The most important thing is this: will he fall in with our arrangements or will he make his own?*

***fall* into one's lap** ⟶ ***drop*/fall into one's lap**

***fall* like flies** ⟶ ***die*/fall/drop like flies**

***fall* off** become less in quantity, intensity, or quality: *Business tends to fall off in the winter months.* **falling-off** *n*: *Customers have recently been complaining about a falling-off in quality.*

***fall* off the back of a lorry** *(humorous, euphemistic)* (of goods) be stolen: *Where did you get these cameras? I bet they fell off the back of a lorry!*

***fall* on/upon sb/sth** *(formal)* attack or seize sb/sth in a fierce, greedy way: *The thieves fell on the old man with sticks and clubbed him to death.*

***fall* on deaf ears** (of a cry for help, warning etc) not be heard or taken notice of: *Repeated requests for a pedestrian crossing at the busy junction fell on deaf ears until there was an accident.*

***fall* on one's feet** ⟶ ***land*/fall on one's feet**

***fall* on hard times** suffer hardship and misfortune: *In the years of famine, the whole country fell on hard times.* Also **fall on evil days.**

***fall* out** *(formal)* occur or happen: *It transpired that everything fell out as had been planned. / As it fell out, the new arrangements proved to be better.*

***fall* out (with sb)** *(informal)* quarrel with sb: *So Ray and Ros have fallen out again, have they? / He seems to fall out with everyone.*

***fall* over backwards to do sth** ⟶ ***bend*/lean/fall over backwards to do sth**

***fall* over oneself to do sth** *(informal)* try very hard to help, please, or satisfy sb: *I was surprised to find when we moved here that people were falling over themselves to be kind to us.*

***fall*/come short (of sth)** be less than the required, satisfactory, or expected standard or amount: *I'm afraid your performance falls far short of what is necessary and you'll have to do much better if you want to continue in this job.*

***fall* through** *(informal)* fail or be discontinued: *The sale of our house fell through at the last moment when the man we thought was going to buy it suddenly decided not to.*

***fall* to sb's lot to do sth** or **fall to sb to do sth** *(formal)* become sb's responsibility: *It fell to my lot (or to me) to devise a new scheme of classifying all the books in the library.*

**the bottom *falls* out of the market** ⟶**the *bottom* drops/falls out of the market**

**the bottom *falls* out of sb's world** ⟶**the *bottom* drops/falls out of sb's world**

**sail under *false* colours** ⟶ ***sail***

**(under) *false* pretences** (by using) lies about your identity, qualifications, financial or social position etc: *He was sent to gaol for six months for obtaining money under false pretences.*

**have (got) a *familiar* ring (about/to it)** ⟶ ***have***

**in the *family* way** *(informal)* pregnant.

**fan the flames (of sth)** ⟶ ***add* fuel to the fire**

**(by) *far* and away** to a very great degree: *That company has (by) far and away the biggest share of the book market in this area.*

***far* and near** (from) everywhere or many places: *People came from far and near to see the exhibition of famous paintings.*

***far* and wide** (to) everywhere or many places: *The missionaries travelled far and wide proclaiming the message of God's salvation. / The police searched far and wide for the missing child but couldn't find anything.*

***far*/miles away** not thinking about your surroundings or whom you are with at all: *'Peter? Peter?' 'Oh, sorry, I was miles away. What did you say?'*

**as/so *far* as . . .** in the way or to the degree that (sb/sth is done, involved, or affected): *I will help you as far as I'm able. / As far as I'm concerned, the whole matter is no longer my responsibility and is now with the police. / His parents both died in the war, so far as he knows.*

**in so *far* as** to the extent that; in the sense that: *In so far as I am a good judge of these* *things, the repairs to the vase have been done very well.* Also **insofar as.**

***far* be it from me to do sth** I do not really have the right or think it appropriate to do sth, such as interfere or disagree (used with a sentence where for example there is interference or disagreement): *Far be it from me to pass judgment, but don't you think she really is right?*

**a *far* cry (from sth)** very different from sth: *Max was so happy now he was adopted and living with a family—this was a far cry from what he was like in the local authority home.*

***far* from (doing sth)** not doing sth expected, but doing sth else instead; certainly not doing sth: *Far from buying vegetables, we now grow all we need ourselves! / 'Isn't he generous with money?' 'Far from it, he spends it all on himself.'*

***far* out** *(slang)* fantastic: *This music's far out, man!*

***farm* sb/sth out (to sb)** give sb/sth to sb else to be responsible for or tackle: *If you can't complete all the work yourself, then you'll have to farm some of it out to people who can do it.*

**after a *fashion*** (do sth) in a limited, not very skilful way: *'Can you skate?' 'Yes, after a fashion.' / He can play the violin after a fashion, but he needs to practise a lot more.*

**not so *fast!*** → ***not***

***fast* and furious** in an exciting, large, and rushed way: *At first there were only a few replies to our advertisement, but now they're coming in fast and furious.*

**play *fast* and loose with sb/sth** → ***play***

***fast*/sound asleep** in a deep sleep: *The children are both fast asleep upstairs.*

**a *fast*/quick buck** *(informal)* money made or earned quickly and easily, especially disregarding other people's interests: *We're going to make a quick buck by selling these jewels at six times the price we paid for them!*

**pull a *fast* one (on sb)** → ***pull***

**a *fast* worker** *(informal)* sb, especially a man, who is good at establishing relations quickly with sb of the opposite sex.

**the *fat* is in the fire** *(saying)* sth unwise has been said or done that is bound to cause anger, fighting, offended feelings, or other trouble.

**a *fat*/precious lot of help, interest** *(informal)* very little help etc: *'Have you told the boss about the problem?' 'That would be no use—I'd get a precious lot of sympathy from him!'*

**live off the *fat* of the land** → ***live***

**the *father* and mother of a row etc** → **the *mother* and father of a row etc**

**like *father*/mother, like son/daughter** *(saying)* a child is similar to its parents concerning a particular aspect of its character: *Young Jim is turning out to be as hard-working as his dad—like father, like son.*

**the wish is *father* to the thought** → ***wish***

**kill the *fatted* calf** → ***kill***

**tidy, conscientious etc to a *fault*** too tidy etc; used to modify an adjective describing something praiseworthy: *Ann was generous to a fault with friends and neighbours and didn't look after her own family properly.*

**in *favour* (with sb)** or **out of favour (with sb)** regarded or not regarded with approval: *I seem to be out of favour with the head of department after my criticism at the meeting.*

**in sb's/sth's *favour*** so as to support, defend, or recommend sb/sth: *I am sure it would help, Headmaster, if you could speak in Tom's favour when his case comes up.*

**come down/out in *favour* of sb/sth** → ***come***

**in *favour* of sb/sth** so as to benefit sb/sth: *The government is going to change how it spends money on education in favour of the universities.*

**be in *favour* of (doing) sth** support or approve an existing or proposed idea, course of action etc: *As far as Joe's suggestion is concerned, I'm all in favour of it. / Some MPs are in favour of restoring the death penalty for major crimes.*

**in/with *fear* and trembling** in a frightened, apprehensive way: *She knew that the headmaster would punish her, so she entered his study in fear and trembling.*

**put the *fear* of God into sb** → ***put***

**go/live in *fear* of one's life** → ***go***

**without *fear* or favour** *(formal)* without bias; according to your understanding of the truth or your responsibility: *In his speech to try to calm both sides in the dispute, Mr Hampden began, 'We shall fulfil our duties to all our citizens without fear or favour.'*

**birds of a *feather* (flock together)** → ***birds***

**a *feather* in one's cap** *(informal)* sth achieved that is a victory or triumph for yourself: *It's a real feather in his cap to be asked to represent the town in next month's trip abroad.*

***feather* one's (own) nest** look after one's own interests by accumulating money or property greedily, selfishly, or sometimes dishonestly: *As a landlord, he's not in the slightest bit interested in looking after his tenants; he only wants to feather his own nest.*

***fed* up (to the back teeth) (with sb/sth)** *(informal)* depressed, annoyed, or bored by sb/sth; have had enough of sb/sth: *I'm fed up with your excuses the whole time. / They were getting fed up to the back teeth with the noise of lorries outside their house at all hours of the day and night.*

***feel* one's age** realize from your failing powers, changed views etc that you are growing old.

***feel* one's ears burning** be aware or think that other people are or have been discussing you: *'We talked about you and Jenny for a long time last night.' 'I thought I felt my ears burning!'* Also **one's ears are burning:** *Some folks' ears must have been burning tonight. I've never heard so much gossip going on!*

***feel* free** please do what you want; you are

very welcome: *Feel free to come and go when you like.*

***feel* sth in one's bones** *(informal)* sense or suspect sth: *That's funny—I felt in my bones that there'd been an accident—and now you tell me there was one today.*

***feel* like (doing) sth** want sth or think that you would enjoy (doing) sth: *Do you know what I feel like at this moment? A nice cup of tea! / As he sat down in the dentist's waiting room he felt like running away.*

***feel*/look like nothing on earth** *(informal)* feel/look very ill or strange: *It's those awful moments when you're just coming round after the anaesthetic, feeling like nothing on earth, that I don't like.*

***feel* lost without sb/sth** → **be/feel *lost* without sb/sth**

**(*feel*) on top of the world** → **(be/feel) on *top* of the world**

***feel*/look small** seem to yourself to be humiliated or despised: *Sue was made to feel small by being told off in front of all the other students.*

***feel* the draught** become conscious of a change that will come soon, especially one that will affect you badly: *People in the North are getting used to unemployment, and even those in the South are beginning to feel the draught.*

***feel* the pinch** suffer from a lack of money: *Schools all over the country are beginning to feel the pinch after the government cut back its spending on education.*

***feel*/be up to (doing) sth** feel or be able, physically or mentally, to do sth; be capable of a task: *I recommend a half-hour's walk every day, or longer, if you feel up to it. / We need a more powerful motor—this little one just isn't up to the job.*

**at sb's *feet*** in a state of admiration and ready to serve sb, because you are influenced by him: *With so many of their records getting to the top of the charts, it seemed as if the whole music world was at their feet.* See also ***sit* at the feet of sb.**

**cut the ground from under sb's *feet*** → ***cut***

**have (got) the ball at one's *feet*** → ***have***

**on one's *feet*** **1** standing up: *Being a shop assistant means that you're on your feet all day long.* **2** (of a business etc) recovered from a period of failure; in a healthy financial state: *Only our party's policies will really get the country on its feet again.*

**take the weight off one's *feet*** → ***take***

**under sb's *feet*** causing inconvenience to sb and stopping sb from doing his work: *It's difficult to do housework with the children under my feet all the time.*

**vote with one's *feet*** → ***vote***

**walk sb off his *feet*** → ***walk***

**sit at the *feet* of sb** → ***sit***

***feet* of clay** a basic weakness in sb/sth which a challenge or attack will reveal.

**have (got) both/one's *feet* on the ground** → ***have***

**at one *fell* swoop** → ***one***

**make one's presence *felt*** → ***make***

**sit on the *fence*** → ***sit***

***few* and far between** small in number and spread out; rarely happening or found; scarce: *Since her illness, the former prime minister's public appearances have become few and far between.*

**a man/woman of *few* words** → ***man***

***fiddle* while Rome burns** behave frivolously or do nothing in a situation that calls for concern and action: *With the world's population growing very fast and millions getting hungrier every day, leaders of the rich nations just seem to be fiddling while Rome burns.*

**a *field* day** a day or time of excitement, important events, or great delight and action: *When anyone brings out a new book on such a controversial subject as abortion, the critics from different sides have a field day.*

***fight* a losing battle** struggle without success to achieve or prevent sth: *The more weeding I do, the more weeds I see that need pulling up. I'm fighting a losing battle!*

**live to *fight* another day** → ***live***

***fight* like cat and dog** *(informal)* (of two people who live or work together) argue and quarrel: *Marriage still has some meaning for them, it seems, although they fight like cat and dog.* **a cat-and-dog life** *n.*

***fight* shy of sb** or ***fight* shy of (doing) sth** avoid sb or (doing) sth; think it wiser or safer to hold yourself aloof from sb or (doing) sth: *I can understand some of you fighting shy of signing the statement. I don't think I'd want to either.*

***fight* sb/sth tooth and nail** fight sb/sth with great energy, boldness, and firmness: *The local people do not want a motorway built through the countryside and so are determined to fight the council tooth and nail.*

***fighting* fit** → **as *fit* as a fiddle**

***fill* in (for sb)** act as a substitute for sb: *The blonde secretary is filling in while our normal girl is on holiday.*

***fill* sb in (on sth)** *(informal)* give sb up-to-date information about sth: *Let me fill you in on the latest developments in the plan.*

***fill* sb's shoes** adequately take over sb's function, role etc: *The old doctor was really loved in these parts. His son's quite a nice chap, but he'll never fill his father's shoes.*

***fill*/fit the bill** be suitable; be all that is required: *This seaside town doesn't exactly fit the bill as the best place to spend a holiday, but it is quite adequate.*

**in the *final*/last analysis** ultimately; most significantly: *He knew he was dying of cancer so he realized that his commitment to his job was not, in the final analysis, of great importance.*

**the final *straw*** → **the *last*/final straw**

***find*/get one's bearings** adjust yourself to have a definite understanding of the position you are in, especially when it is a new situation or place: *When we set foot ashore off the boat, it took a moment or two to find our bearings. / I've only been in this for a week, so I'm still getting my bearings. I'm working out what my priorities will be.*

***find* one's feet** discover what to do in a new job, new surroundings etc; gain a firm purpose in life: *After moving from the civil service to industry, it took her a while to find her feet in a very different job.*

**(not) *find* it in one's heart to do sth** or **(not) find it in oneself to do sth** (not) be able or willing to do sth: *I can't find it in myself to criticize her work after she's tried so hard. / I wish you could find it in your heart to be more polite to our friends, Ralph.*

***find* (sb/sth) out** discover or detect sb's dishonesty or sth wrong: *Do you think the police will ever find us out? / You may get away with it for a while, but sooner or later someone will find out what you've been doing.*

***find* (sth) out** learn by enquiry, study, or calculation: *Please find out which platform the train goes from. / The report found out that children who lived in the countryside were healthier than those who lived in the cities.*

**not to put too *fine* a point on it →*put***

**get sth down to a *fine* art →*get***

**a *fine*/nice/pretty kettle of fish** *(informal)* a disagreeable, muddled, or perplexing state of affairs: *Here's a fine kettle of fish! We've run out of petrol and there's not a garage for miles!* See also **a *different* kettle of fish.**

**in a (*fine*/pretty) pickle** *(informal)* in an awkward or difficult situation: *We'd be in a pretty pickle if we sold all these tickets and then found that there wasn't a coach for us!*

**go over/through sth with a *fine* 'tooth comb →*go***

**have (got) a *finger* in every/the pie →*have***

**have (got) one's *finger* on the pulse (of sth) →*have***

**one's *fingers* are 'all 'thumbs** you are slow and clumsy in doing things with your hands. Also **be 'all 'thumbs.**

**have (got) one's *fingers* in the till →*have***

**work one's *fingers* to the bone →*work***

**at one's *fingertips*** readily available; within the grasp of your thoughts: *He keeps up-to-date with the details of space exploration and has all the information at his fingertips.*

**a/the *finishing* touch** a/the final detail that completes or decorates sth: *Twenty minutes later she was putting the finishing touches to the gateau.*

**set the 'Thames on *fire* →*set***

**the fat is in the *fire* →*fat***

**under *fire*** being attacked, by violence or strong words: *The government's plan to nationalize more industries came under fire again last night.*

***(fire)* a (warning) shot across the/sb's bows →*shot***

***fire* and brimstone** punishment and (God's) anger: *His sermon was solid, biblical, fire-and-brimstone stuff. / The furious car workers emerged from the talks breathing fire and brimstone.*

**go through *fire* and water →*go***

***fire* away** *(informal)* start asking questions: *'Can I ask you something?' 'Yes—fire away.'*

**take a *(firm)* grip/hold on oneself →*take***

**a *firm* hand** strong discipline and control: *What his son needs, if you ask me, is a firm hand!*

***first* and last** *(formal)* completely; when everything is taken into account: *His father wouldn't have done business that way. He was a gentleman, first and last.*

**get to *first* base** or **reach/make first base (with sth) with sth →*get***

***first* come, first served** *(saying)* people will be dealt with, seen etc strictly in order of their arrival or application, with no favouritism being shown: *The rule for going into hospital should be a matter of first come, first served* (or *be on a first come, first served basis*). *But there seem to be some people who want to jump the queue.*

**(in) the *first* flush of youth etc** (in) the freshness or strength of youth at its beginning or best point; (in) the period when a stimulating activity, emotion etc begins or is at its best point: *As you might expect, after twenty years of marriage neither my husband nor myself is in the first flush of romance.*

**at *first* hand** directly; based on your own knowledge, experience, or observations: *I knew at first hand what it was like to be poor; we always had very little money at home.* **first-hand** *adj.*

**of the *first* magnitude** considered as among the best, worst, biggest, most important etc of its kind: *An international crisis of the first magnitude was brewing.*

**(be) the *first*/last (person) to do sth** be very willing/unwilling to do sth: *I'd be the first to admit that I'm not perfect.*

**in the '*first* place → to *begin*/start with**

**have (got) (the) *first* refusal →*have***

**love at *first* sight →*love***

**cast the *first* stone (at sb/sth) →*cast***

***first* thing (in the morning)** early in the morning; soon after you wake up or get up: *I always like a cup of tea first thing in the morning. / Can you lend me some money? I'll pay you back first thing tomorrow.* See also ***last* thing (at night).**

**not know the *first* thing about sth →*know***

**(the) *first*/next thing one knows** *(informal)* then; next; very soon after that: *You'd better stop smoking cigarettes altogether, or, first thing you know, you'll be back to 40 a day.*

***first* things first** the most important or necessary duties or considerations must be attended to before others: *First things first, Susan! Which is more important—pursuing your career or looking after your baby?*

**there's a *first* time for everything** *(saying)* sth must happen or be done for the first time;

because it has not happened or been done before, there is no reason to assume that it never will.

***fish* for sth** → ***angle*/fish for sth**

***fish* in troubled waters** try to gain an advantage in a difficult situation.

***fish* sth out (of sth)** *(informal)* take sth out (of a place) where it has been hidden or lost: *I'm sure we've got copies of the report somewhere in our files. I'll try and fish one out and pass it on to you sometime.*

**(like) a *fish* out of water** (feeling) uncomfortable or awkward, because you are in unfamiliar surroundings: *In his patched jeans and torn leather jacket he felt like a fish out of water amongst the rest of the elegantly dressed party.*

**as *fit* as a fiddle** very healthy and active: *After all that walking on holiday we certainly came back as fit as a fiddle.* Also **fighting fit.**

***fit* (sb) like a glove** (of a coat, dress etc) be exactly the right size and shape for the wearer: *Aren't I lucky? The only dress in the shop that I liked fitted me like a glove!*

***fit* the bill** → ***fill*/fit the bill**

***fit* to drop** → ***ready*/fit to drop**

**in/by *fits* and starts** irregularly, over a period of time; with no pattern of regular occurrence: *He's been trying to learn to play the violin for a number of years, but I keep telling him it's no use learning in fits and starts.*

***fizzle* out** gradually come to the end in a feeble and disappointing way: *The series of evening history lectures began very well, but the audience's enthusiasm soon fizzled out.*

***flag* sb/sth down** stop a moving vehicle by waving your arm, your hand, or a flag: *After the accident we tried to flag down half a dozen cars to get some help but not one of them stopped.*

**keep the *flag* flying (for sb/sth)** → ***keep***

***flake* out** *(informal)* collapse or faint from exhaustion: *When all the guests had gone home and everything had been cleared up, we just flaked out in a couple of armchairs.*

**go up in *flames*/smoke** → ***go***

***flare* up** suddenly begin to burn more brightly or strongly; reach a more violent state: *Trouble in the Middle East flared up again yesterday with heavy losses on both sides.*

**in a *flash*** *(informal)* quickly; suddenly: *People who go round claiming that they can cure you in a flash are deceiving you. / In a flash his whole past lay before him and he realized what sort of a person he really was.*

**a *flash* Harry** *(derogatory)* a man who wears showy clothes and behaves in an extravagant way: *Some flash Harry has just come in here saying he'll buy up all the furniture in the shop—so he can sell it and make a large profit for himself, I bet.*

**a *flash* in the pan** *(informal)* sb/sth that is successful but only for a short time: *His achievements as a player early in the season turned out to be something of a flash in the pan, as we've not seen anything as good since.*

**and 'that's '*flat*!** → ***that***

**in two minutes, ten seconds etc *flat*** *(informal)* in no more than two minutes etc (used to state a surprisingly short time): *She spent nine months writing the first half of the book and did the second half in three months flat.*

**as *flat* as a pancake** *(informal)* (of a landscape) very flat; (of a joke, celebration etc) disappointing and boring: *There are one or two hills but otherwise the land is as flat as a pancake.*

**fall *flat* on one's face** → ***fall***

***flat* out 1** *(informal)* with all the energy, speed, strength etc you have: *If I worked flat out, I reckon I could get all the repairs done by this evening.* **2** *(informal)* exhausted; lying down: *After running in the marathon, Mary was flat out for a week!*

**with a *flea* in her ear** *(informal)* having been criticized strongly, rejected, or humiliated: *When he came to ask for his job back, we sent him away with a flea in his ear and I don't think we'll see him again.*

**a *flea* pit** *(derogatory)* a cheap, sometimes dirty cinema or theatre: *The local cinema is a proper little flea pit.*

**in the *flesh*** in sb's actual bodily presence; in person: *There he was, in the flesh, her son back from the war.*

***flesh* and blood** the human body; the human being; weaknesses, fears etc that all people have: *His illness reminded him that in spite of his great achievements as a scientist he was still flesh and blood. / The pain was more than flesh and blood could stand.*

**one's own *flesh* and blood** → ***own***

**make one's *flesh* creep/crawl** → ***make***

**the spirit is willing but the *flesh* is weak** → ***spirit***

***flex* one's muscles** exercise or show your muscles (before doing sth); display your power, for example as a warning.

**(there are) no *flies* on sb** → ***no***

***fling* sth in sb's face/teeth** → ***throw*/fling sth in sb's face/teeth**

***fling* mud at sb/sth** → ***sling*/fling/throw mud at sb/sth**

**birds of a feather (*flock* together)** → ***birds***

***flog* a dead horse** *(informal)* spend your time and energy on an activity or belief that is already widely rejected, outdated, or accepted: *Pam's flogging a dead horse! Doesn't she know that no one wants to go on the coach outing? Why is she still trying to get people interested?*

***flog* sth to death** *(informal)* talk about or be concerned with a subject so often that interest in it is lost: *The word 'new' has really been flogged to death in advertisements, with the result that no one believes it any more.*

***flood* the market** offer or be for sale through every possible outlet and make/be available in greater quantity than demand really justifies: *Importers flooded the market with cheap toys just before Christmas.*

**a land *flowing* with milk and honey** → ***land***

**(in) the first *flush* of youth etc** → ***first***

***fly* high** be ambitious; achieve a good, powerful position: *So you're opening two new factories and handling your own distribution. That's flying high, isn't it?* **high-flying** *adj*, **high-flyer** *n*: *Is the top stream in the school just for high-flyers?*

***fly* in the face of sth** (of sb, an opinion, decision etc) oppose sth that is reasonable or traditional: *But such a view flies in the face of all the evidence!*

**the *fly* in the ointment** *(informal)* sb/sth that spoils an otherwise good situation or state of affairs: *Life's been just about perfect since we moved here. A spot of local jealousy is the only fly in the ointment.*

***fly* off the handle** *(informal)* lose your temper: *There's no need to fly off the handle!*

**a *fly* on the wall** sb who watches other people and is not noticed himself. **fly-on-the-wall** *adj*: *The idea of the programme was to give a fly-on-the-wall account of life in an ordinary school.*

**with *flying* colours** with very great success: *My son is sure that if he'd not felt ill a few days before the exam, he'd have passed with flying colours.*

**a *flying* start** a very good beginning or advantage that takes you some way towards the completion of a race, journey, or project: *The campaign to raise £100,000 for the heart machine at the hospital got off to a flying start with a gift of £22,000 from local citizens' groups this week.*

**a *flying* visit** a very brief visit: *I'll just have time to pay you a flying visit when I'm passing through London.*

**in a *fog*** *(informal)* being uncertain and confused: *Thank you for your explanation but I must admit I'm still in a fog over what happened.*

**not have (got) the *foggiest* (idea)** → ***have***

***fold* up** *(informal)* collapse with laughter or pain: *His jokes were so funny that the whole audience just folded up.*

***follow* in sb's footsteps** continue the same tradition or do the same job that sb has done before, especially when it has been done well: *He followed in his father's footsteps and joined the navy.*

***follow* one's nose** go straight ahead; act instinctively: *'How do I get to the Post Office?' 'Turn left at the lights, then follow your nose till you get there.'*

***follow* suit** act or behave in the way that sb else has just done: *One of the major oil companies has put up the price of petrol by a penny a litre today. The other companies are expected to follow suit.*

***food* for thought** sth such as an event or remark that stimulates thought or needs to be carefully considered: *I'd not considered it like that before; there's food for thought in what you say. / The lectures had been most interesting and provided much food for thought.*

**a *fool's* errand** a short journey that is unnecessary or brings no advantage: *'That man sounded really ill.' 'He'd better be. I'll be very angry if I've been called out in the middle of the night on a fool's errand.'*

**a *fool's* paradise** a life or state of contentment that is based on deception by yourself or other people: *Since the island was invaded we've become more realistic. We're not living in a fool's paradise any more, although some other people here still are.*

**you could have ˌ*fooled* ˈme!** → ***you***

**my *foot*!** → ***my* eye/foot!**

**on *foot*** walking, in contrast to using other ways of travelling: *It'll take you half an hour on foot, or five minutes in the car.*

**under *foot*** on the ground: *It's rather wet under foot today.*

**have (got) a *foot* in both camps** → ***have***

**a *foot* in the door** → ***have* (got) one's/a foot in the door**

**have (got) one *foot* in the grave** → ***have***

**not put a *foot* right** → ***put*/set a foot wrong**

***foot* the bill** be responsible for paying: *The local council had to foot the bill for all the repairs following last year's extensive floods.*

**put/set a *foot* wrong** → ***put***

***footloose* and fancy-free** not bound to a particular place, routine, or responsibilities; not in love with sb nor occupied by such thoughts.

**follow in sb's *footsteps*** → ***follow***

**. . .*for*. . .** comparing (one thing) with (another): *The packets of washing powder are all different sizes, but, weight for weight, this one is cheapest.*

**be *for* it** → **be for the *high* jump**

**in *force*/strength** (of people) present in large numbers: *The police were out in force to deal with the trouble at the demonstration.*

***force* sth down sb's throat** → ***ram*/force/thrust sth down sb's throat**

***force* sb's hand** compel sb to do sth in a different way or sooner than he intended.

***force* of circumstance** a combination of events and conditions that leaves you with little choice of action: *It was force of circumstances that led to their getting married. There was nobody else of marriageable age on the island, neither of them wanted to leave, and both were lonely.*

**a *force* to be reckoned with** sb/sth that must be treated seriously: *The only way to make this country a force to be reckoned with is to vote for our party at the election.*

**to the *fore*** prominent; publicly or widely known, practised, or discussed; active or useful in a particular situation: *During the long years of unemployment only a few people came to the fore with imaginative ideas.*

**a *foregone* conclusion** a result, consequence, or end that is completely predictable: *It's a foregone conclusion that England will beat Hungary in tonight's match.*

***forgive* and forget** dismiss from your mind all unkind feelings and the desire to blame and punish sb: *He was beaten by Mike, but he says he's prepared to forgive and forget, if Mike lets him win next year!*

***fork* out (sth)** *(informal)* pay money, especially unwillingly: *'I wonder how much I'll have to fork out this time,' I thought as the collection plate came round at the meeting.*

**on/off *form*** acting or working well/badly because sb/sth is in a good/bad physical or mental condition: *She was expected to win but came only third—she'd been ill for a few days and so was rather off form.* A variant of ***on form*** is **in fine/good/great form.**

**in the *form* of** —> **in the *shape*/form of**

***fortune* smiles upon/on sb/sth** be lucky in life, a plan etc: *So we had a fine day for the garden party—I think fortune was smiling on us!*

***forty* winks** *(informal)* a short sleep, especially during the day; nap: *I drew my chair up to the fire and thought I'd just have forty winks before the children came home from school.*

**the *four* corners of the earth/world** the distant regions of the world: *The news of the President's assassination reached all four corners of the earth within minutes of it happening.*

***four*-letter(ed) words** words for the organs or functions to do with sex or the passing of waste matter from the body, especially when used as swear words.

**scatter sb/sth to the *four* winds** —> ***scatter***

***freak* out** *(slang)* behave in an excited, uncontrolled way, for example after taking drugs: *The teenagers really freaked out when the singer came on stage.*

***free* and easy** informal and relaxed in behaviour or towards social conventions: *My parents are very free and easy. There's no need to keep calling them Mr and Mrs Alexander—Donald and Mary are their first names.*

**as *free* as (the) air** or **as free as a bird** with no duties, obligations, ties etc: *It's all right for a bachelor like Mark to travel round the world, but if you've got a wife and children you quite simply are not as free as air.*

**a *free* hand** permission and/or an opportunity to make your own arrangements in an undertaking, your work etc: *My boss gives me a free hand in deciding which outside contractor to use.*

**give *free* rein to sb/sth** —> ***give***

***free* speech** the right to express your opinions publicly on any subject: *Not every country in the world has free speech; in some countries what people can publish is censored by the government.* Also **freedom of speech.**

***freeze* sb's blood** —> **one's *blood* freezes**

***freeze*/chill sb to the bone/marrow** make sb uncomfortably or dangerously cold: *Our new caretaker seems incapable of regulating the heating system. One day we're nearly roasted alive and the next we're all frozen to the bone!* See also **one's *blood* freezes.**

**take *French* leave** —> ***take***

**as *fresh* as a daisy** lively, strong, and healthy: *He was always as fresh as a daisy after his afternoon sleep.*

***fresh* blood** —> ***new*/fresh blood**

**a *Freudian* slip** an action, especially sth said, that was not intended and may reveal an unconscious thought.

**a *friend* in need (is a friend indeed)** *(saying)* a friend who helps you when you need it (is a true friend).

**make *friends* (with sb)** come to like and trust sb: *Roger was new to the district but he soon made friends with the other boys who lived near him. / The best way, we're told, to make friends is to be interested in other people.*

**the *fright* of one's life** a severe fright or shock: *I got the fright of my life when the car suddenly overturned.*

***frighten* sb out of his wits** —> ***scare* sb stiff**

***frightened* of one's own shadow** —> ***afraid*/frightened of one's own shadow**

**have (got) a '*frog* in one's throat** —> ***have***

**on the industrial etc *front*** in the sphere of industry etc: *What happens on the economic front is determined by many other factors.*

***frown* on/upon sth** disapprove of sth: *The committee does not forbid political involvement by club members but frowns upon it strongly.*

**(jump) out of the *frying*-pan into the fire** —> ***jump***

**in *full*** (of money) to a complete amount; (of sth reported or published) with no parts missing: *The loan must be repaid in full within three years. / A summary has already been published; the report itself will be published in full shortly.*

**to the *full*** as completely, thoroughly, or widely as possible: *Once the operation has been successfully completed, you'll be able to live life to the full again.*

**(at) *full* blast** *(informal)* with great power or speed: *Tom must have had his radio on full blast in the next room—I could hardly work it was so loud!*

**come/go *full* circle** —> ***come***

**in *full* cry** at the strongest and most excited point: *In March 1912 the King opened a new museum. At the time, however, the suffragettes were in full cry, and the expectant public was excluded until April.*

***full* of oneself** having a high, especially too high an, opinion of yourself; proud or conceited; talking about yourself all the time: *Now she's gone to university she's so full of herself that she scarcely has time to think about the friends she used to have at home. / When he came out of hospital, he was too full of himself to notice how ill his wife was looking.*

***full* of beans** very lively, active, and happy: *Stan is certainly full of beans again after his illness.*

***full* of the joys of spring** *(informal)* lively; light-hearted: *Why are you so happy? You look full of the joys of spring this morning.*

***full* steam/speed ahead** (let's go, work etc) with as much speed and energy as possible: *We were working full speed ahead to finish the work by the end of April.*

***full* stop** without further qualification; and that is all; I have no more to add: *I don't have to give you any reasons. You're not going to have a motorbike till you're 21, full stop.*

**(be) in *full* swing** at the highest level of activity; operating with full strength; fully started: *The election campaign is now in full swing, and all the politicians and local workers are extremely busy.*

**(at) *full* tilt/pelt** with great speed, force, etc: *The police were chasing him so he ran full pelt down the road.*

**give sb/sth the (*full*, whole etc) works** ⟶ ***give***

**in the *fullness* of time** when (enough) time has passed: *I knew that, in the fullness of time, a new leader with your capabilities would emerge and assume responsibility.*

**in/for *fun*** not seriously; as a joke: *Grandpa didn't mean he was going to eat your ice-cream, you silly girl. He only said it in fun!*

***fun* and games** (*informal*) lively activity or behaviour; playful amusement: *It's not all fun and games at this school—we make our children work hard as well.*

**be sb's (own) *funeral*** (*informal*) be sb's own concern, fault, bad luck etc: *It's his own funeral if he's late; he'll miss all the food!*

***funny* business** (*informal*) sth illegal or not quite straightforward or disapproved of; improper sexual behaviour: *You behave yourself! No funny business!* (or *I don't want any funny business!)*

**nothing could be *further* from sb's mind, the truth etc** ⟶ ***nothing***

# G

***gain*/get/win sb's ear** gain the attention of sb important to influence him or obtain his help: *He knew that somehow he had to gain the ear of the President to win support for his cause.* **have (got) sb's ear** have gained sb's attention.

***gain* ground** (of soldiers) advance in a battle; (of an idea or development) make progress or become more popular: *Our men began to gain ground, forcing the enemy back towards the river.*

**sb's (little) *game*** ⟶ ***little***

***game* for sth** or **game to do sth** (*informal*) prepared or ready for or to do sth: *I'm game to help if I can. What do you want me to do?*

**the *game* is up** (*informal*) an activity, usually fraudulent, has been discovered and will not be allowed to continue: *Mr Sykes, we know that you've been stealing money from the firm; nobody else has the financial knowledge to alter the accounts. The game is up; you've been caught!*

**a *game* that two can play** unpleasant or hurtful behaviour that can cause sb to do the same to you: *Sulking until you get what you want is a game that two can play.* **two can play at that game** (*saying*) if you do that, I or sb else will do it back to you.

**run the *gamut* of sth** ⟶ ***run***

**everything in the *garden* is lovely** ⟶ ***everything***

**lead sb up the *garden* path** ⟶ ***lead***

***gather* dust** be difficult to keep free from dust and dirt; remain unused and neglected: *Why don't you get rid of some of these ornaments? They're only gathering dust on the shelf.* / *The report was left to gather dust and not dealt with for years by the authorities.*

***gather* up the threads** ⟶ ***pick*/gather up the threads**

**run the *gauntlet* (of sb/sth)** ⟶ ***run***

***gear* (sb/sth) up (for sth)** prepare (sb/sth) (for sth), especially to be more efficient: *The political parties' organizations are gearing themselves up for an autumn election.*

***gen* (sb) up (on sth)** (*informal*) teach sb or learn (about sth); receive or give sb facts about sth: *The group genned up on the project so that they could ask questions during their visit.*

**in *general* . . . in particular** without choosing individual cases, in contrast to specifying special examples: *The money is due to come on the 1st of every month; in general it arrives punctually, but at holiday times in particular, it's late.*

**a *gentleman's* agreement** an arrangement between people to do sth, when such an undertaking is not a formal contract or legally binding but is based on mutual trust and honour.

***gently* does it** ⟶ ***easy*/gently/slowly does it**

***get* a lot of stick** ⟶ ***give* sb a lot of stick**

***get* a move on** (*informal*) be fast; do sth quickly: *If you want to get the 8.15 bus, you'll have to get a move on!*

***get* a pat on the back** ⟶ ***pat* sb/oneself on the back**

***get* a/the rise out of sb** ⟶ ***take*/get a/the rise out of sb**

***get* a thick ear** ⟶ ***give* sb a thick ear**

***get* a word in (edgeways)** (*informal*) succeed in saying sth when sb else is talking a lot or when many other people are talking: *You know what Norah is like! She talks so much you can hardly get a word in edgeways.* Note that this is usually used in the negative.

***get*/be above oneself** have too high an opinion of yourself: *He's getting above himself! He's only just joined the firm and already he's giving people orders!*

***get* sth across/over (to sb)** communicate sth to sb; make sth clear to sb: *It takes an experienced salesman only a few minutes to get his message across.*

***get* one's act together** → ***get* it together**

***get* along** live, work, or do sth, especially in a way that is mentioned: *Many couples find it difficult to get along just on the husband's wage, so the wife works as well.*

***get* along (with sb)** → ***get* on/along (with sb)**

***get* along/away/on (with you)!** *(informal)* (an expression of annoyance, disbelief etc): *Get along with you! You don't expect me to believe that story, do you?* Also **go on (with you)!**

***get* an earful/eyeful of this** *(informal)* listen to/look at this: *'I wouldn't have believed it,' he exclaimed to his wife, calling her to the window, 'come and get an eyeful of this!'*

**not *get* (sb) anywhere** → ***get* (sb) nowhere**

***get* around** *(informal)* go to many places and gain experience, especially business or social experience: *You certainly get around! You seem to go to a different continent each month in your job!*

***get* around to (doing) sth** → ***get* (a)round to (doing) sth**

***get*/be at sb** complain often to sb about sth; say sth that (directly or indirectly) criticizes sb adversely: *His mother was always (getting) at him for his untidy ways. / Often, when people are making quite general remarks, she feels she is being got at.* See also ***what* is sb getting at?**

***get* away with sth 1** *(informal)* steal and escape with sth such as money or jewellery: *An armed gang raided a local bank this morning and got away with over £30,000.* **2** *(informal)* escape punishment for sth: *An increasing number of criminals are getting away with the crimes they commit. / I'm not going to let him get away with such outrageous behaviour. He must apologize at once!* **3** *(informal)* receive only a light punishment for sth: *As it was the first time he'd been caught, he got away with just a fine.*

***get* away with (doing) sth** *(informal)* succeed in doing sth: *The council want to close one of the local schools but the parents won't let them get away with it.*

***get* away with (blue) murder** *(informal)* (be able to) do anything extreme and offensive and not be punished for it: *He knows he looks so gentle and harmless that he can get away with murder!*

***get* away from it all** *(informal)* have a short holiday to gain relief from worries, too much work etc: *Why don't you get away from it all and have a weekend in the country?*

***get* back at sb** *(informal)* retaliate or take revenge on sb: *You can't get back at your boss if you think he has treated you unfairly.*

***get*/put sb's back up** *(informal)* make sb angry or offend sb, often by insensitive or clumsy behaviour: *He's completely tactless—his rudeness really gets my back up.* See also **one's *back* is up.**

***get* one's bearings** → ***find*/get one's bearings**

***get* sb's blessing for sb/sth** → ***give* sb/sth one's blessing**

***get* one's breath back** be able to breathe again properly after exercise; recover: *It took him a few minutes to get his breath back after climbing all the stairs. / Once you've done all the exams, it may take you a few weeks to get your breath back.*

***get* by (on sth)** just succeed in doing sth; live or work (on an amount of money etc): *I don't want to do well in the exam. I just want to get by, that's all. / The old man never seemed to have much money but somehow he managed to get by on his pension.*

***get* one's cards** *(informal)* be dismissed from or lose your job: *Where I work, I'd get my cards if I spoke to a customer like that! / 200 have been made redundant already and another hundred can expect their cards before Christmas.* **give sb his cards** dismiss sb. **ask for one's cards** resign from one's job.

***get* carte blanche** → ***give* sb carte blanche**

***get* cold feet** or **have (got) cold feet** become or be nervous or afraid and no longer want to continue what you intended or have started to do: *She had agreed to lead the delegation. Whether she was genuinely ill on the day or simply got cold feet, we'll never know. / I probably wasn't the only one of us with cold feet at that stage but we all still talked as if we were confident of success.*

***get* cracking/weaving** *(informal)* start to move and/or work quickly: *You'd better get cracking on this urgent letter, please, Jane.*

***get*/put sb's dander up** *(informal, becoming old-fashioned)* annoy sb: *There's no need to get your dander up! I only asked you if I could borrow some money!* Also **have one's dander up** be annoyed.

***get* sb down** *(informal)* make sb feel depressed or sad: *Doctor, I don't know how long I can continue like this. The children get me down so much.*

***get* down to (doing) sth** *(informal)* start to do sth, especially a particular job or task, seriously: *I think we've discussed the plans for long enough. Now let's get down to actually carrying them out.*

***get* sth down to a fine art** *(informal)* learn the skill of doing sth perfectly: *Marie's got learning Chinese characters down to a fine art—she does five every morning and goes over them again at night. / Changing nappies was tough at first—but we've got it down to a fine art now.*

***get* down to brass tacks** *(informal)* discuss sth in practical terms: *We must stop being so theoretical and get down to brass tacks. First of all, how much will it cost?*

***get* down to business** start discussing sth seriously, especially after a time of social talk: *Well, time's moving on—I suppose we'd better get down to business now.*

***get* sb's ear** → ***gain*/get/win sb's ear**

***get* even/square (with sb)** retaliate or take revenge (on sb): *For years I listened to his hateful remarks and wanted to get even with him.*

***get*/pull one's finger out** *(informal)* stop behaving in a lazy, inefficient way and begin tackling sth yourself: *Stop criticizing other people! Get your finger out and do something yourself!*

***get* one's fingers burnt** ⟶ ***burn* one's fingers**

**(can) *get* sth for the asking** ⟶ **(can) *have* sth for the asking**

***get* fresh with sb** *(informal)* act or behave in a cheeky, or disrespectful way towards sb, especially sb of the opposite sex: *Don't you get fresh with me, young man! / He was trying to get fresh with her, so she asked her brother to throw him out.*

***get* sb's goat** *(informal)* make sb feel impatient or angry: *You really get my goat! Why do you never listen to what I ask you to do?*

***get* one's hands on sb** *(informal)* seize and hit sb in order to punish or hurt: *Just wait till I get my hands on that child!*

***get* one's hands on sth 1** obtain sth that is important or that you have wanted for a long time: *Do you know where I can get my hands on a reference book on butterflies? I need one to check on something I'm writing.*

***get* hold of sb/sth** *(informal)* obtain sth; reach or contact sb: *Do you know where I can get hold of a telephone directory for France? / I spent all morning on the phone trying to get hold of the manager.*

***get* hold of the wrong end of the stick** *(informal)* misunderstand completely what has been said: *You've got hold of the wrong end of the stick—it's not me who owes him the money, it's him who owes me!*

***get* ideas (into one's head)** *(informal)* have mistaken, unsuitable, or foolish ambitions, notions or urges: *'If I ask you up for a cup of coffee before you drive home,' Linda said to Frank, 'don't go getting ideas, will you?' 'I won't even kiss you goodnight, and that's a promise.'* See also ***put* ideas into sb's head.**

***get* (sb) in on sth** *(informal)* (cause sb to) participate in sth: *It would be good to get in on that new project—I hear that the company is doing well, so the salary should be high.*

***get* in on the ground floor** ⟶ ***come*, get etc in on the ground floor**

***get* in with sb** *(informal)* try to form a relationship with sb: *The only reason she wants to get in with Bob is because he might offer her a job.*

***get* sb/sth into shape** ⟶ ***lick*/knock/get sb/sth into shape**

***get* into one's stride** reach the stage in an action when you are doing it at your best: *When I moved jobs, it took me several months to get into my stride, but now I'm in control of all my responsibilities.*

***get* sth into one's (thick) head** *(informal)* understand sth fully; realize the meaning of: *When will you get it into your head that driving so fast will lead to an accident?* See also ***take* it into one's head (that . . . ).**

***get* sb into trouble** *(informal)* have sexual intercourse with a girl to whom you are not married and make her pregnant: *A few months after he'd got her into trouble they decided to get married.*

***get* it (in the neck)** *(informal)* be criticized strongly or punished; suffer greatly: *The company will get it in the neck whatever happens. If it makes a loss it will be attacked for its failure to be efficient, and if it makes a profit it will be told its prices are too high.*

***get* it together** *(slang)* organize or do sth satisfactorily: *I don't think I did very well in the radio interview. I was too nervous and unsure of myself. Somehow I just couldn't get it together.* Also **get one's act together**.

***get* knotted/lost/stuffed!** *(slang)* go away!; stop annoying me; *'Get lost, Sue! I'm trying to finish my work!'*

***get* sb's monkey up** *(informal)* make sb annoyed: *He really gets my monkey up by boasting all the time about his new car.* Also **sb's monkey is up** sb is annoyed.

***get* (sb) nowhere** *(informal)* (cause sb to) achieve nothing or make no progress: *I've read this pile of books but still have got nowhere in understanding the subject.* Also **not get (sb) anywhere:** *Flattery won't get us anywhere, so let's be honest with each other.*

***get* no/little change out of sb** *(informal)* not be able to persuade or exploit sb; obtain no/little help from sb: *'I imagine the journalists have been here trying to get some information from you.' 'Yes, they have, but they got no change (or they didn't get any change) out of me.'*

**tell sb where to *get* off** ⟶ ***tell***

***get* (sb) off** *(informal)* escape or save sb from punishment or stronger punishment: *Macarthur's a good lawyer. He should be able to get you off. / He got off with just a fine (or got off lightly).*

***get* (sb) off sb's back** *(informal)* (cause sb to) leave sb alone or in peace: *Get off my back, will you, Sarah! Can't you stop chattering all the time!*

***get* sth off one's chest** *(informal)* say sth that you have wanted to say for a long time, so relieving your feelings; *Come on, Mabel, don't just sit there! Something is worrying you, I can tell. The sooner you get it off your chest, the better!*

***get* (sth) off on the right/wrong foot** *(informal)* (cause sth to) make a good/bad start: *When you're interviewed for a job, try your best to get off on the right foot.* Also **start off on the right/wrong foot.**

***get* (sth) off the ground** (cause sth such as a plan to) operate or function properly; reach an advanced stage in development: *Because of a lack of money, the project never really got off the ground.*

***get* (sb) off with sb** *(informal)* (cause sb to) become friendly with sb of the opposite sex: *He went home with a girl he'd got off with at the party. / It's time Jim had a girlfriend. Can't you get him off with one of your friends?*

***get* on 1** perform or fare in a situation: *I don't think I got on very well in the exam. / How did you get on when you went abroad?* **2** be successful in your life; make progress: *You're getting on fine, Mr Turnbull. If you continue taking these pills you'll be well soon. / Parents and teachers usually want their children to get on (in the world).* **3** (of time) become late; (of people) grow older: *It's getting on. I think we must go home soon as we have to be up early tomorrow. / When your parents are getting on, you definitely need to help them more. / He must be getting on for 70.*

***get* on/along (with sb)** live, work, or play together well, be friendly (with sb): *Since we moved to our new house, our two boys have got on very well with the local children.*

***get* on sb's back** *(informal)* bother or harass sb: *'You're late again, Brian!' 'Sir, don't get on my back—the bus never turned up!'*

***get* on (with sb) like a house on fire** *(informal)* live, work, or play together (with sb) very well: *I get on like a house on fire with my Mum, but not so well with my Dad.*

***get* on sb's nerves** annoy or irritate sb: *Marianne really gets on my nerves, the way she only talks about babies all the time.* Also *(informal)* **get on sb's wick**.

***get* on top of sth 1** be able to control or master (a task): *It's taken me months to get on top of all the work caused by the office re-organization, but I've finally done it.* **2** (of work, a difficulty etc) cause worry and too much concern to sb: *Everything's been getting on top of me in the last few weeks, doctor. Can you give me some pills to help me, please?*

***get* out of (doing) sth** avoid (doing) sth: *He always tries to get out of the washing-up.*

***get* out of bed (on) the wrong side** *(informal)* be in a bad mood from the moment when you get up: *What's wrong with Viv? He seems so irritable and touchy this morning. He must have got out of bed the wrong side!*

***get* out of hand** become uncontrollable: *How can we stop increases in prices and wages getting out of hand? / The student teacher could see that the class was getting out of hand, so he had to call for help.*

***get* sb/sth out of one's system** *(informal)* stop yourself being attracted or fascinated by sb/sth: *Susie, why do you look so sad? Can't you get Roger out of your system?*

***get* sth out of the way** deal with and finish sth such as work: *I'll see if I can get the accounts out of the way before lunch.*

***get* over sth 1** recover from an illness, shock, disappointment etc: *The doctor was right. The fever was bad and you will need time to get over it. / She'll never get over her husband's death.* **2** *(informal)* stop being to be surprised, delighted, or offended by sth: *I just can't get over the fact that you've come back to us after all these years.* Note that this is used with ***can't*** and ***couldn't***.

***get* sth over (with)** do sth unpleasant but necessary: *Let's get the work over with and then we can play. / I'll be glad when I've got all my exams over!*

***get* one's own back** *(informal)* retaliate; have revenge on sb: *I'll get my own back on you for what you did to my brother!*

***get*/be past it** *(informal)* be no longer able to do things that you could do at a previous time, especially when you were younger: *I'm afraid the storekeeper, old Arnold, is getting past it. We give him instructions about running the stores, but he just carries on in his own way, taking no notice of what we tell him.*

***get* sb's/the point** ⟶ ***take*/get/see sb's/the point**

***get* round sth** overcome or avoid a problem, difficulty, or obstacle: *The new regulation stops you getting round the tax laws.*

***get* (a)round to (doing) sth** find enough time to do something, especially after a long time: *I'm so busy at the moment I don't know when I'll get round to painting the house.*

***get* round sb (to do sth)** *(informal)* persuade sb to do sth for you: *I can easily get round Dad to lend me some money.*

***get*/be shirty (about sth) (with sb)** *(slang)* become/be bad-tempered (about sth) (with sb): *There's no need to get shirty with me!*

***get* short shrift** ⟶ ***give* sb/sth short shrift**

***get*/be shot of sb/sth** *(informal)* get/be freed from or rid of sb/sth: *'Where can we get shot of the stolen car?' the thieves asked.*

***get* one's skates on** *(informal)* hurry up: *You'd better get your skates on, if you want to catch the train! You've only got ten minutes to get to the station!*

***get* square (with sb)** ⟶ ***get* even/square (with sb)**

***get* sth straight** *(informal)* understand sth clearly and correctly: *Let's get this straight: I'm the boss and I tell you what to do.*

***get*/be stuck in** *(informal)* be involved with sth with great enthusiasm and energy: *You two, Richard and Mike, get stuck in and we'll have the work finished quickly!*

***get* stuffed!** ⟶ ***get* knotted/lost/stuffed!**

***get* one's teeth into sth** *(informal)* tackle sth with determination, concentration etc: *I find that when I get my teeth into a translation, it often isn't as bad as I thought.*

***get* the better of sb** overcome or defeat sb; have your own way when disagreeing or arguing with sb: *Curiosity got the better of him and he just had to ask why he wasn't chosen to be on the committee. / Mary shouldn't allow her brother to get the better of her.*

***get* the bird** ⟶ ***give* sb the bird**

***get* the bit between one's/the teeth** ⟶ ***take*/get the bit between one's/the teeth**

***get* the boot/push** ⟶ ***give* sb the boot/push**

***get* the chop** *(informal)* be sacked from your job, be dismissed or rejected; be killed; (of projects etc) be (formally) discontinued: *In the cutbacks, the workers most recently taken on will be the first to get the chop. / She used to be a violinist in one of the orchestras that got the chop* (or *that were given the chop*) *last year*. Also **be for the chop** be very likely to get the chop.

***get* the cold shoulder** → ***give* sb the cold shoulder**

***get* the feel of sth** *(informal)* become familiar with or accustomed to sth: *When you're learning to drive a car, you'll probably find changing gear difficult, but you'll soon get the feel of it.*

***get* the green light** → ***give* sb the green light**

***get* the hang of sb/sth** *(informal)* understand or appreciate sb/sth or how to do sth: *I still haven't got the hang of all these forms. Which one do I need?*

***get* the jitters/shakes/willies** → ***have* (got) the jitters/shakes/willies**

***get* the message** *(informal)* be certain about what is best, or about what sb thinks or wants to do: *We've worked hard, and I think the voters have got the message all right, so I'm sure we'll win.*

***get* the sack/push** → ***give* sb the sack/push**

***get*/gain the upper hand** gain a position of mastery, power, or control: *I try always to remain calm and sensible, but sometimes my feelings get the upper hand and I lose my temper.*

***get* the wind up** → ***put* the wind up sb**

***get* there** *(informal)* achieve your aim; complete a task by perseverance and patience: *Jones is a slow learner but he gets there in the end.*

***get* (sth) through to sb** communicate sth to sb: *I can't get through to my children any longer. They seem to speak a different language.*

***get* to first base (with sth)** *(informal)* complete the first stage or make significant progress in a project: *The money ran out before we could even get to first base on the plan to open a restaurant.* Also **reach/make first base (with sth).**

***get*/come to grips with sth** begin to tackle or understand a problem satisfactorily: *I really want to get to grips with French so that I can speak it properly when I go to France next year.*

***get* to the bottom of sth** find the cause of or solution to a puzzling situation, problem etc: *The police soon managed to get to the bottom of the mystery.* **be at the bottom of** be the cause of or solution to: *What's at the bottom of his bid for power?*

***get* one's tongue round sth** pronounce a difficult sound or word: *Chinese students find it difficult to get their tongues round some English sounds, especially r and l.*

***get* tough (with sb)** *(informal)* adopt a strict attitude and policy (towards sb): *The police and courts have decided to get tough with young criminals.*

***get* two bites at/of the cherry** → ***have*/get two bites at/of the cherry**

***get* under sb's skin** *(informal)* annoy or irritate sb: *Her constant chattering really gets under my skin.*

***get* oneself/sb up** *(informal)* make yourself/sb look very smart or attractive: *She spent hours getting herself up for the party.* **get-up** *n*: *That's an amazing get-up, Jean. I didn't know you had clothes like that!*

***get* sth up** *(informal)* arrange or organize sth such as a concert or party: *Local parents got up a petition to instal traffic lights at the busy junction.*

***get* up steam** *(informal)* develop the energy to work hard at sth: *It takes me a couple of hours to get up steam in the morning and then I don't want to stop.*

***get*/be up to sth** be planning or doing mischief or sth that is suspected (though perhaps only teasingly) to be silly or wrong: *If you give children enough to do they won't get up to mischief. / He wouldn't be in the premises at night unless he was up to something* (or *up to no good*). */ Now, tell me what you've been up to since we last met.* See also **be *up* to sth.**

***get* weaving** → ***get* cracking/weaving**

***get* wind of sth** hear news about sth in an indirect way: *We must do our best to make sure that the managers don't get wind of our plans to hold a strike.*

***get* one's 'wires crossed** *(informal)* be mistaken about what sb is talking about: *'Sorry—I think we've got our wires crossed. When I said next Tuesday, I was talking about the day after tomorrow.' 'Oh, I thought you meant Tuesday of next week.'*

***get*/be wise to sb/sth** be(come) aware of sb/sth: *She fooled him once or twice, but then he got wise to her* (or *her tricks*). **put sb wise to sb/sth** make sb aware of sb/sth.

***get* word (from sb)** → ***have*/get word (from sb)**

***get* sb wrong** *(informal)* misunderstand sb: *Now don't get me wrong! When I said I was unhappy living here, I didn't mean anything personal.*

**what is sb *getting* at?** → ***what***

**like *getting* blood out of a stone** *(informal)* (especially of trying to get money from sb) extremely difficult: *Persuading some companies to pay you promptly is like getting blood out of a stone.*

**(not) have (got) a '*ghost* of a chance (of doing sth)** → **(not) *have* (got) a cat in 'hell's chance (of doing sth)**

**look a *gift* horse in the mouth** → ***look***

**the *gift* of the gab** *(informal)* the ability to talk fluently and for a long time, especially to persuade you to do sth: *He's a salesman with the gift of the gab and will make you spend your money on things you really don't need.*

***gild* the lily** try to make sth that is already beautiful even more beautiful; spoil a good quality by praising it too much: *Putting such an expensive wrapping paper round those* *presents would be gilding the lily—they are very attractive already.*

**take the *gilt* off the gingerbread** ⟶ ***take***

**a 'ginger group** a group which is connected with or within a political party, popular movement etc and which makes plans and wants action.

***ginger* sb/sth up** *(informal)* make sb/sth such as an activity or movement more lively and interesting: *This 'stop smoking' campaign is so dull—it needs to be gingered up a bit.*

***gird* up one's loins** *(formal, old-fashioned)* prepare yourself for action.

**a *girl* Friday** ⟶ **a *man*/girl Friday**

***give* sb a blank cheque** authorize or allow sb to act and to spend as much money as he chooses in a particular task or situation: *He was given a blank cheque and told to hire the best singers he could.* See also ***give* sb carte blanche (to do sth).**

**(not) *give* a brass farthing etc (about/for sb/sth)** ⟶ **(not) *care*/give a brass farthing etc (about/for sb/sth)**

***give* a dog a bad name (and hang him)** *(saying)* it is difficult to regain a reputation that has been lost; people continue to condemn or suspect sb who has been accused of doing or has done sth wrong.

***give* a good, bad etc account of oneself** perform well, badly etc in sth that needs knowledge, skill etc: *Patrick gave a good account of himself in this year's examination.*

***give*/lend (sb) a (helping) hand** help (sb): *Could you give me a hand to carry the shopping in from the car, please?*

***give* sb a hard time** cause sb difficult work; be in a situation in which people demand too much from you or harass you: *As the parents of ten children, they were certainly given a hard time.* **have a hard time** be given a hard time.

***give* sb a lot of stick** blame or strongly criticize sb, often unfairly: *Their father gives them a lot of stick if they misbehave.* **get/take a lot of stick** be blamed or strongly criticized, often unfairly: *Poor Sharon! She really takes a lot of stick for mistakes that aren't her fault.*

***give* a party (for sb/sth)** ⟶ ***throw*/give a party (for sb/sth)**

***give* sb/oneself a pat on the back** ⟶ ***pat* sb/oneself on the back**

***give* sb a piece of one's mind** *(informal)* bluntly and angrily criticize sb or his behaviour: *If one of my students spoke to me like that, I'd give him a piece of my mind!*

***give* sb a rap on/over the knuckles** ⟶ ***rap* sb on/over the knuckles**

***give* sb a (good) run for his money** *(informal)* provide a strong challenge or close competition for sb: *We may not beat Mr Thomas in the election on 9th June but we'll certainly give him a good run for his money.*

***give* sth a try** use sth as an experiment to see if it works etc well: *I know you don't usually like cabbage—but I've cooked it in a special way today. Why don't you give it a try?* Also *(informal)* **give sth a whirl.**

***give* sb/sth a wide berth** ⟶ ***steer* clear of sb/sth**

***give* oneself airs** ⟶ ***put* on airs**

***give* sb an/the edge (on/over sb/sth)** ⟶ ***have* (got) an/the edge on/over sb/sth**

***give* sb an inch (and he'll take a mile)** *(saying)* if you surrender to sb a little, he will then increase his demands greatly.

***give* and take** (of two people or group) yield to each other's rights and demands: *There will be an answer to the disagreement only if both sides are prepared to give and take.* **give-and-take** *n.*

***give* (sb) as good as one gets** *(informal)* act towards sb or retaliate in an argument, fight etc with as much skill, strength as has been used against you: *The new director knew he was unpopular with his workers but was determined to give as good as he got in disputes.*

***give* sb/sth away** betray sb; reveal sth that is secret: *The couple hid the prisoner for a few weeks, but when their own lives were threatened, they gave him away. / Don't give away where we've hidden the money!* **give-away** *n*: *The blood on his handkerchief was a real give-away.*

***give* birth to sb/sth** produce a baby or young animal or bring sth into existence: *The princess has given birth to a bouncing baby boy. / The country has given birth to many great statesmen.*

***give* sb/sth one's blessing** approve of and commend sb for what he has done, is doing, or proposes to do; approve of a product, project etc and wish or authorize it to be begun or continued: *We're just waiting for the directors to give their blessing to the new scheme before we put it into practice.* Also **have/get sb's blessing for sb/sth; (do sth) with sb's blessing:** *The workers seem determined to take strike action whether they have their union's blessing or not.*

***give* sb his cards** ⟶ ***get* one's cards**

***give* sb carte blanche** authorize or allow sb to do as he chooses in a particular task or situation: *They gave him carte blanche to interview anyone at all in the firm.* Also **get/have carte blanche.** See also ***give* sb a blank cheque.**

***give* cause for sth** arouse or be the reason for sth such as alarm or worry: *The present condition of the Princess's health gives us great cause for concern.*

**(*give*) chapter and verse (for sth)** (supply) an exact reference or source of information and/or full details of the authority you have for stating something: *'Which play is that from?' 'Ask the Professor here. He can give you chapter and verse for almost any line of Shakespeare!'*

***give*/lend colour to sth** make sth appear more truthful, likely, or reasonable by adding details: *This fresh evidence gives colour to his story about what happened.*

***give* (the) credit (to sb) (for sth)** make sure that sb's effort is properly recognized: *It's up* *to publishers to see that authors are given proper credit for all their work. / The credit for the success of the exhibition should be given to the ladies who organized it.* See also ***give* sb credit for sth; *take* (the) credit for sth**.

***give* sb credit for sth** believe that sb has sth such as intelligence or determination: *Joan's results are a sign of greater abilities than I would have given her credit for.* See also ***give* (the) credit (to sb) (for sth); *take* (the) credit for sth.**

***give* sb his due** admit that sb does indeed have some good points, even if they are a few; admit that there are valid reasons for sb's faults: *It was a very difficult job, but to give Sheila her due, she did try very hard.* See also ***give* the devil his due.**

***give* (an) ear/eye to sb/sth** watch or listen to sb/sth, especially when you are occupied with sth else: *You should have given ear to the warnings.*

***give* free rein to sb/sth** allow sb/sth freedom and lack of control: *In a historical novel the author need not keep to the facts, but a history textbook is not the place to give free rein to one's imagination.*

***give*/lose ground (to sb/sth)** retreat (to sb/sth else's advantage); fail to hold your position: *If we cancel the advertising campaign, we shall give ground to our rivals.*

***give* sb ideas → *put* ideas into sb's head**

***give* in (to sb/sth)** yield or surrender to sb or sth: *The battle continued until the enemy finally gave in. / When you're not feeling well, it's easy to give in to self-pity.*

***give* it to sb** *(informal)* attack, scold, or rebuke sb: *The manager will really give it to you when he finds out what you've done.*

***give*/hand it to sb** *(informal)* admire sb; admit or recognize the skill of sb: *I've got to hand it to you, Gwen. You certainly know how to cook us a good dinner. That was superb!* Note that these verbs are always used with ***have (got) to*** or ***must***.

***give* me strength!** *(informal)* (a cry for help and courage to endure sth; used when the speaker is annoyed or impatient): *Goodness me, boy! Can't you even tell me who wrote Macbeth? Give me strength!*

***give* or take a year, ten pence etc** plus or minus a year etc (used in making an estimate): *We've manufactured 30,000 pins this month, give or take a few hundred.*

***give* out** (of strength, a supply etc) come to an end; become used up or spent: *His patience eventually gave out and he got very angry.*

***give* sth out** announce sth: *The news has been given out that the Princess is expecting a baby. / It was given out that seven people had been killed in the air raid.*

***give* sb short change** *(informal)* deal with sb in a brief, impatient, and unsympathetic way: *The deputation was given short change by the Minister.* **get short change** be treated in this way. **short-change sb** cheat or swindle sb.

***give* sb/sth short shrift** deal with sb/sth very quickly and impatiently in a dismissive way: *The minister gave the deputation short shrift, telling its leaders he had no sympathy for a campaign that appealed for public support by means of false statements.* **get short shrift** be treated in this way.

***give* sb something to think about** or **have something to think about** (make sb) think or consider; shock or be shocked; scold or be scolded for doing sth wrong: *The book really gave me something to think about. / If he comes here again, I'll see he has something to think about.*

***give* sb the boot/push** *(informal)* dismiss sb from employment; tell sb he is no longer wanted: *Jack's girlfriend has given him the boot.* **get the boot/push** be treated like this.

***give* sb the bird** *(informal)* hiss or whistle at an actor to make him leave the stage; reject rudely or scornfully: *His act was so terrible that he got the bird on the first night and has never been asked to perform again.* **get the bird:** *We'll probably get the bird, but let's ask these two girls at the far table if we can join them.*

***give* sb/sth the chuck** *(informal)* dismiss sb from his job; break off relations or dealings with sb; reject or discard a plan or goods as being useless or unwanted: *The first TV series he wrote got low audience ratings and was given the chuck after just two episodes.* **get the chuck** be treated in this way.

***give* sb the creeps/horrors/willies** *(informal)* make sb have strong feelings of dislike, revulsion, fear, or nervousness: *I don't know what it is about him that gives me the creeps but I can hardly bear to be in the same room with him.* **get the creeps/horrors/willies** have such strong feelings: *'Are we upsetting you?' 'It's silly of me I know, but I always get the willies when people start talking about illness and death.'*

***give* the devil his due** *(saying)* treat even sb unworthy fairly; recognize the good points of such a person: *You're all saying George is mean, but, to give the devil his due, I've seen him give a lot of help to people in difficulties.*

***give* sb the edge (over sb)** give sb an advantage (over sb else): *Her experience gives her that extra edge over the other girls being interviewed for the job.*

***give* sb the (rough) edge of one's tongue** speak to sb in a rude, sharp, and critical way: *The headmaster has been known to give teachers who don't toe the line the rough edge of his tongue.* **get the (rough) edge of sb's tongue** be spoken to in this way.

***give* sb the elbow** *(informal)* end a relationship with sb; get rid of sb from a job etc: *Girls always give him the elbow after just a couple of weeks.*

***give* the 'game/'show away** *(informal)* betray or reveal sb's plan or intentions: *I wanted to leave without telling my parents, but friends phoned to find out when I was coming and so gave the game away.*

***give* sb the green light** *(informal)* tell sb that he is allowed to do sth: *At its meeting this week, the council gave the green light for work to begin on* (or *gave the green light to build) the new shopping centre.* **get the green light** receive permission to do sth.

***give* sb the horrors** ⟶ ***give* sb the creeps/horrors/willies**

***give* sb the jitters/shakes/willies** ⟶ ***have* (got) the jitters/shakes/willies**

***give* the lie to sth** show sth to be untrue: *Fresh evidence about the Prince's death gives the lie to the story that he died of a heart attack.*

***give* sb the run-around** *(informal)* act deceitfully, cunningly, or evasively towards sb: *He's been hurt a lot by Sue—she's really been giving him the run-around by secretly seeing other men recently.*

***give* sb the sack/push** or **get the sack/push** *(informal)* dismiss sb or be dismissed from a job: *Another 200 men are to get the sack at the steelworks before Christmas.*

***give* sb the slip** *(informal)* escape from sb: *Eight out of the ten prisoners who had escaped were caught, but it was clear that the other two had given the police the slip.*

***give* sth the thumbs-down** *(informal)* make a statement or give a gesture that expresses rejection or disapproval of sth: *I eventually found a publisher to accept my idea for a book after several had given it the thumbs-down.*

***give* sth the thumbs-up** *(informal)* make a statement or give a gesture that expresses acceptance or approval of sth or wishes sb good luck: *We've been given the thumbs-up by the council to open a motorcycle shop.*

***give* sb the willies** ⟶ ***give* sb the creeps/horrors/willies; *have* (got) the jitters/shakes/willies**

***give* sb/sth the (full, whole etc) works** *(informal)* do, say, or provide everything you possibly can do to meet a particular need; treat sb very harshly: *We'll give the car the full works—a new engine, a fresh coat of paint, and so on—you won't recognize it when you come to collect it!*

***give*/hand sth to sb on a plate** *(informal)* offer sth to sb without him having to work hard for it: *You've got to learn that you can't have everything handed to you on a plate in this life but that you've got to make an effort to do things for yourself.*

***give* sb to understand (that . . . )** make sb think that sth is true (often used to state that sb was misled in being made to believe in sth): *I was given to understand by your boss that the money would arrive on the 1st of the month. Could you explain why it hasn't yet come?*

***give* sb up** stop believing that sb will arrive or recover from an illness: *It's lucky you've come! We'd almost given you up and were about to leave! / All the doctors and nurses had given him up when he suddenly started to get better.*

***give* up sth 1** end an attempt, pursuit, or other activity, especially as a sign of defeat: *Rescue workers have given up all hope of finding any more survivors in the earthquake. / I gave up trying to learn French when I discovered how bad my accent was.* **2** withdraw or resign from sth such as a profession or course: *Why did you decide to give up your job after you got married?*

***give* up (doing) sth** renounce a (bad) habit, sutudy, belief etc: *Doug, have you tried to give up smoking?*

***give* up the ghost 1** *(old-fashioned)* die. **2** *(informal)* stop working; stop trying to work, run, study etc: *This old typewriter has finally given up the ghost, so my boss is getting me a new one.*

***give* vent to sth** allow sth such as your feelings to be expressed: *It is much better to give vent to your anger than always to restrain it.*

***give* voice to sth** utter or express sth such as feelings or doubts: *After the speaker had finished, several people gave voice to their objections to the scheme.*

***give* way** collapse; break or fall down: *The bridge gave way under the weight of the heavy lorries.*

***give* way (to sb/sth) 1** allow yourself to be overcome (by sth); yield to the requests (of sb): *Her silence quickly gave way to tears as she realized what had happened. / The employers eventually gave way to the unions' demands.* **2** allow sb/sth else to go first; allow precedence to sb/sth; be replaced by: *Give way to traffic travelling towards you when you drive over the bridge. / Small, local shops are giving way to large supermarkets and out-of-town hypermarkets.*

***give* sb what 'for** *(informal)* punish or scold sb for what he has done: *You thief! I'll tell your father and he'll give you what for!*

**fit (sb) like a *glove*** ⟶ ***fit***

**the *gloves* are off** people are no longer acting with gentleness or mercy, but want to win by fighting, arguing etc: *Up to the present time both sides in the dispute have been cautious but now the gloves are off and a serious confrontation is expected.*

**paint sb/sth in *glowing* colours** ⟶ ***paint***

***glued* to sth** *(informal)* with your eyes fixed to sth such as the television: *She just sat there all evening, glued to the television.*

**a *glutton* for work/punishment** sb who wants to work very hard or endure hardship or difficulties: *You're a glutton for punishment, aren't you? You work all day at the office then come back and write letters for the club every evening. You never have a rest.*

**have (got) sth on the *go*** ⟶ ***have***

**(always) on the *go*** (of people) busy and active: *When you've been on the go all day it's nice to relax in the evenings.*

**no *go*** ⟶ ***no***

**. . . to *go*** (of time or an amount) still to be passed, spent etc: *There's only a few seconds to go before the rocket takes off. / With only two kilometres to go, Max is still first.*

***go* a bundle on sth** *(slang)* like or enjoy sth

very much: *Yes, I've heard that he goes a bundle on that new record.*

***go* a long way** ⟶ ***go* far**

***go* a long way to do sth** or **go a long way towards (doing) sth** help very much to achieve sth: *Offering the workers more money will go a long way towards satisfying them.*

***go*/be about one's business** be busy with your work: *The offices were bustling with people going about their business.*

***go* about (doing) sth** start to do or tackle sth: *This job is easy if you go about it in the right way. / I don't know how to go about organizing a funeral.*

***go*/be after sb/sth** try to obtain sb/sth for yourself, fairly or unfairly: *They were both after the same job. / The question is: Does he like her or is he just after her money?*

***go* against the grain** be contrary to your wishes or the usual practice: *It goes against the grain to pay a higher salary, but he is very experienced, so I think we can make an exception this time.*

***go* ahead** proceed or progress: *Building of the bridge is ready to go ahead as planned.* **go-ahead** *adj* ambitious; enterprising: *a go-ahead young man.* **go-ahead** *n* a decision or permission to proceed: *The government has given the go-ahead to the project.*

***go* all out (for sth)** or **go all out (to do sth)** make a very great effort to obtain or do sth: *We knew that only one of the firms would get the order for computers and so we went all out to get the contract.*

***go* along with sb/sth** agree with sb/sth: *I don't think I can go along with everything that the directors want to do.*

***go* astray** (of things) be lost or stolen; (of people) behave immorally or illegally: *Your letter seems to have gone astray; can you send me a copy of it, please? / A young person can easily go astray in one of our big cities.*

***go*/be at sb/sth hammer and tongs** *(informal)* attack sb or argue with sb or about sth very strongly: *Joe was late again. The boss really went at him hammer and tongs! / The council has been discussing where to reduce spending for several hours and the different sides are still at it hammer and tongs.*

***go* back on sth** fail to keep sth such as a promise; change your mind about (sth) said earlier: *The opposition party thought that the politician had gone back on his word.*

***go* before a fall** ⟶ ***pride* goes/comes before a fall**

***go* begging** be unwanted or unclaimed: *I'll take the last piece of cake if it's going begging.*

***go* behind sb's back** act deceitfully or unfairly: *I feel a bit guilty about going behind his back and complaining about him to the headmaster.* See also **behind sb's *back*.**

**things that *go* bump in the night** ⟶ ***things***

***go* bust** (of a business company) become bankrupt: *In the current recession many firms are going bust every week.*

***go* by sth** use sth as the basis of forming a judgment: *If past experience is anything to go by, the plane will be three hours late.*

***go* by the board** (of an idea, plan etc) be abandoned: *All their plans for the future had to go by the board when they suddenly heard that he had cancer.*

***go* cap in hand** present yourself humbly and respectfully to sb: *Unemployment Benefit isn't something you should go cap in hand for. It's a right you've paid for, yourself, over many years. / The local council have run out of money for the scheme. So now they've had to go cap in hand to the government to ask for more.*

***go* down in history** be remembered for a long time to come: *John Green will go down in history as the man who first won this race in under ten minutes.*

***go* 'down in the world** ⟶ ***come*/go 'down in the world**

***go* down well, badly etc (with sb)** (of a speech etc) be received well etc: *Elaine's article in the magazine went down very well with everyone.*

***go* down with sth** become ill with sth: *Both children have now gone down with measles.*

***go* downhill** *(informal)* (of people, an area, institutions etc) decline or deteriorate: *This restaurant has definitely gone downhill since I last came here.*

***go* Dutch** share the cost of a meal, visit to the theatre etc equally with sb else: *Shall we have a meal together? We'll go Dutch.*

***go* easy on sth** *(informal)* use sth such as food, drink, or paint moderately: *Go easy on the bread! It's all we've got till Monday!*

***go* far 1** last a long time; meet the needs of users adequately: *Whether I earn a small or big amount each week, it doesn't seem to go far these days!* / Also **go a long way:** *Let's have a chicken—that always goes a long way, I find.* **2** rise high in your social position; become very successful: *Donald is an excellent manager. He should go far.*

***go* for sb/sth 1** attack sb/sth physically or with words; rebuke or scold: *Our dog always goes for the postman.* **2** like or be attracted by sb/sth: *I don't really go for wallpaper with pink flowers.* **3** apply to sb/sth: *Do your work, Smith! And the same goes for you, Jones!*

***go* for a Burton** *(slang, becoming old-fashioned)* be ruined, broken, or killed: *Our hopes of winning that contract have really gone for a Burton now that we have just increased our prices.*

***go* for a song** *(informal)* be sold for very little money: *In sales, these old candlesticks go for a song.*

***go* from bad to worse** become clearly or markedly worse than previously: *It was hoped that the world recession had reached its most serious point and that things would now start to get better, but there is disturbing new evidence that suggests that matters may still go from bad to worse.*

***go* from strength to strength** increase your

success, abilities, power etc quickly: *The company has gone from strength to strength since we launched the new brand of pen.*

**go full circle** —> ***come*/go full circle**

**go great guns** *(informal)* do sth energetically or strongly: *'The old chap's going great guns, isn't he?' whispered Ann to me in the middle of his speech. 'He may be old but he can still speak powerfully.'* Note that this is usually used in continuous tenses.

**go halves** share the total amount of sth, such as a cost, equally with sb else: *As you're taking me up to Manchester, we'll go halves on the petrol* (or *when you buy the petrol).*

**go hand in hand (with sth)** be closely connected (with sth else): *Unemployment goes hand in hand with a large number of other social problems in this area.*

**go haywire** *(informal)* become wrong or confused; operate or behave in a crazy, uncontrolled way: *Since the crash on the main line this morning, the timetable has gone completely haywire.*

**go/live in fear of one's life** be constantly afraid that you may be killed, punished etc: *After one attempt to murder him, the President went around in fear of his life.*

**go in (at) one ear and out (of) the other** *(informal)* (of a lesson, warning, or message) not be heeded at all; be totally disregarded: *Halfway through the talk, the lecturer stopped—it was obvious from looking at the audience that what he was saying was going in one ear and out of the other.*

**go it alone** *(informal)* do sth, especially sth difficult, without the help or support of other people: *The mum or dad who has to go it alone in a single-parent family must find it very hard to bring up the children.*

**go like a dream** —> ***work*/go like a dream**

**go like a bomb 1** *(informal)* quickly be a great success: *The bookshop reports that sales of his new books are going like a bomb. / The party went like a bomb.* **2** *(informal)* travel very fast: *My new car really goes like a bomb, doesn't it?*

**go/run like clockwork** (of arrangements etc) proceed without any difficulty or trouble: *The whole meeting went like clockwork—all the preparations were successful, and everything happened very smoothly.*

**go like hot cakes** —> ***sell*/go like hot cakes**

***(go)* like the clappers** *(slang)* (move to do sth) very quickly and vigorously: *It wasn't the usual ambulance that picks up old folk for the out-patient clinic. This one was going like the clappers, lights flashing and siren wailing.*

**go/run like the wind** move very fast: *Harry was on his bike and going like the wind towards the beach.*

**go off 1** (of food and drink) become bad and no longer suitable for eating and drinking: *The milk smells odd. I think it must have gone off in the heat.* **2** become worse in quality; deteriorate: *His books have gone off in recent years.* **3** happen in a way that is mentioned: *How did the ceremony go off?*

**go off at a tangent** leave the main subject under discussion by talking about sth less important: *We were talking about our chances of coming first in the competition this year when Mike suddenly went off at a tangent and started talking about the price of vegetables.*

**go off at half cock** *(informal)* (of a plan, arrangement etc) fail because of poor preparation or because it starts too early. *The scheme to introduce new work schedules went off at half cock since, when it was due to begin, too many people were away ill or on holiday.*

**go off the boil** *(informal)* pass the point of greatest activity or excitement: *The customers were very enthusiastic about our new range of products at first but went off the boil when we eventually quoted prices to them.*

**go off the 'deep end** *(informal)* be very angry: *You should have heard the noise next door! He'd been out late again and she didn't half go off the deep end when he got back!*

**go off the rails** *(informal)* behave in a dishonest or immoral way: *It was after his divorce and when he left his job that he began to go off the rails.* See also ***keep* (sb) on the rails.**

**go on** happen or take place: *What's going on here? / There's something strange going on in that room!* **goings-'on** *n*: *peculiar goings-on.*

**go/be 'on about sb/sth** talk too often or for too long about sb/sth: *She's always on about how poor she is. / You've proved your point. There's no need to go on about it.*

**go/be 'on at sb** keep complaining to sb angrily: *He's always going on at me about the money I spend on drinks.*

**go on record** declare your opinion in public: *As Minister of Defence I'm prepared to go on record as saying that we must use every means to defend our country against all enemy attacks.*

**go on (with you)!** —> ***get* along/away/on (with you)!**

**go one better (than sb)** beat (sb) by improving on what he has done: *Dix & Company have brought out a new car magazine in black and white but we have gone one better by producing one in full colour.*

**go/be out like a light** *(slang)* fall/be fast asleep: *He went out like a light after an exhausting day at work.*

**go out (with sb)** (of two people of different sexes) associate with each other regularly, especially for social functions: *How long have you been going out with Steve? / Mike and Sue had been going out (together) for a couple of years and then decided to get engaged.* Also *(old-fashioned)* **walk out (with sb).**

**go out of the window** *(informal)* (of plans, ideas etc) be rejected: *All our plans for a world cruise had to go right out of the window when Jack lost his job.*

**go out of one's way to do sth** take particular care and trouble to do sth: *Don always goes out of his way to help other people.*

***go* over sth 1** examine or check sth; clean, repair, or correct sth: *I'll just go over these figures again to check that the total is right. / I've asked the garage to go over the car before our holiday.* **going-'over** *n.* See also ***go* over/through sth with a fine-tooth comb. 2** revise or review sth until you know it well: *'Let's go over our lines again to make sure we know them exactly,' said the director.*

***go* over the top** *(informal)* do sth that is more lively, bold, and unrestrained than you usually do: *I'm sorry, I was depressed and did things I shouldn't have done last night. I'm sure I shouldn't have gone over the top as I did.*

***go* over/through sth with a fine-'tooth comb** search or look at sth very closely and thoroughly: *The police went through the field with a fine-tooth comb to try and find the murder weapon.*

***go* overboard (about/for/on sb/sth)** become extremely enthusiastic about sb/sth: *Last month he was keen on jazz; now he's gone overboard on rock music.*

***go* phut** *(informal)* collapse; fail to function: *I'm not sure what happened—there was a bang, some smoke, and then the television just went phut.*

***go* places** *(informal)* become very successful; improve your position in the world: *Mark has only just joined the company, but you can tell from his work that he's the type of person who really wants to go places.*

***go* places (and see people)** *(informal)* visit many exciting places: *Jane is good with people and so wants a job in which she can go places.*

***go* public** (of a private company) issue shares for sale to the public on the stock exchange.

***go* round** be sufficient in numbers or size for everyone to have one or a part: *Are there enough sweets to go round?*

***go* round in circles** keep mentioning the same points, without making any definite progress in a meeting, talk etc: *The discussion just went round in circles, and we didn't come up with any clear answers.*

***go* slow** reduce considerably the speed at which you work, as a protest in industry: *Factory workers voted to go slow for two weeks in support of an increase in pay.* **go-'slow** *n.*

***go* spare** *(slang)* become very upset, annoyed, or puzzled: *Please help me. I'm going spare with worry. / He went spare when I told him I'd lost his money.*

***go* steady (with sb)** (of people of different sexes) have a firm relationship that may lead to marriage: *At 16 I was going steady with a young man—we got engaged at 18 and were married a year later.*

***go* straight** *(informal)* (of a criminal) give up dishonesty or crime as a way of life: *When he came out of prison he decided to go straight.*

***go* the distance** *(informal)* complete an action fully: *The Prime Minister decided not to go the (whole) distance and called an election a year earlier than the rules require.*

***go* the whole hog** *(informal)* go to the full limit of a possible course of action; do sth completely: *They'd painted the kitchen and decided to go the whole hog and redecorate the other rooms as well.*

***go* through fire and water** suffer very great risks and danger, especially in order to help sb.

***go* through the mill** undergo severe discipline, hard training, punishment etc: *In your first few months in the army you really go through the mill.* **put sb through the mill:** *What a ghastly interview! They really put me through the mill.*

***go* through the motions (of doing sth)** pretend to do sth; do sth without thought or sincerity: *The man in the office was just going through the motions of being polite to the public.*

***go* through the roof** *(informal)* (of prices, numbers etc) rise very suddenly to an excessive level: *1983—that was the year the number of people unemployed really went through the roof, wasn't it?*

***go* to bed (with sb)** *(informal)* have sexual intercourse (with sb): *I wouldn't go to bed with just anyone, you know, Mother—I'd want to get to know them first! / After the party he took her home and they went to bed.*

***go* to great etc lengths (to do sth)** do everything that is necessary (to do sth): *The prison staff went to unprecedented lengths to make the prison more secure after a number of prisoners had escaped.*

***go* to great pains (to do sth)** → ***take* pains (to do sth)**

***go* to hell** *(informal)* a strong, offensive expression dismissing or rejecting sb or his wishes, ideas etc. Also *(old-fashioned)* **go to blazes; go to the devil.**

***go* to sb's head 1** (of alcohol) affect sb's judgment and thinking: *I can't drink more than two glasses of beer—it goes to my head.* **2** (of success, fame etc) give sb a wrong sense of importance or abilities: *Don't let your success go to your head!*

***go* 'to it** give your energy and time to doing sth; make an effort to do sth (often used as an encouragement): *Go to it, Goldie! You've nearly finished!*

***go* to pieces** lose your health, sense of well-being, or self-control: *After his wife died, he just went to pieces.*

***go* to pot** *(informal)* be spoilt or ruined: *Since the managing director resigned, the company has really gone to pot; no one knows what he should be doing at all.*

***go* to seed** → ***run*/go to seed**

***go* to show** be a proof or demonstration of sth mentioned: *I don't think about the war at all. It all goes to show how well I've adapted to my new life here.*

***go* to sleep** (of a foot etc) become numb: *I'm sorry, I can't get up. My leg has gone to sleep!*

***go* to the country** hold a general election:

*The Prime Minister may decide to go to the country in the next few weeks.*
***go* to the dogs** *(informal)* become less powerful, efficient etc: *Many people think this country's going to the dogs.*
***go* to the wall** fail; become bankrupt; be defeated: *In the recession several local builders have gone to the wall because of a lack of orders.*
***go* to town** *(informal)* do sth with great energy, imagination, and enjoyment: *She really went to town on the food—it's marvellous!*
***go* too far** exceed what is right or reasonable: *I may have gone a bit too far in suggesting my own plan so strongly.*
***go* under** fail; be overcome by difficulties: *Many large firms have gone under in the recession.*
***go*/come under the hammer** be offered for sale at an auction: *His collection of fine antiques will come under the hammer at Sotheby's next Thursday.*
***go* up in flames/smoke** be destroyed or ruined: *That very dry summer, large areas of woodland went up in flames. / All our hopes for peace have gone up in smoke now that fighting has begun again.*
***go* 'up in the world** ⟶ ***come*/go 'up in the world**
***go* with a bang/swing** *(informal)* be very successful and enjoyable: *The party went with a bang.*
***go* without saying** be so clear that it does not need to be proved and hardly needs to be mentioned: *When you come to our country, it goes without saying that you'll stay with us as our guest.*
***go* wrong 1** make a mistake: *If you read the instructions, you'll see where you went wrong.* **2** (of a machine or plan) fail: *Every time we used the washing-machine it went wrong, so the shop gave us a new one.*
**so help me *God*** ⟶ ***so***
***(God)* bless my soul!** ⟶ ***bless***
***(God)* bless your, his etc soul/heart** ⟶ ***bless***
***God*/goodness/heaven knows 1** I don't know; no one knows: *'What does he hope to achieve by acting like that?' 'God only knows.'* **2** (used to add force to a statement or opinion): *Heaven knows I meant no harm! / I'm no gardening expert, goodness knows!*
***God*/heaven forbid** let me/us hope that sth will never happen or has not happened: *Heaven forbid that Sarah is among the missing children!*
**take *God's* name in vain** ⟶ ***take***
**for *God's* sake** ⟶ **for *goodness'*/God's/heaven's/pity's/Pete's sake**
***God* willing** if that is God's will: *We've had a lovely holiday and will be back again next year, God willing.*
**cleanliness is next to *godliness*** ⟶ ***cleanliness***
**to be *going* on with** ⟶ **to *carry* on with**
**the *going* rate (for sth)** the usual amount of money paid for goods or service: *Some companies try to pay their workers less than the going rate.*
**like *gold* dust** very valuable and scarce: *Toilet paper is like gold dust in some parts of the East!*
**a *gold* mine** a source of great wealth such as a product or idea that earns a large amount of money: *The people who owned the shores near the oil rigs realized they were sitting on a gold mine.*
**the *golden* age (of sth)** the period in which sth is best, happiest, or most prosperous: *This new book looks back on the golden age of steam, and all railway fans will enjoy it immensely.*
**kill the goose that lays the *golden* eggs** ⟶ ***kill***
**a *golden* handshake** a large gift of money given to sb on his retirement or honourable dismissal from a job: *The directors were each given a large golden handshake and a regular pension.*
**the *golden* rule** the best course of action, especially the rule that you should treat others as you would like them to treat you.
**have (been and) *gone* and done it (now/again)** *(informal)* have (unintentionally) caused damage or done or said sth very wrong or surprising: *Oh dear, I've been and gone and done it now! I pressed the wrong button and I've wiped the whole tape. / Peter's gone and done it! After losing six points in the first round he's the winner!*
***gone* on sb/sth** in love or infatuated with sb; greatly or obsessively interested in sth: *John is quite gone on that girl he met at the disco last week.*
**for *good*** permanently; for ever: *I'm going away for good.*
**for sb's (own) *good*** so that sb/sth will benefit: *I don't enjoy criticizing you. I'm only doing it for your own good.*
**be no *good*/use (doing sth)** ⟶ ***no***
**give a *good*, bad etc account of oneself** ⟶ ***give***
***good* and ready, large etc** *(informal)* completely ready, very large etc: *I need to get up good and early to finish my work.*
**as *good* as . . .** almost; for all practical purposes: *I thought the car was as good as sold when the man who wanted it suddenly decided not to buy. / She as good as told me she would come.*
**enough is as *good* as a feast** ⟶ ***enough***
**a nod is as *good* as a wink (to a blind horse)** ⟶ ***nod***
**give (sb) as *good* as one gets** ⟶ ***give***
**as *good* as gold** (of children) very well-behaved: *'How was Rachel this afternoon?' 'She's been as good as gold—she's just sat there and read quietly.'*
**as *good* as one's word** completely reliable and trustworthy: *If he said he would lend you*

*some money to buy a motorbike he will. Jim has always been as good as his word.*

**the *good* book** the Bible: *What does the good book say about this?*

**in sb's *good*/bad/black books** *(informal)* in/out of favour with sb: *What exactly is wrong with this Michael I hear mentioned so often? He seems to be in everybody's black books. / 'Why are you cleaning Mum's shoes?' 'I'm trying to get into her good books!'*

**in *good* company** in the same situation as many able or famous people (often used to comfort and encourage sb when he says he can't or doesn't want to do sth): *You're in good company if you can't speak a foreign language fluently—most of the people I know can't either.*

**a *good*/great deal** much; often: *The boys' father has to be away from home a great deal on business.* Also used with a comparative adjective: *You seem to be a good deal healthier these days.*

**a *good*/great deal (of sth)** a large amount (of sth): *There's been a good deal of unpleasantness about this whole affair, I must admit.*

**one's *good* deed for the day** an action to help sb else that sb (especially a member of the Scout or Guide movement) tries to carry out each day: *On Sunday afternoon he always weeded the garden of the old lady next door. It was his good deed for the day.*

**have (got) a *good* ear for sth** ⟶ ***have* (got) an ear for sth**

***good* egg!** *(slang, old-fashioned)* an expression of delight.

**in *good* faith** sincerely or genuinely: *She recommended him for a job at the bank in good faith and didn't expect that he would steal money from them.* **in bad faith** with insincere intentions.

**a *good* few ((of) sb/sth)** ⟶ **a *good* many ((of) sb/sth)**

***good* for sth** able to last or accomplish (an amount); able to be depended on to provide (sth): *My car is good for a few more years. / He is very rich—good for £50,000.*

***good* for nothing** (of sb) idle, foolish, and bad; (of sth) useless: *A friend of mine says that all foreigners are good for nothing. /* **'good-for-nothing** *n*: *'Their son's old enough to help his father with his work.' 'What? That good-for-nothing?'*

**with (a) *good* grace** showing a willingness but not really wanting to do sth: *He helped his sister with her homework with a good grace, but he'd have preferred to have been playing with his friends.*

***good* gracious/heavens/Lord!** (an expression of surprise or amazement): *Good heavens! It's Suzie Langdon! I've not seen her for years!* Also *(stronger)* **good God!**

***good* grief!** *(informal)* (an exclamation of surprise, dismay, or displeasure; sometimes used with a criticism or objection): *Good grief! How am I going to manage now that I've lost my job?*

**in *good* hands** cared for by capable people: *Don't worry, Jill. Your dogs are in good hands! We'll look after them while you're away.*

**have (got) a *(good)* head for figures** ⟶ ***have***

**have (got) a *(good)* head for heights** ⟶ ***have***

**have had a *good* innings** ⟶ ***have***

**the road to hell is paved with *good* intentions** ⟶ ***road***

**(it's) a *good* job/thing (that)** *(informal)* (it is) lucky or convenient that sth is true, happened etc: *It's a good thing he was here to help us. We couldn't have managed without him. / A good job you came tonight, as we were out last night.*

**you can't keep a *good* man down!** ⟶ ***you***

**a *good* many ((of) sb/sth)** a large or considerable number (of people or things): *We've still a good many replies to receive from our letter.* Also **a good few ((of) sb/sth).**

**have (got) a *good* mind to do sth** ⟶ ***have***

**throw *good* money after bad** ⟶ ***throw***

**the *good* old days** periods in history or in your own life that were, in your opinion, better than the present: *In the good old days you could travel on this route in a steam train!*

**for *good* or ill** whether you think what has happened is satisfactory or not: *For good or ill, she just left home, abandoning her two children—how are they going to live now?*

**take sth in *good*/bad part** ⟶ ***take***

***good* riddance (to bad rubbish)** *(informal)* (an exclamation of relief at having got rid of sb/sth unwanted): *'Mike's leaving on Friday!' 'Good riddance!'*

**give sb a *(good)* run for his money** ⟶ ***give***

**(a) *good* show!** *(becoming old-fashioned)* (a comment on) sth that is a pleasant surprise, lucky, praiseworthy etc: *Everybody put up a good show and can be proud of their efforts.*

**of (*good*, little etc) standing** ⟶ ***standing***

**stand sb in *good* stead** ⟶ ***stand***

**be on to a *good* thing** *(informal)* find a pleasant style of life or occupation: *Dave knows he's on to a good thing, earning that huge salary tax-free!*

**it's a *good* thing (that)** ⟶ **it's a *good* job/thing (that)**

**have a *good* time** ⟶ ***have***

**in *good* time** before an appointed time, so that you can prepare for any difficulties or do sth else: *'What time does the meeting start?' '6 o'clock.' 'OK—I'll be there in good time to get a seat at the front.'*

**do sb a *good*/bad turn** ⟶ ***do***

**(*good*/bad) value for money** ⟶ ***value***

**put in a *good* word for sb** ⟶ ***put***

**(not) have (got) a *good* word to say for sb/sth** ⟶ ***have***

**keep up the *good* work** ⟶ ***keep***

**can say *goodbye* to sth** ⟶ ***say***

**for *goodness'* / God's / heaven's / pity's / Pete's sake** (used to express surprise or annoyance): *He's won, for goodness' sake! / For Pete's sake, leave that thing alone!*

**a wild '*goose* chase** → ***wild***

**kill the *goose* that lays the golden eggs** → ***kill***

**take sth as/for *gospel* (truth)** → ***take***

**be up for *grabs*** *(slang)* able to be obtained/claimed by anyone: *Now that the chairman has resigned, his position is up for grabs.*

**have (got) the *grace* to do sth** → ***have***

**(separate) the *grain* and/from the chaff** → ***(separate)* the chaff and/from the wheat/grain**

**take sth with a *grain*/pinch of salt** → ***take***

**in *grand* style** → **in (great/grand) *style***

**teach one's *grandmother* to suck eggs** → ***teach***

**on/over the *grapevine*** *(informal)* through an unofficial method of passing information or news from one person to another: *I heard on the grapevine that Jack is thinking of leaving the company.*

**(*grasp* an opportunity) with both hands** → **(seize/grasp an opportunity) with *both* hands**

***grasp* at straws** → ***clutch*/grasp/snatch at straws**

***grasp* the nettle** tackle sth, especially a difficult matter, firmly and boldly: *Last time they applied to build a new airport, the application was refused, but the present facilities are so crowded that someone must grasp the nettle soon.*

**(not) let the *grass* grow under one's feet** → ***let***

***grass* roots** a basic level; the popular or natural source from which a movement, especially a political movement, draws its strength: *In those days, there was a lack of contact at the grass roots between the government and the people.* **grass-roots** *adj: a grass-roots movement; grass-roots opinion.*

**turn in one's *grave*** → ***turn***

**the '*gravy* train** *(informal)* an easy way of getting a lot of money and other benefits: *The city with its newly discovered mineral riches was full of people waiting to climb on the gravy train.*

***grease* sb's palm** *(informal)* give sb money to get information from him or to influence his opinion: *'The waiter says all the corner tables are booked.' 'You should have tried greasing his palm.'*

**like *greased* lightning** *(informal)* (of one movement) very fast: *After the phone call, he ran down the stairs like greased lightning, jumped on his bike, and rode off.*

**of (*great*, some, no etc) consequence** → ***consequence***

**a *great* deal (of sth)** → **a *good*/great deal; a *good*/great deal (of sth)**

**go *great* guns** → ***go***

**time is a *great* healer** → ***time***

**go to *great* etc lengths (to do sth)** → ***go***

**go to *great* pains** → ***take* pains (to do sth)**

***great* oaks from little acorns grow** → ***tall*/great/big oaks from little acorns grow**

**no *great* shakes** → ***no***

**set *great* store by sth** → ***set* (no, great, little etc) store by sth**

**in (*great*/grand) style** → ***style***

**the *greatest* thing since sliced bread** *(informal)* sb/sth new or greatly praised: *My husband now uses this glue for all his little repair jobs around the house. He says it's the greatest thing since sliced bread.*

**be (all) *Greek* to sb** → ***all***

**as *green* as grass** inexperienced; naive: *She was as green as grass when she came, but after a few months of sharing a flat with other girls, she began to mature.*

**have (got) *green* fingers** → ***have***

**give sb the *green* light** → ***give***

**little *green* men** → ***little***

***green* with envy** very envious of what sb else has or does: *He turns green with envy every time he sees her talking to someone else.*

**'*grey* matter** mental powers; intelligence; common sense: *Mark's not got much grey matter, but he tries hard.*

**hang/hold on (to sth) like *grim* death** → ***hang***

***grin* and bear it** *(informal)* endure sth unpleasant cheerfully or without complaining: *If your holiday is a disaster, have you any choice but to grin and bear it?*

**wipe the *grin* off sb's/one's face** → ***wipe* the smile/grin off sb's/one's face**

***grin* on the other side of one's face** → ***laugh*/grin/smile on the other side of one's face**

**have an 'axe to *grind*** → ***have***

***grind* to a halt** come to an end or stop working slowly and sometimes noisily: *The machines ground to a halt as the power supply stopped.*

**take a (firm) *grip*/hold on oneself** → ***take***

***grist* to/for the/sb's mill** (of an experience, piece of information etc) useful to sb: *I'm thankful for the help from Peterson's book, which was grist to my own mill when I was writing mine.*

***grit* one's teeth** become determined to do sth difficult or to resist pressure: *When I was a boy I was forced to jump into the water at the swimming baths—I just had to grit my teeth and do it.*

**in(to) a *groove*** → **in(to) a *rut*/groove**

**have (got) both/one's feet on the *ground*** → ***have***

**keep one's ear(s) (close) to the *ground*** → ***keep***

**root sb to the *ground*/spot** → ***root***

**run sb/sth to *ground*** → ***run* sb/sth to earth/ground**

**thin/thick on the *ground*** → ***thin***

**come, get etc in on the *ground* floor** → ***come***

**cut the *ground* from under sb's feet** → ***cut***

***grow* on sb** gradually become more attractive

or appealing to sb: *I didn't like that picture we were given at first, but it's slowly growing on me.*

**money doesn't *grow* on trees** → ***money***

***grow* up** become an adult; act, think, and talk in a mature, sensible way: *Why do you have to behave so foolishly? When will you grow up?* **grown-up** *adj, n*: *When I was young I thought it would be nice to be a grown-up.*

**'*growing* pains** vague aches felt by children; difficulties and problems that occur in the early stages of a new task, activity etc: *The troubles that are affecting the three-year-old republic are more than just growing pains.*

**on/off one's *guard*** prepared/unprepared to face dangers or difficulties: *The prisoners all escaped when the policemen were off their guard.*

**your *guess* is as good as mine** → ***your***

**be my *guest*!** → ***my***

**a *guinea* pig** sb/sth that is used to test sth, for example a new drug or product: *1000 people living in northern England are acting as guinea pigs for research into the common cold.*

**up a *gum* tree** *(slang)* in a very difficult or awkward situation: *What do we do now we've missed the last train back? We're really up a gum tree!*

***gum* up the works** *(informal)* make progress or an activity impossible: *The building was continuing well, but the delay in delivering more bricks has really gummed up the works.*

***gun* for sb** *(informal)* eagerly seek an opportunity to attack or take revenge on sb: *The boss is gunning for people who are lazy and careless. I think he may be gunning for you!*

**have/want sb's *guts* for garters** → ***have***

**have (got) the *guts* to do sth** → ***have***

# H

**one's *hackles* rise** → ***raise* sb's hackles**

**sb *had* better (do sth)** sb ought to do sth: *I'd better see if the baby is all right. / You'd better not try to escape!*

***hail* from sth** have your home in a country or a particular place: *'Where do you hail from?' 'Burma. I was born in Rangoon.'*

**a *hair's* breadth** a very small distance or amount (used when stating that sth is very near): *He escaped death by a hair's breadth—if the other car had been going a bit faster he would certainly have died. / She was within a hair's breadth of winning.* Note that this idiom is always preceded by a preposition.

**sb's '*hair* stands on end** → ***make* sb's 'hair stand on end**

***hale* and hearty** strong and healthy (often used to describe old people): *Being still hale and hearty even in his eighties, my father added to his pension by selling vegetables from his garden.*

**sth and a *half*** *(informal)* sth that is very big, important, or valuable: *Robert is really facing a crisis in his life and has got himself into a mess and a half this time.*

**be too clever etc by *half*** → ***too***

***half* and half** in two equal parts; with an equal amount of two ingredients or feelings: *'Do you like your coffee made with milk or water?' 'Half and half, please.' / 'Are you looking forward to your trip?' 'Half and half really. In some ways I'd like to stay at home, but in other ways I know I'll enjoy it.'*

**be six of one and *half* a dozen of the other** → ***six***

***half* a mo(ment)/tick** *(informal)* (wait) a very short time: *'I'll be with you in half a moment! I've just got a couple more letters to sign.'*

**not *half* be/do sth** → ***not***

**go off at *half* cock** → ***go***

**on the *half*-hour** → **on the *hour*/half-hour**

***half* the battle** an important or the most important part of achieving sth: *When you're ill, wanting to get better is sometimes half the battle.*

***half* the fun, trouble etc of sth** *(informal)* much or a great deal of the enjoyment etc of sth: *Half the pleasure of coming home is to see all the things that have been happening since you left. / 'The department should run well now that they've got a new manager.' 'That's half the trouble; the others want the boss to do all the work and never do anything themselves.'*

***half* the time** *(informal)* very, or too, often: *Do tell me whether you'll be coming home for a meal or not. I don't know where you are half the time.*

**in *half* the time** in a much shorter time than expected: *I don't think much of his woodwork! I could have done the same job in half the time and far better, too!*

**grind to a *halt*** → ***grind***

**a trouble shared is a trouble *halved*** → ***trouble***

**not do sth by *halves*** → ***do***

**go/come under the *hammer*** → ***go***

**go/be at sb/sth *hammer* and tongs** → ***go***

***hammer* sth out** produce an agreement or solution to a problem by long and serious discussion: *Unions and management continued their talks through the night and eventually hammered out a plan to end the strike.*

**at *hand*** near in place or time: *If you have a pen and paper at hand, you can write down the address. / Some people think that the end of the world is at hand.*

**by *hand*** (of a letter etc to be delivered) to be sent by personal messenger rather than through the official postal service; (of an action or process) not using machinery: *The* *letters in the office were marked 'by hand' and it was one of Jack's jobs to deliver them personally. / Several local farmers still milk their cows by hand.*

**eat out of sb's *hand*** → ***eat***

**get out of *hand*** → ***get***

**in *hand*** **1** (the job, task etc) that you are already doing or thinking about: *You have to have a clear mind to tackle the job in hand and not let other things interfere with your work. / Your order is well in hand, sir, and should be ready in a couple of hours.* **2** available for use and in reserve; with time or pay deferred: *The two teams have an equal number of points, but Liverpool have a game in hand. / You pay your rent a week in hand here—you have to pay for two weeks when you begin.*

**off *hand*** without thinking about sth very much: *I can't tell you what last year's sales figures were, off hand—I'll need to check them up.* **off-hand** *adj* not caring or thinking about other people or their feelings: *He has a very off-hand manner.*

**on *hand*** near and available for use, consumption etc: *We've plenty of food on hand if there is a strike.*

**out of *hand*** (of a rejection) immediately and without thinking: *His application was refused out of hand because he had been to prison.* See also ***get* out of hand.**

**to *hand*** within reach; in your possession; readily available: *I don't seem to have my diary to hand at the moment—can I ring you back and make an appointment?*

**wait on sb *hand* and foot** → ***wait***

***hand* sth down/on to** pass sth such as information or skill from one person or generation to a younger or the next one: *The way of making this kind of soup has been handed down from mother to daughter for centuries.*

**have/take a *hand* in (doing) sth** → ***have***

***hand* in hand** (of people) walking, sitting etc next to one another with hands linked as a sign of affection: *The film ends with the happy couple walking hand in hand into the distance.*

**go *hand* in hand (with sth)** → ***go***

***hand* in glove (with sb)** in close co-operation with sb: *Our aim is for the police and army to work hand in glove to maintain order and so make the most efficient use of our resources.*

**put one's *hand* into one's pocket** → ***put***

***hand* it to sb** → ***give*/hand it to sb**

**with one's *hand* on one's heart** very seriously and honestly: *I can tell you, with my hand on my heart, that I've never met him before.*

***hand* sth out** distribute sth; give to different people in turn: *The exam papers were handed out to everyone in the hall. / The government has decided to hand out more money in unemployment pay.* **hand-out** *n* sth distributed such as a gift of money or a leaflet.

***hand* over fist** continuously and quickly (used to describe making profits from business): *Although he only started his business two years ago, he's now making money hand over fist.*

***hand* sb/sth over to sb** give or surrender sb on request or demand to sb such as the police; transfer power or control to sb: *The villagers handed the escaped criminal over to the soldiers. / From next month responsibility for enquiries is being handed over to the Administration Department.*

**bite the *hand* that feeds one** → ***bite***

***hand* to hand** (of fighting) using your own body: *For several minutes they grappled hand to hand on the ground.* **hand-to-hand** *adj: hand-to-hand combat.*

**live (from) *hand* to mouth** → ***live***

***hand* sth to sb on a plate** → ***give*/hand sth to sb on a plate**

**put one's *hand* to the plough** → ***put***

**fly off the *handle*** → ***fly***

***handle* sb/sth with kid gloves** treat sb or a difficult or dangerous situation etc gently, so as not to cause harm, offence, or provocation: *The writers of the book clearly feel that religion is a subject to be handled with kid gloves. The approach is so cautious and one-sided.* **kid-glove** *adj: A kid-glove approach to football violence will gain nothing.*

**at sb's *hands*** (of punishment, blows etc) received from sb: *He had to endure many insults at the hands of his enemies.*

**have (got) sb's blood on one's *hands*** → ***have***

**in sb's *hands*** in the control of sb: *The future of the company now lies in the hands of the government. / I'll leave the matter entirely in your hands.*

**off sb's *hands*** no longer the responsibility of sb: *I'm pleased that, now that the children are off my hands, I've got more time for other things.*

**on sb's *hands*** as the responsibility of sb: *I've enough work on my hands already and don't want any more.*

**out of sb's *hands*** no longer in the control of sb: *I'm afraid the matter has passed out of my hands. You'll have to write to the Area Manager.*

**take the law into one's own *hands*** → ***take***

**time hangs heavy on one's *hands*** → ***time***

**on one's *hands* and knees** with your knees, toes, and hands on the ground: *The tunnel was so low in places that we had to crawl along on our hands and knees.* Also **on all fours.**

**sb's *hands* are clean** → ***have* (got) clean hands**

**win *hands* down** or **beat sb hands down** → ***win***

***hands* off sb/sth** *(informal)* do not touch or interfere with sb/sth; do not criticize sb/sth: *In the demonstration against cuts in money spent on education, several of the banners read, 'Hands off our schools!'*

***hang* about/around** *(informal)* wait or spend your time in a place doing nothing: *Why are you boys hanging around? Shouldn't you be in the classroom?*

***hang*/hold back** (from (doing) sth) be slow, reluctant, or unwilling to do sth, especially because of fear or shyness: *Many companies are holding back from joining the new computer system, to see how many others participate first.*

***hang* by a thread** be in a very uncertain position, especially near to death or ruin: *John's life hung by a thread for several hours, and doctors thought that he wouldn't recover.*

***hang* fire** fail to fire; fail to be carried out and completed because of delay: *Plans to extend the factory had hung fire for years until there were sufficient funds to invest.*

***hang* one's head (for/in shame)** (incline your head forward with a downcast look, especially to avoid the eyes of others because you) feel embarrassed or ashamed: *If I'd been caught reading somebody's private letters I'd be hanging my head in shame, but according to him it's all a huge joke.*

***hang* it (all)!** ⟶ ***damn* (it (all))!**

***hang*/hold on 1** persist or survive; continue to do something or live: *Their food was getting low, but the explorers just managed to hang on until fresh supplies came.* **2** *(informal)* remain, stop, or wait in a place: *Hang on a moment, can you? I must just collect the keys.*

***hang*/hold on (to sth) like grim death** *(informal)* hold on (to sth) very firmly: *As the horse galloped off, you could see poor Sarah hanging on like grim death. / During his innings, Smith slashed one a long way off. It hit Evans right in the stomach, who fell backwards but hung on to the ball like grim death.*

***hang* on sb's lips/words** listen to sb's words with much devoted attention: *The loyal followers hung on their leader's every word.*

***hang* on to sth** hold sth firmly: *The latest television channel is trying hard to hang on to its newly won share of the audience.*

**let it all *hang* out** ⟶ ***let***

***hang* over sb** or **hang over sb's head** be likely to occur to sb: *With the threat of redundancy hanging over the workers* (or *over the workers' heads*)*, this Christmas is unlikely to be a happy one.* Note that this is used in continuous tenses.

***hang* together** have a natural, logical development or link and so form a complete whole or pattern: *I don't think his two statements hang together very well; what he said today is different from what he told us yesterday.*

***hang* up (on sb)** replace the telephone receiver, sometimes in anger and to end the conversation with sb rudely: *She wouldn't let me say that I was sorry—she hung up on me.*

***hang* up one's boots** retire; stop doing your work because you are too old; *I don't think I ever want to hang up my boots—I'm too happy here.*

**I'll be *hanged* if . . .** ⟶ **I'll be *blowed*/damned/hanged if . . .**

**(and/but) thereby *hangs* a tale** ⟶ ***thereby***

**worse/stranger things *happen* at sea** ⟶ ***worse***

**if anything *happens* to sb** ⟶ ***anything***

**(not) *happy* about sth** (not) satisfied with sth: *I'm not happy about leaving little David with a baby-sitter. He hasn't got used to other people yet.*

**as *happy* as a sandboy/king** very happy: *Grandpa's as happy as a sandboy helping the children to fly their kites!*

**a/the *happy* medium** a balance between two things, either of which would be too much by itself: *It can be difficult to strike a happy medium in friendships—you want to get close to people, but not so close that they think you have sexual intentions.*

**many *happy* returns (of the day)** ⟶ ***many***

***hard* and fast 1** (of regulations or categories) fixed and unchanging: *The book gives no hard-and-fast rules about how to start your own business but provides some useful thoughts to set you thinking.* **2** firmly; not able to be moved: *The ice began to melt but it soon got colder again and the ship was stuck hard and fast.*

**as *hard* as iron/steel** physically, mentally, or morally strong: *The school's discipline and academic standards rose greatly while Mr Chester was headmaster. He was a just man, as hard as steel.*

**as *hard* as nails** tough; with great physical energy; ruthless in your dealings with other people: *My stepfather may be ignorant but he's as hard as nails and sly, too.*

**as *hard* as stone/rock/iron** (of ground) very firm; (of sb) having no feelings: *In this cold weather, the earth's as hard as rock. / You'd have a heart as hard as stone not to be moved by his sad story.*

**drive a *hard* bargain** ⟶ ***drive***

***hard* by sth** *(old-fashioned)* situated very close to sth: *Near to the old railway station, hard by the canal, stands a monument to those who died in the war.*

**a *hard* case 1** sb with a harsh, unsympathetic character; sb who has lived a criminal life for many years: *She may turn into a hard case unless someone gives her a loving home very soon.* **2** (sb in) very sad or difficult circumstances: *She was a real hard case—her husband left her years ago and she's brought up four children by herself—I don't know how she's managed.*

***hard* cash** coins and notes, in contrast to cheques or credit cards: *I don't carry that much money on me—not in hard cash. Will you take a cheque?*

***hard* cheese/cheddar** *(slang, old-fashioned)* (an expression showing sympathy, either sincerely or more usually ironically): *'I failed the driving test again!' 'Oh, hard cheese—what did you drive into this time?'*

**the *hard* core (of sth)** the solid, firm, or permanent part of sth: *I'm not sure how many people will come to tonight's meeting, but I* *know we can always rely on the hard core of about 20 of our most committed people.*

***hard* done by** *(informal)* unfairly treated: *I'm afraid you've been rather hard done by—I think someone should come and help you.*

**no *hard* feelings** ⟶ ***no***

**have (got) a *(hard)* job to do sth** ⟶ ***have***

***hard* luck/lines!** ⟶ ***bad*/hard/tough luck!**

**a *hard* 'luck story** a series of events told by sb who wants money, sympathy, or help for himself: *An old chap came to the door and told us some hard luck story, but you could tell he only wanted some money for drink.*

**a *hard*/tough nut to crack** *(informal)* a difficult problem; sb who is very difficult to deal with: *You can try to get him to change his mind, but you'll find him a hard nut to crack.*

***hard* of hearing** deaf: *Your uncle has become rather hard of hearing recently—you'll have to speak more loudly. / The television programme is specially designed for the hard of hearing and has sub-titles.*

**be *hard* on sb** deal with sb strictly or harshly: *I don't like to be hard on old people, but we'll soon have to stop Mrs Smith playing the piano at the social evenings and let one of the younger ladies take her place.*

**be *hard*/close on/upon sb's heels** come immediately or soon after sb/sth in time, prizes etc: *America won the first prize as usual but the Europeans were close on their heels this year.*

***hard* put (to it) to do sth** or **hard pressed to do sth** able to do sth only with great difficulty: *I'd be hard put to it to name all the countries in Africa.*

**the *hard*/soft sell** *(informal)* a sales technique by which the seller forcefully or only indirectly states a product's advantages.

**the *hard* stuff** *(informal)* a drink which contains a lot of alcohol, such as whisky.

**give sb a *hard* time** or **have a hard time** ⟶ ***give***

**fall on *hard* times** ⟶ ***fall***

**play *hard* to get** ⟶ ***play***

***hard* up** poor: *In those days we were so hard up that meat was a real luxury.*

**the *hard* way** the most difficult method of doing, learning, or discovering sth: *I mastered French the hard way—seven years at school in which I learnt almost nothing and then a year in France, when I really picked up a lot.*

***hark* back (to sth)** return to sth that was said or done earlier: *My grandparents loved to hark back to the days when everything was so cheap.*

**not *harm* a fly** ⟶ **not *hurt*/harm a fly**

**out of *harm's* way** safe from causing injury, accident, loss, or misuse: *Most people think that dangerous criminals should be locked up out of harm's way.*

***harp* on (about sb/sth)** *(informal)* mention sth or criticize sb very often so that this causes annoyance: *Why do you have to harp on about the past all the time? Can't you forget old quarrels and face the future?*

**rumour, tradition etc *has* it that . . .** according to rumour etc, it is thought that sth is true: *Local gossip has it that she is expecting a baby.*

**make a *hash* of (doing) sth** ⟶ ***make* a mess/hash of (doing) sth**

**keep sth under one's *hat*** ⟶ ***keep***

**talk through one's *hat*** ⟶ ***talk***

**one's *hat* goes off to sb** ⟶ ***take* one's hat off to sb**

**pass the '*hat* round** ⟶ ***pass***

**a '*hat* trick** gaining three wins, points etc one after the other.

**a '*hatchet* man/job** sb/sth employed to reduce expenditure and especially the number of workers; sb/sth used to attack and criticize opposition: *Politicians see Mr Dowding as the best man to do the hatchet job on the department that the Prime Minister wants.*

***hate* sb's guts** *(informal)* loathe sb very strongly: *I hate your guts, Pete. I never want to see you again!*

***haul* sb over the coals** *(informal)* criticize sb very strongly: *I think we'll be hauled over the coals yet again by the boss for something that isn't our fault at all.*

***have* (oneself) a ball** *(informal)* enjoy yourself very much: *There were only three girls in a class of 27, so they really had a ball!*

***have* a bash (at (doing) sth)** = have a go (at (doing) sth): *I want to have a bash at learning German.*

**not *(have)* a bean** *(informal)* (have) no money at all (with you): *'How much of your pocket money have you got left?' 'Not a bean.' / He arrived home without a bean.*

***have* a, no, some etc bearing on/upon sth** influence; have relevance or a significant effect on sth: *His involvement has no bearing on the matter. If he wasn't there, I still wouldn't join in.*

***have* (got) a bee in one's bonnet (about sth)** *(informal)* have an obsession about sth; be eccentric or slightly insane (about a particular idea or attitude): *Uncle Tom's always opening windows or wanting them opened. He's got a bee in his bonnet about fresh air. / It's not only cranks with bees in their bonnets that are worried about the dangers of nuclear energy.*

***have* a bellyful (of sb/sth)** *(slang)* have as much as, or more than, you want of sth or of sb's company or behaviour: *Tell her I'm not in. I've had a bellyful of that woman and her complaints! / If John's really fond of rock he'll get a bellyful tonight. I believe the performance will last four hours.*

***have* (got) a bone to pick with sb** *(informal)* have sth that you want to complain to sb about: *Ah, there you are, Geoff! I've a bone to pick with you! About last Thursday—why didn't you say anything to me when I saw you in the street?*

***have* (got) a 'bun in the oven** *(slang, old-fashioned)* be pregnant: *She hasn't said so but she's got a bun in the oven, I guess.*

***have*** **a care!** *(old-fashioned)* please be more careful!: *Have a care, Jack! You almost knocked over that vase!*
**(not)** ***have*** **(got) a cat in 'hell's chance (of doing sth)** *(informal)* have (no) chance, hope, or likelihood of doing or obtaining sth: *In that old car he hasn't a cat in hell's chance of overtaking us.* Alternatives to ***a cat in hell's chance*** are ***a chance/hope in hell; a 'ghost of a chance; a 'dog's chance; an earthly (chance).***
***have*** **(got) a 'chip on one's shoulder** believe that people undervalue you or are prejudiced against you because of sth such as a physical handicap or lack of education, leading to you becoming resentful or defiant: *He seems no longer to have a chip on his shoulder that he once had about being adopted.*
***have*** **(got) a clear head** be able to think clearly, either as a characteristic or because you are not affected by tiredness, alcohol etc: *I must have a clear head for the exams—that's why I try to get lots of sleep.*
***have*** **(got) a closed mind (on sth)** be unwilling to think about or accept new ideas or opinions: *He firmly believes in evolution and has a closed mind on other views.*
**not** ***have*** **(got) a clue (about sth)** *(informal)* not know (about) or understand sth at all; lack ability or common sense generally: *'What's the name of that shrub?' 'I haven't a clue.' / She operates the machine but hasn't a clue about how it works.* Also **be clueless (about sth):** *It's a waste of time trying to teach them. They're the most clueless group of students I've ever come across.*
***have*** **(got) a corner in sth** or **make a corner in sth** have a monopoly in an article of trade etc; have (nearly) exclusive rights in sth, an exclusive talent, or the ability to do sth: *'Nobody likes her but she's too valuable to the firm to be got rid of.' 'Rubbish! She hasn't got a corner in her particular expertise. You could find somebody else.' / Since his TV success in* Police *he seems to have made a corner (for himself) in detective roles.*
***have*** **a crack at (doing) sth** *(informal)* = have a go (at (doing) sth): *'Why don't you let me have a crack at selling some of these things? I'm sure I could do better than you!'*
***have*** **(got) a crush on sb** *(informal)* (imagine yourself to) be in love with sb or infatuated by sb (usually used of young people): *Yes, I remember Sybil—used to be in Accounting. I had quite a crush on her for a while.*
***have*** **(got) a familiar ring (about/to it)** sound as if it is already known to you: *That tune has a familiar ring about it! Isn't it the one we kept hearing on holiday last year?*
***have*** **(got) a finger in every/the pie** *(informal)* take part in the planning or completion of many tasks or a task etc (often used to imply that this is really none of your concern): *Poor Aunty Lucy! If she really has to have a finger in every pie, then let her sell the tickets for the party as well! / Pete's got a finger in too many pies and will have to work out how to spend his time.*
***have*** **a/one's fling** *(informal)* enjoy a period of extravagant, unlimited pleasure: *Sandra spent a weekend in Paris a few months before getting married—having a final fling. / Go on—let him have his fling. You're only young once, after all!*
***have*** **(got) a foot in both camps** or **keep a foot in both camps** *(informal)* (be) involved with two separate groups etc that have different ideas: *Don't you see you can't have a foot in both camps? You can't be a moderate and an extremist at the same time!*
***have*** **(got) a 'frog in one's throat** *(informal)* lose the ability to speak, or be able to speak with only a rough voice, for example because you have catarrh: *He began to speak, but it was with a husky, croaking voice: 'I'm sorry, I seem to have a frog in my throat this morning.'*
***have*** **a go (at (doing) sth)** *(informal)* make an attempt to do, win, or achieve sth: *I'm sure I could do it better than that. Let me have a go! / I've got the time so I don't mind having a go at redecorating the house myself. / The police have warned the public against having a go and tackling suspected criminals by themselves.*
***have*** **a go at sb** *(informal)* tease or provoke sb: *The children always seem to enjoy having a go at their teacher.*
***have*** **(got) a good ear for sth** ⟶ ***have*** **(got) an ear for sth**
***have*** **(got) a good mind to do sth** intend to do sth definite or forceful: *I've a good mind to leave you after the way you've treated me.* Also **have (got) half a mind to do sth.**
***have*** **a good time** *(informal)* enjoy yourself, generally, or at a party, on holiday etc: *'Have a good time!' he shouted, as the train pulled out. / When they were younger, their one aim in life was to have a good time on a Saturday evening. / The whole dinner-party went well. People relaxed and mixed well. In fact, a good time was had by all.*
**(not)** ***have*** **(got) a good word to say for sb/sth** dislike or condemn sb/sth completely: *He's not a good word to say for his boss.*
***have*/take a hand in (doing) sth** play a part in an action: *We believe all three of you had a hand in planning the robbery. Now come on, confess it.*
***have*** **a hard time** ⟶ ***give*** **sb a hard time**
***have*** **(got) a (good) head for figures** be clever at arithmetic and calculations: *Dick doesn't need a calculator—he's got a good head for figures already.*
***have*** **(got) a (good) head for heights** be able to stand on a high place without feeling giddy or afraid: *I'm sorry, I've not got a good head for heights. You two go up and I'll stay down here.*
***have*** **(got) a head start** have definite advantages over other people such as competitors: *Being the son of a lawyer gives Mike a head start on the law course.*

***have* (got) a heart of gold** have a very kind and helpful nature: *He has a rough, even unpleasant exterior, but inside, he's got a heart of gold.*

***have* (got) a heart of stone** have a hard, unfeeling, callous nature: *I've never met anyone so pitiless—she's got a real heart of stone.*

***have* (got) a (hard) job to do sth** or **have (got) a (hard) job doing sth** do sth only with great difficulty: *Despite earlier forecasts, it looks as if the government will have a hard job keeping inflation below 5% this year.*

**not *have* (got) a leg to stand on** *(informal)* have no convincing reasons to give to defend or support sb/sth: *Four people say they saw him breaking into the house—so that shows he doesn't have a leg to stand on.*

***have* (got) a lump in one's throat** feel a blockage in your throat caused by strong emotions: *I had quite a lump in my throat as I watched her step off the ship and walk down the gangway to meet me.*

***have* (got) a memory like a sieve** *(informal)* lack the ability to absorb and retain information: *I wouldn't depend on John—he's got a memory like a sieve and has probably forgotten that you ever arranged to meet.*

***have* (got) a mind of one's own** be able to think and decide for yourself: *Stop telling me what I ought to do—I've got a mind of my own!*

**(not) *have* (got) a minute/moment to call one's own** have (no) time to do things that you want to do, especially things that are not work: *As a busy mother of six, she scarcely has a minute to call her own.*

***have* (got) a nerve** *(informal)* be bold or presumptuous in doing sth: *He's got a nerve—using our photocopier when there's one outside his own room!*

***have* (got) a nose for sth** *(informal)* be able to detect sth: *A newspaper reporter must be someone with a good nose for stories with human interest.*

***have* (got) a one-track mind** *(informal)* think about only one subject: *Some people in the electronics club have got a one-track mind. They live and breathe computers all the time!*

***have* (got) a point (there)** say sth in a discussion that is valid and difficult to deny: *You've got a point there. If everyone wanted six children, there'd just not be the room.* Also **have (got) something (there).**

***have* a 'rain check (for/on sth)** ⟶ ***take*/have a 'rain check (for/on sth)**

***have* (got) a screw loose/missing** *(informal)* be slightly mad: *Some people think he's got a screw loose, but he seems harmless to me.*

***have* (got) a second 'string to one's bow** have a second person, commodity, skill etc available as an alternative to a first: *He's mainly an actor, but he does some writing to have a second string to his bow.* Also **have (got) two 'strings to one's bow.**

**not *have* (got) a stitch on (one)** be naked.

**not *have* (got) a stitch/thing to wear** not have enough clothes or not have the clothes you need or want for a particular occasion.

***have* (got) a thing about sb/sth** *(informal)* think and talk a lot about sb/sth; feel strongly about sb/sth: *He's got a thing about blondes. / Mum's got a thing about keeping your shoes clean—she thinks that if people do this then they must be OK.*

***have* (got) a way with sb/sth** be able to treat or deal with sb/sth well: *Julie's certainly got a way with children—they really respond to her care.*

***have* a word with sb** speak to sb to make an enquiry, seek advice, etc: *May I have a word with you, please, James? It's about Maggie—I need your help.*

**not *have* (got) all one's marbles** ⟶ ***lose* one's marbles**

***have* all the answers** ⟶ ***know*/have all the answers**

***have* an 'axe to grind** have an interest or purpose of your own, usually a selfish one, in helping sb, supporting a cause, or accepting public office: *Having no particular political axe to grind, I am standing for election as an Independent. / Only those local people with axes to grind, like building contractors, were in favour of a large military base in the area.* Note that this is usually used in the negative.

***have* (got) an ear for sth** be able to appreciate sth, such as music: *It goes without saying that if you want to be a conductor you must have an ear for music.* Also **have (got) a good ear for sth.**

***have* (got) an/the edge on/over sb/sth** have an advantage over sb/sth: *Max's design is good, but I think Paul has the edge on him* (or *Paul's has a slight edge over his*). **give sb an/the edge (on/over sb/sth)** give sb an advantage (over sb/sth): *Her experience gives her that extra edge over the other girls being interviewed.*

***have* (got) an eye for sth** be able to appreciate sth such as a beautiful picture: *I'm afraid I've not got much of an eye for wallpaper designs.*

***have* (got) an/one's eye on sb/sth** or **keep an/one's eye on sb/sth** watch sb/sth closely, especially in order to take some action: *A cottage that I'd had my eye on for some time was suddenly up for sale. / We've had our eyes* (or *We've kept a careful eye*) *on you for a while, now, Smith, and we've caught you red-handed this time. / The committee's authority extends to keeping an eye on how the money is spent.* Also **keep a close eye on sb/sth.** See also ***have*/keep one eye on sb/sth.**

***have* (got) an eye to/on/for the main chance** do sth concentrating on your own interests or what you think will be profitable.

***have* (got) an idea (that . . . )** think or know that sth is true or may happen: *I've an idea that he's not telling us what really took place. /*

*'Do you think she'll go back to him?' 'I've no idea.'*

***have* (got) an idea of sth** have an impression or understanding of sth: *Now that you've found the cause of the problem you should have an idea of how to solve it.*

***have* (got) an open mind (on sth)** be willing or able to think about or accept new ideas or opinions: *I've got an open mind when it comes to music. I like all different kinds.*

***have* (got) ants in one's pants** *(slang)* be restless; be unable to settle because you are anxious or excited about sth: *There's two hours to go before the play begins, and you've got ants in your pants already!*

***have* (got) one's back to the wall** be unable to retreat or escape from a difficult or dangerous situation; be forced to defend yourself, obtain help, or surrender: *We had known poverty before, but now, in a foreign country without friends or money, we really had our backs to the wall.*

***have* (got) bats in the belfry** *(informal)* be mad or eccentric: *He's not the only one in the family who has (or with) bats in the belfry.*

***have* been around** *(informal)* have had a wide experience of life, especially of social or worldly matters: *The new managing director is only 35, but he's certainly been around.*

***have* sb's blessing for sb/sth** ⟶ ***give* sb/sth one's blessing**

***have* (got) sb's blood on one's hands** be responsible for sb's death: *The General has the blood of the innocent hostages on his hands, as he gave the order for them to be killed.*

***have* (got) both/one's feet on the ground** *(informal)* have common sense; not be likely to do foolish, rash, or dangerous things: *Why are all your girlfriends so dreamy? Can't you find somebody who's got both feet on the ground?*

***have* (got) butterflies (in one's stomach/ tummy)** *(informal)* feel nervous and perhaps slightly sick with anxious excitement: *Even after 20 years as an actor I still have butterflies before going on stage.*

**(can't) *have* one's cake and eat it** *(informal)* (can't) enjoy two benefits, one of which normally excludes the other: *'I'll be broke for months after all this!' 'Well, you're having a fine holiday. You can't have your cake and eat it.'*

***have* carte blanche** ⟶ ***give* sb carte blanche**

***have* (got) clean hands** have committed no crime, done no wrong, or caused no harm: *No country in history has ever had completely clean hands.* Also **sb's hands are clean:** *My hands are clean—you can't blame anything on me.*

***have* (got) cold feet** ⟶ ***get* cold feet**

***have* (got) sb/sth covered** have sb or a place in the direct line of fire from a pistol, gun etc or within the range of a telescope, camera etc: *You will see that I've got you covered. So don't move or I'll shoot!*

***have* (got) sth coming (to one)** *(informal)* be about to experience sth such as a reward, surprise, or punishment: *He's got a shock coming to him when he takes the exams and sees how difficult they are.*

***have* sth coming out at/of one's ears** *(informal)* (a supposed result of consuming or working with sth to excess): *Our kids would eat ice-cream till it came out of their ears if you let them!*

***have* one's day** be important, successful, or useful for a short time only: *The canals of this country have had their day, I'm afraid—they cost too much to maintain. / It looks as if those shoes you're wearing have had their day.*

***have* (got) designs on/upon sb/sth** *(informal)* want to take, win, or control sth such as a position in a company or sb of the opposite sex: *You'd better watch out, Mike. I think Pete's got designs on your job! / He looks as if he has designs on Jackie, that new girl in the office.*

***have* (got) sb's ear** ⟶ ***gain*/get/win sb's ear**

**walls *have* ears** ⟶ ***walls***

***have* egg on one's face** *(informal)* be shown to be foolish: *If I turn up for the rehearsal and find that there isn't one, I'll have egg on my face, won't I? / Let's think this out carefully—I don't want to end up with egg on my face!*

***have* (got) enough etc on one's plate** *(informal)* have enough etc that you are responsible for: *I don't want any extra work, thank you. I've got enough on my plate already.*

***have* (got) everything going for one** *(informal)* have everything working in your/its favour; be extremely lucky in respect of circumstances or opportunities: *I don't believe it was suicide. Why would a young chap of 25 with everything going for him do a thing like that? / All the social and economic pressures support us, while your country has nothing going for it except strong national feelings.*

***have* (got) eyes in the back of one's head** *(informal)* seem to be able to see all around you and know what is going on: *If you ask me, you've got to have eyes in the back of your head to make sure that Pete doesn't get up to anything.*

***have* (got) one's finger on the pulse (of sth)** or **keep one's finger on the pulse (of sth)** *(informal)* have an up-to-date knowledge of sth; be fully aware of sth: *A successful politician is one who keeps his finger on the pulse of the changing mood of the voters.*

***have* one's 'fingers burnt** ⟶ ***burn* one's fingers**

***have* (got) one's fingers in the till** *(informal)* steal, especially small amounts of money, from the shop or small business where you work: *The report says that an alarming proportion of shop assistants have their fingers in the till.*

***have* (got) (the) first refusal** be given the opportunity to buy sth before it is offered generally or to other people: *A trusted friend* *of mine has the first refusal. If he doesn't want it, I'll let you know.*

***have*** **(got) one's/a foot in the door** or **get one's/a foot in the door** have gained or gain a first introduction to an organisation, action etc, especially where this is difficult: *Don't you see that if I can just get a foot in the door of the company they'll begin to take some notice of me?*

**(can)** ***have*****/get sth for the asking** (can) obtain sth, simply by asking for it, without payment or persuasion: *If you know anyone who wants an old piano they can have it (or it's theirs) for the asking.* Also **be sb's for the asking.**

***have*** **(got) green fingers** be able to grow flowers, plants etc successfully; be a good gardener: *Potted plants always die on me. I'm afraid I've not got green fingers.*

***have*** **got sb/sth taped** *(informal)* know all about sb/sth and often also be able to influence or control sb/sth: *I've certainly got June taped. I know where she is at every hour of the day and night.*

***have*****/want sb's guts for garters** *(informal)* scold sb severely; defeat sb soundly in a fight or argument: *It's the boss's car, not mine. She'd have my guts for garters if she knew I'd lent it to you last night.*

***have*** **had a few** *(informal)* have had too much to drink: *He always feels merry after he's had a few.*

***have*** **had a good innings** *(informal)* have lived for a long time or enjoyed a period of fame, power etc: *'How old was Jack?' '87. He'd had a good innings. It was only a pity he had to die as he did.'*

***have*** **had one's chips** *(slang, becoming old-fashioned)* be dying or dead; suffer a great loss in your reputation or position: *Old Mac's had his chips, I fear. He was very rude to his boss last week, and he's leaving on Friday.*

***have*** **had enough (of sb/sth)** not be able to bear any more of sb/sth: *I've had enough! I'm going home! / We've had enough of this talk of failure. You're going out there to win!* Also **have had one's fill (of sb/sth):** *If you've had your fill of this sort of music, we could ask to hear something different.*

***have*** **had it** *(informal)* have come to the end of your life or career; be unable or unwilling to continue an activity or relationship: *I've had it with your kind of people. You make promises about contracts, but I know nothing will happen.*

***have*** **(got) half a mind to do sth** → ***have*** **(got) a good mind to do sth**

***have*** **(got) one's hands full** be extremely busy: *I've got my hands full looking after four children, helping at the social club on Tuesdays and Fridays, and working with the youth group on Saturdays.*

***have*** **(got) one's hands tied** be unable to do sth because of your responsibilities or obligations: *I'm sorry I can't help you, but I've got my hands tied. I can only suggest you contact the Area Manager who might be able to give you some advice.*

***have*** **(got) one's head in the clouds** *(informal)* live in an unreal, dream-like world; be out of touch with reality and think about other things: *Gill doesn't seem to know what's happening around her and has her head in the clouds most of the time.*

***have*** **(got) one's head screwed on the right way** *(informal)* be sensible, generally or in particular matters: *You can certainly trust Bob with your money. He's got his head screwed on the right way and won't go round wasting it.*

***have*** **(got) high hopes** expect much; be optimistic and ambitious in your expectations: *We've got high hopes of winning the contract—we've spent a lot of time and money on research into the market. / The new students came to university with high hopes.*

***have*** **sth in common (with sb/sth)** have interests, qualities, or characteristics that are shared by other people or things: *Come and meet my cousins, Professor Moore. I'm sure you'll find you have a lot in common. / What do guinea-pigs have in common with human beings that makes them suitable subjects for medical experiments?*

***have*** **(got) sb/sth in mind** think about sb/sth such as an idea or answer: *It's dangerous to discuss with others secret plans that you have in mind. / I had it in mind to warn you about the machines.*

***have*** **(got) itchy feet** *(informal)* want to leave somewhere or a job; want to travel: *I've got itchy feet. I've been here for two years, and I think it's time to move to a better job.*

***have*** **(got) it badly** *(informal)* be very enthusiastic about sb/sth, especially be in love: *Pete's got it badly this time: it's that girl he met in Brighton!*

***have*** **it/things both ways** combine two opposite ways of thinking or behaving; satisfy two opposite demands: *You can't have it both ways—either you can be a career woman or you can be a mother.* Also **want it both ways.**

***have*** **(got) it in for sb** *(informal)* want to make trouble for sb in a determined way: *Some people think that the police have got it in for all foreigners.*

***have*** **(got) it made** *(informal)* continue to be successful: *With three outstanding bestsellers in the market, this excellent author really looks as if he's got it made.*

***have*** **it off/away (with sb)** *(slang)* have sexual intercourse (with sb), especially secretly: *She discovered that on her husband's so-called business trips he was having it off with different women.*

***have*** **kittens** *(informal)* be alarmed, surprised, and worried: *The film is about a young teenage couple—the girl excited and happy and the boy having kittens at the thought of being a dad.*

***have*** **(got) (too) many etc irons in the fire** have (too) many etc interests, activities etc at the same time, hoping that one will be successful: *One of the firms I applied for a job with rejected my application, but I've still got a few other irons in the fire.*

***have* (got) mixed feelings (about sb/sth)** think in two opposite ways about sb/sth: *I've got mixed feelings about leaving college—I love it there, but I also know I've got to start a job.*

***have* (got) money to burn** *(informal)* have so much money that you can spend it freely.

***have* (got) more money than sense** *(informal)* spend your money foolishly: *You had more money than sense when you bought that white raincoat. It's always having to be cleaned.*

***have* (got) more than one's fair share of sth** have more than a usual or expected amount of sth: *This cat is so beautiful—it certainly seems to have got more than its fair share of charm!* See also **a/one's *fair* share of sth.**

***have* (got) no business doing sth** or **have (got) no business to do sth** do sth that is not your duty or responsibility by right: *You've got no business going into his office and talking to him like that!*

***have* (got) no, less, more etc call for sth** have no etc need or good use for sth: *Sell or give away any tools you've no call for now.* Also **there is no call for sth:** *'Don't apologize,' said the lawyer. 'If everybody could manage their own affairs there wouldn't be much call for people like me.'*

***have* (got) no, less, more etc call to do sth** have no etc reason or justification for doing sth: *I was perfectly polite—they had no call to take offence.* Also **there is no etc call (for sb) to do sth:** *The children will be quite safe. There's no call for you to worry.*

***have* (got) no time for sb/sth** mock or ridicule sb/sth; consider that spending your time on sb/sth is wasted: *He's got no time for beginners like us, now that he's passed all the exams—he thinks he's superior to us.*

***have* (got) no time to lose** need to hurry in order to do sth or prevent sth happening: *We've no time to lose! If we want to catch the 7 o'clock train, we'd better pack now.*

***have* no truck (with sb/sth)** *(informal)* not want to be concerned with, accept, or recognize sb/sth at all: *The college students seem to think they're superior and don't want to have any truck (or they want no truck) with the local people.*

***have* none of it** refuse to do, become involved in, or agree to sth: *Of course we all knew that a vote would have settled the argument, but Mr Peterson, the chairman, would have none of it.* Note that ***will/would*** is often used with this idiom.

***have* (got) one's nose in a book** *(informal)* be often reading a book: *Jane's studying again! She's always got her nose in a book.*

***have* (got) nothing better to do (than do sth)** be unable to fill your time in a more worthwhile way than an activity that is mentioned: *I had nothing better to do than go along to the meeting.* Variations on this idiom are **for want of anything better to do (than); have better things to do (than); have something better to do (than):** *Some of our youngsters play havoc on the streets for want of anything better to do.*

***have* occasion to do sth** *(formal)* need or find it suitable or convenient to do sth: *We were so preoccupied that we had* (or *there was*) *little occasion to write letters.*

***have* sb on** *(informal)* deceive or trick sb: *Oh Martha! It was just a joke! Grandpa was only having you on!*

***have* (got) sth on sb** *(informal)* have reason or evidence to suggest that sb is to blame: *They left no fingerprints to make sure that the police won't have anything on them.*

***have* (got) sb/sth on the brain** *(informal)* think and talk a lot or too much about sb/sth: *Oh, you! You've got work on the brain. Can't you talk about anything else?*

***have* sb on the carpet** ⟶**be on the *carpet***

***have* (got) sth on the go** have sth happening at the time: *He's becoming a famous lecturer and is often invited to give talks on different subjects, so he always has some lecture on the go.*

**(*have*/keep) one eye on sb/sth** (give) part of your attention to sb/sth while doing sth else: *It isn't easy to keep one eye on a toddler and try to do the housework at the same time.* See also ***have* (got) an/one's eye on sb/sth.**

***have* (got) one foot in the grave** or **with one foot in the grave** *(informal)* (be) so old or ill that you probably will not live much longer: *'Who lives in that small room next door?' 'Some old age pensioner—he's so quiet and lonely—totally forgotten by friends and relatives, with one foot in the grave.'*

***have* one over the eight** *(informal)* have too much to drink: *From the way's he trying to walk, it's obvious he's had one over the eight.*

***have* only (got) oneself to blame/thank** be solely responsible for sth unpleasant which happens to you, because of your own mistake or faults of character: *They sent our soldiers into battle with old equipment—so they've only got themselves to blame for the number of disastrous accidents that happened.*

***have* only (got) sb's word for sth** have only what sb says or promises without having other evidence, written proof etc: *We've only got your word for it that you were driving back from the club at 11 o'clock last night.*

***have* (got) other/bigger fish to fry** *(informal)* have more important, interesting, or advantageous things to do than sth mentioned or suggested: *So you're leaving the project, are you? You've got other fish to fry, no doubt.*

***have* (got) sb over a barrel** *(informal)* put sb in such a difficult position that you can get what you want from him: *The rich oil countries have got many governments over a barrel* *and can tell them what prices they're going to charge.*

**have sth out (with sb)** *(informal)* discuss a matter openly and often angrily with sb, until understanding or agreement is reached: *I'd been annoyed with Pat for days so I finally decided to have it 'out with her. / Isn't it time we had the whole matter out?*

**(have (got)) pins and needles** (have) a prickling feeling in a part of the body when blood flows through it normally again after being stopped by pressure: *I found I'd been sitting on my hand and couldn't write for a bit because I'd got pins and needles.*

**have one's say** be allowed to express your opinion: *One of the principles of a democracy is that everyone can have their say.*

**have (got) something (there)** → ***have* (got) a point (there)**

**have (got) something, nothing etc to lose** risk losing money, your reputation etc by doing sth: *I've got nothing to lose, so I think I'll make contact with your friends in Germany when I go over there.*

**have (got) something etc to say for oneself** be able to explain your behaviour on a particular occasion; talk: *Come on, what were you doing at the factory gates at midnight? What have you got to say for yourself?*

**have (got) something etc to show for it** have real proof of sth or gain or profit from sth: *I spent six hours reading books for the essay but still had very little to show for it.*

**have something to think about** → ***give* sb something to think about**

**have (got) one's tail down/up** *(informal)* be sad and worried or happy and confident: *The team won the semi-final 6–0 and have their tails up for the final.*

**have the advantage of sb** *(formal)* know sth that sb else does not: *'His unfortunate experience at Exeter has made David extremely wary.' 'You have the advantage of me, I'm sorry. Please explain.'*

**have (got) the ball at one's feet** *(informal)* be in a position, and have the means, to succeed: *With their first record in the charts and contracts on both sides of the Atlantic, this group must feel that they now have the ball at their feet.*

**have (got) the best/worst of sth** profit/suffer most from sth: *Of all the countries in the trade agreement, many people think we have the worst of it.*

**have (got) the courage of one's convictions** be brave enough to do or say what you know or believe to be right: *You may not agree with the Prime Minister's economic policy, but at least he has one, and the courage of his convictions as well.*

**have (got) the devil's own luck** be exceptionally fortunate: *He raised his rifle and shot. He'd the devil's own luck and scored a bulls-eye!* Also **have (got) the luck of the devil.**

**not have (got) the foggiest (idea)** *(informal)* have no idea at all about sth: *I haven't got the foggiest idea what to buy Roger for his birthday. / 'Where are we?' 'I haven't the foggiest.'* Alternatives to ***foggiest*** are ***faintest; first; least; slightest.***

**have (got) the grace to do sth** have a sense of what is fitting, polite, or thoughtful and do it: *Fortunately, after the politician's love affair was discovered, he had the grace to resign immediately.* Alternatives to **grace** are: ***courtesy; (good) manners; (common) decency.***

**have (got) the guts to do sth** *(informal)* have enough courage or strength to do sth: *Only a few people have got the guts not to give up when everything is going badly.*

**(not) have (got) the heart to do sth** (not) be willing or able to do sth which could hurt sb else: *I didn't have the heart not to refund the money. He seemed so helpless.*

**have (got) the jitters/shakes/willies** *(informal)* be in a nervous, unsettled state, especially when waiting for or enduring some difficult time: *She's really got the jitters—her driving test's in half an hour!* **get the jitters etc** get into such a state. **give sb the jitters etc** cause sb to be in such a state.

**have the last laugh** *(informal)* be successful at the end of a competition, argument etc after changes in fortune during the competition etc: *They all ridiculed me when I said I was going to write a book. Now look how successful I am—I've certainly had the last laugh!*

**have the last word** speak at the end of a discussion, argument etc to bring it to a close: *As chairman it falls to me to have the last word.*

**have (got) the nerve (to do sth)** *(informal)* be impudent or presumptuous in doing sth: *He's only just come and he has the nerve to tell me how to run the office!* Alternatives to ***nerve*** are: ***cheek; gall.***

**have (got) the patience of Job** have great patience: *I don't know how you manage with four children, Penny—you must have the patience of Job.* Also **(be) as patient as Job.**

**have (got) the time 1** know the correct time of day: *'Have you got the time, please?' 'Yes, it's quarter past three.'* **2** have enough time to do sth: *Old people have the time to help the young mums but lack the energy and inclination.*

**have (got) to do sth** be ordered or forced to do sth; find it necessary to do sth: *'Oh, Mummy,' the twins wailed, 'do we have to go to bed now?' / The Prime Minister explained that the government had set spending targets that had to be reached. / Yes, you can catch this train to Crewe. You'll have to change there to get to Liverpool.*

**have (got) to do with sb/sth** or **be to do with sb /sth** be concerning sb/sth: *'What do you want to see me about?' 'It's to do with the letter you sent.' / I'm not sure exactly what he does for a living but I know it's something to do with telephone exchanges. / 'Are you doing any work for Universal Glazes?' 'Mind your own business! It has nothing to do with you!'*

**have to fly/dash** → ***must* fly/dash**

***have*/get two bites at/of the cherry** have a second attempt at doing sth, especially sth you have failed to do earlier: *We lost that contract with a German firm last year so we probably won't get two bites at the cherry and be able to try again.*

**not *have* (got) two pennies to rub together** *(informal)* have no money at all: *We're absolutely broke—we've not got two pennies to rub together.*

***have* (got) sth up one's sleeve** *(informal)* keep a piece of information etc secret until the best moment to mention it: *I know Max. He's always got some idea up his sleeve that he suddenly brings out to amaze us all!*

***have* (sth) one's (own) way** *(informal)* succeed in doing what you want despite opposition: *Leave me alone—you can have your 'own way. / They were probably a better team, but we didn't want them to have it all 'their way.*

***have* (got) what it takes (to do sth)** *(informal)* have the character, intelligence etc that are required for sth: *I enjoy painting, but I know I haven't got what it takes to be a really good artist.*

***have* (got) one's wits about one** be alert; know exactly what you are doing: *You've got to have your wits about you all the time when you're a nurse.*

***have*/get word (from sb)** receive news or a message (from sb): *'Why didn't Mark tell us he'd passed his exams?' 'He only had word this morning.'*

***have* words with sb** speak angrily to sb; criticize sb: *The boss noticed my error and I was told he wanted words with me.*

***have* (got) one's work cut out** have a lot of work or a very difficult job to do: *'Which class have you been given?' '4D.' 'Poor you! You'll have your work cut out trying to teach that lot.'*

**the *haves* and the have-nots** the rich or privileged contrasted with the poor or underprivileged people.

**watch sb/sth like a *hawk* → *watch***

***hawks* and doves** people who are aggressive in military or political matters contrasted with those who are opposed to war and want negotiation, compromise etc.

**make *hay* while the sun shines → *make***

**a roof over one's *head* → *roof***

**above/over sb's *head*** too difficult for sb to understand: *It was clear from the expression on the faces of the audience that the lecture was above their heads.*

**come to a *head* → *come***

**hit the nail on the *head* → *hit***

***heap* coals of fire on sb's head** be kind to sb who has wronged you in order to make him feel a great sense of shame and remorse.

**knock sth on the *head* → *knock***

**off one's *head*** *(informal)* mad: *He must be off his head if he thinks I'm in love with him.* Also *(slang)* **off one's chump/nut/rocker**.

**over sb's *head*** to a higher level of responsibility than sb: *The new director was appointed over the heads of the senior managers. / He gets angry when you go over his head and talk to his boss.*

***head* and shoulders above sb/sth** very much bigger or greater than sb/sth else: *Sir Winston Churchill stands head and shoulders above other political leaders of our time.*

**on sb's (own) *head* be it** the responsibility is with sb and he will have to suffer any unpleasant effects of his action: *On his own head be it* (or *Be it on his own head) if people don't like him. What can he expect if he behaves like that?*

**need, want etc one's *head* examined/ examining → *need***

**have (got) a (good) *head* for figures → *have***

**have (got) a (good) *head* for heights → *have***

**have (got) one's *head* in the clouds → *have***

**put one's *head* in(to) the lion's mouth → *put***

**bury/hide one's *head* in the sand (like an ostrich) → *bury***

**laugh etc one's *head* off → *laugh***

***head* sb/sth off** cause sb to change direction; prevent sth unpleasant: *Union leaders are meeting the government to try to head off the proposed strike.*

***head* on** with the fronts facing each other; with direct opposition: *The cars crashed head on. / The two political leaders clashed head on in the discussion.* **head-on** *adj*: *a head-on collision.*

**put/lay one's *head* on the block → *put***

**(not) make *head* or tail of sth → *make***

***head* over heels** with your body turning upside down; completely: *The children tumbled head over heels as they played in the snow. / She fell head over heels in love with him.*

**sb's *head* rolls** sb is punished by being dismissed from his job or position: *It is certain that the government will want some ministers' heads to roll when all the spy scandal is known.*

**have (got) one's *head* screwed on the right way → *have***

**have (got) a *head* start → *have***

**sb's *head* swells** sb thinks very highly of himself: *I saw your head swell when they sang your praises!* **swollen-headed** *adj*: *If you go away on one of those courses, we know you'll come back swollen-headed!*

**from *head* to foot/toe** over all your body; completely: *When he came out of the mud bath, he was covered in mud from head to toe!*

**you could *hear* a pin drop** it is/was extremely quiet: *As John told us of his wife's illness we all listened intently—you could have heard a pin drop.*

***hear*! hear!** an expression of agreement and approval, called out at a public meeting: *'It is the wish of this government that both unem-*

*ployment and inflation be reduced to acceptable levels.' 'Hear! hear!'*

***hear* it all** → ***do*/hear/see it all**

**not *hear* of sth** not allow sth to happen (usually used with ***will/would***): *'May I pay for the phone call?' 'Don't be silly! I wouldn't hear of it!'*

**(not/never) *hear*/see the end/last of sb/sth** (not) be finished with sb/sth as the subject of discussion or a matter that affects you: *When will we ever hear the end of that story about what happened to you on the way to Germany?/ Even though he says he's going to emigrate, I don't think we'll ever see the last of him.*

**(not/never) *hear*/see the like (of sb/sth)** (not) hear/see anyone/anything similar or as good, bad, unusual etc (before): *A six-kilo cabbage! In sixteen years of gardening, I've never seen the like of that!*

**can't *hear* oneself think** *(informal)* the surrounding noise is so great that you cannot concentrate: *Can you turn the volume down? I can't hear myself think in here.*

**a man/woman after one's own *heart*** → ***man***

**sb after one's own *heart*** → ***own***

**at *heart*** in your real nature: *At heart she still preferred her former way of life. / Please realize that when I ask you not to do that, I only have your best interests at heart.*

**by *heart*** so that sth learned, such as a poem can be repeated precisely: *There was a time when I knew a lot of Macbeth (off) by heart.*

**with one's hand on one's *heart*** → ***hand***

**(one's) *heart* and soul** ((with) your) total commitment, great devotion, energy, and sincerity: *A conductor must throw himself heart and soul into preparing the music to be performed. / The government and people put their heart and soul into rebuilding the country after the war.*

**one's *heart* bleeds for sb** *(informal)* you feel sorry or pity for sb (often used ironically): *'I have to get up at 6 o'clock tomorrow!' 'Ah—my heart bleeds for you—I have to do that every day!'* Also **one's heart goes out to sb**.

**one's *heart* goes out to sb** → **one's *heart* bleeds for sb**

**one's *heart* is in one's boots** *(informal)* you feel depressed or pessimistic about sth that is to occur or that one must do: *There had been talk of workers being dismissed, so when the manager sent for Dick that morning he went upstairs to see him with his heart in his boots.*

**one's *heart* is (not) in it** you feel (no or little) interest in, enthusiasm for, or identification with sth that you are doing: *In the following year he accepted, for financial reasons, a commission to write a biography, but his heart wasn't in it and it was never finished.* Note that this is usually used in the negative.

**one's *heart* is in one's mouth** *(informal)* you feel sudden fear, worry, or other emotion: *Computer technology was so new in those days that when the managers inspected the research department, our hearts were in our mouths as we weren't sure whether everything would work.*

**one's *heart* is in the right place** you are a kind, worthy person with the right values in life and good intentions: *She's nice, and her heart is in the right place, but she still has rather a weak personality.*

**one's *heart* misses a beat** sudden fear or other strong emotion causes or seems to cause a break in your heartbeat: *For a moment she thought she saw a face looking in through the window and her heart missed a beat.*

**have (got) a *heart* of gold** → ***have***

**in one's *heart* of hearts** in your innermost being: *I know in my heart of hearts that you're right, but I still find it difficult to accept.*

**have (got) a *heart* of stone** → ***have***

**wear one's *heart* on one's sleeve** → ***wear***

**to one's *heart*'s content** as much as or as long as you want: *Don't worry, in this hotel you can eat, drink, and sleep to your heart's content.*

**one's *heart* sinks** you feel suddenly sad, disappointed, or afraid: *My heart sank when I turned the corner and saw the huge number of people in the queue in front of me.*

**not find it in one's *heart* to do sth** → ***find***

***heart* to heart** confidentially, privately, or as between friends. **heart-to-heart** *adj*, *n*: *I had a big heart-to-heart (talk) with my doctor, and she told me how foolish I was to continue smoking.*

**in the *heat* of the moment** when very angry, excited, upset etc, although this is only temporary: *I must apologize for the rude things I said yesterday in the heat of the moment.*

**move *heaven* and earth (to do sth)** → ***move***

***heaven* forbid** → ***God*/heaven forbid**

**(a) *heaven*/hell on earth** a place or set of circumstances where everything is ideal and perfect or exceptionally bad and unpleasant: *The new holiday camp is a real heaven on earth for the area's handicapped children.*

**for *heaven*'s sake** → **for *goodness'*/God's/heaven's/pity's/Pete's sake**

**the *heavens* open** *(informal)* rain falls in torrents: *We were walking back from the bus stop when the heavens opened and we got soaked to the skin.*

**as *heavy* as lead** very heavy; dark and oppressive: *He felt awful—his arms were sore and his legs were as heavy as lead. / It seemed as if a storm was about to break—the sea was gloomy and the clouds were as heavy as lead.*

**with a *heavy* hand** with firm or harsh control: *Old Jake rules the factory with a heavy hand—he knows exactly what everyone is doing.* **heavy-handed** *adj*.

**a *heavy*/light heart** feelings of sadness/joy: *It was with a heavy heart that he left the school gates for the last time—he had been happy there and was sorry to leave.* **heavy-hearted; light-hearted** *adj*.

**time hangs *heavy* on one's hands** → ***time***
**make *heavy* weather of (doing) sth** → ***make***
**a/the *heck* of a . . .** → **a/the *hell*/heck of a . . .**
**one *heck* of a . . .** → ***one* hell/heck of a . . .**
***hedge* one's bets** *(informal)* not commit yourself to a definite course of action: *'Next I might go on stage on Broadway or back to London, I'm not sure.' 'You're hedging your bets, aren't you?'*
**pay *heed* (to sb/sth)** → ***pay***
**at sb's *heels*** following close behind sb: *I managed to make my way through the crowd, with the dog at my heels all the time.*
**be hard/close on/upon sb's *heels*** → ***hard***
**take to one's *heels*** → ***take***
**like *hell*/mad** very much, fast etc: *I spent the evening typing like hell to get the work finished.*
**(not) have (got) a *hope* in hell (of doing sth)** → **(not) *have* (got) a cat in 'hell's chance (of doing sth)**
**all *hell* breaks loose** → ***all***
**will/would see sb in *hell* first** → ***see***
***hell* for leather** *(informal)* with the greatest speed and energy: *The rabbits knew they were being hunted and ran hell for leather across the fields. / The managers of the new television channel were told not to go hell for leather for big audiences but to offer good entertainment.*
**a/the *hell*/heck of a . . .** *(informal)* sb/sth that is very special, impressive, or remarkable: *You were with a hell of a girl last night, Ray!* See also ***one* hell/heck of a . . . .**
**one *hell*/heck of a . . .** → ***one***
**for the *hell* of it** *(informal)* because of the brief excitement that sth brings (usually used of actions against the law or social conventions): *The youths had nothing to do so went round breaking windows just for the hell of it.*
**(a) *hell* on earth** → **(a) *heaven*/hell on earth**
**come *hell* or high water** → ***come***
**(not) have (got) a cat in '*hell's* chance (of doing sth)** → ***have***
**there'll be '*hell* to pay** → ***there*'ll be the devil to pay**
**to *hell* with sb/sth** *(informal)* sb/sth does not matter; you do not want to bother with sb/sth: *'You should finish off your work before you go out to play!' 'To hell with my work! I'm going out now!'*
**can't *help* (doing) sth** find that you cannot avoid (doing) sth: *A kleptomaniac is someone who can't help stealing things. / 'I'm sorry, I can't help it,' she said bursting into tears, 'it's Jack's death—I'm still so upset.'*
**so *help* me God** → ***so***
**give/lend (sb) a *(helping)* hand** → ***give***
***hem*/hum and haw** *(informal)* hesitate when speaking or making a decision: *When we asked for the money back, he hemmed and hawed for a few minutes, but eventually gave it back.* Also **um and aah.**
**a '*hen*/'stag party** a social occasion to which only women/men are invited.

***here* and there** at, to, or from several places in an area; scattered in a random way: *Here and there in the crowd I saw someone I recognized.*
***here* below** in this life, contrasted with heaven, thought to be above.
***here,* there, and everywhere** in, to, or from many different places: *I think you should buy a filing cabinet instead of having your papers here, there, and everywhere.*
***het* up** *(informal)* excited, angry, or worried: *Don't get so het up!*
***hide* one's head in the sand (like an ostrich)** → ***bury*/hide one's head in the sand (like an ostrich)**
***hide* one's light under a bushel** conceal your abilities or achievements; be too modest: *We didn't know you could play the guitar! You've been hiding your light under a bushel all this time!*
**see neither *hide* nor hair of sb/sth** → ***see***
***high* and dry** above a water or tide line; abandoned or ignored: *She was jilted—left high and dry on her wedding day.*
***high* and low** everywhere; in every possible place: *We searched high and low for the ring but still couldn't find it anywhere.*
***high* and mighty** arrogantly thinking that you are more important than other people: *Why is he always so high and mighty? He never thinks he needs anyone's help.*
**with a *high* hand** without caring for other people's feelings or opinions. **high-handed** *adj*: *Mary is one of the most high-handed people I know—she's so rude and tactless and never thinks about anyone except herself.*
**smell/stink to *high* heaven** → ***smell***
**have (got) *high* hopes** → ***have***
**sb's *high* horse** a state of being proud, arrogant, and easily offended: *I know you think you shouldn't be suspected, but why don't you come down off your high horse and answer some questions?*
**'*high* jinks** *(informal)* fun; lively enjoyment: *The children certainly had some high jinks at the party.*
**be for the '*high* jump** *(informal)* be due to suffer a scolding, punishment, or ordeal: *They haven't found who did it yet, but when they do he'll be for the high jump.* Also **be 'for it.**
***high* on sth** exhilarated or influenced by a drug or sth like a drug: *'I'm sure you could get high on this stuff,' Dad said, putting his medicine back on the shelf.*
**in *high* places** at the top level of government or administration: *I've got friends in high places—I'm sure one of them could get you a job.*
***high* spirits** great happiness, liveliness, confidence etc: *Now that he'd got older, it was noticeable that his high spirits had gone.*
**come hell or *high* water** → ***come***
**be *high*/about time (that . . . )** the time is long overdue when sth should happen: *It's high time you put up those shelves that you've*

*been talking about for months. / Don't you think that it's about time we had a talk about our future?*

**over the *hill* 1** in the later part of your life; old: *Some people think if you're over 30, you're over the hill!* **2** past the hardest part of sth: *I've done four out of the six exams so I think I'm over the hill.*

**up *hill* and down dale** to, from, or in many places: *I wish you'd told us where you were going and then we need not have gone up hill and down dale trying to find you!'*

**talk the *hind* legs off a donkey** → ***talk***

***hinge* on/upon sth** be influenced or decided by sth: *The success of the project hinges on Peter's contribution.*

**go down in *history*** → ***go***

***hit* and miss** guesswork; random methods which are partly a success and partly a failure: *The advertisements were rather hit and miss and not based on market research.* **hit-and-miss** *adj: The lie detector tests are largely based on a hit-and-miss technique.*

***hit* and run 1** a motor vehicle accident in which a driver leaves the place where the accident happened without stopping to give help, leave his name etc. **hit-and-run** *adj: a hit-and-run accident; a hit-and-run driver.* **2** an attack or raid in which guerrillas, hooligans etc strike sb/sth suddenly and then quickly leave. **hit-and-run** *adj: hit-and-run tactics.*

***hit*/knock sb for six** *(informal)* defeat or have a serious effect on sb: *Being made redundant really knocked him for six.*

***hit* sb/sth hard** have a strong and bad effect on sb/sth: *Small businesses have again been hard hit by the recent increase in bank interest rates.*

***hit* sb in the eye** *(informal)* be very obvious or striking: *The clash of colours hits you in the eye as you go into the room.*

***hit* it off (with sb)** *(informal)* form or enjoy a good relationship with sb: *Right from the moment when I first met the girl who became my wife, we always hit it off. / How well does he hit it off with his bank manager?*

***hit* on/upon sth** think of a plan or an answer, especially suddenly: *A teacher from London has hit upon the idea of compiling a book of his students' mistakes.*

***hit* the bottle** *(informal)* drink too much as a habit or over a period of time: *I suppose most people know of someone who starts to hit the bottle early in life and stays that way for years.*

***hit* the hay/sack** *(informal)* go to bed: *I think it's time to hit the hay.*

***hit* the headlines** *(informal)* become a prominent part of the news: attract a lot of public attention: *His reputation has suffered a lot since the scandal over his love affair hit the headlines.*

***hit* the jackpot** win a lot of money at poker from the jackpot; unexpectedly make or inherit a large amount of money: *He's really hit the jackpot with this new game—orders for it have been pouring in!*

***hit* the nail on the head** *(informal)* say sth in exactly the right way: *'They never were suited to each other,' she remarked. 'You've hit the nail right on the head, there,' he agreed.*

***hit* the road** *(slang)* begin a journey: *Well, we'd better hit the road, we've got a long way to go.*

***hit* the roof/ceiling** *(informal)* lose your temper suddenly: *At the mere mention of Jill's name, Sam used to hit the roof.*

***hive* sth off** transfer part of a business, operation etc to a different company, place etc: *The government plans to hive off further sections of the nationalized industries to make separate firms.*

**(ride) one's/a *hobby*-horse** → ***ride***

***Hobson's* choice** the choice of taking what is offered or nothing at all; in reality no choice at all.

**be *hoist* with one's own petard** be caught by a plan etc with which you had wanted to catch sb else: *He tried to blow up the building but the explosion went off early, killing him—he was hoist by his own petard.*

**cannot *hold* a candle to sb/sth** not be good enough to be compared with sb/sth: *When it comes to production efficiency, we can't hold a candle to our foreign competitors.* Also **not be fit/able to hold a candle to sb.**

**(*hold* sb/sth) at arm's length** → **(*keep*/hold sb/sth) at arm's length**

***hold* sb/sth at bay** → ***keep*/hold sb/sth at bay**

**hold back** → ***hang*/hold back**

***hold* one's breath** not breathe, because you are under water or because your attention is gripped by sth: *The check-up began with the doctor asking her to hold her breath for a few seconds. / Everyone held their breath as the tightrope walkers stepped onto the high wire.*

***hold*/keep/play one's cards close to one's chest** *(informal)* keep your plans or activities very much to yourself; not let others know what you are engaged upon until it is accomplished: *Despite his readiness to talk generally about the difficulties of his people, the nationalist leader kept his cards close to his chest and said nothing of any substance.*

***hold* court** lead or be in charge of functions at a monarch's court; *(often humorous or derogatory)* be the main admired or respected figure in a meeting: *Kings of old once held court here and received guests from distant lands. / There was Professor Johnson, holding court as usual in the students' coffee bar.*

***hold* down a job** *(informal)* be able to stay in one job for a long time: *Rex has always found it difficult to hold down a job. / You'd have to be a superman to hold down this job!*

***hold* fast to sth** remain firmly attached to sth such as a principle or theory: *She knew that whatever happened in her life, she would hold fast to her religious beliefs.*

***hold* one's fire** not fire a gun immediately; not say or do sth important until you know more or until the right moment comes: *Pete was getting more and more impatient. 'Why* *didn't Daniel telephone if he knew he was going to be late?' 'Hold your fire—he may have had an accident,' his wife tried to calm him.*

***hold* forth (about/on sth)** speak in front of other people for a long time about sth: *The politician held forth on the importance of living in a society free from social injustice.*

***hold* good/true** be or remain valid or applicable: *This principle holds true in every case.*

***hold*/stand one's ground** defend and maintain your position in a battle or argument: *Although the elephants were running towards us, we stood our ground and for some reason they left us alone. / The witness firmly held his ground when confronted by all the questions put to him.*

***hold* sb's hand** clasp or grasp sb's hand; support or comfort sb in difficulty: *Hold Granny's hand while we cross the street. / The industry can't expect the Minister to come and hold its hand every time it has financial problems. / When you're in trouble it can be a great help if someone comes to hold your hand.*

***hold* hands** (of two people sitting or walking) link the nearest hands, as a sign of affection: *Do you remember the first time we held hands?*

***hold* one's head high/up** act with confidence in your worth, abilities etc: *Have you noticed that since she passed all her exams she feels she can hold her head high again?*

***hold* one's horses** *(informal)* go or work more slowly; think about your actions (often used as a request to wait): *Tell him to hold his horses! I'm not yet ready!*

***hold* sb/sth in check** → ***keep*/hold sb/sth in check**

***hold* sb/sth in contempt** scorn or despise sb/sth: *As the election campaign draws to a close, the political leaders of all the parties are holding one another more and more in contempt.*

***hold* no brief for sb/sth** not support, or feel no sympathy for sb/sth: *Why are you surprised I'm so shocked about their behaviour? You know I hold no brief for anarchists.*

**take a (firm) grip/*hold* on oneself** → ***take***

***hold* on (to sth) like grim death** → ***hang*/hold on (to sth) like grim death**

***hold* out 1** (of a store of sth) last or be sufficient for a purpose: *I don't think our coal supply will hold out through the winter.* **2** continue to resist an attack, behaviour, poverty etc: *The soldiers had plenty of weapons and so managed to hold out until reinforcements came.*

***hold* out sth** offer or present a possibility or hope: *We never held out much hope that she would get better.*

***hold* out for sth** refuse a proposed offer, sale etc, hoping for a better one: *The unions refused a 3% increase offered by the management and are holding out for 10%.*

***hold* out on sb** refuse to give sth such as information to sb who is entitled to have it: *I'm not holding out on you. I honestly don't know where he is.*

***hold* sth over** delay or postpone the discussion of sth: *As it was getting late, the matter of future developments was held over until the next meeting.*

***hold* one's own** keep your present position or level of popularity; not be overtaken by your competitors: *Despite much opposition from foreign imports, this country has managed to hold its own in the field of computers.*

***hold* sway** (of a movement, person, idea etc) be the ruling force: *We used to think that the caretaker, Jim, was the one who really held sway in the college, while all the lecturers came and went after a few years.*

***hold* the floor** talk to an audience for a long time; talk so much that you do not allow other people to share in a conversation: *Several politicians gave their proposals briefly, but it was the French delegation that really held the floor, and their plan was eventually accepted.*

***hold* the fort** *(informal)* be responsible for caring for or controlling sth, especially while the usual person responsible is absent: *It's been great to know that while I've been away, you've been holding the fort so well here at the office!*

***hold* the purse strings** *(informal)* be the person who controls the amount of money spent: *In this organization, I'm the one who holds the purse strings, and you must come to me if you want any more money.*

***hold* sb to account** → ***call*/bring/hold sb to account**

***hold* sb to ransom** keep sb in a prison, room etc until money has been paid for their release; try to force sb to do what you want: *The miners are holding the country to ransom over their pay—they won't go back to work until they get a 10% increase.*

***hold* one's tongue** say nothing; stay silent: *We don't want anyone to know what's happened, so you'd better hold your tongue—do you understand?*

***hold* sb/sth up 1** delay the progress of sb/sth: *Production of new tyres has been held up by a shortage of rubber.* **hold-up** *n*: *Road works are causing big traffic hold-ups on the motorway.* **2** try to steal money from a bank, security van etc, using guns: *A group of six armed men today held up a post office in the city centre and escaped with £100,000.* **hold-up** *n*: *This is a hold-up! No one move or we'll shoot!*

***hold* water** *(informal)* be sound; be capable of withstanding investigation: *I think you'll find that this theory holds water—we've tested it against the results of several years' experiments.*

**not *hold* with sth** not approve of sth such as a principle or habit: *She doesn't hold with the idea of men and women living together before they get married.*

**there is no *holding* sb** → ***no***

**be left *holding* the baby** → ***left***

**with no *holds* barred** → ***no***
**money burns a *hole* in sb's pocket** → ***money***
**need/want sth like (one needs/wants) a *hole* in the head** → ***need***
***holier*-than-thou** self-righteous; pretending to be very holy and religious and morally very good: *a holier-than-thou attitude.*
**take *(holy)* orders** → ***take***
**a *holy* terror** *(informal)* sb who is very difficult to deal with or causes a lot of trouble for other people: *I've never met such a rude and naughty child! She's a holy terror!*
**at *home*** **1** in the place where you live or lived; in your own country, not abroad: *At home a large apple tree grew in the garden. / There has been a sudden boom in sales, both at home and abroad.* **2** comfortable and familiar with sth, as if you really were in your own home; relaxed: *The giraffe feels more at home in these natural surroundings than in a cage. / Make yourself at home while I just finish getting the dinner.* **3** (of a sports match) played on your own ground: *This week they're playing at home, next week they're away.*
***home* and dry** safe and successful after a struggle or negotiation to gain sth: *When we've won four out of the six games, we'll know that we're home and dry.*
**a *home* bird** sb who spends most of his time at home because he is happiest there: *Sheila's a home bird really. She likes to spend her free time around the house. But Dave is the opposite—he wants to be out on his motorbike all the time!*
**a *home* from home** a place where you feel as comfortable, happy etc as in your own house: *They used to stay in their father's flat in Brighton every holiday. It was a real home from home!*
***home* truths** frank, open, and honest criticism or assessment of sb, said to show sb his faults: *It's time someone told you a few home truths, my boy!*
**make an *honest* woman of sb** → ***make***
***honest* to God/goodness** honestly; truthfully: *I can assure you, honest to God, he did it!* **honest-to-God, honest-to-goodness** *adj* real; genuine: *This book is an honest-to-God attempt to describe life as a political leader.*
***hook*, line, and sinker** *(informal)* (accept or believe sth) completely, because you have been deceived or because you believe things too easily: *Up to that time, I had swallowed all the teaching I'd ever received, hook, line, and sinker. But then I began to question it.*
**by *hook* or by crook** by any available method, whether this is honest or not: *Don't worry—we'll have the money ready for 4 o'clock, by hook or by crook.*
***hooked* on sth** *(informal)* dependent on or obsessed with sth: *He was only 16 and he was already hooked on drugs.*
**catch sb on the *hop*** → ***catch***
**'some '*hope*(s)!** → ***some***
***hope* against hope (that . . . )** continue to hope that sth will happen etc, even though this seems useless or foolish: *It was over a couple of days since the explosion occurred, but the family were still hoping against hope that their son was safe.*
**what a *hope*!** → ***'some* 'hope(s)!**
***hope* for the best** want everything to go well, especially when there are doubts that it will: *The doctors can't give her any more medicine, I'm afraid; all we can do is hope for the best.*
**cross my heart (and *hope* to die)** → ***cross***
***hopping* mad (about/over sth)** *(informal)* extremely annoyed and angry about sth: *Old Jake will be hopping mad when he hears you've broken the window again.*
**a (small) cloud on the *horizon*** → ***cloud***
**take the bull by the *horns*** → ***take***
**(on) the *horns* of a dilemma** (faced with) (two or more) different actions, opinions etc, one of which must be chosen, but both of which seem equally unsatisfactory, disagreeable, or dangerous: *I was on the horns of a dilemma. If I didn't go for help, the boy would certainly die, and if I did go, the snow would certainly bury him.*
**eat like a *horse*** → ***eat***
**put the cart before the *horse*** → ***put***
***horse* about/around** *(informal)* play or have fun in a wild, noisy way: *Can you children stop horsing about? I'm trying to read this book.*
**a *horse* of another colour** or **a horse of a different colour** a person, matter, point etc of a quite different kind: *You can't have friends sharing your room for the same rent, but if you want your brother to stay for a few days, then that's a horse of a different colour.*
**(straight) from the *horse*'s mouth** *(informal)* directly from the person best or alone qualified to give certain information: *I don't believe it.' 'Well, the boss is in, you can go upstairs and get it straight from the horse's mouth if you like.'*
***horses* for courses** people or things (are) used for the purpose for which they are most suitable: *I'm thinking of horses for courses by creating a new department: producing specialist books for specialists in a subject.*
**not so/too *hot*** → ***so***
***hot* air** impressive words and promises that mean little and will not be put into action: *Her boasting about her business trips overseas is a load of hot air—she's never been abroad once! / He spoke for a good hour, but most of it was just hot air.*
**(all) *hot* and bothered** *(informal)* worried and upset by the need to hurry, too much work etc: *Officials at the Defence Ministry are getting all hot and bothered about secrets getting out.*
**blow *hot* and cold** → ***blow***
***hot* at (doing) sth** *(informal)* accomplished or able at a particular skill, activity etc: *Fay's got quite hot at playing the piano recently, hasn't she?*
**like a cat on *hot* bricks** → ***cat***

**sell/go like *hot* cakes** ⟶ ***sell***
**more sth/often than sb has had *hot* dinners** ⟶ ***more***
**a 'hot line (to sb)** ⟶ a special, secret telephone link to an important person, such as a prime minister: *The President of the United States spoke on the hot line with the Prime Minister to try to stop the invasion.*
***hot* on sth** *(informal)* enthusiastic and well-informed about sth: *I'll ask my brother. He's hot on the latest developments in electronics. / He did quite well in the literature exam but wasn't so hot on the language one.*
**a *hot* potato** *(informal)* a matter that is considered too dangerous to tackle or become involved with: *The reason why he resigned is a real hot potato—we mustn't let the newspapers find it out.*
**the '*hot* seat** *(informal)* a position in which you are open and vulnerable to questions, criticism, and attack: *Our phone-in today is on transport, and the Minister of Transport will be in the hot seat, ready to answer your questions.*
**a '*hot* spot** a country or area where there may soon be a war or other trouble: *As a journalist, I get sent to one hot spot after another.*
**too *hot* to handle** ⟶ ***too***
***hot* under the collar** *(informal)* annoyed, embarrassed, and excited: *Even Bill gets hot under the collar if you keep on ignoring him for long enough.*
***hot* up** *(informal)* become faster or more intense: *The race is really beginning to hot up now as the runners enter the last stage.*
**in *hot* water** *(informal)* in serious trouble: *She got into hot water for being late. / The new clerk found he was in hot water when he forgot to ask for a receipt for the money.*
**on the *hour*/half-hour** exactly at 5 o'clock, 6 o'clock etc or 5.30, 6.30 etc: *Buses leave here for Altrincham on the hour.*
**at/till all *hours* (of the night)** ⟶ ***all***
**on the *house*** given to a customer free by the hotel, restaurant, bar etc where he is: *Drinks are on the house tonight!*
**eat sb out of *house* and home** ⟶ ***eat***
**(like) a *house* of cards** an imaginative plan that is too ambitious and cannot be fulfilled: *The trouble with such a complicated deceit is that if someone finds out one small detail, the whole thing falls down like a house of cards.*
**get on (with sb) like a *house* on fire** ⟶ ***get***
**a *household* name/word** the name of a widely-used product or a famous politician that has become extremely well-known: *His invention meant that he became a millionaire, and he was soon a household name throughout the country.*
**shout (sth) from the rooftops/*housetops*** ⟶ ***shout***
**and *how*!** ⟶ ***and***
***how*/what about sb/sth? 1** *(informal)* what is your opinion of sb/sth?; have you heard about sb/sth?: *How about our team winning again last night, eh? / What about Tom being knocked down by a lorry? It's awful, isn't it!* **2** *(informal)* (used to ask for an explanation of or decision about sb/sth, and often to remind sb): *'I always return my library books on time!' 'Always? What about that time you kept* English for Engineers *for three months too long?'*
***how*/what about (doing) sth?** *(informal)* (used to introduce a suggestion): *How about going to town this afternoon? / What about another cup of tea?*
***how*/what about that!** *(informal)* (used to express surprise, praise, great respect, etc): *'Have you heard Jane's off to America tomorrow?' 'Well, how about that, then!'*
***how* come?** *(informal)* how does/did it happen (that)?; what is the explanation of sth? (often expressing surprise): *If he was a spy, then how come none of us ever found out?*
***how* dare sb (do sth)?** *(informal)* how can sb be so rude (as to do sth)? (a shocked way of reacting to sth wrong, too bold, or defiant): *How dare you talk to me like that? You must say you're sorry immediately! / How dare he treat his parents like that?* Note that usually pronouns, not names, are used in this idiom.
***how* do you do?** (a polite form of greeting used when being introduced on a first meeting): *'Susan, this is Mr Green whom I've told you a lot about. Mr Green, this is Miss Nelson.' 'How do you do?' said Mr Green. 'How do you do?' replied Susan.* **a (fine) how-do-you-do** or **a (fine) how d'ye do** *n (informal)* a difficult situation.
***how* on earth?** *(informal)* how?; in what way? (used to emphasize the speaker's bewilderment, surprise etc): *How on earth do you expect me to know the answer?* Also **how in the world?**
***how's* your father** *(humorous)* used to talk about something that you do not want to refer to directly such as sex: *I hear a bit of how's your father was going on in the front room last night.*
***how* the hell?** *(informal)* how?; in what way? (used to express the speaker's bad temper, hostility, scorn etc): *How the hell should I know where he is?* Alternatives to ***hell*** are ***blazes, devil, dickens*** (all old-fashioned); ***heck.***
***how* the 'land lies** ⟶ **the *lie*/lay of the land**
***how* the other half lives** the life of people different from your own class, race, occupation, especially those that you think are better than you: *Sheila's next interview for the paper was with a pop star in his apartment by the lake. It made quite a change for her to see how the other half lived.*
***hue* and cry** opposition and shouts of alarm and protest: *There was a great hue and cry among the parents when it was announced that the school was to close.*
***hum* and haw** ⟶ ***hem*/hum and haw**
**eat *humble* pie** ⟶ ***eat***
**over the *hump*** *(informal)* past the largest,

worst, or most difficult part of a job, period of time etc: *I'll be over the hump when I've done this exam—then there'll be just two left.*

**a *hundred*/thousand/million and one** *(informal)* very many or too many (things to do, excuses, people to see etc): *I'm so busy—I've got lectures to prepare, a book to finish, and a hundred and one letters to write—I just don't know where to start.*

**be *hung,* drawn, and quartered** suffer a brutal criminal execution; *(humorous)* be very strongly criticized: *I could tell from his reaction to my excuses that he wanted me hung, drawn, and quartered.*

**not *hurt*/harm a fly** *(informal)* be kind and gentle, not wanting to cause injury or pain to anyone (often used with ***wouldn't***): *All my friends were terrified by my landlord, but I knew he wouldn't hurt a fly.*

**it wouldn't *hurt* sb to do sth** *(informal)* it would do sb a lot of good to do sth: *It wouldn't hurt her to walk instead of going in the car all the time.*

***hush*-hush** *(informal)* (of work, documents etc) secret; confidential: *The work going on at the new defence building is very hush-hush.*

***hustle* and bustle** busy, excited activity: *I can't concentrate on my work with hustle and bustle around me.*

**a (Dr) Jekyll and (Mr) *Hyde* → *Jekyll***

# I

***I* dare say** I suppose; it seems probable: *I dare say your story is true, but I'd still like to find out what other people think before I act on it.*

***I'll* eat my hat** *(informal)* (an expression used to show that you think sth is ridiculous, that you do not think sth will happen etc): *They're always late—if they get here a minute before 8 o'clock, I'll eat my hat!*

***I'm* afraid** I'm sorry (used as a polite way of showing regret about refusing something or about something bad that has happened or probably will happen): *I'm afraid I can't come to your party. / 'Can I go now?' 'I'm afraid not.' / I've some bad news, I'm afraid. Jim's had an accident.*

**on *ice*** *(informal)* (of a plan) postponed or deferred: *The scheme to introduce new work arrangements has been put on ice until more money is available.*

**the *icing* on the cake** sth additional that is good, useful etc but not necessary.

**the (very) *idea*!** *(informal)* that is a very unreasonable, ridiculous etc idea, way of behaving etc: *Would I go off to the party and leave you here by yourself? The very idea!*

**sb is 60, 70 etc *if* he's a day** sb is at least 60 etc years old: *'They say Pauline's only 53!' 'Never—she's 60, if she's a day!'*

***if* at first you don't succeed, (try, try again)** *(saying)* if you persevere and are patient, you will eventually achieve your aim.

***if* one has done sth once, one has done it a hundred times** you have been warned, advised etc people very many times: *If I've told you once, I've told you a hundred times. Just shut up!* Variations on ***a hundred*** are: ***a dozen; fifty; a thousand.***

***if* you ˌask ˈme → *ask***

***ifs* and buts** the conditions under which a rule applies and the exceptions to the rule; excuses: *Why are the company's public statements so long? I don't want to hear all the ifs and buts, I just want to know the clear facts.*

**of that *ilk*** of the same kind, quality etc as mentioned: *She goes from one job to another. Girls of that ilk are usually unhappy.*

***ill* at ease** nervous, worried, and embarrassed: *All the candidates for the job were looking very ill at ease as they waited to be asked in for their interviews.*

**the/one's *imagination* boggles → the/one's *mind*/imagination boggles**

***in* between → *betwixt* and between**

**be ˈ*in* for sth 1** have applied for a job or award; compete in a competition: *I hope John gets that university post he's in for. / I'm in for both the 100m and 200m.* **2** be sure or very likely to get or incur sth: *I fear I'm in for a bad cold. / If he thinks he can do what he wants here he's in for a big surprise.*

**something, anything, nothing etc ˈ*in* it** some truth, or some common sense in what is said, rumoured, or advised: *He couldn't go on believing the rumour. He was sure that there was nothing in it. / Was there anything in the suggestion that she was a spy?*

**there's nothing ˈ*in* it → *nothing***

**something, anything, nothing etc ˈ*in* it for sb** money, prestige, or other advantage for sb (to be gained by taking part in sth): *Authors and publishers, who see something in it for them, are in favour of the plan. / If you do what you're told, there's two hundred pounds in it for you.*

**be ˈ*in* on sth** *(informal)* share in or be informed about sth: *I'd like to be in on this project if you'll have me. / Parents aren't always in on what their children are doing.* See also ***let* sb in on sth.**

**every *inch* a man, soldier etc** in all respects a man etc: *He entered the room dressed in a well-cut dark suit and carrying his briefcase and umbrella, looking every inch an important British businessman.*

***industrial* action** a protest, such as a strike or go-slow, against low pay, bad working conditions etc: *The union has not yet decided what form of industrial action to take.*

**under the *influence*** *(informal)* drunk: *He*

*was given a heavy fine for driving while under the influence.*

**as *innocent* as a new-born babe** knowing very little about life; inexperienced and easily deceived: *The comedian's jokes contained some rather rude comments, but Sue, innocent as a new-born babe, didn't really understand them.*

**the *ins* and outs (of sth)** the complex details of sth: *I can never understand the ins and outs of how our legal system works.*

**an *inside* job** (of a crime) arranged by sb who works in the organization or building where the crime takes place: *No one outside the company knew where the money was kept, so the raid must have been an inside job.*

**know sth *inside* out** → ***know***

**turn sth *inside* out** → ***turn***

**take sth in the spirit in which it is *intended*** → ***take***

**to all *intents* (and purposes)** → ***all***

**be *into* sth** *(informal)* have a keen interest in and some experience or knowledge of an art, sport etc: *There weren't many people into real American jazz when we bought these records years ago.*

**the *Iron* Curtain** the western boundary of the group of East European countries that belong to the Warsaw Pact: *A trade delegation from behind the Iron Curtain arrived today on a fact-finding mission.*

**strike while the *iron* is hot** → ***strike***

***iron* sth out** *(informal)* solve a problem or difficulty by discussion, compromise etc: *The meeting was called to try to iron out some of the difficulties in the new school timetable.*

**have (got) (too) many etc *irons* in the fire** → ***have***

**at *issue*** being discussed; relevant to the discussion: *What is now at issue is not what sort of books we should publish, but whether we should publish books at all.*

***itch* to do sth or itch for sth** *(informal)* have an urgent desire or need to do sth or for sth: *I'm just itching to tell them my news! / He was itching for a chance to show off his French.*

**scratch where sb *itches*** → ***scratch***

**have (got) *itchy* feet** → ***have***

**an *ivory* tower** a way of life, especially academic study, that is separated from direct experience of life: *Many people think that university lecturers, living in their ivory towers, should have the harsh realities of life brought home to them.*

**the *Ivy* League** the group of older United States universities, including Harvard, Yale, Princeton and Columbia, which have academic and social prestige.

# J

***jack* sth in** *(informal)* stop doing sth, such as a job: *He didn't like his college course so jacked it in after only a few days.*

**a *jack* of all trades (and master of none)** *(informal)* sb who can do very many different kinds of work, especially crafts (but none of them very well): *They were looking for a worker who wasn't expected to be an expert at anything in particular but a jack of all trades who was prepared to do any odd jobs on the building site.*

***jack* sth up** *(informal)* increase a price, figure etc: *The company's profits were so good that everybody's wages were jacked up by 5%.*

**before you can say *Jack* Robinson** → ***say***

**want *jam* on it** → ***want***

**sb's *jaw* drops** your face shows surprise, especially at something unpleasant: *He insisted on paying for the meal, but his jaw dropped when he saw the bill.*

**and all that *(jazz)*** → ***all***

***jazz* sth up** *(informal)* make sth more exciting and attractive: *Our exhibition stand was dull and boring last year—can't we jazz it up a bit this time?*

**a (Dr) *Jekyll* and (Mr) Hyde** sb who has a dual personality or shows two opposite aspects of his character.

**the '*jet* set** *(informal)* people who for business and/or pleasure travel widely and live in an expensive luxurious way: *I hear your job takes you abroad, Max! You're really one of the jet set now, aren't you?* **'jet-setter** *n* a person who belongs to the jet set.

**lie down on the *job*** → ***lie***

**have (got) a (hard) *job* to do sth** → ***have***

**a *Job's* comforter** sb who means to sympathize with a depressed or unhappy person but in reality depresses him further: *'You should take that medicine—my cousin was in hospital for months with a cough like yours!' 'Thanks very much! You're a real Job's comforter, aren't you?'*

***jobs* for the boys** the giving of paid employment to favoured groups because of friendships or connections with important people: *Jobs for the boys, is it? I suppose you gave Sam and Dave the work just because you know them.*

***jockey* for sth** move about in an attempt to obtain sth, especially an important position: *The election is still three months away, but already some of the members are jockeying for the position of chairman.*

***jog* sb's memory** remind sb of sth; stimulate sb to remember sth: *So you don't remember Mary Woodson? Well here's a photo of you and her at Brighton that will jog your memory perhaps.*

***join* battle (with sb/sth)** fight sb: *A group of local parents have decided to join battle with* *the Council's decision to close two of the town's schools.*

***join* forces (with sb/sth)** add your strength, support etc to those of sb else: *The tourist offices in the regions have agreed to join forces with the office in the capital to try and attract more interest and also to reduce costs.*

***join* issue with sb/sth** → ***take*/join issue with sb/sth**

***join* the club!** well done! (said when sth, especially sth bad, that has already happened to you now happens to sb else: *'I failed the exam again!' 'Join the club! Pete, Sarah, and I have as well—so don't worry!'*

***join* up** become a member of a country's military force; enlist: *I joined up before the war because I knew that I'd be called up anyway when it came.* See also ***call* sb up.**

**beyond a *joke*** no longer funny; now serious: *This has got beyond a joke! Open this door and let me out at once!*

**no *joke* → *no***

**you must be *joking*! → *you***

**keep up with the *Joneses* → *keep***

**not a/one *jot*/tittle** not (in) the smallest degree: *It doesn't matter a jot what you say now—your mistake has ruined everything and you can't change that.*

**a *jot* or tittle** the smallest or least item or detail: *Every year the award ceremony was the same—it seemed that not a jot or tittle ever changed.*

**full of the *joys* of spring → *full***

***juggle* with sth** change or revise facts, especially numbers, often with the intention of cheating sb: *He spent hours juggling with the figures to make it appear that the company made a profit.*

**stew in one's own *juice* → *stew***

***jump* at sth** *(informal)* accept an offer, opportunity etc eagerly and with no hesitation: *The children jumped at the chance of visiting the television studios.*

***jump* down sb's throat** *(informal)* speak to sb in a very angry, critical way: *I only asked him if I could go home five minutes early and he really jumped down my throat!*

***jump* on sb** *(informal)* criticize or challenge sb very sharply: *I hated it at school when the geography master used to jump on anyone who wasn't paying attention.*

***jump*/climb on the bandwagon** *(informal)* take part in sth that other people are already doing and that is proving popular and successful: *When one publisher brings out a book on the Royal Family and it becomes a bestseller, you soon find lots of other publishers jumping on the bandwagon and bringing out books on the same subject, in the hope that they'll sell as well.*

***jump* out of one's skin** *(informal)* be very surprised: *The shock of seeing her again made me nearly jump out of my skin!*

***(jump)* out of the frying-pan into the fire** *(saying)* (involve yourself) in a second situation of danger or difficulty by escaping from a first: *This is a classic case of jumping out of the frying-pan into the fire: something which often happens when managements try to turn a bad decision into a good one and fail miserably.*

***jump* ship** leave, without permission, a ship in which you are serving; desert.

***jump* the gun** *(informal)* do sth before the right time: *The men jumped the gun by building the garage before permission had been given.*

***jump* the queue** not wait in a line of people at a bus stop, in a shop etc, but go in front of them: *The local people accused the newcomers of jumping the queue—they'd been waiting for houses for years but these new people had been given them straight away.*

***jump*/rush to conclusions** be too hasty in forming an opinion about sb/sth without considering all the evidence properly: *'I saw you having lunch with Smith. I wouldn't mind betting that he offered you a job.' 'That would be jumping to conclusions.'* Also **jump to the conclusion that:** *You seem to have jumped to the conclusion that because he was last in the office, it was he who stole the money.*

***jump* 'to it!** *(informal)* hurry up!: *You've got to leave in ten minutes to catch the bus. Come on, jump to it!*

***jumped* up → *bumped*/jumped up**

**(not) *just* a pretty face** (not) just sb who looks attractive without other good features, especially abilities: *So you've got 3 'A' levels and an engineering degree—not just a pretty face, are you?*

***(just)* sb dare!** (a way of discouraging sb from doing sth): *So he'd defy my orders, would he? Let him dare!* Also **don't sb dare!** Note that usually pronouns, not names, are used in this idiom.

***(just)* in case (it rains, of trouble etc) → *case***

***just* the job/ticket** *(informal)* exactly the person, thing, situation etc that is needed or wanted: *'Two sugars in your tea, Dave?' 'Yes, that's just the job, thanks!'*

***just* what the doctor ordered** *(saying)* sth that is exactly right or desirable for sb to have or do: *Ah, a long, cool, refreshing drink! Just what the doctor ordered!*

# K

***keel* over 1** (of a ship etc) overturn partially or completely: *The ship keeled over dangerously after the bomb exploded.* **2** *(informal)* lose your balance and fall to the ground: *People who are not used to the heat in this part of the world sometimes keel over if they stay outside for too long.*

**as *keen* as mustard** very enthusiastic, eager, and active: *Roger is just the boy to be our next Scout leader—he's as keen as mustard and very popular with the other boys.*

***keen* on (doing) sth** *(informal)* in love with or infatuated by sb; enthusiastically interested in (doing) sth; in favour of (doing) sth: *Being keen on an older girl or a member of staff is quite common among the younger girls. / Local people aren't at all keen on having the bus service withdrawn.*

***keep* a foot in both camps** → ***have* (got) a foot in both camps**

**you can't *keep* a good man down!** → ***you***

***keep*/maintain a level head** remain calm and sensible; not lose your temper. **level-headed** *adj.*

***keep* a straight face** not laugh or smile at sth you think is funny: *I find it hard to keep a straight face with those two cracking jokes all the time.*

***keep* a tight/loose rein on sb/sth** exercise strict control over sb/sth or allow sb/sth great freedom: *The finance committee has asked all college departments to keep a tight rein on expenditure.*

***keep* an/one's eye on sb/sth** → ***have* (got) an/one's eye on sb/sth**

***keep* an 'eye open (for sb/sth)** → ***keep* one's 'eyes open (for sb/sth)**

**(*keep*/hold sb/sth) at arm's length** (keep sb/sth) at just enough distance to avoid being attacked, interfered with, or forced into a relationship that you do not want: *There's an art in managing to be polite whilst keeping your neighbours at arm's length.*

***keep*/hold sb/sth at bay** cause sb or sth such as an enemy, poverty, or unemployment to remain at a distance and so have no effect on you: *For several days the garrison managed to keep the enemy at bay. / The doctors have successfully held the disease at bay for several years, but they cannot keep it up for much longer.*

***keep* bad, strange etc company** mix or associate with undesirable, strange etc people: *The magistrate said that the boy had a weak character and had been keeping bad company.*

***keep* body and 'soul together** *(informal)* stay alive, but only with difficulty: *The family managed to keep body and soul together somehow on his low wages.* See also ***body* and soul**.

***keep* one's cards close to one's chest** → ***hold*/keep/play one's cards close to one's chest**

***keep* one's 'chin/'pecker up** *(informal)* not lose your courage, hope, optimism etc: *Keep your chin up! We'll soon be home!* Note that this is usually used in the imperative. Sometimes shortened to **chin up!**

***keep* sb company** be a companion for sb for a short time or permanently: *Mary had a friend who kept her company on trips abroad.* See also **the *company* sb keeps.**

***keep*/lose one's cool** *(informal)* not show your anger, impatience etc or show it in an uncontrolled way: *He was very insulting. I don't really know how I managed to keep my cool.*

***keep*/lose count (of sth)** calculate or become confused about the total reached in any process of addition or the point reached in any sequence: *I hope you keep count of what you spend on postage and phone calls in connection with your spare-time employment. It always comes to more than you think./'But this is Friday, mother.' 'Oh dear, I lose count of the days living here. Each one is so much the same as any other.*

***keep* sth dark (from sb)** hide sth; not tell sth (to sb): *When I found out that everyone else in the family had been planning a party for my sister, I wondered why they had all kept it dark.* See also ***keep*/leave sb in the dark (about sth).**

***keep* one's distance** not stand or be too close to sb/sth; not associate with sb; have only a formal relationship with sb: *When driving you should keep your distance between you and the car in front. / On reflection, I don't think I should have kept my distance from other people so much when I was working: I've got so few friends now.* Also **keep sb/sth at a (safe) distance.**

***keep* (on) doing sth** continue to do sth; do sth very often: *The rest of the competitors kept on running after two of the others fell over. / Why do you keep swearing all the time?*

***keep* one's ear(s) (close) to the ground** *(informal)* be well-informed about what is happening and what may happen in the future. *Why not ask Marge what the rest of the students think? She certainly keeps her ears close to the ground.* Also **have (got) one's ear(s) close to the ground.**

***keep* one's 'ears open** listen carefully for sth: *I've been keeping my ears open in case the baby cries, but I've not heard anything.*

***keep* one's 'end up** continue to look happy in a difficult situation; appear to fulfil your part or defend yourself: *That's it—keep your end up! You'll soon feel better and be out of bed in* *no time! / He managed to keep his end up in the conversation, pretending that he knew all about the composers the others were discussing.*

**not be able to *keep*/take one's eyes off sb/sth** not be able to stop yourself looking at sb/sth beautiful etc: *He couldn't keep his eyes off the attractive girl sitting opposite him.*

***keep* one's 'eyes open (for sb/sth)** watch carefully for sth. Also **keep a weather eye open (for sb/sth)** *(old-fashioned)*; **keep an 'eye open (for sb/sth); keep one's eyes peeled/skinned (for sb/sth)** *(informal)*: *Keep your eyes peeled, and if you see anything suspicious, ring the police at once.*

***keep*/lose faith (with sb/sth)** be loyal/disloyal to sb, a principle, or a group of people: *The government has failed to keep faith with the voters by breaking a number of promises it made.*

***keep* one's finger on the pulse (of sth)** ⟶ ***have* (got) one's finger on the pulse (of sth)**

***keep* one's 'fingers crossed (for sb/sth)** wish sb well for a particular event; hope that sth will be successful, sometimes by actually putting one of your fingers over the next one: *There's a possibility that we'll be able to get Joe Gordon over to sing for us next year, so let's keep our fingers crossed that he can make it. / There! I think the light's mended now. Let's try it. Keep your fingers crossed!*

***keep* one's 'hair/'shirt on** *(informal)* not lose your temper (usually used in the imperative): *'That's* my *radio!' 'Keep your hair on—I only wanted to borrow it!'*

***keep* one's 'hand in** retain a skill by using it sometimes, though less frequently than at an earlier time: *Wallace taught history for years at school, and now he's retired he keeps his hand in by giving the occasional lecture.*

***keep* one's 'hands off (sb/sth)** not touch or take sb/sth: *He had always been a thief, it seems. He could never keep his hands off other people's property.* See also ***hands* off sb/sth.**

***keep*/lose one's head** think and act in a calm and sensible or frantic and foolish way when in difficulty: *Everyone lost their heads and panicked when the fire alarm sounded.*

***keep* one's head above water** stay out of debt; just manage all your responsibilities: *The company had great difficulty keeping its head above water in the recession. / It's a real struggle to keep my head above water all the time with so much paperwork to do.*

***keep* one's 'head down** *(informal)* work very hard, with great concentration: *You'll have to keep your head down for several weeks, as you've got so much preparation to do before the exams.*

***keep* house (for sb)** be responsible for the domestic management of a household: *When my grandmother died, Mother went to keep house for her two brothers.* **housekeeper *n*.**

***keep* sb in** make sb, especially a pupil at a school, remain indoors: *If you don't shut up I'll keep the whole class in for half an hour after school.*

***keep*/hold sb/sth in check** prevent further advance or progress of an enemy, illness etc: *Fortunately, the threatened cholera epidemic was kept in check by the authorities.*

***keep*/leave sb in the dark (about sth)** deliberately not tell sb (about sth): *I don't like being kept in the dark about the company's business affairs—so please tell me what's going on.* See also ***keep* sth dark (from sb).**

***keep*/be in touch/contact (with sb)** maintain communication with sb; (of two people) obtain regular information about each other: *While I was at college I kept in touch with my parents by phoning every week.* See also ***lose* touch/contact (with sb).**

***keep* 'in with sb** continue to receive the friendship or favour of sb: *You should keep in with Mr. Salton; he's an important person and will give you advice on your work.*

***keep* one's 'mouth shut** *(informal)* not give information to other people: *I saw you take the money, but I'll keep my mouth shut if you give me £100.* See also ***shut* one's mouth.**

***keep* mum** *(informal)* say nothing about sth: *He always found it difficult to keep mum when people told him secrets.*

***keep* one's 'nose clean** *(informal)* not get into trouble by breaking the law, disregarding rules etc: *I'll tell him to keep his nose clean when he leaves prison, but I know he'll commit some crime or other.*

***keep* one's nose to the grindstone** work hard and persistently: *You'll have to spend a lot of time keeping your nose (or with your nose) to the grindstone if you want to succeed in life.*

***keep* one's nose out of sth** *(informal)* not involve yourself in matters that do not concern you: *Keep your nose out of my business. It's got nothing to do with you!*

***keep* on (about sb/sth)** *(informal)* mention sth or criticize sb very often so that this causes annoyance: *I wish you wouldn't keep on about that coat you want to buy!*

***keep* (sb) on the rails** or **stay on the rails** *(informal)* (cause sb to) observe the conventions of society: *His parents tried to keep him on the rails while he was at school, but now he was at college he did just as* he *wanted.* See also ***go* off the rails.**

***keep* on the right side of sb** *(informal)* avoid offending sb, often to gain a favour: *I advise you to keep on the right side of the boss over the next few weeks—he's thinking about whom to recommend for promotion.*

***keep* on the right side of the law** not break the law: *You can get the information in any way you like, as long as you keep on the right side of the law.*

***keep* sb on his toes** *(informal)* make sb remain alert and ready for action: *There's a lot of excitement in a policeman's job—enough to keep you on your toes all the time.*

***(keep)* one eye on sb/sth** → ***(have/keep)* one eye on sb/sth**

***keep* open house** be willing to receive visitors, especially at any time: *Bill virtually keeps open house—he always seems to have at least one visitor.* Also **open house:** *It's open house at Bill's place.*

***keep* one's own counsel** form your own ideas, plans etc and not talk about them, so that other people are not sure of what you plan to do: *He listened to other people's suggestions and opinions, took a few notes, and kept his own counsel.*

***keep* sb posted** continue to provide sb with the latest news on sth: *That's all for now, but if there are any further developments, we'll keep you posted.*

***keep* smiling** show courage and cheerfulness in a time of discouragement: *There are so many difficulties facing the world at the moment that it is very hard to keep smiling.*

***keep* tabs on sb/sth** *(informal)* know about sb's movements, the progress of sth etc: *Your job, Jones, is to keep tabs on every suspect in this murder case.*

***keep* the 'ball rolling** → ***set/start/keep* the 'ball rolling**

***keep* the 'flag flying (for sb/sth)** do sth or behave in such a way that shows that you support an opinion, principle, or group: *A large delegation of exporters bravely kept the flag flying for us at the international trade exhibition.* See also ***show* the flag (for sb/sth).**

***keep* the peace** (cause sb to) observe the requirements or laws of a court, country etc: *The judge bound him over to keep the peace for a year. / The United Nations sent a force of soldiers to keep the peace in the area.* **peace-keeping** *adj*: *a peace-keeping force.*

***keep* the 'pot boiling** sustain sb's interest or an activity: *It looks as if we've won the contract, but to keep the pot boiling, I want to see the Managing Director this week.*

***keep* the wolf from the door** *(informal)* earn or be enough to feed yourself and your family: *Pete knew that the money wasn't very good, but at least it was a job and it kept the wolf from the door.*

***keep* oneself to oneself** be secretive; not meet or join other people socially: *I've tried to get Rodney to play football with the rest of us after work, but he likes to keep himself to himself all the time.*

***keep* sth to oneself** not tell others about sth: *I can't understand why you kept the news to yourself for so long. I'd have been keen to tell someone.*

***keep/lose* track of sb/sth** know or become unaware of the progress or movement of sb/sth: *Our computer keeps track of all the monthly payments made. / The suspect was known to be in New York last week but has since been lost track of.*

***keep* sth under one's hat** *(informal)* not tell other people about sth: *We've won the contract for the new tax computer, but keep it under your hat until it's announced officially.*

***keep* sth under wraps** or **stay under wraps** (cause sth to) remain hidden or silent: *The old documents that give details of the political meetings are too controversial and will stay under wraps for a further ten years.*

***keep* up sth 1** maintain sth such as a house in a good condition: *The cottage was so old that it was very difficult to keep up.* **upkeep** *n*: *The upkeep of the house was hard work.* **2** continue a skill, study, or activity: *I wish I'd kept up my French—I need it now for this job.*

***keep* up appearances** continue to present an unchanged appearance in public, especially after something, often bad, has happened: *Neil and Sarah's marriage was breaking up, but they were able to keep up appearances in front of their family and friends.*

***keep* up the good work** persevere in your useful activity or effort: *'I've sold over 50 tickets.' 'Excellent! Keep up the good work!'*

***keep* up with the Joneses** *(informal)* maintain the same material standards as your neighbours: *Wanting to keep up with the Joneses probably explains most of the new cars in our road.*

***keep* up with the times** adapt your way of life to be modern, not old-fashioned: *Every home and office needs the latest electronic equipment to keep up with the times.*

***keep/break* one's word** do or not do as you have promised to do: *He can be trusted to keep his word. / You've broken your word already by arriving late.*

**in/out of *keeping* with sb/sth** like/unlike or agreeing/not agreeing with sb/sth: *This document on dealing with overseas students is hardly in keeping with the policy adopted up to now.*

**for *keeps*** *(informal)* permanently; for ever: *'Oh Mummy! Is she really ours?' exclaimed Sarah, stroking the cat. 'Yes, she's ours, for keeps!'*

**the company sb *keeps*** → ***company***

**beyond/outside one's *ken*** not within your knowledge or understanding.

**the pot calls the *kettle* black** → ***pot***

**a different *kettle* of fish** → ***different***

**a fine/nice/pretty *kettle* of fish** → ***fine***

***kick* oneself** *(informal)* blame yourself or be angry with yourself for sth you have done or failed to do: *Later that day I thought about my refusal to join him in his work, and I (could have) kicked myself for missing such a good opportunity.*

***kick* against the pricks** strongly oppose sth that you can do nothing about, often harming yourself in the process: *'I hate it! I'm not going to school today!' 'You've got to go, dear, I'm afraid. It's no use kicking against the pricks.'*

***kick* sth around** *(informal)* discuss sth such as an idea in an informal way: *We'll begin the meeting by kicking around a few possibilities* *on how we might raise the money, then we'll make some decisions.*

***kick* sb downstairs/upstairs** *(informal)* demote/promote sb to a position of less power: *We can get rid of poor old Joe by kicking him downstairs to Administration. / Mr Smith, the former Minister of Housing, has been kicked upstairs to the House of Lords.*

***kick* one's heels** *(informal)* having nothing in particular to do; wait about idly, especially because of delays caused by other people: *The interviews were running very late, and I spent most of the afternoon just kicking my heels before it was my turn.*

**a *kick* in the pants** or **a kick up the backside** *(slang)* strong criticism: *What he needs is a good kick up the backside. Then he'll do some work.* **kick sb in the pants** criticize sb strongly.

***kick* sb in the teeth** *(slang)* treat sb brutally without thinking about his feelings: *He had been a faithful chairman for many years, but the club members really kicked him in the teeth* (or *really gave him a kick in the teeth) by voting him out of office.*

***kick* off** start, for example in a game of football, but also generally: *The match is due to kick off at 3.00. / At the meeting we'll kick off with the notices, then we'll get down to business.* **kick-off** *n*: *Kick-off is at 3.00.* **for a kick-off** *(informal)* as the first point in an argument: *'Why don't you take the children with you?' 'Well, we couldn't afford it, for a kick-off, and anyway we don't want them to miss school.'*

***kick* over the traces** reject and disobey the rules, especially of your parents: *I never agreed with my Mum. I kicked over the traces as I grew up, but somehow she still loved me.*

***kick* the bucket** *(slang)* die: *He said if he kicked the bucket his deputy could run the business as well as he had.*

***kick* up a fuss, row etc** *(informal)* create a great noise and trouble: *I remember as a child kicking up a great big fuss about wearing a particular cardigan because I didn't like its colour.*

***kick* up a stink** —> ***create*/raise a stink**

**for *kicks*** *(informal)* in order to get excitement and pleasure, sometimes of a dangerous or perverse kind: *When asked why they used to beat up old ladies, the teenagers said that they did it just for kicks.*

**handle sb/sth with *kid* gloves** —> ***handle***

**'*kids'* stuff** a very easy task: *'Aren't you worried about the general knowledge exam?' 'No, that's kids' stuff—I know all the sorts of things that they might ask.'*

**be in at the *kill*** —> **be in at the *death*/kill**

***kill* oneself (laughing)** *(informal)* laugh greatly with much enjoyment: *He didn't realize how funny he looked, but I was killing myself.*

***kill* oneself doing sth** *(informal)* spend a great deal of effort doing sth: *It would be good to leave at 7 o'clock, but don't kill yourself getting here by then. We can leave a bit later if we need to.* Note that this is usually used in the negative.

***kill* sth stone dead** *(informal)* completely destroy sth, making it unable to continue: *The scandal in his private life killed all possibility of his becoming a politican stone dead.*

***kill* the fatted calf** give a very friendly, hospitable welcome, treating sb in the best possible way: *When she returned from abroad, the family put on a party—they really killed the fatted calf for her, in fact.*

***kill* the goose that lays the golden eggs** destroy the source of your profit or success: *The government may be killing the goose that lays the golden eggs by putting a tax on the country's oil and gas resources.*

***kill* time** try to make a period of waiting pass as pleasantly as possible: *That's all right—do stay and chat. I'm only killing time till I go home. / Breaking my flight at Frankfurt, I found I had a couple of hours to kill.*

***kill* two birds with one stone** do two things or achieve two aims with one action: *'When you're next in London, come and see me.' 'Yes, I will—I'll do some shopping and kill two birds with one stone.'*

**in *kind*** **1** (of a payment) in the form of goods or services, not money: *He gets a good wage every week as well as what he receives in kind—a rent-free cottage, food and so on.* **2** (of an answer or retaliation) with the same type of treatment, language etc as you have received: *There's only one thing to do—pay your attacker back in kind with your own two fists.*

**of a *kind*/sort** existing, but not very satisfactory: *There's a road of a kind from the lakeside to the hut. A jeep could do it but not that car you have there.* Also **of sorts.** Note that these idioms come after the noun.

**of a *kind*/piece (with sb/sth)** similar (to), belonging to the same kind or class (as); consistent (with sb/sth): *He told them some rather rude stories, very much of a kind with the stories any teenage boy tells.*

***kind*/sort of sorry etc** *(informal)* rather; to some extent (often used to make an expression sound less definite): *You'll have to explain it kind of gently to her. / The colour of the wallpaper was hard to describe—sort of pink, I suppose.* Note that ***kind/sort of*** may qualify an adjective, adverb, or verb.

**the *King's*/English** —> **the *Queen's*/King's English**

**blow, send etc sb/sth to *kingdom* come** —> ***blow***

**till/until *kingdom* come** for a very long time (often used to imply that any effort spent will be wasted): *You could talk to him till kingdom come but he'll never change his mind.* See also **till/until the *cows* come home.**

**the *kiss* of death** an action that destroys or spoils sb/sth: *Many people think that television has given live entertainment and even the art of conversation the kiss of death.*

**the *kiss* of life** a method of getting an injured etc person breathing again by blowing into his mouth; action that gives life to an organization, business etc: *A teenage girl was given the kiss of life and taken to hospital yesterday after she had stopped breathing at a pop concert. / Our country's economy needs the kiss of life and we're looking to the Minister of Finance to give it.*

***kit* sb/sth out** provide sb/sth with clothes, equipment etc: *It certainly costs a lot of money to kit four children out with new school uniforms!*

**everything but the *kitchen* sink** → ***everything***

**one's *kith* and kin** members of your family: *He'd worked abroad for a long time but longed to return home to his own kith and kin.*

***knee*-high to a grasshopper** *(informal)* still only a small child: *I remember the first time I saw you—when you were just knee-high to a grasshopper—and look what's happened to you since!*

**on one's *knees*** kneeling down; humbly or begging for sth: *I saw him get down on his knees and pray. / The stationery department is so mean that if you want any files you practically have to go down on your knees and beg for them.*

**sb's *knees* are knocking** *(informal)* feel great nervousness and fear: *It was the first time I'd ever spoken in public, and my knees were really knocking!'*

**under the *knife*** *(informal)* having a surgical operation: *She's under the knife next week, I hear. Is it true she's got cancer?*

**(on) a *knife*-edge** (in) a very uncertain state: *The outcome of talks between the workers and the managers is balanced on a knife-edge tonight; if a settlement isn't reached, the national strike will begin at midnight.* Also **(on) a razor-edge.**

**like a *knife* through butter** easily; meeting no resistance or difficulty: *'There you are—like a knife through butter,' said the demonstrator as the powered shovel swung back with its load.*

**a *knight* in shining armour** *(informal)* a gentlemanly, gallant, and brave man, especially one who is seen as a lover, rescuer, or defender: *Her car had broken down, and here he was, a knight in shining armour rescuing a damsel in distress.*

***knit* one's brows** draw together your eyebrows as you think deeply about sth: *He looked serious, his brows knit, as he listened intently to the news of the disaster.*

***knock* sb's block off** *(slang)* hit sb very hard (used as a threat): *If I catch that lad coming in our workshop again, I'll knock his block off!*

***knock* sb cold** *(informal)* cause sb to be unconscious or greatly shocked: *The news that their daughter had been killed in the car accident knocked them cold.*

***knock* sb down** make sb lower the price of sth: *It's very expensive—can't you knock him down a pound or two?* **knock-down** *adj* very low: *knock-down prices.*

***knock* sth down** sell sth at an auction: *The carpet was knocked down for a record £8500.*

***knock* sb down with a feather** → ***you* could have knocked sb down with a feather**

***knock* sb for six** → ***hit*/knock sb for six**

***knock* sb's heads together** *(informal)* force two quarrelling people to behave sensibly by actually knocking their heads together or doing sth equally forceful: *If you children don't stop squabbling, I'll knock your heads together!'*

***knock*/beat sb/sth into a cocked hat** *(informal)* defeat sb/sth completely; be much better than sb/sth else: *All your work knocks my little effort into a cocked hat—well done!*

***knock* sb/sth into shape** → ***lick*/knock/get sb/sth into shape**

***knock* it in/off** *(informal)* stop doing sth (often used as an imperative): *Knock it off, will you? I'm trying to work.*

***knock* off** *(informal)* stop work: *What time do you knock off on Fridays?*

***knock* sb off** *(slang)* kill sb: *They say that the policeman got knocked off because he saw the raiders' faces.*

***knock* sth off 1** *(informal)* write, draw etc a story, article etc very quickly: *I'll knock off a rough sketch for you in a few minutes.* **2** *(slang)* rob a bank, shop etc; steal sth: *The two men got drunk and told stories about how they knocked off a post office the previous day. / Where did you knock off the jewellery?*

***knock* sb off his perch/pedestal** *(informal)* make sb humble and realize that he is not as important, clever etc as he thought he was: *Stories about the politician's private life knocked him off his pedestal.*

***knock*-on effect** an inevitable consequence of some cause: *The reduction in tax should have a knock-on effect on prices.*

***knock* sth on the head** *(informal)* cause sth not to be fulfilled; make sth seem absurd: *The increase in prices has firmly knocked our plan to buy a house on the head.*

***knock* on wood** → ***touch* wood**

***knock* sb out 1** cause sb to become unconscious by hitting him on the head or giving him a drug: *In the boxing last night the champion knocked his challenger out in the first round.'* **2** *(informal)* surprise or delight sb greatly: *Your new dress just knocks me out!* **knock-out** *n*: *That new film of his is a real knock-out!*

***knock* sb out (of sth)** remove or eliminate from a competition: *Altrincham were knocked out of the competition last night, and Aylesbury go into the next round.*

***knock* sb sideways** → ***throw*/knock sb sideways**

***knock* spots off sb/sth** *(informal)* be very much better than sth else: *His performance as Romeo knocked spots off all the others in the cast.*

***knock* the bottom out of sth** (suddenly)

remove the basis of sb's life, hopes, an argument etc: *The steelworks closing down really knocked the bottom out of all our plans for the future. / Recent discoveries seem to knock the bottom out of the theory of evolution, according to some scientists.*

***knock* the living daylights out of sb** → ***beat*/knock the living daylights out of sb**

**tie sb/oneself (up) in *knots*** → ***tie***

**in the *know*** *(informal)* having information not known by or not available to people generally: *Oh, don't worry. I'm not being indiscreet by talking in front of Jack—he's in the know too!*

**you never *know* (with sb/sth)** → ***never***

***know*/have all the answers** have considerable knowledge; believe that you have more knowledge than you do: *He's spent three years at college so he thinks he knows all the answers.* Also **know it all.**

**not *know* any better** not be able to behave well, for example because of a bad upbringing: *They show great patience towards the teenage hooligans. As one teacher said, 'After all, they don't know any better, do they?'*

***know* (sth) as well as I do** → ***know* (sth) very well**

***know* sth backwards** know sth such as a story thoroughly: *He was the son of a preacher so he thought he knew the Bible backwards.*

***know* best** know what should be done, thought etc better than any other person: *'I want to get up.' 'But the doctor said you were to stay in bed, and he knows best.'*

***know* better (than to do sth)** be wiser, more sensible, or better informed (than to do sth): *The changes in local schools were introduced by bureaucrats in the capital who should have known better.*

***know* sb by sight** be able to recognize sb but have no personal acquaintance of him: *'Have you ever met Dr. Galston?' 'No, but I know him by sight, of course.'*

***know* different** *(informal)* have an opinion, information, or evidence that is contrary to sth mentioned or suggested: *The members try to take notice of the club's traditions, but our superior, self-satisfied chairman thinks he knows different and wants to run things his own way.*

***know* for certain/sure that . . .** know with complete certainty that sth is correct: *I know for sure that I locked all the doors and windows. I just don't understand how anyone could have got in.*

**not *know* sb from Adam** not know at all who sb is: *I think you'd better explain to Mr Stott who I am, as he won't know me from Adam.*

***know* sth inside out** know or be skilled in every part of sth: *You've read that book so often that you must know it inside out by now.*

**not *know* one is born** *(informal)* live in such happy, comfortable circumstances that you do not realize your good fortune: *In my country you have to queue for two days to see a doctor. With the government health service here, people don't know they're born.*

***know* it all** → ***know*/have all the answers**

***know* sth like the back of one's hand** know sth such as a place very well: *Thanks, I don't need you to tell me how to find my way around that part of London. I lived there for years, so I know it like the back of my hand.*

***know* no bounds** be unlimited in scope, intensity, extent etc: *Your generosity knows no bounds! How can I ever repay you for all the kindness you've shown us?'*

**not *know* one end of sth from the other** *(informal)* know absolutely nothing about sth such as a machine or skill: *Of all the crazy things, him—a motorbike fanatic—going off with a young girl who didn't know one end of a screwdriver from the other!* Also **can't tell one end of sth from the other.**

***know* one's onions/stuff** *(informal)* understand and be skilled at your work: *The training was led by three experienced ladies who certainly knew their stuff.*

***know* one's own mind** know what you want to do and be able to make decisions: *'Well,' her mother replied, 'you are 25 after all. So you're old enough to know your own mind.'*

***know* one's place** know your position in society or employment and act in an appropriate way (often used of subordinate or inferior positions): *In Victorian days, a servant knew his place and worked just to carry out his master's orders.*

**not *know* the first thing about sth** have absolutely no knowledge of sth: *I'm sorry, I can't help you. You see, I don't know the first thing about computers.*

**not *know* the meaning of sth** have no experience of sth: *Work!—You don't know the meaning of it* (or *the word*)*—you just sit around all day doing nothing!*

***know*/learn the ropes** be/become familiar with how an institution, community etc works and know/discover what to do: *It'll take you a few months to learn the ropes, but I don't think you'll find it very difficult.* Also **show sb the ropes** teach sb: *Graham went back to his old job for a week to show the new man the ropes.*

***know* the score** *(informal)* know the real state of affairs: *I think I now know the score: things are worse than I thought, and you'll need a lot of money to get you out of this mess.*

***know* (sth) very well** be aware of sth, in spite of a claim that you do not: *You know very well what I mean; stop pretending that you don't.* Also **know (sth) as well as I do.**

***know* one's way about/around (sth)** be familiar with a place or a procedure: *Fortunately, I'd been to the library before so I knew my way about and managed to find the book I wanted quite quickly.*

***know* what one is doing/about** *(informal)* understand the nature and purpose of your actions; do sth deliberately: *Mother, I do know what I'm doing. I am 25, remember!*

***know* what is good for one** know what will

produce success or other favourable results: *If you know what's good for you, young man, you'll work harder in the future.*

**not *know* what one is missing** not realize how good sth that you dislike or do not want really is: *I now regret all the years I could have enjoyed classical music. But I was ignorant, you see; I just didn't know what I was missing!*

***know* what one is talking about** have the knowledge or experience of sth to support or justify your statement or opinions about it: *'I wouldn't stand any of their nonsense, I can tell you.' 'Oh, John, you don't know what you're talking about. You've never had to teach in that kind of school.'*

***know* what it is to be/do sth** have personal experience of being/doing sth, such as being ill: *I know what it is to lose your husband, Sarah, so try and take heart.*

***know* what's what** (*informal*) know what should be known of the facts, procedures, rules of behaviour etc in a certain situation or of things in general: *He's written several successful books, so he knows what's what in the literary world.*

**not *know* what to do with oneself** not know how to spend your time; feel embarrassed: *If I was at home all day, I wouldn't know what to do with myself. / The other two were cuddling in a corner, and he didn't know what to do with himself.*

***know* where one is/stands** know exactly what you are required or allowed to do, obtain, or accept within a social, political, or business framework; know the state of your own affairs: *You worry a lot about money but you never seem to know exactly where you stand.*

***know* where one is going** knowing clearly your purpose in life or in a particular activity: *Everyone else around me seems to know where they're going—but I'm so uncertain and hesitant.*

**not *know* where one's next meal/penny is coming from** live without security; live near to starvation or poverty: *They invited a few local down-and-outs to the Christmas party, people who usually didn't know (*or *weren't sure) where their next meal was coming from.*

**not *know* whether one is coming or going** (*informal*) be confused about what you are doing, because you are doing too many things: *I've got so much work to do that I don't know whether I'm coming or going.*

***know* which side one's bread is buttered (on)** know what to do for your own advantage or gain: *I'm sure Ray will make a special effort to please the new supervisor—he knows which side his bread is buttered!*

**not *know* which way to look** or **not know where to look** (*informal*) be embarrassed and self-conscious: *When the girl started breastfeeding her baby in the carriage it was obvious that some of the other people didn't know which way to look.*

**not *know* which way to turn** or **not know where to turn** not know what to do to obtain help, which course of action to follow etc: *I honestly don't know which way to turn now that Roy's left me.*

***know* who's who** (*informal*) know the identity of important people: *He's done business in that country for years, so he really knows who's who and should be able to get us the contract easily.*

**there is no *knowing*/saying/telling . . . ⟶ *no***

**have *known* better days ⟶ have *seen*/known better days**

**one never *knows* (with sb/sth) ⟶ you *never* know (with sb/sth)**

***knuckle* down (to sth)** (*informal*) concentrate on your work: *The exams are in two weeks, so isn't it time you knuckled down to your revision?*

**near the *knuckle* ⟶ near the *bone*/knuckle**

***knuckle* under (to sb)** (*informal*) submit to sb in authority: *The students refused to knuckle under and continued their protest in spite of great pressure.*

**rap sb on/over the *knuckles* ⟶ *rap***

# L

**a *labour* of love** a task that requires hard work and commitment and is not undertaken for necessity or profit but out of devotion: *Cleaning out the stables each day was a real labour of love to the farmer's son.*

***labour* the point** continue to repeat or explain further sth already mentioned: *I think you've said enough—there's no need to labour the point.*

**(it's) not for want/*lack* of trying, being told etc ⟶ *want***

**a '*ladies*' man** (*old-fashioned*) a man who enjoys the company of women: *Jim had always been a bit of a ladies' man but didn't get married till he was 45.*

***laid* back** (*informal*) relaxed; casual: *He has a very laid-back approach to life—never lets anything worry him.*

**be *laid* up with flu etc** be inactive and confined to your bed because of illness or injury: *He's been laid up for weeks with a broken leg.*

**as/like a *lamb* to the slaughter** appearing not to realize that you are about to suffer death or meet with danger, great difficulty, etc: *Thousands of young men followed the call of the country's leaders when war broke out and were led like lambs to the slaughter.*

**in two shakes (of a *lamb*'s tail)** ⟶ ***two***

**a *lame* duck** a business organization that cannot work well because of financial difficulties: *The government cannot go on baling out lame ducks much longer*. See also **a *dead* duck.**

**a *land* flowing with milk and honey** a place where life is enjoyable and resources are plentiful: *The country has become a land flowing with milk and honey now that rich supplies of oil and gas have been discovered.*

**in the *land* of Nod** asleep: *'Father's in the land of Nod, I think.' 'Well, leave him—he's had a tiring day!'*

**in the *land* of the living** leading a normal life, especially after illness, isolation, or sleep: *Ah—so you're back in the land of the living, Mike! It's so good to see you looking better again!*

***land*/fall on one's feet** *(informal)* make a quick recovery after sth such as an illness or business failure, often through good luck: *'He had no money at all after the war but soon got a job.' 'Yes, some people have a knack of falling on their feet, don't they?'*

***land* sb with sth** *(informal)* cause sb to take, accept, or receive sth that he does not want: *I've too much work already and now I've been landed with more jobs to do.* Note that this is often used in the passive.

**drop/fall into one's *lap*** ⟶ ***drop***

**in the *lap* of luxury** in very comfortable surroundings: *He's very rich and enjoys living in the lap of luxury.*

**in the *lap* of the gods** uncertain; not in your control: *It's in the lap of the gods who will win—we've no idea at all.*

***lap* sth up** *(informal)* accept or absorb sth such as flattery or knowledge eagerly: *Terry said all sorts of nice things about her, and she just lapped them up. / I've never known anyone as quick to learn as Ros. She simply laps up information.*

**at *large*** **1** escaped; set free without proper authority; undesirably at liberty: *Three weeks after the gaol break the escaped prisoners were still at large.* **2** taken as a whole group: *The president spoke a few words to the leaders standing near him then addressed the crowd at large.*

**loom *large* (in sth)** be or appear large or important in sth such as an economy, a programme, or sb's thoughts: *Heating costs loom large in their expenditure.*

**as *large* as life** seen as sb really is: *'But your uncle doesn't go to nightclubs!' 'Well, I saw him in that disco, large as life, dancing with a girl half his age.'*

***larger* than life** larger in size, importance etc than the person/thing represented; exaggerated so as to appear very impressive: *In the book, your grandfather really is larger than life, but I expect he was quite an ordinary sort of man to know.*

**be up with the *lark*** or **rise with the lark** ⟶ ***rise***

***lash* out (on sth)** spend a lot of money on sth: *They really lashed out on their daughter's wedding—they must be very rich.*

***lash* out at sb/sth** attack sb/sth very strongly: *The young man lashed out with both fists as the police tried to arrest him.*

**at *last*** at the end of a period of waiting, trying etc: *After nine months' gestation, at last the baby is born.* Also (stronger) **at long last.**

**at the *last*** during the final period of sth, especially sb's life: *He suffered terribly from the cancer but was peaceful at the last.*

**in the *last* analysis** ⟶ **in the *final*/last analysis**

**(and) *last* but not least** or **(and) last but by no means least** (used to introduce the final item in a list to show that this is no less important than the others previously mentioned): *He thanked everyone by name for the help: Mrs Watkins for preparing the food, Miss Smith for the flowers, Mr Jackson for his speech, and last but by no means least Mr Donnan for arranging the furniture.*

**play one's *last* card** ⟶ ***play***

**the *last* ditch** *(informal)* the final resource or effort that you can use to avoid defeat or to be safe. **last-ditch** *adj*: *a last-ditch attempt / last-ditch efforts.*

**the/one's *last* gasp** your last few breaths before death; a last burst of action or effort before the end: *Some people wait until their last gasp to make their peace with God. / The old machines in the factory worked well right up to the last gasp.*

**the *last* lap (of sth)** the final circuit in a race; final stage of a journey, competition, course of study etc: *As they entered the last lap, Jackman was still in third place. / It's been such hard work completing this contract! Thank heavens we're on the last lap now!*

**have the *last* laugh** ⟶ ***have***

**on one's *last* legs** not likely to live, continue, function, be wearable etc much longer: *'Do you know how old his dog Raffles is?' 'Fourteen,' she replied. 'He's on his last legs.' / It was only when it was discovered that the heating and ventilating system was on its last legs that action was taken.*

**(not/never) hear/see the end/*last* of sb/sth** ⟶ ***hear***

**the *last* person/thing sb wants** sb/sth highly unlikely, unsuitable, or disagreeable: *The last thing you want to see when you're feeling sick is a plate of greasy food.*

**as a *last* resort** as a means of help or supply only to be used when every other means has been used: *I want to spend our savings only as a last resort.*

**the *last*/final straw** an additional misfortune, defeat etc that finally overcomes you: *After he was made unemployed he was depressed, but it was the final straw when his wife left him.*

***last* the course** ⟶ ***stay*/last/survive the course**

***last* thing (at night)** immediately before going to bed or to sleep: *Last thing at night* *they always had a cup of cocoa to drink.* See also ***first* thing (in the morning)**.

**(be) the *last* (person) to do sth** → **be the *first*/last (person) to do sth**

**have the *last* word** → ***have***

**the *last* word (in sth)** the best, most fashionable etc of its type: *The advertisers claim that this new car is the last word in luxury.*

**sb's *last* word (on/about sth)** sb's final decision or statement on sth: *I tell you again, I won't compromise—and that's my last word on the subject.*

***latch* on (to sth)** grasp or understand sth: *Joe knew nothing about sailing but quickly latched on to his cousin's instructions.*

***latch* on to sb** attach yourself to a person or group of people, especially when uninvited: *In the cathedral Jean and Mike latched on to a group of tourists so as to listen to their guide.*

**of *late*** recently: *You've been very irritable of late. If you feel tired or unwell, perhaps you should see a doctor.*

***late* in the day** *(informal)* too late to bring good results or achieve what is right or pleasant: *It's a bit late in the day to change your mind now about joining us on holiday! You should have said you didn't want to come ages ago!*

**for a *laugh*** or **for laughs** for the sheer fun and amusement: *When the boys were asked why they threw stones at cars from the bridge over the motorway, they said they did it just for a laugh.*

***laugh* all the way to the bank** *(informal)* not care what people think of the way you make your money so long as you make plenty of it: *He paid them that much? They'll be laughing all the way to the bank.*

***laugh* etc one's head off** *(informal)* laugh etc very noisily: *You'll laugh your head off at the two new comedy series we've planned for you on this channel.* Other verbs are possible, such as ***cry, howl, roar, scream,*** and ***shout***.

***laugh* in sb's face** *(informal)* reject sb scornfully: *When I asked him to give me back the money, he just laughed in my face.*

***laugh* like a drain** *(informal)* laugh in a rough, noisy way: *He sat in front of the television, watching the rather rude jokes and laughing like a drain.*

***laugh*/grin/smile/on the other side of one's face** *(informal)* be made to appear ridiculous because your supposed reason for being happy etc is shown to be wrong: *If Pete thinks he's tricked the physics teacher again, then he'll get a surprise! Mr Parsons will make him laugh on the other side of his face!*

***laugh* sb/sth out of court** *(informal)* dismiss sb/sth scornfully as false or ridiculous: *The charge that the museum was more interested in making money than showing and preserving items of historical interest was simply laughed out of court by its directors.*

***laugh* up one's sleeve** *(informal)* find sth amusing but not show your amusement: *He could feel that his former colleagues were laughing up their sleeves at his dismissal.*

**be *laughing*** *(informal)* be in a fortunate position with no worries: *If you get that amount of money in your new job, you'll be laughing!*

**no *laughing* matter** → ***no***

**rest on one's *laurels*** → ***rest***

***law* and order** the laws under which the people of a country are governed and protected, and the controlling influence of laws in general: *The police are concerned with the maintenance of law and order.*

**take the *law* into one's own hands** → ***take***

**the *law* of the jungle** the principle that no civilized laws apply in a situation but that the strongest, most violent, or most unscrupulous will survive, be successful, etc: *The only law that is effective in this factory is the law of the jungle—the most powerful group, in this case the union leaders, are the ones who win.*

**a *law* of the Medes and Persians** any established practice or rule that is always followed: *They could be more flexible. After all, it's not a law of the Medes and Persians that they have tea at 4 o'clock exactly every day.*

**a *law* unto oneself** sb who does what he wants, without considering the rules of the group of people, society etc he is in: *He's a law unto himself—he doesn't care what anyone else thinks about the way he behaves.*

***lay* a finger on sb** *(informal)* harm or molest sb in some way (usually used in the negative): *The foreman knows which one of the workers is damaging the cars, but he can't lay a finger on him or everyone will go on strike.* / *Honestly, I tell you I didn't lay a finger on her.*

***lay* sth at sb's door** put the blame, responsibility, or guilt for sth on sb: *The report laid the blame firmly at the door of the parents—they should have looked after the children properly.* **lie at sb's door** (of blame etc) be borne by sb.

***lay* sth bare** expose sth fully to the eye or so that it can be fully known: *The commission's report laid all the facts of the proposal bare to the public.*

***lay* (all) one's cards on the table** → ***put*/lay/place (all) one's cards on the table**

***lay* down one's arms** stop fighting: *Tell your men to lay down their arms—the war's over.*

***lay* down one's life (for sb/sth)** sacrifice your life (on behalf of your country, king etc): *Thousands of young men laid down their lives for the cause of peace.*

***lay* down the law** *(informal)* talk with authority, whether you really have this authority or not: *In the pub, a self-styled expert was laying down the law on the country's future, and a group gathered round.*

***lay* eyes on sb/sth** → ***clap*/set/lay eyes on sb/sth**

***lay* (one's) hands on sb** place your hands on sb to bless or heal them: *At the end of the service, several people went forward to the altar, and the ministers laid their hands on them.* **ˈlaying-ˌon of ˈhands** *n.*

***lay*/put one's hands on sth** find sth that you are looking for; obtain and use sth: *Why can I never lay my hands on a pen when I want to write down a phone message? / If we could put our hands on £2 million then the future would be transformed!*

***lay* one's head on the block** → ***put*/lay one's head on the block**

***lay* into sb** *(informal)* attack sb very strongly: *I saw Jack lay into a man half his size outside the pub.*

***lay*/pile it on (thick)** *(informal)* exaggerate, especially when praising sb/sth: *'That's the most marvellous film I've ever seen. It was absolutely fantastic!' 'That's laying it on rather. I thought it was just all right.'* Also **lay it on with a trowel.**

***lay* it on the line** *(informal)* state an order, opinion etc with great force: *Finally, the headmaster came in and really laid it on the line—I've never seen the students turn so quiet!* See also ***lay* sth on the line.**

***lay* sb/sth low** weaken or destroy sb/sth: *The whole family was laid low by the flu last week.*

**the *lay* of the land** → **the *lie*/lay of the land**

***lay* off (it)** or **lay off (doing) sth** *(informal)* stop doing sth harmful, irritating etc: *Lay off it, will you! I'm tired of you interfering with my work!*

***lay* sb off** dismiss an employee from work: *Worst hit is the steel works in Hartlepool, where 1000 men are to be laid off.*

***lay* on sth** supply or organize sth: *It was years before gas was laid on to the village. / The city laid on a splendid reception to greet the winning team when they arrived home.*

***lay* sth on the line** *(informal)* risk sth important such as your reputation or money: *I'm even prepared to lay my own job on the line—either you give these men their jobs back or I leave as well.* See also ***lay* it on the line.**

***lay*/leave oneself (wide) open to sth** invite or expose yourself to criticism, ridicule etc: *By not saying anything in your defence, you leave yourself wide open to all sorts of accusations.*

***lay* out sb, a corpse, a body etc** prepare sb's corpse for burial: *Father was laid out in the front room.*

***lay* out sth** spend (a lot of) money: *The committee decided to lay out all their budget on redecorating the college.* **outlay** *n*: *There has been considerable outlay on furnishings for the new hall.*

***lay* sb to rest** bury sb: *In a simple ceremony, the body of their former colleague was laid to rest in the churchyard.* See also ***lay* sth to rest.**

***lay* sth to rest** finally remove sth such as a rumour or uncertainty; allay: *An official statement from the bosses laid to rest any remaining worries about the future of the company.* See also ***lay* sb to rest.**

***lay* up sth 1** prepare a stock or store of sth such as fuel or food for use: *There was no ammunition laid up in the storehouses.* **2** take sth such as a car or ship out of use for a long time: *The car's been laid up for weeks—I can't afford to have it repaired.*

***lay* up trouble etc for oneself** cause trouble etc for yourself in future by pursuing a certain course of action: *You're laying up trouble for yourself if you don't look after your body and get enough physical exercise.*

***lay* sth waste** destroy sth such as houses, crops etc: *The soldiers made their way across the country, laying waste all the land in their path.* Also **lay waste to sth.**

***lead* sb a dance** *(informal)* make sb follow you from place to place, causing him great worry: *As an expert on strategy, he led the navy a lively dance before they finally sank his ship.*

**you can take/*lead* a horse to water but you can't make him drink** → ***you***

***lead* sb astray** tempt sb to do wrong; mislead: *Young people are easily led astray.*

***lead* sb on** encourage sb to believe, do etc sth, often by deceiving him: *The washing-machine salesman led his customer on with promises of special discounts and after-sales service.*

***lead* sb to believe (that . . . )** make sb think that sth is true, often wrongly: *We were led to believe that there was a guarantee on this clock—and now the shop has told us that because it was in a sale there wasn't one.*

***lead* sb to the altar** *(old-fashioned)* marry a woman.

***lead* sb up the garden path** *(informal)* mislead or deceive sb: *Stop leading us up the garden path with such a silly story—tell us the truth!*

**a *leading* light (in/of sth)** sb who plays an important position in a community, profession etc: *Professor Tipp, a leading light in the movement to restore capital punishment, will be giving a lecture on 'The Future of our Society'.*

**a *leading* question** a question that is so worded that you are encouraged to give a particular answer, such as: *Don't you think it's cheap?*

**the blind *leading* the blind** → ***blind***

**one thing *leads* to another** → ***one***

**take a *leaf* out of sb's book** → ***take***

***lean* on sb 1** need or depend on sb for support or help: *It's fortunate that his cousin lives locally—he leant on her a lot in those first few weeks after his wife's death.* **2** *(informal)* try to force sb to do sth, possibly by means of threats: *If you lean on him, he'll tell us where the safe is.*

***lean* over backwards to do sth** → ***bend*/lean/fall over backwards to do sth**

**a *leap*/shot in the dark** an action, answer, idea etc that is risked in the hope that it is correct: *For many people, believing in God is a leap in the dark. / His suggestion that the company had sold 3 million pens in the last year was a shot in the dark rather than an exact figure.*

**by/in *leaps* and bounds** *(informal)* very much; very quickly: *My knowledge of Ger-*

*man increased by leaps and bounds when I lived in Germany for a year.*

***learn* one's lesson** learn, from sth that you have done or that has happened to you, what (not) to do in similar circumstances: *He used to think that everyone was as honest as himself, but now his wallet has been stolen he's learnt his lesson.*

***learn* the ropes** ⟶ ***know*/learn the ropes**

**a new *lease* of life** ⟶ ***new***

**at *least*** **1** as a minimum number or amount: *There were at least 300 people at the concert.* **2** this much, if nothing more: *He might at least have telephoned if he knew he was going to be late.*

**(not) in the *least*** (not) at all; (not) in any way or in any degree: *She wasn't in the least afraid—her Dad was with her. / If you are in the least doubtful about what to do, then ask for help.*

**the (very) *least* one can do** an action that is the (absolute) minimum that politeness, thankfulness, duty etc demands of you: *They were so kind to us when we were ill, the very least we can do is give them some help now they're in difficulty.*

**the *least* said (about sb/sth), the better** ⟶ **the *less*/least said (about sb/sth), the better**

***leave* a lot, much etc to be desired** be unsatisfactory or inadequate: *Your standard of work has gone down, Smith. In fact it leaves a great deal to be desired.*

***leave*/let sb/sth alone** not take, touch, or interfere with sb/sth: *The museum attendant told the children to leave the exhibits alone.* See also ***let* alone**.

***leave*/let sb/sth be** not interfere with sb/sth: *Oh, leave Mary be! She's in one of her moods again and doesn't want to talk.*

***leave* sb/sth behind** forget to take sb/sth with you: *I realized I'd left my umbrella behind on the train.*

***leave* sb/sth (far) behind** be very much better than sb/sth; outstrip: *Their country leaves ours far behind when it comes to business efficiency.*

***leave* sb cold** not interest, excite, or amuse sb: *Classical music leaves me absolutely cold, but I love rock.*

***leave* sb in the dark (about sth)** ⟶ ***keep*/leave sb in the dark (about sth)**

***leave* sb in the lurch** put sb in a difficult situation: *The party organizers were left in the lurch when their candidate resigned two days before the election.*

***leave* one's mark (on sb/sth)** have an influence on sb/sth that can be noticed and recognized: *She left her mark wherever she worked—the effects of her quiet efficiency were remarkable.*

***leave* no stone unturned** try to find every possible solution to a problem: *'Surely you don't suspect me, Inspector?' 'Well in my business I must leave no stone unturned. Someone committed the crime, after all.'*

***leave* of absence** *(formal)* time spent absent from official duty: *Several of my colleagues at work have had leave of absence to go on training courses.*

**take *leave* of one's senses** ⟶ ***take***

***leave* oneself (wide) open to sth** ⟶ ***lay*/leave oneself (wide) open to sth**

***leave* sb out in the cold** be excluded from or neglected or ignored by a community, group, or activity: *Of the country's three political party leaders, two were invited to take part in the programme but the third was left out in the cold.*

***leave* sth over** leave sth, especially the worse part of sth, as a remainder: *The dogs eat up what we leave over from our food.* **left-overs** (plural only) *n*: *The dogs ate the left-overs.*

***leave* sb speechless** astonish, delight, or anger sb (so much that he cannot properly reply, object etc): *Your kindness leaves me somewhat speechless, I confess.*

***leave* sb/sth standing** *(informal)* greatly exceed sb/sth in speed, skill, worth etc: *As regards the quality of his work, he leaves the others standing.*

***leave* the door open (for/on sth)** make it possible for sth to happen or be done: *The door was left open for further negotiations as the bosses were not completely stubborn at the end of talks.*

***leave* sb 'to it** *(informal)* allow sb to proceed with a task without help or interference: *Oh well, we'll leave you to it, Derek—you seem to be managing very well by yourself.*

***leave* sb to his own devices** allow sb to look after himself or solve a problem himself: *The children's free time was not all completely organized and structured—they were left to their own devices for a while every so often.*

***leave*/let well alone** not interfere with an arrangement, statement etc that is already adequate: *My advice to anyone wanting to tamper with the club constitution is to leave well alone—it is all so complicated that if you make one change, you'll have to change many other things as well.*

***leave* word (with sb)** leave a message with sb: *They left word with the porter that she had had to go into hospital during the night.*

***leaven* the whole lump** have a transforming effect on a complete group, community etc: *It's good for slow learners to be in a class of mixed ability. A few clever students leaven the whole lump.*

**one's *left* hand does not know what one's right hand is doing** you act secretly or in a way that conflicts with other behaviour: *It was clear that the company's left hand didn't know what its right hand was doing—one department was advertising for more workers while another was saying that the whole firm was soon going to close down.*

**be *left* holding the baby** *(informal)* be left as the person who is responsible for dealing with a difficulty or problem or for organizing sth: *The finance company cancelled the loan on the car, and I was left holding a very* *expensive baby. / That's just like Sue—saying she'd arrange the party and then going off to leave me holding the baby.*

***left*, right, and centre** everywhere; in every way: *Posters appeared left, right, and centre advertising the new product. / I seem to have disappointed them left, right, and centre recently.*

***left* to oneself/itself** when not helped, hindered, guided, or interfered with: *You can put a bandage on the cut if you like, but it'll heal just as quickly left to itself.*

**with one's tail between one's *legs* ⟶ *tail***

***lend* (sb) a (helping) hand ⟶ *give*/lend (sb) a (helping) hand**

***lend* one's/an ear (to sb/sth)** listen to sb/sth as a response to a request: *Most people find that their doctor lends an ear when they need help.*

***lend* colour to sth ⟶ *give*/lend colour to sth**

***lend* itself to sth** be suitable for a particular use: *The book lends itself magnificently to being adapted into a play.*

**at *length* 1** after a long time; eventually: *The explorer waited for supplies to come, and when at length they arrived he had nearly starved.* **2** fully; in great detail: *The headmistress explained the new teaching methods at length to try to persuade her teachers to adopt them.*

**the *length* and breadth of sth** all or most of the area of land: *I've walked across the length and breadth of Britain but I've never seen such beautiful scenery as here.*

**the *leopard* cannot change his spots** *(saying)* basic human nature cannot change itself.

**the *less*/least said (about sb/sth), the better** sb/sth is unpleasant, unfavourable etc so we do not want to talk about it for a long time: *I think the less said about your performance in the concert the better—it was not one of your good days, I'm afraid.*

**the *lesser* of two evils** (of two alternatives, especially unattractive ones) sth that is less bad or a little better than sth else: *If you don't agree with either political party you'll just be voting for the lesser of two evils.*

***let* alone** and most certainly (not); how much less likely or probable (it is that you would do, find etc sth than what has been mentioned): *I wouldn't speak to him, let alone trust him and lend him some money.* Note that this is usually used in the negative. Also **never mind.** See also ***leave*/let sb/sth alone.**

***let* sb/sth alone ⟶ *leave*/let sb/sth alone**

***let* sb/sth be ⟶ *leave*/let sb/sth be**

***let* bygones be bygones** allow old quarrels or grievances to be forgotten: *They quarrelled over a girl, but she didn't marry either of them, so why can't they let bygones be bygones?*

***let* sb down** disappoint sb by not keeping a promise or not doing what was expected: *We've been let down so many times by the importers, who always seem to be late delivering the goods.* Also *(becoming old-fashioned)* **let the 'side down.**

***let* fly (at sb/sth) (with sth)** express your criticism (of sb/sth) without restraint; throw or aim sth (at sb/sth) strongly or recklessly: *She really got annoyed! I've never seen anyone let fly at their mother like that before!*

***let* oneself go** be completely relaxed and uninhibited; allow free expression of your feelings: *The students really let themselves go at the party after their exams.*

***let* oneself/sth go** allow the appearance of yourself, a garden, house etc to deteriorate: *The new residents have really let the greenhouse go—it's almost overgrown already.*

***let* one's 'hair down** *(informal)* relax and enjoy yourself: *Go on—let your hair down—it is your birthday!*

***let* sb in on sth** tell sb a secret: *We don't want to let other people in on our ideas for the party.* See also **be *in* on sth.**

***let* it all hang out** *(slang)* act in a very uninhibited or uncontrolled manner, without taking any notice of embarrassment caused: *Adrian's party last year was great—we really let it all hang out.*

***let* it go (at that)** not say or do anything further which could cause more thought or lead to closer examination: *I paid too little for the pens, but I decided to let it go since they'd charged me too much last time I bought something in that shop.*

***let* sb off (sth)** excuse sb from a punishment or a difficult task: *He's lucky—the judge let him off. / She's been let off the drying-up again.*

***let* off steam** *(informal)* release great energy, strong feelings, suppressed tension etc: *They took their lively three-year-old to the park every day so he could let off steam.*

***let* sb off the hook** *(informal)* free sb from punishment or sth unpleasant, difficult, or embarrassing: *We'll let you off the hook this time—but if you break another window, my lad, then you'll be out of a job!*

***let* sb off with sth** give sb a lighter sentence than the law allows: *The Judge let him off with a fine rather than send him to prison.* Also **let sb off lightly.**

***let* on (that . . . )** allow sth to be known: *Don't let on that you can speak French or you'll be asked to lead the school trip to France next month.*

***let* sth out** reveal or disclose sth: *Who let out the exam results? They were supposed to be confidential until tomorrow.* Also **let (it) out that . . . .**

***let* sleeping dogs lie** *(saying)* it is better not to disturb or interfere with sb/sth that is giving no trouble: *There seemed to be no reason to provoke unnecessary panic about the disease, so the authorities decided to let sleeping dogs lie and not make any public statements.*

***let* the cat out of the bag** *(informal)* unintentionally and carelessly disclose a secret or make sth, planned as a surprise, known too soon: *She hadn't told anyone she was taking driving lessons. It was her instruc-*

*tor phoning to change an appointment that let the cat out of the bag.* **the cat is out of the bag** the secret has been made known: *He's hoodwinked the public for a long time, but the cat's out of the bag now.*

***let* the dead bury their dead** *(saying)* it is better to be concerned with present life and work than always remembering the past and people, institutions etc that are dead or finished.

**(not) *let* the grass grow under one's feet** (not) be inactive or waste time when there are things that need to be done.

***let* the 'side down** ⟶ ***let* sb down**

***let* up** relax, slacken, ease off: *You've worked so hard on the report that you can't let up now. There's about another two days' work and then you'll have finished it.* **let-up** *n*: *The storm continued for three hours, with no let-up.*

***let* well alone** ⟶ ***leave*/let well alone**

**to the *letter*** literally; in every detail: *If you didn't follow all the rules to the letter, you were severely punished.*

**the *letter* of the law** a literal and strict enforcement of the law, contrasted with its general purpose or intended effect (**the spirit of the law**): *If I were to adhere to the letter of the law, you would certainly be punished severely, but in view of all your circumstances I shall merely caution you.*

**on the *level*** *(informal)* honest; genuine; sincere: *In any dealings with him you always felt that he was on the level.*

**do/try one's *level* best** ⟶ ***do***

**keep/maintain a *level* head** ⟶ ***keep***

***level* pegging** (in a state of) equality between two or more competitors: *There's ten minutes left, and the teams are still level pegging.*

**take the *liberty* of doing sth** ⟶ ***take***

**at *liberty* to do sth** free to do sth: *If you don't like the way I'm doing it, you're quite at liberty to say so.*

***lick* sb's boots** *(informal)* obey sb who has authority over you, usually in a pretended, humble way: *If he thinks that I'm going to spend the rest of my life licking his boots, he's very much mistaken! / Politicians who want to get on seem to have to lick their leaders' boots all the time.*

***lick*/knock/get sb/sth into shape** *(informal)* raise sb such as a recruit or sth such as a scheme to the proper standard of skill, efficiency etc: *I don't think that the group who volunteered to join the football team are very promising, but our trainer will, I'm sure, soon lick them into shape.*

***lick*/smack one's lips** *(informal)* show great enjoyment or excitement at sth or the prospect of sth: *The children looked on, licking their lips greedily, as mother cut the cake.*

**a *lick* of paint** a coat of fresh paint, especially when put on quickly and not thoroughly: *All this house needs is a good clean and a lick of paint in a few places.*

***lick* one's wounds** *(informal)* (try to) comfort yourself, after a defeat, injury, or loss: *The university administrators are still licking their wounds after last month's big cutback in the money they receive from the government.*

**take the *lid* off sth** ⟶ ***take***

***lie* at sb's door** ⟶ ***lay* sth at sb's door**

***lie* behind sth** be the explanation or reason for sth: *Greed lay behind his desire for power.*

***lie* down on the job** *(informal)* not do a job properly: *We expect our employees to put all their efforts into their work—there's no lying down on the job here.*

***lie* in** stay in bed for a long time in the morning: *We never lie in now that we've got children—there are so many things to do.* **lie-in** *n*: *I like a good lie-in at weekends.*

***lie* in state** (of (the body of) a very important dead person) be placed on public view before burial: *The dead statesman's body will lie in state for five days so that the common people may pay their last respects.*

***lie* in wait (for sb/sth)** hide, preparing to meet sb/sth, especially in an attack: *The gang lay in wait for the security van which contained money for the bank.*

***lie* low** remain in hiding or inactive for a short time: *The thieves lay low for a few days in a farmhouse, then tried to leave the country with the money.* Also *(informal)* **lie doggo.**

**the *lie*/lay of the land** the features and details of sth or the attitudes, thoughts etc of people used to help make a decision: *I wanted to give him some business, so first, to find out the lie of the land, I asked him if he was busy.* Also **how the 'land lies.**

***lie* through one's teeth** *(informal)* tell lies boldly without any shame: *He's lying through his teeth—he says he's never cheated anyone, but I've seen him steal several times.*

**there *lies* the rub** ⟶ **there is/lies the *rub***

**in *lieu* (of sth)** *(formal)* instead (of sth): *You don't get paid for working overtime, but we'll give you time off in lieu.*

**for one's *life*** with the greatest speed (used sometimes when your life is actually in danger): *They heard the gunshots and ran for their lives.*

**(a matter of) *life* and/or death** sth that determines whether you live or die; sth very important that affects the survival of sth: *Whether to go by train or bus is hardly a matter of life and death, so why are you making such a fuss?* **life-and-death** *adj*: *a life-and-death decision.*

***life* and/or limb** your survival and/or your preservation from accident or injury: *Firemen risk life and limb to save people from burning buildings.*

**the *life* and soul of the party** *(informal)* sb who is self-confident, stimulating, witty, and who keeps other people at a party lively: *It was rather dull till Patrick came—he really was the life and soul of the party!*

**take one's *life* in/into one's hands** ⟶ ***take***

**not for the '*life* of one** despite every attempt; not possibly: *I can't for the life of me understand why you're marrying Sheila.*

**(not) *lift*/raise a finger to do sth** (not) bother to make the slightest effort to do sth, especially to help sb: *Even though he knew some of the tenants were suffering greatly, the landlord was so hard that he didn't lift a finger to help them.*

**(not) *lift* one's hand against sb** →**(not) *raise*/lift one's hand against sb**

***lift* oneself up by one's own bootstraps/bootlaces** →***pull*/lift oneself up by one's own bootstraps/bootlaces**

**be/go out like a *light*** →***go***

**as *light* as a feather** very light in weight: *'Are those clothes heavy?' 'No, they're as light as a feather.'*

***light* at the end of the tunnel** success, happiness etc after a long period of difficulty or hardship: *After years of perseverence to find a cure for the disease, it looks as if there's light at the end of the tunnel at least.*

**a *light* heart** →**a *heavy*/light heart**

**in the *light* of sth** according to the way of seeing or understanding sth: *In the light of recent discoveries, scientists are having to think again about theories on the origin of life.*

**make *light* of sth** →***make***

**in the cold *light* of day** →***cold***

**the *light* of day** daylight; the state of being seen or seeing; stage at which a difficulty becomes clarified or solved: *The design for the new car never saw the light of day because of research cutbacks.*

***light* on/upon sth** *(formal)* discover sth, especially by chance: *The explorers suddenly lit upon an entrance to a secret chamber.*

**hide one's *light* under a bushel** →***hide***

**many hands make *light* work** →***many***

**make *light* work of (doing) sth** →***make***

**and the *like*** and so on; together with things or people of a similar kind: *We bought some meat—pork, lamb, and the like—in preparation for the party.*

**(not/never) hear/see the *like* (of sb/sth)** →***hear***

**(not/never) see sb/sth's *like* again** →***see***

**as *like* as two peas** or **as like as peas in a pod** *(informal)* very similar in appearance: *We haven't met before but you must be Alex Bannerjee's brother from Wolverhampton—you're as like as two peas!'*

***like* it or lump it** *(informal)* whether you like sth or not: *I've explained already. While you're staying with your grandparents, you go to church on Sundays, like it or lump it.* See also **lump it.**

**as *likely* as not** probably; with an equal chance of occurring or not occurring: *I can't be sure, of course, but as likely as not Louise will get into university.*

**the *likes* of sb** *(informal)* people like sb; anyone who is as privileged, criminal, humble, intellectual etc: *'The judge gave him a six-month sentence.' 'That's not long enough! Society ought to be protected against the likes of him.'*

**out on a *limb*** *(informal)* in a risky and often isolated position: *The success of one of the two companies in the field has left the other out on a limb. / I know most people think it unlikely, but I'm going to go out on a limb and predict a victory for Blackburn.*

**in the *limelight*** or **out of the limelight** in or out of a place of public attention or notice: *The union leader kept out of the limelight yesterday after rumours about his resignation began to circulate.*

**the (absolute) *limit*** →***absolute***

**in *line* for sth** likely to receive sth such as a job or position: *He's doing so well that he's in line for a directorship soon.*

**lay it on the *line*** →***lay***

**somewhere etc along the *line*** at some point etc during the process of development, manufacture etc: *There always seems to be a strike on in one of the factories in the car industry that holds up production at one point along the line.*

**the *line* of least resistance** the course of action that gives the least difficulty: *Don't give up and follow the line of least resistance, Polly! There's a better way, even though it's harder!*

***line* one's pockets** *(informal)* make or gain a lot of money for yourself, especially by cunning or dishonest methods: *The directors discovered that the workers were lining their pockets by selling the company's products secretly themselves.*

**in/out of *line* with sb/sth** agreeing/disagreeing with the opinions, rules etc of other people: *He is the type of politician who likes to be out of line with others in his party.*

**read between the *lines*** →***read***

**on/along the *lines* of sth** in the style or way of sth: *I'd like to make you a dress along the lines of what you are wearing now. What do you think?*

**put one's head in(to) the *lion*'s mouth** →***put***

**the *lion*'s share (of sth)** very much the largest part of sth: *The national broadcasting company again took the lion's share of television audiences this Christmas.*

**pay *lip*-service to sth** →***pay***

**hang on sb's *lips*/words** →***hang***

**one's *lips* are sealed** *(informal)* you will not say anything to anyone on a particular subject: *I can't disclose the source of my information, I'm afraid. My lips are sealed.*

***lit* up** *(informal)* drunk, merry: *Last New Year's Eve we were all pretty lit up.*

**. . . with a *little* a, b, c etc** →**with a *small*/little a, b, c etc**

**a *little* bird told me** I have heard about sth in a way that I do not want to reveal: *A little bird told me it was your birthday—so here's a present!*

**(God) bless your, his etc *(little)* cotton socks** →**(God) *bless* your, his etc soul/heart**

**twist sb (a)round one's *little* finger** →***twist***

**a *little* fish in a big pond** → ***a big* fish in a little pond**
**sb's *(little)* game** *(informal)* sb's trick, plan, or purpose: *So that's your little game—getting me moved to a different office and then doing my job for me.*
***little* green men** beings from outside the earth.
**of *little* moment** → **of (some, no, little etc) *moment***
**make *little* odds** → ***make* no/little odds**
***little* short of disastrous, deception etc** → ***nothing*/little short of disastrous, deception etc**
**set *little* store by sth** → ***set* (no, great, little etc) store by sth**
**it is *little* wonder (that . . .)** → **it is *no*/little/small wonder (that . . .)**
***live* and learn** gain useful experience as you grow older: *I left my car unlocked outside my house and someone stole a tape-recorder, but you live and learn—I'll never do that again!*
***live* and 'let live** *(saying)* tolerate the ways of other people and not try to direct or run their lives: *Life's a matter of live and let live, isn't it—if you want to be happy.*
***live* (from) hand to mouth** live poorly; use all the money you receive to support yourself without being able to save any: *Although we get unemployment pay, we're really living from hand to mouth.* **hand-to-mouth** *adj*: *a hand-to-mouth existence.*
**be/*live* in clover** *(informal)* live very comfortably and happily: *She married a rich young man and thought they'd be living in clover for the rest of their lives.*
***live* in fear of one's life** → ***go*/live in fear of one's life**
***live* in sin** → ***live* together**
***live* it up** lead an easy life filled with pleasure: *He spent three months in the U.S.A., living it up on his winnings from betting.*
***live* off the fat of the land** *(informal)* enjoy the best food, drink etc; live a materially prosperous life, with plenty of money, food and drink, and entertainments: *Our society has many people living off the fat of the land, while others have scarcely enough to live on.*
***live* on borrowed time** live for a longer time than you are expected to: *The doctors say he's living on borrowed time and will probably die soon.*
***live* to fight another day** have a further chance to be in a fight, competition etc, especially when you have not been too badly beaten: *It looks as if old John will live to fight another day—he only lost the chairmanship by two votes.*
***live* to see the day** survive until the time when sth, especially sth unpleasant, happens: *May I never live to see the day when these fields are turned into building plots.*
***live* to tell the tale** survive an experience so that you can tell other people what happened: *Nobody who was put in that concentration camp lived to tell the tale.*
***live* together** live in the same house, room etc, as if husband and wife, but without being married: *Ruth and Ray lived together for six years before they got married.* Also **live in sin** *(old-fashioned)*; **live with sb.**
***live* up to sth** reach or fulfil a particular standard: *This car will certainly live up to all your expectations if you buy it, sir.*
**a *live* wire** a wire through which electric current passes; a lively, active person: *Don't touch the live wires! / Roger's a real live wire—he's always keen to be involved in anything new.*
**beat/knock the *living* daylights out of sb** → ***beat***
**in/within *living* memory** at or during a time that people living can still remember: *These are the worst floods in this country in living memory.*
***lo* and behold** see!; notice! (used to express or invite surprise): *Who came in the room next? Lo and behold, it was Aunt Bertha, who everyone thought was still in Australia!*
**a *load* of (old) rubbish/cobblers** *(slang, old-fashioned)* nonsense: *I've never heard such a load of old cobblers in my life!*
**a *load* off sb's mind** relief from anxiety: *It took a tremendous load off my mind when I knew that my daughter wasn't on the plane that crashed.*
***load* the dice against sb** prejudice sb's/sth's chance of success: *In school work, the dice are really loaded against children who get no encouragement at home.*
***local* colour** social, geographical etc details that make a novel etc seem more real; customs that are typical of a place: *Macaulay used local colour in his historical writings—he'd travelled widely through the areas he wrote about.*
**the *local* talent** *(informal)* the girls or young men in a town, village, etc who are available to be befriended: *I guess all the boys will be at the disco tonight looking over the local talent.*
**under *lock* and key** locked up, for example in prison: *The escaped prisoners are now safely back under lock and key.*
***lock* horns with sb** argue or fight with sb: *The lawyers said that they did not want to lock horns with the judge but suggested that there was a difference of opinion.*
***lock* sb out** prevent workers from entering their place of work: *Employees have been locked out until they accept the management's offer.* **lock-out** *n.*
***lock*, stock, and barrel** the whole of sth mentioned or implied: *He was emigrating so wanted to sell all his possessions, lock, stock, and barrel.*
***lock* the stable door after the horse has bolted** take precautions too late to be effective: *We decided to fit security locks on all the windows and doors only after the house was broken into—locking the stable door after the horse had bolted.*
**at *loggerheads* (with sb)** in dispute; quar-

relling or arguing (with sb): *The teachers are at loggerheads with the students on how much homework should be set.*

**plough a *lone*/lonely furrow** ⟶ ***plough***

**so *long* (for now)** goodbye until we next meet: *'So long, Ann—see you on Thursday.' 'Yes, see you, Sarah.'*

**the *long* and the short of it** *(informal)* the essential information about a situation, event etc: *The committee discussed the matter for some time, but the long and short of it is that they won't give us any money.*

**the *long* arm of the law** ⟶ **the *strong*/long arm of the law**

**as *long* as** provided that: *I don't mind where I sit as long as it's in the shade.*

**as *long* as one's arm** (of a list) containing very many items: *I've got a list as long as my arm of things to do today.*

**not by a '*long* chalk/shot** *(informal)* not at all or only by the very smallest amount (used to emphasize the previous statement): *Were the critics satisfied with changes in the proposed law? Not by a long chalk!* See also **a '*long* shot.**

***long* drawn out** (of an argument or talks) too lengthy or extended: *The negotiations over reductions in nuclear arms are becoming long drawn out.* **long-drawn-out** *adj*: *a long-drawn-out legal battle.*

**a *long* face** a sad, disappointed, or disapproving expression on your face: *She came in with a long face, as if she was about to burst into tears. / Why the long face, Adrian? I've never seen you look so depressed.*

**not *long* for this world** likely to die soon: *Aunt Madge is getting very weak and isn't long for this world, so the doctors tell us.*

***long* in the tooth** old: *Jack is getting a bit long in the tooth to play football every week.*

**at *long* last** ⟶ **at *last***

**in the '*long* run** over a long period of time; finally; considering everything: *The pills will help him get better in the long run. / In the long run it's cheaper to hire a car just when you need one than to own one.* See also **in the '*short* run; in the '*long*/'short term.**

**a '*long* shot** an attempt to achieve sth that will probably be unsuccessful: *Try to ring him at home. It's a long shot, I know, but he might just be there.* See also **not by a '*long* chalk/shot.**

**of *long* standing** having existed, been established, or been practised continuously for a long time: *The custom of celebrating the beginning of Spring is of long standing. / He is a teacher of German of many years' standing.*

**to cut a *long* story short** ⟶ ***cut***

**in the '*long*/'short term** planning for or looking a long/short way into the future: *We can put the refugees in simple accommodation temporarily, but in the long term we'll need to find them something permanent.* **long/short-term** *adj*: *Things will be all right in a few years' time, but have we made any short-term arrangements?* See also **in the '*medium* term; in the '*long* run; in the '*short* run.**

***long* time no see** *(informal)* (an expression used when you greet sb you have not seen for a long time).

**go a *long* way** ⟶ ***go* far**

***look* a gift horse in the mouth** *(informal)* be critical or complain about sth that is offered freely: *I hear that the club refused the money the local council offered them. Why do you think they looked such a gift horse in the mouth?*

***look* after sb/sth** take care of sb/sth: *Don't worry, Martha, we'll look after the children while you're in hospital.*

**to *look* at** from the outward appearance: *She's not much to look at but she has a very gentle nature. / To look at him, you'd never think he was one of the world's experts on banking.*

**not *look* at sth** refuse to consider or accept sth: *They wouldn't even look at our suggestions.* Note that this is usually used after ***will*** or ***would.***

**a cat can/may *look* at a king** ⟶ ***cat***

**never/not *look* back** continue to prosper: *He's not looked back since he won that big contract three years ago.*

***look* bad** not be right according to convention and likely to make other people think badly of you: *It looks bad not going to your own mother's funeral, doesn't it?* Also **not look good.**

***look* bad (for sb)** suggest probable failure, death, disaster etc: *Things are looking bad for our team, I'm afraid. They're beating us 4–0, and there are only ten minutes left.*

***look* before one leaps** not act hastily without thinking what the results may be.

***look* black** show no signs of hope or improvement: *I know things look black at the moment, son, but you're sure to get a job soon.*

***look* daggers at sb** look at sb very angrily but not say anything: *She looked daggers at Pete for his rude comments.*

***look* down on sb/sth** *(informal)* despise; consider sb/sth as inferior: *Everyone looks down on you, just because you've not got a job.*

***look* down one's nose (at sb)** *(informal)* show that you feel superior (to sb): *Why do you always look down your nose at people who aren't dressed as smartly as you?*

***look* for trouble** ⟶ ***ask*/look for trouble**

***look* forward to sth** await sth eagerly and with excitement: *The children are looking forward very much to seeing their grandparents in the holiday.*

**not *look* good** ⟶ ***look* bad**

**not *look* sb in the eye/face** not look at sb without a sense of guilt, shame, or fear: *I don't think I could ever look him (straight) in the face again after what's happened.*

***look* in (on sb)** pay a short call or visit: *I'll look in on you again sometime, Mary! 'Bye for now!*

***look* into sth** investigate sth: *Thank you very*

*much for the information, sir. I'll get one of our detectives to look into the matter.*

***look* like nothing on earth** → ***feel*/look like nothing on earth**

***look* on** stand at a distance from sth, watching, but not becoming involved: *A whole group of people just looked on while the men fought each other.* **'onlooker** *n.*

***look* on/upon sb/sth as . . .** regard or consider sb/sth as: *He is looked upon as a great authority on the tax system.*

**be sb's ('own) *look*-out** *(informal)* be sb's concern or responsibility: *It's 'his look-out if he's late.*

***look* out (for sb/sth)** be alert to see sb/sth: *If you're catching the same train as me, I'll look out for you.* **look-out** *n* **1** a guard; sb who watches: *Norman will be look-out while we rob the bank.* **2** the act of looking out: *Keep a look-out for Paul, we don't want to miss him.*

***look* out (for sth)** be careful; guard (against sth): *Look out! There's a bull coming! / When you're eating fish, look out for the bones.*

***look* small** → ***feel*/look small**

***look* the other way** not look at sb/sth, especially deliberately in order to avoid having to greet sb or become involved with sth: *When I saw Jan in the street, she just looked the other way.*

***look* up** *(informal)* improve: *Things are looking up for small businesses now that the government has lowered some taxes.*

***look* sb up** pay a visit to sb: *I'll look you up when I'm passing this way again.*

***look* sth up** find out or check a fact or piece of information by reference to a book or document: *If you don't know the meaning of a word, look it up in a dictionary.*

***look* up to sb** admire sb; regard sb with great respect: *He was always taught to look up to older people.*

***look* what the cat's brought/dragged in!** *(informal, humorous)* an expression used when sb who looks untidy, bedraggled, or very wet enters a room etc): *'Look what the cat's brought in!' cried his brothers as Ray came into the sitting-room soaking wet from the storm.* **like something the cat's brought/dragged in** (appear) in this condition.

**like *looking* for a needle in a haystack** extremely difficult to find: *That list must be in these boxes somewhere—but it's like looking for a needle in a haystack.*

**on the *loose*** escaped from a prison, asylum, zoo etc: *A tiger is still on the loose this morning after escaping from London Zoo last night.*

**at a *loose* end** having nothing to do: *I'm at a bit of a loose end this afternoon—do you fancy a game of tennis?*

**the *loose* ends/threads** minor matters that need to be dealt with to bring a project etc to a neat conclusion: *Now that we've done the report, there are just a few loose ends to tie up and then the whole investigation will be over.*

**keep a *loose* rein on sb/sth** → ***keep* a tight/loose rein on sb/sth**

***loose* talk** careless statements, gossip etc about people or affairs: *We must take sure that this loose talk doesn't develop into a serious leak of secret information.*

***lord* it over sb** *(informal)* behave in a superior way towards sb: *He's just been promoted to supervisor and enjoys lording it over his former workmates.*

**have (got) something, nothing etc to *lose*** → ***have***

**not *lose* any sleep over sth** *(informal)* not be very anxious about: *There are a few changes we are going to make to the timetable, but there's nothing very serious, so there's no need to lose any sleep over them.*

***lose* one's bearings** be without a clear understanding of the position you are in, especially when this happens suddenly: *She'd lost her bearings after lying unconscious for a few moments, and it took a while for her to know where she was.*

***lose* one's cool** → ***keep*/lose one's cool**

***lose* count (of sth)** → ***keep*/lose count (of sth)**

***lose* face** suffer a humiliating loss of respect: *How can we give up our rights as a nation without losing face?*

***lose* faith (with sb/sth)** → ***keep*/lose faith (with sb/sth)**

***lose* one's grip** release your grasp on sth; cease to keep your skill to understand and deal with sth: *Gradually, the old maths master lost his grip, and his teaching got worse.*

***lose* ground (to sb/sth)** → ***give*/lose ground (to sb/sth)**

***lose* one's head** → ***keep*/lose one's head**

***lose* heart** feel your courage, hope, or enthusiasm becoming weaker: *The committee lost heart when money given by supporters fell by 50% in three months.*

***lose* one's heart (to sb/sth)** become very fond of sb/sth: *The children were very sad when they had to give the rabbits back. They had quite lost their hearts to the dear little animals!*

***lose* one's life** die in a natural disaster, war, etc: *Sixty people lost their lives in the air crash.* **loss of life** *n*: *Fortunately there was little loss of life in the battle.*

***lose* one's marbles** *(slang)* cease to keep your senses: *Poor Jack's getting old now and acting rather strangely—I think he's beginning to lose his marbles.* Also **not have (got) all one's marbles.**

***lose* one's nerve** cease to keep your self-control; panic: *Try not to lose your nerve in the exams.*

***lose*/waste no time (in doing sth)** do sth very quickly, with no delay: *As soon as the contract had been signed, Rod lost no time in assembling a team to work on the project.*

***lose* out (to sb)** be defeated or overtaken in popularity by sb: *In the election he lost out to a younger man.*

***lose* out on sth** suffer the loss of sth: *The new regulations mean that you won't lose out on a pension even if you did not pay money to the government while you were working.*

***lose* the thread of sth** fail to follow and understand sth such as a logical line in an explanation: *The professor went into so much detail that most of his students lost the thread of his argument.*

***lose* one's touch** *(informal)* cease to keep an ability that you have: *Margaret used to make lovely cakes every week, but she seems to have lost her touch now that she rarely does any baking.*

***lose* touch/contact (with sb)** no longer be in regular communication with sb: *I was friendly with many people at college, but I've lost touch with most of them now.* Also **be out of touch/contact with sb.** See also ***keep*/be in touch/contact (with sb).**

***lose* track of sb/sth** → ***keep*/lose track of sb/sth**

**fight a *losing* battle** → ***fight***

**at a *loss* (for sth/to do sth)** *(informal)* not knowing what to do, how to do sth, etc: *We're at a loss to know how the money disappeared.*

**at a *loss* for words** not knowing what to say: *He's never at a loss for words; in fact it's difficult sometimes to stop him talking!*

***loss* of life** → ***lose* one's life**

**there's no love *lost* between sb and sb** → ***no***

**a *lost* cause** a project or aim that sb has devoted himself to supporting, but which is not likely to receive or has not received enough support: *How she loved to support lost causes! She would come in and make sweeping changes, and in no time at all the charity would be back on its feet!*

**be *lost* on sb** be wasted on sb; be unnoticed by sb: *The quotations from Shakespeare were completely lost on the students—they weren't familiar with his plays.*

**be/feel *lost* without sb/sth** *(informal)* be unable to work or live efficiently, happily etc; without sb/sth: *These days, most people would be completely lost without a telephone. / I left my watch at home and feel lost without it.*

**take a *lot* of doing** → ***take* some doing**

**give sb a *lot* of stick** → ***give***

**a *lot* of water has passed under the bridge (since . . . )** or **much water has passed under the bridge (since . . . )** *(informal)* much time has passed and many things have happened since something happened: *Why do these people continue to give us their impressions of life when they were children? So much water has passed under the bridge since then.*

**it's a *lot* to ask (of/from sb/sth)** → **it's *asking* a lot (of/from sb/sth)**

***loud* and clear** public(ly) and unambiguous(ly): *The government was overwhelmingly defeated in the election—and the prime minister got the message loud and clear from the voters.*

**actions speak *louder* than words** → ***actions***

**for *love*** without payment or other reward, because you like the work or the person you are working for: *These people are really committed—they devote their spare time to helping run the youth club and do it all for love.*

**all's fair in *love* and war** → ***all***

***love* at first sight** falling in love at the first meeting: *I'd never really believed in love at first sight, but we certainly both felt something when we were introduced to each other.*

***love* is blind** *(saying)* when you are in love with sb it blinds you to his or her faults.

**there's no *love* lost between sb and sb** → ***no***

***love* me, love my dog** *(saying)* true affection and care for sb should reach everyone and everything connected with him.

**not for *love* or money** *(informal)* however hard you try; not at all: *I couldn't spend the night alone in the house for love or money. / After his heart attack he found he couldn't get any life insurance for love or money.*

**(at) a *low* ebb** at a point when there is little interest or activity: *Having just lost the election, the fortunes of the party are at a low ebb at the moment.*

**a *low* profile** an attitude, way of behaving etc that does not assert itself greatly or attract much public notice: *The former leader of the party kept a low profile so that all the attention would focus on the new leader.*

***lower*/raise one's sights** be content to achieve less or be determined to achieve more than you had originally wanted: *The club had hoped to collect enough money to redecorate all six rooms, but they had to lower their sights and only do four.*

**down on one's *luck*** → ***down***

**(just) for *luck*** in order to bring good fortune (sometimes the supposed reason for doing something again): *When a couple leave for their honeymoon it's custom to tie an old boot or shoe to the back of the car just for luck. / 'That was a nice goodbye kiss,' he said to his little granddaughter. 'Let's have another one, for luck!'*

**just one's *luck*** *(informal)* (sth is) annoying or inconvenient to you: *'The plumber called while you were out.' 'That's just my luck—I waited all morning for him to call, and I only slipped out for a few minutes!'*

**as *luck* has it** fortunately or unfortunately: *He had just the qualifications they wanted, and as luck would have it, they happened to have a vacancy. / She went to see him, but as luck had it, he was out.*

**one's *luck* holds** you continue to be fortunate: *'I've not seen a doctor for over 20 years.' 'Well, let's hope your luck holds for another 20!'*

**one's *luck* is in** you are fortunate: *His luck was in and he managed to find a place to park his car in the busy streets.*
**the *luck* of the devil → *have* (got) the devil's own luck**
**the *luck* of the draw** *(informal)* the fact that chance or fortune sometimes decides what people are, do, get etc: *'I wish I wasn't in Mary's team.' 'That's the luck of the draw, I'm afraid—you'll just have to accept it.'*
**a *lucky* dip** a box at a party, fair etc of different kinds of wrapped articles which are taken by sb; a situation where what happens may be useful, pleasing etc or not.
**sb's *(lucky)* number comes up → *number***
**thank one's *lucky* stars → *thank***
**have (got) a *lump* in one's throat → *have***
***lump* it** *(informal)* accept a situation without complaining: *If you don't like the food here then you'll just have to lump it, that's all; there's nothing else.* See also **like it or lump it.**
***lunatic* fringe** a small group in society, community etc who are extreme, radical, or fanatical: *Most of the employees here don't want any trouble; it's only the lunatic fringe that give the company a bad reputation by trying to disrupt production all the time.*
**leave sb in the *lurch* → *leave***

# M

**like *mad* → like *hell*/mad**
**be *mad* about/on sb/sth** *(informal)* be very enthusiastic about or obsessed by sb/sth: *Rachel's mad about that new boy at the youth club at the moment. / My uncle's mad on trains.* Also **be nuts/wild about sb/sth.**
**as *mad* as a hatter** or **as mad as a March hare** not normal in behaviour; foolish, eccentric, or insane: *I'm staying with my Aunt Grizelda; she's 87 years old, has three pet monkeys, and eats only fish and oats—she's as mad as a hatter!* Also *(informal)* **as nutty as a fruitcake.**
***mad* at sb** *(informal)* very angry with sb: *Sheila was mad at me for not telling her I was going to be late.*
**(not) *made* of money** *(informal)* (not) very rich: *That's not my Rolls Royce! I'm not made of money, you know!*
***made* to measure** (of a suit etc) cut specially to fit the person it is for. See also **off the *peg*.**
**wave a *(magic)* wand (and do sth) → *wave***
**have (got) an eye to/on/for the *main* chance → *have***
***maintain* a level head → *keep*/maintain a level head**
**on the *make*** *(slang)* trying to make a profit, beat sb, or find a sexual partner: *Most of the boys at school are all right, I suppose, but some of them are on the make the whole time.*
***make* a bee-line for sb/sth**
***make* a bolt/dash for sth/it** *(informal)* hurry to catch a bus, keep an appointment etc; escape from captivity: *If I make a dash for the 8 o'clock train, I might just make it. / The prisoners made a bolt for it while the police van was left unguarded for a moment.*
***make* a bomb → *cost*/earn/make/pay/spend a bomb**
***make* a break for it** *(informal)* try to escape from captivity: *While the guards were out of sight for a moment, two of the prisoners decided to make a break for it.*
***make* a change** cause an alteration, especially an improvement; be a great difference or relief from sth that usually happens: *A week's holiday by the seaside made a welcome change from working in the factory.*
***make* a clean breast of sth** confess in full to sth: *Joe and Phil were caught actually stealing the money, so they decided to make a clean breast of it and tell the police everything.*
***(make)* a clean sweep (of sth) → *clean***
***make* a day, night etc of it** spend the whole day etc doing sth: *We only needed a morning in Manchester, but we were enjoying ourselves so much we made a day of it.*
***make* a dent/hole in sb/sth** *(informal)* considerably reduce an amount or sb's reputation: *Having to pay out unexpectedly for car repairs made a dent in their savings. / Being told off in public seems to have made quite a dent in his pride.*
***make*/pull a face** have an expression on your face that shows dislike or defiance or is used to frighten sb: *There's no need to pull such a face! Didn't you know that you'd have to work ten hours a day?* Also **make/pull faces.**
***make* a fool of sb/oneself** make sb look or feel ridiculous: *She made a complete fool of herself at the party, but she didn't seem to mind at all. / The children loved to make a fool of their teacher. / No one likes being made a fool of in public.*
***make* a go of (doing) sth** *(informal)* cause sth, such as a relationship, to succeed: *He was determined to make a go of his second marriage.*
***make* a man of sb** help sb to behave like a man: *Two years in the army will make a man of you.*
***make* a meal of sth** *(informal)* treat sth as more important than it really is; do sth to excess; put too much effort into sth: *I thought John was going to say he was sorry quickly but he seems to be making a meal of it.*
***make* a mess/hash of (doing) sth** *(informal)* handle or manage sth badly: *The travel agents made a complete mess of the arrangements for our holiday.*
***make* a mountain out of a molehill** *(informal)* be very anxious about insignificant

things: *You're making a mountain out of a molehill, Marianne. I don't know why you're so worried! Sheila is only borrowing your video recorder, not stealing it!*

***make* a move** move; go away or leave; start a task or duty: *I think we'd better make a move, darling, as it's getting late. Thanks for a lovely evening! / If we don't make a move soon, we'll never get the job done.*

***make* a nuisance of oneself** cause other people to be angry by making a noise, interrupting etc; risk unpopularity by criticizing people in authority etc: *Harriet, stop making a nuisance of yourself! / If we continue to make a nuisance of ourselves with the council, they may eventually give in to our demands.*

***make* a pass at sb** act in a flirtatious way towards a member of the opposite sex: *I saw you making a pass at the waitress just then!*

***make* a pig of oneself** *(informal)* be extremely greedy; eat and drink too much: *They all made pigs of themselves at the party and felt very sick afterwards.*

***make* a pig's ear (out) of sth** *(informal)* do sth very badly: *The printers made a pig's ear of printing the leaflet.* **a pig's ear** a mess.

***make* a/one's pile** *(informal)* accumulate a large amount of money: *He made a pile by buying old bits of metal, cleaning them up, and then selling them as modern sculptures.*

***make* a point of (doing) sth** take particular care to do sth: *He always made a point of helping old ladies cross the road.*

***make* a rod for one's own back** do sth that will cause you harm or suffering in the future: *Sheila's making a rod for her own back by not telling the tax office she's got two jobs—they'll find out sooner or later.*

***make* a scene** show publicly that you are angry etc in a noisy, unpleasant, or embarrassing way: *Ruth, there's no need to make a scene here in the restaurant with everyone looking at us!*

***make* a song and dance about sth** *(informal)* become excessively worried or excited about sth: *Mary's parents always make a song and dance about her coming home late, so we'd better be going soon.*

***make* a splash** *(informal)* gain much attention by showing your abilities, possessions etc in a showy way: *One radio disc jockey made quite a splash with his frequent appearances on television quiz shows.*

***make*/take a stand** resist an attack and adopt a firm attitude of defence against sb/sth: *The women's purpose in camping outside the air base is to make a stand against the use of nuclear weapons.*

***make* 'all the 'difference** have a great, especially good effect on sth: *Your saying sorry makes all the difference. / A new coat of paint makes all the difference to this room, doesn't it?*

***make* allowance(s) for sb/sth** consider certain factors, especially difficulties or deficiencies, and so be less strict when assessing or judging sb/sth: *The court was asked to make allowances for his age. / It would be sensible to add a further £200 to the budget to make allowance for inflation.*

***make* amends (to sb) (for sth)** repay or compensate sb for sth you have failed to do in the past: *And if you've stolen anything, you'd better make amends for it as soon as you can.*

***make* an attempt on sth** try to break or exceed a record for the fastest time, longest distance etc: *Barrie Dunbar will make another attempt on the land speed record later in the year.*

***make* an attempt on sb's life** try to kill a famous person: *Several attempts were made last year on the President's life.*

***make* an example of sb** punish sb for a mistake, crime etc in order to deter other people from doing the same: *The headmaster made an example of Jones to try to stop misbehaviour by the other pupils.*

***make* an exhibition of oneself** behave in a showy, vulgar way that draws attention to yourself: *Why did you have to make such an awful exhibition of yourself at the party?*

***make* an honest woman of sb** *(informal)* (of a man) marry a woman, especially when he has had a sexual relationship with her for some time: *They've been living with each other for a year—when is he going to make an honest woman of her?*

***make* believe that . . .** pretend or imagine sth imaginary: *Let's make believe that we're Red Indians.* **'make-believe** *adj, n*: *There's no need to be worried, it's only a make-believe gun. / He told his parents he'd got a job but it was only make-believe.*

***make* bold to do sth** →**be/*make* so bold (as to do sth)**

***make* bricks without straw** try to do a piece of work without the necessary materials, equipment, information etc: *Mark couldn't find the books he needed to write his essay, so he was making bricks without straw.*

***make* capital out of sth** use sth to one's own advantage; exploit, sometimes unscrupulously: *The media made great capital out of his careless remarks in the interview.* Also **capitalize on sth.**

***make* sb's day** make sb feel very happy: *Thanks for sending me those flowers. It really made my day!*

***make* do (with sth)** manage with sth, accepting it, although it is not fully satisfactory: *I didn't have time to go to the shops today, so I suppose we'll have to make do with what is left from yesterday's meal.*

***make* (both) ends meet** match the money you spend to the money you earn: *However much money you earn, it's still difficult to make ends meet.*

***make* eyes at sb** *(informal)* look at sb of the opposite sex in a way that tries to attract his or her interest and attention: *Just look at Maria! There she goes making eyes at Ray again!*

***make* faces** → ***make*/pull a face**
***make* first base (with sth)** → ***get* to first base (with sth)**
***make* one's 'flesh creep/crawl** *(informal)* cause you to feel fear, disgust, or hatred: *His black clothes, his stare and grin—indeed his whole sinister manner—made my flesh crawl.*
***make* for sb/sth 1** move towards sb/sth, especially in a definite way: *As the mother came into the room, her little girl made straight for her.* **2** move towards sb/sth, especially in an attack or to get hold of sth: *He made for me with his fists. / I expected him to make for the parcel I was carrying.*
***make* for sth** help sth to happen or develop; promote or facilitate: *Frankness and honesty make for good industrial relations.*
***make* free/bold with sth** use sth too much and often without permission: *Your friends at the party who made so free with the drinks weren't even invited!*
***make* friends (with sb)** become friendly (with sb): *Chuck's made friends with several people at work.*
***make* fun of sb/sth** ridicule sb/sth; treat sb/sth unkindly: *People enjoy making fun of the clothes I wear, though they seem all right to me.* Also **poke fun at sb/sth.**
***make* good** succeed in life and business, especially if you have come from a low social or economic group or been a criminal or idle person: *The story is the traditional one of a local boy from a poor background who dreams of glory and eventually makes good.*
***make* good sth 1** compensate for or repair damage or an injury: *How can we possibly make good the waste and loss to society of thousands of unemployed young people? / You must make good the rusted area before you can paint it.* **2** fulfil or carry out sth such as an intention or threat: *The government still has to make good many promises it made at the last election.*
***make* great etc strides** progress, develop, or improve very quickly: *Johnny has made tremendous strides since he went to a different school.*
***make* sb's 'hair stand on end** cause sb to feel extreme fear or horror: *Steve and Jack talked about their trip to the North Pole. It was very interesting, but hearing about the dangers they faced made my hair stand on end.* Also **set sb's 'hair on end. sb's 'hair stands on end** sb feels extreme fear or horror: *It was very dark, and when a dog howled my hair stood on end!*
***make* haste** *(old-fashioned)* move quickly: *The shepherds made haste to gather their sheep before dark.*
***make* hay while the sun shines** *(saying)* make the best use of opportunities and favourable conditions while they last.
**(not) *make* head or tail of sth** *(informal)* not understand sth at all: *I can't make head or tail of this picture—it's too abstract!* Note that this is usually used in the negative; then an alternative to ***or*** is ***nor.***
***make* headway** move forward; progress further towards success or completion: *The government's not making much headway in the battle against inflation.*
***make* heavy weather of (doing) sth** *(informal)* make a task seem more difficult than it really is: *You seem to be making heavy weather of a very simple calculation.*
***make* history** do sth that has never been done before and may be recorded in the history of a country, sport etc: *Joe Blondell has made history tonight by becoming the first man to regain the northern regional championship.*
***make* it** *(informal)* achieve or do what you want, plan, or hope to do: *The bus goes in ten minutes—you must hurry or you won't make it. / It's natural to have dreams of success and fame, but only a few people in this world actually make it.*
***make* it one's business to do sth** want to do sth very much; do sth in a determined or careful way: *Mrs Brown makes it her business to know what's going on in her street.*
***make* it snappy** *(informal)* be quick to do sth: *Jack slapped the money onto the counter. 'Two beers please,' he called out, 'and make it snappy!'* Note that this is usually used in the imperative.
***make* light of sth** treat sth such as discomfort or pain as unimportant or slight: *In fact, she suffered great inconvenience, but she made light of the whole affair when I asked her about it.*
***make* light work of (doing) sth** do sth with ease: *The team of men were so skilled that they made light work of building the garage.*
***make* love (to sb)** have sexual intercourse with sb: *He'd made love to several women before he finally got married and settled down.*
***make* one's mark** be successful and famous in a job or in art, science, sport etc: *Norman quickly made his mark and was the company's top salesman.*
***make* mincemeat of sb/sth** *(informal)* demolish or destroy sb/sth completely: *Top-of-the-league Manchester United made mincemeat of Wolverhampton Wanderers last night, beating them 5–0.*
***make* sb's mouth water** (of (the thought, smell, or prospect of) food) cause saliva to flow in the mouth: *Just looking at these cookery books is enough to make my mouth water!* **'mouth-watering** *adj*: *mouth-watering recipes.*
***make* much of sth** emphasize sth; consider sth as important: *He makes much of his upper-class background when you talk to him. / Don't make too much of Sally's harsh manner—she's really quite gentle once you get to know her.*
***make* one's name** gain a reputation (in a particular field); become famous: *He came to London and soon made his name as a fashion expert.* Also **make a name for oneself.**
***make* no bones about (doing) sth** not hesitate to act or say sth in a frank and forceful way: *He made no bones about criticizing the*

*new play strongly in his review. / I'll make no bones about it—I think this is the worst piece of work I've ever seen.*

***make* no mistake (about sth)** do not allow appearances to mislead you: *Alison looks very quiet and shy, but, make no mistake about it, she's a very determined career woman.* Note that this is used in the imperative.

***make* no/little odds** or **not make much odds** not/hardly affect a matter, result, decision, argument etc: *With talented children it makes very little odds how you teach them; they'll learn anyway.*

***make* noises about sth** *(informal)* make known your thoughts, feelings etc about sth: *He's always making noises about resigning from his job. / The publishers have made encouraging noises about my suggestions for a book.*

***make* nothing, something etc of sb/sth** understand nothing, something etc about sb/sth: *I looked through his diary but I couldn't make much of all his scribbles. / What do you make of Annie? She seems impenetrable to me.*

***make* off** *(informal)* leave or escape quickly: *The thieves ran out of the jeweller's and made off in a stolen car.*

***make* off with sth** *(informal)* steal and hurry away with sth: *The robbers made off with £10,000 in used bank notes.*

***make* or break sb/sth** be crucial in making sb/sth either a success or a failure: *The council will make or break the future of the local theatre this week—it'll either decide to increase the money it gives or withdraw all its support.* **make-or-break** *adj*: *a make-or-break chance.*

***make* or mar sth** be crucial in making sth either a success or failure: *The weather will either make or mar this afternoon's athletics match.*

***make* out** *(informal)* manage, survive, progress, or fare: *How did you make out in the interview?*

***make* out sb/sth** manage to decipher or read sth or understand sb: *I can't make out what that sign says—it's still too far away. / I never could make Janet out. Why does she always annoy people who try to help her?*

***make* out that . . .** claim or assert that sth is true: *He's trying to make out that his firm is very successful, but we know that it's nearly bankrupt.*

***make* one's peace with sb** settle a quarrel with sb: *Has Philip made his peace with Rosemary or are they still arguing?*

***make* one's presence felt** make others aware of your presence or existence by sth such as the force of your personality, superior ability, or aggressive behaviour.

***make* oneself scarce** go away, because it is wise or tactful to do so: *The thieves made themselves scarce well before the police arrived.*

***make* short work of (doing) sth** deal with or get rid of sth quickly: *Those hungry youngsters certainly made short work of the chocolate biscuits!*

**be/*make* so bold (as to do sth)** dare, offer, or attempt to do sth that needs courage (used in polite requests to do or say sth): *Might I make so bold as to suggest that you ask for help?* Also **make bold to do sth.**

***make* sth stick** *(informal)* prove, substantiate, or make effective sth said about or against sb/sth: *You've accused him of corruption but can your charge be made to stick?*

***make* strange bedfellows** (of very different things or people) be unexpectedly associated together: *The humour and horror in this book make rather strange bedfellows.*

***make* the best of sth** do the best one possibly can in a difficult situation: *With the government cutbacks, the hospital will just have to make the best of the limited resources at its disposal.* There are variations on this idiom: **make the best of a bad job; make the best of things.**

***make* the grade** *(informal)* reach a required or desired standard in ability, education etc; succeed: *Whoever makes the grade at the end of the three-week course will get a job.*

***make* the most of sth** derive as much experience or other benefit from (doing) sth; use sth to the full: *The doctors have told him he's only got six months to live, so he's making the most of them.*

***make* the running** set the pace that other competitors must keep if they hope to win; satisfy the standard or requirements set by others; take the lead in a course of action, conversation etc, encouraging or forcing others to join or compete: *Johnson made the running for the first part of the race but was too tired by the end so came fifth. / Our company has always made the running in the field of stationery products, and all the other firms follow our lead.*

***make* tracks (for sth)** *(informal)* go away (to somewhere): *It's getting late; I think we must make tracks for home. Thank you for a lovely evening!*

***make* sb up** put powder, lipstick, special paint etc on sb's, especially your own face to make it look more attractive or for an appearance on television, in a theatre etc: *She spent two hours making herself up before the party.* **make-up** *n*: *Alison looks after the actors' wigs and does their make-up.*

***make* sth up 1** invent sth such as a story, false account, or example: *He's very good at making up songs.* **2** form, compose, or constitute sth: *The regional committee is made up of representatives of the local committees.* **make-up** *n.*

***make* (it/sth) up** settle a quarrel: *Why don't you two kiss and make up? / Has Ray made it up with Ros yet?*

***make* up for sth** compensate for sth; repay sb for a bad action: *His strong personality makes up for his ugly appearance. / Your kind behav-*

*iour now more than makes up for your rudeness last week.*

***make* up one's mind** decide sth: *Look, I've thought about it a lot, and now I've made up my mind—you can borrow my car! / He wants someone to make up his mind for him.*

***make* oneself useful** do useful work, especially a small task to help sb: *If you want to make yourself useful you could do the washing-up.*

***make* way (for sb/sth)** allow sb/sth to pass: *The crowd made way for the ambulance men to reach the injured driver.*

**as you ˌ*make* your bed, so you must ˈlie on it** *(saying)* you must suffer the results of your own actions: *I told you it was a silly thing to do, but you didn't take my advice, and as you make your bed, so you must lie on it.*

**what *makes* sb tick →*what***

**in the *making*** evolving or in the process of being made or becoming: *He's always been interested in government. Maybe he's a politician in the making.*

**be a *man*** behave like a man; show courage, independence, courtesy, etc: *You don't have to do what all the other boys tell you. Be a man and say no!*

**like a *man*** in the manner of a brave, courageous, and strong man: *You took your punishment like a man, Fred!*

**to a *man*** without exception: *They agreed to a man that I should be the group's representative.* See also **as *one* man.**

**a *man*/woman after one's own heart** sb who is exactly the kind that matches your view of an ideal person: *John's a man after my own heart: he likes music, poetry, wine, and long-distance walking in the mountains.*

***man* and/or beast** the human race and/or all animals: *The nuclear waste washed up on beaches is fatal to both man and beast.*

***man* and boy** for all or most of your life: *He worked with the BBC, man and boy, for over 40 years.*

**a *man*/girl Friday** sb who does all different kinds of jobs in an office etc: *Wanted: Girl Friday to help small, busy, friendly company.*

**the *man* in the street** the average citizen who does not have any special skills or knowledge: *It's difficult to understand all the implications of the Finance Minister's statement, so now in the studio one of our experts will explain it all for the man in the street.* Also **the man on the Clapham omnibus.**

**every *man* Jack (of sb) →*every***

**a *man*/woman of few words** sb who does not talk much: *Admiral Blanchard was always a man of few words, so his speech at the dinner was quickly finished.*

**a *man*/woman of his/her word** sb who keeps a promise: *You're a woman of your word, I see. Most people wouldn't have visited a grumpy old man like me in such bad weather as this.*

**a *man* of letters** *(formal)* a writer of essays, poetry, novels etc, especially ones of good quality: *Samuel Johnson, one of the most respected men of letters, worked here for many years.*

**a *man*/woman of many parts** sb with a wide range of abilities and interests: *A social worker must be someone of many parts—able to act quickly in an emergency, good at listening, and, at the right, time, able to give advice.*

**a *man*/woman/person of substance** sb who owns a lot of land, money etc: *He is a person of substance, with five farms in the north, and well-known in the area.*

**a *man*/woman of the world** sb with great experience of life, public affairs, business: *You're a man of the world, aren't you, Roger? I need some practical advice on what to do regarding my relationship with a certain young lady.*

**the *man* on the Clapham omnibus →the *man* in the street**

**ˈno *man*'s land →*no***

**one *man*'s meat is another man's poison →*one***

**(as) *man* to man** (speaking) honestly and frankly: *We spoke man to man about the state of our marriages.* **man-to-man** *adj*: *a man-to-man talk.*

**(every) *man*, woman, and child** every living person: *We may be faced with a situation in which every man, woman, and child will meet their death.*

***all* manner of** all kinds of: *The warehouse was stocked with all manner of goods.*

**in a *manner* of speaking** *(informal)* in a kind of way; as a way of expressing it would be: *She is, in a manner of speaking, my wife—we live together, but we've not had the actual wedding ceremony.*

**ˈ*many* a long day** *(becoming old-fashioned)* a very long time: *I've not read such a good book for many a long day.*

**ˈ*many* a time, man etc** *(becoming old-fashioned)* many times etc: *That post-box has always been there. You must have passed it many a time.*

***many* hands make light work** *(saying)* a task is done easily if a lot of people share the work.

***many* happy returns (of the day)** (a way of greeting sb on his/her birthday): *'Many happy returns of the day, Susie,' the group called out as she came into the room.*

**have (got) (too) *many* etc irons in the fire →*have***

***many* moons ago** a very long time ago: *'Have you two met before?' 'Yes, we knew each other many moons ago—in Oswestry, was it?'*

**a man/woman of *many* parts →*man***

**not in as/so *many* words** not clearly; not in exactly the same words as are claimed or reported to have been used: *'Have you told her definitely that you can't come?' 'No, not in so many words, but I hinted strongly that I might not.'*

**put sth on the *map* →*put***

**as mad as a *March* hare** → ***as mad* as a hatter**
**(you can) tell that to the *marines*** → ***tell***
**quick/slow off the *mark*** → ***quick***
**up to the *mark*** equal to the required standard: *Your work hasn't been up to the mark this term, Jones. Why not? / I'm not feeling quite up to the mark today.*
***mark* my words** take note of what I am telling you: *Mark my words, Sheila, he'll be back—he never stays away for long!*
***mark* time** make no advance or take no action, waiting until a suitable moment arrives: *Business is fairly slow; we're just marking time till the economy improves.*
***mark* you** → ***mind*/mark you**
**a *marked* man** sb who is noted as one who must be killed or avoided: *When they discover you're a spy, you're a marked man.*
**price oneself out of the *market*** → ***price***
**the bottom drops/falls out of the *market*** → ***bottom***
**freeze/chill sb to the bone/*marrow*** → ***freeze***
**for 'that *matter*** (used to give an additional item that is equally relevant to sth just mentioned): *Universities—and all different types of college, for that matter—don't exist just to perform academic research.*
**something etc is the *matter* (with sb/sth)** something etc is wrong (with sb/sth): *What's the matter, Gail? You look ill. / John's been very quiet recently. I wonder if anything is the matter with him. / 'Are you all right?' 'Yes; nothing's the matter, thanks.' / Something's the matter with this machine. / What's the matter with smoking? It's allowed, isn't it?*
**as a *matter* of course** according to the usual or natural procedure: *These days, we take the development of a child to a mature adult as a matter of course.*
**as a *matter* of fact** and that is a fact (used to emphasize a statement or contradiction, often implying that a listener etc might not believe what has been said): *'Who's going to be the next chairman of the committee?' 'As a matter of fact, I am.'* **matter-of-fact** *adj*: unemotional.
**as a *matter* of form** in a way that is correct or polite but not essential: *The new constitution was being drawn up, and Roger asked the former secretary for his views as a matter of form.*
**(a *matter* of) life and/or death** → ***life***
**a *matter* of opinion** sth about which opinions differ: *Who will win this afternoon's game is a matter of opinion.*
**a *matter* of time** sth inevitable; sth that will happen sooner or later: *She tries to keep cheerful and hopes she's getting better, but we all know it's only a matter of time before she dies.*
**no *matter* who, what etc** → ***no***
**not know where one's next *meal*/penny is coming from** → ***know***
**make a *meal* of sth** → ***make***
**a '*meal* ticket** *(informal)* a person, organization, or situation that can be relied upon to give a source of regular livelihood or income, without asking anything in return: *She'll have to get a job one day—she can't go on thinking of her boyfriend as a meal ticket for life.*
***mean* business** be serious in your intentions; be determined to do what you have planned to do: *By sending their top people to meet our leaders at the summit conference, they really showed they meant business.*
**no *mean* feat, performer, etc** → ***no***
***mean* it** be completely serious when making a promise or threat or announcing an intention, warning etc: *If you tell the police I was here, I'll kill you. I mean it!*
**a *mean* trick** → **a *dirty*/rotten/mean trick**
**'*mean* well** have kind intentions, even though you may offend other people: *Your mother means well, I know, but why does she have to keep interfering in our marriage?*
**by 'all *means*** of course; certainly (used to agree to a request): *'May I smoke?' 'By all means—go ahead.'*
**by 'no *means*** *(formal)* of course not; certainly not: *It has by no means been proved that the theory of evolution is the correct explanation for the development of the world.*
**made to *measure*** → ***made***
***measure* up (to sth)** show skills, qualities etc that reach a required standard: *The job is difficult, but I think he'll measure up (to it) all right.*
**a law of the *Medes* and Persians** → ***law***
**in the '*medium* term** (of a policy, action etc) planning for or looking into neither the immediate nor the distant future, but in between. **medium-term** *adj*: *Our medium-term aim is to replace four out of the six lorries with more modern vehicles, and, looking to the future, do the other two as well.* See also **in the '*long*/'short term.**
**as *meek* as a lamb** humble and submissive; without protest: *They thought he would resist arrest, but he accompanied the detectives to the police station as meek as a lamb.*
***meet* sb halfway** compromise with sb; (of two people) each give the other person part of what he wants: *The two sides finally met halfway—the workers gave up their pay claim but got the cut in working hours that they wanted.*
***meet* one's maker** die or be destroyed (sometimes used humorously): *And when I finally go to meet my maker, I'll talk about all the good deeds I've done, so he'll have to let me into heaven, won't he?*
***meet* one's match** encounter sb who has equal strength, abilities etc in a competition or argument: *The chap wasn't as weak as he looked, and I began to wonder if I had finally met my match.*
***meet* one's Waterloo** suffer defeat or failure: *Many readers and interpreters of the writer Tortill meet their Waterloo in 'Kensington Terrace', his most difficult novel.*
**more (. . .) than *meets* the eye** more than

you might at first think: *There's more to this business than meets the eye. I shall have to investigate further*.

**butter wouldn't *melt* in sb's mouth** → ***butter***

**in/into the *melting* pot** in/into a process of change and often also confusion: *The future of football on television went back* (or *was thrown back*) *into the melting pot last night when the leaders of the football clubs rejected the television companies' latest offer*.

**down *memory* lane** thinking about the past in a fond way: *We're taking a trip* (or *We're going*) *down memory lane this evening as Mary Smithson looks back at her fifty years in show business.*

**have (got) a *memory* like a sieve** → ***have***

**sort out the *men* from the boys** → ***sort***

**on the *mend*** improving in condition, health etc: *'How is Marianne?' 'She's on the mend now, thanks. She should be back at work next week.'*

***mend* one's ways** improve your behaviour, attitudes etc: *If you don't mend your ways soon, my boy, then we'll send you away to boarding school.*

**don't *mention* it** *(informal)* (a polite reply to an expression of thanks or apology): *'Thank you, Constable, for your help.' 'Don't mention it, madam, that's what we're here for!'*

**be off (the *menu*)** → ***off***

**throw oneself on sb's *mercy*** → ***throw***

***mess* about** behave or work in a casual, often playful or silly way: *We spent the afternoon just messing about on the boat.*

***mess* sb/sth about** treat sb/sth in a rough way that causes hurt or inconvenience: *The hospital have really messed him about—he had to wait months for an appointment, and when he finally got there, they'd lost the notes of his illness.* Also **mess about with sb/sth.**

**make a *mess*/hash of (doing) sth** → ***make***

***method* in sb's madness** a pattern or purpose in sb's unusual behaviour or suggestion: *I don't understand Josephine at all—she seems so illogical—but other people tell me there's method in her madness.*

**on one's *mettle*** determined to show your best abilities and skills: *The enthusiastic new workers have really put the older employees on their mettle.*

**when the cat's away the *mice* will play** → ***when***

**take the *mickey* out of sb** → ***take***

***middle*-of-the-road** moderate; not extreme: *The new chairman is middle-of-the-road—he isn't strongly connected with any political party and so has no special policies to support.*

**burn the *midnight* oil** → ***burn***

**the pen is *mightier* than the sword** → ***pen***

**a miss is as good as a *mile*** → ***miss***

**can see/tell a *mile* off** → ***see***

***miles* away** → ***far*/miles away**

***miles* better, bigger etc (than . . . )** *(informal)* very much better etc than sb/sth else: *He likes his new job miles more than his old one.*

**a land flowing with *milk* and honey** → ***land***

***milk*/suck sb/sth dry** obtain from sb/sth all the money, help, support etc that is available: *I spent an evening with the old man in his home and milked him dry of every last historical detail for my research.*

**the *milk* of human kindness** kindness, affection, and sympathy towards other people.

**go through the *mill*** or **put sb through the mill** → ***go***

**a *million* and one** → **a *hundred*/thousand/million and one**

***mince* (one's) words** make what you say softer or more moderate to please people: *Sir John Dray, not a man to mince his words, spoke frankly and critically of the government's present economic policies at a dinner in London last night.* Also **mince matters.** Note that these idioms are usually used in the negative.

**be (all) in the *mind*** *(informal)* be imaginary, not true or real: *'I'm sure Harriet is in love with me.' 'It's all in the mind!'*

**bored, scared etc out of one's *mind*** extremely bored etc: *I always get bored out of my mind by Professor Pipe's lectures.* See also **out of one's *mind*.**

**drive sb out of his *mind*/wits** → ***drive***

**out of one's *mind*** mad; very angry, anxious etc: *The noise in here is driving me out of my mind!* See also **bored, scared etc out of one's *mind*.**

**stoned out of one's *mind*** → ***stoned***

**the/one's *mind*/imagination boggles (at sth)** *(informal)* you cannot imagine or conceive an idea, supposed incident etc: *The mind boggles at the amount of money it will cost to rebuild the library after the fire.* **'mind-boggling** *adj.*

**have (got) a *mind* of one's own** → ***have***

***mind* out (for sb/sth)** *(informal)* be careful to avoid sb/sth that is dangerous: *Mind out—the dish is hot!* Note that this is often used in the imperative.

***mind* over matter** the power of thought, your will etc is stronger than a bodily weakness or material difficulty: *Getting up in the morning to go to work is a real case of mind over matter.*

***mind* one's own business** concern yourself with your own affairs, work, or life, without being over-concerned or curious or interfering with other people: *'How's that new contract with Smiths coming on?' 'Mind your own business!'*

***mind*/watch one's p's and q's** *(informal)* be very careful to be correct in behaviour, speech, or procedure: *The headmistress will be at the dinner tonight, so you'd better mind your p's and q's.*

**in one's *mind's* eye** as viewed mentally: *I can see it all in my mind's eye now—hot sunshine, sandy beaches, lovely girls—I am looking forward to the holiday!*

***mind* one's step** —› ***watch*/mind one's step**
***mind*/mark you** note what I'm saying (used to emphasize, develop, or disagree with sth that has just been said): *'We spent a lot of money last month.' 'Yes, but mind you, it was Christmas, and we did have all the presents to buy.'*
**up to the *minute*** most recent: *And now with an up-to-the-minute report on the latest developments we go over to our reporter at the Space Control Centre.*
**any *minute*, day etc now** —› ***any***
**(not) have (got) a *minute*/moment to call one's own** —› ***have***
**drag sb/sth's name etc through the mud/ *mire*** —› ***drag***
**as *miserable* as sin** very unhappy: *I don't think Peter should visit his grandparents unless his cousins go too—he'd be as miserable as sin without company of his own age.*
**put sb out of his *misery*** —› ***put***
**not/never *miss* a trick** *(informal)* notice and deal with every tiny detail: *Tony's an expert designer. You can rely on him never to miss a trick whatever the problem is.*
**a *miss* is as good as a mile** *(saying)* narrowly missing success, danger etc has the same practical result as doing so by a wide margin: *'You couldn't have failed the exam by much, according to this list.' 'A miss is as good as a mile. I've got to do the whole year over again.'*
***Miss* Right** —› ***Mr*/Miss Right**
***miss* the boat/bus** be too late or fail to take advantage of an opportunity: *The trade fair has come and gone and we've missed the boat because nobody knew about it.*
**one's heart *misses* a beat** —› ***heart***
**and no *mistake*** *(informal)* there can be no doubt about it: *This is the best medium-sized car on the market, sir, and no mistake!*
**make no *mistake* (about sth)** —› ***make***
***mix* sb/sth up (with sb/sth)** confuse two or more things so that you do not know which is which; be unable to distinguish one person/ thing from another: *The airline staff mixed my luggage up with yours. / People are always mixing me up with my twin brother.* **mix-up** *n*: *There's been a mix-up, I'm afraid. You've got the wrong tickets.*
***mix* one's drinks** consume different kinds of alcoholic drink at a party etc: *No gin for me, Bob. I'll stay with whisky, thanks—I don't want to mix my drinks.*
**a *mixed* bag/bunch/lot** *(informal)* a large number of different kinds of people or things: *This year's new students are a proper mixed bag.*
**a *mixed* blessing** sth that seems to have pleasant effects but also unpleasant ones: *Her coming early was a mixed blessing; it was nice to see her, but it meant I did less work.*
**have (got) *mixed* feelings (about sb/sth)** —› ***have***
***mixed* up** *(informal)* (of people) muddled in thoughts or feeling: *Mary's all mixed up at the moment; she needs to go away for a few months to get herself sorted out. / The book is all about crazy mixed-up kids who are trying to work out what they want out of life and who rebel against their parents.*
**at the *moment*** now; at the present time: *At the moment we've only a few subscriptions, but I'm sure we'll have some more soon.* The variation ***at this moment in time*** is considered to be a cliché by many careful speakers.
**for the *moment*** temporarily: *We are quite happy living in Oxford for the moment, but there may come a time when we want to move.* Also **for the present; for the time being.**
**of (some, no, little etc) *moment*** *(formal)* of some etc importance: *This matter is of great moment, Jones, so listen carefully.*
**the *moment* of truth** the point when the reality of the condition of a person or sth such as an economy has to be faced: *The moment of truth for this country is approaching fast. Will our own supplies of energy be exhausted before new resources can be found?*
**at a *moment's* notice** —› **at *short* notice**
**(not) have (got) a minute/*moment* to call one's own** —› ***have***
**in the *money*** *(informal)* rich: *With my pay rise and that new job Susan has got, we'll really be in the money.*
**for 'my *money*** —› ***my***
***money* burns a hole in sb's pocket** sb is eager to spend money or spends it quickly or extravagantly (as if it were something dangerous to have or carry about).
***money* doesn't grow on trees** *(saying)* it isn't easy to obtain money; it has to be worked for.
***money* for old rope** *(informal)* money or profit earned or obtained from a task that is little or no trouble: *Being paid for cleaning the office once a week is money for old rope—it only takes me half an hour.* Also **money for jam.**
***money* is no object** —› ***expense*/money is no object**
**spend *money* like water** —› ***spend***
***money* talks** *(saying)* if you are rich then you can be treated favourably, exert political pressure etc.
**have (got) *money* to burn** —› ***have***
***monkey* about/around (with sth)** *(informal)* play or interfere with sth in a mischievous or clumsy way: *Stop monkeying about with the fire extinguisher!*
**'*monkey* business** *(informal)* mischievous, boisterous, or fraudulent action or behaviour: *If that's all the profit that's shown in the accounts, there must have been some monkey business going on somewhere.*
**get sb's/one's *monkey* up** —› ***get***
**(not in) a *month* of Sundays** *(informal)* (not in) a very long time: *I haven't seen her in a month of Sundays. / It'll take you a month of Sundays to finish that job.*
**over the *moon*** *(informal)* very happy and

excited: *The whole team is absolutely over the moon. They're really thrilled that they won.*

**do a *moonlight* (flit)** → ***do***

**a *moot* question/point** an undecided matter; subject on which there is disagreement: *Whether she'd be less depressed if she had more to do is a moot point; I personally doubt it.*

***moral* support** sympathy, public approval or just sb's presence, rather than financial or practical help: *Will you stay and give me some moral support while I explain to Connie why I'm late?*

***more* haste, less speed** *(saying)* if you try to do something quickly, you are more likely to make mistakes and so take a longer time than if you had not rushed.

**have (got) *more* money than sense** → ***have***

***more* sth/often than sb has had hot dinners** *(informal)* very many or very frequently: *You can't tell me anything about motorbikes—I've had more motorbikes than you've had hot dinners! / Will you stop ordering me about? I've organized dog shows more often than you've had hot dinners!* Note that the preceding verb is always in a perfect tense.

***more* or less** approximately or roughly; virtually or practically: *The road runs more or less parallel to the High Street. / By September we knew more or less what our income would be for the whole year.*

***more* power to sb's elbow** (used to approve of what sb is doing and to encourage him to continue): *I think the action groups are a good idea. More power to their elbow, I say!*

***more's* the pity** unfortunately; it is even more to be regretted when you consider sth previously mentioned: *'I hear that a lot of the old town was demolished to allow the shopping centre to be built.' 'And the new buildings are not nearly as nice, more's the pity.'*

***more* than a bit/little drunk, excited etc** quite or considerably drunk etc: *To be honest, Pete was more than a little disappointed not to get the job.*

***more* than anything (else) (in the world)** very much; especially, most importantly: *He wanted to marry her more than anything else in the world.*

**bite off *more* than one can chew** → ***bite***

***more* than one can say/tell** very deeply: *I shall miss you more than I can possibly say.*

***more* than one can say for/of sb/sth** or **more than can be said for/of sb/sth** certainly not true of or applicable to sb/sth: *John's not afraid of hard work, which is more than can be said of some of his friends.*

**have (got) *more* than one's fair share of sth** → ***have***

***more* than glad, ready etc to do sth** extremely glad (about sth); very ready (to do sth): *If you want any help moving the furniture, I'll be more than willing to help you.* Also **only too glad etc to do sth.**

***more* than likely** very probable; very probably: *Frost and snow are more than likely on higher ground tonight.*

***more* ( . . . ) than meets the eye** → ***meets***

***more* than welcome** warmly received into sb's home etc; greatly appreciated (often used in an invitation): *I wish you'd come and see us in Cornwall. I need hardly say that you'd be more than welcome. / I enclose a rough copy of the play, and any comments you care to make will be more than welcome.*

**the *more* the merrier** *(saying)* the enjoyment of a group of people grows as the number of people involved increases (often used as an invitation): *'You'll bring Mr and Mrs Parsons, won't you?' 'Yes, and can Mrs Dale come as well?' 'Of course; the more the merrier!'*

**there is *more* to sb than that etc** → ***there***

***more* to the point** more important(ly) and more relevant(ly) to the matter or situation: *He knew that his intentions were wrong and, what is more to the point, dangerous as well.* See also **to the *point*.**

***more* trouble than one/it is worth** cause more inconvenience than is compensated for by the benefit or pleasure sth gives: *If you're cooking just for yourself, then electric food mixers and processors are probably more trouble than they're worth.*

**at (the) *most*** not more than sth mentioned: *'I'll be away for ten days at the most, probably only a week.'*

**the *most* (that) one can say (for sb/sth)** or **the most that can be said (for sb/sth)** the only praise that can be given for sb/sth, and this is not much: *His lecture was one of the most boring I've ever heard. The most I could say for it was that it only lasted 20 minutes.*

**for the '*most* part** mostly; largely; most frequently; most extensively: *His early writings were for the most part short stories. / The motorway wasn't built to withstand such heavy use and it has had to be rebuilt for the most part.*

**the *mother* and 'father of a row etc** *(informal)* a great example of sth noisy or unpleasant such as a row: *If the government intervenes to stop the broadcast then there'll be the mother and father of a fuss about it.* Also **the father and 'mother of a row etc.**

**like *mother,* like daughter** → **like *father*/mother, like son/daughter**

**necessity is the *mother* of invention** → ***necessity***

**tied to his *mother's*/wife's 'apron strings** → ***tied***

**a '*mother's* boy** *(derogatory)* a boy or man whose character and behaviour are influenced too much by his mother.

**set sth in *motion*** → ***set***

**go through the *motions* (of doing sth)** → ***go***

**make a *mountain* out of a molehill** → ***make***

**if the *mountain* will not come to Mohammed, Mohammed must go to the mountain** *(saying)* if people or circumstances will not change or adjust to suit you, then you yourself must change or adjust to suit them.

**down in the *mouth* ⟶ *down***

**one's heart is in one's *mouth* ⟶ *heart***

**put words in(to) sb's *mouth* ⟶ *put***

**take the words out of sb's *mouth* ⟶ *take***

**one's *mouth* waters ⟶ *make* sb's mouth water**

**on the *move*** travelling from one place to another; developing or making progress; active: *In former times, families would go on the move in search of gold. / The economy is on the move again after the recession.*

***move* heaven and earth (to do sth)** make every effort, use all your influence and power (to achieve or obtain sth): *We shall move heaven and earth to try to stop the factory closing down.* Also **move mountains (to do sth).**

***move* mountains (to do sth) ⟶ *move* heaven and earth (to do sth)**

**the *moving* spirit** the person who begins and usually leads an activity in a group, enterprise, reform etc: *The moving spirit behind the revival in this type of art was a dealer in East London, a Mr Driberg.*

***mow* sb down** kill sb, often a large group of people, especially with gunfire: *The soldiers were mown down as soon as they came over the top of the hill.*

***Mr* Big** *(informal)* the most important person in a group, area etc: *Harry Cheesman, considered the local Mr Big in his connections with the criminal world, was today found dead in his house in Wandsworth.*

***Mr*/Miss Right** *(informal)* the ideal person to marry: *I'll know when Mr Right comes along—but I'm still waiting!*

**a *Mrs* Grundy** a narrow-minded person who looks critically at other people's behaviour.

**a *Mrs* Mop** *(informal)* a woman who cleans a house or office.

**as *much*** exactly that: *'I think Brown has let us all down badly.' 'Well, I hope you'll say as much to him.' / 'They've decided to get married.' 'I thought as much.'*

**as *much* as (to) do sth** do/say sth in intention and effect, if not literally: *He as much as told me I'd got the job. / That's as much as to say you don't trust me.*

**'so *much* for sb/sth ⟶ *so***

**not make *much* odds ⟶ *make* no/little odds**

***much* of a muchness** not greatly different from one another in ability, especially poor ability: *The students' exam performance seems much of a muchness again this year.*

**not *much* of a musician, help etc ⟶ *not***

***muck* about/around** *(informal)* behave or play in a lazy, silly, or foolish way: *When are you going to stop mucking about and start doing some serious work?*

***muck* sb/sth about/around** *(informal)* treat sb/sth in a rough way that causes hurt or inconvenience: *Listen—stop mucking my sister around or you'll end up in a fight!* Also **muck about/around with sb/sth.**

***muck* in (with sb)** *(informal)* work well together; put yourself on close, friendly terms with the people you work with: *If we all muck in, we'll get the job finished more quickly.*

***muck* sth up** *(informal)* spoil sth; do a job badly: *The delay to the trains really mucked up all our holiday arrangements.*

**drag sb/sth's name etc through the *mud*/mire ⟶ *drag***

***muddle* along/through** proceed, live a life, or manage to do sth, but only in a disorganized, inefficient way: *Without a definite plan for national recovery, this country will continue just to muddle along.*

**a '*mug's* game** *(informal)* a habit or practice that does no good to yourself and is sth only a foolish person does: *The aim of the campaign is to try to persuade young people that smoking is a mug's game.*

***mug* up (on) sth** *(informal)* learn sth thoroughly for a test etc by studying hard for a short period of time: *We've got the French exam tomorrow so I'd better mug up irregular verbs.*

***mull* over sth** think about sth carefully and for a long time: *The committee has just finished mulling over the results of the survey into members' interests, and some changes will be proposed soon.*

**cover a *multitude* of sins ⟶ *cover***

**keep *mum* ⟶ *keep***

***mum's* the word** *(informal)* keep silent; say nothing about sth: *When we get to the gate, remember mum's the word until I give you the signal.*

**(like) *music* to sb's ears** *(informal)* sth that is pleasant to hear: *How I hated biology! Hearing the bell ring at the end of the lesson was music to my ears!*

***must* fly/dash** or **have to fly/dash** *(informal)* have to leave immediately, especially to go to an expected appointment: *Just look at the time! I'm sorry—I'll have to fly!* Note that the subject is usually in the first person.

***must* needs (do sth) ⟶ *needs* must (do sth)**

***mutton* dressed as lamb** *(informal)* a middle-aged or old person, especially a woman, who dresses, uses hairstyles etc in a manner suitable for sb much younger.

***my* eye/foot!** *(informal, old-fashioned)* what nonsense! (an expression of scornful rejection of what sb else has just said): *'It's too expensive.' 'Too expensive, my eye! I know you can afford it!'* Note that often the rejected words are repeated. Also *(old-fashioned)* **all my eye and Betty Martin!**

**be *my* guest!** please do as you like (used as an invitation or a reply to a question): *'May I borrow your calculator?' 'Be my guest!'*

**for '*my* money** *(informal)* in my opinion: *The star of the show is Cecilia Ashton, who for my money is our country's best actress at the moment.*

# N

**a *nail* in sb's/sth's coffin** *(informal)* sth that makes the death, end, or failure of sb/sth quicker or more certain: *The government stopped the money it gave to the theatre, thereby driving another nail into the coffin of arts in the region.*

**hit the *nail* on the head** ⟶ ***hit***

**on the *nail*** *(informal)* (of payments) made immediately at the time of purchase: *You have to pay cash on the nail at that store—they want to be certain they get their money.*

***nail* one's colours to the mast** make your opinions on a subject known and support an organization or course of action: *The Prime Minister nailed his colours firmly to the mast on the question of nuclear disarmament.*

***nail* sb down** *(informal)* get sb to say exactly what his intentions, beliefs etc are: *Try to nail him down on a time when he can come to see us.*

**with the *naked* eye** with only the eye, without any scientific apparatus: *You shouldn't ever look at the sun with the naked eye.*

**sb's *name* is mud** *(informal)* sb is disliked or resented, though perhaps only for a short time: *You know how important it is to go to the wedding. Your name will be mud if you don't!*

**you *name* it (he's got it etc)** ⟶ ***you***

***name* (no) names** (not) identify by name sb you are describing, accusing, or praising: *The prime minister has decided who she wants to be the new defence secretary, but she has no intention of naming names yet.*

**in the *name* of sb/sth** representing sb or sth such as freedom or justice (often used as a reason for an action or request): *There have been more wars and persecutions undertaken in the name of religion than in any other cause. / Open up in the name of the law!*

**by the *name* of sth** known as sth; called: *The story is about a fellow by the name of Higginbottom.*

**the *name* of the game** *(informal)* the real nature of sth: *Survival is the name of the game in the jungle.*

***name* the day** choose the date for a wedding: *They're engaged but they've not yet named the day.*

**. . . , who/which shall be *nameless*** *(informal)* (sb/sth) that will not be referred to by name: *'How do you know?' 'On good authority, I assure you. But the person who told me shall remain nameless.'*

***narrow* sth down to sth** reduce or limit a number of people, places etc to a smaller number: *At the first interview the number of candidates for the job was narrowed down from twelve to three.*

**a *narrow* escape** an injury, danger, or failure that is just avoided: *Commuters had a very narrow escape when a stone thrown by vandals shattered the window just by their seats.* Also **a near miss/thing.**

**a *narrow* shave/squeak** ⟶ **a *close* shave/thing**

**a *nasty* piece of work** *(informal)* an unpleasant, dishonest, dangerous etc person: *I would avoid Philip if I were you; I hear he's a nasty piece of work.*

**set sth at *naught*** ⟶ ***set***

***near* and dear (to sb)** physically and emotionally close to sb: *Fortunately, Rose, a near and dear friend, helped me a lot while Mother was ill.*

**as *near* as dammit** *(informal)* very nearly: *It's 5 metres high, as near as dammit.*

**as *near* as makes no difference/odds/matter** so close that any differences are not important: *This spot, or as near as makes no difference, is where the famous Doctor Jones was born.*

**a *near* miss** an attempt to hit, reach, or achieve sth that only just fails: *'4000 kilometres?' 'That's such a near miss,' the quizmaster said, 'that I think we'll give you the mark. The correct answer is 3982.'*

**a *near* miss/thing** ⟶ **a *narrow* escape**

***near* the bone/knuckle 1** so close to the truth as to offend or embarrass sb; accurate but unkind: *It was a bit near the bone to accuse him of copying.* **2** (especially of a joke) coarse or rude: *We don't want anything near the knuckle, lad. There'll be ladies present.*

***near* the mark** approximately or very nearly accurate in a description, diagnosis etc: *Your boss was near the mark when he said the job would take six months to complete—in fact, it took five.*

**one's *nearest* and dearest** your family: *Christmas is traditionally a time that you spend with your nearest and dearest.*

**. . . or (the) *nearest* offer** or the highest price offered below the one mentioned (abbreviated, for example in newspaper advertisements, to **o.n.o.**): *For all these pieces of furniture, I'll take £100 or nearest offer.*

**a *necessary* evil** sth undesirable, imperfect or harmful that is for practical reasons indispensable: *Many people think of nuclear energy as a necessary evil; if it didn't exist, we would suffer more than we do at the moment.*

***necessity* is the mother of invention** *(saying)* a lack or need of sth produces the will to provide it.

**a pain in the *neck*** ⟶ ***pain***

***neck* and neck (with sb/sth)** in an equal position in a race, in popularity etc: *With only ten metres to go, Jackson and Waite are neck and neck.*

**up to one's *neck* in sth** → **up to one's *ears*/eyeballs/eyes/neck in sth**

**in your, this etc *neck* of the woods** *(informal)* in the place where you live, this is etc: *I see you're the representative from Manchester. How's business in your neck of the woods?*

***need,* want etc one's head examined/examining** *(humorous)* (in sb's opinion) show oneself to be stupid in behaviour, attitudes etc: *If you think we'll win this afternoon's game, you need your head examining!*

***need*/want sth like (one needs/wants) a hole in the head** *(informal)* consider sth completely unnecessary: *We need yet another committee like we need a hole in the head. What we really want is action!*

**like looking for a *needle* in a haystack** → ***looking***

***needless* to say** obviously: *Rachel is always punctual, so, needless to say, she arrived at 3 o'clock exactly. / He wanted to pour petrol on the lawn, but he wasn't allowed to, needless to say.*

***needs* must (do sth)** or **must needs (do sth)** *(formal)* must necessarily (do sth): *It was clear that as the next director of the Art Institute he must needs have more than a superficial knowledge of the various schools of art.*

***neither* here nor there** of no importance or relevance: *The fact that he's rich is neither here nor there—he's still an unpleasant person.*

**have (got) the *nerve* (to do sth)** → ***have***

**a *nervous* wreck** sb whose mental and psychological state has collapsed: *Years in gaol by himself had left him a nervous wreck, incapable of mixing with other people or concentrating on any task.*

**a/sb's '*nest* egg** money saved (by sb) for future use: *They've got a nice little nest egg in reserve for their retirement.*

***never* a dull moment** *(informal)* no lack of interesting and exciting things happening; life is very busy: *We've four children at home, so there's never a dull moment!*

**not/*never* darken sb's door again** → ***darken***

**you *never* know (with sb/sth)** or **one never knows (with sb/sth)** it is impossible to judge or guess what sb/sth is likely to be or do: *'On Thursday night, I've got to dine with a man in Downham. We shall only be talking business; you wouldn't be interested.' 'You never know, I might be.' / He's like the weather; you never know what he plans to do.*

***never* mind** → ***let* alone**

***never* mind (doing) sth** forget about sth; stop, or don't start, doing sth: *Never mind about the washing-up—let's go out now!*

**on the *never*-never** *(informal)* using the hire-purchase system, agreeing to pay for sth in instalments but having the right to use it immediately: *They bought their new furniture on the never-never because they hadn't yet saved up the full price.*

***never* say die** *(informal, becoming old-fashioned)* don't lose your courage; keep trying: *Come on, Gloria, don't despair. It'll all be finished soon! Never say die!*

***new*/fresh blood** additional, different people who make a fresh and lively contribution to a group and so make it more effective: *What this committee really needs is some new blood.*

**as innocent as a *new*-born babe** → ***innocent***

**a *new* broom (sweeps clean)** sb who has just started in a job (who) makes major and thorough reforms in an organization: *The rest of the firm considered her to be a real new broom—and her energetic programme of changes in office practices wasn't particularly welcome, either.*

**turn over a *new* leaf** → ***turn***

**a *new* lease of life** a renewal of or improvement in sb's health, strength etc; further opportunity of success: *Looking after two young children has given Granny a new lease of life.*

**see sb/sth in a *new* light** → **see sb/sth in a different/better/new light**

**(like) a *new* man/woman** sb who has gained or regained health and happiness: *When she came out of hospital she felt like a new woman.*

**be a *new* one on sb** be sth that was not previously known to sb: *That joke's a new one on me, Jake! How did it go again?*

**as clean as a *new* pin** → ***clean***

**the '*new* school** → **the '*old*/'new school**

**you can't teach an old dog *new* tricks** → ***teach***

**put/pour *new* wine in(to) old bottles** → ***put***

**no *news* is good news** → ***no***

**be *news* to sb** be surprising and interesting or significant information: *Did you say the company was employing more people? That's news to me—I thought they were closing down.* Also **come as news to sb.**

**the *next* best thing (to sb/sth)** the most satisfactory substitute for sb/sth: *The committee invited the daughter of the famous artist Sue Kirkpatrick to give a speech as the next best thing to Sue Kirkpatrick herself, who couldn't come.*

***next* door** at, in, or to the building, house etc that is adjacent: *They live in the house next door.* **next-door** *adj*: *our next-door 'neighbours.*

**as . . . as the *next* man etc** just as . . . as any other man etc: *If you have always thought that one electric cooker was as good as the next one, then it's time you visited our showroom. / I'm as honest as the next man, but I don't see why the government should have this much of my wages in tax.*

**one's *next* of kin** the closest member or members of your own family: *In emergency, please contact next of kin.*

**(the) *next* thing one knows** → **(the) *first*/next thing one knows**

**(in) *next* to 'no time** (in) very little time: *He'll be here in next to no time.*

***next* to nothing** almost nothing; a very small amount: *I admit I knew next to nothing about teaching although I knew a lot about chemistry when I first became a science teacher.*
**the *next* world** life after death, especially heaven: *In the next world we will all be completely free from suffering and illness.*
**a *nice* kettle of fish** ⟶ **a *fine*/nice/pretty kettle of fish**
***nice* and warm, easy etc** *(informal)* pleasantly warm etc: *It was nice and cool in the room. / I like my coffee nice and strong.*
**in the *nick* of time** *(informal)* at exactly the right time; just in time not to miss sth, to do sth etc: *It was lucky that you were nearby when the accident happened and you could save Jackie in the nick of time.*
**the *nigger* in the woodpile** *(informal, old-fashioned)* the person who is responsible for spoiling sth, causing trouble etc. Note that ***nigger*** is now widely considered offensive.
***night* and day** ⟶ ***day* and night**
**a *night* on the town** an evening of social enjoyment away from your home, for example at a restaurant, public house, or dance-hall: *The students all had a night on the town after the exams were over.* Also **a (big) night out.**
**a *night* owl** sb who stays up late at night and who is more lively during the night than the day: *He's a night owl and finds he can study best in the early hours of the morning.*
**a cat has *nine* lives** ⟶ ***cat***
***nine* times out of ten** almost always: *My Dad tells us that he's always right, and the truth is that nine times out of ten he really is!*
**a *nine* days' wonder** sb/sth that attracts a lot of attention, but only for a short time: *Yes, she was a nine days' wonder, wasn't she? Who remembers her now?*
**(dressed, made up etc) (up) to the *nines*** *(informal)* wearing fine clothes, a lot of make-up etc as is suitable for a special occasion: *The sisters left for the party done up to the nines.*
**(talk etc) *nineteen* to the dozen** *(informal)* talk etc a lot and very quickly: *They'd not seen each other for months, so when they met they spent the afternoon chattering away nineteen to the dozen.*
**a *nine*-to-five job, mentality etc** regular, routine work as an employee, especially in an office, shop, or factory: *She left school and got a nine-to-five job but quickly found it boring.*
***nip* sth in the bud** stop sth from going any further: *It's a pity that this awful scheme wasn't nipped in the bud or at least reduced in scale in the early days of its operation. / Their friendship was soon nipped in the bud when Sheila had to go away to college, leaving Rob by himself at home.*
***nit*-picking** *(informal)* finding or pointing out small, unimportant faults, mistakes etc.
**the *nitty* gritty** *(informal)* the basic, especially practical, facts of a matter, decision etc: *In this new series of programmes we want to get down to the real nitty gritty of what life is like in a city these days.*
***no* bother** ⟶ ***no* trouble, bother, problem etc**
**in '*no* case** never; not for any reason: *Even if we had the drug in stock we would in no case supply it to anyone without a doctor's prescription.* Note that this is much more emphatic than **not (do sth) in any case.**
***no* chicken** *(informal)* quite old; no longer young: *I'm no chicken, but I still go for regular walks in the country.*
**of *no* consequence** ⟶ **of (great, some, no etc) *consequence***
***no* dice** *(slang)* (an expression used when refusing to do sth or when sb has had no success or luck): *'Can you lend me some money till after the weekend?' 'Sorry, Pete, no dice!' / We tried to see the film, but no dice. Since we'd last been to the cinema, it had been turned into a bingo hall!*
***no* end** greatly: *Your visit pleased her no end.*
***no* 'end of people, a fuss etc** a lot of people etc: *Mixing with those friends of his has done him no end of harm.*
***no* fear!** *(informal)* no; certainly not (used to say no emphatically to a request or suggestion): *'Did you see Robert off at the station?' 'What, at half-past six in the morning? No fear! We said goodbye last night.'* **there is no fear of . . .** there is no or little likelihood of (sth happening).
**(there are) *no* flies on sb** sb is clever and unlikely to make a foolish mistake: *When it comes to selling their goods, there are no flies on Johnson's.*
***no* fool** ⟶ ***nobody*'s fool**
***no* go** not possible or desirable: *A child could wriggle through the gap, but it was clearly no go for a man of his size.*
**a *no*-'go area** an area in which the police have no control, and into and out of which movement is restricted: *Terrorists have turned this part of town into a no-go area.*
***no* good** nothing good; no good results: *No good will come of this plan—it will upset everybody.*
**come to *no* good** ⟶ ***come***
**be *no* good/use (doing sth)** be of no value at all; having no effect: *It's no use crying—it won't make any difference. / It's no good, I can't continue.*
**it's *no* good/use crying over spilt milk** *(saying)* worrying, complaining, or feeling upset about damage, a mistake, or loss which cannot be put right has no value at all: *Oh well, the vase is broken now and it's no use crying over spilt milk. So forget about it, will you?* Also **there's no point/use in crying over spilt milk.**
***no* great shakes** *(slang)* not very good, efficient, suitable etc: *He's no great shakes as a French teacher.*
***no* hard feelings** no resentment or bitterness about sth done or said to you by sb else: *He thought I was wrong and said so. I bear him no hard feelings for it.*

**there is *no* holding sb** sb cannot be prevented from doing sth: *There was no holding him once he started talking about his life in India.*

**with *no* holds barred** *(informal)* with free use of any methods in an argument, competition etc; with no regard for conventions of behaviour, fairness etc: *In this game it's no holds barred. All the rules have gone!*

***no* joke** a difficult or unpleasant task, experience etc: *Trying to find a job these days is no joke, as any young person will tell you.*

**there is *no* knowing/saying/telling . . .** you cannot be sure about (what will happen): *There is no telling what he may do when he gets angry.*

***no* laughing matter** a subject which is serious and should not be treated lightly or with amusement: *And you can stop smiling, too, Smith! A bad accident is no laughing matter, believe me!*

**there's *no* love lost between sb and sb** *(informal)* two people dislike each other: *Everyone knows that there's no love lost between Roger and his boss—you can see how they hate working together.*

**'*no* man's land** land between the boundaries of two countries or between two opposing armies; disputed or desolate land; conditions of life where you feel you have no purpose.

***no* matter who, what etc** it is not important who etc: *No matter when he comes, I won't see him. / I'll always love you, no matter what (happens).*

***no* mean feat, performer, etc** a considerable feat etc: *He saved himself by walking along the window ledge, which was no mean achievement for a man of 75.*

**,*no* news is 'good news** *(saying)* if you do not hear information about sb/sth, then it is likely that things are going all right, no trouble has occurred, or no help is needed.

**make *no* odds** → ***make* no/little odds**

***no* picnic** *(informal)* an unpleasant task or experience: *Looking after a house of eight children is no picnic, I can tell you.*

***no* problem** → ***no* trouble, bother, problem etc**

**(there is) *no* question . . .** there is no doubt about sth: *This town's my home, there's no question of that, but I can't get any work here.*

**be *no* respecter of persons** not show more regard for one person than for another; not be influenced by class, wealth, fame etc: *The plague was no respecter of persons—rich and poor, young and old, thousands died in the epidemic.*

***no* room to swing a cat** *(informal)* a restricted or overcrowded space in which to live or work: *There's no room to swing a cat in here, Mark. How do you manage?*

***no* secret** sth that many people know: *It's no secret that they argue all the time and are getting divorced.*

**be ,*no* skin off 'sb's nose** *(slang)* not have an unpleasant effect on sb, cause upset, or seem important to sb: *It's no skin off my nose if he's too proud to accept help. Let him carry on by himself.*

**(there is) *no* smoke without fire** *(saying)* signs of sth such as a scandal always have a basis or cause for their existence: *A rumour circulated in the press about the royal couple, and two weeks later it was confirmed when they announced their divorce. There's no smoke without fire.*

***no* sooner said than done** sth that you have been asked to do will be done immediately after the request has been made.

***no* stranger to sb/sth** well-known to sb; familiar with sth: *Tonight we welcome back Harold Harowitz, who is no stranger to the London theatre, to star in the new production of 'Swallow Court'.*

**by *no* stretch of the imagination** however much you wish sth to be good, right etc: *You can't by any stretch of the imagination call that factory beautiful!*

**in ,*no* time (at 'all)** extremely quickly: *If you get one of the new fast trains, you'll be in London in 'no time.*

**have (got) *no* time for sb/sth** → ***have***

**(there is) *no* time like the present** *(saying)* now is the best time to do sth.

**have (got) *no* time to lose** → ***have***

***no* trouble, bother, problem etc** no or very little worry or inconvenience: *'I expect you'd like me to look after the children.' 'No, they're no trouble in the afternoons. They usually play quite happily together.' / 'Can you repair these shoes for me by tomorrow?' 'No problem—they'll be ready by 4 o'clock this afternoon if you want.'* Also *(slang)* **no sweat.**

**(there are) ,*no* two ways a'bout it** *(informal)* there is only one way to act or think: *There are no two ways about it—someone who steals is a thief and should be prosecuted.*

***no* way** *(informal)* no possibility; definitely no/not: *There is no way that all the people outside will fit into the hall. / 'Will you continue racing after this accident?' 'No way—I've had enough.'*

**it is *no*/little/small wonder (that . . . )** it is not surprising that . . . : *It's no wonder that you can't find the notes you want. Why don't you file things away properly?*

**be *nobody*'s business** → **be *none* of sb's business**

**like '*nobody*'s business** *(informal)* with great intensity, frequency etc: *I don't know where the money's come from, but he's been spending it like nobody's business for the last three months.*

***nobody*'s 'fool** a wise person who is not easily deceived by anyone: *I'm sure you won't be able to trick Jack into helping you with the robbery or anything else illegal—he's nobody's fool.* Also **no fool.**

***nod* one's head** move your head up and down to show agreement or approval.

**a *nod* is as good as a wink (to a blind horse)** *(saying)* a hint or suggestion can be accepted and acted upon without further elaboration.

***nod* off** *(informal)* fall asleep: *I'm sorry, I was nodding off—what did you say?*

**a *nodding* acquaintance** sb that you know slightly; occasional casual contact or knowledge (of sb/sth): *'Who was that?' 'Mrs Jones—just a nodding acquaintance. We see each other sometimes and exchange a "Good morning" across the street.' / The police knew that he had more than a nodding acquaintance with importers of illegal drugs.*

***noise* sth abroad** *(formal)* announce sth: *It was noised abroad that he would be assuming the chairmanship of the company from January.*

**make *noises* about sth** ⟶ ***make***

***non*-U** ⟶ ***U*/non-U**

**be *none* of sb's business** not concern sb at all: *'Who's staying here?' Jill asked inquisitively. 'That's none of your business,' Tony replied angrily.* Also **be nobody's business; be no one's business; not be anyone's/anybody's business.**

**have *none* of it** ⟶ ***have***

**be *none* the better/worse for sth** ⟶ **be (all, none etc) the *better*/worse for sth**

***none* the wiser, worse etc for sth** no wiser etc because of sth: *I'll go and hear Dr Smithson's lecture, but I know I'll be none the wiser* (or *I know I won't be any the wiser) afterwards.*

***none* too clever, quickly etc** not very clever etc: *I agreed, none too happily, to join in their plans to steal the money.*

***none* too soon** (almost) too late: *They were discovered by the pilot of the helicopter, and none too soon, because they'd eaten all their food.*

***nooks* and crannies** small spaces, subdivisions etc in a room or building: *Are you still looking for your ring? Have you looked in all the nooks and crannies?*

**look down one's *nose* (at sb)** ⟶ ***look***

**pay through the *nose* (for sth)** ⟶ ***pay***

**turn up one's *nose* (at sb/sth)** ⟶ ***turn***

**under sb's *nose*** *(informal)* obvious and visible; unnoticed: *'Have you a match to light the gas with?' 'There's a box of matches right under your nose.' / The trouble with the country's leaders is that they can't see what's happening under their very noses.*

**have (got) a *nose* for sth** ⟶ ***have***

**have (got) one's *nose* in a book** ⟶ ***have***

**rub sb's *nose* in it** ⟶ ***rub***

***nose* sth out** discover sth by smell or a careful search: *If there's any truth in the rumour then you can rely on Peter to nose it out.*

**keep one's *nose* to the grindstone** ⟶ ***keep***

**a *nosey* Parker** *(informal)* sb who interferes in other people's affairs.

**(and) *not* before time** and this is sth that ought to have happened a long time ago: *John has been promoted, and not before time, considering the amount of work he does.*

***not* half be/do sth** *(informal)* be/do sth wholly or to a very great degree: *He may be a nice dog but he won't half be a nuisance on holiday. / You don't half like the sound of your own voice, Rachel! Can't you be quiet for a moment?*

***not* in as/so many words** ⟶ ***many***

***not* likely!** certainly not!: *'Jenny will do my work for me, won't you?' 'Not likely!'*

***not* much of a musician, help etc** not a very good musician etc: *I'm not much of a mechanic, I'm afraid, but I'll have a look at your car if you like.*

***not* so fast!** *(informal)* a request to sb to wait a moment, often used when you think sth is wrong: *Not so fast, young man! Let me see your ticket!*

***not* to mention** and also; and perhaps more importantly: *The final report did not justify all the time, not to mention all the money, that was spent on the investigation.* Also **to say nothing of.**

***not* to worry** *(informal)* I'm not going to worry too much; don't worry (sometimes used to suggest to sb that he need not worry for you): *'I'm sorry to make you listen to all my troubles.' 'Not to worry, I'm in no hurry.'*

**have (got) *nothing* better to do (than do sth)** ⟶ ***have***

**the truth, the whole truth, and *nothing* but the truth** ⟶ ***truth***

***nothing* could be further from sb's mind, the truth etc** sth just mentioned is an opinion, wish etc that you definitely do not have, agree with, think true etc: *'Did you go to his room with the intention of killing Mrs Samson?' 'Honestly, nothing could have been further from my mind—I just went there to collect a parcel.'*

***nothing* doing** *(informal)* no; I refuse to do what is requested; I/you cannot do sth: *'Can you give me a room for tonight?' 'Sorry, nothing doing.' / I tried to get the stain off my shirt, but nothing doing.*

***nothing* (else) 'for it (but . . . )** no other action possible or right in the circumstances except sth: *There was nothing for it: I had to see Peter even if it meant waiting all day.*

***nothing* if not active, an optimist etc** be noticeably active etc: *Miss Janes, the headmistress, considered herself nothing if not just, and she was always extremely careful in disciplining the girls.*

***nothing* 'in it** ⟶ **something, anything, nothing etc '*in* it**

**there's *nothing* 'in it** the competitors in a race are very close to each other: *As they come up to the last hundred metres, there's nothing in it, and any of the five runners could win.*

***nothing* 'in it for sb** ⟶ **something, anything, nothing etc '*in* it for sb**

***nothing* is sacred** *(saying)* even noble or important subjects or situations are treated frivolously and with disrespect.

***nothing* like** far (from); not at all (near): *We need to sell at least 60,000 copies of the* *books and so far we've sold nothing like (or we've not sold anything like) that number. / The bottle is nothing like empty—why did you buy a new one?'* Also **nowhere near.**

**there's *nothing* like sth (for doing sth)** or **there's nothing like sth to do sth** there is nothing that is as effective in achieving a result as sth: *There's nothing like a good novel to help you forget your troubles.*

***nothing* of the kind/sort** not at all what has been suggested, supposed etc: *Valerie claimed that she was descended from the King, but she was nothing of the kind. In reality, she was the daughter of a local farmer!*

**feel/look like *nothing* on earth** ⟶ ***feel***

***nothing* out of the ordinary/usual** ⟶ ***ordinary***

***nothing*/little short of disastrous, deception etc** completely or nearly disastrous etc: *The closure of petrol stations in country areas would be little short of disastrous for people who live in villages.*

***nothing* succeeds like success** *(saying)* success brings confidence in yourself and respect from others that lead to greater success.

**there's *nothing* to choose between A and B** there is no or very little difference between (two things): *It's only the gold lettering on the front of this book that makes it more expensive. Otherwise there's nothing to choose between them.*

**(there's) *nothing* 'to it** a task is easy: *This machine isn't very complicated. All you have to do is pull these two switches and it starts. You see, there's nothing to it!*

***nothing* to shout about** or **nothing to write home about** sb/sth that is not exceptional in any way: *The play was OK, I suppose, but nothing much to write home about.*

***nothing* ventured, nothing gained** *(saying)* you cannot obtain or achieve anything except by making an effort and risking failure, loss, or a rebuff.

**as of *now*** *(informal)* from this moment or date onwards: *I haven't time for all this! As of now, anybody who wants a cooked breakfast makes it themselves. / So as of now, we're engaged!*

**(every) *now* and again/then** occasionally; at irregular times: *We see each other now and again, but we're not close friends.* Also **every so often.**

***now* or never** sth must be done immediately or there will be no further opportunity to do it: *I knew I had to decide. It was now or never. So I chose to marry her.*

***nowhere* near** ⟶ ***nothing* like**

**(to) the *nth* degree** *(informal)* (to) the greatest amount, number etc that is possible: *That girl's so efficient—she's got her whole life organized to the nth degree!*

***null* and void** *(legal)* not valid, binding, or enforceable; cancelled: *The result of the election was declared to be null and void after it was found that some votes had been counted twice.*

**any *number* (of)** ⟶ ***any* amount/number (of)**

**without *number*** extremely numerous; too many to count or keep count of: *In the hot, damp weather, gardening became a constant battle against slugs without number.*

**sb's (lucky) *number* comes up** *(informal)* sb is very lucky in a major competition: *And when my number comes up, then, we'll go on a round-the-world cruise!*

**sb's *number* is up** *(informal)* sb is going to die: *I believe I'll have a feeling inside me when my number is up.*

***number* one** *(informal)* yourself: *All he does in life is look after number one.*

**sb's/sth's days are *numbered*** ⟶ ***days***

**off one's *nut*** ⟶ **off one's *head***

**be *nuts* about sb/sth** ⟶ **be *mad* about/on sb/sth**

**the *nuts* and bolts (of sth)** the essential or practical details of a procedure, undertaking etc: *The directors will discuss the overall schedule and costs, and leave the nuts and bolts of the detailed planning to us.*

**(put sth) in a *nutshell*** *(informal)* (express sth) in a few words: *Unemployment is rising, prices are increasing; in a nutshell our economy is in a bad state.*

**as *nutty* as a fruitcake** ⟶ **as *mad* as a hatter**

# O

**rest on *one's* oars** ⟶ ***rest***

**be off one's *oats*** *(slang)* not feel well.

**an '*object* lesson** sth learned or taught by the study and use of the actual things; practical demonstration of a principle etc as an example or warning: *Watching the first team win 5–0 was a real object lesson in successful scoring tactics for the second and third teams.*

**(as) stubborn/*obstinate* as a mule** ⟶ ***stubborn***

**on *occasion*** sometimes; not very often: *Such a big orchestra is needed to play the symphony that it has only been performed on occasion in this country.*

**take (the) *occasion* to do sth** ⟶ ***take***

**an *odd* bird/fish** *(informal, becoming old-fashioned)* an eccentric person; sb whom other people find hard to understand or tolerate: *Henry's a bit of an odd fish; his neighbours say he keeps canaries in his kitchen!* Also **a queer fish.**

***odd* jobs** different tasks, especially small, practical ones: *I've got a few days' holiday and want to try to do a few odd jobs around the* *house; there's the wall light to repair and the bedroom door to be painted for a start.* **odd-'job man** *n* sb who is employed to do odd jobs in a house, garden, school etc.

**(the) *odd* man/one out** an extra person, male or female, or thing when others are put into pairs or groups; a peson who is different from or not comfortable socially with others in a group: *Nine was an awkward number for a weekend of bridge games because it meant that one of us was always the odd man out.*

**against all the *odds*** despite a strong disadvantage, great opposition etc; with little or nothing in your favour: *Against all the odds this little-known man succeeded in becoming President.*

**make no/little *odds*** ⟶ ***make***

**over the *odds*** *(informal)* higher/more than the usual price: *I don't mind how much the machines cost. I'm prepared to pay over the odds if you can deliver them quickly.*

***odds* and ends** ⟶ ***bits* and pieces**

**the *odds* are (that . . .)** it is (very) probable that: *I don't think we can come. The odds are that we won't be able to get a baby-sitter—not on Christmas Eve.* Also **it's 'odds 'on (that . . .)**

**the *odds* are against sth** sth is (very) improbable: *You might even have a calm and comfortable crossing, although in January the odds are against it.*

**it's '*odds* 'on (that . . .)** ⟶ **the *odds* are (that . . .)**

**at *odds* with sth** disagreeing with sth; not conforming with sth: *The deputy chairman's statement about nuclear energy is greatly at odds with the chairman's—which one should we believe?*

**be *off* (the menu)** be no longer available (that day): *'Steak pie is off, I'm sorry,' the waitress told him.*

***off* and on** sometimes; occasionally, not continuously or regularly: *It rained off and on during the night.* Also **on and off.**

**on the '*off* chance (that)** *(informal)* because you hope, if you are lucky, that: *I called at their house on the off chance that they'd let me stay, but they weren't at home. / We thought it was unlikely that they'd have any rooms left for the summer holiday, but we wrote on the off chance and they said they had!*

**in the *offing*** likely to happen soon: *The company say that because an increase in wages is in the offing, they might have to raise their prices soon.*

**as *often* as not** about as many times as not: *'You're always up until after midnight, and it's not good for you.' 'That's not true—as often as not I'm in bed well before then.'*

**like *oil* and water** incompatible; unable to work well etc together: *The new man soon found it was impossible to work with his boss; they were like oil and water—they just didn't mix.*

**pour *oil* on troubled waters** ⟶ ***pour***

**of *old*** *(formal)* at an earlier or past time: *In days of old, an order of knights lived in this castle.*

**as *old* as the hills** very old, ancient: *Many of the tribe's customs and rituals are as old as the hills.*

**rake over *old* ashes** ⟶ ***rake***

**an *old* bag** *(slang)* an old woman (often used to refer to her loss of good looks, poor figure etc): *Some old bag came here complaining that we'd charged her too much.*

**a chip off the *old* block** ⟶ ***chip***

**put/pour new wine in(to) *old* bottles** ⟶ ***put***

***old* boy/girl** *(informal)* (a friendly or familiar way of talking to) a man/woman, often, but not always, middle-aged or elderly, or an animal: *I'm sorry I'm late, old boy, but the car broke down outside Hemel Hempstead. / The old boy had been a fighter pilot in the Second World War and still sported a fine moustache. / Come on, old girl, eat up your biscuits, and then we'll go for a walk.* Also (for males) **old chap/man;** (for males or females) **old thing.**

**'*old* boy/girl** a former pupil of a secondary school, especially a school not supported by government money and where education is paid for by parents: *The Old Boys' reunion will take place in the Great Hall on Saturday 2 July.*

**the *old*-'boy network** the unofficial system of giving jobs, information etc to people you know, especially from school: *I just don't know anybody who works there, and the only way to get in seems to be by the old-boy network.*

**the '*old* brigade/guard** *(informal)* the senior members of a profession etc, whose standards and practices are being challenged or superseded: *Jack's one of the old brigade—he insists on doing a job thoroughly. It's a pity there aren't more people like him today!*

**an *old* chestnut** *(informal)* a joke or story that has been repeated often.

**you can't teach an *old* dog new tricks** ⟶ ***teach***

***old* enough to be sb's father/mother** too much older than sb for a marriage, relationship etc to be suitable: *Peter and Helen are getting married? That's ridiculous! He's old enough to be her father!*

**an *old* flame** *(informal)* a previous boyfriend or girlfriend: *His third wife was an old flame, Mary, who he'd first met 20 years earlier.*

**an *old* fogey** *(informal)* a dull, old-fashioned, and reactionary person, especially an old person: *I'm not such an old fogey that I don't remember what it was like being a teenager.*

**an *old* hand at (doing) sth** sb who is experienced at doing a certain job, activity etc: *Mr Jackson is an old hand at negotiating our contracts—he's been with the firm for nearly twenty years, so he knows all the procedures.*

***old* hat** *(informal)* already known, accepted, or practised and not new or original: *Let me state again the main events in the history of the* *war, though I expect this will be old hat to many of you.*

**an *old* head on young shoulders** the wisdom, caution, and tastes that are usually associated with older people, but found in a young person: *He has an old head on young shoulders—one of the most mature 25-year-olds I know.*

**an *old* maid** a woman, especially an old woman, who is not married and probably never will be: *'I've been too busy in my life to think about love,' Miss Mellings answered in a superior tone. And there spoke a real old maid!*

**the *old* man** *(informal)* a man in authority over other people, for example a headmaster or boss: *The old man wants to see me in his office.*

**the/one's *old* man/woman/lady/girl** *(informal)* one's husband/wife or father/mother: *'It's a bargain,' said my brother Jack. 'Let's buy it between us and keep it for the old girl's birthday!'*

**the *old* one-two** *(slang and old-fashioned)* an ogling look that shows a sexual interest or invitation: *From the photograph I could easily imagine him as my mother described, giving the old one-two to the maids.*

**money for *old* rope** ⟶ ***money***

**the 'old/'new school** those following former/present practices, standards etc: *Mother was one of the old school who didn't like to accept help from anyone, especially the government—she said she always wanted to be independent.*

**the *old* story** ⟶ **the *same* old story**

**'any *old* time, place/where, how etc** ⟶ ***any***

**for '*old* times' sake** because of warm, sentimental memories of your past: *I'd never been to Inverness before, but I decided to visit the Gordons for old times' sake—we'd known each other in India many years ago.*

**an *old* 'wives' tale** a story, recommended practice, or piece of information, that is unsupported by fact or is supposed to have been given from one generation to the next: *Eating carrots to help you see in the dark is an old wives' tale—it doesn't make any difference at all.*

**an *old* woman** sb, male or female, who is fussy, timid, and very cautious: *Stop being such an old woman, Dave! I've never known anyone to worry over such little details!*

***olde* worlde** *(humorous)* belonging to or like a past period of history in appearance, style, or sentiment: *This village has a real olde worlde feel to it—it all looks straight out of the 17th century!*

**the *oldest* profession** prostitution.

**an '*olive* branch** a token of peace; peaceful intentions: *Unions held out an olive branch to management last night in their offer of a new basis for talks.*

**not be *on*** ⟶ **be *out***

**go/be '*on* about sb/sth** ⟶ ***go***

***on* and off** ⟶ ***off* and on**

**go/be '*on* at sb** ⟶ ***go***

**at *once*** **1** immediately: *I'm sorry but there's been an emergency; I must ask you to leave at once.* **2** *(formal)* simultaneously; at the same time as sth else: *The noise was more of a cry for help, at once firm and urgent.*

**(just) for *once*** on this/that occasion, if at (almost) no other time (used to imply that sth should be done more often): *You're early for once—thank heavens!* Also **(just (for)) this once:** *I don't normally drink alcohol, but just this once I think I could have a glass of beer.*

**,*once* a . . . , 'always a . . .** sb will always be sth, in spite of changes in circumstances: *He's been retired for years but he still carries on teaching!' 'Yes—once a teacher, always a teacher!'*

**,*once* and for 'all** at this one time and from this time forward: *Understand this once and for all, will you—you're here to learn and I'm here to teach!* **once-and-for-all** *adj*: *a once-and-for-all payment.*

***once* bitten, twice shy** *(saying)* if something has gone wrong on one occasion, then you will be very careful about being involved in a similar matter again: *'Would you like to help arrange the school play this year, Michael?' 'No, thanks; I'd rather not. Doing last year's play meant that life was so hectic for weeks. It's a case of once bitten, twice shy, I'm afraid.'*

***once* in a blue moon** *(informal)* very rarely: *I'm very healthy and thankfully only have to go and see a doctor once in a blue moon.*

***once* in a lifetime** (probably) only once in the life of any one person: *It's only once in a lifetime that you get the chance to see someone as famous as one of the Beatles—so I made sure that I did.* **once-in-a-lifetime** *adj*: *a once-in-a-lifetime experience.*

***once* in a while** occasionally: *There's not much cleaning to do—I just dust the furniture and vacuum the carpets once in a while.*

***once* too often** once again but on that occasion with unpleasant or disastrous consequences (often used as a warning): *You've often dozed off with a lighted cigarette between your fingers. One day when I'm not here you'll do it once too often!*

***once* upon a time** a long time ago (used to introduce a story or fairy tale for children): *Once upon a time there lived a princess in a big castle in a faraway land.*

**at *one* (with sb/sth)** *(formal)* united (with sb/sth), forming or seeming to form a whole; agree with sb/sth: *Out here on the mountains, I feel a strange sense of being at one with nature.*

***one* and all** *(informal)* everybody: *The boss came in and wished us a happy Christmas, one and all.*

***one* and the same** ⟶ ***all* one (to sb)**

**(like) a/*one* big happy family** a group of persons who live or work together without disagreement, where no member is made to feel superior or inferior to another: *The old cliché of being just like one big happy family* *was pretty true of the television cast through the whole series.*

**'one day** at some time, especially in the future: *One day I'll be famous!*

***one* degree under** *(informal)* feeling slightly unwell: *I was feeling one degree under when I got up, but by lunch-time I was all right again.*

**go in (at) *one* ear and out (of) the other** → ***go***

**(have/keep) *one* eye on sb/sth** → ***have***

**at *one* fell swoop** by means of a single action or effort: *It would be a foolish politician who promised to lower the rate of inflation and unemployment at one fell swoop.*

***one* for (doing) sth** *(informal)* sb who very much likes (doing) sth: *He's a great one for early-morning walks. If you go and stay with him he'll get you out in the fresh air to see the sun rise!*

***one* for the road** *(informal)* a last drink before going home: *'How about one for the road?' 'No thanks—not unless it's a strong black coffee!'*

**on (the) *one* hand . . . on the other (hand)** (used to show contrasting facts, opinions etc): *On the one hand, Richard knew he really couldn't afford to build the extension; on the other, he knew that if he didn't decide to do it then, he never would.*

***one* hell/heck of a . . .** *(informal)* an exceptional, especially a bad example of sth: *I'd been drinking the previous night and woke up with one hell of a hangover.* / *They had one heck of a quarrel and she packed her bags and left him.* See also **a/the *hell*/heck of a . . . .**

***one* in the eye for sb** *(informal)* a serious setback or disappointment for sb: *A further by-election defeat is one in the eye for the government.* Also **a smack in the eye for sb**.

**as *one* man** (of people) acting with one mind, doing the same thing: *As one man, the natives fled from the hunters.* / *The crowd rose as one man, demanding the execution of the prisoner.* See also **to a *man*.**

***one* man's meat is another man's poison** *(saying)* what is good or pleasing for one person may be bad or unsuitable for another.

**a *one*-night stand** a single performance of a concert etc as one of a series in different places; sexual relationship lasting only a single night.

**'one of these days** at some time in the future: *It's been nice talking to you. We must meet up again one of these days.*

***one* of those days** *(informal)* a day on which many things go wrong: *'Oh dear, it looks as if it's going to turn out to be one of those days,' cried Sarah, dropping her breakfast bowl on the kitchen floor.*

***one*-off** *(informal)* happening, carried out, made etc only once: *a one-off job.*

***one* or two** a few: *I've got one or two things to do this morning, like clean the carpet, wash the car, and do the shopping.*

**have *one* over the eight** → ***have***

**kill two birds with *one* stone** → ***kill***

***one* swallow does not make a summer** *(saying)* one fortunate event should not be taken to mean that the general situation has improved.

**for *one* thing, . . . , (and for another, . . .)** this is one reason, example etc to support my argument, . . . , (and this is another): *Your mother and I are dissatisfied with your behaviour. For one thing, you've stopped telling us when you're coming home at nights, and for another, you're so rude when you are here.*

**,one thing and a'nother** *(informal)* several different items, tasks, topics etc: *What with the cleaning, the washing, and one thing and another, I've not had a moment's rest all day.*

***one* thing leads to another** sth said or done, which is in itself perhaps not very important, starts a sequence of events: *I met Jack in a bar in Kansas City. One thing led to another and he offered me a job as his assistant.*

**have (got) a *one*-track mind** → ***have***

**(be) *one* up on sb** *(informal)* (be) in a better, more prosperous etc position than sb: *Rachel likes to be one up on her neighbours.*

**'one up to sb** (an exclamation showing approval to sb who has acted skilfully, wisely etc): *One up to the BBC for organizing a competition that gave audiences so much pleasure.*

**with *one* voice** unanimously, expressing everyone's agreement: *It's very rare to find the unions and managers speaking with one voice, but on the question of safety at work there is complete agreement.*

***one* way or the other** whichever of two possible events happens; however things develop: *I don't mind one way or the other whether I go to the party or not.*

**(not the *only* etc) pebble on the beach** → ***pebble***

***only* too glad, ready etc to do sth** → ***more* than glad, ready etc to do sth**

***oodles* of** *(informal)* a lot of: *They've got oodles of money.*

**an *open*-and-shut case** *(informal)* a legal case or other matter in which there should be no doubt about the verdict, outcome etc: *The Inspector knew he had an open-and-shut case against Markson as soon as the fingerprints had been checked.*

**with *open* arms** receiving sb warmly and eagerly: *Not all Londoners dislike foreign tourists. 'I welcome them with open arms,' said one ice-cream seller in Hyde Park enthusiastically.* / *The modern housewife rushes with open arms at anything that saves time in the kitchen.*

**an *open* book** sb/sth that has nothing mysterious about him/it; sb/sth that is easily understood: *Her mind was an open book—she couldn't deceive anybody.* / *The secret workings of the civil service are anything but an open book to the general public.*

***open* sb's eyes (to sth)** cause sb to become aware of facts or circumstances previously unnoticed or not fully understood: *The trip to third-world countries really opened the eyes of*

the delegation. **eye-opener** *n*: *The trip was quite an eye-opener.*
***open* fire (on sb/sth)** start firing guns etc (at sb/sth): *The general gave the order to open fire on the enemy.*
**with an *open* hand** generously. **open-handed** *adj.*
***open* house** ⟶ ***keep* open house**
**an *open* letter** a letter, especially a letter of protest to sb famous, that is made public, for example by being printed in a newspaper.
**have (got) an *open* mind (on sth)** ⟶ ***have***
***open* one's (big) mouth** *(informal)* say something when you should not: *Trust you to open your big mouth and let out the secret!*
**an *open* question** a matter that cannot be answered or decided at the moment: *Whether it is better to hang murderers or put them in prison for life remains an open question.*
**an *open* secret** sth that is supposed to be a secret but is generally known: *It's an open secret that they're getting married.*
***open* the door to sb/sth** allow sb/sth to begin; give sb/sth a chance to do sth: *The success of the operation on his legs opened the door to a whole new life for him.* / *The government are afraid that if the country opens its doors to potential immigrants, there'll be a flood of people wanting to come in.*
***open* the floodgates (of sth)** release a great force of feeling, destruction, rebellion etc that had previously been controlled: *Now that the workers have agreed a pay increase that is higher than the government's target, the floodgates will certainly be opened for other higher wage demands.*
***open* to sb** available and accessible to sb and obtainable by sb; not restricted: *The park is open to the public until 8 o'clock.* / *This book is a useful guide to the opportunities open to school-leavers.*
***open* to sth 1** willing to accept a suggestion, offer, correction etc: *I'm open to any advice you want to give me.* **2** vulnerable or susceptible to sth such as criticism or infection; not protected; exposed: *The suggestion is open to misinterpretation unless you make it clearer.* / *How they will react to this accusation is open to question. I just don't know.*
**lay/leave oneself (wide) *open* to sth** ⟶ ***lay***
***open* up** become less shy and talk more freely: *After a few drinks he really opened up and told us all his problems.*
**an *open* verdict** the conclusion of an enquiry by a jury into sb's death stating that they cannot decide the reason for the death: *The jury returned an open verdict because they couldn't decide whether Miss Jones' death was an accident or suicide.*
**sb's *opposite* number** sb who has the same or very similar position as sb in a different country, company, or other group; counterpart: *The American Secretary of State will have talks with his Soviet opposite number at the conference.*
***opt* out of sth** choose not to do sth or take part in sth: *Why does he always opt out of his responsibilities at the most important point?*
***or* else!** or sth terrible will happen! (used after a command as a threat or warning): *Do what I say, or else!*
**in *order* 1** neatly, tidily, or consecutively arranged; planned or ready to function properly: *It'll take a couple of hours to get the house in order again after the party.* **2** appropriate or permissible: *Would it be in order for us to take the decision in your absence, sir?*
**out of *order* 1** not neatly, tidily, or consecutively arranged: *I checked the papers that were to be printed and noticed that one or two were out of order.* **2** not function or work properly: *Because the lift was out of order, we had to walk up the stairs.* **3** be inappropriate, unsuitable, or impermissible: *Such remarks are too personal and strictly out of order.*
**the *order* of the day** the procedure or business for a named day, such as in the House of Commons; an accepted or usual feature or practice: *Until fairly recently, coal fires were the order of the day in most homes.*
**something/anything/nothing out of the *ordinary*/usual** a person, thing, event, opinion, remark etc that is or is not different or unusual: *I've read this novel and it really is something out of the ordinary.* / *He's a healthy, intelligent boy but nothing out of the usual.*
**A.N. *Other*** an unnamed person (used for example in a list of a team, to show that a place needs to be filled).
**on (the) one hand . . . on the *other* (hand)** ⟶ ***one***
**turn the *other* cheek** ⟶ ***turn***
**the *other* day/morning/afternoon/evening/night** only a few days ago: *It was only the other day we were talking about you, and here you are!* Also **the other week** recently, but more than just a few days ago.
**have (got) *other*/bigger fish to fry** ⟶ ***have***
**the boot is on the *other* foot/leg** ⟶ ***boot***
**how the *other* half lives** ⟶ ***how***
**laugh/grin/smile on the *other* side of one's face** ⟶ ***laugh***
**the *other* side of the coin** the contrasting aspect of a matter: *You get a full five-year guarantee and insurance with this product, but the other side of the coin is that it costs more than the others.*
***other* things being equal** provided that outside circumstances remain the same: *'Wouldn't you like your husband to earn another £5000 a year?' 'Of course I would, other things being equal. But not if he has to go to Singapore, which is what this new job would mean.'*
**in *other* words** expressed in a different way: *He earns twenty times as much as I do. In other words he's very, very rich!*
**be *out*** *(informal)* not be allowed, tolerated, or condoned: *In your state of health, smoking is strictly out, though an occasional drink won't do you any harm.* Also **not be on:** *He*

*must learn that turning up for work an hour late is simply not on.*

***out* and about** travelling around out of doors, working normally, visiting friends etc: *You should get out and about more instead of always sitting reading or watching television.*

**an *out* and out scoundrel, disaster etc** a complete, thorough scoundrel etc: *We won one or two minor concessions from him, so the meeting wasn't an out and out failure.*

***out*-herod Herod** be even more wicked than the most wicked person imaginable: *Reports are reaching us of acts of brutal cruelty by the invading army who seem to want to out-herod Herod to an inconceivable degree.* Other names can be substituted for ***Herod*** to mean to exceed sb in a particular quality: *In ambition and arrogance the new military dictator already out-napoleons Napoleon.*

**be/go *out* like a light** → ***go***

**be *out* of sth** → ***run/be out of sth***

***out* of sight, out of mind** *(saying)* sb/sth that is no longer present or visible tends to be soon forgotten.

**be *out* to do sth** or **be out for sth** intend to do or get sth: *They're out to improve relations between workers and employers. / I'll sell if the price is right, but I warn you I'm out for as much as I can get.*

**at the *outside*** at the highest estimate of a possible number, amount of time, money: *I don't think the factory produces more than 10,000 units per year at the outside.*

**the *outside* world** places, people etc that are without contact with a separate group or community: *Some remote farms are still cut off from the outside world because of heavy snowfall. / He spent 15 years lecturing at university and then got a job in the outside world.*

**have (got) a 'bun in the *oven*** → ***have***

***over* and above** besides sth; in addition to sth: *The basic cost will be £1000. Over and above this there will be my expenses—say another £300. / If the report recommends that higher safety standards are needed over and above the existing requirements, then we will implement them.*

***over* and done with** finished; never to be used, thought about etc again: *When the job is properly over and done with, we can all go home.*

***over* and over (again)** repeatedly; on many occasions: *The doctor has warned him over and over again to stop smoking, but he doesn't take any notice.*

***over* to you** *(informal)* the responsibility is now yours; it's your turn: *'You're doing it in completely the wrong way.' 'OK—over to you, then, if you think you know how to do it!'*

***overshoot*/overstep the mark** exceed the permitted limits in a competition, language or behaviour; do sth very inaccurately: *Don't overstep the mark, son! You can't talk to us as if we were your slaves! / He clearly overshot the mark in his estimate of how long the job would last.*

**(think) the world *owes* one a living** → ***world***

**come into one's *own*** → ***come***

**on one's/its *own*** **1** alone: *A bowl of thick vegetable soup can be a meal on its own. / Why are you sitting all on your own?* **2** without help; independently: *I don't need your advice, thanks. I can do it on my own!*

**at one's *own* expense** → ***at sb's expense***

**stand on one's *own* (two) feet** → ***stand***

**one's *own* flesh and blood** (members of) your own family: *In times of suffering, you must help your own flesh and blood, mustn't you?* See also ***flesh and blood***.

**for sb's *(own)* good** → ***good***

**on sb's *(own)* head be it** → ***head***

**sb after one's own *heart*** sb of the ideal kind or that sb likes best: *But why not ask Rodney? There's a man after my own heart! Quietly and efficiently, he gets on with the job.*

**(be) one's *own* man/woman** (be) capable of independent judgment: *She's very much her own woman, and often she and her husband disagree.*

**(be) one's *own* master/mistress** (be) in control of your own affairs: *The chairmen of nationalized industries are no longer their own masters—they have to obey the government's orders.*

**a dose/taste of one's *own* medicine** → ***dose***

**for one's ('*own*) part** → ***part***

**in one's/its *own* right** because of what sb/sth is in itself, by nature, achievements etc, not because of connections with sb/sth else: *The packaging of goods for sale has become an industry in its own right.*

**under one's *own* steam** independently, with no help from other people: *You'll have to get to the meeting under your own steam, but I can give you a lift home.*

**do one's *own* thing** → ***do***

***own* up (to sth)** admit responsibility (for sth such as a mistake): *The teacher asked whoever had broken the window to own up.*

**one's *own* worst enemy** sb/sth whose own faults are worse than other bad things that have affected him; the cause of your misfortunes: *The publishing industry is again predicting its downfall. It is something of its own worst enemy because it does so so often and nothing happens.*

# P

**put sb through his *paces* → *put***

***pack* one's bags** *(informal)* leave, because you are annoyed and disappointed: *If there's no future for this university, we might as well pack our bags and try our luck somewhere else.*

***pack* it in** *(informal)* stop doing sth: *That noise is awful. Pack it in immediately!*

**a *pack* of lies** an account of sth that is totally untrue: *The police discovered that the suspect's story was a complete pack of lies.*

***pack* sb off** send sb away, often quickly without much care: *If we could pack all the children off to boarding-school, then we'd have much more time for our own work.*

***pack* the house** attract a full audience; fill a theatre, concert hall etc: *The Christmas pantomime doesn't pack the house these days as it used to.* / *The youth band still plays to packed houses.* Also **pack them in.**

***pack* up** *(informal)* (of a machine) stop working or functioning properly: *The washing machine has packed up again.*

***packed* like sardines** (of a large number of people) sitting, standing etc very close together in a confined space: *We travelled back in the rush hour and were all packed like sardines in the train.*

***packed* out** *(informal)* (of a theatre etc) full: *The concert hall was packed out to hear the famous orchestra.*

***pad* sth out** make a report, story etc fuller by adding more material, especially unnecessary material: *The book seemed very padded out—I could have written all that was there in a quarter of the space!*

**a *pain* in the neck** *(informal)* sb/sth that is disliked, annoying, or tiresome: *I find writing letters a real pain in the neck.*

**on *pain* of death** with the risk that you will be killed if you disobey: *Civilians were forbidden to give food or shelter to enemy soldiers on pain of death.*

**be at *pains* to do sth** take great care to do sth: *The chairman was at (great) pains to emphasize that because one factory was closing down, it did not mean that the others would also.*

***paint* sb/sth in glowing colours** describe sb/sth in such a way that suggests it deserves praise, is very good, pleasant etc: *You paint Devon in such glowing colours, Terry, that we really must go and see if it is as beautiful as you say it is.*

***paint* the town red** *(informal)* enjoy a lively, exciting time in a restaurant, night club etc: *The sailors went ashore and really painted the town red that night.*

**not as/so black as one/it is *painted* → *black***

**beyond the *pale*** (of sb or sb's words, action etc) socially unacceptable or inferior: *Such remarks are completely beyond the pale and will not be tolerated.*

**as *pale* as death** very pale, because of shock, illness etc: *She suddenly went as pale as death and I thought she was going to faint.*

**in the *palm* of one's hand** completely under your control and influence: *I now have you in the palm of my hand, and you are totally at my mercy.*

***palm* sth off (on sb)** *(informal)* get rid of sth that you do not want by persuading sb to accept it: *He palmed his old car off on his nephew even though he knew it needed some repairs.*

***palm* sb off with sth** *(informal)* dishonestly persuade sb to accept sth: *'Why weren't you punished for not coming punctually?' 'Oh, I palmed Mr. Hartley off with some excuse that the trains were late.'*

***pan* out** develop: *See how the day pans out, and if you've got time, come and see us.*

**a kick in the *pants* → *kick***

**have (got) ants in one's *pants* → *have***

**catch sb with his *pants*/trousers down → *catch***

**scare/frighten the *pants* off sb → *scare* sb stiff**

**on *paper*** in theory, in contrast to practice; when considered only on written evidence: *The idea sounds good on paper, but I'm not sure whether it will really work.*

***paper* over the cracks** *(informal)* hide disagreements, faults, or difficulties, sometimes quickly or carelessly: *The writers of the government report came to different conclusions, but the final text contained recommendations that tried to paper over the cracks.*

**a *paper* tiger** a person, group etc that is less powerful than he/it thinks, claims etc: *Chairman Mao claimed that all reactionaries were paper tigers.*

**above/below *par* → *above***

***par* for the course** *(informal)* what you would expect to happen: *'There's been another military coup in Africa.' 'The third this year—well, I suppose that's about par for the course.'*

**on a *par* with sb/sth** equal in rank, importance etc to sb/sth: *Our company's export record is now on a par with the best in any other industry.*

***pardon* my French → *excuse*/pardon my French**

**'*parrot* fashion** (learnt, repeated etc) without understanding the meaning: *I don't know any French so I'll just have to learn a few phrases parrot fashion before I go to France.*

**for one's ('own) *part*** in your (own) opinion;

your own contribution is: *Some people want to send all immigrants back to their own countries. For 'my part, I think we should welcome them and make them feel at home here.*

**on sb's *part*** (of sth such as a refusal or miscalculation) made or done by sb: *The delay in payment was an error on the part of the accounts office.*

***part* and parcel of sth** an integral part of sth: *Do I allow my children out on their own? Do I let them talk to strangers? How should I discipline them? These decisions are all part and parcel of being a parent today.*

***part* company (with sb/sth)** leave sb; no longer hold the same beliefs etc as sb and separate oneself from him, a group etc: *The two colleagues parted company after working together for over ten years./We agree on most matters, but we part company on the issue of nuclear disarmament.*

***part* of the furniture** sb/sth thought of as permanently occupying an office, institution etc: *The bank messenger had been there so long he seemed to be part of the furniture. No one ever thought he had a home to go to, or that he might fall ill, or die, or want to retire.*

**in general . . . in *particular* → *general***

**a/the *parting* of the ways** a place where a road etc divides into two; a point when you must follow one course of action or another: *I'd come to the parting of the ways—was I to continue as a teacher or devote my remaining years to writing, which is what I really wanted to do? I knew I had to make up my mind.*

**a *parting* shot** an action, gesture, comment etc, especially one that is critical, made at the moment of leaving: *Sue and Ray had quarrelled. As Ray walked out the door, his parting shot was, 'I hope I'll never see you again!'*

**the *party* line** the official policies of a political party: *Ministers in the government are expected to follow (or toe) the party line.*

**a/sb's '*party* piece** a particular song, act etc that sb can perform well enough to be able to perform it at a party etc: *James hasn't done his party piece yet. Come on, James, we can't let our visitors go without letting them hear a real Scots song!*

**be (a) *party* to sth** take part in, approve, or condone an action: *Six people are accused of having been responsible for, or been party to, the murder.*

**make a *pass* at sb → *make***

***pass* away/on** *(euphemistic)* die: *Miss Kettering passed away peacefully in her sleep last night.*

***pass* for sb/sth** seem to be sb/sth though in fact not be this: *Your English is so good that you could pass for a native speaker.*

**(like) ships that *pass* in the night → *ships***

***pass* sb/sth off as sb/sth** represent sb/sth falsely as sb/sth: *The manufacturers are trying to pass off their new car as a completely different model, but we all know that it's just the old one with a few small improvements.*

***pass* out** become unconscious: *It gets so hot in this lecture hall that I sometimes think I'm going to pass out.*

***pass* sb over** not consider for promotion sb who is or thinks he might be eligible: *When the new appointments were made, Peter was passed over in favour of a younger man.*

***pass* the buck (to sb)** *(informal)* shift the responsibility for sth (to sb else): *By asking me to take care of planning the meeting, Terry is quite neatly passing the buck.* See also **the *buck* stops here.**

***pass* the 'hat round** *(informal)* collect money, for example for a celebration or a present for a colleague who is ill: *They passed the hat round to pay for the refreshments for the office party.*

***pass* the time** make a period of boredom, waiting etc less tedious: *They passed the time telling each other jokes while they waited for the next train.* See also ***pass* one's time (doing sth).**

***pass* the time of day** say a short greeting such as 'Good morning!': *I don't know any of the neighbours very well. We just pass the time of day occasionally.*

***pass* one's time (doing sth)** spend your time usefully or positively (doing sth): *I passed my time in the army learning French.* See also ***pass* the time.**

***pass* water** discharge urine from your body.

**a lot of water has *passed* under the bridge (since . . .) → *lot***

***past* history → *ancient*/past history**

**get/be *past* it → *get***

***pat* sb/oneself on the back** praise or congratulate sb: *Government ministers have really been patting themselves on the back for their generosity to some charities.* Also **give sb/oneself a pat on the back:** *It would be nice if people gave you a pat on the back and told you how good you were more often, wouldn't it?* **get a pat on the back** be praised or congratulated.

**not (be) a *patch* on sb/sth** not (be) nearly as good, bad, beautiful etc as sb/sth: *She's growing up into a very nice girl, but her looks aren't a patch on her mother's.*

***patch* up sth** settle a quarrel or argument: *Fortunately they patched up their disagreement before it got to a fight.*

**the world beats a *path* to sb's door → *world***

**we/our/their *paths* cross → *cross* sb's path**

**have (got) the *patience* of Job → *have***

**(be) as *patient* as Job → *have* (got) the patience of Job**

**the *patter* of tiny feet** (the sound of) young children around you in your home: *I don't want to have children as soon as I'm married but all the other girls in the office can't wait for the patter of tiny feet.*

***pave* the way (for sb/sth)** prepare for sb/sth or make the arrival of sb/sth easier: *A small test project into the effects of the drug has paved the way for a large national investigation.*

**the road to hell is *paved* with good intentions** → ***road***

**the streets are *paved* with gold** → ***streets***

**there'll be the 'devil to *pay*** or **there'll be 'hell to pay** → ***there***

***pay* a bomb** → ***cost*/earn/make/pay/spend a bomb**

***pay* a/the price (for sth)** suffer a loss or disadvantage when sth else is gained or as a penalty for sth wrong: *The cabinet minister had to pay the price for his disloyalty to the government and resign.*

***pay* attention (to sb/sth)** listen carefully (to sb); take notice of sb/sth: *Pay attention while I give you the instructions. / Economists are paying close attention to the latest developments in the Middle East.*

***pay* sb back (for sth) 1** punish sb who has done sth wrong or bad to you: *We'll pay them back for their insults one day.* **2** repay sb for a kind act he has done; repay what you owe sb: *It was so nice to spend the weekend with you and the family. We'll pay you back when we've got a home of our own.*

***pay* sb back in his own coin** punish sb for treating you badly, by treating him in the same way: *She used to snub him a lot in public—it was her way of paying him back in his own coin for the way in which he scorned her at home.*

***pay* court to sb** treat sb with great respect and admiration, such as would be shown to a princess: *Soon after the young, attractive Miss Brown arrived at the office, the young men were all dangling around her, paying court to her and trying to win her affections.*

***pay* heed (to sb/sth)** take careful notice (of sb/sth): *Pay no heed to her rude behaviour—she does it just to attract attention.*

***pay* lip-service to sth** say that you are loyal to sth, support sth etc, but in reality not do this: *Many people just pay lip-service to the ideals of love and the brotherhood of man and in fact lead totally selfish lives.*

***pay* off** be useful or successful: *The preparations for the meeting were hard work, but they certainly paid off and it was a great success.*

***pay* sb off** pay sb in full and then discharge him from employment: *Some of the ship's crew were paid off at the end of the voyage.*

***pay* one's respects to sb** express your good opinion of sb; make a visit to sb on a polite social call: *The crowd filed past the body of the dead general, paying their last respects to the great hero of the war.*

***pay* the earth (for sth)** → ***charge*/pay the earth (for sth)**

***pay* through the nose (for sth)** *(informal)* have to pay too high a price for sth: *Why pay through the nose? Come to Smith's for good quality car repairs at prices you can afford!*

***pay* one's/its way** maintain yourself/itself from money earned from work or services: *The division is being made into a separate company and will be expected to pay its own way within five years.*

**he who *pays* the piper calls the tune** *(saying)* the person who provides the money for sth should control how it is spent.

**it (always/never) *pays* to do sth** you will gain a benefit if you are sensible or wise enough to do or not to do sth: *It never pays to believe that you are cleverer than your opponent.*

**you *pays* your money and you takes your choice** → ***you***

***peace* and quiet** freedom from noise or other disturbances: *We drove out of the big city into the countryside to get some peace and quiet for a few hours.*

***peace* of mind** freedom from worry, fear etc: *I like to know that the children are all home before I go to bed, for my own peace of mind.*

**cast *pearls* before swine** → ***cast***

**the *pearly* gates** *(informal)* the entrance to heaven, at which traditionally St Peter is thought to stand: *When my time is up, I hope I'll find St Peter welcoming me at the pearly gates.*

**as like as *peas* in a pod** → **as *like* as two peas**

**(not the only etc) *pebble* on the beach** *(informal)* just one of many people or things that are equally available, suitable, or desired: *'While you're wondering whether that caravan's worth the price, someone else may come and buy it!' 'I don't mind; it's not the only pebble on the beach.'*

**a/the *pecking* order** an order of importance among a group of people or things: *The invasion last year was a painful reminder that a pecking order still exists among the nations of the world today.*

**put/set sb on a *pedestal*** → ***put***

**a *peeping* Tom** sb who secretly looks at women undressing, people having sexual intercourse etc.

**off the *peg*** (of a suit etc) ready to wear; not cut specially to fit the person it is for. See also ***made* to measure.**

**take sb down a *peg* (or two)** → ***take***

***peg* out** *(informal)* faint or collapse from exhaustion; die: *Several of the runners pegged out at the end of the marathon.*

**a *peg* to hang sth on** or **a peg on which to hang sth** a topic, occasion etc used as an opportunity or excuse to express your opinions: *Whatever subject the professor speaks on, he always makes it a peg to hang his own political views on.*

**the *pen* is mightier than the sword** *(saying)* statesmen, writers, philosophers etc have a greater effect on history than conquerors, leaders of armies etc; laws and persuasion can influence people more than use of armed force.

***pennies* from heaven** unexpected or incidental benefits, especially money: *We need more money but we can't rely on pennies from heaven. We'll just have to work harder.*

**not have (got) two *pennies* to rub together** → ***have***

**the *penny* drops** *(informal)* you now understand sth that was unnoticed or puzzling before: *There was a long silence on the stage, and then the penny finally dropped—I was supposed to be speaking!*

**a *penny* for your thoughts** *(informal)* say what you are thinking about (said to sb who is deep in thought): *A penny for your thoughts, Hugh! You've not said anything all evening!*

**in for a *penny*, in for a pound** *(saying)* having spent some money or time, gone to some trouble etc, it will be worth spending still more in order to do sth: *The new carpet made everything else look so shabby that it was a case of in for a penny, in for a pound, and we bought new wallpaper and curtains as well!*

**not know where one's next meal/*penny* is coming from** → ***know***

***penny* wise and pound foolish** *(saying)* cautious in spending little on small things, but reckless on larger, unnecessary items.

**a ˈ*pep* talk** *(informal)* a talk designed to inspire confidence or increase co-operation or production: *Just before the exams began, our teacher came in and gave us all a pep talk on what good students we were—it really encouraged us!*

***pepper*-and-salt** having small spots or areas of black and white mixed together, giving a grey appearance: *a pepper-and-salt jacket/beard.*

***pepper* sb/sth with sth** *(informal)* strike sb or provide sb/sth with a great number of sth such as shots or questions: *His book was peppered with quotations from the Bible.*

***peppercorn* rent** a very small rent.

**at one's *peril*** at the risk of serious danger: *You'll be climbing the mountain at your (own) peril if you go in this bad weather.*

**in *peril* of sth** risking sth such as your life: *He walked through the streets of the city in peril of his life.*

***perish* the thought!** *(informal and becoming old-fashioned)* may it never happen; I hope it will not happen: *They may make us sit and watch the films of their holiday again, perish the thought!*

***perk* up** become more cheerful, lively etc: *He seemed depressed, but he perked up when I suggested (or at the idea of) going out for a meal.*

**in *person*** **1** physically present, in contrast with being simply known: *We were invited to the television studios and met in person the people we've seen on the screen.* **2** yourself personally, in contrast with sb else acting as a substitute or representative: *I'm sorry I won't be able to come to the party in person, as I shall be on a business trip, but I'm sending my deputy.*

**a *person* of substance** → **a *man*/woman/person of substance**

**for *Pete*'s sake** → **for *goodness'*/God's/heaven's/pity's/Pete's sake**

***peter* out** gradually come to an end: *The climbers' hopes of reaching the summit began to peter out when they realized that the storms were getting worse.*

**a *photo* finish** the finish of a race, competition etc in which the contestants are so close to one another that a photograph is taken to decide the winner; such a race.

***pick* a fight/quarrel (with sb)** deliberately look for a reason or excuse to have a fight or argument (with sb): *Why do you always pick a fight with boys who are smaller than you?*

***pick* and choose** choose from a number of alternatives in a very fussy way: *You can't pick and choose what job you want nowadays; you must be satisfied with what you're offered.*

***pick* at sth** take small or very few mouthfuls of food, because you are fussy or unwell: *Stop picking at your food, Janet! Eat it all up or you won't have any pudding!*

***pick* sb's brain(s)** ask sb questions to obtain information, ideas etc which you can then use for yourself: *Do you mind if I pick your brains for a moment? I've got this idea for a new book and I need some help.*

***pick*/shoot holes in sth** or **pick a hole in sth** *(informal)* criticize or make adverse comments about sth: *It's easy for you, as a newcomer, to pick holes in this scheme, but you're not aware of the months of planning that we've done.*

**the *pick* of the bunch** →**the *best*/pick of the bunch**

***pick* on sb** choose sb, especially unfairly, to do an unpleasant task, or for criticism; criticize or attack: *Why doesn't he pick on people his own size if he wants a fight?*

***pick* sb's pocket** steal money or small articles from sb's pocket: *'He'll get his pocket picked,' Larry said, looking at the man at the counter stuffing a wad of notes into his jeans and turning back to the bar again.* **pickpocket** *n* sb who picks pockets.

***pick* up** **1** (of sth such as sales or exports) improve: *The report gives evidence that the economy is slowly picking up after the recession.* See also ***pick* (sb) up.** **2** (of an engine) start to function again; increase speed: *The car engine spluttered for a few seconds then picked up.*

***pick* (sb) up** (help or cause sb to) recover health: *Catherine was feeling very ill yesterday but has picked up a lot today.* **pick-me-up** *n*: a drink that helps your health recover. See also ***pick* up 1.**

***pick* sb up** *(informal)* **1** find and arrest sb; call for questioning: *The main suspect in the murder case was finally picked up by police in London yesterday.* **2** make the acquaintance of sb with a view to a sexual relationship: *He went home with a girl he'd picked up at the disco.* **pick-up** *n* sb who is picked up or the act of picking sb up.

***pick* sth up** **1** acquire a skill, or knowledge of sth, especially without undertaking a special study of it: *I knew no German when I went to*

*Germany but I picked up quite a bit in the short time I was there.* **2** *(informal)* buy sth cheaply or be lucky to find sth that you buy: *That picture was a real bargain! Where did you pick it up?* **3** *(informal)* earn (money): *How much does he pick up each week?* **4** continue telling (a part of) a story etc after an interruption: *This is a point I'll pick up later on in the lecture.* **5** hear or gather a piece of news, information etc: *They picked up some rumour that the firm was going to close down.*

***pick* up the pieces** put matters right again after a failure, defeat, state of confusion etc: *The People's Party has already begun to pick up the pieces after its recent defeat in the election.*

***pick*/gather up the threads** *(informal)* readjust to a job, way of life etc after sth such as the separation of a husband and wife; make a new start in a relationship: *Sue is trying hard to pick up the threads of normal life again after her husband's death. / It's lovely to be able to pick up the threads of our friendship after 20 years.*

**have (got) a bone to *pick* with sb** ⟶ ***have***

**in a (fine/pretty) *pickle*** ⟶ ***fine***

**no *picnic*** ⟶ ***no***

**put sb in the *picture*** ⟶ ***put***

**the *picture* of health etc** completely or extremely healthy etc: *Fred and Jane looked the very picture of happiness on their wedding day.*

***pie* in the sky** *(informal)* (the promise or hope of) very good conditions of life at a time in the future, especially when you know these cannot be fulfilled: *Most voters know that the promises of the different parties before an election are all just pie in the sky.*

**of a *piece* (with sb/sth)** ⟶ **of a *kind*/piece (with sb/sth)**

**a *piece* of cake** *(informal)* (of a task etc) very easy to do successfully or well: *After climbing mountains in the Swiss Alps, going up English hills is a piece of cake.*

**give sb a *piece* of one's mind** ⟶ ***give***

**(buy) a *pig* in a poke** ⟶ ***buy***

***pig*/piggy in the middle** *(informal)* a person or group who is in a helpless position between others or who is made use of by others.

**make a *pig* of oneself** ⟶ ***make***

**make a *pig*'s ear (out) of sth** ⟶ ***make***

**sb's *pigeon*** *(informal)* sb's concern or responsibility: *Sales figures aren't 'my pigeon. Ask Miss Rowsham in the Trade Department about them.*

**put/set the cat among the *pigeons*** ⟶ ***put***

***pigs* may/might fly** *(saying)* wonderful and impossible things might happen (used when you do not believe sth will happen): *'He might let you have it cheaply, since you're a relative.' 'Yes, and pigs might fly!'*

***pile* it on (thick)** ⟶ ***lay***

***pile* on the agony** *(informal)* give a description of an event that emphasizes the pain and suffering felt: *He always piles on the agony when he has a slight cold and makes it sound as if he's going to die!*

***pile* up** (of cars etc travelling close behind each other) crash into each other: *Several cars and lorries piled up on the motorway in thick fog this morning.* **pile-up** *n.*

**a *pillar* of society etc** sb on whom society etc depends for its security; a reliable supporter or helper of a group, family etc: *Mr Jones, widely regarded as one of the pillars of local politics for years, has died at the age of 78.*

**from *pillar* to post** from one place to another; in/to many directions: *European MPs have to rush from pillar to post between their home constituencies and various meetings in different parts of Europe.*

***pin* sb down** force or persuade sb to say what he really thinks, intends to do etc: *Terence is a very difficult man to pin down. He often says one thing one day and contradicts himself the next.*

***pin* sth down** define, describe, or find sth exactly: *There's something in his character that I don't like, though I can't quite pin it down.*

**you could hear a *pin* drop** ⟶ ***hear***

***pin* one's faith on sb/sth** put your trust in sb/sth: *Some people pinned their faith on the revival of the country's economy, others on the rise of a new political leader.*

***pin* one's hopes on sb (doing) sth** have your hopes depend on sb/sth: *The bosses are pinning their hopes on the workers' accepting (or acceptance of) their new offer to end the strike.*

**'*pin* money** *(informal)* money earned by a woman for her personal use, as separate from a regular income: *I haven't got a job, but I do teach a little French from time to time, just for pin money.*

**at a *pinch*/push** if circumstances make it necessary, but with some difficulty: *I think we could manage to run a car at a pinch, but I'd rather have a little extra spending money at the moment.*

**take sth with a grain/*pinch* of salt** ⟶ ***take***

**in the *pink* (of health etc)** *(informal)* in the best, highest etc condition (of health etc).

**see *pink* elephants** ⟶ ***see***

**(have (got)) *pins* and needles** ⟶ ***have***

***pip* sb at the post** defeat sb in a race, activity etc when very near to the finish, a decision etc: *We thought we'd won the contract, but we were pipped at the post by a rival firm who offered a lower price at the last moment.* Note that this is often used in the passive.

**put that in your *pipe* and smoke it** ⟶ ***put***

***pipe* down** *(informal)* be quiet: *Oh, pipe down, will you! I've still got some work to do!*

**a '*pipe* dream** a hope, belief, plan etc that will probably never come true: *The museum's director has a pipe dream of buying all the waste land by the railway and building a new gallery there.*

***pipe* up** begin to speak: *A small voice piped up*

*from the back of the room, 'I didn't understand the question, sir!'*

**in the *pipeline*** (of a suggestion, plan, or things) being processed or developed; about to be delivered; receiving attention: *Agreements to build cars worth a total of £20 million were still in the pipeline at the end of the year.*

**he who pays the *piper* calls the tune** → ***pays***

***piping* hot** extremely hot: *Piping hot soup served here.*

***pit* one's strength etc against sb/sth** set or match your strength etc in competition against sb/sth: *In this part of the contest, all the competitors work together to pit their wits against a question sent in by a listener.*

***pitch* and toss** (especially of a boat) move or be swung and thrown about in all directions: *The boat pitched and tossed in the rough seas.*

***pitch* in** attack sth in a strong, forceful way; begin working or eating in an eager, enthusiastic way: *It's good to see everyone in the office pitching in; I think we'll manage to send the work off punctually.* Also **pitch into sth.**

***pitch* in (with sth)** give or offer sth such as help or support: *A colleague pitched in with some statistics when he saw I was having difficulty in the negotiations.*

**for *pity*'s sake** → **for *goodness*'/God's/heaven's/pity's/Pete's sake**

**in *place*** or **out of place** appropriate/inappropriate: *Such a rude remark would be most out of place at a formal occasion.*

**put oneself in sb's shoes/*place*** → ***put***

**put sb in his *place*** → ***put***

***place* (all) one's cards on the table** → ***put*/lay/place (all) one's cards on the table**

**(not) be sb's *place* to do sth** (not) be within sb's responsibilities, authority, terms of employment etc to do sth: *It's not my place to give orders, sir. That would be most presumptuous. I am merely here to obey your instructions.*

**avoid sb/sth like the *plague*** → ***avoid***

***plain* and simple** → ***pure*/plain and simple**

**as *plain* as a pikestaff** clearly visible, obvious: *There's a big sign saying 'No Entry—Private Road' as clear as a pikestaff at the entrance. You can't miss it.*

**(in) *plain* clothes** (of policemen, soldiers etc) (wearing) ordinary civilian clothes, not a uniform: *Policemen in plain clothes mingled with the crowd as the President drove past.* **plain-clothes** *adj*: *a plain-clothes policeman.*

**a *plain* Jane** a girl or young woman who is not very attractive.

**(be) (all) *plain* sailing** (be) a matter of simple, straightforward procedure and progress: *We may be successful now, but I can assure you that developing this business hasn't been all plain sailing.*

**have (got) enough etc on one's *plate*** → ***have***

**a game that two can *play*** → ***game***

**come into *play*** → ***come***

***play* all one's cards** *(informal)* use every means, argument, resource etc in your power: *I've played all my cards. There's nothing more I can do to persuade him.*

***(play)* a cat-and-mouse (game) (with sb)** *(informal)* (keep sb in) a state of uncertain expectation, treating him alternately cruelly and kindly: *The government has accused the water workers of playing cat-and-mouse with the country—first they called a national strike; then they called it off; and then they wanted to strike again.*

***play* sb along** pretend to agree with or want sb for a short time, especially for your own advantage: *They're just playing you along. They want to hear how you'd tackle the problem and then they'll discuss it with another company.*

***play* along with sb/sth** agree to cooperate with sb or conform to sth, especially temporarily: *We're prepared to play along with the new scheme for three months, but then we'll want to review our position.*

***play* ball (with sb)** *(informal)* work or act in agreement with others so that things continue without difficulties : *So he won't play ball, eh! He'll soon realize he can't manage without us.*

***play* (sth) by ear** play music which you have heard or remembered but not seen written down: *She could listen to a tune once or twice and then just sit down and play it. I wish I could play by ear like that!* See also ***play* it by ear.**

***play* one's cards close to one's chest** → ***hold*/keep/play one's cards close to one's chest**

***play* one's cards well, badly etc** *(informal)* use well etc the means at your disposal to fulfil your wishes: *If you play your cards right, you'll take over from your boss when he retires in a few years.*

***play* sth down/up** make sth appear less/more important than it really is: *Another crisis is developing in the United Nations, but the politicians are trying to play it down.*

***play* fair/straight (with sb)** play a game according to the rules; act justly and honestly with sb: *He never played fair with anyone—that's why he was always in trouble.*

***play* fast and loose with sb/sth** *(informal)* act in an insincere, deceitful way towards sb or sb's feelings: *He played fast and loose with several women's affections.*

***play* for time** try to delay sth such as a defeat, an embarrassing admission, or a decision: *I knew they were just playing for time and hoping that the delay would bring about some advantage for them.*

***play* sb's game** or **play the same game** co-operate with sb to promote your own interests, or try to do better than sb, by using methods similar to his: *When a second television channel began to attract large audiences, controllers of the first channel decided to play the same game and fought back with more popular programmes.* See also ***play* the game.**

***play* gooseberry** *(informal)* be the unwanted single person in a group of couples, especially the third person with one couple: *Oh, you two go by yourselves! You don't want me coming along playing gooseberry.*

***play* hard to get** *(informal)* pretend to be less interested than you really are in sb of the opposite sex; try to set a high value on yourself by not accepting an offer of employment etc quickly: *She's playing hard to get, but I know she's in love with me.*

***play* havoc/hell with sb/sth** *(informal)* disturb, upset, or trouble sb/sth greatly: *These storms play havoc with our television reception.* Also **play the devil with sb/sth.**

***play* into sb's hands** do exactly what sb, especially an opponent, wants you to do, without knowing it: *The thieves played right into the hands of the police by leaving the scene of the crime in a conspicuous car.*

***play* it by ear** *(informal)* work out how to deal with sth as it happens, without making plans in advance: *You can't really prepare for the questions he's going to ask you—you'll just have to play it by ear, I'm afraid.* See also ***play* (sth) by ear.**

***play* it cool** *(informal)* not become excited, worried, angry etc: *The police play it cool when there's trouble on the streets—they don't want things to develop into a riot.*

***play* one's last card** *(informal)* use the only means, argument etc that remains: *I've just one last card left to play—I'll try pleading ignorance of the new rule and hope he'll let me off paying the extra money.*

***play* off sb against sb** oppose one person to another, for your own personal advantage: *A good way of winning more customers would be to play off our two main competitors against each other.*

***play* on sb's weaknesses, generosity etc** exploit sb weaknesses etc: *He played on her good nature and managed to borrow some money from her.*

***play* possum** pretend to be dead, unconscious, asleep etc in order to protect yourself from attack or to avoid having to do sth.

***play* (it) safe** avoid a risk; take a course of action on which there seems to be least danger, although another course could be more successful: *I should play safe and take out insurance even though it seems expensive.*

***play* second fiddle (to sb)** *(informal)* be inferior or subordinate in your position or job to sb: *I was asked to stay on as housekeeper after he got married, but I couldn't bear the idea of playing second fiddle to another woman.*

***play* straight (with sb)** ⟶ ***play* fair/straight (with sb)**

***play* the devil with sb/sth** ⟶ ***play* havoc/hell with sb/sth**

***play* the fool** ⟶ ***act*/play the fool**

***play* the game** act in a way that is right and honourable; do what is expected of you as a loyal supporter: *Rupert told the teacher what had happened—but all his friends thought he had been unfair and that he hadn't played the game properly.* See also ***play* sb's game; a *game* that two can play.**

***play* to the gallery** behave ostentatiously or disrespectfully in order to gain the attention of other people: *The meeting was disappointing—the speaker seemed more interested in playing to the gallery than giving a serious talk.*

***play* truant/hookey** be absent from school, work etc without permission or good reason.

***play* one's trump /winning card** *(informal)* do or say sth that you have kept secret until the most suitable moment: *'Sarah, I don't mind if you're not going to the party, then,' Mark said, and, playing his winning card, he added, 'There'll be lots of other nice girls there.' At this Sarah suddenly had a change of mind!*

**play up** ⟶ ***act*/play up**

***play* up to sb** *(informal)* flatter or encourage sb in order to gain an advantage for yourself: *He's always playing up to the pretty girl students.*

***play* with fire** take unnecessary and dangerous risks: *He loved driving fast, even though he knew he was playing with fire.*

***played* out** very tired, having no vitality etc: *I'm always played out by the time I finish work on Fridays.*

**what is sb *playing* at?** ⟶ ***what***

**as *pleased* as Punch** delighted: *He claims he doesn't mind what the critics say about his books, but he's really as pleased as Punch when one of his books is well received.*

**there are *plenty* more (good) fish in the sea** or **there are plenty of other (good) fish in the sea** *(informal)* there are many other people/things that are as good: *'He never did love me,' sobbed Tina. 'There, there, try to forget Pete. Remember there are plenty of other fish in the sea.'*

***plight* one's troth** *(old-fashioned)* make a promise of marriage.

**the *plot* thickens** *(humorous)* the plot of a novel etc or a situation in real life is becoming more complicated and intriguing.

***plough* a lone/lonely furrow** perform your work alone: *The new Leader of the movement is Jack Spencer, who for years ploughed a lonely furrow working amongst teenagers in Liverpool.*

***pluck* up courage** force yourself to be brave: *He spent hours plucking up enough courage to ask her to marry him.* Also **screw up one's courage.**

**a *plum* job, part etc** *(informal)* a very good job etc, especially one that is well paid and not too difficult: *I hear Jim's really got a plum job—four hours a day for twice the money that I earn!*

***plump* for sb/sth** *(informal)* choose sb/sth from a number of things or people; support: *I plump for Harrison—he's the right man for the job.*

***ply* one's trade** perform a skilled occupation: *The old workshop where Grandad had plied his trade as a blacksmith for years was eventually demolished.*

**(be) in/out of *pocket*** make a profit/loss on a transaction etc: *They came back from a day at the races £100 out of pocket.*

**beside the *point*** not directly concerned with the matter being discussed; not relevant: *How much it costs is beside the point—I'll pay you any amount if you can be certain that this parcel will arrive in London tomorrow.*

**to the *point*** relevant(ly): *The editor deleted a few sentences from the article that weren't altogether* (or *strictly*) *to the point before he sent it off to the printer.* See also ***more* to the point.**

***point* a/the finger at sb** accuse sb: *When interviewed by the police, all the witnesses pointed the finger at poor old Ian.*

**make a *point* of (doing) sth** → ***make***

**(be) on the *point* of (doing) sth** (be) about to do sth: *I was on the point of telephoning you when you arrived.*

**in *point* of fact** → **in *fact***

**the *point* of no return** the stage in an undertaking at which it is only possible to continue; a level of commitment, success, or failure that has been reached and cannot be reversed: *A monk reaches the point of no return on the day he makes his vows.*

**a/one's *point* of view** an opinion about or assessment of sb/sth; general attitude: *'What's your point of view, Harriet? Do you agree with Jack that we must stop the business?' 'I think that if we're losing money then we must close down.'* Also **viewpoint.**

***point* out sth** mention or draw attention to sth: *The Finance Minister pointed out that the increase in unemployment was due to reasons beyond the control of the government.*

**a *poison*-'pen letter** an anonymous letter that accuses, maligns, or slanders sb: *As editor of this magazine, I've received many poison-pen letters over the years.*

***poke* fun at sb/sth** → ***make* fun of sb/sth**

***poke* one's nose into sth** *(informal)* involve yourself in matters that do not concern you: *I wish he'd stop poking his nose into my private affairs! They're none of his business!*

**up the *pole*** *(informal)* crazy or mad: *You must be up the pole if you believe that story!*

**'*poles*/'worlds apart** completely dissimilar: *Politically, the two leaders are poles apart.*

***polish* sth off** *(informal)* finish sth such as a meal or a task: *They were so hungry it took them only a few minutes to polish off the pie and chips!*

***polish* sth up** improve sth such as your knowledge of a language, a skill, or a performance: *I'll have to polish up my Spanish before I go to Spain this summer.*

**a *political* football** an institution, policy, group of people etc that is run or treated in a different way depending on the political party in power: *The railways of this country have been a political football for too long, to be kicked around according to the fancies of the party in power without a thought being given to the general public.*

**as *poor* as a church mouse** having or earning barely enough money for your needs: *He was always as poor as a church mouse while he was a student, but he's now doing better.*

**the *poor* man's sb/sth** sb/sth that is an inferior substitute for a well-known person, expensive food, institution etc: *'What's on these biscuits?' 'It's something out of a tin—a sort of poor man's 'caviare.'*

**a *poor* relation** a poor member of a family; sb/sth with less respect, prestige, power than others: *Short stories have for too long been the poor relations of literature.*

**(a) *poor* show!** → **(a) *bad*/poor show!**

**take a dim/*poor* view of sb/sth** → ***take***

***pop* along/(a)round/in** *(informal)* visit sb casually: *I'll just pop round and see Pete and Janet—I want to borrow a book from them.*

***pop* off** *(informal)* die: *Stop talking about who's going to inherit my money! I've no intention of popping off just yet!*

**sb's eyes nearly *pop* out of his head** → ***eyes***

***pop* the question** *(old-fashioned)* make a proposal of marriage to a woman: *He was going out with her for years before he popped the question.*

**a *port* of call** a port at which a ship stops temporarily on a voyage; place where you stop for a short time, for example to make a visit or have refreshments: *I'm on a tour of universities in the south-east to visit our authors.' 'Where's your next port of call, then?'*

**pip sb at the *post*** → ***pip***

**keep the *pot* boiling** → ***keep***

**the *pot* calls the kettle black** *(saying)* sb criticizes another person for a fault which he has himself: *'You've not done any work all morning!' 'Neither have you—talk about the pot calling the kettle black!'*

**take *pot* luck** → ***take***

**(demand etc) one's *pound* of flesh** (claim insistently) the full amount of sth due to you legally or by rights, whatever suffering etc may result: *It would have cost Brown less to forget the debt than to claim the money back from the people who'd left the hotel without paying, but he was determined to get his pound of flesh.*

***pour* a quart into a pint-pot** → ***put*/pour a quart into a pint-pot**

***pour* cats and dogs** → ***rain*/pour cats and dogs**

***pour*/throw cold water on sth** *(informal)* discourage or try to prevent a plan, suggestion etc from being carried out: *If you want to go to Italy for the summer, don't let your family pour cold water on the idea.*

***pour* new wine in(to) old bottles** → ***put*/pour new wine in(to) old bottles**

***pour* oil on troubled waters** calm a disagreement, violence etc: *There were angry* *scenes outside the factory today between striking and non-striking workers, but local union officials poured oil on troubled waters and managed to stop a fight.*

**the *poverty* trap** a situation in which the total income of a family, couple etc decreases, because an increase in earnings above a certain level means a decrease in the money received from the government.

**the *power* behind the throne** the person who really controls an organization, country etc, in contrast to the person who has the title of leader, ruler etc: *You don't want to speak to Mr Bush about it—he may be one of the directors, but his deputy is the real power behind the throne.*

**do sb/sth a *power*/world of good** → ***do***

**more *power* to sb's elbow** → ***more***

**the *powers* that be** the people who control a country, organization etc: *I'm not sure whether we're allowed to leave the office early without permission or whether we have to ask the powers that be.*

**for (all) *practical* purposes** practically considered; in all practical aspects: *There are five types made, but one is almost impossible to get, so for all practical purposes there are just four.*

**in *practice*** what really happens is that: *The king or queen is the head of the country, but in practice the prime minister makes the decisions.*

**in *practice* or out of practice** having developed/lost a skill: *I've not played tennis for a couple of years, so I'm a bit out of practice.*

***practice* makes perfect** *(saying)* if you repeat an exercise, task etc, you will greatly develop your skill.

***practise* what one preaches** live the way that you advise other people to live: *You ought to practise what you preach! You say you should always be kind to people who are in worse situations than yourself, but I saw the nasty way you spoke to that old man today.*

***preach* to the converted** talk to people who already hold the views and ideas being communicated: *The meeting was rather a farce. It was supposed to be a rally for people with any political views but the speaker found himself preaching to the converted.*

***precious* few/little** *(informal)* very few/little: *I had precious little choice—I didn't want to give a speech, but my firm had given me such a generous leaving present that I had to say a few words.*

**a *precious* lot of help, interest etc** → **a *fat*/precious lot of help, interest etc**

**at a *premium*** having a special value or importance; wanted by many people and therefore difficult to obtain: *The job is very demanding and requires the rare skills of tact, negotiating skill, and keen intelligence, which are at a premium with today's young people.*

**put a *premium* on sb/sth** → ***put***

***presence* of mind** the ability to remain calm and do the right thing in a crisis: *A ten-year-old girl from Leeds showed remarkable presence of mind yesterday when she threw four of her younger brothers out of a window of their burning house to be caught by her father below.*

**for the *present*** → **for the *moment***

***present* company excepted** (used as a polite comment to show that a critical statement does not apply to the people there on that occasion): *My impressions are that the people in this town, present company excepted of course, are rather unfriendly.*

**(not) just a *pretty* face** → ***just***

**a *pretty* kettle of fish** → **a *fine*/nice/pretty kettle of fish**

**(come to) a *pretty* pass** → ***come***

**cost (sb) a *pretty* penny** → ***cost***

**in a *(pretty)* pickle** → **in a (*fine*/pretty) pickle**

***prevention* is better than cure** *(saying)* it is wise to prevent a trouble such as illness in order to avoid having to cure it.

**(not) at 'any *price*** (not be/do sth) regardless of any consideration: *My career is important to me, but not at any price.*

**at a *price*** by paying (too) large an amount of money; by spending or sacrificing (too) much effort, time, security etc: *He knew he could be a very successful businessman, but at a price—he wouldn't see (or but at the price of not seeing) his wife or children very often.*

**beyond/without *price*** extremely valuable: *These paintings are without price; they couldn't possibly be replaced if they were damaged or stolen.*

**cheap/dear at the *price*** → ***cheap***

**not at 'any *price*** *(informal)* absolutely not at all: *She'd like to go, but her father won't allow it at any price.*

**pay a/the *price* (for sth)** → ***pay***

**a *price* on sb's head** a reward for the capture, defeat etc of sb: *There's a price on the heads of those criminals who robbed the wages van this afternoon.*

***price* oneself out of the market** set your price so high that no one buys your goods: *If you charge so much, you'll soon price yourself out of the market.*

***prick* the bubble (of sth)** reduce the apparent size, importance etc of sb/sth to its true amount: *Failing his exams badly pricked the bubble of his own self-importance.*

***prick* up one's ears** (of a person) pay attention; (of an animal) raise its ears as a sign of listening: *'And the winner is . . . ' His ears pricked up. ' . . . Michael Poole.' No, he'd lost again!*

**kick against the *pricks*** → ***kick***

**sb's *pride* and joy** sb/sth that sb is very proud and pleased to have, do, or be associated with: *He was a very skilled artist—he said that drawing and painting every day was his pride and joy.*

***pride* goes/comes before a fall** *(saying)* if you behave proudly, then you are likely soon to meet a difficulty that will make you humble.

***pride* of place** the best position: *All the entries are very good, but pride of place must go (or be given) to Cynthia Jones' daffodils.*

**in *principle*** (considered) as a general idea, theory etc, not considering the details: *The idea sounded fine in principle but it didn't work in practice. / In principle I agree with you; we do want to employ more people. But how can we pay them?*

**on *principle*** because of a moral or reasoned code of behaviour: *I dislike going out for meals in restaurants on principle; why should you pay so much more money for food that you could prepare yourself?*

**a *private* eye** *(informal)* sb who is paid to investigate the affairs of sb else; private detective: *The only way he could find out if they were having an affair would be to hire a private eye.*

**a *prize* ass, fool etc** *(informal)* sb/sth that is outstandingly good/bad: *You made me look a prize idiot, didn't you, calling me by my sister's name in front of all those people?*

**no *problem*** ⟶ ***no* trouble, bother, problem etc**

**the *prodigal* son** sb who leaves a home, community etc to follow a life of pleasure or extravagance or to return to a former way of life or loyalties.

***prolong* the agony** make an unpleasant experience, tense situation etc last longer than necessary: *Why do judges in competitions have to prolong the agony? We just want to hear who's won, not all their comments on how high the standard is again this year, and so on!*

***promise* (sb) the earth/moon** *(informal)* make an extravagant, rash promise: *People are fed up with politicians promising the earth and then not keeping their word.*

**a/the *promised* land** a situation where there is happiness and security: *No one really expects that economists and politicians will bring us quickly and prosperously into the promised land.*

**the *proof* of the pudding is in the eating (of it)** *(saying)* the real value of sb/sth can be judged only by practical experience and not from appearance or theory.

**a *proper*/right Charley** *(informal)* a stupid person: *He made me look a right Charley when I couldn't answer the question in front of all those people.*

**a *prophet* of doom** sb who holds and spreads pessimistic views about the present and future conditions of the world etc: *The newspapers are full of prophets of doom who predict that things can only get worse.*

**the *pros* and cons** the different points in an argument in favour of and against sb/sth: *The aim of this new television series is to give the pros and cons of issues of topical interest.*

**under *protest*** while complaining, objecting etc; unwillingly: *The children will only go to bed at night under protest.*

**as *proud*/vain as a peacock** self-important; clearly pleased and proud: *When I passed my English exam, my Mum was as proud as a peacock and told all the neighbours about it!*

**the exception *proves* the rule** ⟶ ***exception***

**in the *public* eye** well known in the community generally: *He's been in the public eye since he appeared in that quiz programme on the television.*

***puffed* up with sth** filled with conceit etc: *He's been puffed up with a sense of his own importance since he was promoted.*

***pull* a face** ⟶ ***make*/pull a face**

***pull* a fast one (on sb)** *(informal)* carry out sth quickly before sb realizes he is being deceived or has time to object: *He thinks too clearly and isn't the sort of person you could pull a fast one on.* Also **put one across sb; put one over on sb.**

***pull*/take/tear sb/sth apart** criticise sb/sth strongly; find serious faults in sb/sth: *The critics tore his play apart.* Also **pull sth to pieces; tear sb-sth to bits/pieces/shreds:** *He just didn't know his subject well enough and got torn to shreds.* See also **tear sb/sth apart 1; *pull*/take sth to pieces.**

***pull* in** move towards the side of or just off the road etc: *The lorry driver pulled in to get a cup of tea and some chocolate.* **pull-in** *n* a café on the roadside.

***pull* sb in** *(informal)* arrest sb: *The police pulled in those youths for questioning after the robbery.*

***pull* sb's leg** *(informal)* say sth in a joking way to tease, deceive, or slightly annoy sb: *'You came first! You've won the prize!' 'Really? Have I won?' 'No, I was just pulling your leg!'*

***pull* sth off** *(informal)* succeed in sth: *Jones has pulled off some remarkable shots so far in the competition.*

***pull* out all the stops** *(informal)* use all your power, resources etc to achieve an aim: *After they'd won the contract to do the repair work in only two weeks, the whole team pulled out all the stops and just managed it.*

**(not) *pull* one's punches** *(informal)* (not) describe, criticize, or rebuke sb less strongly than would be possible: *The reviewer didn't pull any punches. He didn't think that the new comedy show was at all funny.*

***pull* rank (on sb)** make use of your place in a society or at work to gain advantages to which you are not really entitled: *The tickets have all been sold, but as a local councillor he thinks he can get in by pulling rank.*

***pull* (sb) round** (help sb to) regain consciousness: *It took her a few hours to pull round after the operation.*

***pull* one's 'socks up** *(informal)* take command of yourself; become more purposeful; improve your behaviour: *You really must pull your socks up if you want to beat Jackie in the competition.*

***pull* (the) strings/wires** *(informal)* manipulate other people, use influential friends, indirect pressure etc to obtain an advantage: *You can often achieve more by pulling strings rather than writing letters or trying to persuade people of your point of view.*

***pull* the carpet/rug (out) from under sb's feet** *(informal)* take the help or support away from sb suddenly: *He was about to give his secretary a big pay rise when she pulled the carpet from under him by saying she wanted to resign.*

***pull* the wool over sb's eyes** *(informal)* hide your real actions or intentions from sb; deceive sb: *Stop trying to pull the wool over my eyes! I know you're joking! Why did you really come here?*

***pull* (sb) through** (help sb to) recover (from an illness); (help sb to) survive a danger or crisis: *The doctors think he has a good chance of pulling through. / Their courageous spirit pulled them through the dark days of the war.*

***pull*/take sth to bits/pieces** separate a machine etc into the parts of which it is made: *The electrician had to take the television to pieces to find out what was wrong with it.* See also ***pull*/take/tear sb/sth apart.**

***pull* sb to pieces** → ***pull*/take/tear sb/sth apart**

***pull* together** act, work etc, with efforts combined in a well-organized way: *People often pull together in a crisis.*

***pull* oneself together** take control of yourself, your feelings etc and begin to behave with purpose: *Stop crying and pull yourself together! You're not a baby any more!*

***pull* (sth) up** stop (sth such as a vehicle): *A lorry pulled up as I was walking along the footpath, and the driver asked me the way to the soft drinks factory.*

***pull* sb up** check or correct sb: *His wife has to pull him up sometimes to criticize his old-fashioned ideas.*

***pull*/lift oneself up by one's own bootstraps/bootlaces** *(informal)* try to improve your position by your own efforts and without the help of sb else: *Because the firm couldn't borrow any more money to escape bankruptcy, there was only one thing they could do—pull themselves up by their own bootstraps.*

***pull* sb up short/sharply** → ***bring*/draw/pull sb up short/sharply**

***pull* one's weight** do your fair share in a joint undertaking; do the best you can: *Only if each one of us in the team pulls his weight will the project be successful.*

**have (got) one's finger on the *pulse* (of sth)** → ***have***

***pump* sth out of sb** get sb to tell you sth when he does not want to: *We pumped all the information out of him gradually.*

***pure*/plain and simple** exactly; neither more nor less: *It was greed, plain and simple, that made them want to eat all that food.* Note that this idiom follows the noun it modifies.

**as *pure* as the driven snow** innocent; chaste; very pure morally: *Don't tell us she's as pure as the driven snow because we won't believe you!*

**on *purpose*** deliberately; not accidentally: *I didn't break the window on purpose!*

**hold the 'purse strings** → ***hold***

**at a *push*** → **at a *pinch*/push**

***push* along/off** *(informal)* (of a guest or visitor) leave your house: *It's late; I think we ought to be pushing along now.* Also *(more informal)* **shove off.**

***push* one's luck** *(informal)* risk sth in a bold and often foolish way, hoping that your good fortune will continue: *Don't push your luck—I know the boss paid you more money last week but he doesn't have to always.*

**a *push*-over** *(informal)* an easy task, job etc; sb who is easily persuaded or influenced: *I'm not worried about the history test. It'll be a push-over.*

***push* the boat out** *(informal, and becoming old-fashioned)* hold a cheerful, noisy party with drink, singing etc; have a good time: *It was the end of term so we decided to really push the boat out.*

***push* up daisies** *(informal)* be dead and in your grave: *I'm not thinking about what's going on now—it's what happens when I'm pushing up daisies that worries me.*

***pushing* forty, fifty etc** approaching the age of 40, etc: *It's not when a man's pushing 65, but long before, that he should think about retirement.*

***put* a brave, bold etc face on it** behave bravely etc, while in reality you are disappointed: *Although it was obvious that the trade unions had done better in the deal, the management were determined to put a brave face on it.* Also **put on a brave, bold etc face/front.**

***put* a damper on sb/sth** make sb/sth less happy: *The news of the bride's mother's death put a damper on the whole wedding proceedings, and no one really enjoyed it.* Also **put the dampers on sb/sth.**

***put*/set a foot wrong** make a mistake: *According to the biography she had written of her husband he had never put a foot wrong.* Also **not put a foot right:** *I don't seem to be able to put a foot right this morning.*

***put* a premium on sb/sth** make sb/sth seem important; set a special value or importance on sb/sth: *We put a high premium on old-fashioned virtues like punctuality and honesty in this job.*

***put*/pour a quart into a pint-pot** *(informal)* do sth impossible, such as place sth very big into sth smaller: *You know you'll never be able to fit all those clothes into your suitcase—it's like trying to put a quart into a pint-pot!*

***put* a sock in it** *(slang, becoming old-fashioned)* be quiet; stop what you're doing: *Put a sock in it! I'm trying to get some sleep while you all are chattering away.*

***put* a spoke in sb's wheel** *(informal)* cause sb difficulty; delay sb's plans: *I hear that Freda* *wants to be the new secretary, but I think we can put a spoke in her wheel and stop her.*

***put* sth about** spread sth such as a rumour, gossip etc which is often false: *They put it about that the firm was closing down.*

***put* all one's eggs in/into one basket** *(informal)* risk all your money, time etc on one single opportunity, or give all your attention to one matter, instead of many: *It may be better to invest a little amount of money in several firms than put all your eggs in one basket and invest in just one.*

***put* sb at his ease** make sb stop feeling nervous or anxious, especially with other people: *The vicar found that having a dog helped put visitors at their ease. / The specialist telling him that the illness wasn't so bad after all put his mind at ease.*

***put* sb away** confine sb in a prison, mental hospital etc: *You wouldn't put your own mother away even if she were getting senile, would you?*

***put* sth away** eat a lot of food; drink a lot: *He's so slim—I don't know how he puts it all away without getting fat like me!*

***put* sth away/by** save money, goods etc for future use: *He's very rich—he must have put a lot of money away in the last few years.*

***put* one's back into sth** *(informal)* do sth with all your strength: *I really had to put my back into finishing off cementing the path this afternoon.*

***put* sb's back up** ⟶ ***get*/put sb's back up**

***put* sth behind one** not allow sth that has happened in the past to affect you any longer: *He failed his exams but succeeded in putting all that behind him and became an influential businessman.*

***put* one's best foot forward** *(informal)* hurry; work as hard, go as fast etc as possible: *If we put our best foot forward we may just finish the work by Friday.*

***put*/lay/place (all) one's cards on the table** *(informal)* declare (all) your intentions and thoughts openly: *Negotiators in a business deal don't begin by putting all their cards on the table at the beginning of discussions. / I think it's time I lay my cards on the table. I'm not very rich, and I'm not sure I can really afford all the money you're asking.*

***put* sb's dander up** ⟶ ***get*/put sb's dander up**

***put* sb/sth down** destroy or kill sb/sth, especially an animal, because it is old or sick: *The cat became very ill and had to be put down.* Also **put sb/sth to sleep.**

***put* down roots** adopt a settled way of life: *But we've put down roots here now—we've bought our own house and started a family!*

***put* sth down to sth** consider sth as the cause or explanation of sth: *The broadcasting company puts the success of the English-language programme down to the expansion of tourism, which has made the learning of English very important.*

***put* one's feet up** *(informal)* relax or rest, especially in a chair etc, though not necessarily by having your feet supported: *After a hard day at the office, the first thing I like to do when I come in is put my feet up for half an hour.*

***put* one's finger on sth** *(informal)* point to sth such as a source of trouble in an exact way: *I can't quite put my finger on what's wrong. / You've put your finger on a very important matter.*

***put* one's foot down 1** *(informal)* go faster in a car etc by pressing the accelerator down: *If you put your foot down, we might be home by 7 o'clock.* **2** *(informal)* state or declare sth strongly, especially that you do not want sth to happen: *Without due warning Kate told her parents she wanted to leave home, but her Dad put his foot down and wouldn't let her. / I think we'll have to put our foot down now or Robert will soon ask for even more money.*

***put* one's foot in it** *(informal)* say or do sth that upsets, offends, or embarrasses sb: *Why did you have to go and tell her about her birthday party? You fool, it was supposed to be a surprise! You really put your foot in it this time, didn't you?*

***put* sth forward** suggest an idea or plan for discussion: *The students put forward new proposals on the running of the college to the College Education Committee.*

***put* one's hand into one's pocket** pay for something: *One of our colleagues is retiring, so I expect they'll want us to put our hands into our pockets for a present.*

***put* one's hand to the plough** work with great effort.

***put* one's hands on sth** ⟶ ***lay*/put one's hands on sth**

***put* one's head in(to) the lion's mouth** deliberately put yourself into a very dangerous situation.

***put*/lay one's head on the block** risk defeat or failure; expose oneself to blame, criticism etc: *The government is really laying its head on the block by saying that if it loses this vote in parliament tonight it will call an election.* Other nouns apart from ***head*** may be used: *Miners are spending time thinking about the call to strike before they put their standard of living on the block.*

***put* one's (own) house in order** organize your (own) affairs, work methods, etc efficiently: *A government minister warned the newspaper industry to put its own house in order before it started to tell other industries how they should be run.*

***put* ideas into sb's head** *(informal)* make sb have too high an opinion of himself, expectations that cannot be fulfilled etc: *Don't go putting ideas into his head! Just because he's passed the exam, it doesn't mean he's one of the world's experts!* Also **give sb ideas.** See also ***get* ideas (into one's head).**

***put* in a good word for sb** speak favourably of sb, for example in a recommendation: *His uncle put in a good word for him and he got the job.* Also **say a good word for sb.**

**(*put* sth) in a nutshell** ⟶ ***nutshell***
***put* in an appearance** *(informal)* appear, especially for a short time, at a party, etc because you feel a sense of duty to attend: *We'll stay for quarter of an hour, just to put in an appearance, and then we'll go home. / The director had much more urgent business to deal with, but he did at least put in an appearance at the office party.*
***put* (sb) in for sth** enter (sb) for a competition, job etc: *We're thinking of putting Rachel in for the 100 metres.*
***put* sb in his place** remind sb of his inferior position, status etc: *The headmaster used his authority to put all the boys in their place.*
***put* oneself in sb's shoes/place** consider what you would do or think if you were in the position of sb else: *Put yourself in his shoes! If your mother had just died, how would you feel?*
***put* sb in the picture** *(informal)* give sb information about sth: *Let me put you in the picture on the latest developments, as things have changed a lot since you came here last.*
***put* sb/sth in the shade** *(informal)* be far more successful than sb/sth: *We thought the first two groups were good, but this third one has really put the others in the shade.*
***put* sth into effect** make sth such as a plan happen; implement: *The recommendations of the government report will be put into effect without delay.*
**(to) *put* it mildly** (to) describe sth in less strong terms than it probably deserves; (to) make an understatement: *You were a fool, to put it mildly, to go there so late at night. / To say that she was surprised is putting it mildly; in fact she was completely flabbergasted.* Also **to say the least (of it).**
***put* it on** ⟶ ***put* on airs**
**not *put* it/sth past sb** *(informal)* consider sb quite able or likely to do sth, especially sth unpleasant or wrong: *I wouldn't put it past him to steal money from his own mother.* Note that this idiom is used with ***would.***
***put* it to sb that . . .** suggest sth to sb: *'I put it to you, Prime Minister, that not all the facts have yet been revealed,' the journalist went on.*
***put*/set one's mind to (doing) sth** give your full attention to (doing) sth: *If you put your mind to it, young Smith, you could pass all your exams easily.*
***put* one's money on sb/sth** *(informal)* confidently expect sb/sth to happen, succeed etc (and so support it with your money): *I'm putting my money on Jane Havergill to be the next leader.*
***put* one's 'money where one's 'mouth is** *(informal)* not only say that you support sth but also show your support in a practical way, especially by giving money: *The trade unions say they're in favour of equal opportunities for men and women, but they should put their money where their mouth is and do something as well.* Note that ***mouth*** is always singular.
***put*/pour new wine in(to) old bottles** try to contain or adapt new ideas, methods etc in an old, unsuitable framework.
***put* one's oar in** *(informal)* interfere in sb's affairs or interrupt a discussion: *Why did you have to come and put your oar in? We don't want your help, thank you!*
***put* sb off 1** make excuses to sb, especially to try to avoid a responsibility; evade: *The insurance man calls tomorrow, but I've got no money, so how can I put him off?* **2** discourage, displease, or disconcert sb: *I was hungry, but the smell of rotten food put me off. / Don't be put off by his appearance, he's nice when you get to know him.* **off-putting** *adj*: *His appearance is off-putting.*
***put* sb off (doing) sth** cause sb to lose interest in (doing) sth such as learning a language or to stop enjoying a meal etc: *The crash put her off driving. / I tried to learn English, but the teacher wasn't very good and put me right off it.*
***put* sth off** delay sth such as an event or a decision to a later time; postpone: *The concert had to be put off because the main singer was ill.*
***put* sb off his stride/stroke** disturb the steady progress of sb's work or activity: *All the interruptions put him off his stride, and he did very little work.*
***put*/set sb on a pedestal** treat sb as though he were morally perfect, very knowledgeable etc: *The trouble with being a famous television personality is that ordinary people tend to put you on a pedestal.*
***put* on airs** behave in a way that makes you seem more important or better than other people: *She puts on airs all the time to try to impress new acquaintances.* Also **give oneself airs; put it on.**
***put* sth on the map** *(informal)* make sth prominent or widely known: *Television has really put some games and sports such as snooker and basketball on the map.*
***put* one across sb** ⟶ ***pull* a fast one (on sb)**
***put* one foot before the other** or **put one foot in front of the other** *(informal)* walk (usually used in the negative): *The old lady was so crippled with arthritis that she could hardly put one foot in front of the other.*
***put* one over on sb** ⟶ ***pull* a fast one (on sb)**
***put* our/your/their heads together** *(informal)* combine our etc thoughts to solve a problem: *If we all put our heads together, we might find the answer to our difficulties.*
***put* sb out** be a nuisance to sb; cause sb trouble: *I hope it won't put you out too much if we stay to tea.*
***put* out feelers** *(informal)* discover first thoughts and reactions to a plan: *The government is putting out feelers to the unions to see if there is a possibility of a peaceful settlement in the dispute.*
***put* sb out of his misery** stop sb's worry; satisfy sb's curiosity: *Come on—put us out of misery—did you pass your driving test or not?*
***put* paid to sth** destroy or stop sth: *Days of*

*continuous rain really put paid to their hopes of a quiet, sunny holiday on the beach.*

***put* pen to paper** begin to write sth: *It often takes me some time to put pen to paper but when I do, I write a lot.*

***put* one's shirt on sb/sth** *(informal)* risk everything, especially all your money, in the hope that sb/sth will succeed: *I'm willing to put my shirt on Daredevil to win the next race.*

***put* the boot in** *(slang)* attack sb cruelly and unfairly: *Max was already badly bruised even before the gang of thugs put the boot in. / The firm cut their wages by 10% and then six months later put the boot in by giving them all the sack.*

***put* the cart before the horse** *(informal)* reverse the proper order of events, causes etc: *Working out what you'd do if you won all that money is putting the cart before the horse, isn't it?*

***put*/set the cat among the pigeons** *(informal)* arouse strong feelings, especially of shock, dismay, or anger: *I then told them that the whole schedule had been brought forward by two years, and that really set the cat among the pigeons.*

***put*/turn/set the clock back** return to the past, especially to traditional institutions and values: *Many people see the call to reintroduce capital punishment for murder as putting the clock back 100 years. / You can't turn the clock back to the good old days all the time.*

***put* the dampers on sb/sth** →***put* a damper on sb/sth**

***put* the fear of God into sb** *(informal)* frighten sb very much; force sb to obey you in a certain way: *The first thing you find when you join the army is that your superiors put the fear of God into you.*

***put*/set the record straight** provide a correct version, explanation of events, facts etc: *Let's put the record straight—we don't owe you £5000:* you *owe* us *£5000.*

***put* the screws on sb** *(informal)* persuade sb by force to do sth, especially to pay money: *The rest of the gang will put the screws on me if we don't give them their share of the money soon.* Also **put/turn the heat on sb.**

***put* the skids under sb** *(informal)* make sb hurry; cause sb difficulty: *Tell him he'll get the sack if he doesn't finish the work by tonight—that'll put the skids under him!*

***put* the stoppers on sth** *(informal)* cause sth to stop: *The company installed a new machine to check phone calls to put the stoppers on unnecessary conversations.*

***put* the tin lid on sth** *(informal)* stop or ruin sth finally: *The refusal of our grant application really puts the tin lid on our plans to expand the club.*

***put* the wind up sb** cause sb to be afraid: *Hearing the air-raid siren really put the wind up me.* **get the wind up** be afraid.

***put* that in your pipe and smoke it** *(informal)* think about what I've said; you will have to accept the unpleasant fact: *We've got no more money, so you can't spend any more. Put that in your pipe and smoke it!*

***put* one's 'thinking cap on** *(informal)* think carefully about a problem: *I'll put my thinking cap on and see what ideas I can come up with.*

***put* sb through his paces** test the ability of sb: *The purpose of the weekend is to put the new recruits through their paces.*

***put* sb through the mill** →***go* through the mill**

***put*/set sth to rights** settle or restore sth such as an injustice: *It will take years to put to rights all the wrongs caused by the dictator's rule.*

***put* sb/sth to shame** make sb/sth appear insignificant or of little value by comparison: *This new man with no real experience of selling methods has put the older salesmen to shame by his great achievements.*

***put* sb/sth to sleep** →***put* sb/sth down**

**not to *put* too fine a point on it** to speak frankly and honestly: *Not to put too fine a point on it, we're most dissatisfied with the low standard of your work.*

***put* two and two together** *(informal)* draw the obvious conclusion from the stated facts: *I saw Peter holding Janet's hand and put two and two together, and assumed they'd started going out with each other.* **put two and two together and make five** draw the wrong conclusion.

***put* sb up** provide sb with temporary lodgings, overnight hospitality etc: *Yes, we can put you up for a night or two.* See also ***put* up at etc.**

***put* up at etc** stay temporarily at a place: *We put up at a small boarding-house on our way to Scotland.* See also ***put* sb up.**

***put* sb up for sth** propose or nominate sb as a candidate in an election: *We'll put him up as the next secretary.*

**a *put*-up job** sth that is dishonestly or craftily arranged in advance in order to deceive sb.

***put* sb up to sth** encourage sb to behave in a mischievous or illegal way: *They put me up to it! It wasn't my idea to make trouble!*

***put* up with sb/sth** tolerate or bear sb/sth: *I don't think I can put up with their bad behaviour much longer.*

***put* upon sb** trouble sb; take unfair advantage of sb: *He's so generous that he is often put upon by friends who want to borrow money.* Note that this is often used in the passive.

***put* sb wise to sb/sth** →***get*/be wise to sb/sth**

***put* words in(to) sb's mouth** suggest that sb has said sth when he has not: *You're putting words in my mouth! I've never said anything about changing my job.*

**a *Pyrrhic* victory** an unprofitable victory or success, where the losses are greater than is justified by the gains: *You may have won your case, but to have to pay the court costs makes it rather a Pyrrhic victory for you, doesn't it?*

# Q

**on the *QT* → on the *quiet*/sly**
**put/pour a *quart* into a pint-pot → *put***
***Queen* Anne is dead** *(saying, old-fashioned)* everyone already knows what you've just said; your news is stale.
**the *Queen*'s/King's English** standard English, in contrast to dialect, colloquial language, or slang: *When we speak of the Queen's English as distinct from dialects, we must remember that there is nothing in the dialects that makes them inferior.*
**a *queer* fish → an *odd* bird/fish**
***queer* sb's pitch** or **queer the pitch for sb** put obstacles in the way of sb's success: *I'm not sure whether Clive is seriously interested in Anne, but if he is, then his money and good looks could easily queer your pitch.*
**in '*Queer* Street** in difficulty, especially having little or no money: *You work hard for years but suddenly lose your job and find yourself in Queer Street—this is a common experience in a recession.*
**beyond/without *question*** not to be doubted; without doubt: *His honesty is beyond question. / She is without question the best person for the job.*
**in *question*** doubted or suspected: *His sincerity is not in question; we all know he means what he says.*
**out of the *question*** unthinkable or impossible, totally unsuitable or inadvisable: *An expensive holiday abroad was out of the question on his salary. / I had completed three-quarters of my journey, so to turn back would have been out of the question (*or *it would have been out of the question for me to turn back).*
**the sb/sth in *question*** sb/sth involved or already being discussed: *'Gerald is arranging the sale for her.' 'Well I hope she realizes what she's doing. The gentleman in question isn't always very reliable.'* Note that the noun is usually a general one (e.g. ***gentleman, young lady, matter***) rather than one named specifically.
**there is no *question* . . . → *no***
**cut sb to the *quick* → *cut***
**the *quick* and the dead** living and dead people: *The Bible says that Jesus Christ will come again to judge the quick and the dead.*
**as *quick* as a flash** very fast or suddenly: *I didn't mean to let the dog out, but he ran past me, as quick as a flash, when I opened the door.* Also **as quick as lightning.**
**a *quick* buck → a *fast*/quick buck**
***quick*/slow off the mark** fast/slow to act, seize an opportunity etc: *You must be quick off the mark if you want to apply for the job—they will accept the first person who comes.*
***quick*/slow on the uptake** mentally fast/slow to grasp information, a suggestion etc: *Jackie's always been a bit slow on the uptake. You have to say something a few times before she understands what you're talking about.*
**a *quick* one** *(informal)* a single drink, especially an alcoholic drink: *'Would you like another beer?' 'Yes, I've just got time for a quick one before I catch the train.'*
**on the *quiet*/sly** *(informal)* privately; secretly: *I warned a few of my regular customers on the quiet that there wouldn't be any more petrol at the weekend so they'd better fill their tanks before then.* Also **on the QT.**
**as *quiet* as a mouse** saying very little; making very little noise: *Bob's sister seems rather shy, as quiet as a mouse. I've only seen her once when I've been at his house.*
**as *quiet*/silent as the grave/tomb** (of sth) very still; noiseless; (of sb) not speaking: *I do miss the children. The house seems as quiet as the grave without them.*

# R

***rack*/beat one's brain(s)** think very hard in an effort to solve a problem, or to remember or invent sth: *I've been racking my brains for a week to think of some way of raising the money.* See also ***beat* one's 'brains out.**
***rack* and ruin** a state of disrepair and decay or very bad organization, caused by neglect: *The cottage is going to rack and ruin; a builder will have to come and repair it soon.*
**on the *rack*** in a state of anxiety, distress, pain etc.
**the '*rag* trade** the business of designing, making, and selling women's clothes.
**a *rag*-and-'bone man** sb who buys and sells old clothes, household waste, or discarded goods.
**from *rags* to riches** from great poverty to wealth. **rags-to-riches** *adj*: *a rags-to-riches story.*
**on the *rails* → *keep* (sb) on the rails**
***rain*/pour cats and dogs** rain very heavily: *We spent two weeks in North Wales, but we hardly did anything—it rained cats and dogs all the time.*
**take/have a '*rain* check (for/on sth) → *take***
**come *rain* or (come) shine → *come***
**it never *rains* but it pours** *(saying)* difficul-

ties, problems etc tend to come together in large numbers or quickly one after the other.

**for a *rainy* day** (of saving money) providing for future needs or an unforeseen emergency: *'Don't spend it all at once,' the boss said, smiling at him. 'Put it into the bank and save some of it for a rainy day.'*

**(not) *raise* a finger to do sth** ⟶ **(not) lift/raise a finger to do sth**

***raise* a stink** ⟶ ***create*/raise a stink**

***raise* an eyebrow** cause sb to express disapproval, sometimes by an actual facial gesture: *Yes, you're right—what the chairman had to say in his speech certainly did raise a few eyebrows.*

***raise* Cain/hell** *(informal)* complain, protest, or show your authority in an angry or very strong way: *Your Dad will raise Cain if he catches you here.*

***raise* one's/a glass to sb/sth** say words to sb or about sth that express loyalty, admiration, good wishes etc and then lift your glass and drink from it: *Ladies and gentlemen, let us raise our glasses to our host this evening. / Glasses were raised to the success of the new bookshop in Warminster at the official launch party recently.*

***raise* sb's hackles** cause sb to feel and show anger, resentment etc: *His constant sarcastic remarks really raise my hackles.* **one's hackles rise** feel and show anger, resentment etc.

**(not) *raise*/lift one's hand against** (not) threaten to attack or hit sb: *My husband hasn't raised his hand against me once in all our forty years of marriage.*

***raise* one's hat (to sb)** lift your hat slightly as a sign of courtesy or respect (towards sb): *The old man raised his hat as the lady went by.*

***raise* one's hat to sb** ⟶ ***take* one's hat off to sb**

***raise* its (ugly) head** ⟶ ***rear*/raise its (ugly) head**

***raise* one's sights** ⟶ ***lower*/raise one's sights**

***raise* the roof** *(informal)* make a lot of noise by shouting, singing, clapping etc: *A festival of brass bands from the whole county really raised the roof in the town hall last night.*

***rake* it in** *(informal)* make large profits: *Sales of the new computer game increased rapidly before Christmas, and the company has really been raking it in.* Also **rake the money in.**

**a *rake*-off** *(informal)* a share of profit etc, especially in an illegal deal: *Jack may be a good person to be one of the gang, but he wants a rake-off of 30%.*

***rake* over old ashes** discuss memories, especially of unpleasant events: *I don't want to rake over old ashes, Margaret, but whatever happened to Roger? I know you were very friendly with him at one time.*

***rake* through sth** search sth carefully to try to find a particular item: *The police raked through his papers to try to find a will.*

***rake* up sth** *(informal)* try to revive a past grievance, enmity, scandal etc that is better forgotten: *Why did you have to rake up his criminal past? He's a different man since he left prison.*

***rally* round (sb/sth)** come together to support sb/sth in a time of crisis: *All her friends rallied round when her husband died.*

***ram*/force/thrust sth down sb's throat** *(informal)* repeat sth often in the hope of impressing it on the hearer: *Oh shut up! I'm tired of having religion rammed down my throat all the time!*

**(the) *rank* and file** ordinary members of a group, organization etc, in contrast to the leaders: *There is a new sense of participation among the rank and file of the trade unions.* **rank-and-file** *adj*: *the rank-and-file membership.*

***rant* and rave** complain, protest, or enthuse in a noisy way: *An old man stood on the platform ranting and raving about the high cost of tickets and the lateness of the trains.*

***rap* sb on/over the knuckles** *(informal)* reprimand or criticize sb for sth: *Th boss complained about my laziness and rapped me severely over the knuckles.* Also **give sb a rap on/over the knuckles.**

**a *rare* bird** sb/sth that is only seldom seen or met with: *He's a top scientist and also a famous artist—something of a rare bird these days.*

***raring* to do sth** very eager and ready to do sth: *The company's policy is to employ students who've just left university, as they are raring to put into practice all that they've learnt at college.*

***rat* on sb/sth** *(informal)* tell secret information about sb/sth; abandon an agreement or undertaking: *Jack ratted on his friends and told the police who had stolen the money.*

**the '*rat* race** a constant, competitive struggle to be more successful than other people in business, a profession, social status etc: *Chris and Elizabeth decided to leave the rat race in the city and got jobs and bought a house out in the country.*

**at 'any *rate*** whether for this or another reason; this much, if no more: *I thought Susan quite liked me; at any rate, I know she didn't like me going out with Jane.*

**at 'that/'this *rate*** if that/this is so; according to that/this way of behaving: *'You've been on radio and television. . . . At this rate,' his father went on, 'you'll be more famous than anyone else in the family.'*

**at a *rate* of knots** *(informal)* very fast: *You must have marked all those exam papers at a rate of knots—you only started them an hour ago!*

***rattle* sth off** say or repeat sth quickly and easily from memory or reading: *He rattled off a list of all the kings and queens of England.*

***rave* it up** *(slang)* enjoy yourself wildly, especially at a party. **rave-up** *n*: *The party was a real rave-up.*

**in the *raw*** unrefined; not made to appear more pleasant, acceptable etc than it really is:

*The television programme is about new soldiers who begin to experience army life in the raw.*

**a *raw* deal** unjust or harsh treatment; insufficient pay or reward: *Many retired people feel they are getting a raw deal from the State: they pay money towards a pension for all their working life but discover it isn't worth much when they retire.*

**a *ray* of hope** a possibility of sth good happening that will improve an unsatisfactory, unpleasant etc state of affairs: *There's a ray of hope on the economic front with the level of unemployment down slightly this month.*

**(on) a *razor*-edge** ⟶ **(on) a *knife*-edge**

***reach* first base (with sth)** ⟶ ***get* to first base (with sth)**

***read* between the lines** take a meaning from a text, statement etc that is not actually stated but is implied: *Reading between the lines, it was clear that the poor man was very worried about his wife's health.*

***read* sth into sth** understand or assume more than was intended by a remark, article etc: *Stop reading things into what he said! The Minister said that the economy would get better, but he didn't say when it would.*

***read* sb like a book** understand the character, behaviour etc of sb thoroughly: *He may try to hide things from his parents, but they can read him like a book.*

***read* sb's mind/thoughts** know what sb is thinking, planning etc: *I can't read your mind! If you don't tell us what's worrying you, we can't help you.*

***read* the 'riot act** declare, with authority, that a course of action, behaviour, argument etc, must stop: *Our teacher heard the noise in the classroom and came in and really read the riot act to us.*

**at the *ready*** held, prepared for use: *The students sat with their pens at the ready, eager to write down notes from the lesson.*

***ready*/fit to drop** *(informal)* exhausted: *By the time they'd walked back all the way from town, they were fit to drop.*

**for *real*** *(informal)* not pretended; not in a pretended way: *She pinched herself. It was for real, all right! Here she was at Buckingham Palace, about to meet the Queen.*

**(in) *real* life** (in) life as most people live it, in contrast to life, behaviour, or situations in books, on television etc: *On Saturday evenings, she's Cynthia Wentworth, Birmingham's champion ballroom dancer. In real life, she's Doreen Ruddle, a waitress in a café.* **real-life** *adj*: *a real-life family.*

**the *real* McCoy** sb/sth that is absolutely genuine: *'It was probably one of those sparkling wines that looks like champagne but isn't.' 'No, it was the real McCoy—champagne, all right.'*

**be a *real* ringer for sb/sth** ⟶ **be a *dead*/real ringer for sb/sth**

***rear*/raise its (ugly) head** become apparent; show itself: *Famine still rears its ugly head every so often in many parts of the world.*

**within *reason*** reasonable, reasonably; not extravagant(ly) or ridiculous(ly): *I'll do anything you want, within reason. / People think that if you smoke and drink within reason, your health won't be affected.*

**by *reason* of sth** *(formal)* because of sth: *The judge stated that by reason of their neglect of their daughter, her life was in danger.*

**on the *rebound*** still recovering from a rejection or disappointment, especially the ending of a boyfriend/girlfriend relationship: *She was on the rebound when she met John, fell in love with him, and married him soon afterwards.*

***reckon* on sth** expect that sth will happen; depend on sth happening: *I didn't reckon on your coming early—we aren't quite ready yet.*

***reckon* with sb/sth** consider or treat sth seriously; carefully include sth in your thoughts, calculations etc: *You should reckon with all the possible difficulties before signing the contract.*

**a force to be *reckoned* with** ⟶ ***force***

**for the *record*** so that it should be recorded; used to refer to a statement etc that is officially or publicly made: *Just for the record, I'd like to state that I disagree with our chairman on the following points . . . .*

**off the *record*** unofficial(ly); confidential(ly): *One of the committee members told John off the record that he had got the job.* **off-the-record** *adj*: *an off-the-record statement.*

**put/set the *record* straight** ⟶ ***put***

**in the *red*** or **out of the red** in or not in debt; not having or having money in one's account: *Most of the time my bank account seems to be in the red!* See also **in the *black*.**

**as *red* as a beetroot** with red cheeks, from anger or embarrassment: *I could feel myself turning as red as a beetroot when the teacher praised my essay and read it out to the whole class.*

**the *red* carpet** a strip of red carpet for an important visitor to walk on from a car, plane etc to a building; a respectful welcome: *Well, I didn't expect such red carpet treatment—I'm most flattered.*

**a *red* face** an embarrassed or guilty expression on your face: *I'm certain he's ashamed of what he did. He certainly had a red face for a few days after it happened! / I was doing imitations of the boss, when he came in! He just stood there for a moment and then went off without saying anything, but was my face red!*

**a *red* herring** a topic, incident etc that diverts your attention from the main subject or purpose: *Don't get sidetracked by any red herring when interviewing people.*

**a *red*-'letter day** a very special day because sth important or pleasant takes place then: *3 August is a red-letter day—it's when we're getting married.* Also **the day of days.**

**the *red*-'light district, quarter etc** a district

within a city where there are brothels, often showing red lights.

**(like) a *red* rag to a bull** *(informal)* (sth) very likely to provoke a strong reaction, especially resentment or an attack: *Any mention of unions at a board meeting used to be like a red rag to a bull.*

***red* tape** the formalities of business and administrative procedures: *All this red tape! Why do I have to fill in five forms just to order some new stationery for the department?*

**a *redeeming* feature** ⟶ **a *saving* grace**

***Reds* under the bed** *(humorous)* Communists or left-wing activists considered as instigators of industrial unrest and a threat to democracy.

***reel* sth off** say or repeat sth quickly and easily from memory, especially a list: *Sarah learnt several of Wordsworth's sonnets and loved to reel them off to her family.*

***reflected* glory** the fame and attention obtained from association with sb/sth that is famous or greatly respected or admired: *He worked for a famous designer but was not content to bask in someone else's reflected glory and so set up his own business.*

**a (sad) *reflection* on sb/sth** something which brings discredit on sb/sth: *The high rate of divorce is a sad reflection on the state of family life today.*

**as *regular* as clockwork** occurring at set times in a way that can be depended upon: *The postman comes at 8.40 in the morning, as regular as clockwork.*

***relieve* sb of sth 1** free sb from a duty, obligation etc: *The manager was relieved of the responsibility of looking after the factory at Milton Keynes following the reorganization.* **2** dismiss sb from a job: *The General was relieved of his command because of his offensive remarks about the Royal Family.* **3** *(humorous)* steal sth from sb: *Some scoundrel relieved him of his wallet.*

**something to *remember* sb by** ⟶ ***something***

**in *respect* of sth** *(informal)* with special reference to sth such as a period of time or the cost of sth: *Substantial increase can now be expected in respect of gas and electricity prices.* Also **with respect to sth:** *With respect to your enquiry on the new pension scheme, I have pleasure in enclosing our explanatory leaflet.*

**be no *respecter* of persons** ⟶ ***no***

**pay one's *respects* to sb** ⟶ ***pay***

***rest* assured that . . .** be completely certain or confident that: *Mike, you can rest assured that no one blames you in the least.*

***rest* on one's laurels** pause to enjoy your achievements: *You shouldn't be content to rest on your laurels but should work even harder and become still more successful.*

***rest* on one's oars** have a rest after a period of hard work or great activity.

***return* the compliment** do or say the same thing that someone else has done or said, for example to invite sb to your house when you have visited his: *Thanks for a lovely evening! We'll try and return the compliment very soon.*

***return* to the fold** come back to a group or community such as a church or club after leaving it: *Pat was glad to return to the fold—she liked the people at the church and had missed them while abroad.* Other verbs used in this idiom are: ***accept, receive, welcome***: *Steve was grudgingly accepted back into the fold—but only as an observer, not as a full member.*

**many happy *returns* (of the day)** ⟶ ***many***

***reveal* one's hand** ⟶ ***show*/reveal one's hand**

**neither/no *rhyme* nor reason** no sense at all: *I can see neither rhyme nor reason in his actions.*

**that's *rich*** ⟶ ***that***

**take sb for a *ride*** ⟶ ***take***

***ride* for a fall** *(becoming old-fashioned)* act in such a reckless way that disaster, failure etc is likely: *To invest money in a company that is near bankruptcy is really riding for a fall.*

***ride* high** be successful or confident of your own abilities etc over a period of time: *Politically, he is riding high at the moment, being a minister in the government and a close adviser to the Prime Minister.*

***(ride)* one's/a hobby-horse** (talk about and try to win support for or get others interested in) a cause, way of life, method of working etc about which one has strong feelings: *There goes Jack on his hobby-horse again! When will he realize we're not interested in his brand of socialism?*

***ride* out the storm** ⟶ ***weather* the storm, crisis etc**

***ride* roughshod over sb/sth** treat sb/sth in a harsh, unsympathetic way: *The parents complained to the council about the closing of two schools, but the authority rode roughshod over their protests and ignored them completely.*

***rig* sb/oneself out** provide sb/oneself with clothes, equipment etc: *The children were rigged out in their smart new uniforms.*

**as of *right*** according to what you are entitled to, especially according to the law: *A third of your mother's money comes to you as of right, you know, whether she left a will or not.*

***right* and proper** correct and suitable or appropriate; conforming to the accepted standard: *My views on how to tackle the problem weren't considered right and proper.*

**as *right* as rain** in good health; satisfactory: *You need some fresh air and good food, then you'll soon feel as right as rain again.*

***right*/straight away** immediately: *'When do you want me to start?' 'Right away, if you can.'*

**a *right* Charley** ⟶ **a *proper*/right Charley**

***right* enough** ⟶ ***sure*/right enough**

**get (sth) off on the *right*/wrong foot** ⟶ ***get***

**sb's *right*-hand man** sb's chief assistant, especially when thought of as capable and indispensable: *I'm very lucky to have Norman* *as my right-hand man. He runs the department here when I'm abroad on business.*

**not *right* in the head** ⟶ ***soft*/wrong in the head**

**in one's *right* mind** sensible: *No one in his right mind would choose to live in such filth.*

***right* on!** *(slang)* (an expression of agreement, approval etc): *'You played very badly today, Pete,' said Dick. 'Right on there, Dick,' Pete replied.*

**the *right* people** people of a high social or professional standing, especially when thought of as being influential: *In business, it's important to know the right people—they can give you useful contacts.*

**one's heart is in the *right* place** ⟶ ***heart***

***right* royal** very fine and splendid: *Granny is 80 on Thursday, and the whole family is organizing a right royal celebration for her.*

**keep on the *right* side of sb** ⟶ ***keep***

**on the *right*/wrong side of 40 etc** aged less/more than 40 etc. *He's still on the right side of 50.*

**keep on the *right* side of the law** ⟶ ***keep***

**take sth in the *right* spirit** ⟶ ***take* sth in good/bad part**

**do the *right* thing** ⟶ ***do***

***right* you are** *(informal)* I agree with what you say; I will do it: *'Two teas, please.' 'Right you are!'*

**by *rights*** according to what should happen or what you would expect: *Yes, I know Marge should be here by rights, not me. But why should she always come?*

**put/set sth to *rights*** ⟶ ***put***

**throw one's hat into the *ring*** ⟶ ***throw***

***ring* a bell** cause a vague memory to be remembered: *I can't recall too clearly that we've already met, although your name rings a bell.*

***ring* out the old (year), ring in the new** celebrate the end of one year and the beginning of the next.

***ring* the changes (on sth)** keep changing your choice (from a limited selection of things) to give variety: *After two weeks going to the restaurant, I found I'd rung the changes on the whole menu.*

***ring*/bring the curtain down (on sth)** mark the end of an event: *The steam engine left London at 10 o'clock this morning on its last journey to the north, so bringing the curtain down on the age of regular steam locomotion in this country.*

***ring* true/false/hollow** seem or sound, genuine/untrue/insincere: *His story of intense adolescent self-analysis does somehow ring true.*

**don't *ring* us, we'll ring you** ⟶ **don't *call* us, we'll call you**

**run *rings* (a)round sb/sth** ⟶ ***run***

**a *ringside* seat** a seat in the front rows round a boxing, circus etc ring; position from which you can observe and experience what is happening very closely.

**read the '*riot* act** ⟶ ***read***

***rip* sb off** *(informal)* cheat sb; get money from sb by deceit; charge very high prices: *Don't buy a car from that garage. They really rip you off!* **rip-off** *n.*

***rip* sth off** *(informal)* steal sth; get sth by dishonesty or cunning; steal from sth: *A gang ripped off the local post office last week.*

**a '*ripe* old age** a full or more than averagely long span of life: *My great-grandmother lived to the ripe old age of 96.*

***rise* and shine** *(informal, becoming old-fashioned)* wake up; get up; get dressed and ready quickly: *I know they're on holiday, but go and tell him to rise and shine if they want some breakfast.*

***rise* to the bait** act in response to sth that is aimed at attracting your interest: *I knew he was trying to get me annoyed, but I didn't rise to the bait.*

***rise* to the occasion** show the imagination, courage, eagerness etc which are suitable for a particularly challenging time, especially one that is unexpected and difficult: *When the main singer became ill, Cathy had to take her place. Everyone thought she rose to the occasion magnificently.*

***rise* with the lark** or **be up with the lark** get up very early: *I heard it on the 6 o'clock news this morning!' 'You must have been up with the lark! I didn't get up till 8!'*

***rising* 20 etc** nearly 20 etc years old: *I don't know how old he is exactly, but he must be rising 35.*

***risk* one's neck** *(informal)* chance losing your life in an accident that is caused by foolishness or courage; be liable to incur any penalty, danger etc: *The car in front was moving from side to side over the road—I think the driver must have been drunk—and I wasn't going to risk my neck trying to overtake him.*

**sell sb down the *river*** ⟶ ***sell***

***rivet* sb to sth** fix or hold sb firmly to sth with great attention, fascination, amazement etc: *The sight of the awful monster riveted the children to the spot.*

**the *road* to hell is paved with good intentions** *(saying)* good motives which are not put into practice or have bad results bring blame or punishment.

**on the *road* to ruin, success etc** following a way, course of action etc that will lead to ruin etc: *The doctors say that the operation was successful and Jill is now well on the road to recovery.*

**a *roaring* success** a very great success.

**do a *roaring* trade** ⟶ ***do***

***rob* Peter to pay Paul** borrow money from sb to pay the debts you owe to sb else; manage to do one thing but only by spoiling another.

**(at) *rock* bottom** (at) the lowest possible level: *Audiences at the local cinema have now reached rock bottom, and it may have to close down.* **rock-bottom** *adj*: *rock-bottom prices.*

***rock* the boat** do sth which spoils or disturbs a situation that has been pleasant and comfortable: *Managers and workers were* *working well together until Sheila started to rock the boat and urged us all to go on strike.*

**off one's *rocker* ⟶ off one's *head***

**on the *rocks*** **1** *(informal)* in danger of being destroyed or ruined: *Everyone knows that Jake and Judy's marriage is on the rocks.* **2** (of an alcoholic drink) served with ice.

**make a *rod* for one's own back ⟶ *make***

**rule (sb/sth) with a *rod* of iron ⟶ *rule***

**a *rod*/stick to beat sb with** a fact, argument etc that is used against sb in order to blame or penalize him: *The report critical of the government's handling of the crisis gave the opposition party another stick to beat the government with.*

**a *rogues'* gallery** a collection kept by the police of portraits, files, photographs etc of known criminals.

***roll* in the aisles** laugh uncontrollably; think sth very funny: *That comedian at the playhouse really had them rolling in the aisles! / It seemed as if the whole theatre was rolling in the aisles at his jokes.*

***roll* on Friday, the end of term etc!** *(informal)* may Friday etc come quickly; used as a wish: *Roll on next month! The exams will all be over then!*

***roll* up** *(informal)* arrive: *The whole family rolled up to welcome her home from her stay abroad. / 'Roll up, roll up! Come and see the greatest show on earth!' shouted the man outside the circus.*

***roll* up one's sleeves** *(informal)* prepare yourself for future work: *It's time you rolled up your sleeves, young man, and started earning your living.*

**set/start/keep the 'ball *rolling* ⟶ *set***

**(be) '*rolling* in it/money** *(informal)* (be) very rich: *Terry can lend me some money; he's rolling in it.*

**a *rolling* stone (gathers no moss)** *(saying)* sb who moves from one place, job etc to another (does not accumulate property, friends etc).

**fiddle while *Rome* burns ⟶ *fiddle***

**(when) in *Rome,* do as the Romans do** *(saying)* you should adjust your habits to suit or conform to the customs of the place you live in or the people you live with.

***Rome* was not built in a day** *(saying)* it takes time, patience, and hard work to do a difficult or important job.

**'*romp* home** be a clear winner in a race: *Sizewell romped home in the 3 o'clock at Epsom this afternoon.*

**go through the *roof* ⟶ *go***

**under one *roof*** or **under the same roof** in the same house etc: *I'm not sleeping under the same roof as Linda. We're not talking to each other since we had our argument.*

**a '*roof* over one's head** a place to live in; house of your own: *You can live in this flat for a while. It may not be much but at least it would be a roof over your heads while you find the house you're looking for, and it would be cheaper than a hotel.*

**shout (sth) from the *rooftops*/housetops ⟶ *shout***

**no *room* to swing a cat ⟶ *no***

***root* and branch** wholly; completely; utterly: *The communist government wants to destroy every trace of religion in the country, root and branch.*

***root* for sb/sth** encourage or support sb strongly, especially sb in a competition or struggle: *'You know we're all rooting for you, Hugh,' his family had told him before the race.*

***root* sb to the ground/spot** cause sb to stand fixed and unmoving: *The explosion rooted them to the spot for a moment, and then they all ran away, screaming.*

***rope* sb in** *(informal)* persuade sb to join an activity, club etc: *He tried to rope me in to organize the office party but I refused.*

**a *rose* by any other name would smell as sweet** *(saying)* what matters is what people or things are, not what they are called.

***rose*-coloured/-tinted spectacles** an optimistic view of life; thinking things are better than they really are: *This television play looks at life through rose-coloured spectacles. Everything ends happily, which isn't at all realistic.*

**(not) be *roses* all the way** (of conditions of life or work) (not) be luxurious, pleasant, or easy: *Life is not roses all the way, even if you have a deep philosophical conviction.* See also **a *bed* of roses.**

**the *rot* sets in** *(informal)* a decline or deterioration begins: *The rot really set in when Jackson was appointed chairman, and attendances at our meetings have fallen sharply.*

**a *rotten* apple ⟶ a *bad*/rotten apple**

**a *rotten* trick ⟶ a *dirty*/mean/rotten trick**

***rough* and ready** adequate and acceptable, but not refined or very exact: *I can give you a rough and ready estimate for the cost of the work now and a precise figure later.*

**(the) *rough* and tumble (of . . . )** a fight involving a number of people, but especially where no one is injured; scuffle; competitive conditions of life or work: *Children learn a lot in the rough and tumble of school life.*

**a *rough* diamond** an uncultured, rude person who has good qualities: *He's in charge of the working men's club—a bit of a rough diamond, but a good bloke.*

***rough* it** *(informal)* accept or endure uncomfortable travel, accommodation etc: *If you're prepared to rough it, you can sleep in the side wing of the hostel—there's no heating there.*

***rough* justice** judgments, punishment, or rewards not based on exact legal principles, not carefully considered etc: *'That's rough justice,' complained Bill, after he'd been dismissed from his job by his boss without, so he thought, a fair hearing.*

**a *rough*/smooth passage** a difficult/easy time: *The bill was given* (or *enjoyed) a smooth passage through Parliament.*

**a *rough* ride** a hard or painful experience:

*My boss really gave me a rough ride this morning when he complained about my bad work.*

**take the *rough* with the smooth** —> ***take***

**a square peg in a *round* hole** —> ***square***

**go *round* in circles** —> ***go***

***round* sth off** finish or complete sth in a suitable way: *The politicians rounded off their tour of the country with a big rally in the capital.*

***round* on/upon sb** attack sb physically or with words: *The Prime Minister rounded on his critics last night and insisted that the government would continue with its policies.*

**a *round* robin** a letter, especially of petition or protest, which is signed by many people.

***round* the bend/twist** —> ***bend***

***round* sb/sth up** collect a group of animals, people, or things in one place: *The sheepdog rounded up the sheep on the hillside.*

**. . . in a *row*** (of a number of events etc) (happening) successively, one after the other: *That's the fourth win in a row for Cambridge.* Also **. . . running**: *The young couple had no sleep for two nights running because of their baby.*

**there is/lies the *rub*** that is where there is a difficulty: *There's the rub! People complain about traffic jams in cities, but they aren't really prepared to leave their cars at home and travel by bus or train.*

***rub* along (together)** have a satisfactory relationship with sb: *She and her husband have rubbed along nicely for years.*

***rub* it in** *(informal)* constantly remind sb of sth he wants to forget: *All right, don't rub it in! I know I'm a failure without you having to tell me every five minutes!*

***rub* sb's nose in it** *(informal)* remind sb forcibly of sth wrong or unpleasant he has done: *I know that we were disappointed at Peter's poor exam results, but you don't need to rub his nose in it all the time.*

***rub* off on sb** pass from one person to another as a result of close contact: *My wife is Burmese and I'm British—so some of her cultural background has rubbed off on me.*

***rub* 'salt into the wound** deliberately increase the sense of shame, injury, sorrow etc that sb feels: *James criticized his wife in front of their children, and then, to rub salt into the wound, humiliated her in front of his friends as well.*

***rub* shoulders (with sb)** live, work, or associate with sb closely: *In this club, the famous and the unknown rub shoulders with each other quite freely.*

**not have (got) two pennies to *rub* together** —> ***have***

***rub* sb up the wrong way** *(informal)* do sth that annoys or offends sb: *I think someone has rubbed Michael up the wrong way this morning. He's in an awful temper!*

**a *rude* awakening** a sudden awareness that things are very different from, especially much worse than, what sb thought they were: *Criticism of his latest play came as a rude awakening after the great success of all his others.*

***ruffle* sb's feathers** cause sb to show annoyance or lose self-assurance: *Everyone knew her as a woman of great calm, but the rumours going round the village about her private life certainly ruffled her feathers.*

**pull the *rug* (out) from under sb's feet** —> ***pull***

**as a *rule*** almost always: *It's lucky for you that I'm still up. As a rule, I'm in bed by eleven.*

**work to *rule*** —> ***work***

**a *rule* of thumb** a rough means of measuring or assessing sth that is based on past experience or practice rather than precise scientific calculation: *It's difficult to calculate exactly how much paint you need to decorate a room, but as a rule of thumb, you'll need a litre of paint to every 12 square metres of wall.* **rule-of-thumb** *adj*: *a rule-of-thumb guide.*

***rule* sb/sth out of court** exclude; say that sb/sth cannot be considered to take part in an activity: *The new member's ideas were ruled out of court by the chairman.*

***rule* the roost** be the person who directs others in a business, community etc: *It's Dad who rules the roost in this house—and we're punished if we don't do what he says.*

***rule* (sb/sth) with a rod of iron** govern, control, or manage with great firmness and discipline: *The boss rules his department with a rod of iron—he always criticizes you strongly if you don't follow his instructions.*

**on the *run*** escaping from arrest or prison: *Four men broke out of gaol last night. Three were caught, but one is still on the run.*

***run* a temperature** or **have (got) a temperature** have a body temperature that is higher than normal: *He had a slight fever and was running a temperature.*

***run* a mile (from sb/sth)** *(informal)* be careful to avoid or escape from sb/doing sth: *The poor cat is so nervous that she'll run a mile if you try to go near her.*

***run* across sb/sth** —> ***come*/run across sb/sth**

***run* amok** go about in a wild, uncontrolled state, liable to attack or kill people; be or get out of control: *A man ran amok in a commuter train yesterday—he struck two railway staff and smashed several carriage windows.*

***run* an eye (on/over sth, to the left, etc)** —> ***cast*/run an eye (on/over sth, to the left etc)**

**(not) *run* away with the idea/notion (that . . . )** *(informal)* (not accept) or be misled by an idea, especially one that has no real foundation: *Don't run away with the idea that you're going to be famous just because you've appeared once on television.*

**(try to) *run* before one can walk** (try to) do sth at an advanced level before you have mastered its basic skills: *No wonder she wasted such a lot of material! She should have chosen an easier pattern to start her dressmaking. She was trying to run before she could walk!*

**still waters *run* deep** —> ***still***

***run* down** tired and in poor health: *Jackie's*

*been working too hard for the last few weeks and feels rather run down.*

**a *run*-down** *(informal)* a description or analysis: *Mr Evans is here to give us all a run-down on the latest developments in the political situation.*

***run* (sth) down** (cause sth such as a factory to) decline in output, employees etc: *The company is running down the steelworks as it is to be closed next year.* **run-down** *n*: *There has been a sharp run-down in traditional manufacturing industries recently.*

***run* sb down/over** knock sb to the ground, killing or injuring him: *A car ran down two pedestrians outside the town hall this morning.*

***run* sb/sth down 1** criticize sb/sth unkindly; belittle or disparage: *He's always running his wife down in front of other people. I'm very surprised she tolerates it.* **2** find sb/sth after a long search or enquiry: *The police spent hours looking for the escaped convict and eventually ran him down in a wood.*

***run* for it** *(informal)* escape from a danger by moving very quickly: *Run for it! There's a bomb in here!*

**give sb a (good) *run* for his money** ⟶ ***give***

***run* sb in** *(informal)* arrest and take sb to a police station: *Theodore was run in for drunken driving.*

***run* sth in** prepare a car engine etc for full use by driving it slowly for a certain distance: (sign on back window of car) *Running in—please pass.*

***run* in the family** (of a physical or moral feature) keep appearing in successive generations of the same family: *He and his dad have long noses—it runs in their family. / He knew he was going to become a lawyer—the tradition ran in the family.*

***run* into sb** ⟶ ***bump*/run into sb**

***run* its course** happen or be done and then stop, without interference: *The long, hot summer ran its course, and we thought autumn would never come.* **let sth take its course** allow sth to happen naturally: *The doctors agreed to let the disease take its natural course.*

***run* like clockwork** ⟶ ***go*/run like clockwork**

***run* like the wind** ⟶ **go/run like the wind**

***run*-of-the-mill** average in quality or kind: *You can only submit new, large projects for the competition, not small, everyday, run-of-the-mill matters.*

***run* sb off his feet** ⟶ ***rush*/run sb off his feet**

***run* out** become less until there is no more left: *Time is running out for a peaceful settlement in this area.* See also ***run*/be out of sth.**

***run*/be out of sth** finish or exhaust a supply of sth or ideas: *I'm sorry but we've run (or we're) out of that book at the moment. We're expecting our next delivery on Monday.*

***run* out of steam** *(informal)* lose the original driving force or energy that started a movement, operation etc: *The campaign to visit every home in the area to tell them about the new community centre began well but soon ran out of steam.*

***run* rings (a)round sb/sth** *(informal)* perform so skilfully that your opponent is made to look clumsy and foolish: *I can't debate this with him in public! He'll run rings around me—he's far too clever.*

***run* riot** behave or do sth without discipline, control, or restraint: *His imagination ran riot as he thought about what he would do if he had a million pounds!*

***run*/be short (of sth)** have little/few (of sth) left: *We're running short of milk—we've only one carton left till Monday.*

***run* the gamut of sth** experience or include everything in a range of sth: *His feelings ran the whole gamut of human emotions, from great joy to intense sorrow.*

***run* the gauntlet (of sb/sth)** accept and have to endure attack or criticism (from sb/sth): *The Prime Minister's car had to run the gauntlet of a large group of demonstrators outside the hall.*

**(not) *run* to sth** (not) be sufficient for sth: *The funds were reduced this year, so our budget didn't run to an office party at Christmas.*

***run* sb/sth to earth/ground** find sb/sth after a long, difficult search: *I spent years hunting for this book on butterflies and was so pleased when I eventually ran it to ground in a second-hand bookshop in London.*

***run*/go to seed** stop flowering as seed is produced; become careless of your appearance and clothes; get worse in appearance, standard etc: *It used to be such a nice hotel—good food, friendly staff, and a nice atmosphere—but it's really gone to seed since the old owner sold it.*

***run* sth up** make or construct quickly, especially using a sewing-machine: *My daughter was in the school play, so I had to run up a costume for her last week.*

***run* wild** indulge in unrestrained activity: *The children from the city run wild for an hour or two when they first arrive at the recreation centre in the country.*

**on the lowest, top etc *rung* of the ladder** at the most junior, senior etc position in an organization etc: *Everyone has to start on the lowest rung of the ladder and they can gradually work their way upwards.*

**. . . *running* ⟶ . . . in a *row***

**take a *running* jump** ⟶ ***take***

***rush*/run sb off his feet** *(informal)* make sb work very hard, especially doing a lot of work or moving a lot: *In the last few days before Christmas the sales assistants were completely rushed off their feet.* Note that this is usually used in the passive.

***rush* one's fences** be too rash or quick about tackling a task and problem, and so often be inefficient or fail: *His calm wisdom has stopped me rushing my fences on many occasions.*

***rush* to conclusions** ⟶ ***jump*/rush to conclusions**

***rustle* sth up** prepare sth such as a meal for

an unexpected guest; collect or provide support, help etc, for a special need: *It's nice of you to pay us a visit. I'll go and see if I can rustle up a snack in the kitchen.*

**in(to) a *rut*/groove** in(to) a fixed routine or pattern of life: *I'm bored; I want some adventure! I'm stuck in a rut! Whatever happened to my ambitions?*

# S

***sackcloth* and ashes** (symbols of) a public display of penitence and sorrow for your wrongdoing.

**a *sacred* cow** sb/sth that is greatly respected and admired, especially by a particular group, so that criticism is not tolerated: *Some of the social sciences such as psychology and sociology seem to have become sacred cows that cannot be attacked by modern society.*

**a *(sad)* reflection on sb/sth** → ***reflection***

**in the *saddle*** in a position of responsibility and control: *A new man is in the saddle now and we hope there'll be some improvements in the company's position.*

***saddle* sb with sth** give sb the responsibility for sth, especially when he does not want it: *I'm always being saddled with extra duties.*

***safe* and sound** not harmed: *The climbers returned safe and sound from their expedition in the mountains.*

**as *safe* as houses** secure; not dangerous; not likely to result in a loss: *'Do you think that wooden bridge will bear our weight?' 'Yes—the farmer takes his cows over it every day—it's as safe as houses.' / Investing your money with this company is as safe as houses.*

**a *safe* bet** a project, method etc that is almost sure to be successful; opinion that is almost sure to be correct: *If you want a cheap holiday with lots of sunshine, then Spain is a safe bet.*

**on the '*safe* side** cautious; to avoid risk or danger: *I don't think it will rain, but I'll take my umbrella just to be on the safe side.*

**better (to be) *safe* than sorry** → ***better***

***safety* first** (a slogan or policy that is aimed at preventing accidents on roads, at work, and at home; policy that makes avoidance of risks more important than chances of gain or improvement).

***safety* in numbers** better protection against bad luck if you are in a group of people: *The troops realized that they couldn't escape and that there was safety in numbers, so they kept their position.*

**when all is *said* and done** → ***all***

**you('ve) *said* it!** → ***you* can say 'that again!**

***sail* close to the wind** do or say sth that comes very near to breaking a law, offending a moral principle etc: *'That's sailing a bit close to the wind, isn't it, Rodney—using such bad language when your mother is here?'*

***sail* under false colours** pretend to have a certain character, hold certain beliefs etc that you do not really have: *Everyone found out that the politician had been sailing under false colours—he'd misused his position to get money for himself.*

**take the wind out of sb's *sails*** → ***take***

**one's '*salad* days** *(becoming old-fashioned)* when you are young, innocent, inexperienced etc; when an organization etc is new: *I used to walk to and from school every day—a total of eight miles—in my salad days.*

***salt* sth away** save sth, especially money, for use in the future: *When you're young, it's good to salt part of your income away for your old age.*

**rub '*salt* into the wound** → ***rub***

**the *salt* of the earth** people, especially ordinary people, whose character and actions are thought to be very valuable: *These young people are the salt of the earth, in my opinion—I admire them for visiting and helping the elderly in their homes.*

**(the) *same* again** a request for or an invitation to have another drink or dish of the same kind as the previous one: *'The same again, dear?' 'Yes, please!'*

**in the *same* boat** *(informal)* in the same, especially difficult or unpleasant, position or circumstances: *Making a living is tough these days. But everyone is in the same boat.*

**in the *same* breath** together (with sth else), as if the two were the same or equally important, interesting etc: *James may be an excellent fellow in other respects, but as for his business competence, I wouldn't mention him in the same breath as his father* (or *him and his father in the same breath*).

**be tarred with the *same* brush** → ***tarred***

***same* here** *(informal)* I agree; so am/are/do/have I/we: *'I'm nearly falling asleep.' 'Same here—I think I'll put my books away now and go to bed.'*

**the *same* old story** the usual, expected tale of events that has been heard or experienced many times before: *'It's the same old story with Pete—a youngster comes from the provinces to try to get a job in London but can't find one and gets hooked on drugs—I've seen dozens of similar cases.* Also **the same/old story.**

**(be) not in the *same* street (as sb/sth)** *(informal)* (be) very different (from sb/sth): *Their books aren't in the same street as ours—ours are far better.*

**come to the *same* thing (as sth)** → ***come***

**at the *same* time 1** not at a different time; together in time: *She gets up at the same time every morning. / You can't do your homework and watch television at the same time!* **2** also to be considered; in spite of sth already known or mentioned: *There's not much to do up here, but at the same time at least we're away from home.*

**(and) the *same* to you** I wish you the same thing (said in reply to a greeting or insult): *'Merry Christmas!' 'And the same to you!'*

**by the *same* token** following logically from the same circumstances or argument: *It is clear that the universities need more money. But by the same token, all other kinds of institutions in higher education can claim the same right.*

**(be) on the *same*, a different etc wavelength** ⟶ ***wavelength***

**bury/hide one's head in the *sand* (like an ostrich)** ⟶ ***bury***

**the *sands* of time are running out (for sb/sth)** there is very little time left for sb/sth to survive, or in which sth can be done: *Commentators say that the sands of time are running out for the country. If an agreement is not reached soon between the different races, then a civil war is inevitable.*

**packed like *sardines*** ⟶ ***packed***

**(what's) *sauce* for the goose is sauce for the gander** *(saying)* what is thought suitable treatment for one person should be so for another person.

***save* one's/sb's bacon** *(informal)* avoid death, injury, punishment etc: *I had to tell a lie, just to save my bacon, but it gave me the chance to escape.*

***save* one's breath** *(informal)* not waste time talking, as you are not having any effect: *He won't follow your advice and stay here, so you might as well save your breath.*

***save* (sb's/one's) face** prevent sb from or avoid suffering a humiliating loss of respect: *It's a matter of pride. I'm not going to say I did it just to save your face.* **face-saving** *adj*: *face-saving measures.*

**to *save* one's life** *(informal)* at all; under any circumstances: *I wouldn't work with him to save my life! / He couldn't fire a gun to save his life!*

***save* sb's/one's (own) neck/skin** *(informal)* rescue sb or escape from death, punishment etc: *He only wants to save his own skin—he doesn't care if someone else is punished in his place.*

***save* the day** turn a likely defeat or failure into victory or success: *Your coming here really saved the day—we couldn't have mended the puncture by ourselves.*

***save* the situation** solve a political, business, social, etc difficulty: *A policeman arrived at the crucial moment and saved the situation.*

**be *saved* by the bell** be rescued from an awkward or embarrassing situation at the last possible moment (often used as an exclamation): *'Well, for the third time, why didn't you tell me what really happened?' John asked Margaret insistently. Just then the phone rang and John had to leave. 'Saved by the bell!' yelled out her friend.*

**a *saving* grace** sth which prevents sth from being thought of as completely bad: *No one is completely evil—everyone has at least some saving grace.* Also **a redeeming feature.**

**can't *say*/tell** be unsure about or not know: *'Did you ask how much the repairs would cost?' 'Yes, but the manager wasn't there, and the mechanic couldn't say.'*

**you don't *say* (so)** ⟶ ***you***

***say* a good word for sb** ⟶ ***put* in a good word for sb**

**would not *say* boo to a goose** *(informal)* be very shy and afraid of upsetting people: *Poor Mike's an only child. And he's never really mixed with other lads—he wouldn't say boo to a goose.*

***say* cheese** (said by a photographer) pretend to say the word 'cheese' and so smile for a photograph: *Come on, everybody, say cheese!*

**have (got) something etc to *say* for oneself** ⟶ ***have***

**(not) have (got) a good word to *say* for sb/sth** ⟶ ***have***

**can *say* goodbye to sth** (can) give up or forget about sth: *You'll have to say goodbye to your ambition of becoming a doctor if you can't pass your exams.*

**before you can *say* Jack Robinson** *(informal)* very quickly or suddenly: *Let me fetch your newspaper for you. I'll run down to the shop to get it and be back before you can say Jack Robinson!*

**can't *say* no** not have the strength of mind or the good sense to refuse an invitation, proposal etc: *You know me—when people ask me to go round to their home I just can't say no.*

**to *say* nothing of** ⟶ ***not* to mention**

***say* one's piece** make formal statement of your opinion, thanks, protest etc: *Molly was very nervous, but when she said her piece at the meeting it was well received.*

**you can *say* that again!** ⟶ ***you***

**to *say* the least (of it)** ⟶ **(to) *put* it mildly**

**(just) *say* the word** just state your request, wishes etc and they will be immediately and willingly fulfilled: *If you need any help, just say the word and we'll come!*

**there is no *saying* . . .** ⟶ ***no***

**the *scales* are weighted against sb/sth** there is a special disadvantage or obstacle working against sb/sth: *Even though it is now legal for a Roman Catholic to become head of state, in an officially Protestant country the scales are weighted against such a possibility.*

**the *scales* fall from one's eyes** you suddenly realize and understand the truth about sth, or the true nature of sb/sth that was judged wrongly before: *I had never thought he was a very good actor, but the scales fell from my eyes when I saw his marvellous performance last night.*

***scare* sb stiff** frighten sb very much: *I was scared stiff when I gave my speech in front of such a large audience.* Also **scare/frighten sb out of his wits; scare/frighten the pants off sb.**

***scatter* sb/sth to the four winds** *(formal)*

send sb/sth off in all directions: *After the great man was shot, his band of followers was scattered to the four winds.*

**((not) be) sb's *scene*** *(informal)* (of surroundings, company etc) ((not) be) sth suited to sb's temperament or abilities: *The holiday wasn't really our scene. We wanted more freedom to do what we liked, rather than be told where to go all the time.*

**set the *scene* for sth** → ***set***

**behind the *scenes*** (in a theatre) behind the main stage, where the audience cannot see; in private, not seen by the public. **behind-the-scenes** *adj*: *Behind-the-scenes talks took place yesterday in an attempt to settle the dispute between the newspaper and its journalists.*

**throw sb off the *scent*/track/trail** → ***throw***

**tell tales out of *school*** → ***tell***

***scissors* and paste** the assembling of existing items of news, entertainment etc for further presentation without adding anything new or drawing new conclusions. **scissors-and-paste** *adj*: *There's only time to do a quick scissors-and-paste job for this week's article—we'll find some photographs and old material we've used before and put something together.*

**on 'that *score*** for that reason: *'Don't you think Stuart wastes our money?' 'No—I'm not angry with him on that score.'*

***score* (a point) off sb** defeat sb; make sb appear stupid, for example by a witty remark: *That television presenter enjoys scoring points off the people he interviews by making clever retorts to their answers.*

***scot*-free** not punished or harmed: *Somehow the man was found not guilty so he got off scot-free.*

***scrape* along/by** manage to live for some time with very little money: *We scrape along somehow, but it's very difficult since Pete lost his job.*

***scrape* (the bottom of) the barrel** *(informal)* choose sb/sth of the poorest quality because it is the only one remaining or available: *'There's no-one left to ask but Mark.' 'You're really scraping the barrel, aren't you?'*

**from *scratch*** from the beginning, having no help, preparation etc at all: *If I have to start the book from scratch, it'll take me two years to write, but if I can use Bill's material then it'll only take me nine months.*

**up to *scratch*** at the required or expected standard: *The level of safety in the power station was brought up to scratch after the enquiry found that there were some defects.*

***scratch* a living** earn, grow, or produce only just enough to survive: *The villagers managed to scratch a living somehow during the three years of drought.*

***scratch* one's head** wonder or be puzzled about what to do, think etc, often accompanied by lightly scratching or rubbing your head: *We're all scratching our heads for an answer to the problem.*

**you *scratch* my back and I'll scratch yours** → ***you***

***scratch* the surface (of sth)** give sth a brief, slight, or superficial study or treatment: *I've spent a couple of weeks reading material for my essay on butterflies, but I realize I've only scratched the surface and I need to spend a lot more time on it.*

***scratch* where sb itches** *(informal)* be appropriate or relevant to sb's needs: *This book really scratches where I itch—it's very helpful.*

***scream*, cry etc blue murder** *(informal)* shout very loudly, making much noise and fuss, because you disagree very strongly with sth: *Larry will scream blue murder if Keith gets promoted and he doesn't.*

**have (got) a *screw* loose/missing** → ***have***

***screw* up one's courage** → ***pluck* up courage**

**have (got) one's head *screwed* on the right way** → ***have***

**by the *scruff* of one's/the neck** (seize or hold sb) by gripping the back of his neck, coat collar etc; (pick up etc an animal) by the loose skin of its neck: *The policeman stopped the fight by grabbing hold of the bigger lad by the scruff of the neck and taking him outside.*

**the *scum* of the earth** a group of people thought to be worthless or despicable: *'The scum of the earth—that's what you are,' said one of the wives to the men on strike outside the factory gates, 'where's the money coming from to feed our children?'*

**between *Scylla* and Charybdis** *(formal)* threatened by two dangers, of which, if you avoid one, you are more likely to be harmed by the other: *It's very difficult to steer a course between the Scylla of being too polite and the Charybdis of being very casual.*

**(all) at *sea*** confused or very puzzled in your mind: *The professor's lecture was very technical and left most of the students all at sea.*

**set the *seal* on sth** → ***set***

**a *sealed* book (to sb)** → **a *closed*/sealed book (to sb)**

**come/fall apart at the *seams*** → ***come***

**the '*seamy* side (of life etc)** the unpleasant or immoral aspects of life etc: *The television documentary clearly described the seamy side of life in the capital—with its alcoholics, tramps, and prostitutes. / I suppose even the world of entertainment has its seamy side.*

***search* one's heart/soul** closely examine your feelings or motives. **heart-searching, soul-searching** *n*: *I did a lot of heart-searching before I knew I'd accepted the job for the right reasons.*

**'*search* 'me** *(becoming old-fashioned)* I don't know; I've no idea: *'Why doesn't he want to go?' 'Search me—I would have thought anyone would have accepted the offer of a free holiday abroad immediately.'*

**a/one's *second* childhood** a period in life, especially in old age, when you act, feel etc as you did when you were a child: *She repeats* *herself quite a lot. It's a sign that she's in her second childhood.*

**play *second* fiddle (to sb)** → ***play***

**at *second* hand** not directly; not based on your own knowledge, experience, or observations: *I should tell your Dad that you were in a fight; he'll hear about it at second hand anyway, so it's better to tell him yourself.*

**second-hand** *adj* **1** known, discovered, or experienced not directly: *Second-hand evidence is not good enough—you must have seen the events yourself.* **2** not new, but with one or more previous owners: *We can't afford a new car so we'll have to buy a second-hand one.*

**(be) *second* nature (to sb)** (be) an ability or habit that sb has learned or practised for such a long time that it comes as easily as if he had been born with it: *Driving a car has become second nature to me—I've been doing it for over forty years.*

***second* sight** the supposed ability to see or know about events taking place in the future or somewhere else: *'I don't know why I telephoned you.' 'It's good that you did! You must have second sight! I've never felt as lonely as this and I just had to talk to someone!'*

**have (got) a *second* string to one's bow** → ***have***

***second* thoughts** further thoughts leading to a different opinion or decision from one previously held: *I'd planned to resign from my job but had second thoughts and didn't* (or *but on second thoughts changed my mind*).

***second* to none** equal with any other and better than most: *The aeroplane's safety record is second to none.*

**no *secret*** → ***no***

**can *see*/tell a mile off** can easily and quickly perceive sth: *You could tell a mile off that he was lying!*

***see* about (doing) sth** deal with or start to do sth: *I must see about lunch soon. / If you want to go abroad, you ought to see about getting a passport.*

**cannot *see* beyond/past the end of one's nose** *(informal)* not plan for the future: *He was so taken up with day-to-day administration that he couldn't see beyond the end of his nose.*

***see* eye to eye (with sb) (about/on sth)** have the same viewpoint as sb else on sth: *He's not always seen eye to eye with the boss about everything, and I think that's maybe why he's leaving.* Note that this is often used in the negative.

***see* fair play** → ***fair* play**

***see* fit (to do sth)** consider it correct or acceptable (to do sth): *The magazine didn't see fit to publish my article but returned it to me with a brief note.*

***see* sb/sth in a different/better/new light** have a different, especially more favourable, opinion about sb/sth: *This book has helped me see the problems of handicapped people in a different light.*

**will/would *see* sb in hell first** *(informal)* very strongly reject the idea of doing or agreeing to what sb wants: *So you think I'd work for the man who made me bankrupt! I'd see him in hell first!*

***see* it all** → ***do*/hear/see it all**

***see* life** experience or observe various ways of living, especially those that are different from your own: *Martha's son Gary has joined the navy, and he certainly seems to be seeing life—he's travelled to all sorts of exotic places and met lots of exciting people.*

***see* light** see a solution or end to a difficulty or problem: *I'm beginning to see some light. The answer might be to lower our prices for just a short time to win some customers back.* See also ***see* the light.**

**(not/never) *see* sb/sth's like again** or **not/never see the like of sb/sth again** (probably not) find anyone/anything as outstandingly good, able etc as sb: *You were lucky to hear the Beatles at a concert—you'll never see their like again.* See also **(not/never) *hear*/see the like (of sb/sth).**

***see* neither hide nor hair of sb/sth** find no trace of the existence or presence of sb/sth: *'Have you seen Jill?' 'No, I've seen neither hide nor hair of her all day.'*

***see* sb off** accompany sb to the place where he leaves on a journey: *I'll come to the station and see you off.*

***see* sb/sth out** last, live, or remain for a period of time: *There'll be enough coal to see out the winter* (or *to see us out for the winter*). / *Granny is getting weaker, and I don't think she'll see out another week.*

***see* over/round sth** visit and view a place, such as a house or estate: *I must see round the house before I decide whether to buy it or not.*

***see* pink elephants** *(informal)* imagine things that aren't real, when one is drunk: *Terry has a drink problem but just laughs it off. 'The time to worry is when I start seeing pink elephants,' he says.*

***see* sb's/the point** → ***take*/get/see sb's/the point**

***see* reason/sense** think or act sensibly after considering the facts or taking advice: *I think he'll see reason. If we give him all the information, then I'm sure he'll change his mind.*

***see* red** become very angry: *Coming in very late at weekends really makes my Mum and Dad see red!*

***see* sb (all) right** *(informal)* look after sb's interests, material needs etc: *If your wife dies, then the money from her insurance will see you and the children all right for quite a few years.*

***see* stars** *(informal)* be blinded for a few moments, with flashing sensations, for example by a blow on the head: *There was a bang. I saw stars and then the next thing I knew I was on the floor of the hut.*

***see* the back of sb/sth** get rid of or be free of sb/sth: *I really am pleased to see the back of all the tourists now that summer's over—we can enjoy our town by ourselves once again.*

***see* the colour of sb's money** *(informal)*

actually see sb's money, before a decision is reached (used when you are not sure that sb really has the money or will pay): *'I'll give you £1000 for it.' 'Let's see the colour of your money first!'*

**live to *see* the day** ⟶ ***live***

**(not/never) *see* the end/last of sb/sth** ⟶ **(not/never) *hear*/see the end/last of sb/sth**

***see* the light** realize that you were mistaken before and decide to follow a new way in life, especially in religion or politics: *One of the most committed Christians I know was a very strong atheist before he saw the light.* See also ***see* light.**

**(not/never) *see* the like (of sb/sth)** ⟶ **(not/never) *hear*/see the like (of sb/sth)** See also **(not/never) *see* sb/sth's like again.**

***see* the sights** visit the famous places in a city, country etc: *We spent our first day in London seeing the sights and were very tired by the evening.* **sightseeing** *n* **sightseer** *n*.

**not *see* the wood for the trees** not understand or realize the main subject, issue etc because you are too closely involved with many small details: *The aim of this book is to give an overall view of the history of the country—it's designed for readers who otherwise wouldn't see the wood for the trees.*

***see* the world** travel, live, or work in many different parts of the world: *The company told me I'd see the world when I was interviewed for this job, but all I've done is stay at my desk in the twelve months I've been here.*

***see* through sb/sth** understand the real nature of sb/sth underneath a pleasant and deceptive outward appearance: *You can't fool me: I can see right through you! I know you're only joking!* See also ***see* sb through (sth).**

***see* sb through (sth)** ensure that sb passes safely through a time of great difficulty: *Her neighbours' friendship and support really saw her through the first few months after her husband died.* See also ***see* through sb/sth.**

***see* to it (that . . . )** ensure or take care that sth happens: *Please see to it that Nurse Beattie only works during the day and not at night in her first week back on duty after her illness.*

***see* one's way (clear) to do sth** find that it is possible or convenient to do sth: *If you could see your way clear to remaining silent on this subject, we would be most grateful.*

***see* which way the 'cat jumps** *(informal)* see how sb acts or reacts: *It'll be interesting to see which way the cat jumps now that the local council has said John's business is illegal—will he continue it or stop?*

***see* which way the 'wind is blowing** *(informal)* find out what is likely to happen or what others think or feel: *I think we should wait a while and see which way the wind is blowing before we decide where to invest our money.*

***see* you (later)** ⟶ **I'll/we'll be *seeing* you**

***seeing* is believing** *(saying)* you need to see sth before you can believe it really exists or happens.

**be *seeing* things** *(informal)* think or imagine that you can see sth that does not exist: *I must be seeing things—that looked like my old headmaster who just walked by, but it can't be as he's been dead for years.*

**(I'll/we'll) be *seeing* you** *(informal)* goodbye: *I'll be seeing you, Rod!' 'OK—cheerio!'* Also **see you (later).**

**have *seen*/known better days** have been more successful, more powerful, or better at an earlier time: *This company has certainly seen better days—our income last year was half what it was five years ago.*

**wouldn't be *seen* dead with sb/sth, in sth etc** *(informal)* strongly dislike sb/sth, wearing sth etc: *I wouldn't be seen dead in one of her awful old-fashioned hats!*

**(*seize*/grasp an opportunity) with both hands** ⟶ ***both***

***sell* sb down the river** *(informal)* betray the interests of your own people, trade union etc: *A compromise was reached to settle the strike, but the workers thought that their leaders had sold them down the river.*

***sell*/go like hot cakes** *(informal)* be bought quickly and eagerly by many people: *At the moment, her latest novel is selling like hot cakes.*

***sell* out to sb** betray your principles or your friends to an enemy, for example through a secret agreement: *The union leaders were accused of selling out to the employers.* **sell-out** *n*: *The leaders were accused of a sell-out.*

***sell* oneself/sb/sth short** say or describe yourself or sb/sth in a way that undervalues your/his/its true worth, ability etc: *Don't sell yourself short when you go for an interview.* See also ***sell* sb short.**

***sell* sb short** cheat sb by giving him less than the proper amount: *The market has sold us short—we paid for a kilo of oranges and we've only got 900 grams!* See also ***sell* oneself/sb/sth short.**

***send* a chill/shiver up/down sb's spine** cause feelings of horror, dread, or fear: *The very mention of a cat to my cousin Jack would send a chill up his spine, and if one jumped on his knee he'd probably break out in a cold sweat and scream.* **spine-chilling** *adj*: *spine-chilling horror stories.* Also **send shivers up/down sb's spine.**

***send* sb about his business** tell sb not to interfere in the affairs of other people: *The security officers were always suspicious—anyone found just wandering around the research area was soon sent about his business.*

***send* sb off** say goodbye to sb: *The whole family went to the airport to send her off.* **send-off** *n*: *She got* (or *was given*) *a good send-off.*

***send* sb packing** *(informal)* send sb away or dismiss sb from a job etc quickly and with little consideration: *I'll send him packing if he comes here again trying to sell me books I don't want.*

***send* sb to Coventry** refuse to associate with sb by not speaking to him, as a punishment: *Of all the men in his local railway depot, Jim* *was the only one who drove trains during the strike. So it was hardly surprising that, when it was all over, the other men sent him to Coventry.*

***send* sb/sth to kingdom come** → ***blow,* send etc sb/sth to kingdom come**

***send* sb/sth up** *(informal)* ridicule sb/sth by imitating him/it: *Have you seen how Jill sends up the headmistress of her school? It's hilarious!* **send-up** *n*: *She does a hilarious send-up of her headmistress!*

***send* word (to sb)** send news, a message etc: *The chairman sent word that the meeting would have to be postponed because he was ill.*

**in a *sense*** if understood or thought about in one way rather than in other ways: *That economic analysis is scientific in a sense—at least they've tried to interpret the statistics objectively.*

**bring sb to his *senses*** → ***bring* sb to himself**

**these things are *sent* to try us** → ***things***

***(separate)* the chaff and/from the wheat/grain** (separate) the worthless from the valuable or useful persons, things, or ingredients in a mixed lot: *We received hundreds of entries for the poetry competition. It was easy enough to sort out the chaff from the wheat but difficult to make the final choice.* Also **(separate) the grain/wheat and/from the chaff.** See also ***(separate)* the sheep and/from the goats.**

***(separate)* the sheep and/from the goats** separate the righteous from sinners; separate those thought worthy or unworthy of any moral, social, academic etc criteria: *The exams at the end of the first year usually separate the sheep from the goats.* See also **(separate) the chaff and/from the wheat/grain.**

***serve* sb right** *(informal)* be a just or appropriate penalty or punishment for sb: *'The boss criticized my work today!' 'That serves you right for you criticizing mine yesterday!'*

***serve* time** → ***do* bird/porridge/time**

***set* a foot wrong** → ***put*/set a foot wrong**

***set* sth at naught** consider sth to be unimportant; have disregard or scorn for sth: *All our plans were set at naught when three of our best players resigned within a month.*

***set* sb/sth back** hinder or reverse the progress of sth: *The strike has set back the building work by three weeks.* **setback** *n*: *Plans to extend the shop suffered a serious setback when the council refused building permission.*

***set* sb back £50 etc** *(informal)* cost sb £50 etc: *Their new car set them back over £10,000. / I'm sure his daughter's wedding set him back quite a bit.*

***set* one's cap at sb** *(old-fashioned)* (of a woman) deliberately try to attract a man, especially in order to get him to marry her: *As soon as she came to work here, she set her cap at the only unattached man in the office.*

***set* eyes on sb/sth** → ***clap*/set/lay eyes on sb/sth**

***set* one's face against sth** oppose sth very strongly: *Why did her father set his face against her marriage to Rodney? He seemed quite pleasant to me.*

***set* foot in/on sth** arrive at some place: *Neil Armstrong was the first man to set foot on the moon, in July 1969. / From the moment you set foot in this house you've been grumbling—now what's wrong?*

***set* sb's 'hair on end** → ***make* sb's 'hair stand on end**

***set* one's heart/mind on (doing) sth** long deeply to do or achieve sth: *He set his mind on becoming a doctor. / From a small child, her heart was set on horses.*

***set* sth in motion** or **set the wheels in motion** make sth begin to move; start a project, meeting etc: *The campaign must be set in motion very soon, as the election is only six months away.*

***set* one's mind to (doing) sth** → ***put*/set one's mind to (doing) sth**

***set* off/out** begin a journey: *The group set out early in the morning to climb the mountain.*

***set* sth off** (of sth that makes a background etc) make sth appear more pleasing by contrast: *That dress sets off her jewellery very well.*

***set* (sb/sth) on sb** (cause sb/sth to) attack sb: *They set a dog on the burglar. / He was set on in a dark street.*

***set* sb on a pedestal** → ***put*/set sb on a pedestal**

***set* sth on fire 1** cause sth to burn: *Three youths were accused of setting the house on fire.* Also **set fire/light to sth. 2** arouse great interest and excitement in a place: *Her lively writings had once set the whole of the literary scene on fire.*

***set* one's sights high/low** be ambitious in your life or a project: *Some people are too ambitious, while others don't set their sights high enough.*

***set* one's sights on sth** have sth as your goal or aim: *His sights were set on becoming a professor by the age of 35.*

***set* (no, great, little etc) store by sth** consider sth to have (no, great, little etc) importance or value: *He sets little store by his father's advice and thinks he can live his own life as he wants.*

***set* sb's 'teeth on edge** (of a grating noise such as the scrape of chalk on a blackboard) annoy or irritate sb: *I wish you wouldn't do that! Scraping your fingernails on that metal table really sets my teeth on edge!*

***set*/start/keep the 'ball rolling** start sth, especially a conversation, or keep it going: *Mike, would you like to set the ball rolling and give us your views on the plan? / For some time, nobody else was interested, but I kept the ball rolling and have finally had some success.*

***set* the cat among the pigeons** → ***put*/set the cat among the pigeons**

***set* the clock back** → ***put*/turn/set the clock back**

***set* the scene for sth** prepare for sth: *The scene was set for a deep disagreement when the*

*Prime Minister and Leader of the Opposition met in a live debate on television.*

***set* the seal on sth** mark in an appropriate way the high or final point in the success or progress of sth: *Winning first prize in the competition for the best actor of the year really set the seal on his career in the theatre.*

***set* the 'Thames on fire** *(informal)* be very successful and arouse great excitement: *Her performance in the play was adequate but nothing that would set the Thames on fire.*

***set* the pace** fix a rate of running, walking etc which others try to keep to; take the lead in an activity involving co-operation or competition: *Rod set the pace, and the other boys raced uphill behind him. / The advertisers claim that this new model really sets the pace for small, economical cars.*

***set* to 1** begin to work or do sth energetically: *The children hadn't eaten for hours, so they really set to at tea time.* **2** begin to fight or argue: *When those women set to, it's difficult to stop them.* **set-to** *n*: *What began as a pleasant evening quickly became a serious set-to.*

***set* sth to rights** ⟶ ***put*/set sth to rights**

***set* sb up** *(informal)* make sb feel healthier, stronger etc: *A good holiday by the sea will set you up again nicely after your stay in hospital.*

***set* sth up** establish a committee, office etc: *Special courts were set up at the weekend to deal with all the football hooligans.* **set-up** *n* the structure of a business etc.

***set* oneself up as (being) sb/sth** claim to be sb/sth: *He sets himself up as being an authority on Shakespeare, but his knowledge is only average.*

***set* up house (with sb/together)** start to live together as man and wife, whether married or not: *Noel and Sue liked each other a lot so decided to set up house together.*

***set* up shop** *(informal)* establish a business, profession etc: *He worked for himself for several years, then set up shop as a small publisher.* Note that the business concerned need not just be a shop.

***settle* a(n old) score (with sb)** seek or get revenge for an injury, loss, or offence caused by sb: *His long journey across the deserts lay before him. But first he had a score to settle at home before he could set out on his adventures.*

***settle* up (with sb)** pay the money you owe sb: *I'll just settle up with the hotel reception then get my bags and we'll go.*

**the *seven*-year itch** the boredom, restlessness, and desire for sexual variety that is supposed to come after seven years of marriage.

**the *seventh* heaven** a state of extreme happiness and satisfaction: *Laura's clear preference for Peter's company that evening really put him in the seventh heaven.*

***sew* sth up** *(informal)* complete the arrangements for sth such as a contract: *The deal was sewn up over a few drinks in the bar.*

***sex* appeal** the attraction that sb has for a person of the opposite sex.

***shack* up (with sb)** *(slang)* live in an informal style with sb to whom you are not married: *Her parents would be alarmed if they knew that their darling little Samantha was shacking up with a long-haired unemployed docker.*

**put sb/sth in the *shade*** ⟶ ***put***

**(beyond/not/without) a *shadow* of doubt** (with not) the smallest doubt: *I think Mr Jones is absolutely right beyond a shadow of doubt.*

**a *shaggy* 'dog story** *(informal)* an amusing, rambling tale whose final few words give no meaning to the whole joke.

***shake* down** become accustomed to a new job or way of life: *We'll give the new workers a few weeks to shake down and then see how they're coping with their responsibilities.*

***shake* one's fist (at sb)** hold out your fist in annoyance (at sb): *The angry workers stood outside the factory gates swearing and shaking their fists as the directors drove by, but they couldn't change anything—the factory would never open again.*

***shake* hands (with sb)** take hold of another person's (usually right) hand and move it up and down when greeting, saying goodbye, congratulating, or making peace or an agreement: *When you're first introduced to a man in Britain you usually shake hands (with him)* (or *you usually shake his hand* or *shake him by the hand*).

***shake* one's head** move your head from side to side to show refusal, concern, or disapproval: *Marge shook her head. 'I'm sorry, but I can't let you go to the disco as you're not old enough.'*

***shake* like a jelly/leaf** shake, tremble etc with fear, nervousness or anxiety: *The boys stood outside the headmaster's study, shaking like a jelly, as they waited to be punished.* Also **shake in one's shoes.**

***shake* off sb/sth** get rid of sb/sth, especially by running away: *The gang managed to shake off their pursuers and escaped.*

***shake* off sth** be cured of an illness, depression etc: *My cold isn't too bad—I think I'll shake it off in a few days.*

***shake* sb up** shock or disturb sb mentally, emotionally, or physically: *The accident really shook him up, and he was off work for a couple of weeks.*

***shake* sb/sth up** thoroughly reorganize sb/sth, especially a group of people, an organization etc: **shake-up** *n*: *The administration department needs a good shake-up to make it efficient again.*

***shake* the dust (of sth) off one's feet/shoes** leave a place, trying to rid yourself of its unpleasant associations: *If he wants me to come and work for him, I'll jump at it! I'd be only too pleased to shake the dust of home off my feet!*

**in two *shakes* (of a lamb's tail)** ⟶ ***two***

**put sb/sth to *shame*** ⟶ ***put***

**'*shame* on you!** (an exclamation of reproach said to sb who has behaved badly or said or done sth that he should be ashamed of): *Shame on you! You should be feeling very guilty for giving in to their demands so easily!*

**tell the truth and *shame* the devil** → ***tell***

***Shanks*'s pony** (on) foot: *'How are you getting there?' 'On Shanks's pony—no buses travel that far, and we've not got a car.'*

**in good, bad etc *shape*** in a good physical condition; efficient: *The books certainly left the printers in good shape. They must have got damaged on the way here.*

**out of *shape*** in a bad physical condition; twisted or bent: *I feel a bit out of shape—I've not played tennis for months and need to practise hard before the summer.*

**in the *shape*/form of sb/sth** as; consisting of: *Help soon arrived in the shape of two policemen. / They were planning a huge celebration in the form of a splendid dinner.*

**in any *shape* or form** in whatever form sth appears or is presented in: *He'd never smoked tobacco in any shape or form all his life.*

***share* and share alike** an equal division or use of commodities, facilities etc: *It was share and share alike in the first days after the war when no one seemed to have anything.*

**a *share* of the cake/pie** → **a *slice*/share of the cake**

**a trouble *shared* is a trouble halved** → ***trouble***

**as *sharp* as a needle/razor** very quick to understand things: *You don't need to be as sharp as a needle to see that he's not telling the truth.*

**(a) *sharp* practice** an action which is not illegal but which is intended to deceive other people and make a profit: *There are some sharp practices going on in the double-glazing business and I want to put a stop to them.*

***shed* light (up)on sth** → ***throw*/cast/shed light (up)on sth**

***shed* tears (over sb/sth)** express regrets (about sb/sth), especially when you think they are unnecessary: *You're not going to shed any tears over Sarah, are you, Mark? You're really quite pleased that you're no longer friends, aren't you?* Note that this is usually used in the negative.

**(separate) the *sheep* and/from the goats** → ***separate***

**a wolf in *sheep*'s clothing** → ***wolf***

**on the *shelf*** (of an unmarried woman) thought to be past the age of getting married, so staying unmarried: *Some women think that if they've not got their man by the age of 20 they're on the shelf!*

**come out of one's *shell*** → ***come***

***shell* out (for/on sth)** *(informal)* pay or meet the cost of sth: *I'm tired of having to shell out money on car repairs all the time.*

***shift* one's ground** alter one's position in a battle or argument: *Your opponent will try to get you to shift your ground in a debate but you must resist him.*

**come rain or (come) *shine*** → ***come***

**when one's *ship*/boat comes in** *(informal)* when you hit the jackpot; when you have a lot of money to spend: *Perhaps, when our boat comes in, then we'll be able to sail around the world.*

**(like) *ships* that pass in the night** (like) people or groups who meet briefly and perhaps for the only time in their lives: *They'd fallen in love but knew they were destined to be like ships that pass in the night. They'd never see each other again.*

**(all) *shipshape* (and Bristol-fashion)** in good order; tidy, well-organized, and fully equipped: *We'll have to clear up after the office party and get everything shipshape again before our first customers come in after Christmas.*

**in one's '*shirt* sleeves** not wearing a jacket: *It was so hot that even the King took his jacket off and listened to the concert in his shirt sleeves.*

**get/be *shirty* (about sth) (with sb)** → ***get***

***shiver* me/my timbers** *(old-fashioned)* (an exclamation of astonishment or amusement).

**send a *shiver* up/down sb's spine** → ***send* a chill/shiver up/down sb's spine**

**(where) the *shoe* pinches** *(informal)* (in which way) a situation proves difficult, especially financially: *Any housewife with a family to feed knows where the shoe pinches without having to be an expert economist.*

**in sb's *shoes*** *(informal)* in sb's position: *If I were in 'his shoes, I'd resign immediately.*

**put oneself in sb's *shoes*/place** → ***put***

**on a *shoestring*** with very little money or resources: *The government is trying to run this department on a shoestring, but it's impossible to do it well.* **shoestring** *adj*: *on a shoestring budget.*

***shoot* a line** *(old-fashioned)* suggest by your remarks that your position, work etc is better or more important than it really is: *When I tried to tell people how rich my parents were, they all thought I was shooting a line.*

***shoot* one's bolt** make a final attempt to attack sb, defend yourself, or achieve an aim: *It was clear that with ten minutes still to go in the match, their team knew they had shot their bolts and realized we would win.* Note that this is usually used in a past tense.

***shoot* sb/sth down (in flames)** *(informal)* defeat sb, or his argument, in a discussion: *Why do you always shoot me down in flames whenever I think of a good idea? / My latest proposal was quickly shot down, but I only suggested it to get people thinking.*

***shoot* holes in sth** → ***pick*/shoot holes in sth**

***shoot* one's mouth off** *(informal)* speak in a loud, indiscreet, and boastful way: *Why did you have to go and shoot your mouth off? We wanted to keep the party a secret!*

***shop* around (for sth)** go from one shop, dealer etc to another until you find the best value for money; examine the claims of different places etc before committing yourself: *It's wise to shop around a bit first before you* *decide where to buy something big like a new washing-machine.*

***short* and sweet** lasting too short a time but still welcome and pleasing; short, even if good in no other way: *His visit was short and sweet—just a couple of hours. / If you're giving an after-dinner speech, it's best to keep it short and sweet.*

***short* back and sides** a haircut for men where the hair is cut very short around the ears and above the neck: *Do you remember the days when all soldiers in the army had a short back and sides?*

**give sb *short* change** ⟶ ***give***

**a *short* cut (to sth)** a shorter way than usual to cross a field, achieve success etc: *Mark took a short cut behind the post office to get to college more quickly. / There are no short cuts to a rapid recovery, I'm afraid—you'll just have to get plenty of rest over the coming months.*

**at *short* notice** without much warning; without much time to get sth done: *I'm willing to go anywhere you want, even if it's at short notice.* Also **at a moment's notice.**

***short* of sth 1** less than sth; below a particular level: *The car's performance was far short of what he'd been led to expect.* **2** ⟶ ***run*/be short of sth**

***short* of (doing) sth** except (doing) sth: *I'll try anything to get a job, short of breaking the law.*

**nothing/little *short* of disastrous, deception etc** ⟶ ***nothing***

**as thick as two *short* planks** ⟶ ***thick***

**in the '*short* run** over a short period of time: *In the short run the pills will make him worse, but in time he'll feel better.* See also **in the '*long* run; in the '*long*/'short term.**

**give sb/sth *short* shrift** ⟶ ***give***

**in the 'short term** ⟶ **in the '*long*/'short term**

**make *short* work of (doing) sth** ⟶ ***make***

**like a *shot*** immediately; with great speed: *I'd be off like a shot if he offered me a job abroad.*

**(fire) a (warning) *shot* across the/sb's bows** (make) the first move in a quarrel, fight, contest etc: *The annual battle to get more money than other departments in the college has begun again, with the heads of departments firing shots across the bows to make their intentions clear to one another.*

**a *shot* in the arm** an injection from a hypodermic syringe; sth that has a short, stimulating or restorative effect: *The economy needs more than a quick shot in the arm; it needs to be fundamentally changed.*

**a *shot* in the dark** ⟶ **a *leap*/shot in the dark**

**get/be *shot* of sb/sth** ⟶ ***get***

**straight from the *shoulder*** ⟶ ***straight***

**a *shoulder* to cry on** sb who listens to your troubles and offers sympathy and kindness: *When you're depressed, all you want is a shoulder to cry on (or all you want to do is cry on someone's shoulder).*

***shoulder* to shoulder (with sb)** in mutual support, co-operation, endeavour, or agreement (with sb): *Scientists, standing shoulder to shoulder with the politicians, devised a number of weapons that helped us to win the war.*

**nothing to *shout* about** ⟶ ***nothing***

***shout* sb down** shout so loudly that sb finds it impossible to continue speaking: *The Finance Minister was shouted down twice when he tried to talk to students at Manchester University this evening.*

***shout* (sth) from the rooftops/housetops** *(informal)* tell sth to everyone: *The exams are over—I could shout from the rooftops how happy I am!*

***shove* off** ⟶ ***push* along/off**

**for *show*** only to attract attention and impress people: *Don't take any notice of his behaviour. It's done just for show.*

***show* (sb/sth) a clean pair of heels** get ahead of sb/sth very quickly; make much better progress than a competitor: *Ian waited for the starter's gun. He knew he was the fastest runner in the race and was ready to show all the others a clean pair of heels.*

***show* one's (true) colours** reveal your real and usually bad character or beliefs: *We thought he was kind and generous, but he really showed his true colours when we heard that he'd refused even to buy his wife a birthday present.* Also **show oneself in one's true colours.**

***show* a leg** *(slang, old-fashioned)* rise from bed or sleep: *'Come on, you lazy ones,' said Brian, lifting the tent flap, 'show a leg!'*

***show* one's face** (of a person) appear briefly: *I think it would be tactful at least to show my face at the office party before I go home. / He made such a fool of himself last time, I doubt if he'll even show his face there again.*

**have (got) something etc to *show* for it** ⟶ ***have***

***show*/reveal one's hand** let other people know your intentions, capabilities etc: *He was a skilled negotiator, used to showing his hand at the right time to get the best deal for his company.*

**a *show* of hands** a vote in which each person shows his opinion by raising his hand: *Let's have a show of hands to decide if we should go on the outing or not.*

***show* off** display your possessions, abilities etc to impress people; act in a way that tries to attract attention: *Stop showing off, children! No one is impressed by your behaviour!* **show-off** *n*: a person who shows off.

***show* sb/sth off** display sb/sth; draw attention to sb/sth: *James had been to college, and his mother liked to show him off in front of her friends.*

***show* the door to sb** *(informal)* ask or cause sb to leave, especially after a quarrel or when negotiations are no longer useful: *Do you think you'll have any success when you present your report, or will the Board of Directors show you the door?*

***show* the flag (for sb/sth)** make clear that

you loyally support a country, party, or principle: *At the charity fair, the women's group was there as usual, showing the flag for the ladies of the town.* Also **fly the flag (for sb/sth).** See also ***keep* the flag flying (for sb/sth).**

***show* up** *(informal)* appear or arrive, especially after some delay: *We waited an hour for him to show up but he didn't come.*

***show* (sb/sth) up** be or make easily visible: *Close examination of the metal shows up a number of small cracks.*

***show* sb up** *(informal)* make sb feel embarrassed by behaving badly in his company: *We can't take you anywhere, James; we're always afraid you'll show us up in public!*

***show* willing** let sb know that you are willing to do sth whether actually required or not: *I think Jane's got plenty of helpers for the exhibition stand, but I'll go along and show willing.*

***shrug* sth off** dismiss sth as unimportant; not be worried by sth: *He has such a high opinion of himself that he shrugs off any criticism as completely unimportant.*

***shrug* one's shoulders** raise, then drop your shoulders, usually to show your indifference or sometimes helplessness: *'I don't care whether you go or not,' Pete said, shrugging his shoulders, 'I'm not at all interested in what you do.'*

***shudder* to think (that . . . )** *(informal)* hate or be afraid to think (that . . . ): *I shudder to think when he last had a bath—his clothes are so dirty and he smells awful!*

***shut* one's eyes to sth** —> ***close*/shut one's eyes to sth**

***shut* one's mouth** *(informal)* stop speaking; not start to speak: *'Shut your mouth,' Roger said rudely, 'or I'll kick you out.'* Other nouns that can be used instead of ***mouth*** are: ***trap, face,*** or ***gob.*** See also ***keep* one's mouth shut.**

***shut* (sb) up** (cause sb to) stop talking or make a noise: *For heaven's sake, shut up! You've been talking all morning!*

***shut* up shop** close a business of any kind: *The family had had a small grocer's for years, but the two sons decided to retire and finally shut up shop last week.*

***shut* the door ((up)on sb/sth)** or **shut the door in sb's face** —> ***close*/shut/slam the door ((up)on sb/sth)**

***shy* away from (doing) sth** avoid or move away from sth unpleasant: *Delegates at the conference shied away from demanding a total shutdown of all factories but said that they would protest by refusing to work overtime.*

**as *sick* as a dog/parrot** *(informal)* vomiting a great deal; deeply concerned or worried, often because of a lost opportunity: *I'd felt some nausea all day so went to bed early. But I was up six times in the night, as sick as a dog.* / *I saw an ad in the paper for just the car I was looking for. I was as sick as a parrot when they told me it had just been sold!*

***sick* at heart** very unhappy and worried because of sorrow, disappointment, fear, or doubt: *He'd killed so many men in the battle that he returned home feeling completely sick at heart.*

***sick* (and tired) of sb/sth** *(informal)* wearied, bored, or annoyed by sb/sth: *I'm sick and tired of Dave Wright coming in here telling us to work harder. When is he going to do more work, that's what I'd like to know!* Also **be sick to death of sb/sth.**

***sick* of the sight/sound of sb/sth** *(informal)* wearied, bored, or annoyed by sb/sth that you have seen/heard too often: *I'm sick of the sight of kids! After teaching them all week I've had more than enough of them!*

***sick* to death of sb/sth** —> ***bored,* sick etc to death of sb/sth**

**a bit on the *side*** —> ***bit***

**(a bit) on the cold, small etc *side*** rather cold etc: *We looked around the house. It was quite pleasant but a bit on the cold side. We want something more modern that will be easier to look after.*

**on the *side*** *(informal)* as an activity that is additional to your main job, sometimes done secretly without telling the tax authorities: *He was employed fulltime by a firm of local builders but did some odd decorating and home repair jobs on the side.* See also **a *bit* on the side.**

**know which *side* one's bread is buttered (on)** —> ***know***

**come down/out on the *side* of sb/sth** —> ***come* down/out in favour of sb/sth**

**time is on the *side* of sb** —> ***time***

**laugh/grin/smile/on the other *side* of one's face** —> ***laugh***

**on the right/wrong *side* of 40 etc** —> ***right***

**on the *side* of the angels** holding correct, accepted, or moral opinions; behaving correctly or morally: *The policemen in Scobie's crime novels are not always on the side of the angels.*

**(on) this *side* of the grave** —> ***this***

***side* with sb** put yourself on the same side as sb: *He always sides with the group he thinks will win because he doesn't like losing.*

**know sb by *sight*** —> ***know***

**a *sight* better, worse etc (than . . . )** very much better etc (than sb/sth): *He didn't like being a prisoner but it was a sight better than being dead.*

**a *sight* for sore eyes** sb/sth that is welcome and that you are relieved to see.

***sign* in/out** record your arrival/departure in a hotel etc by writing your name: *We signed in, and then a porter took our bags to our room.*

**a *sign* of the times** sth that shows the nature of or changes in the political, economic, or social values of a particular period: *'Letters seem to take ages to be delivered these days.' 'Ah, it's a sign of the times—not even the postmen work as efficiently as they used to.'*

***sign* off** announce or mark in some way the end of a radio or television programme, especially at the end of the day: *The radio* *station signs off every night by playing the national anthem.*

**sign (sb) on** register your/sb's name, when unemployed or when joining the armed forces: *600 people signed on last week when the biscuit factory closed down.*

**sign on the dotted line** write your signature on a legal document; state firmly your commitment to sth: *All you have to do is sign on the dotted line and the video recorder will be yours—and your monthly payments won't begin until February.*

**sign/take the pledge** swear or promise formally that you will not drink alcohol: *When I went to work for them many of them were often drunk, but I made them take the pledge. It wasn't easy but they coped eventually.*

**sign (sb) up** (cause sb to) join a club, for example a football club, or enrol for a course: *Manchester United have just signed up a star player from Wolverhampton Wanderers for over £1 million.*

**signed, sealed, and delivered** (of a legal document) with all the formalities completed, and presented to the relevant person.

**(speech is silver but) silence is golden** *(saying)* it is desirable, and may be more effective, not to say anything.

**as silent as the grave/tomb** ⟶ **as quiet/silent as the grave/tomb**

**the silent majority** people who lack the ability or interest to make their opinions or reactions known in public, for example through television, organized demonstrations, or pressure groups.

**the 'silly season** the period in the late summer when trivial items occur in the news media, because people are still on holiday and few important things happen.

**every cloud has a silver lining** ⟶ ***every***

**born with a silver 'spoon in one's mouth** ⟶ ***born***

**simmer down** become calmer after being angry or very excited: *It's no use trying to discuss anything with him when he's in such a rage. You'll just have to wait till he's simmered down a bit.*

**as simple as falling off a log** ⟶ **as *easy* as ABC**

**the 'simple life** a simple, independent way of life, especially in the country, in contrast with the stress and complications of life in a city: *The family got tired of the rush of life in the big city so moved out to the country, to enjoy the simple life.*

**live in sin** ⟶ ***live* together**

**sing a different song/tune** (be made to) change your opinion about or attitude towards sb/sth: *'Anne says she wants to have a large family.' 'She'll soon sing a different tune when she's had one or two children!'*

**sing sb's/sth's praises** praise or commend sb/sth enthusiastically and often: *The new doctor won't like you if you continually sing the praises of his predecessor.*

**sink one's differences** agree to forget or suspend hostility or disagreements: *Let's sink our differences and see if we can work together.*

**sink in** be fully absorbed and understood: *Gradually the truth began to sink in—he'd be married in a week's time!*

**sink like a stone** sink straight down immediately: *I don't think that old life jacket would help you. You'd probably sink like a stone if you fell into the sea!*

**sink or swim** perish or survive; fail or succeed: *The government's attitude to this company is to leave it to sink or swim without offering any help at all.*

**sink, vanish etc without trace** disappear, leaving no sign of having been in a place: *Some people thought that the treasure chest must have come from a ship that had sunk without trace long ago.*

**a/that sinking feeling** a sensation of panic, fear, or helplessness: *I had a sinking feeling as soon as I saw Chris. I knew she'd only have come if something was wrong.*

**for one's sins** *(humorous)* used when you consider sth slightly unpleasant or as a form of mild punishment: *Yes, I've got to mark that whole pile of books by tomorrow morning, for my sins!*

**your sins will find you out** *(saying)* your wrongdoing will be discovered.

**sit at the feet of sb** learn from an expert or sb in authority (sometimes used humorously): *In his student days he had sat at the feet of Professor Jackson and listened eagerly to his lectures.* See also **at sb's *feet*.**

**sit back** *(informal)* relax and take no action: *We can't afford just to sit back and do nothing while millions of people are starving in the third world.*

**a sit-down strike, demonstration etc** a form of protest in which demonstrators sit down in a building, public place, or place or work: *The students decided to stage a sit-down strike in the administration offices to show their opposition to the increase in fees.*

**sit down under sth** endure or suffer sth unpleasant without protest or complaint: *I can't sit down under such insults any longer—I must do something.*

**sit in** sit on the floor or occupy the building where you are employed etc as a protest: *Students are sitting in at the university again this week to complain about the increase in rents.* **sit-in** *n.*

**sit in (for sb)** take the place (of sb) at a meeting etc: *Mr Jones will sit in for me at the council meeting next week as I'm abroad on business then.*

**sit in on sth** attend a meeting, conference etc as an observer: *Will you let me sit in on the investigation? I'd like to see how you tackle it.*

**sit on sb** *(informal)* rebuke sb strongly who has behaved disrespectfully; force sb to be quiet or inactive: *If a junior boy addressed a teacher by his first name, then he would be firmly sat on.*

***sit* on sth 1** *(informal)* keep sth; not part with sth: *We'll sit on the stolen jewels for a few months until we can sell them safely.* **2** *(informal)* suppress information; delay action on sth: *The committee have been sitting on our application for a couple of months—it's time they dealt with it!*

***sit* on the fence** not decide between two opposite courses of action, beliefs etc: *A good umpire cannot sit on the fence and be neutral in determining who is right.* / *Why is the council sitting on the fence and taking such a long time to make up its mind about building the by-pass?*

***sit* tight** remain in the same place, for example when hiding; do nothing in order to avoid making a mistake or to wait for the best opportunity: *If your car breaks down on the motorway, the police advise you to sit tight until a repair vehicle arrives.*

***sit*/wait up** stay awake and out of bed until past your usual bedtime, for example while waiting for sb: *Don't sit up for me—I'll be home very late.*

***sit* up (and take notice)** *(informal)* become suddenly alert, aware, and interested: *Coming bottom of the class certainly made Jill sit up and take notice. She's thought about her work a lot more since then.*

**a *sitting* duck/target** sb/sth that is easy to attack, criticize, or exploit; sb/sth that can be easily hit: *The report concluded that the firm was a sitting duck, just waiting for other companies to take its business.* / *Putting those rockets on fixed sites would make them sitting targets for the enemy.*

**be *sitting* pretty** *(informal)* be in a pleasant, advantageous, and enviable situation: *If you make £10,000 profit when you sell this house, you'll really be sitting pretty!*

***six* feet under** dead and buried in the ground.

**be *six* of one and half a dozen of the other** (of two people or things) have no difference; be of equal value or weakness: *I've tried both routes and as far as I can see it's six of one and half a dozen of the other.* / *Patrick says his neighbours are too noisy, but if you ask me it's six of one and half a dozen of the other—you should hear how loud he plays his radio!*

***six* of the best** *(old-fashioned)* being hit six times with a cane or strap as a school punishment.

**at *sixes* and sevens** in a state of disorder and confusion: *Everything's been at sixes and sevens since the rooms were decorated. We'll have to tidy everything up soon.*

**a *sixth* sense** a special sensitivity beyond the normal five senses of sight, hearing, smell, taste and touch, believed to warn you of danger, help you understand other people etc: *She'd have left the meeting halfway if she'd not had some kind of sixth sense that told her it would be useful to stay.*

**the *sixty*-four thousand dollar question** the most important question or matter: *The $64,000 question for many people is 'Has life any real meaning?' Is there a purpose to it all?*

**cut sb/sth down to *size* ⟶ *cut***

**that's about the *size* of it** *(informal)* that is a fair account, description etc of the matter or situation.

**(*skate*) on thin ice ⟶ (be/skate) on *thin* ice**

**a *skeleton* in the cupboard** sth criminal or shameful in your own past or in your family history which is kept hidden: *Most people have some skeleton hiding in the cupboard if you look hard enough for it.*

**a *skeleton* staff** the smallest possible number of people needed to provide the most necessary services at a place of work: *Over the Christmas holiday, we have just a skeleton staff on duty to undertake essential maintenance work.*

***skin* and bone** very or too thin: *You're already just skin and bone! You don't need to go on a diet!*

**by the *skin* of one's teeth** narrowly; by a small margain: *He escaped death by the skin of his teeth.* / *Our car broke down on the way so we thought we would miss the ferry but we caught it by the skin of our teeth.*

**be ˌno *skin* off ˈsb's nose ⟶ *no***

**the *sky*'s the limit** there is no limit to what can be achieved, obtained, charged etc: *For an ambitious young man with his qualifications, the sky's the limit.*

**take up the *slack* ⟶ *take***

**slam the door ((up)on sb/sth)** or **slam the door in sb's face ⟶ *close/shut/slam* the door ((up)on sb/sth)**

**a *slap* in the face** a harsh rejection or refusal: *Bill assumed he would be the next editor of the newspaper. So he got a real slap in the face when an outsider was appointed.*

***slap* sth on (sth)** *(informal)* add sth to the price of sth, especially a lot or unfairly: *We'd only been in the flat two months when the landlord slapped £50 a month on the rent.*

**a *slap*-up meal etc** *(informal)* an excellent meal etc: *They treated us to a slap-up meal in a restaurant.*

**not *sleep* a wink** not get any sleep: *I didn't sleep a wink last night as I was worrying about my driving test today.*

***sleep* around** *(informal)* (especially of a woman) to have sexual intercourse with different people; be sexually promiscuous.

***sleep* like a log/top** sleep soundly: *Yesterday evening I was exhausted but last night I slept like a log so now I feel refreshed.*

***sleep* on it** have a night's sleep before making a difficult decision: *The situation is so serious that we suggest you take our offer away, sleep on it, and give us your considered response tomorrow morning.*

***sleep* rough** sleep out of doors: *As a tramp, he was used to sleeping rough in the park or under a railway bridge.*

***sleep* tight** *(informal)* I hope you sleep well (said to sb about to go to bed, or already in bed): *Goodnight, Pat, sleep tight!*

***sleep* with sb** *(informal)* have sexual intercourse with sb to whom you are not married: *Her parents have brought her up strictly, so I'm sure she would never sleep with her boyfriend.* Also **sleep together:** *I'm sure they've not slept together.*

**let *sleeping* dogs lie** → ***let***

**have (got) sth up one's *sleeve*** → ***have***

**laugh up one's *sleeve*** → ***laugh***

**wear one's heart on one's *sleeve*** → ***wear***

**roll up one's *sleeves*** → ***roll***

**a *slice*/share of the cake** a share of sth valuable such as profits or benefits: *Third-world countries are discovering how their natural resources have been exploited by the rest of the world and now want a bigger slice of the cake.* Also **a share of the pie.**

**the greatest thing since *sliced* bread** → ***greatest***

***sling* one's hook** *(slang, old-fashioned)* go away; leave.

***sling*/fling/throw mud at sb/sth** *(informal)* speak rudely and unfairly about sb/sth: *The politican was accused of slinging mud at his opponent in the election.* **mudslinging** *n.*

**let sth *slip*** say sth stupidly or carelessly; say sth casually or indirectly but hoping that it will be noticed: *Don't let it slip that you were here last night. / She let slip a remark about not having enough money to pay for her new car.*

***slip* sb's memory/mind** be forgotten by sb, especially for a short time: *I know their phone number, but it's just slipped my memory for the moment.*

**a '*slip* of a boy/girl** just a young boy or girl; adult who is thin and does not look strong: *Jack's a mere slip of a boy—he's only about 12, isn't he?*

**a *slip* of the tongue/pen** sth that you did not mean to say/write: *My mistake was just a slip of the tongue; I'm sorry.*

***slip* on a banana skin** make a foolish mistake: *Several government ministers have slipped on banana skins recently and caused a lot of embarrassment to the Prime Minister.*

***slip* through one's fingers** escape or be passed or missed: *Although the police set up road blocks after the prisoner had escaped, it was clear that he had slipped through their fingers. / I wouldn't let such an opportunity as this slip through your fingers—it may never come again.*

***slip* up** make a mistake: *Someone must have slipped up badly—we ordered only 10 books and they've sent us 80!*

**as *slippery* as an eel** (of objects) very difficult to grasp; (of people) devious, untrustworthy, and dishonest: *Don't do any work for Mr Jacks. I hear he's as slippery as an eel and that he'll get you to do the work but will never pay you for it.*

**the *slippery* slope** a situation that could quickly lead to a great danger, error, moral decline etc; process of such a decline: *Some people think that the odd occasion when the police have been given guns marks the start of the slippery slope towards arming them permanently.*

***slope* off** *(informal)* go away, rather secretly, especially to avoid doing sth unpleasant: *Why does he always slope off when there's the washing-up to do?*

***slow* off the mark** → ***quick*/slow off the mark**

***slow* on the uptake** → ***quick*/slow on the uptake**

***slowly* but surely** gradually; steadily: *The world of communication is changing slowly but surely—dull books in black and white are gradually being replaced by ones with lots of colourful pictures.*

***slowly* does it** → ***easy*/gently/slowly does it**

**on the *sly*** → **on the *quiet*/sly**

**a *smack* in the eye for sb** → ***one* in the eye for sb**

***smack* of sth** have a slight taste or suggestion of sth: *That deal smacks of dishonesty.*

***smack* one's lips** → ***lick*/smack one's lips**

**. . . with a *small*/little a, b, c etc** (used for emphasis to indicate 'unimportant'): *If this is art at all, then it's art with a very small a.* See also **. . . with a *capital* A, B, C etc.**

***small* beer** sth that has little importance and value, in comparison with sth much greater: *I've got 60 shares in the company, but that's small beer compared with my father's thousands.*

**a *(small)* cloud on the horizon** → ***cloud***

**'*small* fry** people in a group or organization who are thought not to be important; small, unimportant businesses: *These little local firms are mere small fry compared with huge international companies.*

**(in/into etc) the *small* hours** (in/into) the first few hours after midnight, as an extension of the day before: *The discussions to avoid a strike lasted into the small hours, and at 3 o'clock in the morning union leaders and managers left the building very tired, but having reached an agreement.*

**be thankful for *small* mercies** → ***thankful***

**the *small* print** the parts of a legal document, contract etc that contain warnings or exclusions printed in small type and are therefore difficult to read and easily overlooked: *Make sure you read the small print before you sign the lease.*

**'*small* talk** light, superficial conversation about unimportant matters, used to establish a friendly relationship.

**the '*small* time** → **the '*big*/'small time**

**in a *small* way** → **in a *big*/small way**

**it is *small* wonder (that . . .)** → **it is *no*/little/small wonder (that . . .)**

**it's a *small* world** *(informal)* (used when you meet someone you know or have some connection with in an unexpected place): *When I got on the train at Milan, the other passenger in the compartment was a neighbour of ours in Manchester. 'Well, well, it's a small world,' I said as we shook hands.*

**a '*smart* alec(k)** *(informal, derogatory)* sb

who tries to show that he is cleverer than everybody else: *Some smart aleck will get himself killed at that bend if we don't ban overtaking there.* Also **a 'clever Dick.**

**a *smash*-and-'grab raid** a theft from a shop carried out by breaking a window and taking the goods inside: *Thieves escaped with television and video equipment valued at thousands of pounds in a smash-and-grab raid in Chester last night.*

***smell* a rat** *(informal)* be suspicious that sth is wrong: *A green car drove slowly past the bank several times. He smelt a rat so jotted down the registration number.*

**a rose by any other name would *smell* as sweet** → ***rose***

***smell*/stink to high heaven** *(informal)* have a very strong and unpleasant smell: *When was the last time you cleaned out the dog kennel? It smells to high heaven.*

**wipe the *smile*/grin off sb's/one's face** → ***wipe***

**smile on the other side of one's face** → ***laugh*/grin/smile on the other side of one's face**

**go up in *smoke*** → ***go***

**put that in your pipe and *smoke* it** → ***put***

***smoke* like a chimney** *(informal)* smoke cigarettes very frequently, or almost continuously: *He smokes like a chimney when he's worried or upset—over 60 cigarettes a day.*

***smoke* sb out** drive sb from hiding using smoke or some cunning means: *They used a piece of pipe connected to the exhaust of the car to smoke the rats out.*

**a '*smoke* screen** temporary cover of smoke in a battle to help an escape etc; behaviour or talk that prevents observation or understanding of what you are doing: *Some smoke-bombs provided a smoke screen that allowed the ship to leave the battle unnoticed. / The council officers were accused of putting up a smoke screen of deception to try to hide their corrupt activities.*

**(there is) no *smoke* without fire** → ***no***

**as *smooth*/soft as a baby's bottom** *(informal)* looking or feeling very soft and smooth: *If you wash your hands with this new soap, then they'll feel as smooth as a baby's bottom.*

**as *smooth* as a 'billiard table** (of a flat surface such as a lawn or floor) very smooth: *It takes many years of careful cutting and rolling to get a lawn as smooth as a billiard table.*

**as *smooth* as velvet** very soft to the touch, ear, or taste, or in appearance: *That brandy goes down as smooth as velvet, but it's very strong!*

**a *smooth* passage** → **a *rough*/smooth passage**

**at a '*snail*'s pace** very slowly: *Granny may drive her car at a snail's pace, but she's never had an accident.*

**a *snake* in the grass** sb who appears friendly but is harmful and dangerous.

***snap* one's fingers (at sb/sth)** *(informal)* treat sb/sth with contempt; (make a sound with your fingers, attracting sb's attention, and) have sth done (by him) immediately: *In their final months at school, the students just snap their fingers at all the rules. / He goes to expensive restaurants, so he's used to snapping his fingers at waiters.*

***snap* sb's head/nose off** → ***bite*/snap sb's head/nose off**

***snap* 'to it!** *(informal)* hurry up; start working or doing sth: *Snap to it! You've got to finish this work by five o'clock.*

***snatch* at straws** → ***clutch*/grasp/snatch at straws**

**not *sneeze*/sniff at sth** *(informal)* consider sth as important or worthy of attention: *His offer may not be as much as you'd hoped, but nevertheless it's not to be sneezed at.*

**(be) *snowed* under by/with sth** *(informal)* (be) overwhelmed by a large amount of work, documents etc: *When you set up your own company, you may quickly get snowed under with papers dealing with insurance and pensions if you're not careful.*

***snuff* it** *(informal)* die: *Old Jack was over 90 when he finally snuffed it.*

***snuff* sb/sth out** kill sb or suppress opposition: *The government snuffed out the rebellion very quickly to avoid a civil war.*

**as *snug* as a bug in a rug** *(informal)* very comfortable: *He'll get a good pension from the government when he retires, and he's bought a little cottage in the country so when he's old he'll really be as snug as a bug in a rug.*

**'*so*-and-so 1** *(informal)* sb/sth that does not need to be named: *Ask old Mr So-and-So—he'll know the answer.* **2** *(derogatory)* an unpleasant person: *Jill's a right little so-and-so! She gets you to tell her all your intimate secrets, then gossips about you to her friend.*

**not (*so*/too) bad** → ***bad***

**in *so* far as** → ***far***

***so* far as . . .** → ***far***

***so* far, so good** sth has gone well up to now but is not yet finished: *'How's it going?' 'So far, so good—we've built six out of eight.'*

***so* help me God** *(informal)* with the help of God; *(informal)* I'm sure: *I promise to tell the truth, the whole truth, and nothing but the truth, so help me God. / I'll get revenge on him one day, so help me.* In the informal sense, ***God*** is often omitted.

**not *so*/too hot** *(informal)* not very good, healthy etc: *'How do you feel today?' 'Not so hot.'*

***so* long (for now)** goodbye until we next meet: *'So long, Ann—see you on Thursday.' 'Yes, see you, Sarah.'*

**'*so* much for sb/sth** sb/sth deserves little respect: *So much for his promise to pay me by the end of February! It's now 3rd March and we've not yet had anything!*

***so* there!** *(informal)* that's the position and there's no need to argue (usually said in defiance): *I'm not letting you watch any more television, so there!*

***so* to speak** → ***as* it were**
***so* what?** *(informal)* what is important or relevant about that?: *You say that the universe was created by some Supreme Being. So what?* Also *(more formal)* **what 'of it?**
***soak* sb to the skin** make sb's clothes completely wet through to his body: *The storm burst while they were walking home from the bus stop and they got soaked to the skin.* Note that this is usually used in the passive.
***soak* up sth** assimilate or absorb sth: *I've never known such a keen student! He just soaks up all that we can teach him!*
**a '*soap* opera** a series of programmes on radio or television about domestic life and the fortunes of a family or community: *Soap operas that have lasted for years like 'Dallas' still attract very many viewers.*
***sob* one's eyes/heart out** → ***cry*/sob one's eyes/heart out**
**a '*sob* story** *(informal)* a story or account of circumstances etc intended to arouse the listener's sympathy: *He told us some sob story just to get us to give him some money.*
**as *sober* as a judge** not at all drunk; very serious or solemn: *It's odd that he had his accident when he was as sober as a judge—the police could have caught him for drunken driving many times.*
***sober* down** *(informal)* become calm and serious after a period of lighthearted or frivolous behaviour: *When you sober down a bit, I've got some news to tell you.*
***sober* (sb) up** *(informal)* (cause sb to) recover from a drunken state: *He drank several cups of strong black coffee to sober up after the party.*
**as *soft* as a baby's bottom** → **as *smooth*/soft as a baby's bottom**
**a *soft* option** an easier course of action, study etc than others: *We don't want the students to think of the course in linguistics as a soft option, just because there's no exam in it at the end of the year.*
***soft*-'pedal (on) sth** *(informal)* mention or deal with a matter in a quiet, unemphatic way so as to minimize its importance: *The chairman soft-pedalled on the plan to cut costs because it was bound to be unpopular.*
**the *soft* sell** → **the *hard*/soft sell**
***soft* soap** *(informal)* flattery; behaviour designed to make someone do you a favour; behave in such a way: *He knew he would have to soft-soap people to try to persuade them to give him some business.* When this is a verb, it is usually hyphenated.
**a *soft* spot for sb/sth** a special fondness for sb/sth, especially in a sentimental way; weakness for sb/sth: *I've always had a soft spot for my little cousin Clare. / I was impressed by her soft spot for people who are sick or disabled.*
**a *soft*/easy touch** *(informal)* sb easy to borrow or steal money from or to overcharge: *He met him only once and quickly realized that he was an easy touch, so he managed to get £5 out of him.*
***soft*/wrong in the head** *(informal)* mentally subnormal; weak, sentimental, or foolish in your opinions or actions: *Lotty's a bit soft in the head. She thinks she's Josephine, Napoleon's wife.* Also **not right in the head.**
***soften* sb up** weaken the resistance of sb you want to persuade etc: *The salesman spent some time softening up the housewife and managed to sell her a new vacuum cleaner.*
***softly*, softly** gentle, gradual, and cautious: *The softly-softly approach to hooliganism has failed, so the court will have to take firmer action with offenders.* Note that this is hyphenated when used before a noun.
**be *sold* on sth** *(informal)* be enthusiastic about sth, especially in an uncritical way: *I'm completely sold on the idea of extending the lounge so that we'll have more room for parties.*
***soldier* on** continue working, trying etc, in spite of difficulties: *I soldiered on, lonely and wretched, and eventually reached the camp at eleven o'clock at night.*
**of (*some*) consequence** → **of (great, some, no etc) *consequence***
**'*some* 'hope(s)!** *(informal)* there is little or no chance of sth happening: *Some hope you becoming manager—you're far too lazy!* Also **what a hope!**
***some* men etc are more equal than others** *(saying)* although members of a particular group, society etc may appear equal in status, some members in fact receive favoured treatment.
**of *some* moment** → **of (some, no, little etc) *moment***
**'*some* 'party, 'tennis-player etc** *(informal)* a remarkably good party etc: *That was some game—you did very well to beat them by so much!*
**. . . or *something*** *(informal)* or some similar thing, person, activity etc: *You don't have to spend a lot of money on a present. Just get her a bunch of flowers or something.*
***something* 'in it** → **something, anything, nothing etc '*in* it**
***something* 'in it for sb** → **something, anything, nothing etc '*in* it for sb**
***something* like sth** approximately or roughly sth; (of an emotion, attitude etc) very similar to sth: *Something like a dozen people turned up for the meeting. / The second suggestion was less outrageous than the first and met with something like approval.*
***something*/somewhat of a sth** quite or rather a sth: *He's something of an authority on butterflies.*
***something* out of the ordinary/usual** → ***ordinary***
**there is *something* to be said for sth** → ***there***
***something* to remember sb by** a gift given at a time of parting or as a memento of sb recently dead; *(humorous)* blow, punishment, or scolding: *He said I was to have his gold watch as something to remember him*

*by. / The thief got away but not before I'd given him something to remember me by.*

***something* to think about** a situation, subject etc that provides material for, or stimulates, thought; shock or rebuke: *The meeting had been unusually interesting and really gave me something to think about.*

**go for a *song* → *go***

**make a *song* and dance about sth → *make***

**would as *soon* do A (as B)** *(informal)* would as willingly or more willingly do sth (as sth else): *Susan can have my ticket since she wants to see the show. I'd as soon stay at home anyway.* Also **would sooner do A (than B).**

***sooner* A than B** *(informal)* I'm glad, relieved etc that it is A and not B who has to do sth: *'I've got to get up at 5.30 tomorrow morning to get my plane!' 'Sooner you than me!' / He's the best at that sort of job, so if it has to be done, sooner him than anyone else.*

***sooner* or later** at some time; inevitably: *I think you should tell your parents you're pregnant. They'll find out sooner or later.*

**no *sooner* said than done → *no***

**a sight for *sore* eyes → *sight***

**like a bear with a *sore* head → *bear***

**a *sore* point (with sb)** a matter which causes feelings of anger or resentment with sb or among a group of people: *The constant increases in the tax on cigarettes and petrol have become a sore point with many people.*

**stand/stick out like a *sore* thumb → *stand***

***sorry* for oneself** pitying oneself: *Stop feeling sorry for yourself all the time, Olive!*

**of a *sort* → of a *kind*/sort**

***sort* of sorry etc → *kind*/sort of sorry etc**

***sort* out the men from the boys** separate people with great skill, knowledge etc from those without: *The weekend training course is designed to sort out the men from the boys so that we can see who will make the best leaders.*

**it takes all *sorts* (to make a world) → *takes***

**of *sorts* → of a *kind*/sort**

**(be) out of *sorts*** not in your normal good health: *He wasn't used to Chinese food, so the next day he felt a bit out of sorts.*

**upon my *soul*/word!** *(old-fashioned)* **1** certainly; truly (used to emphasize a comment, promise, or threat): *I wish I were dead, upon my word I do.* **2** (used to express delight, astonishment etc): *Upon my soul! I never thought I'd see my son wearing a smart suit like that!*

***sound* (like) sb/sth** seem to be sb/sth: *'Shall we go swimming tonight?' 'That sounds like a very good idea.'*

**as *sound* as a bell** in good condition physically: *'You're as sound as a bell. There's absolutely nothing to worry about,' the doctor said after finishing his examination.*

***sound* asleep → *fast*/sound asleep**

***sound* off (about sth)** *(informal)* talk noisily and boastfully (about sth); speak loudly and pompously on sth: *I wonder when he'll stop sounding off about his new job.*

***sound* sb out** (on/about sth) try to discover sb's feelings or opinions on a subject: *Hal spent some time sounding us out on the plan to extend the club building.*

***sound* the (death) knell of sb/sth** be the reason for sb/sth ending, going out of fashion, or being replaced: *The arrival of large supermarkets has sounded the death knell of the local corner shop.*

**(be) in the *soup*** *(informal)* (be) in trouble or difficulties: *I'll be really in the soup when I get home—I've forgotten to buy anything for tea.*

***soup* sth up** *(informal)* improve the performance of a car by modifying its engine: *Mike drives around in some fast car that the garage souped up for him.*

***sour* grapes** (an expression of disapproval said to comfort yourself about what you would like but cannot have): *He said that it really wasn't worth showing pictures at that exhibition, but that was sour grapes because his pictures weren't accepted and mine were.*

***sow* the dragon's/dragons' teeth** do sth that causes trouble, arguments etc at a future time, though this is not your intention.

***sow* (one's) wild oats** go through a youthful period of careless pleasure-seeking.

**throw a '*spanner* in the works → *throw***

***spare* sb's blushes** *(informal)* avoid making sb look embarrassed, awkward, or foolish: *We'll spare his blushes for the moment and not ask Mr Randall here why he came last in the election.*

***spare* no expense, trouble etc** not economize in money, trouble etc: *The village spared no expense to make sure that the visit of the President was a complete success.*

***spare* the rod and spoil the child** *(saying)* a child has to be physically punished when necessary so that he will learn to behave properly or know what is right.

***spark* sth off** cause sth; start sth, sometimes sth violent: *The remarks in his speech on the church and the state remaining separate have sparked off a major row between the country's religious and political leaders.*

**(the) *sparks* fly** *(informal)* there is sharp disagreement, argument, or quarrelling: *Sparks have been flying between the Prime Minister's office and the Department of Foreign Trade about the reception of foreign trade delegations.*

**so to *speak* → *as* it were**

***speak* for itself** *(informal)* sth is so clear and impressive that no further comment is necessary: *Our record of export achievement speaks for itself, and I think you'll agree if you look at the figures.*

***speak* for yourself!** *(informal)* that's your opinion, and I disagree with it: *I think we've had enough to eat, thank you.' 'Speak for yourself, Mary, I'm going to have some more!'*

**actions *speak* louder than words → *actions***

***speak* of the devil (and he appears) → *talk*/speak of the devil (and he appears)**

***speak*/talk to sb 1** talk to sb in the hope of obtaining a favour or service: *Something is wrong with the roof. I'll have to speak to the landlord about it.* **2** *(informal)* scold or reproach sb to try to get him to improve his behaviour: *Those children will have to be spoken to, George—I'm not letting them trample over my flowers like that again.*

***speak*/talk the same language** or ***speak*/talk a different language** share or not share a way of expressing yourself; draw or not draw upon common experiences, training, ideas etc, that make real communication and understanding possible: *The unions and managers are at last beginning to speak the same language.*

***speak* volumes for sb/sth** *(informal)* show a great deal about the nature of sb/sth: *His courageous behaviour on that occasion speaks volumes for his character.*

**on *spec*** *(informal)* as a speculation, guess, or gamble: *They told me on the phone that all the tickets for the concert had been sold, but I went along on spec and got two that had been returned.*

***spell* sth out** explain the meaning of sth in full: *The managing director has written to all employees spelling out the implications of the proposed take-over.*

***spend* a bomb** ⟶ ***cost*/earn/make/pay/spend a bomb**

***spend* a penny** pass urine.

***spend* money like water** *(informal)* spend money as freely as if it were in endless supply: *You can't go on spending money like water. We just can't afford it!*

**variety is the *spice* of life** ⟶ ***variety***

***spick* and span** fresh, clean, and tidy in every way: *It's lovely to go into a hotel bedroom and find everything spick and span—the beds nicely made, clean towels, and everything smelling fresh.*

***spill* over** be greater than can be accommodated by a town or city: *The population of the crowded cities is spilling over into new towns out in the country.* **overspill** *n*.

***spill* the beans** *(informal)* tell a secret, news, or other piece of information before one should: *That's just like Marcia to spill the beans and tell Pete we're having a party for him!*

**cry over *spilt* milk** ⟶ **it's *no* good/use crying over spilt milk**

***spin* a yarn/tale** tell a fanciful story, especially one intended to mislead or impress sb: *She came an hour late and spun some yarn about her car breaking down.*

**a *spin*-off** a useful product or result that is derived incidentally from a prophet: *Some modern household gadgets were originally spin-offs from space research programmes.*

***spin* sth out** make sth last as long as possible; extend or prolong sth: *We've not got a lot to discuss so we'll have to spin the meeting out somehow to last the full hour.*

**send a chill/shiver up/down one's *spine*** ⟶ ***send***

***spirit* sb/sth away** make sb/sth disappear quickly and mysteriously: *The government minister was spirited away even before the journalists had had a chance to talk to him.*

**take sth in the *spirit* in which it is intended** ⟶ ***take***

**the *spirit* is willing but the flesh is weak** *(saying)* sb's intentions and desires are good, but laziness, love of pleasure etc may prevent them from being put into action.

**as/if/when the *spirit* moves/takes sb** according to sb's inclination or eagerness: *'Doesn't your husband work in the garden at all?' 'Oh yes, he does sometimes, but only when the spirit moves him.'*

**the *spirit* of the law** the general purpose or intended effect of the law, contrasted with its strict literal meaning (**the letter of the law**).

***spit* and polish** meticulous or excessive cleaning and polishing: *This cabinet needs a lot of spit and polish to make it look new again.*

***spit* in sb's eye** *(informal)* do sth very contemptuous to sb, though not necessarily actually spitting at sb: *Why did the unions bother to come to the meeting if all they were going to do was spit in the management's eye?*

**cut off one's nose to *spite* one's face** ⟶ ***cut***

**the *spitting* image of sb/sth** sb/sth exactly or extremely like another: *She's the spitting image of her mother.* Also **the spit and image of sb/sth.**

***splash* down** (of a spacecraft) strike the surface of the sea: *The astronauts expected to splash down at six o'clock local time.* **splash-down** *n*.

***splash* out on sth** spend a lot of money on sth, especially in an impulsive, carefree way: *She went and splashed out on a new dress for the party.*

***split* hairs** argue about minor points: *Quarrelling about whether authors should get money from photocopies of their publications is much more than splitting hairs—it's very important!* **hair-splitting** *n*.

***split* on sb** *(informal)* give information about sb that will get him into trouble: *Don't split on me if I'm not at school tomorrow! We've got a French test so I think I'll be ill!*

**a *split* second** a measure of time, either calculated very exactly or too short to calculate: *It took one minute to the split second for the mechanics to change a wheel on a racing car.* **split-second** *adj*: *split-second timing.*

***split* one's sides laughing** or ***split* one's sides with laughter** laugh extremely heartily: *A group of people stood there, splitting their sides with laughter as they watched the clowns practise their act.*

***split* the difference** come to an agreement by choosing an amount halfway between two others: *You want £100 for it, I've offered you*

*£60 so far—so why don't we split the difference and agree on £80?*

**too many cooks *spoil* the broth ⟶ *too***

**spare the rod and *spoil* the child ⟶ *spare***

**be *spoiling* for a fight etc** be eager to fight: *The youths looked aggressive and seemed to be spoiling for a fight.*

**put a *spoke* in sb's wheel ⟶ *put***

***spoken* for** reserved or allocated; committed or engaged: *'Could I have the last copy of that book, please?' 'I'm sorry, but that one's already spoken for. I can give you the next one we get, though.'*

***sponge* (sth) from sb** *(informal)* get money etc from sb without intending to give anything in return: *You can't keep sponging from your parents! Their money won't last for ever.* Also **sponge on sb (for sth):** *If I lose my job I'll have to sponge on friends for a few months.*

**on the *spot* 1** at the place and time that sth happens or is needed or asked for: *We go now to our reporter on the spot, Max Davies, for his latest report of the disaster. / If a policeman asks to see your driving licence you should show it to him on the spot.* **2** in a difficult situation: *I was really put on the spot when the chairman of the meeting suddenly asked me to give a speech.*

**root sb to the ground/*spot* ⟶ *root***

**(a) *spot* check** a test or investigation made randomly without warning; test in such a way: *Some oranges were found to be rotten when spot checks were made at the harbour, and the whole cargo had to be destroyed.* When this is a verb, it is usually hyphenated.

**a *spot* of bother/trouble** *(informal)* a small difficulty: *You can expect a spot of bother on the motorway this morning, as there are some roadworks going on.*

***spot* on ⟶ *bang*/spot on**

**up the *spout*** *(slang)* lost or ruined: *All our plans are now completely up the spout since Jack lost his job.*

**a *sprat* to catch a mackerel/whale** *(saying)* sth of relatively small importance that is sacrificed, risked, or offered in the hope of gaining sth much greater.

***spread* like wildfire** travel with great speed: *Rumours about a possible take-over of the company spread like wildfire through the financial institutions yesterday.*

***spread* one's wings** extend your activities and interests: *You'll be ready to spread your wings soon, Russell. You've proved you're a successful artist—you could now try to do some sculpture, couldn't you?*

***spring* a leak** crack etc so that a liquid, especially water, comes in or out; *(informal)* cause or allow secret information to be released: *This government's so-called secret service sprung another leak yesterday when a highly confidential document was found lying in a railway carriage in London.*

***spring* clean** clean and tidy thoroughly; freshen: *You can't always sweep the dust under the carpet and just slap paint onto rotting wood. You've got to spring clean some time.* **spring-clean, spring-cleaning** *n.*

**on the *spur* of the moment** as soon as you think of (doing) sth; impulsively: *I've accepted the offer of a job abroad. I decided on the spur of the moment to go, without thinking.*

***spur* sb on** encourage sb to achieve more, try harder etc: *The crowd spurred the athletes on in the final stage of the race.*

***spy* out the land** assess a situation: *The manager wants to send Mark to Scotland to spy out the land and report on whether there are possibilities for sales there.*

**(be) (all) *square* (with sb)** (be) equal in amount of points etc in a game or competition; (by repayment) (be) clear of any debt or obligation: *At half-time the teams were all square: the score was 2–2. / I've just repaid his loan so I'm square with him at last.*

**on the *square*** honestly and fairly: *You must always act on the square when negotiating for contracts.*

**a *square* deal** just and fair treatment, exchange of goods etc, value for money etc.

**(back to) *square* one** ((be put or have to go) back to) the beginning or starting point and try to do sth all over again: *Rejecting the plan could put the two-year process of choosing a new design back to square one.*

**a *square* peg in a round hole** sb whose character and abilities are not suited to his position or job: *I'm like a square peg in a round hole in this job. Everyone else in the office seems much cleverer than me and they make me feel so inadequate.*

***square* up (with sb)** pay the money you owe before leaving a hotel, restaurant etc: *I'll square up with the waiter while you get our coats.*

***square* with sb** tell sb directly and honestly: *Let me square with you, Peter. I'd like to give you the job but we can't pay the salary you'd want.*

***square* sth with sb** get sth approved by sb: *You'll have to square your idea with your commanding officer before you go ahead with it.*

***stab* sb in the back** *(informal)* attack the position, reputation etc of sb who is trusted, by acting in a strongly disloyal way: *The President felt that he'd been stabbed in the back when a leading member of his party joined the opposition.* **a stab in the back** *n*: *To his former colleagues it was a real stab in the back.*

***stack* the cards/odds against sb** *(informal)* make it unlikely that sb will succeed (usually used in the passive): *Let's be realistic—the cards have always been stacked against Andy from the start. He came from a broken home and never had the love he needed.*

**the *staff* of life** bread or another food that supports life in a particular society.

**a '*stag* party ⟶ a '*hen*/'stag party**

**at *stake*** being risked; able to be lost etc, depending on what happens: *The team must* *win the game on Saturday if they want to remain in the competition. With so much at stake, you must see that they are all fit.*

***stake* (out) a claim to sb/sth** declare a special interest in sb/sth: *Each department is staking out a claim to the largest amount of money in next year's budget.*

***stake* (out) one's claim to sth** declare or make known that you have a special right to own sth: *As the time to allocate funds for the coming year drew near, the various departments in the college all staked out their claims to more money.*

***stamp* out sth** stop, eliminate, or get rid of sth by force: *The government acted quickly to stamp out the rebellion.*

**sb's '*stamping* ground** the place where sb lives, is active, or is often found: *His favourite stamping ground when he was a boy was the city's docks—he'd spend hours wandering round looking at the ships.*

***stand* a chance (of (doing) sth)** have the possibility of achieving sth: *You stand a very good chance of passing the exam if you work hard.*

***(stand)* at ease** (a military order to soldiers to) stand in a relaxed position, with the feet apart.

***stand* by 1** be present at the scene of sth but not do anything: *A crowd of people stood by and watched while the man had a fit—no one helped him.* **bystander** *n.* **2** be ready for action if needed: *Emergency vehicles are standing by in case flood waters rise.* **stand-by** *n* a useful article, commodity etc that is available if needed: *We eat mostly fresh food but keep a few tins as a stand-by.*

***stand* by sb** support or be loyal to sb: *She stood by me even when my depression was at its worst—she was a real friend to me.*

***stand* by sth** be faithful to a promise, statement etc: *I shall stand by my principles even if it means losing my job.*

***stand* down** leave a position, team etc or withdraw from an election: *The bad publicity lessened Jones' chances of being elected, but he refused to stand down.*

***stand* for sth** represent; denote: *The initials BBC stand for British Broadcasting Corporation.*

**(not) *stand* for sth** (not) allow or tolerate sth: *I won't stand for such rude behaviour in my house.*

***stand* one's ground** → ***hold*/stand one's ground**

***stand* in for sb** take the place or job of sb for a short time: *The Queen was met by the President's wife, who was standing in for her husband.*

***stand* sb in good stead** serve sb well; be valuable to sb: *Your experience of working on different projects will stand you in good stead when you want to change your job.*

**(not) *stand* in sb's way** (not) prevent sb from doing sth, sth happening etc: *If you want to be a policeman, then we won't stand in your way. In fact we'd encourage you.*

***stand* on ceremony** be very formal in your behaviour: *Come on—don't stand on ceremony! Start eating or the food will get cold!*

***stand* on one's dignity** say firmly that you should be treated with respect, as your status, age etc deserve: *In some universities, lecturers stand on their dignity and insist on eating separately from the students.*

***stand*/turn sth on its head** turn sth upside down; suggest the opposite side or meaning of sth: *He stood the argument on its head, saying that the plan wouldn't save money but would in fact cost more.*

***stand* on one's own (two) feet** (of a person, country, or economy) be independent or self-sufficient; not need the help of other people etc: *Son, you've got to learn to stand on your own two feet—your mother and I can't keep on lending you money all the time.*

***stand* or fall by sth** succeed or fail, survive or perish, or be judged good or bad on the basis of sth: *This theory of economics stands or falls by whether it works in practice or not.*

***stand*/stick out a mile** be striking or very noticeable: *His rudeness sticks out a mile. He never even tries to be polite.*

***stand*/stick out for sth** refuse a proposed offer, sale etc, hoping for a better one: *Union leaders have been offered a 4% pay increase but are sticking out for 8%.*

***stand*/stick out like a sore thumb** *(informal)* be obvious or conspicuous and often unpleasing: *The new modern office block stands out like a sore thumb among the older buildings in town.*

***stand* still** not progress, develop, or take positive action: *Medical knowledge has not stood still in recent years, and some doctors believe that a cure for cancer may be found soon.*

***stand* the pace** be able to maintain the same rate of running etc that sb sets: *I couldn't stand the pace. The others were too fast for me!*

**can't *stand* the sight/sound of sb/sth** *(informal)* not like or be very upset by actually seeing/hearing sb/sth: *If you can't stand the sight of blood you won't make a very good nurse!*

***stand* the test of time** prove to be of more than temporary use or value: *He sells his pictures for quite a lot of money, but I'm not sure they'll stand the test of time.*

***stand* to gain, lose etc (sth)** be likely to gain etc: *The firm stands to gain considerable prestige if we get this contract.*

***stand* up and be counted** make openly known what political, social, religious etc group you are a member of, or what opinion you hold in a controversial matter: *I want to stand up and be counted. There are lots of people who feel like me that society is becoming immoral. That's why I've organized the petition.*

***stand/*stick up for sb/sth** defend sb in a quarrel or fight; support a particular cause: *He always stuck up for his younger brother at school. / Our MP has always stood up for women's rights.*

***stand* up to sb** resist sb boldly: *You must learn to stand up to the school bully.*

***stand* up to sth** remain healthy, in a good condition etc despite severe or harsh treatment: *The car has been specially painted to stop it going rusty so it should stand up to the worst weather conditions.*

**of (good, little etc) *standing*** having an established (good etc) reputation or position: *Because the criticism came from men of standing in the community, the council acted quickly.*

***standing* on one's head** *(informal)* easily, without effort: *I could run the shop standing on my head if the boss should die suddenly.*

**it *stands* to reason (that . . . )** it is to be expected; it follows naturally that sth is the case: *It stands to reason that the price will go up if the tax is increased.*

**(be) *staring* sb in the face** (be) obvious or clearly suitable, but not noticed by sb: *I was wondering where the bank was, and then I saw it was opposite me, staring me in the face all the time! / The answer to their problems is staring them in the face if only they'd realize!*

**ˌ*stark* raving/staring ˈmad/ˈbonkers** *(informal)* insane; wildly angry: *The boss must have gone stark raving mad! He says we can finish work an hour early today!*

***start* off on the right/wrong foot →*get* (sth) off on the right/wrong foot**

**start the ˈball rolling →*set*/start/keep the ˈball rolling**

**(be) in a *state*** (be) in a nervous, worried, or excited condition: *I never saw anyone in such a state as he was—he was so upset.*

**lie in *state* →*lie***

**above/below one's *station*** behaving, acting etc in a superior/inferior way that your social level does not entitle you to: *Some older academics still believe that workers should not be educated above their station.*

***stave* off sth** prevent sth undesirable or harmful, especially temporarily: *The European Commission has a plan to stave off the financial collapse of the European Community.*

***stay* one's/sb's hand** *(old-fashioned)* restrain or hold back an action done in anger: *God cannot stay his hand against the nation's wrongdoing.*

***stay* on the rails →*keep* (sb) on the rails**

***stay* put** remain where you are; not travel, escape, seek promotion etc: *Council house rents are so cheap that some families stay put instead of buying their own homes.*

***stay*/last/survive the course** continue running, working etc until the end of a race or any activity: *Will the Chairman stay the course of his one year in office? Considering he was elected by the smallest majority in the club's history, I somehow doubt it.*

***stay* under wraps →*keep* sth under wraps**

**as *steady* as a rock** very firm or reliable; very loyal: *'Is that wooden bridge safe?' 'Yes—it's as steady as a rock!'*

***steady* ('on)!** be more careful; stop doing sth so fast: *Steady on, you two, you'll be hurting each other in a minute!*

***steal* a march (on sb)** do sth before sb else, so gaining an advantage over him: *They stole a march on us by publishing a new dictionary just before ours.*

***steal* the cream →like the *cat* that stole the cream**

***steal* the show** receive more applause, notice, etc than sb who is expected to receive the most attention: *The royal couple appeared on stage, but it was their baby who completely stole the show.*

***steal* sb's thunder** spoil the effect of sb's attempt to do sth by doing it before him: *He had planned to announce his invention at the September meeting, but his deputy stole his thunder by talking about it in August.*

**run out of *steam* →*run***

**(all) *steamed* up** *(informal)* very excited or angry: *He's all steamed up about the delay to the trains again.*

***steel* oneself (for/against sth)** or **steel oneself to do sth** prepare oneself for sth difficult or unpleasant: *Motorists ought to steel themselves against further possible increases in the tax on petrol.*

***steer* clear of sb/sth** avoid going near or meeting sb, using sth etc; shun: *The council advise you to steer clear of the beach because of the oil slick.* Also **give sb/sth a wide berth.**

**in/out of *step* (with . . . )** in or not in agreement or harmony with sb/sth: *The building methods in this country are out of step with more modern techniques used elsewhere in the world.*

***step* down** resign, especially to let someone take your place: *The chairman was getting very old so decided to step down to let his son take over.*

***step* in** intervene to help or hinder sb: *The government stepped in with an offer that saved the company from bankruptcy.*

**a *step* in the right direction** sth done to bring a desired objective, especially an improvement, nearer: *Unemployment is so bad in this area that the opening of a small factory is at least a step in the right direction.*

***step* into sb's shoes** assume or take control of a responsible task or job: *Mike stepped into his father's shoes when his father retired as chairman.*

***step* into the breach** take the place of sb who is absent or unwilling: *Patrick couldn't give the opening speech as his mother had just died, but John stepped into the breach and did it for him.*

***step* on it** or **step on the gas** *(informal)* press down the accelerator of a car etc to increase speed; hurry: *Tell the driver to step on it—our train goes in ten minutes!*

***step* up sth** increase sth in number, speed etc; improve: *The car manufacturers are stepping up production of their new model in the autumn.*

**a ˈ*stepping* stone** a way of reaching a higher professional, social, or educational level: *I want someone who sees the job of manager as more than a stepping stone to something better.*

**in a *stew*** *(informal)* in a difficult or worrying situation: *He'd lost all his money and got himself in a right stew.*

***stew* in one's own juice** *(informal)* bear the unpleasant effects of your own actions without anyone helping you: *Let Laura stew in her own juice. She caused all the difficulties in the first place.*

***stick* around** *(informal)* remain in a place waiting for sth to happen, sb to arrive etc: *If you stick around, then I expect someone will give you a lift into town.*

***stick* at nothing** → ***stop*/stick at nothing**

**a *stick*-in-the-mud** sb who does not like changes and who has fixed, unimaginative habits or ideas. **stick-in-the-mud** *adj*: *stick-in-the-mud attitudes.*

***stick* in sb's throat** be difficult to accept: *Telling John he couldn't come swimming with the rest of the boys because he was late really stuck in my throat. I knew he'd walked all the way from home. But we must keep to the rules.*

***stick* it/sth out** endure sth unpleasant: *He hated his job, but he knew he had to stick it out because it brought money to support his family.*

***stick* one's neck out** *(informal)* behave in a bold, adventurous way; take risks that may lead to trouble for you: *I'm prepared to stick my neck out and say that I think the Prime Minister is wrong.*

***stick* out a mile** → ***stand*/stick out a mile**

***stick* out for sth** → ***stand*/stick out for sth**

***stick* out like a sore thumb** → ***stand*/stick out like a sore thumb**

***stick* them/'em up** *(informal)* raise your hands above your head (said for example by bank robbers): *All of you, stick 'em up and move away from the safe!*

***stick* to sth** not abandon your principles, beliefs etc: *You should stick to your decision once you have made it.*

**a *stick* to beat sb with** → **a *rod*/stick to beat sb with**

***stick* to one's guns** *(informal)* stubbornly refuse to surrender your rights, opinion etc: *The government should stick to its guns and keep firmly to what it believes is the right way to handle the economy.*

***stick* up for sb/sth** → ***stand*/stick up for sth**

**the ˈ*sticking* point** the limit beyond which you cannot be persuaded to go: *The sticking point in the negotiations is whether to start the new system immediately or wait till January.*

**a *stickler* for sth** sb who is fussy about particular behaviour in himself and other people: *Miss Jamison is a stickler for accuracy and will always criticize you if you spell a word wrongly.*

**out in the *sticks*** in the isolated or more remote parts of a country.

***sticks* and stones may break my bones but words will never hurt me** *(saying)* insults in words cause you no physical injury.

**come to a *sticky* end** → ***come***

**(be on) a *sticky* wicket** *(informal)* be in a difficult situation because you cannot justify or defend a wrong that you have done: *You have in effect stolen their idea, so you'll be on a sticky wicket if they take you to court over it.*

**as *stiff* as a board** (of things) very stiff; fixed and rigid.

**as *stiff* as a poker** completely straight in the way you stand, walk etc; very formal in the way you behave: *The old lady was sitting upright in her chair, as stiff as a poker, unlike some younger members of her family.*

**as *stiff*/straight as a ramrod** completely straight in the way you stand, walk etc: *The captured general kept his dignity to the end, walking as straight as a ramrod to his execution.*

**a *stiff* drink** a drink that contains a lot of alcohol: *Give him a stiff drink—he's just heard he's failed his exams again.*

**a *stiff* upper lip** great self-control; complete control over your feelings and thoughts, especially in a difficult or dangerous situation: *'How's he reacted to the news?' 'Badly, I think, although he's trying to keep a stiff upper lip.'*

**a *still* small voice** your sense of right and wrong; the expression of your conscience: *A still small voice inside me told me that what I was planning to do was wrong.*

***still* waters run deep** *(saying)* a quiet person can have much knowledge, deep feelings etc.

**a *sting* in the tail** an unsuspected and unpleasant feature or result: *The pay for the job abroad sounded very attractive—£20,000 a year tax free—but there was a sting in the tail: you couldn't bring the money back into this country.*

**like *stink*** *(slang)* very hard, strongly, fast etc: *If you're willing to work like stink, you might just pass the exam.*

***stink* to high heaven** → ***smell*/stink to high heaven**

***stinking* rich** *(informal)* extremely rich, perhaps to an offensive degree: *The family who've moved into the house are stinking rich. They actually own three Rolls Royces!*

***stir* sb's blood** arouse sb's enthusiasm, excitement etc: *The speaker at the young people's rally really stirred many of the listeners' blood.*

**a *stitch* in time saves nine** *(saying)* if you act immediately when sth goes wrong, it will save you a lot of work later: *'Must you stop to mend that now?' 'I prefer to—a stitch in time saves nine.'*

**not have (got) a *stitch* on (one)** → ***have***

**not have (got) a *stitch*/thing to wear** → ***have***

**in *stitches*** (of laughter) laughing uncontrollably: *The whole audience was in stitches.* / *The comedian had the whole audience in stitches.*

**sb's ˌ*stock*-in-ˈtrade** the qualities and methods sb uses as part of his profession, trade etc: *Friendly persuasion is the stock-in-trade of every salesman.*

**on the *stocks*** in preparation; being built, developed etc: *The new encyclopaedia was on the stocks for several years before it was finally published.*

**can't/won't *stomach* sb/sth** *(informal)* cannot tolerate sb/sth: *I can't stomach his rudeness much longer.*

**like getting blood out of a *stone*** → ***getting***

***stone* cold 1** (of things that should be hot) very cold: *I'm not drinking that tea! It's gone stone cold.* **2** (of people) unfeeling or callous.

***stone* cold sober** completely sober; not drunk at all: *Honest, Mum! I didn't have anything to drink. I was stone cold sober all evening!*

**kill sth *stone* dead** → ***kill***

***stone* deaf** completely or extremely deaf: *He's just turned 90 and is now stone deaf.*

***stone* me!** → ***damn* me!**

**a ˈ*stone*'s throw** a (very) short distance: *Their new house is just a stone's throw from the park.*

***stone* the crows** *(informal, old-fashioned)* (used to express surprise or disbelief): *Stone the crows! What are you doing here? I thought you were in India still!*

***stoned* out of one's mind** *(slang)* very much under the influence of drugs or alcohol.

**fall between two *stools*** → ***fall***

***stop*/stick at nothing** behave in a completely ruthless, unscrupulous way to achieve sth: *He's so ambitious he'd stop at nothing to reach the top.*

***stop* (sb) (dead) in his tracks** (cause sb to) stop suddenly: *Seeing the snake on the path ahead stopped him dead in his tracks.*

***stop* off** break a journey to pay a visit to friends etc: *We stopped off in Birmingham to see some friends on our way up to Scotland.*

***stop* over** break a journey by air for a short time: *They stopped over in Bombay on their trip to Australia.* **stopover** *n.*

***stop* short** not complete something such as a distance or statement: *He ran down the road but stopped short when he saw the police car.*

***stop* short of (doing) sth** not go as far as doing sth: *He criticized him very strongly for his bad work but stopped short of dismissing him from his job.*

***stop* the rot** bring to an end a process of deterioration, especially in social or industrial practices or standards: *Productivity was falling lower and lower until a new board of directors took control of the company to try to stop the rot.*

***stop* the show** attract so much attention, applause etc from an audience that proceedings are halted. **show-stopper** *n*: *The star's costumes were a real showstopper.*

**set (no, great, little etc) *store* by sth** → ***set***

**take sb/sth by *storm*** → ***take***

**a *storm* in a teacup** *(informal)* a lot of fuss; great disturbance about sth that is or proves to be unimportant: *The politician described the row over the incident as a storm in a teacup.*

***stow* away** hide aboard a ship or aeroplane to try to travel free to another country: *At the age of 15, he stowed away in a cargo-boat bound for Africa.* **stowaway** *n.*

**the *straight* and narrow (path)** a morally upright life; a way of life that conforms strictly to certain religious, moral, or political standards: *He kept to the straight and narrow while he lived with his parents but soon turned to crime when he left home.*

**as *straight* as a die** in a straight line or direction; honest; not ambiguous: *If anyone's stealing from the till it must be one of the new assistants—Jones has been with us for years and I know he's as straight as a die.*

**as *straight* as a ramrod** → **as *stiff*/straight as a ramrod**

**as *straight* as an arrow** in a straight line or direction: *You can't get lost if you follow this track. It's as straight as an arrow and runs right through the middle of the wood.*

**straight away** → ***right*/straight away**

**keep a *straight* face** → ***keep***

***(straight)* from the horse's mouth** → ***horse***

***straight* from the shoulder** directly; frankly; forcefully: *What's the matter with me, doctor? Tell me honestly, please, straight from the shoulder.*

***straight* up** *(slang)* completely frank and honestly: *I'm telling you this straight up! I saw the gang break into the jeweller's and steal the jewels!*

***strain* at a gnat (and swallow a camel)** *(saying)* worry about doing or allowing sth slightly wrong but not about sth very wrong.

***strain* at the leash** want freedom from some restrictions such as at home: *The deputy sales manager strained at the leash for several years and eventually left to start his own company.*

**make *strange* bedfellows** → ***make***

**truth is *stranger* than fiction** → ***truth***

***stranger* things happen at sea** → ***worse*/stranger things happen at sea**

**no *stranger* to sb/sth** → ***no***

**make bricks without *straw*** → ***make***

**a *straw* in the wind** an incident, rumour or opinion that shows the development of a situation, changes that are planned etc.

**a *straw* poll/vote** an unofficial poll or vote.

**the man in the *street*** → ***man***

**(right) up sb's *street*/alley** *(informal)* what sb knows or likes: *I got this book out of the*

*library for you. I know you're interested in butterflies so it's right up your street.*

**'*streets* ahead of sb/sth** *(informal)* far better or more efficient, intelligent etc than sb/sth: *Our foreign competitors are streets ahead of us—when are we going to improve our products?*

**the *streets* are paved with gold** *(saying)* it is a place, especially a city, where you can get rich quickly.

**in *strength* → in *force*/strength**

**on the *strength* of sth** using sth as your main reason, argument etc for doing sth: *He was offered a job as a computer salesman on the strength of only two months' experience in selling.*

**go from *strength* to strength → *go***

***strengthen* sb's hand** increase sb's power to do sth in the face of opposition or competition: *The recommendations in the report will strengthen the hand of those fighting to keep the country's railway system intact.*

**at a *stretch*** (of periods of time) at a time; without a break: *I'm getting old and find that I can't read a book for more than a couple of hours at a stretch.*

***stretch* a point** extend a regulation or definition to cover sb/sth not normally included; make a concession that is not usually made: *'When is his birthday?' 'Not till next week, 23rd February.' 'Oh, I think, we could stretch a point and call him 16 now.'*

***stretch* one's legs** walk about after sitting, lying etc for a long time: *The long-distance coach stopped at the motorway service station so that the passengers could have something to eat and stretch their legs.*

**by no *stretch* of the imagination → *no***

***(strictly)* for the birds → *birds***

**put sb off his *stride*/stroke → *put***

**take sth in one's *stride* → *take***

***strike* a blow for sth** *(informal)* perform a strong and courageous act as part of an attack for sth: *The workers were determined to strike a blow for freedom by calling a series of demonstrations against government policies.*

***strike* a chord** produce a mental or emotional response in sb: *The poem that was read out struck a familiar chord in my mind. Later, I remembered I'd memorized it years earlier.*

***strike* a light!** *(slang, old-fashioned)* (an exclamation of surprise or protest): *'Have you got those sandwiches ready?' 'Strike a light, Jim! It's only two minutes since you asked me to make them!'*

***strike* sb dumb** astonish, bewilder, or terrify sb so much that he is silenced: *Faced with such an awful choice he was struck completely dumb.*

***strike* it rich** become rich suddenly: *He found he'd struck it rich when he unexpectedly inherited some money from his aunt.*

***strike* lucky** be lucky by finding sb/sth that you are looking for or of a kind that you hope for: *If you spend your money betting on horses, you may strike lucky one day.* **a lucky strike** *n*: *That was a lucky strike, finding one so soon!*

***strike* me dead/pink!** *(slang, old-fashioned)* (an expression of surprise, disbelief etc).

***strike* up** begin to play: *The band struck up and started playing a waltz.*

***strike* while the iron is hot** make immediate use of an opportunity; do sth while conditions are favourable: *He seems in a good mood. Why don't you strike while the iron is hot and ask him right now?*

**within '*striking* distance** near enough to be reached or hit: *In one minute, enemy aircraft will be within striking distance.*

***string* sb along** *(informal)* mislead or deceive sb into believing or doing sth: *That young man has been stringing Rosie along for years; he carries on going out with other girls.*

***string* along with sb** *(informal)* stay with sb; work, play, or go with sb: *While his other friends were on holiday, Mike strung along with Sandy.*

**have (got) a second *string* to one's bow** or **have (got) two strings to one's bow → *have***

***string* sth together** combine words or sentences together to form units: *He said he'd been learning German for two years but he could hardly string a complete sentence together.*

**(no) *strings* attached** (no) special conditions which limit the use or enjoyment of sth: *You can ask for a demonstration of our new video recorder in your own home with no strings attached. There's absolutely no obligation to buy it.*

**tear a *strip* off sb/sth** or **tear strips off sb/sth** or **tear sb off a strip → *tear***

**at a/one (single) *stroke*** with one action and often suddenly: *It is very doubtful if the number of people unemployed could be reduced at a stroke.*

**not do a *stroke* (of work) → *do***

**put sb off his *stroke* → *put***

**on the *stroke* of eight, midnight etc** at exactly eight o'clock etc: *He always starts work on the stroke of nine.*

**the *strong*/long arm of the law** the authority of the police and other law-keeping forces: *The long arm of the law will be raised against the strikers if they don't stop their illegal demonstrations.*

**as *strong* as a horse** having great muscular strength and able to do heavy physical work: *He had to carry heavy loads around the building site, so this quickly made him as strong as a horse.* Also (usually used only of men) **as strong as an ox.**

***strong* language/words** immoderate speech, using swear words or very forceful expressions: *Saying he's the worst prime minister for 100 years is certainly very strong language.* See also ***bad* language.**

**a '*strong* point** an ability, quality etc that sb excels in: *Writing letters has never been my* *strong point—I prefer to ring people up and talk to them.*

**(be) *strung* up** *(informal)* (be) tense or nervous: *Phil seemed all strung up just before he gave his big speech.*

**(as) *stubborn*/obstinate as a mule** very difficult to persuade to do or think differently: *He just wouldn't understand our views. He was as stubborn as a mule.*

**be *stuck* for sth** *(informal)* lack or need something: *If ever you're stuck for transport, let me know and you can come in my car.*

**get/be *stuck* in** → ***get***

**be *stuck* with sb/sth** *(informal)* have to accept sb/sth unpleasant or unwanted: *I suppose we're stuck with your father-in-law for the rest of the holiday, aren't we?*

***stuff* and nonsense** foolish or false beliefs, ideas etc; often used to express strong disagreement: *'They say he's the best boxer in the district!' 'Stuff and nonsense—Joe's far better!'*

***stuff* him, that etc!** *(slang)* an impolite expression of strong contempt and disapproval: *Stuff you! I'm fed up with your rudeness! I never want to see you again!*

***stumble* across/(up)on sth** discover sth by chance: *I stumbled across this old manuscript in the attic.*

***stumble* over/through sth** say words, a speech etc with mistakes, much hesitation etc: *The little boy stumbled over his lines in the school play.*

**a '*stumbling*-block** an obstacle; sth that gets in the way or prevents sb from doing sth: *He's well qualified for the job, but his age is the stumbling-block.*

***stump* up (for sth)** *(informal)* pay a necessary sum of money, especially when you do not want to: *I'm getting tired of stumping up for school outings every term.*

**in (great/grand) *style*** on a very lavish scale: *They're used to living in style. They've got a very comfortable home that's tastefully decorated and has lots of expensive furniture.*

**if at first you don't *succeed*, (try, try again)** → ***if***

**nothing *succeeds* like success** → ***nothing***

***such* as it/sth is** although sth is only of poor quality, very small etc: *You're welcome to borrow the lawn-mower, such as it is, at any time you want it.*

***suck* sb/sth dry** → ***milk*/suck sb/sth dry**

**teach one's grandmother to *suck* eggs** → ***teach***

***suck* up to sb** *(informal)* try to please sb important or powerful by doing favours, praising him etc: *I hate the way he always sucks up to all the teachers.*

**a *sudden* death play-off** an additional contest in sports to decide between people or teams who have achieved equal results, especially after a given period of extra time: *If the two teams are equal at the final whistle, they compete in a sudden death play-off.*

**(not) *suffer* fools gladly** (not) tolerate or be patient with stupid or foolish people.

***sugar*/sweeten the pill** try to make sth unpleasant or unwelcome seem less so: *To sweeten the pill of higher charges, the bank is giving its services free to new customers for one month.*

***suit* sb (right) down to the ground** be perfectly suitable for sb: *The timetable you've arranged for the lecture tour suits me right down to the ground: two days of lectures and three days of rest!*

**under the *sun*** in the world; anywhere; of any kind that you can think of: *She's the kindest woman under the sun.*

**make hay while the *sun* shines** → ***make***

**one's *Sunday* best** your smartest clothes: *Years ago, people used to put on their Sunday best when they went to church or visited relatives.*

**(and) 'that's for *sure*** → ***that***

**as *sure* as death/fate/hell** certain to happen; used especially in predictions, promises, or threats: *It's as sure as death to rain, with all these heavy clouds in the sky.*

**as *sure* as eggs is eggs** *(informal)* certainly: *If he goes on driving like that, he'll end up in hospital, as sure as eggs is eggs.*

**as *sure* as I'm sitting/standing here** without any doubt: *You might not think she'd be so rude, but those were her exact words, as sure as I'm sitting here.*

***sure*/right enough** *(informal)* exactly as you had expected, as had been forecast etc: *I always thought those two would get married, and sure enough they now have.*

**a *sure*-fire method etc** *(informal)* a certain, reliable method etc: *Being rude to your boss is a sure-fire method of losing your job!*

**know for certain/*sure* that . . .** → ***know***

***sure* thing** *(informal)* of course; yes: *'You'll come tonight?' 'Sure thing!'*

***surprise*, surprise!** this is a surprise: *Surprise, suprise! I'm back and I've got a present for you!* Note that this is also used ironically to mean 'this is really no surprise.'

***survive* the course** → ***stay*/last/survive the course**

***sus* sb/sth out** *(informal)* find out what sb/sth is like: *He was trying to trick me, but I sussed him out.*

**strain at a gnat (and *swallow* a camel)** → ***strain***

**one *swallow* does not make a summer** → ***one***

***swallow* one's pride** humble yourself, as in admitting a mistake or your guilt or in order to do or obtain sth: *He found it difficult to swallow his pride and ask for help.*

**sb's '*swan* song** sb's last work, appearance, or performance.

***swap*/change horses in mid-stream** change your opinion and course of action while in the middle of doing sth; suddenly transfer your loyalty and support from one person or group to another: *'I don't believe in changing horses in mid-stream,' his doctor* *told him. 'Give this treatment a chance before you think of trying something else.'*

***swear* blind (that . . . )** *(informal)* say emphatically or obstinately (that sth is the case): *Peter's the kind of person to slip a few pounds into my handbag if he knew I was short of money. But he'd swear blind he hadn't.*

***swear* by sth** have great confidence in the value of a product: *Julie swears by that new washing powder. She says her clothes have never been as white!*

***swear* like a trooper** *(informal)* use many swear words: *He swore like a trooper before he met Anne—but he's been a changed person ever since.*

**in/into a *sweat*** *(informal)* in/into a state of worry or anxiety: *I'm not surprised he's in such a sweat! The exams start tomorrow, and he's not done any revision yet!*

**no *sweat* ⟶ no *trouble*, bother, problem etc**

***sweat* blood** *(informal)* **1** work very hard, especially in pain: **2** be very worried or fearful: *I sweated blood waiting to hear if Mary and the baby had survived the crash.*

***sweat* it out** *(informal)* suffer and endure an unpleasant situation: *The work may be long and boring, but it's better to stay in your job and sweat it out than be unemployed.*

***sweat* like a pig** *(informal)* sweat very much: *I've never seen anyone so nervous. He was sweating like a pig as he waited for the result of the interview.*

**by the *sweat* of one's brow** through hard work and great effort: *It's not been easy to get to the top of the company. I've only been able to achieve it by the sweat of my brow.*

***sweep* sb off his feet** *(informal)* impress and excite sb with great enthusiasm; cause sb, especially a girl, to fall in love with you: *There's no point in waiting for some nice young man to come along and sweep you off your feet—you've got to go out and meet people yourself, you know.*

***sweep* the board** win all or most of the prizes: *In Hollywood last night Britain swept the board with the Oscar awards. / The new car swept the board in the rally, winning six out of the eight major prizes.*

***sweep*/brush sth under the carpet** *(informal)* hide or forget sth that might cause difficulty, trouble, or a scandal for yourself: *The report's findings are clear—they will either have to be disproved or accepted—the government can't just sweep the matter under the carpet.*

**a new broom (*sweeps* clean) ⟶ *new***

**as *sweet* as honey** very sweet in taste; very pleasant in speech and behaviour and sometimes insincere: *I can't drink this tea. It's as sweet as honey! / He's the kind of person who's as sweet as honey to your face but says nasty things about you to other people.*

***sweet* Fanny Adams** or ***sweet* f.a.** *(slang)* nothing at all; nothing important: *What's been happening while I've been out?' 'Sweet f.a.'*

***sweet* nothings** pleasant but unimportant things said to sb you love: *The couple sat in the back of the taxi, and he whispered sweet nothings in her ear all the way home.*

**be *sweet* on sb** be fond of or in love with sb: *I hear that Mark's sweet on Debbie at the moment.*

**a *sweet* tooth** a fondness for sweet foods and drinks: *Hannah is the only one of us with a sweet tooth. If it weren't for her, I wouldn't make any puddings.*

***sweeten* the pill ⟶ *sugar*/sweeten the pill**

***sweetness* and light** harmony and reason: *His period as head of department at the college was not all sweetness and light, I can assure you! At times, his colleagues found him completely unbearable.*

**in the *swim*** socially active; up to date; fashionable: *If you want to keep in the swim, you'll have to go to all the parties in town.*

***swim* against/with the tide** act in a way that opposes/conforms to the general trend: *Britain's largest bank yesterday decided to swim against the tide by holding its interest rate at the existing level; all the other major banks lowered theirs two days ago.*

**go with a bang/*swing* ⟶ *go***

**no room to *swing* a cat ⟶ *no***

***swings* and roundabouts** *(saying)* you lose in some respects but gain in others; the disadvantages balance the advantages in a particular course of action.

***switch* off** stop listening or enjoying yourself; become dull, lifeless, or unresponsive: *They started discussing accountancy again so I just switched off.*

***switch* sb on** *(informal)* make sb lively and responsive: *Pop music really switches her on.*

**get sb/sth out of one's *system* ⟶ *get***

# T

**to a *T*/tee** *(informal)* exactly; in every detail: *One of the nurses was giving an imitation of what Matron is like when she gets angry. It was the old girl to a T!*

**drink sb under the *table* ⟶ *drink***

**on the *table*** *(informal)* (of a suggestion or amount of money) offered for discussion or negotiation: *One of the resolutions on the table for the meeting calls for money to be given to the third world. / The Steel Corporation can put a further £10 per week on the table only if the workers agree not to strike.*

**put/lay/place (all) one's cards on the *table* ⟶ *put***

**with one's *tail* between one's legs** *(informal)* feeling humiliated or dejected, as when surrendering: *He hopes I'll come back and apologize to him with my tail between my legs.*
**have (got) one's *tail* down/up** —> ***have***
**(at) the *tail* end** (at) the final or last part or position: *I came in only at the tail end of the discussion so I don't know what they were talking about.*
***tail* off** decrease in quantity, degree, loudness etc, especially gradually: *Business tails off in the summer with so many people away on holiday.*
**the *tail* wags the dog** *(informal)* a part of something controls the whole; sb/sth dictates the course of action for sb/sth more important.
***take* a back seat** *(informal)* change to a less important role or function: *After forty years in the business it's time for me to take a back seat and let someone younger come in with fresh ideas.*
***take* a chance (on sth)** or **take chances (on sth)** try to do sth knowing that the result may be injury, loss, disgrace etc; take a risk or risks: *When overtaking, it's wise never to take chances. / The thieves took a chance on the house being unguarded—but it wasn't.*
***take* a coach and horses through sth** —> ***drive*/take a coach and horses through sth**
***take* a dim/poor view of sb/sth** *(informal)* think that sb/sth is bad or wrong; disapprove of sb/sth: *I take a dim view of you sending Hugh home by himself when you knew he was very ill.*
***take* a (firm) grip/hold on oneself** *(informal)* calm yourself, especially your feelings, in a difficult situation: *Take a firm grip on yourself! When do you last remember having your keys? Surely they must be here somewhere—you can't really have lost them!*
***take* a hand in (doing) sth** —> ***have*/take a hand in (doing) sth**
***take* a hint** understand and do what sb has suggested indirectly: *She yawned and said, 'Goodness, it must be late.' 'OK,' Pete said, 'I can take a hint. I'll be going home.'*
**you can *take*/lead a horse to water but you can't make him drink** —> ***you***
***take* a joke** *(informal)* accept teasing, playful tricks etc in good humour: *The children sometimes say some rude things to their teacher without meaning them, but she can't take a joke and gets very angry.*
***take* a leaf out of sb's book** copy sb's action and learn from him; base your behaviour on what sb does: *If you're having trouble controlling the children, you should take a leaf out of Sandra's book. She knows how to discipline them.*
***take* a lot of beating** —> ***take* some beating**
***take* a lot of doing** —> ***take* some doing**
***take* a lot of stick** —> ***give* sb a lot of stick**
**give sb an inch (and he'll *take* a mile)** —> ***give***
***take* a pew** *(informal, becoming old-fashioned)* sit down: *Take a pew, old chap, while I get you a drink.* Note that this is usually used in the imperative.
***take* a poor view of sb/sth** —> ***take* a dim/poor view of sb/sth**
***take*/have a 'rain check (for/on sth)** *(informal; mainly US)* postpone the acceptance (of an offer or invitation) to a later date: *Thanks for the invitation—I'm afraid we're busy at the moment, but could we take a rain check on it?*
***take*/get a/the rise out of sb** *(informal)* make sb angry by making fun of him: *He didn't mean it—he was just trying to take a rise out of you!*
***take* a running jump** *(informal)* go away (used as a rude expression when you are angry with sb): *I'm fed up with you this morning! Go and take a running jump!*
***take* a shine to sb** *(informal)* start to like sb: *Why has Jim taken a shine to Sally? I don't know what attracts him to her.*
***take* a stand** —> ***make*/take a stand**
***take* a turn for the better/worse** become better/worse: *Her illness took a turn for the worse in the morning, and she died later that day.*
***take* sb aback** shock or surprise sb: *When he came out onto the balcony, he was greatly taken aback by the crowd's angry response.*
***take* account of sth** —> ***take* sth into account**
***take* advantage of sb** use your own strength and another person's weakness to get what you want; seduce a woman: *The salesman took advantage of the old lady's kind nature and went away with her life savings. / He took advantage of her while she was drunk.*
***take* advantage of sth** make good use of sth such as an opportunity or benefit: *He took full advantage of the sports centre and practised in it every day. / It has come to my notice that proper advantage is not being taken of the facilities of the library.*
**(not) *take* all day/morning/afternoon/evening/night** —> **(not) be/take *all* day/morning/afternoon/evening/night**
***take* sth amiss** be offended by sth that was not intended to cause offence: *Please don't take it amiss if I said I'd prefer you not to come to the station to say goodbye.*
**take sb/sth apart** —> ***pull*/take/tear sb/sth apart**
***take* sth as/for gospel (truth)** believe sth without questioning it or where there is no real proof: *There's no need to take everything the doctor says as gospel truth; he's not infallible, you know.*
***take* sb/sth as he/it comes** accept or tolerate sb/sth without wishing him/it to be different from his/its present state: *My Dad always said you should take life as it comes and be willing to overcome any difficulties that may happen to you.*
***take* sth as read** think that sth will very probably happen: *I assume we can take it as read that prices will continue to rise.*
***take* sb/sth at (his/its) face value** treat or

consider sb/sth as it seems to be from the outward appearance: *You should take what he says about your achievements at face value and not try to read into it things that weren't intended.*

***take* sb at his word** believe exactly what sb says: *He's always kept his promises before, so I think we should take him at his word now.*

***take* sth back** withdraw sth such as a remark or accusation: *I apologize and take back my rude comments about you.*

***take* sb's breath away** make sb surprised or filled with wonder or awe: *Our friends' help and generosity really took our breath away.* **breathtaking** *adj*: *a breathtaking view.*

***take* sb/sth by storm** defeat a town etc suddenly by force; have a great effect on sb/sth: *His performance in the Olympics took the whole sporting world by storm.*

***take* care of sb/sth** make sure that sb is well and happy; take the responsibility for or look after sb/sth: *I don't want your help. I can take care of myself quite well, thank you.* / *You needn't worry about the children while they're in the creche. They'll be taken good care of.* / *My husband takes care of paying all the bills in this house.*

***take* chances (on sth)** ⟶ ***take* a chance (on sth)**

***take* coals to Newcastle** ⟶ ***carry*/take coals to Newcastle**

***take* one's courage in both hands** decide to be very bold and courageous: *The young boy was screaming for help in the swimming pool. I took my courage in both hands and jumped in to try to save him from drowning.*

**let sth *take* its course** ⟶ ***run* its course**

***take*/break cover** find or come out of a place of hiding or shelter: *He had nipped into a telephone kiosk to take cover from the freezing wind and I nearly missed him.*/*When they saw that the game was over, the children broke cover into the sunlight and went back home.*

***take* (the) credit for sth** be recognized as the person who has done sth: *The managers shouldn't take all the credit for the team's victory in the competition.* See also ***give* sb credit for sth; *give* (the) credit (to sb) (for sth).**

***take* sb down a peg (or two)** *(informal)* humble sb who is arrogant and very proud: *She's very conceited and needs to be taken down a peg or two.*

***take* effect 1** become law; actually happen: *The new regulations take effect at 0001 hours on 1 January next year.* **2** (of a drug, alcohol etc) produce an expected or desired effect: *It takes a little while for the medicine to take effect, but when it does, you'll feel much better.*

***take* exception to sth** be very offended by a charge or accusation: *I take strong exception to your suggestion that this action was done for financial gain.*

**not be able to *take* one's eyes off sb/sth** ⟶ **not be able to *keep*/take one's eyes off sb/sth**

***take* French leave** leave your work, duty etc without permission; go away without telling anyone.

***take* sb's fancy** ⟶ ***catch*/take sb's fancy**

***take* sb for sb/sth** think, wrongly, that sb/sth is sb/sth else: *He speaks Spanish so well that people often take him for a Spaniard.* / *Of course I didn't steal the money! What do you take me for?*

***take* sb for a ride** *(informal)* deceive or cheat sb: *I think the training scheme takes people for a ride, to be honest. It's supposed to give work experience to people, but the pay is very low.* / *You're telling me you paid £600 for that car! You've been taken for a ride!*

***take* sth for gospel (truth)** ⟶ ***take* sth as/for gospel (truth)**

***take* sth for granted 1** assume sth is fair or reasonable and act accordingly: *We took it for granted that there would be some rooms available at the hotel.* **2** assume that sb will act or react in a certain way and treat him in an unimportant way, showing no care or thankfulness: *Most people take their parents for granted—it's only when they start their own family that they realize everything their parents did for them.* / *I think you should have asked me before making those arrangements. I don't like being taken so much for granted.*

***take* God's name in vain** use the name of God without proper reverence, for example in a curse. See also ***take* sb's name in vain.**

***take* sth hard/lightly** be greatly/little worried, disappointed etc by sth: *Try not to take it too hard if you fail your driving test. You've only been learning for a short time.*

***take* one's 'hat off to sb** *(informal)* express admiration for sb: *I take my hat off to the excellent team of nurses at the hospital—they do difficult work for long hours and are paid very little money.* Also **raise one's hat to sb; one's hat goes off to sb.**

***take* heart (from sth)** be encouraged by sth: *You can take heart from the fact that over 90% of the girls you taught passed their exams.*

***take* holy orders** ⟶ ***take* (holy) orders**

***take* home £100 etc** receive £100 etc as pay after all taxes, national insurance etc have been paid. *In 1983 the average employed worker in Britain took home £108 a week.* **take-home** *adj*: *take-home pay.*

***take* sb in** deceive, cheat, or delude sb: *The door-to-door salesman really took Mary in and easily persuaded her to buy a vacuum cleaner from him.*

***take* sth in** observe, listen to, or read sth carefully, or understand it fully: *It was clear that the students weren't taking the material in, so the teacher stopped and explained things again more slowly.* / *I can hardly take it in! Have we really won £1 million?*

***take* sth in good/bad part** accept or respond to sth with tolerance/resentment, displaying good humour/bad temper: *A few people were offended by the comedian's rude jokes, but* *most people took them in good part.* Also **take sth in the right/wrong spirit.**

***take* sb/sth in hand** control or discipline sb, to try to show him how to behave; control sth to try to improve it: *Someone should take her youngest child firmly in hand—I've never seen anyone so unruly!*

***take* sth in one's stride** deal with a difficulty easily: *First his car was stolen, and then he lost his job, but he seemed to take it all in his stride.*

***take* sth in the right/wrong spirit** ⟶ ***take* sth in good/bad part**

***take* sth in the spirit in which it is intended** accept sth said, done, or given by sb in a way that matches his (good) motives and intentions: *He is obviously a great joker, so people take his rather insulting remarks in the spirit in which they are intended.*

***take* sb into one's confidence** confide in sb; share confidentially your problems, plans etc with sb: *I decided to take my boss into my confidence and ask his advice on what I should do.*

***take* sth into account** consider sth; include sth in your calculations: *Where I think Harris' book is inadequate is that he has failed to take into account the factors that led to the war.* Also **take account of sth:** *We mustn't forget to take account of the increase in petrol prices when we work out our revised costs.*

***take*/join issue with sb/sth** disagree with sb/sth: *Three members of the committee took issue with the chairman on the matter of members' expenses.*

***take* it** *(informal)* tolerate or withstand pain, stress, criticism etc: *I can't take it any more! You annoy me all the time and I'm leaving you!*

***take* it (that . . . )** assume (that sth will happen, is true etc): *You'll be there, I take it? / 'I take it that you won't be back for lunch,' said the receptionist as we left the hotel.*

***take* it easy** *(informal)* go or do sth more slowly; not become excited, angry etc: *'If you leave at 11 you should be there by midday.' 'I'd rather leave earlier and take it easy.' / Take it easy, Jack! There's no need to get so annoyed!*

***take* it from me etc (that . . . )** *(informal)* you may assume or believe on my authority (that sth is true, will happen etc): *Take it from me that the worst is over. / You can take it from me, I don't think he'll bother us any more.*

***take* it in turns to do sth** ⟶ ***take* (it in) turns to do sth**

***take* it into one's head (that . . . )** or **take it into one's head to do sth** *(informal)* form the idea that sth is true, will happen etc; decide to do sth (often used to imply that the thought or action is foolish): *Somehow she'd taken it into her head that her husband was trying to poison her.* See also ***get* sth into one's (thick) head.**

***take* it or leave it** *(informal)* accept or reject sb/sth offered, without a further alternative being offered: *'I'll give you £20 for your old car,' said the salesman, 'take it or leave it.'*

***take* it out of sb** *(informal)* make sb very tired: *Looking after four children all under the age of five really takes it out of you!*

***take* it/sth out on sb/sth** *(informal)* make sb/sth else suffer for sth you have done or suffered: *I know you're disappointed but there's no need to take it* (or *your anger) out on me.*

**not *take* kindly to sb/sth** resent, reject, or oppose sb/sth: *The natives didn't take kindly to the suggestion that their customs and language are primitive.*

***take* leave of one's senses** behave in a wild, crazy, and irrational way; go mad: *He must have taken leave of his senses to be so rude to his father.*

***take* liberties with sb/sth** act too freely towards sb/sth: *This is a very rough translation, and I think that the translator has taken liberties with the original text.* See also **take the liberty of doing sth.**

***take* one's life in/into one's hands** *(informal)* run a serious risk of being killed: *The swimmers are taking their lives into their hands every time they enter these deep waters.*

***take* sth lightly** ⟶ ***take* sth hard/lightly**

**(not) *take* sth lying down** *(informal)* (not) accept or suffer sth passively or weakly without fighting back, objecting, or arguing: *The union is not taking the threat of redundancies lying down and has started a campaign to fight the cuts.*

***take* one's medicine** *(informal)* submit to sth unpleasant: *When the other boys were caught, he admitted he'd helped them and took his medicine with the rest of them.*

***take* sb's name in vain** *(humorous)* mention sb's name, sometimes disrespectfully, without his knowledge: *Pete turned to see who was talking about him. 'I thought I heard my name being taken in vain,' he said.* See also **take God's name in vain.**

**not *take* no for an answer** be stubbornly determined, ignoring all objections or refusals, to do or obtain what you want: *Will you come to dinner? I know you're busy, but I won't take no for an answer!*

**sit up (and *take* notice)** ⟶ ***sit***

***take* (the) occasion to do sth** *(formal)* make use of a suitable time or opportunity in order to do sth: *The President spoke about foreign relations but took the occasion also to mention his country's economic crisis.*

***take* off 1** (of a plane, helicopter etc) leave the ground: *The airliner took off from Rome Airport half an hour ago.* See also **touch down. 2** *(informal)* (of an idea) become very successful or popular; (of profits, sales etc) rise very quickly: *Sales of books on computers have really taken off in the last few years.*

***take* sb off** *(informal)* imitate or copy the appearance, speech, behaviour of sb in a funny way: *Gerry can take off the headmaster perfectly!*

***take* on** become upset, sad etc: *Don't take on so! The doctor said you're not seriously ill.*

***take* sb on 1** give a job to sb; employ: *The computer company took on 50 extra workers last month.* **2** accept sb as an opponent in a fight, quarrel, or competition: *The mine workers are determined to take on the government in this dispute.*

***take* sth on** undertake or agree to do a task; assume responsibility for sth: *I'm very busy already, so I don't want to take on any more work.*

***take* sth on board** accept or adopt an idea or suggestion: *We will listen to your views and take on board your comments and opinions about what you want to see in this new magazine.*

***take* sth on the chin** *(informal)* accept sth unfortunate, such as a disappointment, with courage: *Losing his job after years at the firm was a great blow to him, but it was typical of Ted to take it right on the chin.*

***take* (holy) orders** (of a priest, monk etc) become admitted into the service and work of the Church.

***take* sb out of himself** make sb forget his worries and become less concerned with himself, his thoughts etc: *A holiday would help her a lot at the moment. It would take her out of herself after her daughter's death.*

***take* sb/sth over** acquire control of a business company: *The attempt to take over the 150-year-old family firm failed.* **take-over** *n.*

***take* over (from sb)** continue a job in the place of sb else: *I've been asked to take over leading the team from Jenny.*

***take* pains (to do sth)** or ***take* pains over sth** be very careful or involve yourself in much work, effort etc (to do sth): *She's an excellent teacher and always takes pains to explain things clearly. / He takes great pains over planting the flowers in the garden.* **painstaking** *adj*: *painstaking work.* Also **go to great pains (to do sth).**

***take* part in sth** be involved with sth; help in sth: *I decided not to take part in the strike. / He takes an active part in the local Scout troop.*

***take* one's pick** choose or select sth: *There are eight different types of shampoo on sale at the chemist's, so you can take your pick.*

***take* place** happen; occur: *The sports meeting took place on a hot summer Saturday in London.*

***take*/get/see sb's/the point** understand and appreciate sb's reasons or argument, though not necessarily agree with them: *I take your point (or Point taken), but I don't share your opinion.*

***take* pot luck** *(informal)* accept whatever is available or offered, for example a type of meal or entertainment: *You're welcome to come and have something to eat with us any evening if you're happy to take pot luck.*

***take* root** (of ideas etc) become firmly fixed in people's minds: *You seem to have given them some good advice. I only hope your words of wisdom will take root.*

***take* shape** acquire a recognizable or organized form: *The large new entertainment centre in the city is slowly beginning to take shape.*

***take* sb's side** support sb against another person in a fight, dispute etc: *I decided to take Rosy's side—she was more likely to win the argument than Roger, I thought.* Also **take sides.**

***take* some beating** or ***take* a lot of beating** be very good and difficult to improve on: *For imagination and romance her novels take a lot of beating!*

***take* some doing** or ***take* a lot of doing** be very good and difficult to perform or accomplish: *Starting a new life in this country after emigrating from Burma took a lot of doing, I can tell you.*

***take* steps (to do sth)** act in order to achieve a desired result: *The government has decided to take steps to prevent a further leak of nuclear waste from the power station.*

***take* stock (of sth)** assess sth such as a situation, progress, or prospects: *We've been working on this project for two months now, so let's stop and take stock of our present position.*

***take* the air** *(old-fashioned)* go outdoors, especially for a walk: *After a large lunch, Fitzsimmons and his wife liked to take the air and walk round the gardens of their country house.*

***take* the biscuit** *(informal)* be a very bad or good example of sth: *For unpleasantness, your old cow of a mother really takes the biscuit.*

***take*/get the bit between one's/the teeth** *(informal)* begin doing sth, especially sth difficult, in a strong, determined way: *I didn't think John would do at all well back at school after being ill for six months, but he's really taken the bit between the teeth and caught up quickly with the rest of the class.*

***take* the bull by the horns** *(informal)* handle a difficult or dangerous situation by tackling it directly and boldly: *Just sitting here thinking about the problem isn't helping. You've got to take the bull by the horns—so go on, face her and settle your differences right away!*

***take* the credit for sth** → ***take* (the) credit for sth**

***take* the edge off sth** lessen the force of sth such as criticism or hunger: *I find that the bright sun on a winter's day tends to take the edge off the cold.*

***take* the floor 1** stand up to talk to the audience at a meeting: *Next, the chairman invited the Chief of Defence Staff, Sir Robin Fortescue-Smith, to take the floor.* **2** begin dancing on a dance-floor.

***take* the gilt off the gingerbread** *(informal)* reduce or cancel the effects or feelings of good news, a happy event etc: *It rather takes the gilt off the gingerbread when you go back to your job after a refreshing holiday and find a lot of extra work to do.*

***take* the law into one's own hands** act in a way that you think is right against an injustice, not wanting help from the police etc: *Groups of local citizens have decided to take the law into their own hands and fight the terrorists themselves—because they think the police and army aren't having any effect.*
***take* the liberty of doing sth** do sth presumptuously; act without the permission of sb: *I have taken the liberty of giving your name to Mr Jones as someone who will help with the games at the Christmas party; I hope you don't mind.* See also ***take* liberties with sb/sth.**
***take* the lid off sth** *(informal)* reveal the truth about sth that has been secret: *The company with the biggest interest in this area has decided to take the lid off the study it commissioned and make its findings public.*
***take* the mickey out of sb** *(informal)* ridicule or imitate sb in a mocking way: *Every time the new student teacher goes into his class, the pupils take the mickey out of him.*
***take* the occasion to do sth** ⟶ ***take* (the) occasion to do sth**
***take* the pledge** ⟶ ***sign*/take the pledge**
***take* the plunge** *(informal)* finally do sth about which you have been undecided or hesitant: *The company saw the opportunity for sales in Canada so took the plunge and appointed a team of salesmen.*
***take* the point** ⟶ ***take*/get/see sb's/the point**
***take* the rap (for sb/sth)** *(informal)* accept the blame and/or punishment for a mistake, crime etc: *I'd confess if I thought someone else would have to take the rap for what I'd done.*
***take* the rise out of sb** ⟶ ***take*/get a/the rise out of sb**
***take* the rough with the smooth** *(informal)* accept difficulties as well as pleasant times: *You may be happy now, but life isn't always easy—you'll have to learn to take the rough with the smooth.*
***take* the weight off one's feet** *(informal)* sit down and relax: *After standing serving in the shop all day, I really need to take the weight off my feet in the evening.*
***take* the 'wind out of sb's sails** *(informal)* end sb's overconfidence or pride: *John kept on saying that he would win the match. So Sheila, who really is rather inexperienced, quite took the wind out of his sails by beating him.*
***take* the words out of sb's mouth** say exactly what sb else had intended to say: *You've taken the words right out of my mouth! How amazing! And I didn't even know you felt the same way as I do.*
***take* one's time (doing/over sth)** not hurry (in doing sth): *It's an important decision, Cathy, so take your time thinking about it.*
***take* to sb/sth** begin to feel a liking or affection for sb/sth: *I took to Rachel from the moment I first met her.*
***take* to (doing) sth** begin to form a habit of doing sth: *Now he's unemployed he's taken to lying in bed till lunchtime.*
***take* sth to bits/pieces** ⟶ ***pull*/take sth to pieces**
***take* sth to heart 1** be deeply affected by sth: *Don't take it so much to heart! You shouldn't let what she wrote worry you.* **2** consider sth seriously: *Naturally I'm pleased that they took my suggestions to heart and followed my advice.*
***take* sb to one's heart** show affection for sb: *The town really took the group of Vietnamese boat people to its heart and helped them settle in this country.*
***take* to one's heels** *(informal)* run away very quickly: *The robbers took to their heels when they heard the police arrive.*
**(*take* to sth) like a duck to water** (be able to do sth) very readily and easily: *'Do the children like living in the country?' 'They've taken to it like a duck to water* (or *like ducks to water*). *They've never been happier!'*
***take* sb to task (for sth)** criticize or reprimand sb for an error or failure: *The government has taken the newspaper to task for its coverage of the elections.*
***take* sb to the cleaners** *(slang)* cause sb to lose or spend a lot of his money, especially by cheating him: *He got into the wrong company, and his so-called friends really took him to the cleaners.*
***take* its toll (of sth)** damage; reduce the strength or numbers of sth: *Her depression is now beginning to take its toll of her health.*
***take* (it in) turns to do sth** share a task, duty etc: *My brother and I take it in turns to phone up Aunty. He rings up one week and I ring up the next.* Also **take a/one's turn to do sth.**
***take* umbrage (at sth)** be offended (by sth): *You can't have an ordinary conversation with her—she always takes umbrage at something you say.*
***take* sb unawares** ⟶ ***catch*/take sb unawares**
***take* sb under one's wing** give help, guidance, or protection to sb: *When our new worker arrives, I'll let Jack take him under his wing for a few days to show him what to do.*
***take* sth up** adopt sth as a study, hobby etc; accept an offer, challenge etc: *Our neighbours have taken up squash to keep fit.*
***take* sb up (on sth)** accept sb's offer, challenge etc: *Thanks for the invitation; we'll take you up on it sometime.*
***take* up the cudgels** begin to fight: *The local council would certainly take up the cudgels against the government if they were refused the money.*
***take* up the slack** pull a sagging rope tight; make full use of people and machines in industry which were idle or under-used before: *The government's decision to expand the economy will mean taking up the slack that there is at the moment.*
***take* up with sb** become friendly with sb, often sb thought to be unpleasant: *She's taken up with some long-haired, left-wing fellow she met at college.*

***take*** **sth with a grain/pinch of salt** not wholly believe sth; accept sth only with reservations or scepticism: *I think you should take his account of what happened with a grain of salt, as he's well known for inventing fanciful stories.*

***take*** **sb's word for it (that . . . )** accept sth on sb's authority: *'The matter really isn't very important,' Mike advised. 'OK, I'll take your word for it,' John said, 'Let's talk about something else then.'*

**be** ***taken*****/caught short** have a sudden need to go to the lavatory.

**it** ***takes*** **all sorts (to make a world)** *(saying)* different people like different things; different people have different characters and abilities: *'I don't understand Bill. How can anyone spend so much time fiddling with a car?' 'Well, it takes all sorts, you know—he probably thinks you're crazy spending every Saturday afternoon at a football match.'*

**have (got) what it** ***takes*** **to do sth** → ***have***

**(and/but) thereby hangs a** ***tale*** → ***thereby***

**tell** ***tales*** **out of school** → ***tell***

***talk*** **a different language** → ***speak*****/talk the same language**

***talk*** **about sth!** *(informal)* (used to reinforce a statement about sth saying that it is either a very good or bad example): *Talk about 'rudeness! I've never known anyone be so unpleasant!*

***talk*** **sb down** bring sb who controls an aeroplane down to land by giving him instructions; persuade sb who is on top of a building to come down: *The pilot had fallen ill, so the airport's control tower had to talk one of the passengers down. Fortunately, he'd flown a plane before and landed safely.*

***talk*** **down to sb** *(informal)* address sb as though he were inferior: *Try not to talk down to children when you're teaching them.*

***talk*** **one's head off** *(informal)* speak for a very long time: *The girls hadn't seen one another for months, so they really talked their heads off when they met.*

***talk*****/speak of the devil (and he appears)** *(saying)* (used when sb who has just been mentioned appears unexpectedly). *They were talking about Peter when he came in. 'Talk of the devil!' several of them burst out.*

**the** ***talk*** **of the town** sb/sth that is the subject of great local interest: *Stella's performance in the opera is the talk of the town—everyone thinks she was fantastic!*

***talk*** **shop** discuss matters concerned with your trade or profession at a time when more general conversation would be more suitable: *Are you two talking shop again? I'd have thought you had enough of farming during the day without talking about it during the evening as well!*

***talk*** **the hind legs off a donkey** *(informal)* be able to talk endlessly: *He would obviously make a good politician—he can talk the hind legs off a donkey!*

***talk*** **the same language** → ***speak*****/talk the same language**

***talk*** **through one's hat** *(informal)* talk nonsense: *He must be talking through his hat! I don't believe a word of what he's said!*

***talk*** **through the back of one's head/neck** *(informal)* talk nonsense: *'Why don't you try discussing it with her?' 'You're talking through the back of your head—you know she won't listen to me.'*

***talk*** **to sb** → ***speak*****/talk to sb**

***talk*** **to a brick wall** *(informal)* speak but gain no response from your intended audience: *I might as well be talking to a brick wall: are you listening to me?*

***talk*** **turkey** discuss sth frankly and seriously: *Let's talk turkey, and the matter will soon be settled.*

***tall*****/great/big oaks from little acorns grow** *(saying)* everything has to have a small beginning, and then it may grow to be very big: *'He set up a business many years ago in just one little shop in London. Now he's got lots of shops all over the country.' 'Tall oaks from little acorns grow!'*

**a** ***tall*** **order** sth asked or expected that is very difficult to do or provide: *Finishing my thesis by April is certainly a tall order, but I'll do my best.*

**a** ***tall*** **story/tale** an account of events that seems unlikely: *I don't believe what he said for a moment—it sounds a pretty tall story to me.*

***tan*** **sb's hide** *(informal)* beat sb soundly: *If you come into our garden again to take apples from the tree, I'll tan your hide!*

**go off at a** ***tangent*** → ***go***

**on** ***tap*** ready for use: *I've got plenty of people on tap to help when we need them*

**have got sb/sth** ***taped*** → ***have***

**be** ***tarred*** **with the same brush** have the same faults (as sb else or as each other): *As far as I am concerned every lecturer is lazy—they're all tarred with the same brush.*

***tart*** **oneself/sb/sth up** *(informal)* make yourself/sb/sth attractive, especially in a tasteless, showy way: *She tarted herself up to meet her new boyfriend.* / *The house was far nicer before it was all tarted up—I think the decorations are very vulgar.*

**a** ***taste*** **of one's own medicine** → **a** ***dose*****/taste of one's own medicine**

**not for all the** ***tea*** **in China** *(informal)* not (do sth) no matter how great the reward is: *I'm not going back to that house. The neighbours are so rude and nasty I wouln't live there again for all the tea in China.* Also **not for the world:** *The ice-skating was fantastic! I wouldn't have missed it for the world.*

***teach*** **sb a lesson** or **teach sb to do sth** make plain to sb, especially by means of punishment or an unpleasant experience, that he has done sth wrong: *So you were sick after eating all Pat's chocolates, were you? That will teach you a lesson (or not to take things that aren't yours)!*

**you can't *teach* an old dog new tricks** ⟶ ***you***

***teach* one's grandmother to suck eggs** *(informal)* tell or show sb how to do sth that he can do very well already: *I don't want to teach my grandmother to suck eggs, but may I make a suggestion?*

***tear* a strip off sb/sth** or **tear strips off sb/sth** *(informal)* criticize sb/sth; scold sb: *Poor Anne was late again, and the teacher really tore a strip off her when she came in.* Also **tear sb off a strip.**

***tear* sb/sth apart 1** cause sb to suffer great pain or sorrow: *The fight between what was right and what she wanted to do almost tore her apart.* **2** ⟶ ***pull*/take/tear sb/sth apart**

***tear* oneself away from sth** *(informal)* leave or stop doing sth unwillingly: *I found the book so fascinating that it was difficult to tear myself away from it!*

***tear* one's hair out** *(informal)* be very worried, anxious, or exasperated: *Why were you so late? We were tearing our hair out wondering where you were!*

***tear* into sb/sth** attack sb/sth violently, either physically or with words: *The dog was starving so really tore into the meat that was offered.*

***tear* sth off** write or draw sth very rapidly: *He tore off a quick letter to his family while waiting in the airport lounge.*

***tear* sb/sth to bits/pieces/shreds** ⟶ ***pull*/take/tear sb/sth apart**

**to a *tee*** ⟶ **to a *T*/tee**

**armed to the *teeth* (with sth)** ⟶ ***armed***

**kick sb in the *teeth*** ⟶ ***kick***

**lie through one's *teeth*** ⟶ ***lie***

**take/get the bit between one's/the *teeth*** ⟶ ***take***

**in the *teeth* of sth** fighting against sth: *We'd be quicker trying a zig-zag course than rowing in the teeth of this wind.*

**set sb's *teeth* on edge** ⟶ ***set***

**'*teething* troubles** difficulties and setbacks when new: *If a new car is having teething troubles, then your local garage can usually put everything right.*

**can't *tell*** ⟶ **can't *say*/tell**

**can *tell* a mile off** ⟶ **can *see*/tell a mile off**

***tell* it how/like it is** *(slang)* describe sth in exact detail and with complete honesty: *Tell it like it is, Rachel. We want to know all the facts, however unpleasant they are.*

***tell* sb off (for (doing) sth)** scold or reprimand sb (for doing sth wrong): *The boss told the workers off for their careless work.*

***tell* on sb** (especially among children) report sb for sth he has done wrong: *Please don't tell on me! I'll never do it again!*

***tell* on sb/sth** have a bad effect or put a strain on the health of sb or condition of sth: *The long hours and heavy responsibilities of his job are beginning to tell on him.*

**can't *tell* one end of sth from the other** ⟶ **not *know* one end of sth from the other**

***tell* tales** *(informal)* spread information about sb's secrets, faults etc: *Someone had been telling tales! How else could he have known that I helped her to get the job?* **telltale** *n* sb who tells tales; *adj* revealing sth such as sb's thoughts or activities.

***tell* tales out of school** *(informal)* talk about private matters in places or to people that are outside a certain group or profession.

**(you can) *tell* that to the marines** *(old-fashioned)* I don't believe it: *Police at the entrance to the football ground saw Jones trying to hide something under his jersey. One officer stopped him and he produced a wooden club, claiming it was to protect himself. 'You can tell that to the marines!' the policeman replied.*

**live to *tell* the tale** ⟶ ***live***

***tell* the truth and shame the devil** *(saying)* tell the truth, especially where there seem to be good reasons or strong temptations not to do so.

***tell* sb where to get off** *(slang)* criticize or rebuke sb very strongly, especially when you can no longer tolerate his behaviour: *I'm tired of him boasting! It's time someone told him where to get off.*

**to *tell* you the truth** speaking frankly and honestly: *'Does it hurt?' 'To tell you the truth, it's very painful.'*

**there is no *telling* . . .** ⟶ **there is *no* knowing/saying/telling**

**you're *telling* me!** ⟶ ***you* can say 'that again!**

***tempt* fate/providence** do sth that is thought likely to bring bad luck.

**be *ten*/two a penny** *(informal)* be numerous and easily obtainable; not be very valuable: *You'd think that with so many people unemployed, good secretaries would be ten a penny, but no.*

***ten* to one** very probably: *The clouds look very dark. Ten to one it'll rain!*

**stand the *test* of time** ⟶ ***stand***

***test* the water** try to discover whether sth is likely to succeed, by asking a few people for their opinions or by trying to sell a few examples of a new product: *Your idea might offend some people, so I should test the water, if I were you, before you go ahead with it.*

**set the *Thames* on fire** ⟶ ***set***

**have only (got) oneself to blame/*thank*** ⟶ ***have***

***thank* goodness/God/heaven(s)** (an expression of thankfulness or relief): *'It's only her leg that's hurt.' 'Thank goodness for that.'* Also **thank the Lord.** Note that the idioms with *God* or *the Lord* are avoided by some speakers as they are thought to show a lack of respect towards God.

***thank* one's lucky stars** *(informal)* be specially or unexpectedly fortunate: *You can thank your lucky stars you've got a home to live in, even if it is rather plain. Millions of people in this world haven't even got a room of their own!*

**be *thankful* for small mercies** be grateful

for minor benefits or encouragements, which, though not good, could be worse: *I suppose we ought to be thankful for small mercies. A 2% increase in the money we receive may be less than the rate of inflation, but it's better than having our grant cut altogether.*

***thanks* to sb/sth** because of the good or bad influence or actions of sb/sth: *A week ago I didn't know anything about computers, but thanks to the book you lent me, I'm beginning to understand the subject. / Thanks to the traffic jam on the way to the airport, I missed my plane.*

**in '*that* case** since that is so; if that were so: *'I've eaten enough. I don't want the pear.' 'In that case, I'll have it myself.' / 'Perhaps they changed their minds about coming?' 'They should have let me know in that case.'*

***that* (all) depends** —> **it/that all *depends***

***that* 'does it** *(informal)* **1** some task is now finished: *He put the meat into the casserole, added onion, carrots, and potatoes, covered it all with water and put the dish into the oven. 'There, that does it—a good stew for me!'* **2** that is the limit of my patience: *That does it! I can't take any more of your cheek! I'm leaving!*

**(not) (all) *that* good, easy etc** (not) so very good etc: *Life really isn't all that easy for us just now. / Is the job that good that you don't mind the poor salary?*

***that* is (to say)** (used to clarify or explain further what has just been said): *He was happy until this evening, that is, until he discovered a note from his wife saying that she'd left him.*

***that*'ll be the day** *(informal)* that will really be an important day when it happens (used to show that you do not really believe that sth will happen): *'When I'm rich, I'll buy you a new car.' 'That'll be the day!'*

**and *that*'s a fact** *(informal)* what has just been mentioned really is true, even if it is extraordinary or unbelievable: *I don't know who he is or where he came from, and that's a fact!*

***that*'s about 'it** *(informal)* that is virtually everything: *That's about it, then. I think we've discussed everything; all we've got to do now is to decide the date of our next meeting.*

***that*'s all 'I can say** *(informal)* this is my opinion; this is my most suitable comment, whether you like it or not: *'This is just an average day for us.' 'Then I wouldn't like to be here on a busy one, that's all I can say!'*

***that*'s all right** —> **that's/it's *all* right**

***that*'s as (it) 'may be** —> ***be* that as it may**

***that*'s done/torn it!** *(informal)* (of a misfortune, accident, or mistake) that has spoiled sth or made a plan useless!: *'I hear she's resigned as chairwoman!' 'That's torn it now—we really needed her to give us a good lead in the year ahead!'*

**and '*that's* 'flat!** *(informal)* that is my final decision (used to emphasize usually a negative statement such as a refusal): *I'm not going out with you, and that's flat!*

**(and) '*that*'s for sure** you can be certain of that: *Well, now he's got his money, you'll never see him again, that's for sure!*

***that*'s life** *(informal)* that is the kind of thing that often happens or that you have to learn to accept: *It's a pity that Rachel and Mike got divorced, but then that's life.*

***that*'s rich** *(informal)* that is amusing or ridiculous: *He told you the best way to get there? That's rich—he's never been there in his life!*

**(and) *that*'s that** sth is over and finally decided, arranged etc: *We'd planned to go on a luxury holiday in Spain, but now Steve's been made redundant we can't go, and that's that!*

***that* will do** that is enough (used as an instruction that sth should stop; often as a command to stop behaving in some way): *'That will do, you two! How many more times do I have to tell you not to do that?' said Jackie irritatedly to the children. / That will do—I don't think it needs another coat of paint.*

**it/*that* will never/won't do** *(informal)* (a comment on an unsatisfactory situation that needs to be improved; often used to show sympathy): *You say you've not got a suit to go to your brother's wedding in? That will never do!—I'll go out and buy one for you now!*

***them* and us** the upper or ruling classes, bureaucrats, employers etc, contrasted with ordinary working people, (often used to imply mistrust or resentment of the first group).

***there* and then** at the first opportunity: *I had to see him urgently and eventually found him in the canteen so spoke to him there and then.* Also **then and there.**

**(*there* are) no flies on sb** —> ***no***

***there* are plenty more (good) fish in the sea** or **there are plenty of other (good) fish in the sea** —> ***plenty***

***there* is more to sb than that etc** the description, reasons etc given do not give a complete or adequate account of sb: *There's more to Jane than just good looks, you know.*

***there* is something to be said for sth** there are reasons to recommend or approve of sth: *Yes, now that I've thought about it, I'm sure there's something to be said for Peter's point of view. / There is still much to be said for the old-fashioned exercise of walking.*

***there* is/lies the rub** —> ***rub***

**(but) *there* it is** that is the position; those are the facts (often used to show resigned acceptance of a situation that you do not like and that you would change if you could): *I don't like my job—it's the same dull routine day after day, but it does give me some money, so there it is.* Also **(but) there we/you are.** See also ***there* you are!**

***there*'ll be the 'devil to pay** or **there'll be 'hell to pay** *(informal)* you'll have to face trouble, blame etc as a result of some action:

*There'll be the devil to pay if they find out where the money's gone to.*

***there's* none so blind/deaf as those who will not see/hear** *(saying)* people will not see/hear what they are stubbornly determined to avoid seeing/hearing.

***there* you are!** *(informal)* (used to show that you are right and sb else is wrong or to mark the successful completion of a task): *There you are! I told you he'd refuse to come with you.* See also **(but) *there* it is.**

**(and/but) *thereby* hangs a tale** there is a story connected with or illustrating sth just mentioned that is unusually surprising or interesting.

***thick* and fast** in large numbers or great quantity: *Replies to the advertisement are now pouring in thick and fast. / By midnight on Christmas Eve, snow was falling thick and fast.*

**through *thick* and thin** through good times and bad times; persistently, loyally etc: *I promise to stay with you always, through thick and thin.*

**as *thick* as thieves** spending a lot of time in each other's company and having the same interests: *I've never met such a close family before; they're all as thick as thieves!*

**as *thick* as two short planks** *(informal)* very stupid: *It's hopeless trying to explain anything to him—he'll never understand it; he's as thick as two short planks!*

**a *thick* head** *(informal)* an aching head; brain that is dulled or confused by alcohol, drugs, a blow etc: *It's the morning after the college reunion and a lot of people have got thick heads.*

**get sth into one's *(thick)* head ⟶ *get***

**in the *thick* of it** or **in the thick of (doing) sth** in the busiest, most active, intense etc. part of sth such as a task or fight: *They were in the thick of checking all the material for the book so I didn't disturb them.*

***thick* on the ground ⟶ *thin*/thick on the ground**

**a *thick*/thin skin** little/great sensitivity towards criticism, reproach etc: *As a manager you have to learn to grow a thick skin and not let people's insults affect you.* **thick-/thin-skinned** *adj.*

***thick* with sb/sth** full of sb/sth: *The air was thick with rumours of redundancies after the government announced its economies.*

**blood is *thicker* than water ⟶ *blood***

**like a *thief* in the night** unexpected(ly) and not observed.

**out of *thin* air** or **into thin air** from/to nowhere: *Ideas for new products don't just come from out of thin air, you know. You have to sit down and work at them! / Where can I have put that key? It can't just have disappeared into thin air!*

**as *thin* as a rake** very thin: *He was as thin as a rake in spite of his enormous appetite.*

**the ˌ*thin* end of the ˈwedge** an apparently small event that develops into something widespread and significant: *This man is just the thin end of the wedge—there are thousands who will want to leave if he gets permission.*

**(be/skate) on *thin* ice** (be in) a difficult, risky, or uncertain situation: *You're skating on thin ice when you say it's often cheaper to photocopy a friend's book than to buy one. What does the law say?*

***thin*/thick on the ground** few/numerous; sparse/dense: *Jobs in publishing are very thin on the ground at the moment.*

***thin* on top** with little hair on your head; becoming bald: *Max is only 30 but he's already getting a bit thin on top.*

**a *thin* skin ⟶ a *thick*/thin skin**

**a *thin* time** a period of poverty, poor health etc: *The small independent shops have had a thin time in recent years.*

**have (got) a *thing* about sb/sth ⟶ *have***

**ˌone *thing* and aˈnother ⟶ *one***

**one *thing* leads to another ⟶ *one***

**a *thing* of the past** sth that is old-fashioned: *Are qualities like modesty and humility things of the past?*

**a ˈ*thing* or two** much that is useful, interesting, or important: *He thinks he knows a lot about carpentry, but I'm sure I could teach him a thing or two.*

**not have (got) a stitch/*thing* to wear ⟶ *have***

**these *things* are sent to try us** *(saying)* difficulties are intended (by God) to test our patience, courage etc.

***things* that go bump in the night** *(humorous)* strange or supernatural noises or events.

**give sb something to *think* about** or **have something to think about ⟶ *give***

***think* again** reconsider sth, with a view to changing your opinion and action: *The unions hope that the Prime Minister will think again about her decision to close the factory.*

***think* aloud** speak what you are thinking: *Let me think aloud for a moment—if we reduce the size of the book, then the cost of paper should be less.* Also **think out loud.**

**not *think* anything ˈof sth** think that sth is not important: *Now you come to mention it, I did see someone going into the Pershores' house, but I didn't think anything of it.* Also **think nothing ˈof sth.**

***think* better of sth** reconsider a possible action and decide not to do it: *He was about to say something, then thought better of it and kept quiet.*

**who does sb *think* he is? ⟶ *who***

***think* nothing ˈof sth ⟶ not *think* anything ˈof sth**

***think* nothing of (doing) sth** not consider (doing) sth to be unusual or special in some way: *He thinks nothing of exercising for an hour before breakfast every day.*

***think* nothing of it!** (said as a polite reassurance to sb who thinks he has been rude or as a response to an expression of thanks): *'I really am very sorry for forgetting your wife's name just now.' 'Oh, think nothing of it—it happens to all of us!' / 'Thank you very much for all* *your efforts in helping me find this book!' 'Oh, that's quite all right! Think nothing of it!'*

**not *think* of (doing) sth** refuse to consider or accept (doing sth): *'Will you let me pay for the meal?' 'I wouldn't think of it!'*

**a '*think* tank** a group of people who give advice to a government on matters such as policy and management.

**to *think* that . . .** how surprising, exciting, sad etc it is to think that (sth happened): *I can still hardly believe it! To think that the President actually stayed at my hotel!*

***think* the world of sb/sth** have a very high opinion of sb/sth: *The young people in the youth club think the world of the club leaders.*

**(*think*) the world owes one a living** ⟶ ***world***

**(not) *think* twice about doing sth** (not) pause for reflection before doing sth: *If they offered me a job, I wouldn't think twice about accepting it!*

**put one's '*thinking* cap on** ⟶ ***put***

**the *third* degree** long and intensive interrogation, possibly including torture, to make sb reveal information or confess. **third-degree** *adj.*

***third* time lucky** *(saying)* the third attempt to do sth is or will be successful.

**the *Third* World** the countries of Africa, Asia, and South America, especially when thought of as developing and not aligned with either the East or the West.

***this* and/or that** a number of different activities, subjects etc: *'What are you doing these days, Mary?' 'Oh this and that—all sorts of things. I keep myself busy, you know.'* Also **this, that, and the other.**

**to *this* day** up to and including this present time from the time when sth happened: *To this day we don't know what really happened to old Grandpa Hopcraft. Some of the family think he died because he drank too much—others think something more sinister took place the night he was found dead.*

**in *this* day and age** nowadays (often used when giving an opinion about modern conditions, beliefs, or behaviour): *Who'd ever work 40 hours a week for that amount of money in this day and age?*

**(on) *this* side of the grave** in this world; in your lifetime: *Learning is a continuous process that goes on all the time this side of the grave.*

**a *thorn* in the flesh** sb/sth that annoys another person or group or weakens their well-being, health, or authority: *Unprofitable coal mines are a thorn in the flesh for the National Coal Board at the moment.*

***those* were the days** that was a pleasant, exciting etc time to be alive: *'They bought the house for £600 in 1930.' 'Ah, those were the days!'*

**it's the '*thought* that counts** *(saying)* the affection, goodwill etc that lie behind an action or gift are more important than the action or gift itself.

**a *thousand* and one** ⟶ ***a hundred*/thousand/million and one**

**hang by a *thread*** ⟶ ***hang***

**pick/gather up the *threads*** ⟶ ***pick***

***three* bags 'full, sir!** *(humorous)* (an expression used when you do sth that sb has rather unreasonably demanded of you): *'Could you get my newspaper off the desk, please?' Max asked his wife. 'Yes, sir, three bags full, sir! Is there anything else you want me to do?'*

***three* cheers (for sb/sth)** (an expression of approval of sb/sth; a cheer-leader calls out 'Hip, hip,' and everyone shouts, 'Hurray'; this all happens three times): *At the end of the game, the captain of the winning side called out, 'Three cheers for United—hip, hip, hurray; hip, hip, hurray; hip, hip, hurray!'*

**the *three* Rs** reading, writing, and arithmetic, considered as the first essentials in education: *Many teachers are now beginning to go back to traditional patterns of teaching, concentrating on the three Rs in the early years at school.*

***thrilled* to bits** *(informal)* very excited and delighted: *We're thrilled to bits that you two are getting married!*

**have (got) a lump in one's *throat*** ⟶ ***have***

**ram/force/thrust sth down sb's *throat*** ⟶ ***ram***

**(be) at each other's *throats*** or **(be) at one another's throats** fighting or quarrelling fiercely with each other: *Within months of their marriage, Sue and Rodney were at one another's throats.*

**the power behind the *throne*** ⟶ ***power***

***through* and through** completely; in every detail: *I've only known her for a few days but I feel I know her through and through.*

***throw* a fit** have a fit; become very excited or angry: *Karen hasn't thrown a fit for years now; I think she's cured. / Your father will throw a fit when he sees you've broken another window!*

***throw*/give a party (for sb/sth)** arrange a party (for sb/sth): *Her parents threw a party to celebrate her engagement.*

***throw* a 'spanner in the works** *(informal)* spoil sth or prevent the success of sth by making a damaging suggestion or demand: *Everything had been well organized for the holiday until Terry threw a spanner in the works by saying he wouldn't come unless he could bring his girl-friend.*

***throw* a veil over sth** ⟶ ***draw*/throw/cast a veil over sth**

***throw* caution/discretion to the winds** act very boldly: *You must decide whether to support this project with your money. I'd throw caution to the winds, if I were you, and back it.*

***throw* cold water on sth** ⟶ ***pour*/throw cold water on sth**

***throw* down the gauntlet** issue a challenge; invite a fight, defence etc: *The government have thrown down the gauntlet to the unions to see if they will act responsibly in their wage demands.*

***throw* good money after bad** spend more money while trying (and failing) to recover money already lost: *The government can't just keep pouring money into all these industries that will never make a profit; it's throwing good money after bad.*

***throw* one's 'hand in** give up any attempt: *After failing to be a successful dancer she threw her hand in and went back to teaching.*

***throw* one's 'hat into the ring** *(informal)* declare your intention to take part in a competition, especially an election: *With two candidates standing for election, the result seemed certain, but when a third threw his hat into the ring, everything became unclear.*

***throw* sb in at the deep end** *(informal)* introduce sb to the most difficult part of an acitivity, especially one for which he is not prepared: *On the first day of her new job, Sue was thrown in at the deep end by having to do all the director's correspondence as the regular secretary was ill.*

***throw*/fling sth in sb's face/teeth** reproach and humiliate sb by reminding him (again or often) of sth, especially a fault or past wrong or foolish action: *After twenty years of respectable living Sybil's past was suddenly thrown in her face.*

***throw*/cast in one's lot with sb** *(formal)* become a partner, associate etc of sb or a group to share their fortunes in life, work etc: *He left his old firm to throw in his lot with a new company.*

***throw* in the towel** (in boxing) admit defeat; give up any attempt to do sth: *It's a bit early to throw in the towel—you've only just started work on the project!* Also **throw up the sponge.**

***throw* oneself into (doing) sth** involve yourself enthusiastically in (doing) a task: *They really threw themselves into the project to extend the club buildings, and within 18 months they had a new hall!*

***throw*/cast/shed light (up)on sth** make sth clearer, by giving new information; explain: *His new book throws new light on the events in the battle.*

***throw* mud at sb/sth** → ***sling*/fling/throw mud at sb/sth**

***throw* sb off his balance** confuse, shock, or surprise sb: *'I need a little time to answer you,' the speaker replied, and you could see that the question had thrown him off his balance.*

***throw* sb off the scent/track/trail** to do sth that prevents sb from following you: *The police believed the man's description, and it threw them off the track for a while.*

***throw* oneself on sb's mercy** rely entirely upon sb's kindness; beg for lenient treatment: *Patrick was clearly guilty; all he could do was throw himself on the mercy of the court.*

***throw* sb/sth overboard** reject or discard sb/sth: *Michael threw all his hesitation overboard and decided to ask Ruby to marry him.*

***throw*/knock sb sideways** shock or confuse sb: *He was really thrown sideways when he heard he'd lost the vote; everyone thought he'd win easily.*

***throw* the baby out with the bathwater** *(informal)* lose sth essential or valuable when getting rid of sth undesirable: *There are some good points to nuclear power, and if we were to reject it all because of its disadvantages, we'd be throwing the baby out with the bathwater.*

***throw* the book (of rules) at sb** *(informal)* remind sb strongly of the correct way of doing sth: *I know I'm throwing the book of rules at you but if you want to spend more than the allowed sum you have to get my permission.*

***throw* up** vomit; be sick: *He got very drunk and spent the whole night throwing up.*

***throw* up one's hands/arms in horror, despair etc** show or express great horror etc: *When I told my neighbours we were going to live in the jungle, they threw up their hands in horror!*

***throw* up the sponge** → ***throw* in the towel**

***throw* one's weight about/around** behave in an arrogant, authoritative way, so that others are made to feel unimportant: *Ever since he was put in charge of a bigger group of workers he's been throwing his weight around, so it's not surprising he's lost most of his old friends.*

***thrust* sth down sb's throat** → ***ram*/force/thrust sth down sb's throat**

**be under sb's *thumb*** *(informal)* be under the control of sb or at the mercy of sb: *The head of department really has all the lecturers under his thumb.*

**a *thumbnail* sketch/portrait (of sb/sth)** a brief, concise description (of sb/sth) in words.

**on *tick*** *(informal)* delaying (full) payment for some small item until a later time, with no formal agreement: *She's very understanding: if I've not got any money in the middle of the week she always lets me have a few groceries on tick till I get paid on Friday.*

***tick* sb off** reprimand sb: *The teacher ticked the boy off for being late again.*

***tick* over** live or work at a steady rate with nothing unexpected or very important happening: *Now it's summer, things are just ticking over at the office. It's not until the autumn that our major work begins.*

***tickle* sb's fancy** → ***catch*/take sb's fancy**

***tickle* sb's ribs** *(informal)* amuse sb: *We've a host of comedy acts lined up for tonight's show, ladies and gentlemen, and they'll all tickle your ribs!* **rib-tickler** *n* a joke.

***tickled* pink** *(informal)* very pleased or flattered: *I know it's a long way, but we'd both be tickled pink if you could make the journey to come to our wedding.*

**swim against/with the *tide*** → ***swim***

***tide* sb over** help sb to live through a difficult period: *A loan of £500 would tide me over nicely till June.*

**the *tide* turns** the course of events or the trend of opinions or feelings is changing, especially for the better: *At last the tide seems* *to be turning in our favour; I think we now have a chance of winning.*

***tie*** **sb hand and foot (to sb/sth)** ⟶ ***bind*****/tie sb hand and foot (to sb/sth)**

***tie*** **sb's hands** restrict the power, authority, or activities of sb: *Police fear that the new bill on citizens' rights will tie their hands. / I'm sorry I can't do anything about it; my hands are tied.*

***tie*** **sb/oneself (up) in knots** confuse sb greatly: *He tied himself up (*or *He got tied up) in knots trying to explain why he had lipstick on his face.*

***tie*** **sb up** keep sb busy or occupied: *Can you ring back later? I'm a bit tied up at the moment. / Finishing this work will tie me up till Friday.*

***tied*** **to his mother's/wife's 'apron strings** *(of a man or boy)* dependent on and controlled by his mother or wife: *Although he's over 30, he's still very much tied to his mother's apron strings.*

**in a *(tight)* corner/spot** an awkward or dangerous situation that is difficult to escape from: *We've always managed to get out of tight corners, Jim and I, in our service overseas.*

**keep a *tight*/loose rein on sb/sth** ⟶ ***keep***

***tighten*** **one's belt** *(informal)* not spend so much money; reduce your standard of living: *The Prime Minister has asked everyone to tighten their belts to help the country get out of the economic crisis.*

**on the *tiles*** *(informal)* enjoying yourself in a wild manner, dancing, drinking etc: *After the exams were over, all the students had a night on the tiles.*

**have (got) one's fingers in the *till*** ⟶ ***have***

**at/*till* all hours (of the night)** ⟶ ***all***

***till*****/until kingdom come** ⟶ ***kingdom***

***till*** **the cows come home** ⟶ ***cows***

***tilt*** **at windmills** attack imaginary enemies, thinking that they are real: *Arguing amongst themselves is tilting at windmills—we should be working to bring the government down.*

**at a *time*** in sequence; separately: *The children ate their ration of rice a few grains at a time to make it last longer.*

**at the *time*** then; when sth that is mentioned happened or happens: *I remember watching Neil Armstrong set foot onto the moon on television. I was only 6 at the time.*

**be high/about *time* (that . . . )** ⟶ ***high***

**born before one's *time*** ⟶ ***born***

**in *time*** **1** soon enough for a time, date, purpose that is mentioned: *He arrived in time to catch the bus.* **2** eventually: *All traces of the wound will disappear in time.*

**in sb's *time*** ⟶ **in sb's *day*/time**

**in ˌno *time* (at 'all)** ⟶ ***no***

**on *time*** punctually: *I'm pleased the books have arrived on time. If they'd have come after your lecture, they'd have been useless!*

***time*** **and (time) again** very often; repeatedly: *His theory has been disproved time and time again, but he still believes it.* Also **time after time.**

***time*** **and tide wait for 'no man** *(saying)* natural processes will continue whatever you do; it is important not to postpone a favourable opportunity while it is offered: *Gill saw some rare geese and wanted to take a photograph of them. 'The camera is at the bottom of the rucksack and the light will be better in the morning,' Mike told her. But when they came back the next day, the geese were no longer there. Time and tide wait for no man.*

**for the *time* being** ⟶ **for the *moment***

***time*** **flies** *(saying)* time seems to pass very quickly: *How time flies! I've got to go now. Thanks for a lovely afternoon!*

**there's a first *time* for everything** ⟶ ***first***

**there's a *time* (and a place) for everything** *(saying)* there are times, (places,) circumstances etc in which sth may be done, and others in which it should not.

***time*** **hangs heavy on one's hands** time seems to pass very slowly because you are bored, do not have enough to do etc. Also **time drags.**

**from/since *time* immemorial** from/since longer ago than anyone can remember; from an undated time of origin: *The furniture in this hotel looks so old that it must have been here since time immemorial!*

***time*** **is a great healer** *(saying)* pain, sorrow etc come to be less strongly felt as time passes. Also **time heals**: *When Sheila broke off our engagement, I felt awful for months but everyone around me said that time would heal, and it has.*

***time*** **is money** *(saying)* time is valuable; wasting it is like wasting money.

***time*** **is on the side of sb** the more that time passes, the more sb will be helped etc: *Time is on the side of the police in the siege at the embassy—the longer they wait, the more likely the terrorists are to surrender.*

**(there is) no *time* like the present** ⟶ ***no***

**pass the *time* of day** ⟶ ***pass***

**the *time* of one's life** a very enjoyable occasion such as a party or holiday: *We've just got a postcard from our parents on their world cruise. They're having the time of their lives!*

**from *time* to time** occasionally; irregularly: *I only drink alcohol from time to time.*

***time*** **'was when . . .** there once was a time when (sth happened, especially sth that does not still happen): *Time was when I could buy a box of chocolates for my wife and have some change from £1!*

***time*** **(alone) will tell** it is only in the future that you can be certain of sth: *Time alone will tell whether his decisions as Prime Minister were wise or not.*

**be behind the *times*** live, work etc in an old-fashioned way; not adapt to modern ideas: *Her teaching methods may be a bit behind the times, but her students are nevertheless successful.*

***times*** **change** *(saying)* the values and conditions of life change: *Times have changed. What people used to think was wrong—strong* *violence and things like that—is now shown quite often on television.*

**as *timid* as a mouse** very shy; lacking courage: *You can't expect Arthur to protect his own interests—he's as timid as a mouse.*

**put the *tin* lid on sth** → ***put***

**the patter of *tiny* feet** → ***patter***

**the *tip* of the iceberg** the small, visible, and often measurable part of sth known to be much greater: *The few people who are caught not paying their taxes are just the tip of the iceberg—many more get away with it.*

**on the *tip* of one's tongue** on the point of being remembered so that it can be said: *What's her name? You know, that short blonde girl—it's on the tip of my tongue: yes . . . Claudia, that's it!*

***tip* sb off** warn sb that sth will happen; tell the police that a crime is to be committed: *The Police had been tipped off about the robbery and so were at the bank to catch the gang.* **tip-off** *n*: *The newspaper office received a tip-off this morning that a bomb would explode outside the palace.*

***tip* the balance/scales** affect or finally settle a result, decision, or choice: *What really tipped the balance in favour of giving the job to Rodney was his experience. Apart from that, the two candidates seemed equally capable.*

***tit* for tat** a trick, injury etc as a response to one received: *Tom pushed Polly off her chair. Then she got up and gave him tit for tat by pushing him off his.*

**not a/one *tittle*** → **not a/one *jot*/tittle**

**on one's *tod*** *(informal)* alone; without other people present or helping: *If you won't come with me to the party, then I'll go on my tod.*

***toe* the line** conform to the regulations, conventions, or orders of the group to which you belong; do as sb expects or requires you to do: *The Prime Minister is angry because some members of his government are not toeing the line.*

**on one's *toes*** → ***keep* sb on his toes**

**tread/step on sb's *toes*** → ***tread***

**can't do sth for *toffee*** *(informal)* lack the natural or practical ability to do sth such as sing or draw: *Max is hopeless at sports. He can't play tennis for toffee!*

**take its *toll* (of sth)** → ***take***

**(every/any) *Tom*, Dick, and/or Harry** *(informal)* all different sorts of people; anyone at all (often implying that the people are ordinary and unsuitable): *The problem is that any Tom, Dick, or Harry can set up a company to give advice on legal matters—they don't have to have had special training.*

***tomorrow* is another day** *(saying)* there will be another opportunity to do sth: *Don't worry if you don't finish tonight—tomorrow's another day.*

**come down on sb like a *ton* of bricks** → ***come***

***tongue* in cheek** not meant to be taken seriously or literally; meant ironically: *The nuclear weapons store is very close to the town, and some of the residents, tongue in cheek, are calling their town the safest place on earth.* Also **with one's tongue in one's cheek.**

**(it's) *too* bad** → ***bad***

**not *(too)* bad** → **not (so/too) *bad***

***too* big for one's boots** too conceited; feeling that you are much better than other people: *Sue's really been getting too big for her boots since she became the Managing Director's secretary.*

**be *too* clever etc by half** *(informal)* be far too clever etc (used in a critical way of sb): *That lad is too clever by half! He tries to pretend he's ill whenever he doesn't want to go to school, but we know what he's up to!*

***too* close for comfort** so near that you become afraid or anxious: *Phew! That was a near miss! That lorry came a bit too close for comfort just then!*

***too* funny, sad etc for words** extremely funny etc: *The scene in the garden, when everyone had saucepans on their heads, was too funny for words!*

***too* good to be true** too favourable to be believed: *The news of Brian's recovery is just too good to be true. Only last week they said he'd have to stay in hospital for weeks.*

**not *too* hot** → **not *so*/too hot**

***too* hot to handle** *(informal)* too dangerous to tackle or become involved with: *The book deals with issues that people have fierce arguments about—matters that are often thought to be too hot to handle.*

***too* many cooks spoil the broth** *(saying)* a job will be mismanaged and the result will be unsatisfactory if too many people try to do it together.

**have (got) *(too)* many etc irons in the fire** → ***have***

***too* right/true!** unfortunately what has been described is true: *'There's too much sex and violence on television these days.' 'Too true!'*

**the *tools* of one's/the trade** the tools, implements, and other aids that are needed for or associated with a trade, profession, or other activity: *If you set up your own business, you'll have to spend quite a lot of money just on the tools of your trade.*

**long in the *tooth*** → ***long***

**fight sb/sth *tooth* and nail** → ***fight***

**come out on *top*** → ***come***

**(the) *top* brass** *(informal)* people of the highest rank, position, or authority: *The local top brass all attended the banquet for the new mayor.*

***top* dog** a person, group, country etc considered to be superior and to have advantages over others.

**(out of/from) the *top* drawer** (from or belonging to) the higher social classes or a professional, artistic etc elite: *Cicero was born of a long-established and wealthy family which, however, was not quite from the top drawer.* **top-drawer** *adj*: *a top-drawer dinner-party by candlelight.*

**off the *top* of one's head** *(informal)* without having time to think or prepare exactly or properly: *Off the top of my head I'd say it'll cost £100 to do the repairs.*

**on *top* of that/sth** additionally; besides: *He broke his arm and, on top of that, caught glandular fever.*

**the *top* of the tree/ladder** the highest position in your profession or job: *'Every apprentice has the chance to get to the top of the tree in this firm,' the managing director told the new employees on their first day at work.*

**(be/feel) on *top* of the world** (be) extremely happy: *The whole team felt on top of the world after winning first prize in the competition.*

**at the *top* of one's voice** extremely loudly: *'Look out!' she screamed at the top of her voice as the rocks came down the hillside.* Note that the plural is either ***at the top of their voices*** or, more usually, ***at the tops of their voices.***

***top* secret** (of information etc) extremely confidential, especially on an international, governmental, or military level: *Make sure no one else sees the defence plans—they're top secret!*

***top* the bill** be the most important performer in a theatre etc: *The Majestics will be playing tonight; Susie Saw will be singing, and topping the bill, we have the Crazy Ducks.*

**from *top* to bottom** in or throughout every part of sth: *The police searched the house from top to bottom, looking for drugs.*

**be *torn* between . . .** be divided in your feelings or mind between two conflicting aims, impulses, or emotions: *Poor Edith! She's torn between staying on at college for a further year to get higher qualifications and going out and getting a job now to earn some money.*

**that's *torn* it! ⟶ *that*'s done/torn it!**

***toss* a coin** decide by spinning a coin in the air sth such as who begins a sports game. Also **toss (up) (for) sth:** *We'll toss for who bats first.*

***toss* and turn** move restlessly from one side to the other on your bed: *I didn't sleep at all; I was tossing and turning the whole night thinking about today's exams.*

***toss* sth off** *(informal)* produce or create sth such as a poem or story very quickly and without much thought: *He was an experienced writer and could toss off a thousand-word article in half an hour.*

**keep/be in *touch*/contact (with sb) ⟶ *keep***

**lose *touch*/contact (with sb) ⟶ *lose***

***touch* and go** a situation in which death, disaster, or failure will only be narrowly avoided: *He was so badly injured it was touch and go whether he would survive or not.*

***touch* down** (of a plane, spacecraft etc) land; come back to the ground: *The Space Shuttle is due to touch down in an hour.* See also **take off.**

***touch* sb for a loan, £10 etc** *(slang)* borrow money from sb, especially when you do not intend to pay it back: *He's very careful with his money and not the sort of chap you could touch for a few pounds.*

**a *touch* of class** a superior quality: *I don't like these new office blocks—the large old-style buildings had a real touch of class. / He's got a touch of class all right—a real gentleman.*

***touch* on/upon sth** mention sth briefly: *Later in the lecture I'll touch on the causes of unemployment, but I want to spend most of the time talking about its effect.*

**touch sth off ⟶ *trigger*/touch sth off**

***touch* up sth** change the appearance or content of sth slightly by adding or removing small details: *I've almost finished the painting—it just needs to be touched up in one or two places.*

**not *touch* sb/sth with a barge-pole** *(informal)* feel a strong aversion to or dislike of sb/sth; refuse to have anything to do with sb /sth: *'I think she's trying to get off with you.' 'That scruffy little girl! I wouldn't touch her with a barge-pole!' / Six months ago Tony was telling me how wonderful it was to get married, and you were telling me not to touch a wedding-ring with a barge-pole.*

***touch* wood** (an expression that is said while touching sth made of wood in order to bring or continue good luck or to avoid bad luck): *We've had no serious illnesses or accidents in our family, touch wood.* US equivalent: **knock on wood.**

**as *tough* as leather** or **as tough as old boots** (of meat or other food) very difficult to chew and swallow; (of people) physically strong and able to bear difficulties or able to withstand criticism: *I wish I'd ordered chicken. This steak is as tough as leather. / She's as tough as old boots! Strong words of abuse don't affect her at all.*

**a '*tough* guy** *(informal)* a determined, ruthless, and unfeeling man difficult to oppose or persuade.

***tough* luck! ⟶ *bad*/hard/tough/luck!**

**a *tough* nut to crack ⟶ a *hard*/tough nut to crack**

**in *tow*** following behind; with you: *Mrs Durrbridge arrived at the playgroup with her four children in tow.*

**a *tower* of strength** sb who can always be depended on for support, practical ability, encouragement etc: *My neighbour Valerie was a real tower of strength to me in the first few months after my husband died.*

**a night on the *town* ⟶ *night***

**paint the *town* red ⟶ *paint***

***toy* with sth** consider sth, though not in a serious way: *Norman and Denise toyed with the idea of emigrating but decided not to.*

**sink, vanish etc without *trace* ⟶ *sink***

**kick over the *traces* ⟶ *kick***

**throw sb off the scent/*track*/trail ⟶ *throw***

**a '*track* record** *(informal)* sb's successes and failures in the past: *We want someone for this job who has a good track record in selling our sort of products.*

**make *tracks* (for sth)** ⟶ ***make***

**stop (sb) (dead) in his *tracks*** ⟶ ***stop***

***trade* on sth** use sth such as sb's kindness to gain an unfair advantage.

***trade* sth in** use sth to pay for sth else in part: *If you trade in your old gas cooker, the gas company will give you £20 off the price of a new one.* **trade-in** *n* the article traded in; the transaction itself; *adj*: *a trade-in price.*

**throw sb off the scent/track/*trail*** ⟶ ***throw***

***trail* one's coat** express your views in a way that is deliberately intended to produce argument, anger etc: *Perhaps I go too far, trailing my coat on purpose by being too offensive.*

***tread* a tightrope (between sth and sth)** ⟶ ***walk*/tread a tightrope between sth and sth**

***tread*/walk on air** be very happy: *When she got the letter offering her the job she was treading on air for the rest of the week.*

***tread*/step on sb's toes** *(informal)* behave without proper regard for other people's feelings: *I've only just started in this job and I don't want to tread on anyone's toes, but there must be more efficient ways of packing boxes than having three people do it.*

**. . . a *treat*** *(informal)* very well, successfully, effectively etc: *Your new dress suits you a treat! / The hot soup went down a treat.*

***treat* sb like (a piece of) dirt** behave towards sb as if he were completely unimportant: *I've got as much right to be there as anyone else, but they treat me like dirt.*

**by *trial* and error** by correcting your mistakes until you find the best method: *No one taught me how to cook, so I've had to learn by trial and error.*

***trials* and tribulations** many difficulties and hardships: *Life is rarely easy. Most of us at some time or other have to go through trials and tribulations.*

**in a *trice*** very quickly; in one short, swift movement, action, or decision: *In a trice, the gang had disappeared with all the jewels.*

**the *tricks* of the/one's trade** skilled and effective methods of doing sth developed within a trade or profession: *He's been a carpenter for over 20 years so he's learnt all the tricks of the trade.*

***trigger*/touch sth off** cause a strong action or reaction: *The arrival of the police triggered off further violence, the demonstrators claimed.*

***trip* sb up** cause sb to make a mistake or error: *Be careful—some of the interviewer's questions are designed to trip you up.*

**a *Trojan* horse** a disguised means of introducing sth harmful: *The new factory is to be run by robots—and so it could be a Trojan horse, destroying more jobs than it creates.*

**on the *trot*** **1** one after the other: *The bus has been punctual for five days on the trot! Is this a record?* **2** very busy and active: *I've been on the trot all day so I'm very tired.*

**no *trouble*, bother, problem etc** ⟶ ***no***

**a *trouble* shared is a trouble halved** *(saying)* if you talk with sb about your worries, they will seem less.

**fish in *troubled* waters** ⟶ ***fish***

**pour oil on *troubled* waters** ⟶ ***pour***

**carry all the *troubles* of the world on one's shoulders** ⟶ ***carry* the weight of the world on one's shoulders**

**catch sb with his pants/*trousers* down** ⟶ ***catch***

**so rich, ignorant etc it isn't *true*** *(informal)* extremely or unbelievably rich etc: *We've just got a new boss—he's so efficient it isn't true!*

***true* blue** uncompromising in principles, loyalties etc (often used to describe a supporter of the British Conservative Party): *The Prime Minister was sure of support, speaking to an audience of staunch, true-blue Tories.*

**show one's *(true)* colours** ⟶ ***show***

***true* to form** consistent with previous experience or practice or the character or nature of sb/sth: *The candidate's speech ran true to form—he spent most of the time criticizing the other parties' policies and only briefly mentioned his own party's solutions to the country's problems.*

**play one's *trump*/winning card** ⟶ ***play***

***trump* up sth** invent sth false such as evidence or a charge: *They say the authorities trumped up some charges to get the man convicted.*

**turn up *trumps*** ⟶ ***turn***

***trust* sb/sth to do sth** *(informal)* as expected, sb/sth has managed to do sth: *Trust Jack to come and help—he's a good chap! / Trust it to rain today!*

**tell the *truth* and shame the devil** ⟶ ***tell***

***truth* is stranger than fiction** *(saying)* the events of real life are more surprising than those imagined by writers.

**the *truth*, the whole truth, and nothing but the truth** (part of the statement made by sb before he gives evidence in a court of law); the absolute truth.

**(the) *truth* will 'out** *(saying)* the truth about an event or a situation cannot remain hidden for ever.

***try* anything once** be interested and open-minded enough to go through any experience or activity: *'Would you have eaten it if you'd known it was sheep's brains?' 'Why not—I'll try anything once!'*

***try* one's damnedest (to do sth)** or **try one's damnedest for sb** ⟶ ***do*/try one's damnedest (to do sth)**

***try* one's hand (at (doing) sth)** find out, by trying it, if you can do or like doing sth: *I've always wanted to try my hand at carpentry. I'll make something small to start with.*

***try* it on (with sb)** *(informal)* act in a bold or impudent way to see if your behaviour is accepted (by sb): *Stop trying it on! I won't take any notice of you!* **try-on** *n*: *I don't think he'll carry out his threat—it was just a try-on!*

***try* one's level best** ⟶ ***do*/try one's level best**

***try* one's luck** attempt to do or obtain sth, hoping that you will succeed: *At the sugges-*

*tion of my Uncle Michael I decided to try my luck as a window cleaner.*

**if at first you don't succeed, (*try*, try again)** ⟶ ***if***

***tuck* in** or **tuck into sth** eagerly start to eat a meal, snack etc: *The boys really tucked into their dinner after their long walk in the country.*

***tug* at sb's heartstrings** *(informal)* move sb's feelings deeply (often used ironically): *The story of all his problems really tugged at my heartstrings.*

**to the *tune* of £5000 etc** *(informal)* at the cost of a particular sum of money, especially a large sum: *The state coal industry receives subsidies from the government to the tune of £1 million per day.*

**in/out of *tune* with** in or not in agreement with: *The policeman's statement is clearly out of tune with the local police committee's policy.*

***turf* sb out** *(informal)* ask or force sb to leave a place or resign from a job: *The landlady will turf you out if you get drunk.*

**done to a *turn*** ⟶ ***done***

***turn* a blind eye (to sth)** pretend not to see sth: *The council agreed to stop turning a blind eye to illegal parking.*

***turn* a deaf ear to sth** pretend not to hear sth such as complaints; deliberately ignore sth: *In teaching you'll have to learn to turn a deaf ear to your children's constant questions at times.*

**not *turn* a hair** not show a strong emotion such as fear, dismay, or excitement in circumstances when such a reaction might be expected: *He didn't turn a hair as the judge sentenced him to 20 years' imprisonment.*

***turn* one's back on sb/sth** reject sb/sth; refuse to face a problem or have further contact with sb/sth: *Why do you always turn your back on difficulties just when you're needed? / His parents finally turned their backs on Tony when he didn't invite them to his wedding.*

***turn*/change one's coat** transfer your loyalty or commitment from one group, such as a country or political party, to another: *That's exactly like your head of department! He's the sort of person to turn his coat and join the other side just to suit his own purposes.* **turncoat** *n.*

***turn* sb/sth down** refuse sb who applies or sth such as an application or invitation: *There was only a limited number of vacancies, so most of the people interviewed had to be turned down. / The opportunity is too good for me to turn it down!*

**take a *turn* for the better/worse** ⟶ ***take***

***turn* in** go to bed: *It's getting late. I think I'll turn in now.*

***turn* in one's grave** *(informal)* (of sb who is dead) be likely to be offended or displeased: *Beethoven would turn in his grave if he knew that the melodies of his symphonies had reached the top twenty in the pop-music charts!*

***turn* sth inside out** search a place thoroughly: *I've turned my desk inside out, but I still can't find the right paper.*

**a *turn* of events** a change or development in circumstances, especially when this is not foreseen or is beyond your control: *A fortunate turn of events meant that he could be present on such an occasion.*

**a *turn* of phrase** a way of expressing, defining, or describing sth: *He's a very pleasant lecturer to listen to—he has quite an amusing turn of phrase, really.*

***turn* sb off** *(informal)* make sb lose interest; cause dislike or nausea: *The desire for money was the main value that the young people noticed in their parents, and it turned them right off.*

***turn* on sb** attack sb, physically or with words: *Even friendly dogs can turn on you if you tease them!*

***turn* on sth** *(formal)* depend on or be conditioned by sth; have sth as its main topic: *A true understanding of the text turns on the precise meaning of this one sentence. / The discussion constantly turned on the need to provide more money.*

***turn* sb on** *(informal)* excite or stimulate sb, especially sexually: *Short skirts really turn me on!*

***turn* sth on its head** ⟶ ***stand*/turn sth on its head**

***turn* on one's heel** leave suddenly: *Quite unexpectedly he turned on his heel and ran off.*

***turn* out 1** be present: *A crowd of 20,000 turned out to welcome the royal couple.* **turn-out:** *n*: *There was a very large turn-out.* **2** develop or progress in a particular way: *We need not have worried; everything turned out well in the end./We'll have to see how things turn out.*

***turn* out sth** (especially of a factory) produce or manufacture sth: *The factory turns out over 100 cars a day.*

***turn* sb out** dress sb smartly: *I admire the way she turns her kids out.* Note that this is often used in the passive: *She wanted to be well turned out whenever she was seen in public.*

***turn* out to be sb/sth** prove eventually to be sb/sth: *The beautifully dressed lady turned out to be the agent of a foreign power. / All the telephone calls turned out to be hoaxes.*

***turn* over a new leaf** improve your behaviour: *He turned over a new leaf after he left prison and has never been in trouble with the police since.*

***turn* sb's stomach** cause sb to be revolted or disgusted: *If you don't like violence, then don't watch 'Bloodbath' tonight—it'll really turn your stomach.*

***turn* tail** run away because of defeat, timidity, or fear: *As soon as the robbers saw the police, they turned tail and fled.*

***turn* the clock back** ⟶ ***put*/turn/set the clock back**

***turn* the corner** be successfully past a danger or a crucial point in an undertaking or your health or finances: *Most of the profits are* *swallowed up by the mortgage. Once we've got that paid off I'll feel we've turned the corner.*

***turn* the heat on sb** → ***put* the screws on sb**

***turn* the other cheek** not retaliate or complain when attacked, criticized, or punished (and be ready to accept further humiliation): *Jesus told his followers to turn the other cheek, but very few people are able to do this in practice.*

***turn* the tables (on sb)** gain an advantage (over sb) after having been at a disadvantage: *I'll turn the tables on you one day and punish you for all the wrongs you've done to my family.*

***turn* to** begin to work with great effort: *If we all turn to, we'll get the work finished by this evening.*

***turn* to sb** go to sb for help, advice, information etc: *I'm pleased I had one or two friends to turn to when I needed sympathy after my husband's death.*

**take a/one's *turn* to do sth** → ***take* (it in) turns to do sth**

***turn* turtle** (of a ship or boat) turn upside down.

***turn* up** *(informal)* (of people) appear or arrive, sometimes after a delay; (of things) be found, become available: *I'm sure Gill will turn up soon. She's not usually late. / His wallet eventually turned up—but all the money had been stolen.*

**a *turn*-up for the book(s)** *(informal)* sth that is very unexpected or unusual: *It's incredible! Everyone thought John would easily beat Ray in the election, but Ray won. That's a real turn-up for the book!*

***turn* up like a bad penny** appear unwantedly: *You can't get rid of Tom so easily; you always think he's got a job a long way away and then he turns up again like a bad penny.*

***turn* up one's nose (at sb/sth)** *(informal)* behave in a superior way (towards sb/sth); consider sb/sth to be not good enough: *There's no need to turn up your nose at simple plain home cooking, dear, after all your grand business lunches.*

***turn* up trumps** *(informal)* help sb, especially by being generous or reliable: *When I lost my job, I didn't think I could afford the holiday, but my parents turned up trumps at the last minute and paid for me to go.*

**sb's back is *turned*** → ***back***

**a '*turning* point** sth that marks the beginning of a new trend in sb's life, a course of events, a project etc: *The capture of the mountain ridge ranked as the turning point in the battle.*

**take (it in) *turns* to do sth** → ***take***

***twiddle* one's thumbs** do any unimportant thing just to pass time: *Don't think I've been sitting around twiddling my thumbs all day while you've been out at work! I've been very busy!*

**a *twinkle* in sb's eye 1** an eager or mischievous look on sb's face: *I could tell from the twinkle in his eye that he didn't mean what he said.* **2** a vague idea or plan: *We had dreams of you becoming a musician when you were just a twinkle in your father's eye* (= before you were born). / *At the moment the scheme is still only a twinkle in John's eye, so to speak, but I think it will work.*

**in the *twinkling* of an eye** instantaneously; very quickly: *Her mood can change in the twinkling of an eye.*

**round the *twist*** → **round the *bend*/twist**

***twist* sb's arm (to do sth)** *(informal)* persuade sb to do sth, but not by using physical force: *He has a lot of commitments at the moment, but I think I can twist his arm to write the article for us.*

***twist* sb (a)round one's little finger** *(informal)* persuade sb, especially a man, to do what you want, by means of charm or flattery: *He'll agree all right; she knows she can twist her dad round her little finger.*

**be *two* a penny** → **be *ten*/two a penny**

**have/get *two* bites at/of the cherry** → ***have***

**a game that *two* can play** → ***game***

**stand on one's own *(two)* feet** → ***stand***

***two* heads are better than one** *(saying)* two people who work together are likely to achieve a better result than one person on his own.

**in *two* minds (about sth)** unsure (about sth); not able to reach a decision about sth: *He was in two minds about whether to marry Ursula or not.*

**not have (got) *two* pennies to rub together** → ***have***

**for *two* pins** *(informal)* with very little persuasion or very slight provocation: *You just give me the chance! For two pins I'd be out of this house and never come back again.*

***two*'s company, three's a crowd** *(saying)* two people, especially a boyfriend and girlfriend, are happier on their own than with sb else.

**in *two* shakes (of a lamb's tail)** *(informal)* quickly and easily: *It's just a loose connection in the plug—I'll fix it for you in two shakes of a lamb's tail!*

**as thick as *two* short planks** → ***thick***

**as cross as *two* sticks** → ***cross***

**have (got) *two* 'strings to one's bow** → ***have* (got) a second 'string to one's bow**

**cut *two* ways** → ***cut* both/two ways**

**(there are) no *two* ways about it** → ***no***

***two* wrongs don't make a right** *(saying)* you cannot justify a wrong action by saying that sb else has done something similar or that sb has done sth wrong to you.

# U

***U/non-U*** (used to describe language and social habits thought to be upper class or non-upper class): *At one time it was thought U to say 'lavatory' and non-U to say 'toilet'.*

**as *ugly* as sin** exceptionally ugly: *The house itself is as ugly as sin, though it stands in a very pleasant setting.*

**an *ugly* customer** *(informal)* sb who is or might be dangerous, violent, or difficult to control or deal with: *He looks a real ugly customer! I think I'll stay clear of him!*

**an *ugly* duckling** a child, puppy etc who at first is less attractive, clever etc than other members of the family but who later surpasses them.

**rear/raise its *(ugly)* head** ⟶ ***rear***

***um* and aah** ⟶ ***hem*/hum and haw**

***unheard* of** unknown; without an example of in the past: *Today's instant international communication systems were unheard of a few years ago. / It's unheard of that a boy from his village should go to college!*

**an *unknown* quantity** sb/sth that you have no experience of, or whose actions etc cannot be predicted accurately: *We've planned everything for the garden party—it's just the weather that is an unknown quantity now.*

***until* kingdom come** ⟶ ***till*/until kingdom come**

***until* the cows come home** ⟶ **till/until the *cows* come home**

**an *unwritten* law** a long-established custom or tradition that is difficult to break or disobey: *There's no caretaker in the block of flats, and according to some unwritten law, whoever lives in the ground-floor flat is responsible for keeping the main front-door area clean and tidy.*

***up* (with) sb/sth!** (an exclamation of approval of sb/sth): *Up the workers!* See also ***down* with sb/sth!**

***up* and about** *(informal)* out of bed after sleeping or being ill: *I'm glad to see he's up and about again after his illness.*

***up* and coming** *(informal)* likely to increase in success, popularity etc: *The aim of the festival is to give an opportunity to up-and-coming music groups to perform in front of a large audience.*

***up* and doing** active or vigorously engaged in general or in a particular task or duty: *Strong feeling against the scheme isn't enough. You have to be up and doing—you need to arrange protest meetings and organize petitions to make any impact at all.*

***up* and down** (of sb's mood or spirits) good at time but bad at others: *Sarah's not been completely healthy for months—she's up and down all the time.*

***up* and down (sth)** across (a room etc); in one direction (on a street etc), then another: *Joe paced up and down the hospital waiting room, anxious for news of his wife in the operating theatre.*

***up* and leave, do sth etc** surprise or annoy sb by leaving etc: *We were having a pleasant discussion when suddenly John upped and left, without a word.*

**on the *up-and-up*** *(informal)* improving steadily: *It looks like his career's on the up-and-up—now his book has been published, he's been asked to work on a new television series on wildlife in different countries.*

***up* against sb/sth** strongly opposed or confronted by sb/sth: *Remember that you will be up against a more experienced player. / In selling their product, the company was up against fierce competition.*

***up* against it** faced with great difficulties: *It is when he is really up against it that a man's true quality shows.*

***up* in arms** ⟶ ***arms***

***up* to sb** sb's responsibility or duty: *It's up to the doctor to decide whether he goes into hospital or not. / Structural repairs are up to the landlord, surely?*

**feel/be *up* to (doing) sth** ⟶ ***feel***

***up* to sth** aware of and therefore more able to deal with sth such as sb's plans, tricks, or deceit: *After 20 years in the classroom I'm up to most of my pupils' dodges.*

**get/be *up* to sth** ⟶ ***get***

***up* to one's ears/eyeballs/eyes/neck in sth** ⟶ ***ears***

**not *up* to par** ⟶ **above/below *par***

***up* yours, his etc!** *(taboo)* (a rude expression telling sb to be quiet or go away).

**an *uphill* task, struggle etc** a difficult task etc, either in itself or because of opposition: *He never has much to say; sustaining a conversation of more than a few minutes with him is a real uphill struggle.*

**the *upper* crust** *(informal)* the aristocracy; people who think themselves or who are thought by others to be on a high social level.

**get/gain the *upper* hand** ⟶ ***get***

***ups* and downs** good, happy times, and also sad times of failure: *I suppose every marriage has its ups and downs.*

***upset* the apple-cart** *(informal)* do sth that spoils carefully made plans or steady progress: *The police have an arrangement with a local garage to tow away the cars, so they don't* *want anyone else doing that or it will upset the apple-cart.*

**quick/slow on the *uptake* →*quick***

**be no good/*use* (doing sth) →*no***

***use* one's head/loaf** *(slang)* think properly and sensibly: *Use your loaf! You can stack more bottles into that box if you put the top layer in upside down!*

**something/anything/nothing out of the *usual* →something/anything/nothing out of the *ordinary*/usual**

# V

**as *vain* as a peacock →as *proud*/vain as a peacock**

**(good/bad) *value* for money** (really or not really) worth the price paid: *That stereo system I bought eight years ago was good value for money—it's always worked very well.*

**a '*value* judgment** a personal opinion of the value, usefulness, significance etc of sb/sth, not based on any evidence or experience: *Lacking solid evidence, the court had to make a value judgment on what the law meant by 'reasonable' behaviour.*

***vanish* without trace →*sink*, vanish etc without trace**

***variety* is the spice of life** *(saying)* new or different things to do or experience make life more interesting.

**draw/throw/cast a *veil* over sth →*draw***

**in a 'lighter, 'different etc *vein*** in a less serious etc mood, manner, or style; dealing with less serious etc subject matter: *The evening took the form of a series of commendations to the retiring chairman. The new chairman gave a long, appreciative speech and there were several shorter tributes in a similar vein.*

**with a *vengeance*** *(informal)* to an extreme degree: *After a pause of a few months, terrorists have returned to the city's streets with a vengeance: six bombs exploded in three hours last night, killing a total of twelve people.*

**nothing *ventured*, nothing gained → *nothing***

***very* 'good, (sir/madam)** (a polite form of agreement, especially in accepting an order or request from an employer, customer etc): *'Please see that the car is ready to pick me up at eight o'clock!' 'Very good, sir!'*

**the *(very)* idea! →*idea***

**the *(very)* least one can do →*least***

***very* well** (an expression of acceptance or agreement, often unenthusiastic or reluctant): *'No, I won't let you pay for my fare! I insist—I'll pay.' 'Very well, then, if that's what you want, you can!'*

**a *vested* interest (in sth)** a right or privilege of a person or group, allowed in law; a deep personal concern for sth, especially one that leads to private gain: *Now I know why he wanted to delay the change-over from oil to gas; he's got a vested interest in oil as he's a director of the oil company!*

**a *vicious* circle/spiral** a situation in which an effect leads back to the original cause and makes the whole process continue: *Wage increases lead to higher prices which in turn lead to wage increases—it's a vicious circle.*

**in *view* of sth** because of sth; considering sth: *In view of the growing need for treatment in the new city, the council have decided to build another hospital.*

**with a *view* to (doing) sth** with the intention and hope of (doing) sth: *Attempts are being made to call a conference for beekeepers with a view to establishing an international association.*

**by *virtue* of sth** *(formal)* because of sth; by the influence of sth: *He said he deserved more pay by virtue of his long service.*

**one's '*voice* breaks 1** a boy's voice changes from the higher voice of a child to the lower voice of a man: *He used to sing in the cathedral choir until his voice broke.* **2** strong feeling prevents you from speaking evenly or without interruption: *I don't think I'll be able to give my farewell speech without my voice breaking.*

***vote* with one's feet** reject sth by leaving a place: *We don't want to repeat what happened at last year's conference, when, as you may remember, many members voted with their feet and the committee had to resign.*

# W

***wade* into sb/sth** *(informal)* start what you mean to do vigorously and without delay; fight, attack, or scold sb strongly: *This was no good-natured scrap such as boys often enjoy. The twins were really wading into each other!* Also **wade in:** *If I wade in as soon as I get to the office, I can usually deal with the day's mail by 10.30.*

***wade* through sth** read, study, search or examine a long, boring, or difficult book, set of papers or accounts etc: *Can't you tell me the main points? I haven't got the time to wade through a 40-page report on such a difficult subject.*

**on the *wagon*** *(informal)* not drinking any alcohol: *Once this holiday's over I'm going on* *the wagon for a few weeks to give my liver a chance to recover!*

**the tail *wags* the dog** → ***tail***

***waifs* and strays** homeless people, especially children in a big city; lost or abandoned cats and dogs.

**lie in *wait* (for sb/sth)** → ***lie***

***wait* and see** wait to find out what will happen or what sb else will do (before taking action or forming an opinion yourself): *'What are you getting for your birthday?' 'I don't know. I asked my Mum but she said "Wait and see." ' / 'They'll never eat all that!' 'Won't they? Just you wait and see!'*

**can't *wait* for sth** or **can't wait to do sth** *(informal)* long or be impatient for the time when you will have sth or be able to do sth: *John should be home quite soon. I can't wait to see his face when I tell him he's got the job!*

***wait* for it 1** *(informal)* don't do sth, move, or speak until the right moment has come: *'Wait for it!' Jack warned the eager boys as he held up the starting-pistol.* **2** *(informal)* (said in order to emphasize a pause before the most amusing or surprising part of a story, joke etc you are telling): *This young copper had just finished his Safety First talk to the children when, wait for it, he stepped right off the platform and broke his ankle!*

***wait* on sb hand and foot** do almost everything for sb, especially those things which he might well be able to do for himself: *In former times, men of all classes, however hard they worked, expected to be waited on hand and foot in their homes.*

***wait* one's turn** not try to do sth before other people who are entitled to do it first: *Here, you! You can't push in like that! Go to the back of the queue and wait your turn!*

***wait* up** → ***sit*/wait up**

**could *wake*/waken the dead** (of a sound) be very loud: *He must be awake—his alarm clock could wake the dead.* Also **be enough to wake/waken the dead:** *The noise of his motorbike is enough to wake the dead.*

***wake* (sb) up to sth** (cause sb to) realize or become aware of sth: *It took me a few weeks to wake up to the fact that somebody was fiddling the accounts.*

***wakey*, wakey!** *(informal)* wake up and get out of bed!

**(try to) run before one can *walk*** → ***run***

***walk*/tread a tightrope (between sth and sth)** try or hope to avoid disaster or failure in a situation where you can neither act freely nor afford to make a mistake: *Any hostage knows he is walking a tightrope between life and death.*

***walk* all over sb 1** *(informal)* thoroughly defeat sb in a competition: *We thought we'd sent out a strong team on the tour, but the other side walked all over us.* **walk-over** *n* an easy or decisive victory; sth easy (for sb) to do. **2** *(informal)* domineer over sb with no consideration for his opinions or wishes: *This is your chance to assert yourself, Bob. If you don't, Muriel will think she can walk all over you for the rest of your life.*

***walk* away with sth** win a competition, game, or prize decisively or easily: *In a home final, Liverpool walked away with the Cup, winning 6–0.* Also *(informal)* **waltz off with sth.**

***walk* (right/straight) into sth** not be careful enough to avoid a danger, trap, or trick or an unwelcome consequence of sth you do or say: *No scouts were sent ahead to check the route, and so all the soldiers just walked straight into the ambush.*

**a/sb's *walk* of life** a/sb's occupation and/or social position: *The students came from all walks of life, the children of earls and plumbers.*

***walk* sb off his feet** *(informal)* make sb walk so quickly that he is exhausted: *She may be over seventy, but I'm sure she could walk some of you younger ones off your feet.*

***walk* off with sth** deliberately steal, or accidentally take away, sth that does not belong to you: *Don't put your handbag on the floor beside you when eating in a restaurant. Somebody may walk off with it.*

***walk* on air** → ***tread*/walk on air**

***walk* out** (of workers) leave a place of work as a form of striking: *This morning thousands of employees at the car factory walked out as a protest at the management's decision to dismiss one man for drunkenness.* **walk-out** *n.*

***walk* out (of a meeting etc)** leave a meeting, conference etc as a form of protest or disapproval: *It was quite absurd to call the talks 'negotiations'! The other side wouldn't give way on anything, so we walked out.* **walk-out** *n.*

***walk* out (with sb)** → ***go* out (with sb)**

***walk* out on sb** *(informal)* leave or abandon sb who is depending on your help or co-operation: *'Why did Harry leave his first wife?' 'He didn't.* She *was the one who walked out on him.'*

***walk* tall** behave self-confidently, believing that your abilities, good character etc deserve respect: *You're as good as anybody else, so stop acting humbly and walk tall!*

***walk* the plank** go or be sent to death or destruction: *You might as well ask a man to walk the plank as drive in this fog!*

**a *walking* dictionary etc** *(informal)* sb who can perform the functions of sth such as a dictionary very well: *You should see all the tools and things he carries around with him—he's a walking hardware shop!*

**drive sb up the *wall*** → ***drive***

***wall*-to-wall carpets/carpeting etc** carpeting that covers the whole floor; sth in abundance; people or things in large numbers: *Talk about being rich—they've got wall-to-wall butlers!*

***walls* have ears** sb (in or near a building) may be listening: *'Tell me more.' 'Not just now. Walls have ears. Let's take a walk in the park.'*

**a *Walter* Mitty** a day-dreamer who imagines himself the hero in important, dangerous, or romantic situations: *He'd rather sit up in his room planning the future than make an effort to cope with the present. He's a real Walter Mitty.*

**what more could one ask/*want*?** ⟶ ***what***

***want* a hole in the head** ⟶ ***need*/want sth like one needs/wants a hole in the head**

***want* a thick ear** ⟶ ***give* sb a thick ear**

***want* sb's blood** or **be after sb's blood** want to kill sb; want revenge on or to punish sb; be extremely angry with sb: *There are people who are after the President's blood for personal as well as political reasons, so assassination is an ever-present threat.*

***want* for sb/sth** need or lack sb/sth: *We had to live very simply when we first started a family, but we were never so poor that we wanted for food. / Cheerful, unselfish people seldom want for friends.*

**not *want* for sb/sth** have plenty or too much/many of sb/sth: *Our journey turned out to be far more than a pleasure trip—we certainly didn't want for excitement!*

***want* sb's guts for garters** ⟶ ***have*/want sb's guts for garters**

***want* one's head examined/examining** ⟶ ***need*, want etc one's head examined/examining**

***want* it both ways** ⟶ ***have* it/things both ways**

***want* jam on it** *(informal)* want (for your own greater ease, pleasure or profit) sth in addition to what you are given or have a right to expect: *'Well, it's good of you to let me borrow your mower. When can you bring it over?' 'You want jam on it, don't you?' said his brother. 'Come and fetch it yourself!'*

***want* sth like (one wants) a hole in the head** ⟶ ***need*/want sth like (one needs/wants) a hole in the head**

**(it's) not for *want*/lack of trying, being told etc** (it is) not because you haven't tried, etc: *He's had no success in finding another job, though not for want of trying.*

***want* the moon** ⟶ ***cry*/ask for the moon**

**not *want* to know** deliberately avoid contact with or information about sb/sth that might upset, trouble, or inconvenience you: *When I grew up, neighbours were always willing to give help; nowadays if you're ill or in trouble, people just don't seem to want to know.*

**a *war* of nerves** a contest in which each of the opposing people, groups, or countries tries to frighten or exhaust the other by threats, harassment, strategies, or psychological pressures: *A war of nerves followed, conducted mainly by means of lawyers' letters, as neither tenant nor landlord felt sure of winning their case if actually brought to a court of law.*

***warm* the cockles (of sb's heart)** make sb feel pleased and happy: *The delightful story of how the sailor met his wife is enough to warm the cockles of your heart!*

***warm* to/towards sb/sth** take a liking to, or sympathetic interest in, sb/sth; become fond of sb/sth: *We met your brother Paul at a reception the other night. Such a nice young man! We warmed to him at once!*

***warm* to sth** become lively or active as you proceed with a task: *Once he warmed to his subject, the speaker lost his initial shyness and ended up holding his audience spellbound.*

***warm* up 1** (of machines, car engines etc) reach the point of functioning properly because the parts are warm and working smoothly: *I keep telling you not to leave the choke out once the engine has warmed up.* **2** exercise before taking part in a race, football match, etc: *There's a substitute warming up on the sidelines. I wonder whose place he's going to take.* **warm-up** *n.*

***warm* (sb) up** (cause sb to) become more lively, interested, or cheerful: *'This party's dragging a bit, isn't it?' 'Never mind, it'll warm up after the guests have had a few more drinks.'*

**(fire) a *(warning)* shot across the/sb's bows** ⟶ ***shot***

**on the *warpath*** *(informal)* preparing to show anger about sth: *The unions are on the warpath—they're getting ready for battle with the government following threatened redundancies among their members.*

**(have been) in the *wars*** *(informal)* (especially of children) (be) hurt as a result of fighting or quarrelling: *What happened, Martha? You look as if you've been in the wars!*

***warts* and all** mentioning all sb's/sth's faults: *This current affairs programme is renowned for its coverage of contemporary issues—it believes in presenting a complete picture of a topic—warts and all.*

**come out in the *wash*** ⟶ ***come***

**won't/wouldn't *wash* (with sb)** *(informal)* not be accepted as valid, reasonable, likely etc (by sb): *Such an excuse won't wash with me, young man! You just tell me what really happened!*

***wash* a meal down with sth** *(informal)* drink sth after or at the same time as eating a solid meal: *We ate roast chicken and washed it down with a fine French wine.*

***wash* (one's) dirty linen in public** *(informal)* talk or write publicly about errors, scandals etc that can or should be dealt with privately in the family or business circle where they occur: *The scandal was exposed, and in the trial, several leading politicians were forced to wash their dirty linen in public.*

***wash* one's hands of sb/sth** say or show that you no longer want to be involved with or responsible for sb/sth: *Now that I realize you intended to break the law to get that contract, I wash my hands of the whole affair. I don't want anything at all to do with it!*

***washed* out** *(informal)* very tired: *So, he had to stay up all night looking after his wife, did he? I thought he looked a bit washed out this morning.*

***waste* (one's) breath (on sb/sth)** speak (about sb/sth) but not have any effect: *The majority of delegates were quite content to be rushed through a busy agenda with a minimum of discussion. One felt that the real professionals there were wasting their breath. / He looked at me with hatred, but obviously decided not to waste his breath on me.*

***waste* no time (in doing sth)** → ***lose*/waste no time (in doing sth)**

***waste* not, want not** *(saying)* if you never waste anything, such as food or money, you're not likely to lack what you need: *My grandmother's motto was always 'Waste not, want not', and she never allowed anyone to leave the table without having eaten all the food up.*

***watch*/mind one's step** *(informal)* be careful how you act or speak in order to avoid danger, criticism etc: *You'd better watch your step, Jackson. I don't like young lads who are disrespectful towards their elders.*

**not *waste* words** speak very briefly and relevantly, especially when this is also effective: *I hear the new Managing Director doesn't waste words. He's supposed to be very businesslike and efficient.*

***watch* every penny, word etc** consider carefully before committing yourself to spending money, talking etc: *She gets offended so easily that you've really got to watch every word you say.*

***watch* it!** *(informal)* a warning to sb to be careful: *Watch it, young Smith! If you keep being cheeky, I'll send you to the Headmaster.*

***watch* sb/sth like a hawk** keep sb/sth under close and constant observation: *I don't like living near a busy road when our daughter's so young. You have to watch her like a hawk to make sure she doesn't run out into the traffic.*

***watch* out!** *(informal)* be careful!: *Watch out! Don't go too near to the edge or you'll fall into the water.*

***watch* one's p's and q's** → ***mind*/watch one's p's and q's**

***watch* the clock** *(informal)* be careful not to work longer than the required hours; check very often how much time you still have to work: *Someone who spends all his time watching the clock is usually not a good worker.* **clock-watching** *n.*

***watch* the 'world go by** observe what is happening around you; lead a withdrawn, self-sufficient life: *Many old people have no choice but to sit in their rooms by themselves and watch the world go by.*

**a *watched* kettle/pot never boils** *(saying)* waiting attentively for sth to happen makes it seem to take longer: *Don't you know a watched kettle never boils? Looking out of the window all the time won't make them come any more quickly!*

***water* sth down** make sth such as a philosophy or principles weaker: *Some modern theologians water down Christianity as it is found in the Bible.*

**a lot of *water* has passed under the bridge (since . . .)** → ***lot***

**like *water* off a duck's back** making little or no impression or effect: *I keep telling the boys not to bang the doors, but it's like water off a duck's back—they carry on banging them just the same!*

***wave* a (magic) wand (and do sth)** find a means of doing, easily and quickly, sth that is difficult or impossible: *You've got to overcome this problem yourself. I'm sorry, but I can't just wave a magic wand and sort it out for you.*

**be on the same, a different etc *wavelength*** *(informal)* have the same etc thoughts, feelings, opinions etc: *Josephine and I are on the same wavelength. We really understand each other.*

***wax* and wane** increase and then decrease: *Politicians must accustom themselves to the fact that they will wax and wane in popularity throughout their careers.*

**in a *way*** not exactly or wholly; if you think about some aspects of a situation: *In a way, I'm happy about not going to France. If I'd gone, I wouldn't have had enough time to prepare for the exams at the beginning of next term. / In some ways I agree with your interpretation.*

**by the *way*** (used to introduce a comment or question that is only indirectly related, if at all, to the main subject of conversation): *I'm not surprised he's ill. Some people—and that, by the way, includes you—are too lazy to look after themselves properly. / Oh, by the way, Mary—and excuse me interrupting you—your husband wants you to phone him before you leave here.*

**get sth out of the *way*** → ***get***

**no *way*** → ***no***

**out of the *way*** remote; far from a town or city: *They've gone to live in some out-of-the-way little village in Cornwall.*

**pave the *way* (for sb/sth)** → ***pave***

**(not) stand in sb's *way*** → ***stand***

**under *way*** having started and made progress: *The project is now well under way.*

**where there's a will there's a *way*** → ***where***

***way* ahead (of), way behind etc** a long way or far ahead (of), behind etc: *In mathematical ability, he's way ahead of his fellow students. / By mid-January, production was already way below target.*

**by *way* of sth 1** *(formal)* via; by a route which includes a place that is mentioned: *Travellers to London by way of Dover are warned of delays caused by engineering works on the railway.* **2** as a kind of sth: *What are you thinking of doing by way of a holiday this year? / By way of introduction to our lecture tonight, ladies and gentlemen, I'd like to explain something of the historical background.*

**in the *way* of sb/sth** as regards sb/sth:

*There'll be little in the way of rain in southern districts this afternoon.*

**by 'way of being sth** considered to be sth mentioned: *She's very fond of visiting art galleries and is by way of being something of an artist herself.*

**a/sb's way of life** the normal pattern of social or working life of sb or a group: *Foreigners take some time to adjust to our way of life.*

**the way of the world** what many people do and are used to seeing done: *Cheating your employer seems to be the way of the world these days.*

**'one way or the other** ⟶ ***one***

**way out** *(informal)* very unconventional: *Karen loves to wear way-out clothes!*

**on the way out** becoming unfashionable or obsolete: *Short skirts are definitely on the way out now and longer ones are in again.*

**that's the way the 'cookie crumbles** *(informal)* that is the state of affairs and nothing can be done about it (used when sth unfortunate has happened): *I'm sorry you're going to be away when we come to Germany, but that's the way the cookie crumbles.* Also **that's the way it goes.**

**the way to a man's heart is through his stomach** *(saying)* a woman can win a man's affection by giving him food that he enjoys.

**go out of one's way to do sth** ⟶ ***go***

**see one's way (clear) to do sth** ⟶ ***see***

**laugh all the way to the bank** ⟶ ***laugh***

**ways and means** methods and resources for doing sth: *I know the rules forbid it, but the man said that there were still ways and means of getting into the college at night.*

**fall by the wayside** ⟶ ***fall***

**as weak as water** very weak: *The doctor told me the infection had cleared up but not to be surprised if I felt as weak as water for a few days. / This beer's as weak as water!* Also (of people) **as weak as a kitten.**

**weak at the knees** *(informal)* temporarily weak and trembling from illness, strong emotion etc: *'How do you feel?' 'Fine, really; a bit weak at the knees, but that will soon pass.'* **weak-kneed** *adj.*

**the weaker sex** ⟶ **the *fair*/weaker sex**

**not have (got) a stitch/thing to wear** ⟶ ***have***

**not wear sth** *(informal)* not tolerate, allow, or accept sth: *Len won't wear that excuse! You'll have to think of something else!*

**wear and tear** deterioration from ordinary use: *Most insurance policies cover you against damage or loss but not against wear and tear.*

**wear one's heart on one's sleeve** allow your emotions, especially love, to be seen.

**wear off** (of a feeling or an effect) gradually disappear: *The feeling of strangeness of having moved to the new area soon wore off as they made friends.*

**wear one's official, a different etc hat** *(informal)* act in an official etc role or capacity: *As a friend I can help you, but you must remember that when I'm wearing my hat as chairman of the governors I couldn't possibly do so.*

**wear on** (of time) proceed, especially slowly: *As the evening wore on, she grew more and more bored.*

**wear sb out** exhaust sb: *Don't let the children wear you out, Sally! / I feel quite worn out after all those exercises!*

**wear sth out** make sth unusable through continuous wear, handling etc: *Growing children wear clothes out very quickly.*

**wear the trousers** *(informal)* be the dominant partner in a marriage: *Who wears the trousers in your house?*

**wear thin** become exhausted or less effective or acceptable: *My patience is beginning to wear a bit thin, so you'd better watch out!*

**under the weather** *(informal)* slightly unwell or unhappy: *Bill was off work for two weeks with flu and is still feeling a bit under the weather.*

**keep a weather eye open for sth** ⟶ ***keep* one's 'eyes open (for sb/sth)**

**weather the storm, crisis etc** survive a storm etc: *Unemployment and inflation are running very high, the government has just resigned, and there's been a military coup—will the country be able to weather the storm?* Also **ride out the storm.**

**weed out sb/sth** get rid of sb/sth from a collection or group: *Let's have a look at the applications and see if we can weed out the unsuitable ones.*

**weigh a ton** *(informal)* be extremely heavy to hold or carry: *This case weighs a ton, Adam! What have you put in it?*

**weigh against sb/sth** or **weigh in favour of sb/sth** count in judgment against or in favour of sb/sth: *His years in prison weighed heavily against him whenever he tried to get a job.*

**weigh anchor** raise the anchor(s) of a ship; prepare to leave the place where a ship is docked or moored.

**weigh sb down** lower sb's spirits, making him anxious, sad, or depressed: *Financial problems have weighed us down for years. / Mark seems very weighed down by all his additional responsibilities at the moment.*

**weigh in with sth** join in a discussion or argument with a suggestion or criticism: *Just as it seemed Peggy and Rex had decided what to do, Bob weighed in with a proposal that really upset both of them.*

**weigh on one's mind** (of a responsibility) make you worried and anxious: *The safety of the missing children weighed heavily on their parents' minds.*

**weigh sb/sth up** try to assess or understand sb/sth before reaching a conclusion: *He weighed up all the facts and decided he could make a success of the project.*

**weigh one's words** choose carefully the words you speak or write: *Hamilton was always known as someone who weighed his words thoughtfully; he never wanted to give offence to anyone by what he said.*

**worth one's *weight* in gold** → ***worth***
**carry (the *weight* of) the world on one's shoulders** → ***carry***
**take the *weight* off one's feet** → ***take***
**the scales are *weighted* against sb/sth** → ***scales***
***weird* and wonderful** cleverly made or original but strange: *We don't want any of your weird and wonderful educational theories here—just teach the students to pass the examinations, that's all.*
**you're *welcome*** → ***you***
**(all) *well* and good** that is all right; that is good or satisfactory: *If you refuse to follow our advice, well and good, but don't say we didn't warn you.*
***well* and truly** completely: *There was nothing they could do. They were well and truly lost.*
**be '*well* away 1** be making progress: *So you've got all that furniture! You're well away in settling down in your own home.* **2** (of people) be talking, arguing etc easily and probably continuing for some time: *'Jack and George are well away tonight, aren't they?' 'Yes, once they start talking about their army days, you can't stop them!'*
***well*, did you ever?** *(informal)* (an expression of surprise or amazement): *Well, did you ever! So Sheila's coming back here after all! I said she'd never enjoy emigrating to Australia.*
***well* done!** (a comment of approval and congratulation): *Well done, lads—the football challenge cup has come back to our town for yet another year!*
***well* heeled** *(informal)* obviously rich: *This restaurant caters for well-heeled tourists from America.*
***well*, I never (did)!** *(informal)* (an expression of surprise): *Well, I never did! Foreigner or not, you certainly speak English well!'*
***well*/badly off** in a fortunate or unfortunate situation, especially financially: *We're quite well off really, I suppose.*
***well*/badly off (for sth)** well or poorly supplied (with sth): *I'm badly off for cookery books—I need a few more.*
***well*-oiled** *(slang)* drunk.
***well* to do** quite rich.
***well* up** (of tears, or other strong emotion) flow freely: *He couldn't stop the tears welling up as he gave his farewell speech to his colleagues.*
**be *well* up in sth** be very knowledgeable about sth: *Ask John—he's well up in the latest developments in computers.*
***wend* one's way** *(old-fashioned)* go or travel: *Slowly, he wended his way home. He knew he'd never see her again.*
***wet* behind the ears** *(informal)* inexperienced or immature: *There always seems something odd about final-year students having to obey a new teacher who's still wet behind the ears.* Also **not dry behind the ears.**
**a *wet* blanket** sb who is gloomy or boring and so prevents other people from enjoying themselves: *Terry's such a wet blanket—we don't want to ask him to the party!*
***wet* one's whistle** *(informal, old-fashioned)* have an alcoholic drink.
**a/the *whale* of a . . .** *(informal)* a very good, large example of sth: *We had the whale of a time on holiday. / The show was a whale of a success!*
***what* a hope!** → ***some* hope(s)!**
***what* about sb/sth?** → ***how*/what about sb/sth?**
***what* about (doing) sth?** → ***how*/what about (doing) sth?**
***what* about that!** → ***how*/what about that!**
***what* did you etc do with sth?** where did you etc put, lose, or hide sth? (usually used in perfect and simple past tenses): *Miss Jones, what have you done with the file of last month's invoices? / What did you do with my coat?*
**(well) *what* do you know?** *(informal)* (an expression introducing or commenting on an interesting or surprising piece of information): *'Dave tells me he's getting married to Jane next month.' 'Well, what you do know? The pair of them have kept it all very dark, haven't they?'*
**(and/or) *what* 'have you** *(informal)* (and/or) similar people, things, places etc: *If you add up the cost of petrol, oil, insurance, repairs, and what have you, running a car these days certainly isn't cheap.*
***what* is sb/sth doing, (doing sth)?** why is sb/sth doing sth, in that particular place etc? (used to show annoyance, puzzlement, suspicion etc): *What is she doing (sitting) in my chair? / What's a nice girl like you doing in a dump like this?' / What do you think you're doing, throwing stones at the window?*
***what* is sb driving at?** *(informal)* what is sb trying to say or do?: *What are you driving at? You must explain yourself more clearly!*
***what* is eating sb?** *(informal)* why is sb so worried, unhappy etc?: *Larry looks rather depressed today. I wonder what's eating him.*
***what* is sb getting at?** what is sb suggesting in an indirect way?: *I think I now understand what you're getting at.*
**(and) *what* is more** (and) more importantly; furthermore: *I don't think the council will give us permission to build an extension, and what is more we probably can't afford it anyway.*
***what* is sb playing at?** *(informal)* (an expression showing anger, bewilderment etc at sb's behaviour): *What on earth does the Prime Minister think he's playing at, reducing the amount of money spent on education?*
***what* is the world coming to?** *(informal)* (an expression used to complain about changes in living conditions, moral attitudes etc): *What is the world coming to? What with strikes, rising prices, high unemployment—where's it all leading?* Also **I don't know what the world is coming to.**
**for *what* it/sth is worth** however much or little value or importance sth has (used when

the speaker is not sure about this): *I think he may be the best man for the job. But that's just my opinion, for what it's worth.*

**have (got) *what* it takes (to do sth)** ⟶ ***have***

***what* makes sb tick** *(informal)* what motivates sb and makes him live, act, react as he does: *Sheila's a very mysterious person. I don't know what makes her tick at all.*

***what* more could one ask/want?** this is surely an ideal arrangement, state of affairs etc: *A stable marriage and a contented family life—what more could you ask?*

**and 'what not** and other (similar) things: *The shop sells screws, nails, hammers, and what not.*

***what* 'of it?** ⟶ ***so* what?**

***what* on earth?** *(informal)* what? (used to emphasize the speaker's bewilderment, surprise etc): *What on earth are you doing here?* Also **what in the world?**

***what* price sth** *(informal)* how likely is it that sth will happen or be done?; what is the value of sth?: *What price freedom of speech if the government bans all public meetings? / What price a successful career if it ruins your marriage?*

***what*'s all this/that ( . . . )?** why is this/that happening?; tell me more about this/that: (said in an annoyed tone): *What's all this noise for? / What's all this I hear about you wanting to leave?*

***what*'s cooking?** *(informal)* what is being planned or done?: *What's cooking in here then? You all look very guilty!*

***what*'s sth in aid of?** what is the purpose of sth?; why is sth as it is?: *'What's all this in aid of?' asked Andrew, pointing to the mass of wires behind the tape-recorder. / 'What's this new car in aid of, then?' 'I've got a new girlfriend!'*

***what*'s the big idea?** *(informal)* what is the reason for such behaviour? (used to imply that there is no reason): *What's the big idea? I've already given you these details on my application form. Why do you want them all again?*

***what*'s the damage?** *(slang)* how much does sth cost?: *Thanks for mending the motorbike. Now what's the damage?*

***what*'s the odds?** *(informal)* what does it matter?; one action, choice etc is as good as another: *What's the odds? I can go on Thursday or Friday; I've not got anything planned for either day yet.*

***what*'s up?** *(informal)* what's the matter?; what is wrong?; what is happening?: *What's up, Raymond? You look worried!*

**know *what*'s what** ⟶ ***know***

***what* the eye doesn't see (the heart doesn't grieve over)** *(saying)* you can't/shouldn't be troubled by sth you don't know exists.

***what* the hell!** *(informal)* (an exclamation showing defiantly that you do not care): *What the hell! It's the last day of term. I can be late at school for once!*

***what* the hell?** *(informal)* what? (used to expressed the speaker's bad temper, hostility, scorn etc): *What the hell has it got to do with you? Mind your own business!* Alternatives to ***hell*** are: ***blazes, devil, dickens*** *(all old-fashioned)*; ***heck.***

***what* with . . .** *(informal)* because of (sth): *What with the bad weather this spring and being ill for a month, I've not done much gardening. / What with one thing and another today, I've not even had time to read the newspaper.*

**(separate) the *wheat* and/from the chaff** ⟶ ***(separate)* the chaff and/from the wheat/ grain**

**at/behind the *wheel*** *(informal)* controlling sth: *The new man behind the wheel at the company is an ex-Army officer.*

***wheeling* and dealing** *(informal)* clever, often immoral, political or commercial negotiating and bargaining.

**set the *wheels* in motion** ⟶ ***set* sth in motion**

***wheels* within wheels** a complicated-looking network of influences, centres of power and decision-making etc that makes quick decisions difficult: *The ordinary citizen may feel that some matters of international politics can be easily agreed but there are always wheels within wheels.*

***when* all is said and done** ⟶ ***all***

***when* the cat's away the mice will play** *(saying)* when the person in charge of children, pupils, or workers is absent, they do as they like, enjoy themselves, or stop working.

***where* it's at** ⟶ ***where* the 'action is**

***where* on earth?** *(informal)* where?; whereabouts? (used to emphasize the speaker's bewilderment, surprise etc): *Where on earth have I put my keys?* Also **where in the world?**

***where* the 'action is** *(informal)* where the most exciting events are happening: *He wants to live in London because he thinks that's where the action is.* Also **where it's at.**

***where* the hell?** *(informal)* where?; whereabouts? (used to express the speaker's bad temper, hostility, scorn etc): *Where the hell do you think you're going? Stay here while I'm talking to you!* Alternatives to ***hell*** are ***blazes, devil, dickens*** *(all old-fashioned)*; ***heck.***

***where* there's a will there's a way** *(saying)* if you are sufficiently willing or determined, then difficulties will be overcome and a way to do or obtain sth will be found: *'We've not got enough seats—I don't know how they'll all fit in!' 'Oh, where there's a will there's a way. We'll manage somehow.'*

**tell sb *where* to get off** ⟶ ***tell***

**see *which* way the cat jumps** ⟶ ***see***

**see *which* way the wind is blowing** ⟶ ***see***

***while* away the time, an hour or two etc** make the time pass: *He writes a lot of poetry to while away the time.*

***whip* up sth** arouse or excite sth such as anger

or enthusiastic support: *I can't whip up any interest in the coach outing.*

**a '*whipping* boy** sb who takes the punishment that is due to sb else who really is responsible: *The government always finds a whipping boy to pay the penalty for its mistakes.*

**by a *whisker*** *(informal)* narrowly; only just: *In the crash, she escaped death by just a whisker.*

***whistle* for sth** *(informal)* ask for sth, especially money, with no hope of getting it: *John borrowed £100 and as far as he's concerned, I can whistle for it.*

**'*whistle* stop** a short stop on a journey to meet and talk to the general public, voters etc. **whistle-stop** *adj*: *The Prince and Princess went on a whistle-stop tour round Australia.*

**as *white* as a sheet/ghost** very pale in appearance, as a result of illness, fear, a shock etc: *June came in, as white as a sheet, to say she'd seen an accident at the corner of the lane.* Also **as white as chalk.**

**as *white* as snow** very white: *I scarcely knew him when we met again. His hair had gone as white as snow.* **snow-white** *adj*.

**a *white*-collar job, worker etc** professional or business work etc. See also **a *blue*-collar job, worker etc.**

**a *white* elephant** sth that is never or hardly ever used but has cost a lot of money: *The theatre turned out to be an expensive white elephant—so few people go there that it's not worth maintaining it.*

**a *white* lie** a lie that does no harm and is merely more convenient or polite than telling the truth: *I had to tell him a white lie—that there wasn't any more beer in the house—just to get him sobered up.*

***who* does sb think he is?** *(informal)* sb has no right to give orders, behave in a superior way etc: *Who does Mr Drayton think he is? The boss or something? He should knock before he comes into my office!*

***who* on earth?** *(informal)* who?; which one? (used to emphasize the speaker's uncertainty etc): *Now, who on earth is going to break the news to his mother?* Also **who in the world?**

**know *who's* who** ⟶ ***know***

***who* the hell?** *(informal)* who?; which person? (used to express the speaker's bad temper, hostility, scorn etc): *Who the hell told you that? It was supposed to be a secret!* Alternatives to ***hell*** are ***blazes, devil, dickens*** *(all old-fashioned)*; ***heck.***

**on the *whole*** generally speaking: *On the whole we're happy living here, but it is a long way away from my parents' home.*

**go the *whole* hog** ⟶ ***go***

**leaven the *whole* lump** ⟶ ***leaven***

**the truth, the *whole* truth, and nothing but the truth** ⟶ ***truth***

**give sb/sth the (full, *whole* etc) works** ⟶ ***give***

**the *(whole)* world 'over** ⟶ ***world***

***whoop* it up** *(informal)* celebrate in a cheerful, noisy way: *Groups of revellers were still whooping it up right through till the early hours of New Year's Day.*

***why* don't . . . ?** (used in making a request, invitation etc): *Why don't you come and sit next to me?*

***why* on earth?** *(informal)* why?; for what reason? (used to emphasize the speaker's bewilderment, surprise etc): *Why on earth do we have to go and see your mother? I'd much rather stay at home.* Also **why in the world?**

***why* the hell?** *(informal)* why? (used to express the speaker's bad temper, hostility, scorn etc): *Why the hell did you go and tell John that I'm taking Sandra out to dinner tonight? Don't you know he's keen on her too?* Alternatives to ***hell*** are ***blazes, devil, dickens*** *(all old-fashioned)*; ***heck.***

**the *whys* and wherefores** the reasons for sth; purposes, causes etc of sth: *Let's not worry about all the whys and wherefores of the different methods of advertising. Let's just get on and choose one of them!*

**give sb/sth a *wide* berth** ⟶ ***steer* clear of sb/sth**

***wide* of the mark** inaccurate in a description, diagnosis etc: *Their estimate of the cost of building the new extension was wide of the mark. They originally said it would cost £100,000, but it turned out to be nearly £300,000!*

**lay/leave oneself *(wide)* open to sth** ⟶ ***lay***

**tied to his mother's/*wife*'s apron strings** ⟶ ***tied***

**be *wild* about sb/sth** ⟶ **be *mad* about/on sb/sth**

**a *wild* 'goose chase** a search for sb/sth who can or will not be found; a useless investigation: *I hope this doesn't turn out to be a wild goose chase like the time you sent me into town to try to find a chemist's that was open on Sunday.*

**sow (one's) *wild* oats** ⟶ ***sow***

**a *wildcat* strike** a strike that is suddenly called by a group of workers without the approval of a trade union.

**beyond one's *wildest* dreams** *(informal)* (in a way that is) very much greater than you expected: *The success of the new play was beyond everyone's wildest dreams: the theatre's been full every night for weeks!*

**at *will*** as you wish; when and how you want: *Discipline was non-existent. Students roamed about the campus at will, as if there had never been such a thing as a timetable.*

**a *will* of iron** the firm determination to achieve what you want or think right: *You don't need to have a will of iron to slim—just the desire and some discipline.*

**a *will* of one's own** sufficient determination and independence of thought to do what you want: *Julia's only two, but she's already got a will of her own and won't do some things if she doesn't want to.*

**where there's a *will* there's a way** ⟶ ***where***

**you can't *win* ⟶ *you***
***win* sb's ear ⟶ *gain*/get/win sb's ear**
***win* hands down** or **beat sb hands down** win etc without effort or by a clear lead: *Liverpool won the competition hands down; their nearest rivals were ten points behind them.*
***win* the day ⟶ *carry*/win the day**
**go/run like the *wind* ⟶ *go***
**see which way the '*wind* is blowing ⟶ *see***
**take the *wind* out of sb's sails ⟶ *take***
***wind* up (doing sth) ⟶ *end*/wind up (doing sth)**
***wind* sb up** make sb excited: *Whenever we talk about politics, he always gets very wound up.* Note that this is usually used in the passive.
**go out of the *window* ⟶ *go***
***wine* and dine (sb)** have, share, or entertain sb to a meal with wine, as a social or formal occasion: *The job offered plenty of scope for wining and dining.*
***wine,* women and song** a man's social pleasures.
**take sb under one's *wing* ⟶ *take***
**a nod is as good as a *wink* (to a blind horse) ⟶ *nod***
***wink* at sth** *(old-fashioned)* decide to ignore or overlook sth.
**play one's trump/*winning* card ⟶ *play***
***wipe* sb/sth off the face of the earth** *(informal)* remove completely, especially by force: *In the event of war, whole areas would be wiped off the face of the earth.* Also **wipe sb/sth off the map. disappear off the face of the earth** disappear completely.
***wipe* the floor with sb** *(informal)* defeat other competitors decisively: *The German Democratic Republic wiped the floor with their opponents, picking up 26 of the 30 major prizes.*
***wipe* the slate clean** forget past faults or offences: *Since we're both to blame, why don't we forgive each other and wipe the slate clean?* See also **a *clean* slate/sheet.**
***wipe* the 'smile/'grin off sb's/one's face** *(informal)* stop sb smiling/grinning: *This is serious, so you can wipe the smile off your face, young Gerald, for a start!*
**get one's '*wires* crossed ⟶ *get***
**be *wise* after the event** know what should have been done in connection with sth, but only after it has happened: *It's no good being wise after the event! We should have taken measures to prevent the fire happening in the first place.*
**get/be *wise* to sb/sth ⟶ *get***
**the *wish* is father to the thought** *(saying)* you think that sth is true or likely because you wish it to be so.
***wish* sb/sth on(to) sb** *(informal)* pass to sb sb/sth unpleasant that you do not want yourself: *I wouldn't wish my grumpy old Dad on my worst enemy!*
***wishful* thinking** persuading yourself that sth is true or will or could happen, because it is what you would like: *When government ministers predict in an election year that the economy is on the verge of a boom, they are quite naturally suspected of wishful thinking.*
**to *wit*** *(formal)* that is; more specifically: *'They should have appointed a more reasonable person.' 'To wit, yourself, I suppose?'*
**be '*with* sb** *(informal)* understand sb's explanation, reasoning, or instructions: *I'm not with you, I'm sorry. Could you repeat that? / Are you all with me so far? Does anybody want to ask a question?*
**drive sb out of his mind/*wits* ⟶ *drive***
**scare/frighten sb out of his *wits* ⟶ *scare* sb stiff**
**have (got) one's *wits* about one ⟶ *have***
**at one's *wits'* end** not knowing what to do in a difficulty; extremely confused: *I've no idea what to do. I'm at my wits' end. Can you help me, please?*
***woe* betide sb** sb mentioned will surely be punished, reprimanded etc: *Mr Matthews would get us to learn our French irregular verbs every week, and woe betide anyone who got them wrong!*
**keep the *wolf* from the door ⟶ *keep***
**a *wolf* in sheep's clothing** sb who appears friendly and harmless but is really an enemy or evil-doer.
**a '*wolf* whistle** a whistle made by a man to a woman especially in a street or other public place, to show that he sees her as physically attractive. **wolf-whistle** *vb* make a wolf whistle.
**a *woman* after one's own heart ⟶ a *man*/woman after one's own heart**
**a *woman* of few words ⟶ a *man*/woman of few words**
**a *woman* of her word ⟶ a *man*/woman of his/her word**
**a *woman* of many parts ⟶ a *man*/woman of many parts**
**a *woman* of substance ⟶ a *man*/woman/person of substance**
**a *woman* of the world ⟶ a *man*/woman of the world**
**it is no *wonder* (that . . . ) ⟶ *no***
***wonders* will never cease** *(informal)* (a comment expressing surprise and pleasure at sth, often sth trivial): *'Where's Johnny?' 'Round the back, washing the car!' 'What! Wonders will never cease!'*
**out of the *wood*(s)** *(informal)* free from difficulties, danger etc: *The company's financial position has improved slightly after last year's disastrous performance, but we're still not out of the wood yet.*
**not see the *wood* for the trees ⟶ *see***
**the nigger in the *woodpile* ⟶ *nigger***
**pull the *wool* over sb's eyes ⟶ *pull***
**a man/woman of his/her *word* ⟶ *man***
**in a *word*** briefly; in as few words as possible (often used to summarize or express differently what has gone before): *You certainly picked the right person for that job, James. In*

*a word, Barbara was the best manageress we've ever had!*

**take sb at his *word*** → ***take***

**upon my *word*!** → **upon my *soul*/word!**

**have only (got) sb's *word* for sth** → ***have***

**not be the *word* for it/sth** be inadequate to describe sth fully or strongly enough: *Unkind isn't the word for it! I've never seen anyone treat their pets so cruelly as he does.* Also **there's no other word for it.**

**from the *word* go** *(informal)* right from the start: *Jackson took the lead in the race from the word go and came in ten seconds ahead of the next man. / It's important to realize from the word go that you may not get the job.*

**(have) a *word* in sb's ear** (speak) words to sb in private: *A word in your ear, John, before you meet him; I think there's something you ought to know.*

**a *word* in season** sth that is said, especially as advice or sympathy, at a suitable time: *Sometimes it's right to interfere. A word in season might have saved Bradbury from his own folly.*

**by *word* of mouth** as a spoken message, in contrast to other ways of communication: *I hope you didn't mind getting the news by word of mouth, but I didn't know how else I could contact you.*

***word* perfect** able to repeat sth learnt such as a poem or part in a play with no mistakes at all: *We're all expected to be word perfect for the final rehearsal on Thursday.*

**have a *word* with sb** → ***have***

**hang on sb's lips/*words*** → ***hang***

**too funny, sad etc for *words*** → ***too***

***words* fail me** I cannot express or describe sth (often said because the speaker is too embarrassed, surprised, angry etc): *Words fail me! How can I thank you enough for all the kindness you've shown me?*

**put *words* in(to) sb's mouth** → ***put***

**take the *words* out of sb's mouth** → ***take***

**sticks and stones may break my bones but *words* will never hurt me** → ***sticks***

***work* like a beaver** → ***beaver* away**

***work*/act like a charm** have an immediate desired effect: *Whatever it was she said or did to change his attitude, it worked like a charm.*

***work* one's fingers to the bone** *(informal)* work very hard and for a long time, especially doing manual tasks in a home, shop, or factory: *For years she worked her fingers to the bone at the packing machine, coming home at night exhausted.*

***work*/go like a dream** go with no problems or easily: *All our arrangements went like a dream, and we had a fantastic day!*

***work* like a horse/slave/Trojan** work very hard: *I've been working like a slave all day, but I'm still only halfway through it all!*

***work* out** develop in a suitable way: *I hope your plans work out all right. / We're pleased that things have worked out for them both in America.*

***work* sth out** understand sth: *I can't work out where we are on this map.*

***work* out at sth** → ***come*/work out at sth**

***work* to rule** strictly follow the rules laid down for a job, as a means of industrial protest: *The union's general secretary has called on all members to work to rule from Monday in support of their claim for a 10% increase in wages.* **work-to-rule** *n.*

***work* oneself up** become very excited: *Don't work yourself up (or get (all) worked up) over something that you can't put right yourself.*

***work* up sth** gradually develop sth such as business; arouse sth such as strong emotions: *When I came back from holiday, I found it difficult to work up any enthusiasm for my job again.*

***work*/do wonders/miracles** have an unusually good or marvellous effect: *The advertisers claim that their new washing powder will do wonders on dirty stains.*

**in *working* order** functioning properly: *We are pleased to announce that the escalators are now in working order again.*

**give sb/sth the (full, whole etc) *works*** → ***give***

**gum up the *works*** → ***gum***

**throw a spanner in the *works*** → ***throw***

**come down in the *world*** → ***come***

**not for the *world*** → **not for all the *tea* in China**

**out of this *world*** very fine, beautiful, unusual etc: *All her cooking is good, but the steak and kidney pudding she makes is really out of this world!*

**the bottom drops/falls out of one's *world*** → ***bottom***

**all the *world* and his wife** → ***all***

**a '*world* away from sth** → **'*worlds* away from sth**

**the *world* beats a path to sb's door** everyone wants to share, benefit from, buy etc what sb has to offer: *If you can invent a better tyre, the world will beat a path to your door!*

**watch the '*world* go by** → ***watch***

**the *world* is one's oyster** you are able to enjoy all the pleasures and opportunities of life that you want: *When they leave college, many young people feel the world is their oyster.*

**a/the *world* of difference, truth etc** *(informal)* a very great difference, a lot of truth etc: *There's a world of difference between the first small steam engines and today's large, sleek electric locomotives.* See also **do sb/sth a power/world of good.**

**carry (the weight of) the *world* on one's shoulders** or **carry all the troubles of the world on one's shoulders** → ***carry***

**the (whole) *world* 'over** everywhere; in any place in the world: *People are basically the same the whole world over.*

**(think) the *world* owes one a living** (think that) you are entitled to be well supported or provided for because you deserve it or simply because you exist: *The world doesn't owe you* *a living you know. Why don't you go out and get a job for yourself?*

**'*worlds* apart** ⟶ **'*poles*/'worlds apart**

**'*worlds* away from sth** very different from or far away from sth in space or time: *His multimillion-pound business is worlds away from the day twenty years ago when he arrived in this country as a penniless refugee!* Also **a 'world away from sth.**

**change (sb/sth) for the better/*worse*** ⟶ ***change***

**take a turn for the better/*worse*** ⟶ ***take***

**be (all, none etc) the better/*worse* for sth** ⟶ ***better***

**be the *worse* for wear** be worn, damaged, tired or drunk: *I always carry my diary in my back pocket, so by the end of the year it's a bit the worse for wear. / We had to change trains several times, and it was all so dirty and noisy! Eventually we arrived at Margaret's, a little the worse for wear, I can tell you.*

***worse* luck** *(informal)* which is unfortunate or a pity (said as a comment on sth previously mentioned): *'We'll see you at Robin's party, I hope?' 'No, I'm on duty that night, worse luck!'*

***worse* off** ⟶ ***better*/worse off**

**sb's bark is *worse* than his bite** ⟶ ***bark***

**can/could do *worse* than do sth** ⟶ ***do***

***worse*/stranger things happen at sea** *(saying)* things could be worse (said when you have to accept a disappointment, failure etc).

**at *worst*** ⟶ **at *best*/worst**

**if the *worst* comes to the worst** if circumstances become too difficult, troublesome, or dangerous; if a plan etc fails: *If the worst comes to the worst and all the hotels are full, you could always come and stay with us.*

**one's own *worst* enemy** ⟶ ***own***

**have (got) the best/*worst* of sth** ⟶ ***have***

**(be) *worth* a try** (be) sufficiently likely to achieve success, a result etc to justify your trying it: *None of the other medicines have worked, but she seemed to think this new one was worth a try.*

**(be) *worth* one's salt** (be) deserving what you earn, fulfilling your function or doing your work well and competently: *Any plumber worth his salt could install a central heating system for you.*

***worth* the name** ⟶ ***worthy* of the name**

***worth* one's weight in gold** extremely valuable or useful: *A reliable car is worth its weight in gold.*

**be ˌ*worth* 'while** having value in itself; sufficiently important, interesting, profitable etc to give a good return for the effort or attention spent: *I always find it worth while taking time to explain a job carefully to a new employee—it saves time later.* **'worthwhile** *adj*: *a worthwhile job.*

**be *worth* sb's while** be profitable or interesting for sb: *I'm sure it'll be worth my while coming to the conference. I always make useful contacts there.*

***worthy* of the name** deserving to be named or defined as sth mentioned: *Any doctor worthy of the name would help an injured man in the streets.* Also **worth the name.**

**rub salt into the *wound*** ⟶ ***rub***

***wrapped* up in sb/sth** completely absorbed by or extremely involved in sb/sth: *I got so wrapped up in the detective story that I didn't notice the time.*

**under *wraps*** ⟶ ***keep* sth under wraps**

***wring* sb's neck** *(informal)* strangle or throttle sb (used as an expression of anger or as a threat): *If he ever comes back here, I'll wring his neck!*

**nothing to *write* home about** ⟶ ***nothing* to shout about**

***write* sb/sth off (as . . . )** *(informal)* consider sb/sth as unimportant, not worth listening to etc: *Just because he didn't pass all his exams at school there's no need to write him off as a failure for the rest of his life.*

***write* sth off 1** damage sth so badly that it has no value and is not worth repairing. **write-off** *n*: *The car was a complete write-off.* **2** accept that sth, especially money, is lost and cannot be recovered: *The firm has had to write off several thousand pounds' worth of bad debts.*

**the *writing* on the wall** clear signs that warn of failure, disaster, or defeat: *Fortunately, the company saw the writing on the wall early on and took action to avoid losing money later.*

**be *written* all over sb's face** or **be written on sb's face** be clearly seen on sb: *Guilt was written all over her face.*

**get hold of the *wrong* end of the stick** ⟶ ***get***

**get (sth) off on the right/*wrong* foot** ⟶ ***get***

***wrong* in the head** ⟶ ***soft*/wrong in the head**

**get out of bed (on) the *wrong* side** ⟶ ***get***

**on the right/*wrong* side of 40 etc** ⟶ ***right***

**born on the *wrong* side of the blanket** ⟶ ***born***

**take sth in the *wrong* spirit** ⟶ ***take* sth in good/bad part**

**bark up the *wrong* tree** ⟶ ***bark***

**rub sb up the *wrong* way** ⟶ ***rub***

# Y

**(from) the *year* dot** *(informal)* (from) a distant time in the past or, less commonly, the future: *The book contained church records going back to the year dot.*

***you* and yours** *(informal)* a person, his wife or her husband, and their children; your family: *Greetings to you and yours!*

***you* bet!** *(slang)* you can be sure!: *'Do you*

*want to come and play outside?' 'You bet I do!'*

**you can say 'that again!** *(informal)* that is absolutely true! I know that already: *'Golly! It's cold!' 'You can say that again!'* also **you're telling me!: you('ve) said it!**

**you can take/lead a horse to water but you can't make him drink** *(saying)* you can give sb the opportunity to do sth, but you will not get him to do it if he does not want to.

**you can't keep a good man down!** *(informal)* sb who is competent, skilled etc cannot be stopped: *'I hear that Maurice is skiing again, in spite of breaking his leg last year.' 'You can't keep a good man down!'*

**you can't teach an old dog new tricks** *(saying)* you can't get old people, who are set in their lifestyle, to change their ideas, ways of working etc.

**you can't win** *(informal)* whatever you choose to do comes to an unhappy conclusion, does not satisfy etc: *If we tell the government we're on strike, they'll reduce the money they pay us; and if we don't tell them, then our income falls below a certain level and we won't get that money anyway. You can't win, can you?*

**you could have ˌfooled 'me!** *(informal)* I wouldn't have thought so: *So you're wearing a wig. You could have fooled me! I thought you had a new hairstyle!*

**you could have knocked sb down with a feather** *(informal)* sb was helpless with astonishment, overcome by surprise etc: *Joe is the last person I would ever have expected to get married. You could have knocked me down with a feather when he told me!*

**you don't 'say (so)!** or **you 'don't say!** *(informal)* (an expression used to show surprise, sometimes ironically): *'I've got a touch of indigestion.' 'That comes from eating too much!' 'You don't say!'*

**you must be joking!** *(informal)* (used to express disbelief): *'Jackie passed her driving test!' 'You must be joking—I thought she only started learning two months ago!'*

**you name it (he's got it etc)** *(informal)* (he has etc) every person, thing, place etc that you can mention: *Snow, floods, hail—you name it, we've had it this winter!*

**you pays your money and you takes your choice** *(informal)* you choose whatever alternative course, explanation etc you want; any one is as good as any other.

**you're only young once** *(saying)* let young people enjoy freedom and fun while they are young, before they have to face responsibilities, work etc.

**you're welcome** *(mainly US, informal)* (a reply after being thanked for a service, information etc): *'You've been most helpful.' 'You're welcome. That's what we're here for.'*

**you scratch my back and I'll scratch yours** *(informal)* if you help, praise etc me, then I'll do the same to you.

**as you were** (an order to return to a former position or situation or what was originally said): *As you were, children! That was a false alarm. / It'll cost £60 . . . no, £80 . . . , no, as you were, £60.*

**an old head on *young* shoulders** → ***old***

**your actual sb/sth** *(informal)* the real person or thing: *This is valuable. It's not any old plate, you know. It's your actual silver. / So this is your actual video-recorder that you've been telling me so much about!*

**your guess is as good as mine** *(informal)* don't ask me, because I don't know the answer either (often implying that no one knows the answer): *'If the government knows how to run the country, why aren't things getting any better?' 'Your guess is as good as mine!'*

**(and) Bob's *your* uncle** → ***Bob***

**yours truly** *(informal)* I/me: *Who'll be taking the children round the zoo? Yours truly, as usual!*